COLETTE

GARLAND REFERENCE LIBRARY
OF THE HUMANITIES
(VOL. 805)

Photograph courtesy of the Bibliothèque Nationale, Paris

COLETTE
An Annotated Primary and Secondary Bibliography

compilation and annotation by

Donna M. Norell

GARLAND PUBLISHING, INC. • NEW YORK & LONDON
1993

Library of Congress Cataloging-in-Publication Data

Norell, Donna M.
   Colette : an annotated primary and secondary bibliography / by
Donna M. Norell.
         p.   cm. — (Garland reference library of the humanities ; vol.
805)
   Includes indexes.
   ISBN 0-8240-6620-0
   1. Colette, 1873-1954—Bibliography. I. Title. II. Series.
Z8182.3.N66   1993
[PQ2605.028]
016.848'91209—dc20

                                                   92-26827
                                                   CIP

Printed on acid-free, 250-year-life paper
Manufactured in the United States of America

To Ken,
at last

CONTENTS

Preface ix
Acknowledgments xix
Introduction: Colette in the World xxi
Abbreviations xxix

WORKS BY COLETTE
Correspondence:
  Book-Length Collections: French 3
  Uncollected Letters: French 13
  Book-Length Collections: English Translations 22
Multi-Volume Collections and Single-Volume Collections of Texts
from Several Works:
  Multi-Volume Collections 25
  Single-Volume Collections of Texts from Several Works: French 29
  Single-Volume Collections of Texts from Several Works: English 31
Memoirs, Chronicles and Reminiscences 49
Novels and Novellas 77
Books of Essays, Articles and Short Stories 157
Theater and Spectacle 237
Theater Criticism 247
Film Writing and Film Criticism 251
Miscellaneous Publications 255

CRITICISM ON COLETTE
Books, Monographs and Pamphlets on Colette 269
Articles on Colette 303

APPENDICES
Appendix A. Special Issues on Colette 509
Appendix B. German Translations of Colette's Works 513
Appendix C. ItalianTranslations of Colette's Works 525
Appendix D. Spanish Translations of Colette's Works 531
Appendix E. Index of Book Titles of Colette's Works 539
Appendix F. Index of Editors, English Translators, Illustrators
             and Other Contributors to Colette's Books 545

PREFACE

Purpose and Scope of the Bibliography

For many years now, the need for a comprehensive bibliography on Colette has been widely recognized, not only by scholars, students and other researchers in the English-speaking world but also by those in France and other European countries. Although it is from the former category that the principal users of this volume are expected to come, it is our earnest hope that both these groups will profit from its publication.

Work on this bibliography was begun some eight years ago, before the first volume of the Pléiade edition of Colette's *Œuvres* came into print. Since then three of the Pléiade's projected four volumes have appeared, the third one just recently. When the fourth and final volume is published the edition will undoubtedly provide for long years to come the most detailed and most extensively documented French bibliography available on Colette's writing. Our compilation is by no means intended to compete with the Pléiade's bibliography, which comprises a long section of each volume as part of the documentation. In the first place, the Pléiade's presentation of works is essentially chronological whereas ours is by genre. Secondly, our primary bibliography, which details both French and English editions, is supplemented by a comprehensive secondary bibliography of books and articles. And, thirdly, all our entries, both primary and secondary, have been annotated so that users may be guided as to their fitness for a particular purpose.

Neither our primary nor our secondary bibliography is intended to be exhaustive. However, we have striven to list and describe, with stated exceptions, all Colette's works published in book form during the years 1900 to 1988, all verified extracts published in periodical or other form after their first book publication up to 1988, and all books and articles published on Colette within that same period. Although the cut-off date of 1988 has been chosen only for practical purposes, the choice of 1900 as the initial date is prompted by logical considerations. Considerable evidence exists that Colette was probably writing music reviews for *La Cocarde* as early as February 1895. Nevertheless her first book, *Claudine à l'école*, came out in print only in 1900.

Our decision to confine the extracts to those published after their first appearance in book form is based on other factors. Most of Colette's works, even the novels, appeared first as a series of separate texts published in weekly or monthly periodicals. Although the known quantity of these is already immense, it is certain that more texts will be turned up by future researchers. During the first few years of the century France had about 3000 newspapers and periodicals, a few dozen of them in Paris alone. Many of these were ephemeral, their issues now lost or impossible to obtain. Since Colette was known to be already active on the fringes of Paris' literary scene before the new century began, it is not unreasonable to conclude that some of these publications will one day be proven to contain some of her texts. Colette's habit of publishing short texts first in non-book form before collecting them within the covers of a book continued right up to her death. Since we found it necessary to set limits on the amount of material we could include, our choice of the date of first publication in book form as the initial entry for a particular work seemed the right one, in that it rendered less troublesome the complications engendered by Colette's publishing history.

The secondary bibliography is subject only to the restrictions of the period chosen. In other words, length has not been a factor in determining inclusion of a book or an article. On the other hand, users should be aware that, for the most part, prefaces in and reviews of Colette's books are listed only in the primary bibliography; only a few of them are annotated in the secondary.

In all decisions taken as to what and what not to include in this book, we have been guided by our prime goals of accuracy and usefulness. We hope that we have not erred too greatly in our endeavors towards this end.

Sources

We have used any and all bibliographical sources available to us.
These include published national bibliographies, such as the *British
National Bibliography* and the *National Union Catalog*, as well as major
ongoing publications such as the *French XX* series, the *MLA
Bibliography* and the *Revue d'histoire littéraire de la France*. Short
specialized bibliographies in editions of Colette's work or in critical
books or articles, as well as those listed in earlier published
bibliographies, have furnished us with many leads. Our researches have
led us into numerous libraries in Canada, the United States, Britain and
France, where we have consulted fiches, card catalogs, bound
bibliographies and computer records. The records of the National Library
of Canada in Ottawa, the Bibliothèque Nationale in Paris, the British
Museum in London, the Library of Congress in Washington, and the New
York Public Library have provided us with much information and
material. We have not hesitated to check our findings against lists
previously published. In particular, the first two volumes of the Pléiade
edition of Colette's *Œuvres* have provided us with much supplementary
detail about primary works up to 1923, as has the Cabeen *Critical
Bibliography of French Literature* for secondary ones.

Every attempt has been made to verify entries by personal inspection,
for both primary and secondary listings. In some cases we have had to
resort for verification to records we made long ago for another purpose. In
others, however, all our efforts to obtain a copy of the desired work have
come to naught, sometimes because no library consulted had or could
obtain a copy of the work in question, sometimes because it was of such
a transient or fragile nature that no copy was ever deposited in permanent
archives. Such is especially the case of some English editions, mostly
paper-back, designed for the mass market, where copies once available in
circulating libraries have long since become worn and been discarded; even
some of relatively recent date have proved unexpectedly elusive. Except in
a few cases, therefore, items whose existence could not be verified by
inspection have been omitted. In exceptional cases, where there was
sufficient information to render the authenticity of an entry certain, we
have provided the known data and added the indication "Not seen." This
applies to both primary and secondary entries, especially to book entries.
Contents of such entries have not been cross-referenced if those contents
are in any way doubtful.

Details about the Primary Bibliography

Excluded material

Public talks, *causeries*, radio broadcasts, and the like are not listed.

Manuscripts are not listed, even those known to have been deposited and catalogued in libraries for research purposes.

Reprints of books are not listed.

As we have already indicated, short pieces or extracts by Colette published in books or periodicals after their initial publication in book form have been included only when they could be verified. There is no doubt that unlisted ones do exist, and we should be grateful for any information that users might provide in locating them, so that they might be listed in a second edition.

Short passages in style studies, student anthologies and the like have been excluded unless the length or treatment of the passage renders them significant. This means that a book containing several pages of Colette text might not to be listed. *Apprendre à écrire*, the excellent student series by Cognet & Janet (Paris: Bellin. Coll. La Classe de français) is a case in point, for, although it does not appear in this bibliography, the 1960 edition contains 8 extracts from Colette's work in the first volume and 13 in the second.

Organization of material

Except in the first two and the last sections, primary entries have been organized by genre. Such a system may at first seem unattractive when dealing with a writer whose work is known to be little susceptible to classification. However, efforts to organize the material in other ways proved to be equally difficult, so that in the end the familiar classification by genre was the one adopted. Many of Colette's titles could logically be placed in two or even three different sections. In such cases, we have simply chosen whatever category seemed the most suitable.

There are nine sections. In the first or "Correspondence" section, the material is divided into three parts: collections of letters from Colette, uncollected letters from Colette arranged alphabetically by recipient, and English translations of Colette's letters. The inclusion of the few English translations in a separate sub-section was made necessary by the fact that the English entries do not correspond in any clear way to the French ones.

The second section also contains three parts. It lists the large collections of Colette's work in several volumes, such as the 1949-1950 Le Fleuron edition of her *Œuvres complètes*, the single-volume collections of pieces taken from several books, such as the *Textes choisis de Colette* prepared by Pierre Clarac, and the English collections. Again, this third, separate sub-section was made necessary because of the existence of several collections of translations of texts from more than one work. For example, the volume *Places* includes texts from six different French works.

The third section, "Memoirs, Chronicles and Reminiscences," includes what we believe to be Colette's most autobiographical works. They are a varied group, however. Among them are the dispassionate and even theoretical *Le Pur et l'impur*, the meditative reminiscences such as *L'Etoile vesper* and *Le Fanal bleu*, the childhood texts of *La Maison de Claudine* and *Sido*, which were long regarded as true but are now known to be partly invention, the probably factual *Noces*, and the controversial account of Colette's years with Willy, *Mes apprentissages*. Colette herself wrote, "L'erreur se prête facilement à l'écrivain qui veut dépeindre sa province et son passé. Il se persuade qu'il confronte ses souvenirs avec la seule vérité.... Il se trompe, il oublie."--The writer who wishes to depict her region or her past falls easily into error. She persuades herself that her memories furnish her with the truth.... She is mistaken, she forgets ("Ces dames anciennes," *Belles Saisons*, 1955). The works placed in this section are, we are convinced, based to a great extent on the details of Colette's life, but in dealing with them one must at no time disregard Colette's own warning.

The fourth section groups together novels and novellas. Colette's own designation of a work as one or the other has often seemed to carry with it a large dose of the arbitrary and bears little relationship to its length or other recognized criteria. We have therefore made no distinction between the two genres, and have placed them both in the same section. At least one novella, *Le sieur Binard*, is so short that it would normally be classified as a short story. Another, *Flore et Pomone*, which is usually published with three novellas but is essentially non-fictional, is not listed with the novellas but has instead been placed in section five.

The fifth section consists of the many volumes of short pieces that do not fall into the previous sections. Its title, "Essays, Articles and Short

Stories," is probably as close as one can get to defining their nature. A few, such as the texts of *La Femme cachée*, are clearly *contes* or short stories. *The Discours de réception* is the text of a public address. *Les Heures longues* is largely a series of reporting articles written during World War I. Many of the other collections of texts are, however, of a hybrid nature. That this is so becomes even more apparent when one discovers the extent to which Colette cut and added pieces for subsequent editions. Her habit of shifting short texts from book to book constitutes a bibliographer's nightmare. A glance at the entries for *La Chambre éclairée* illustrates the difficulties. Only 14 of the original 31 texts published in its first edition were retained for the Le Fleuron *Œuvres complètes* in 1949; during the preceding 29 years Colette had transferred most of the texts to other editions. One inclusion in this category deserves special mention: even though they might at first glance seem to belong to the second section, we have retained in the fifth section the three volumes of extracts about animals, *Bêtes libres et prisonnières*, *Chats de Colette* and *Chiens de Colette*, because they follow the pattern used by Colette herself with such books as *Découvertes* or *Prisons et paradis*, which are comprised of groups of texts on a theme. To this section we have also assigned *L'Envers du music-hall*, arbitrarily, some would say, since it is often classified among Colette's *chroniques*, but following the premise that it is more fictionalized than *La Maison de Claudine* or *Sido*; we hope that this judgment does not prove troublesome to users.

The sixth section consists of Colette's theater writing. The title "Theater and Spectacle" has been used to broaden the category sufficiently to permit inclusion of the libretto for *L'Enfant et les sortilèges*.

The brief seventh section is devoted to Colette's theater reviews, most of the known ones collected under the title of *La Jumelle noire*. English entries are grouped together at the end.

The equally brief eighth section lists together her film writing and her film criticism, both of them known to us chiefly through the Virmaux presentation. English entries are grouped together at the end.

The final section, "Miscellaneous Publications," incorporates all those items that do not fall into any of the other eight categories. It includes prefaces, contributions to collaborative works, publicity pieces, poems and similar material. All entries are arranged alphabetically by title, with English entries grouped together at the end.

Information about individual works

In so far as the parameters previously outlined permit and with already stated exceptions, works have been arranged alphabetically by title.

For each title, the following entries appear, and in this order: French editions arranged chronologically, cross-references to extracts or full inclusion in other entries, annotation, reviews arranged alphabetically by title of periodical, and, finally, English translations with British editions following American ones and both of them including cross-references to extracts and inclusions in other entries. Reviews apply to both French editions and translations, but are usually attached to the French editions. They are attached to the English editions only in those rare cases where the English title was published first or where there is no corresponding French title.

The following data is included for each edition: title; name of author appearing on the cover if not "Colette," in square brackets; place of publication; publisher; year of publication; number of pages; collection of which the volume was a part. Names of translators or illustrators may also be indicated, where pertinent. If the translator is the same for all editions, his or her name may be given in the annotation or, if there is a separate translator for each part of a book, in a section describing the partial contents. Size of book, type of paper and similar facts are not included.

Date of publication given is the one shown on the title page or, if none is shown, the actual date of printing or copyright.

Annotations include whatever information we have deemed most useful for users. Most are descriptive. Judgments made on the shortcomings or merit of specific works reflect our personal opinion and are offered only in a spirit of helpfulness.

Contents of each primary work are indicated where applicable, either in the annotation or in each entry. This information is especially important for works belonging to the fifth section, where there is little likelihood that all editions bearing the same title will have the same contents. One also finds instances of Colette's giving identical titles to two different short texts, as for example those titled "Hirondelles" in *En pays connu* and *Journal à rebours*, and those titled "Là-haut" in *Contes des mille et un matins* and *A portée de la main*. We have attempted to signal such areas of confusion, wherever possible.

The peripatetic history of so many of Colette's short texts has necessitated a fairly extensive network of cross-references. Both number and abbreviated title are used to identify cross-references. For the user's convenience, text titles of contents are sometimes added as well, but may refer either to the initial text title or to the new one, depending on which title will help to make identification of the text easier. Name of translator may also be given, if not easily ascertainable elsewhere.

Details about the secondary bibliography

Excluded material

Doctoral dissertations are not included unless published, because such a list, though useful, would too much extend the scope of this volume.

Encyclopædia-type entries are not listed, even though Colette's renown is such that a section on her is found in most standard encyclopædias.

The same situation obtains for histories of French literature, except in the case of a few passages significant by their length or content.

No correlation has been assumed between the length of an article and its usefulness to researchers. In other words, no minimum length is required for inclusion in this bibliography. A few entries designate only an anecdote or paragraph, though we have attempted to signal such brevity in the annotation.

Reviews are listed only for books and monographs and are generally those that are the most accessible. All have been verified.

The *Bulletin de la Société des Amis de Colette*, an informative newsletter distributed to members of the Société from 1962 to 1973, has not been included, despite its potential usefulness to researchers.

Organization of material

The secondary works have been divided into two sections: those published as independent works and those appearing as part of a longer work. Within those classifications they are arranged alphabetically by author. Several more elaborate systems of classification were tried, by means of which readers might be guided towards criticism on specific primary works or towards that applying a particular methodology or towards titles directed towards a particular public, but under all these systems few of the entries fell easily into their category. We therefore opted for the simplest and, we believe, the most useful system in the end.

Anonymous articles have been listed at the end of the articles section, alphabetically according to journal or newspaper. Although this is contrary to established practice, we believe it to be the most useful arrangement for users of this volume.

Annotations

The annotations of critical books and articles are in most cases descriptive. We have attempted to present them fairly and without bias. Little attempt has been made to assess the merits of the methodology used. Instead, an indication is usually given of the author's intentions, conclusions or opinions, and often the degree of success deemed to have been achieved.

There is no correlation between the length of an annotation and the merit or importance of the critical work it presents.

Annotations of my own articles have been written by Paul Fortier.

Style

In matters of style we have attempted to follow the dictates of the *Chicago Manual of Style*, 13th ed.

Because they are so numerous and in many cases not well known, titles of periodicals have been spelled out in full, except that the definite or indefinite article at the beginning of the title has usually been deleted from those listed in reviews and secondary articles.

In the case of French books, the number of pages indicated includes the page showing the printing justification, usually one or two pages after the table of contents or the last page of text.

In the case of articles or chapters in books, the name of the author is the same for both article and book unless the contrary is specifically indicated.

Numbering of entries is continuous from 0001 to 2271, except that one entry has been added at the last moment with the number 0752a. Entries designated only by the letters xxxx are indicators inserted in a useful place for the purpose of directing the user to information found elsewhere in the bibliography.

Contrary to established practice, we have chosen to provide page numbers for periodical entries, because our own experience has been that its inclusion saves users much time when they are attempting to locate a small text, particularly in newspapers.

Appendices

The lists of translations of Colette's work into German, Italian and Spanish have been compiled from published bibliographies, especially national bibliographies, current book listings and records of library holdings. Only a few of the entries have been verified by inspection. Some of the others have been verified through correspondence with the publisher. Scholars should therefore use these sections with caution.

The other appendices need no explanation.

And finally...

Clarity, accuracy and potential usefulness have been our watchwords during the preparation of this volume. We are resigned to the certainty that it contains errors and omissions, human nature not yet having achieved a stage that would guarantee any project's perfection. Whatever the defects of this bibliography are, however, it is our fervent hope that future users will benefit from its publication and be better able to find their way about among the treasures of Colette's world.

ACKNOWLEDGMENTS

Among the many persons whose names deserve to be mentioned at the beginning of this volume, the following can on no account be omitted:
--Richard Aftanis and Andrea Rinke, for casual assistance in the initial compilation of titles.
--Jocelyn McGuire, for her longer, more intensive and ill-paid labors during the project's early stages.
--Eleanor Reid Gibbard, for permission to use her published list of English editions of Colette's work as a precious base on which to build.
--Elsa Allen, John Allen, Philip Clark, Eugenia Desmond, Rosemarie Finlay, Katherine Horn, Juliette Laureyssens, Abel Martinez, Cristina Povoledo, Ernest Skublics and Kirsten Wolf, for small or great but always invaluable assistance with languages presenting special obstacles.
--librarians in the University of Manitoba Inter-Library Loan Section, especially Barbara Bennell and MaryAnn McCuaig, for their professional expertise, unfailing courtesy and unremitting efforts on my behalf over the past several years.
--Nicole Michaud-Oystryk and Sharon Tully, also of the University of Manitoba Libraries, for their prompt response to specific inquiries.
--Rosemary Dwyer and Father Harold Drake of St. Paul's College Library, for their willing service in filling my frequent and sometimes inconvenient special orders.
--staff members of the Bibliothèque Nationale in Paris, the British Museum Reading Room in London, the Library of Congress in Washington, the National Library of Canada in Ottawa, the New York Public Library and all the many other libraries that not only opened their

doors, but in some cases their stacks, to my searches and dealt generously with my submissions.

--all the unknown and unseen persons who answered my inquiries at the hundreds of other libraries contacted while this project was in process.

--those publishers and organizations that replied to letters requesting information or material, in particular Deborah Blackman of Plaza & Janès in Barcelona and Amy Einhorn of Farrar, Straus & Giroux for the special effort they exerted on my behalf.

--Lawrence Desmond, Paul Fortier and Isabelle Strong, my colleagues, who read the manuscript and offered many worthwhile suggestions.

--St. Paul's College of the University of Manitoba, and the Social Sciences and Humanities Research Council of Canada, for intermittent financial assistance.

--my sister, Jean Margaret Hopper, who has likely forgotten the mounds of pages she once typed on Colette before computers lightened the load.

--Marie Ellen Larcada, my editor, for her patience with a project whose duration seemed to prolong itself with every letter.

--and, finally, André Joubert, my colleague and former mentor, who first unveiled for me the riches of Colette's work, little knowing that it would one day come to this.

To all of these, as well as to the many unnamed persons who have, at one time or another, in one way or another, been instrumental in bringing this project to fruition, I offer immeasurable thanks.

D.N.

INTRODUCTION:
COLETTE IN THE WORLD

It would not be wrong to say that what is in this book represents Colette's world. Almost everything written by and about a writer who lived for eighty years, who never stopped writing for the last fifty of them, and whose glory remains untarnished during the nearly forty years since her death, will of necessity include most of the thoughts she expressed to others, as well as those projected towards her by writers known and unknown. Metaphorically, this means that her work has been like a sun, its rays streaming out through the world to illuminate other minds, which have responded in kind by praise or condemnation. This bibliography is not exhaustive, but it aims to be fairly complete, so it is in this way that what Colette wrote and what others wrote about her reflects a world centered upon her, which is hers alone.

When Colette put pen to paper to write her first novel, *Claudine à l'école*, nearly one hundred years ago, few people, and least of all she herself, anticipated that her renown would reach the world-wide proportions that it has. Indeed, her reputation is still that of a writer who typifies all that is French, one who is therefore by definition difficult for people beyond the French-speaking world to understand fully. For years, English-language critics treated her like an exotic food, a taste of which was a treat but the ingestion of which in large quantities was not to be thought of by any right-thinking person. Yet for all her "Frenchness" and for all the limitations accorded to her even by her compatriots, Colette's books have been translated into many languages and are now sold throughout the western world. There is a paradox here somewhere, and if it does not lie in the situation it must be found in Colette herself.

Who or what was Colette? Few writers have been judged from so many perspectives and with such a variety of results. The hundreds of articles, the thousands of words written on her are witness to this fact. Was she a literary genius, as some have insisted and as her enduring reputation seems to confirm? Or did the splendor of her prose simply gush forth from a pool of instinct like an artesian spring waiting to be tapped? Before modern critical methods began to unseal its secrets, her style was lauded by some as the product of just such a process. And what about the woman herself? Was she, as a few have claimed, a publicity-seeker, calculating, hard-working and ambitious, one who wrote mostly for money and published with an eye to the main chance? Still others have described her character in very different terms, never tiring of repeating that Colette was friend to everybody and everything, as generous with her time and her gifts as she was with words. And there is another question on which much ink has been spent. Was Colette a moral innocent or had she a perverted mind? Was she really, as the great André Gide once wrote, forever tainted by the milieu in which she spent the years of her first marriage? Or was she simply "pagan" and "amoral," the product of deficient maternal training? For decades critics depicted her as a sort of Demeter, an earth-mother bound to sensation, to nature and to animals, knowing and knowledgeable but oblivious of moral precepts current in French or any other civilized society. During those same years only a few braved popular opinion by rejecting the earth-mother thesis, viewing Colette's success instead as the logical product of a quick, discerning intelligence, exceptional in its linguistic sophistication and sense of poetry.

All of these contrary and often extreme views have at one time or another found purchase with Colette's public, for all have some validity in fact. But on one point readers have been in agreement, that of her greatest obsession. Among the faces of this multiple Janus there is one that no hostile critic ever denied: on page after page the young Gabrielle Colette gazes sorrowfully back, mourning her childhood.

"Qui me dira maintenant ce que j'étais alors?" she writes, of her own childish self--who will tell me now what I was then? And the plaintive reply: "Je m'y suis essayée, mais c'est de trop loin que je me vois"--I have tried but I see myself from too far away (*Autres bêtes*). The loss of, and the search for, the unified self has long been recognized as one of Colette's characteristic themes, but it is one on which scholarly study has only in recent years begun to show fruitful results.

During the past two decades Colette criticism has expanded in many directions, most of them with profit. A smattering of articles has focused on her shifting choice of names, detecting in these transitions a reflection not only of Colette's changing fortunes but also of her developing identity. Born Sidonie-Gabrielle Colette, in 1873, in a village in the French provinces, she was married at the age of twenty to a sophisticated, some would say decadent, Parisian many years her senior. Thus she became Madame Henry Gauthier-Villars, for respectable Paris at least. It was a name by which she was less well known, however, than the soubriquet Madame Willy, which echoed her husband's best-known literary pseudonym, the one under which her own first novels were published. In 1900 *Claudine à l'école*, and in succeeding years its three sequels, *Claudine à Paris*, *Claudine en ménage* and *Claudine s'en va*, bore Willy's name alone on the cover. It was only in 1904 that the *Dialogues de bêtes* were published and publicly proclaimed as the first sole work of his wife, Colette Willy.

This was just a beginning. After true authorship of the Claudine novels became known and once she had parted from Willy, the fledgling writer began to express her new-found independence by signing herself Colette (Colette Willy). This resort to parentheses seems a modest gesture to us today, and many have wondered why she continued to sign her books in this way long after 1912, when in private life she became the Baroness Colette de Jouvenel. Only in 1923 did she truly begin to use the two-syllable name by which Colette became a household word. And Colette she remained, even after her marriage with Maurice Goudeket some twelve years later.

Scholars interested in the evolution of Colette's independence have been quick to point out that hers is a recognized given name for a girl, that it seems therefore to represent an affirmation, on Colette's part, of her femininity. It was also her own family name before marriage, and so has been similarly interpreted as an expression of her tie to the masculine. There is no need to hark back to Colette's sentimental attachments to find meaning in this. The usual, and reasonable, conclusion arrived at by most of the scholars who mention it is that the name she finally chose for herself was the subconscious expression of an achieved ideal, of a rare androgyny of mind, and an even rarer synthesis of past and present. This may or may not be so. But there is no doubt that the many faces Colette seems to have shown the world, and the many talents and activities that characterized her life, are echoed in the peripetias of her nomenclature.

What does suggest itself as significant is that the choice of Colette, the one name that nearly all her previous, longer names contained within themselves, expresses a thread of unity which also runs through her writing. A quick look at the titles listed in this book shows that her work is diverse. Novels, short stories, essays, articles, plays and spectacles, journalistic reporting, drama criticism, film reviews, and prefaces, all jockey for room in a chronological listing. Yet these works are amazingly all of a piece. Is it because of her style, or because of her subject matter? Early critics frequently chastized Colette for being too subjective; they complained that she was always talking about herself. Emphasis on this reputedly widespread weakness of women writers, greatly indulged in by Colette, comforted many lesser talents whose names are now forgotten. Recent scholarship has shown, however, that even Colette's subjectivity is in part an illusion; much of the so-called reality that she portrays is actually invention. But the illusion remains, and it continues to be part of a signature that is as clearly inherent in her prose as is that of Chopin in his music. Whether relating fact or fiction, fantasy or boring conformity, Colette always spoke in the same true voice.

That her singular voice is in part the product of her unimpeachable style has at no time been in doubt. Not even her harshest critics have ever denied its perfection, or its uniqueness. In 1927, Jean Larnac, in one of the best early attempts to define her genius, wrote "Elle résiste à l'analyse. On ne peut que l'admirer"--She resists analysis; one can only admire her (*Colette, sa vie, son œuvre* [Paris: Kra, 1927], 225). As late as 1951 her great friend, writer Germaine Beaumont, echoed Larnac's words: "Colette échappe aux méthodes, aux formules, et même aux définitions"--Colette eludes method, formulas, and even definitions (*Colette par elle-même* [Paris: Seuil, 1951], 5). Critics have long made a great thing out of listing the features of Colette's style. It is not difficult to trace its special character to its transparency, to her habit of wedding the style completely to the subject so that the style conveys part of the meaning. Fortunately, modern techniques permit scholars to address themselves to these more enigmatic aspects of her work. Other writers may not be able to emulate Colette's style, but at least they may now understand it better.

For whom does Colette speak, and to whom? Some would say that she has always spoken for herself alone. Many paragraphs have been written interpreting her life's output as the expression of a long search for identity, of a struggle for a psychological unity whose achievement may or may not be reflected in Colette's choice of name. But part of her appeal lies in the fact that her favorite subjects--love, flowers, animals, the past, childhood, and the secret self--are familiar to humble and mighty alike, and to readers of all ages. In 1863, Baudelaire offered posterity one of his several definitions of beauty. "Le beau," he wrote, "est toujours, inévitablement, d'une composition double.... Le beau est fait d'un élément éternel, invariable, dont la quantité est excessivement difficile à déterminer, et d'un élément relatif, circonstanciel, qui sera, si l'on veut, tour à tour ou tout ensemble, l'époque, la mode, la morale, la passion" (*Le Peintre de la vie moderne*). In short, beauty, in literature as in other things, contains at one and the same time something that all the world recognizes as universal, and something topical, ephemeral, or unique to its creator. Colette's success might well be a demonstration of the truth of Baudelaire's statement.

Colette's universal appeal is amply illustrated in the popularity of her books, even in translation. In France, her name was a household word long before her death. Grand Officer of the French Legion of Honor, member of the Goncourt and the Belgian Academies, long touted, though to no effect, as the first female candidate for membership in the French Academy, she was the recipient of many honors on her home ground. Elsewhere, her best-known novels were read from the outset by sophisticated people, in translation as well as in the original. For the most part, however, published criticism conveys the impression that Colette's fame outside of France, especially in the English-speaking world, was for a long time very limited because Colette was just too French to be justly appreciated by other than the Gallic mind.

A careful perusal of these bibliographical listings will turn up facts that challenge this assumption. In France the early Claudines were such a commercial success that they inspired a whole line of Claudine products. Ice cream, collars, hats, ties, cigarettes, lotions, perfumes, cakes, and even photographic paper profited from the vogue there. But these early works were becoming known elsewhere, too, almost concurrently. One national bibliography lists early German translations of all the Claudine novels, under Willy's name of course, one of them, *Claudine in Paris*, actually appearing in 1901, the same year that it was published in French.

Unfortunately, our chances of examining these initial German translations are no longer good. Opposite most of the entries is appended the phrase "Im Deutschen Reiche verboten"--forbidden in the German Reich.

It was under her own name and on another front that Colette first became known in America, and a little later, too. In 1913 Desmond Fitzgerald brought out *Barks and Purrs*, Maire Kelly's translation of the *Sept dialogues de bêtes* for American readers. In England, Charlotte Remfry-Kidd's translation of *La Vagabonde* appeared in 1912, although in many ways it was Colette's animal pieces that created the initial impact there as well, if more modestly. Not only did *La Paix chez les bêtes* provoke at least two long and favorable reviews within a few months of its French publication, it also inspired the translation of one of its texts for the journal *Living Age*: "Mirette, the Story of a 'Too Little Dog'."

This same second decade of the century saw Colette's fame growing in Italy. In 1917, when World War I was still more than a year from over, Colette was in Rome, making the film version of her novel *La Vagabonde*. In fact, she had gone into the film business in a number of ways. She had become both critic and writer. Until 1974 her activities in this field were little recognized, for Colette did not collect her film work for publishing during her lifetime. It was not until the appearance of the Virmaux's splendid *Colette: au cinéma* that the full scope and enthusiasm of her film work finally became evident. Yet she had collaborated with the famous Musidora in a number of silent film ventures, especially in Italy. As early as 1911, moreover, the celebrated Italian critic, G.-A. Borgese, had termed her an "authentic writer," and shortly afterwards Renato Serro had written an article deploring publicity stunts exploiting the Claudine image but praising something treasurable in the early novels, the merit of which he attributed to Colette alone. In short, Colette's flourishing reputation in Italy during the second decade was but a continuation of an earlier beginning, the Claudine novels having appeared in Italian in 1906.

France, England, America, Italy--one scarcely counts the partly francophone Belgium and Switzerland--by 1920 the voice of this very French writer was being heard far beyond her national boundaries. And in the next two decades, generally deemed to be those of Colette's greatest achievements, her fame abroad spread sufficiently that critical articles and translations sprouted up like mushrooms.

These were the years of her conquest of Rumania. Silvia Butureaunu writes that by 1931 Colette's work, mostly in French but with one novel, *La Vagabonde*, already translated into Rumanian, was well known in that country. As a result, Colette visited Rumania, arriving there in March of 1931. She was accorded a lavish reception by both royalty and the press. It is curious that, although Colette wrote freely of her travels to America and North Africa, her Rumanian trip evoked from her very few published lines. On the other hand, it left a legacy with her hosts, for her work is still the focus in Rumania, not only of considerable popular attention, but also of much scholarly application.

The early 1930's saw a veritable flurry of translations into English, both in America and in Britain. In 1924, Princess Alexandre Gagarine's *Cats, Dogs and I*, an English version of *La Paix chez les bêtes*, had already strengthened Colette's reputation in England as an animal writer. During the next few years her novels, too, became immensely popular there, as Phyllis Mégroz, Viola Garvin, Frederick Blossom, Rosemary Carr Benét, and James Whitall successfully brought her work to a wider public. A similar movement occurred in the United States, though much of the rise in Colette's popularity on that side of the Atlantic must be attributed to Janet Flanner, who not only translated *Claudine à l'école* into English in 1930, but for many years publicized both writer and books through her regular "Paris Letter" in the *New Yorker*.

And so it continued. South America, Scandinavia, Africa, Asia: the light from Colette's sun streamed out from France and over the globe. Glancing through the bibliography, one notes a published talk on Colette by Luiz Annibal Falcão of Rio de Janeiro in 1933, a short appreciation by Kikou Yamata of Japan, another by P.S. Kogan of the Soviet Union, all in a very short period of time. In Scandinavia, Colette's influence on writer Cora Sandel, who was also her translator, is well known. In Egypt, Georges Dumani published the text of a long address on Colette in 1943. During World War II, editions of her books were brought out in Montreal, Mexico City, Geneva, Buenos Aires, Brussels and Barcelona. By 1945 the richness of Colette's voice was producing echoes, if sometimes in a small way, in all the inhabited continents of the world. The great flood of post-World War II editions, the spate of books and articles inspired by her centenary in 1973: these are by no means isolated phenomena, but manifestations of her ongoing world-wide popularity.

Given Colette's renown beyond France, it seems incomprehensible that her work has often been viewed as a challenge for translators. Yet its wealth of imagery makes it so. One could say that transposing a Colette book into another language is partly a matter of deciding which of its attractions one can most readily afford to do without. That her books have become popular in so many other languages therefore signifies something of a wonder.

Colette's appeal can be traced in part to a special synthesis of the universal and the particular. A passage on her favorite theme demonstrates this. "Aucun été, sauf ceux de mon enfance, ne commémore le géranium écarlate et la hampe enflammée des digitales," one reads. "Aucun hiver n'est plus d'un blanc pur"--No summer but the summers of my childhood can commemorate the scarlet geranium and the stocks of flaming foxglove; no winter nowadays is so pure a white (*Sido*). The same idea is echoed in dozens of other passages. Every feature of her childhood, she says, made it incomparable, infinitely superior to all other childhoods. Yet elsewhere she confesses that her case was not truly exceptional, for all happy childhoods are unique. In other words, the paradox is not really one, but an illusion. And so it is with every subject she portrays. Whether it be love, childhood or a good lunch, Colette speaks for herself and to herself, awakening at the same time, in the mind of every reader, an echo born of that person's own experience, however different from hers.

In 1950 Joseph Barry deplored the fact that Colette's work was not much known outside of France. That her international reputation has grown since then is true. However, all the evidence points to the fact that Colette has always had something of importance to say, even to those who can never appreciate her command of the French language, and these people have recognized this fact by reading her in translation. That Colette put everything about herself into her books, as so many critics were once wont to declare, is now acknowledged to be untrue, and the so-called autobiographical data that they often seem to furnish have been shown to be unreliable. But that her writing, in conjunction with the immense amount of published criticism about her, represents an ongoing dialogue with her readers, seems to us self-evident. The two main parts of this bibliography can be thought of as representing the dialogue's two voices.

This is the message that we have tried to convey in this introduction and that we hope the users of this bibliography will keep in mind when they consult its pages.

Donna M. Norell
St. Paul's College
University of Manitoba
Winnipeg, Canada

ABBREVIATIONS

Aug.	August
coll.	collection
Dec.	December
ed.	editor(s), or edition(s)
fasc.	fascicle
Feb.	February
front.	frontispiece
illus.	illustrations
introd.	introduction
Jan.	January
n.d.	no date
n.p.	no publisher, or no place of publication
no.	number(s)
non-pag.	non-paginated
Nov.	November
OC	item 0056
OCC	item 0055
OCLF	item 0054
OP	item 0053
Oct.	October
p.	page(s)
pref.	preface
rev.	revised
Sept.	September
trans.	translation
vol.	volume

WORKS BY COLETTE

CORRESPONDENCE

BOOK-LENGTH COLLECTIONS: FRENCH

UNE AMITIÉ INATTENDUE

0001 UNE AMITIÉ INATTENDUE: correspondance de Colette et de
Francis Jammes. Introd. and notes Robert Mallet. Paris: Emile-
Paul, 1945. 77p.

Ten letters from Colette and seven from Jammes, from April 1904
to April 1906, in which one can detect the development of a
reciprocal esteem. Most letters refer to the other's books, their
exchange of photographs and their common love of nature.
Contains Colette's request for Jammes' preface to *Sept dialogues de
bêtes*. Jammes portrays himself as a victim of current literary bias,
and more than once asks both Colette's and Willy's intercession on
his or a friend's behalf. Colette's touching final letter, in which she
proposes breaking off their correspondence because she has become
a theatrical performer, is of special interest, as is Jammes' long

reply, wherein he encourages her to continue writing to him and expresses once more his belief that her inner nature does not correspond to her public persona. Mallet's detailed notes are informative and his introduction valuable for its discussion of Jammes' influence on Colette. Colette's letters to Jammes also in *Lettres à ses pairs*.

EN TOURNÉE...

0002   EN TOURNÉE...: cartes postales à Sido. Pref. Michel del Castillo. Notes Michel Rémy-Bieth. Paris: Persona, 1984. 112p.

Extracts in *Album Masques: Colette* [item 1057], 100-1. Two postcards, one from Naples in Nov. 1910, the other from Tunis in March 1911.

Chiefly postcards from Colette to her mother, from 1905 to 1912, during the years when Colette toured as a music-hall performer. Most contain comments on landscapes, places visited or the hectic pace of the performer's life. Although many are rapidly written and none offer significant material, the collection is fascinating and provides an over-all impression of Colette's travels, activities and personality during one of the most interesting periods of her life. Also contains "Notes de tournées" from *Mes cahiers*. Del Castillo's preface is disappointing because of its evident lack of objectivity.

Reviews:
Esprit créateur 27 (Fall 1987): 101. Françoise-E. Dorenlot.
Figaro, 19 Oct. 1984, 28. Jean Chalon.
Magazine littéraire, no. 212 (Nov. 1984): 54-55. Jean-Louis Hue.

LETTRES A HELENE PICARD

0003 LETTRES A HELENE PICARD. Text established and annotated by Claude Pichois. Paris: Flammarion, 1958. 237p.

0004 LETTRES A HELENE PICARD. LETTRES AU PETIT CORSAIRE. Text established and annotated by Claude Pichois and Roberte Forbin. Geneva: Crémille, 1972. 323p. Contains items 0003 and 0010.

0005 LETTRES A HELENE PICARD, A MARGUERITE MORENO, AU PETIT CORSAIRE. Text established and annotated by Claude Pichois and Roberte Forbin. Pref. Maurice Goudeket. Paris: Flammarion, 1988. 232p.-356p.-153p. [individual pagination]. Contains items 0003, 0006 and 0010.

Also in *OCC*15 [item 0055].

Generally short letters from 1920 to 1942 show Colette working against deadlines, giving advice and encouraging a friend who must cope with failing health and a faltering career as poet. Contains several excellent descriptions of nature and informative details of Colette's financial difficulties of the 1930's. Includes some letters and a poem by Picard, also correspondence with Marguerite d'Escola upon Picard's death. Useful footnotes. Preceded by the final version of Colette's memorial text "Pour Hélène Picard," which was incorporated into *L'Etoile vesper*.

Reviews:
Carrefour, 2 July 1958, 11.
Figaro littéraire, 13 Dec. 1958, 2. André Rousseaux.
Monde, 23 Aug. 1958, 7. Robert Coiplet.

English translations: American

Extracts in *Letters from Colette* [items 0050-51]. Trans. Robert Phelps.

English translations: British

Extracts in *Letters from Colette* [item 0052]. Trans. Robert
Phelps.

LETTRES A MARGUERITE MORENO

0006 LETTRES A MARGUERITE MORENO. Text established and
annotated by Claude Pichois. Paris: Flammarion, 1959. 358p.

0007 LETTRES A MARGUERITE MORENO. Text established and
annotated by Claude Pichois. Geneva: Crémille, 1972. 327p.
Contents identical with those in item 0006.

Also in:
OCC 14 [item 0055]. Includes "Lettres de Colette à Marcel
Schwob," from *Lettres à ses pairs.*
Lettres à Hélène Picard, à Marguerite Moreno, au Petit Corsaire
[item 0005].

Extracts in:
Autobiographie... [items 0057-58].
Marcel Schwob et son temps [item 0046].

Letters date from 1902 to 1948, and include several from actress
Moreno as well as correspondence between Colette and Pierre
Moreno. Intimate in tone and content, these letters witness
Colette's deep friendship with one whom she once called *la moitié
de mon âme* [half of my soul]. Interesting lights on the literary
world of pre-World War I, and on Colette's difficult life during
World War II. References to persons and places in the otherwise
excellent footnotes are sometimes oblique. Preceded by Colette's
essay "A Marguerite Moreno," first published in *Figaro littéraire*
just after Moreno's death in 1948, then in the first edition of *Trait
pour trait*, and finally as part of *Le Fanal bleu.* Also includes item
1037, Colette's préface to Moreno's *Souvenirs de ma vie.*

Reviews:
Bulletin critique du livre français 17 (1962): 369.
Figaro, 16 Sept. 1959, 16. André Billy.
Figaro littéraire, 18 July 1959, 1, 8. Philippe Hériat.
Nouvelle Revue française 7 (Dec. 1959): 1099-1101. Roger Judrin.
Table ronde, no. 143 (Nov. 1959): 154-55. Roger Dardenne.

English translations: American

Extracts in:
Earthly Paradise [items 0082, 0084-85]. Trans. Derek Coltman.
Letters from Colette [items 0050-51]. Trans. Robert Phelps.

English translations: British

Extracts in:
Earthly Paradise [items 0087-89]. Trans. Derek Coltman.
Letters from Colette [item 0052]. Trans. Robert Phelps.

LETTRES A MOUNE ET AU TOUTOUNET

0008 LETTRES A MOUNE ET AU TOUTOUNET (Hélène Jourdan-
Morhange et Luc-Albert Moreau), 1929-1954. Pref. Bernard
Villaret. Paris: Eds. des femmes, 1985. 407p.

Contains many more letters to musician Jourdan-Morhange than to
painter Moreau. A few letters are to and from persons on the
periphery of their long-time friendship with Colette. Most letters
deal with every-day events, especially matters relating to summer
homes at Saint Tropez and vacations elsewhere. Some good
descriptive passages and fair coverage of difficulties during World
War II. Insufficient footnotes. Followed by Colette's preface to
Jourdan-Morhange's *Ravel et nous* and two other texts: "Florilège
(Luc-Albert Moreau vu par ses amis [1950])," and "L'opinion d'une
femme, Sortilèges." The last text is designated as uncollected but

under the title of "Sortilèges" it has been part of *Aventures quotidiennes* since 1924.

Review:
French Review 60 (April 1987): 712-13. Catherine Slawy-Sutton.

LETTRES A SES PAIRS

0009 LETTRES A SES PAIRS. Text established and annotated by Claude Pichois and Roberte Forbin. Paris: Flammarion, 1973. 455p.

Also in *OCC* 16 [item 0055]. Lacks letters to Marcel Schwob [moved to *Lettres à Marguerite Moreno* in *OCC* 14].

Extracts in:
Claudine en ménage [item 0403], 369: letter to Jeanne Muhlfeld.
Cardinal [item 1353], iii-iv: letter to Marcel Schwob.

The least cohesive volume of Colette's correspondence. Contains letters from 1893 to 1953, some previously published, which show Colette in relations with both famous and little-known literary figures and artists, among them Carco, Fargue, Houville, Jammes, Mauriac, Noailles, Proust, Ravel, Schwob, and Valéry. Some refer to Willy's role in Colette's early works. Letters vary in importance but illustrate her growing independence and maturity, both in epistolary style and in attitude to life. Grouped according to correspondent. Includes some letters to Colette from others, as well as extracts from works both by and on her. Pieces by Colette include an excerpt from her *Discours* and three portraits from *Trait pour trait* [Noailles, Mondor, Fargue]. For pieces on Colette by others, see Noailles, Hérriot, Dunoyer de Segonzac, and Fargue. Also index of names.

Reviews:
Books Abroad 48 (Autumn 1974): 728. Marguerite Girard.
Bulletin critique du livre français 28 (July 1973): 832.

Culture française 20 (Nov.-Dec. 1973): 363-64. Luigi Losito.
Esprit 41 (June 1973): 1397-98. Fernande Schulmann.
Figaro littéraire, 18 Aug. 1973, 2. Claudine Jardin.
Monde, 25 Jan. 1973, 20. G.G.-A. [Ginette Guitard-Auviste].
Revue générale 4 (April 1973): 85-87. Arnold de Kerchove.
Times Literary Supplement, no. 3718 (8 June 1973): 647.

English translations: American

Extracts in *Letters from Colette* [items 0050-51]. Trans. Robert
Phelps.

English translations: British

Extracts in *Letters from Colette* [item 0052]. Trans. Robert
Phelps.

LETTRES AU PETIT CORSAIRE

0010 LETTRES AU PETIT CORSAIRE. Text established and annotated
by Claude Pichois and Roberte Forbin. Pref. Maurice Goudeket.
Paris: Flammarion, 1963. 157p.

Also in:
OCC 16 [item 0055].
Lettres à Hélène Picard. Lettres au Petit Corsaire. Item 0004.
Lettres à Hélène Picard, à Marguerite Moreno, au Petit Corsaire.
Item 0005.

Extracts in *Autobiographie...* [items 0057-58].

Chiefly letters to Renée Hamon from 1932 until her premature
death in 1943. Of Breton stock, Hamon had a taste for exotic
travel, hence the title. Reveals Colette's tendency to help others
being reciprocated by Hamon's food shipments to her during the

war. Also contains excerpts from Hamon's journal and notebook, which demonstrate the extent of her obsession with Colette. Preceded by Colette's preface to Hamon's *Aux Iles de la lumière.*

Reviews:
Revue de Paris 70 (May 1963): 37-45. Emmanuel Berl.
Revue des sciences humaines, no. 111 (July-Sept. 1963): 415-17. Francis B. Conem.

English translations: American

Extracts in:
Earthly Paradise [items 0082, 0084-85]. Trans. Derek Coltman.
Letters from Colette [items 0050-51]. Trans. Robert Phelps.

English translations: British

Extracts in:
Earthly Paradise [items 0087-89]. Trans. Derek Coltman.
Letters from Colette [item 0052]. Trans. Robert Phelps.

LETTRES DE LA VAGABONDE

0011 LETTRES DE LA VAGABONDE. Text established and annotated by Claude Pichois and Roberte Forbin. Introd. Claude Pichois. Paris: Flammarion, 1961. 296p.

0012 LETTRES DE LA VAGABONDE. Text established and annotated by Claude Pichois and Roberte Forbin. Introd. Claude Pichois. Geneva: Crémille, 1972. 295p. Contents identical with those in item 0011.

Also in *OCC*15 [item 0055].

Extracts in *Autobiographie...* [items 0057-58].

Letters chiefly to Georges Wague, Colette's music-hall partner, to Léon Hamel, a long-time friend of her music-hall days, and to Léopold Marchand, whose collaboration with Colette began in 1919. Topics discussed are many: money, travel, vacations, pets, theater engagements and personalities, and marital situations. A development toward maturity in Colette's letter-writing style is discernible. Together, the letters, which date from 1906 to 1953, provide valuable insight into Colette's theatrical activity. Useful footnotes. Appendix contains a 1906 article by Fernand Hauser on Colette and "Missy," and three by Colette: a music-hall review of 1913, a portrait of Léopold Marchand, and a brief passage on Wague.

Reviews:
Figaro, 2 Aug. 1961, 3. André Billy.
Nouveau Candide, 6 July 1961, 15. Dominique Aury.
Nouvelles littéraires, 15 June 1961, 1, 7. Edith Mora.
Revue des deux mondes 14 (15 July 1961): 310-11. Gérard d'Houville.
Times Literary Supplement, no. 3126 (26 Jan. 1962): 52.

English translations: American

Extracts in:
Earthly Paradise [items 0082, 0084-85]. Trans. Herma Briffault.
Letters from Colette [items 0050-51]. Trans. Robert Phelps.

English translations: British

Extracts in:
Earthly Paradise [items 0087-89]. Trans. Herma Briffault.
Letters from Colette [item 0052]. Trans. Robert Phelps.

SIDO: LETTRES A SA FILLE

0013 SIDO: LETTRES A SA FILLE. Preceded by unpublished letters
from Colette. Prefaces Bertrand de Jouvenel, Jeannie Malige and
Michèle Sarde. Paris: Eds. des Femmes, 1984. xxiii-523p.
Contains mostly letters to Colette from her mother. Letters by
Colette all date from after her mother's death. However, they do
include a letter to Colette's second husband, Henry de Jouvenel,
one to his first wife, Claire Boas, three to his son Renaud and
one to his son Bertrand. Most of Colette's voluminous
correspondence to her mother was destroyed after the latter's
death in 1912. Despite the paucity of letters from Colette to her
mother and the rarity of footnotes, this volume is an essential
document for those seeking to understand the relations between
Colette and her mother, since Sido's letters humanize the
idealized portrait Colette presents of her in most of her works.
They demonstrate her concern for Colette's welfare, her faith in
her daughter's ability to write, her "modern" ideas on morality
and love, and her own loneliness and courage. Informative
details on relations within the Colette family, on Colette's and
Sido's change of attitude towards Willy, and on the suffering of
Sido's last years are valuable. Some passages are clearly source
material for *Sido* and *La Naissance du jour*. Several letters had
previously been published in item 1422 Sidonie Landoy
Colette, and one in item 1951 Parinaud. See item 1273 Boivin
for index and commentary.

Extracts in *La Naissance du jour* [item 0592], 169-71.

Reviews:
Esprit 10-11 (Oct.-Nov. 1984): 323. Fernande Schulmann.
Esprit créateur 27 (Fall 1987): 101. Françoise Dorenlot.
Figaro, 22 June 1984, 33. Jean Chalon.
French Review 60 (Feb. 1987): 401-2. Joan Hinde Stewart.
Magazine littéraire, no. 212 (Nov. 1984): 54-55. Jean-Louis Hue.
Quinzaine littéraire, no. 423 (1 Sept. 1984): 19. Leïla Sebbar.

UNCOLLECTED LETTERS: FRENCH
alphabetically, by recipient

0014 "Une lettre de Colette Willy à propos de ses débuts comme auteur dramatique, actrice et danseuse." *Le Damier*, no. 2 (April 1905): 26-27. Followed by item 0387 "Lettre de Claudine à Renaud." Authorship slightly doubtful, according to D'Hollander. Colette rejects the suggestion that she has major ambitions in the theater and thanks those who have permitted her to be a success thus far in her own small way. First letter also in item 0002 *En tournée*, 102; item 1058 *Les Albums de Colette: naissance d'un écrivain*, 110; and *Femmes et littérature*, 96B. Romorantin: Martinsart, 1980.

0015 Open letters to readers of *Paris-Théâtre* and *Paris-Journal*. Extracts in item 1057 *Album Masques: Colette*, 59-61. Exchange of letters by Colette and Willy in the public press in the fall of 1909 debated their collaboration on the Claudine novels. Colette insisted that the works were hers and that the scabrous elements were Willy's. *Paris-Théâtre* was favorable to Colette, while *Paris-Journal* took Willy's side of the quarrel. The tone of the letters is very acerbic. See *OP*1, xcix-cix, for Pichois' discussion of the exchange.

0016 Letters to Natalie Clifford Barney. In *Autour de Natalie Clifford Barney*, by François Chapon, Nicole Prévot and Richard Sieburth, under the direction of Georges Blin, 22-24. Paris: Université de Paris (Bibliothèque littéraire Jacques Doucet), 1976. Catalogue lists 20 letters from Colette, from Nov. 1904 to July 1953, and gives text of three. The first letter pre-dates Colette's divorce from Willy and alludes to Barney's move to Neuilly. The second offers suggestions for a house-warming gift. The third acknowledges receipt of a photograph and comments on Danièle Delorme's success as Gigi.

xxxx Letters to Natalie Clifford Barney. In item 1185 Barney, 204-5. Letter of Dec. 1946 thanking Barney for a parcel of food, and one of Jan. 1950 acknowledging receipt of a photograph. Letter of 1950 also in item 0016 Barney, and extract in item 1057 *Album Masques: Colette*, 99.

0017   Letter to Philippe Berthelot. In "Philippe Berthelot," by Daniel
       Langlois-Berthelot. *Nouvelle Revue des deux mondes*, June
       1976, 581. Undated note expressing condolences. The deceased
       person is not identified.

0018   Letters to Pierre Boissie [Roger Valbelle]. In item 1589 Frugier.
       Three letters concerning the "Collection Colette," published
       between 1923 and 1925 by Ferenczi and for which Colette chose
       the selections.

0019   Letters to Pierre Brisson. "C'est terrible d'avoir raison tous les
       deux!" *Figaro littéraire*, 20 Jan. 1973, 15. Presented by Jean-
       François Brisson. Six letters from Colette to Brisson and one
       from Brisson to her. The first letter finds Colette making
       changes in *La Seconde* in Dec. of 1928, for publication in *Les
       Annales*, then directed by Brisson. Those of twenty years later
       find her being reconciled with him after a disagreement. Brisson
       was then director of *Le Figaro*.

0020   Letters to Yvonne Brochard and Thérèse Sourisse. In "Six lettres de
       Colette aux Petites Fermières," by Marie-Thérèse Colléaux.
       Cahiers Colette, no. 10 (1988): 15-34. Colette corresponded
       with the "little farmers," Brochard and Sourisse, from 1933
       until her death. They frequently sent her much-needed supplies
       of food during World War II. In all, 264 letters from Colette to
       the two women are known, all but seven addressed to Brochard
       alone, the others either to Sourisse or to both women. They
       remain unpublished, with the exception of the six letters here,
       dated 27 Feb. 1933, 3 Feb. 1942, 8 July 1942, 26 Sept. 1943,
       5 Feb. 1945 and 30 Aug. 1947. The letters are preceded by a
       brief biography of Brochard and an introduction which
       highlights a feature of much of Colette's correspondence:
       though her epistolary style is familiar in tone, the contents
       rarely go beyond the superficial. The 1942 letter in which
       Colette expresses her joy at Maurice Goudeket's return from the
       concentration camp is a rare exception. Colléaux's commentary
       is excellent.

xxxx   Letters to Claude Chauvière. In item 1072 Chauvière, 121-23. Two
       letters offering advice on writing.

xxxx Letter to Gabriele D'Annunzio. In item 2160 Tosi. Letter of 1915
expressing admiration for D'Annunzio and confirming their new
friendship. Also a telegram of 1928.

0021 "Lettre de Colette à Lucie Delarue-Mardrus." *Les Pharaons*, no. 17
(Winter 1974): 34-35. Facsimile of undated hand-written letter
in which Colette gives her friend advice about writing.

0022 Letters to Queen Elisabeth of Belgium. In "Colette et la Reine
Elisabeth," by Georges-Henri Dumont. *Revue générale*, no. 2
(Feb. 1986): 11-17. Eight letters and partial letters dated from
April 1936 to Feb. 1954. Dumont traces Colette's relationship
with Queen Elisabeth and attempts to define its nature. The two
women struck up a friendship at the time of Colette's election
to the Belgian Academy. When Colette was confined to her bed
with arthritis, she received several personal visits from the
Queen, which are acknowledged in these letters. Followed by
three letters from Maurice Goudeket to the Queen after Colette's
death.

0023 Letters to François Fracchia. "Lettres inédites à un Tropézien." In
item 1060 *Autour de Colette à Saint-Tropez*, non-pag. [11-40].
Ten letters, in facsimile and dating from 1926 to 1936, to the
entrepreneur in charge of renovations to Colette's summer home
at Saint Tropez. One announces the house's change of name
from Tamaris-les-Pins to La Treille Muscate. Most stress the
urgency of completing work. Some furnish information on
financial arrangements; many provide details, even diagrams, of
changes to be made to the building. This collection comprises
valuable biographical material.

0024 Letter to Anatole France [extract]. In "Propos," by Gaston
Palewski. *Nouvelle Revue des deux mondes*, no. 12 (Dec.
1978): 623. Written during the early years of Colette's marriage
to Willy. Colette thanks France for a book and for his kindness
to her during her illness.

xxxx Letters to Maurice Goudeket. In item 1092 *La Douceur de vieillir*.
Memoirs of Colette's third husband contain many passages from
unpublished correspondence between him and Colette, but lack
of specific dates or other documentation renders their usefulness
minimal.

0025   Letter to André Hamard. In item 1058 *Les Albums de Colette: naissance d'un écrivain*, 131-32. Fac-simile of handwritten letter written about a year before Colette's death to a resident of Châtillon-Coligny. Colette nostalgically recalls the time she lived there with her brother.

0026   Letters to Colette de Jouvenel. In item 1072 Chauvière, 249-54. Three fascinating letters to Colette's daughter at school. She offers standard advice on many matters, often admonishing the girl to apply herself to her studies, to refrain from smoking and to write more often. Includes interesting comments on self-discipline and human nature. Although these are not significant letters, they do reveal Colette in an intimate situation and at her most natural.

0027   "Lettres de Colette à Renaud de Jouvenel." *Revue de Paris* 73 (Dec. 1966): 3-19. Letters and excerpts, mostly undated but covering the years 1920-1952. Renaud de Jouvenel's introduction offers fascinating remarks about Colette and Henry de Jouvenel, who was Renaud's father and Colette's second husband. Content is mostly trivial but several letters include comments on Colette's work. The personal tone reveals her real affection for the step-son she called "le Kid."

0028   Letter to Jacques de Lacretelle. In "Jacques de Lacretelle," by André Maurois. *Livres de France* 27:6 (1959): 2-11. Article includes fac-simile of hand-written, undated business letter from Colette, asking Lacretelle to visit her at the offices of *Le Matin*.

0029   "Lettre à M. Yves Le Béchec." *Cahiers Colette*, no. 9 (1987): 3-4. Letter of 28 July 1945 in which Colette thanks Béchec for gifts of butter. A rural schoolteacher, Le Béchec frequently sent her dairy products during World War II.

0030   Letter to François Mauriac. In *François Mauriac*, edited by Jean Touzot, 195. Paris: L'Herne, 1985. Brief letter of 1932, expressing admiration for Mauriac's novels.

0031   Letters to Robert de Montesquiou. In "Colette et Robert de Montesquiou, d'après leur correspondence inédite," by Joy Newton and Jean-Pierre Bruel. *Kentucky Romance Quarterly* 25 (May 1978): 213-24. A discussion of Colette's relations with

writer and esthète Count Robert de Montesquiou, with extracts
from letters written between May 1905 and June 1909, during
one of the most unsettled periods of Colette's life. One finds
Colette exchanging books with Montesquiou, concurring in his
admiration of Beardsley's work, and expressing her concern for
Montesquiou's good opinion. It was at one of Montesquiou's
receptions that Colette met the Countess Anna de Noailles,
with whom she would become good friends.

0032 Letter to Madame Luc-Albert Moreau [extract]. In *Hommages à
Luc-Albert Moreau: exposition de ses estampes et livres
illustrés*, 4. Paris: Bibliothèque Nationale, 1949. Pamphlet for
an exhibition of the works of Moreau, who had died the year
before, contains letter describing Moreau as a born artist and a
great one. A close friend of Colette's, he was one of her favorite
illustrators.

0033 Letters to Marguerite Moreno [extracts]. In item 1986 Pichois, xl-
xli, xlviii-xlix. Letters not included in *Lettres à Marguerite
Moreno* furnish details of Colette's relations with Bertrand de
Jouvenel [26 Aug. 1920 and 22 Oct. 1924] and Maurice
Goudeket [7 May 1925]. Excellent commentary by Pichois
sheds light on Colette's sentimental attachments.

0034 Letters to Pierre Moreno [extracts]. In item 1091 Giry, 172-74. In
one letter, Colette offers Pierre Moreno advice on the raising of
his children. In another, she alludes to the inaccuracy of the
word "complete" to describe the *OCLF*, then in preparation.

0035 Letters to the Marquise de Morny. "Lettres de Colette à Missy." In
item 1057 *Album Masques: Colette*, 96-98. Two undated
letters, with partial fac-simile, to Colette's companion from the
time of her divorce to her involvement with Henry de Jouvenel.
The first expresses a desire to be at Rozven with Missy and
refers to a wrist-watch given her by Auguste Hériot. The other,
written after Colette had met Maurice Goudeket, recounts every-
day events at Saint Tropez, where she and Goudeket were
vacationing.

xxxx Letters to Elie Moroy. In item 1895 Monnier. Three brief letters of
1922, 1928 and 1929, none significant. In one, Colette refuses
to comment on her own work or its place in feminine literature.

0036   Letters to Jeanne and Lucien Muhlfeld. In item 0403 D'Hollander, 367-69. Five letters and cards contain details about the publication of *Claudine en ménage* and its pre-edition, *Claudine amoureuse*. Commentary by D'Hollander provides valuable biographical detail.

0037   Letters to Musidora [pseud. of Jeanne Roques]. "Colette et le cinéma muet (souvenirs de Musidora)." In item 0980 *Colette: au cinéma*, 303-9; item 1188 Barrot, 301-3; and item 1359 Cazals, 195-99. Two letters first published in *L'Ecran français*, 13 Feb. 1950. Colette praises Musidora's acting in the film *La Flamme cachée* (1918), for which she had written the scenario. The film has since been lost, so that Colette's remarks, as well as those by Musidora on Colette's film activities, are extremely valuable to researchers.

xxxx   Letters to Musidora [pseud. of Jeanne Roques]. In item 1917 Musidora. Many letters and extracts, most of them dated from about 1911 to early World War I. Content is trivial but one can follow the development of the friendship between the two women.

xxxx   Letters to Musidora [pseud. of Jeanne Roques]. In item 1918 Musidora. Two short undated notes included in a special homage issue published upon Colette's death. Both are trivial in content, although one refers to the film *La Flamme cachée* and the other to Colette's work as war correspondent at Verdun during World War I.

0038   Letter to Marie Noël. In "Colette et Marie-Noël," by Lucien Hérard. *Mémoires de l'Académie des sciences, arts et belles-lettres de Dijon* 122 (3 June 1973): 465-66. Letter of 16 May 1927 expressing admiration for Noël's *Les Chansons et les heures* and reminding her that they are from the same region. Followed by Noël's "farewell letter," written after Colette's death and saying that she has requested a mass for Colette in her native Puisaye.

0039   Letters to Louis Piérard and to Dufrane Friart. *Trois cent trente-deux lettres à Louis Piérard*, edited by Marianne Pierson-Piérard, 101-3. Paris: Minard, 1971. Four letters to and one about Piérard, all except one undated but written at various periods of

Colette's life. All are brief and acknowledge Piérard's good-will or his efforts at making her work known in Belgium.

0040 Letter to Francis Poulenc. *Revue de Paris* 74 (Oct. 1967): 34. Also in *Correspondance: Francis Poulenc, 1915-1963*, 83-84. Paris: Seuil, 1967. Letter of 1931, commenting on features of poems by Apollinaire. A brief passage on the beauties of Saint Tropez weather witnesses to Colette's flair for spontaneous description.

0041 Letters to Jeanne Pouquet [de Caillavet]. In item 1855 Maurois, 103-4. Three fragments, one dated 13 Feb. 1948, the others undated but possibly 1949. Colette and Willy had been friends of the young Gaston de Caillavet and his bride Jeanne during the 1890's, when they frequented the salon of Gaston's mother, Madame Arman de Caillavet. For over two decades after the quarrel with Madame Arman, they remained estranged from the young couple, but gradually Colette resumed relations with Jeanne. Maurois insists that Jeanne de Caillavet was the model for "La Rose-Chou" of *Claudine en ménage*. In the first letter, Colette declares that she has a clear picture in her mind of Jeanne's youthful beauty, and asks her for a photograph. In the second letter she declares that she often looks at an available picture of Gaston and at the concierge's photograph of Jeanne. Fragment of a third letter thanks Jeanne for a photograph.

0042 Letters to Marcel Proust. "Dixième anniversaire de la mort de Colette: deux lettres inédites de l'auteur de 'Chéri' à Proust." *Figaro littéraire*, 23 July 1964, 1. Two letters, the first tentatively dated by Philip Kolb at May 1895 and the other at July 1921. In the first letter Colette acknowledges receipt of a letter from Proust to Willy, and says how much she and her husband had enjoyed hearing Proust recite his own poetry. The 1921 letter praises Proust's *Sodome et Gomorrhe*; Colette says it may be the definitive work on homosexuality. Also in *Lettres à ses pairs*, all eds.; *Quinzaine littéraire* 159 (1 March 1973): 5. The 1895 letter is also in *Correspondance: Marcel Proust*, edited by Philip Kolb, vol. 1, 383-84. Paris: Plon, 1970.

0043 Letter to Henry Prunières. *Revue musicale*, 1 April 1925, 109. Colette apologizes for being unable to collaborate on that issue because of bronchitis and related problems. Follows Prunière's long and favorable review of *L'Enfant et les sortilèges*.

0044 Letter to Rachilde. In "Le mystère des Claudine enfin éclairci!"
      Figaro littéraire, 20 Jan. 1973, 15. In a letter of 1900, Colette
      acknowledges her authorship of *Claudine à l'école* and Willy's
      role in their completion. In a much longer letter to Rachilde,
      Willy also acknowledges their collaboration and praises his
      wife's talent. These two letters were the subject of a public
      exchange of letters, in which Colette's daughter, Colette de
      Jouvenel, protested that their publication was intended to show
      her mother in an unfavorable light (*Figaro littéraire*, 3 Feb.
      1973, 14). Jean Chalon refuted the protestations in the same
      issue.

0045 Letters to Maurice Ravel. In "'L'Enfant et les sortilèges':
      correspondance inédite de Ravel et Colette," by Arbie Orenstein.
      Revue de Musicologie, 52:2 (1966): 215-20. Traces Colette's
      collaboration with Ravel on their famous opera-ballet. Includes
      letters and extracts from 1919 to 1925, as well as details of the
      project's reception by the public. Ravel is shown to be the
      dominant partner. Three of the Colette letters are reprinted in
      Lettres à ses pairs. One letter is reprinted in item 1500 Druilhe,
      9; and in *Ravel et nous*, by Hélène Jourdan-Morhange, 68, 127.
      Geneva: Eds. du Milieu du monde, 1945; also extracts in item
      1742 Jourdan-Morhange.

xxxx Letter to Louis de Robert. In item 2056 Robert, 278. Letter of
      1910. Colette praises Robert's books and expresses hostility
      towards those who use clichés when talking or writing about
      feminine sensibility.

0046 Letters to Marcel Schwob. In *Marcel Schwob et son temps*, by
      Pierre Champion, 272-85. Paris: Grasset, 1927. Includes some
      of Colette's earliest letters known. The collection covers the
      whole period of Colette's friendship with Schwob, beginning in
      1894 and ending with his death in 1902. The earliest letters are
      interesting because of their youthful exuberance and sometimes
      playful style. Contents are generally trivial, but include
      anecdotes as well as descriptions of animals and landscapes and
      references to Schwob's declining health. The last few letters are
      to Marguerite Moreno, Schwob's wife and Colette's life-long
      friend. Letter of 1894 is also in item 1353 Cardinal, iii-iv; and
      fragments of several in item 1072 Chauvière, 53-54. See also
      Lettres à ses pairs and *Lettres à Marguerite Moreno*.

0047 Letters to Madame Sigrist de Cesti. "Lettres inédites de Colette."
 Europe, no. 631-32 (Nov.-Dec. 1981): 129-31. Five letters and
 a post-card signed Colette de Jouvenel, all written from Lake
 Como, where Colette was staying in the fall of 1916. All deal
 with the sale of Italian rights for the scenario of a film to be
 based on *Claudine à l'école* and *Claudine à Paris*. They show
 Colette to be an astute bargainer. None of the negotations bore
 fruit.

0048 Letter to Lucien Solvay. In item 1058 *Les Albums de Colette:
 naissance d'un écrivain*, 332-33. Fac-simile of handwritten letter
 in which Colette comments on the metamorphosis of *Minne*
 and *Les Egarements de Minne* into *L'Ingénue libertine*.

xxxx Letters to Jean Stévo. In item 2128 Stévo. Fac-simile of hand-
 written letter of 16 Nov. 1952. Affirms Colette's ties with
 Belgium.

0049 Letters to Paule Tondut. "Lecture de lettres inédites à une jeune
 Tropézienne." In item 1060 *Autour de Colette à Saint-Tropez*,
 non-pag. [147-53]. When Tondut was four years old, her parents
 sold Colette the property at Saint Tropez that she would name
 La Treille Muscate. Few of these 8 letters, cards and dedications
 are dated but they were written during the two decades preceding
 1949. Personal in tone, though without significant content,
 they show Colette interested in life at Saint Tropez long after
 she had ceased to hold property there.

xxxx See also item 1072 Chauvière. Includes many passages from letters
 both to and from Colette, with little concern for documentation.
 Complete letters are annotated separately [Schwob, Chauvière,
 Colette de Jouvenel].

xxxx See also item 1109 Malige. Includes many fragments of letters
 published elsewhere.

xxxx See also items 1986-87 Pichois, who quotes many passages from
 letters both to and from Colette. Not all of them have been
 published elsewhere.

BOOK-LENGTH COLLECTIONS: ENGLISH TRANSLATIONS

LETTERS FROM COLETTE

Selection and trans. Robert Phelps. Chosen from *Lettres à Hélène Picard*, *Lettres à Marguerite Moreno*, *Lettres de la Vagabonde*, *Lettres au Petit Corsaire*, *Lettres à ses Pairs*. Arranged chronologically. Some notes.

Reviews:
Best Sellers 40 (Dec. 1980): 338. Sharon J. Kobritz.
Booklist 77 (1 Dec. 1980): 499.
Christian Science Monitor 73 (11 March 1981): 17. Alexandra Johnson.
Guardian Weekly 124 (8 March 1981): 18. Mina Curtiss.
Kirkus Reviews 48 (1 Oct. 1980): 1326.
Library Journal 105 (15 Nov. 1980): 2412. Marcia G. Fuchs.
Literary Review 47 (May 1982): 1-2. Simon Blow.
London Magazine 22 (June 1982): 97-99. Helen Harris.
London Review of Books 5 (6 Oct. 1983): 14-15. Brigid Brophy.
New Statesman 103 (2 April 1982): 23. David Montrose.
New York Review of Books 28 (2 April 1981): 6-9. Diane Johnson. Also in *Terrorists and Novelists*, 58-67. New York: Knopf, 1982.
New York Times Book Review, 16 Nov. 1980, 16. Doris Grumbach.
New Yorker 56 (29 Dec. 1980): 69-72. John Updike.
Progressive 45 (March 1981): 61.
Publishers' Weekly 218 (24 Oct. 1980): 38.
Punch 282 (5 May 1982): 749. Mary Anne Bonney.
Quarto, no. 27 (April 1982): 7. Anne Caulkin.
Time 117 (26 Jan. 1981): 76. Gerald Clarke.
Virginia Quarterly Review 57 (Autumn 1981): 126.
Washington Post Book World, 18 Jan. 1981, 4. Mina Curtiss.
Washington Post Book World, 4 Sept. 1983, 12.

American editions

0050 LETTERS FROM COLETTE. New York: Farrar, Straus & Giroux, 1980. xii-194p.

0051 LETTERS FROM COLETTE. New York: Ballantine, 1983. xii-194p.

British editions

0052 LETTERS FROM COLETTE. London: Virago, 1982. x-214p.

MULTI-VOLUME COLLECTIONS
and
SINGLE-VOLUME COLLECTIONS OF TEXTS FROM SEVERAL WORKS

MULTI-VOLUME COLLECTIONS

0053 ŒUVRES. Paris: Gallimard, 1984- . Coll. Bibliothèque de la
Pléiade, nos. 314 and 327 [2 vols. of projected 4]. Published
under the direction of Claude Pichois. Collaborators on vol. 1:
Alain Brunet, Léon Delanoë, Paul D'Hollander, Jacques Frugier,
Michel Mercier and Madeleine Raaphorst-Rousseau.
Collaborators on vol. 2: Bernard Bray, Alain Brunet, Léon
Delanoë, Maurice Delcroix, Jacques Dupont, Jacques Frugier,
Michel Mercier, Madeleine Raaphorst-Rousseau and Yannick
Resch. Only two of the four eventual volumes in this compact,
beautifully bound and carefully documented series were
published before 1988. Footnotes and an up-to-date primary
bibliography are provided for each work, as well as extensive
appendices, maps, notes on variants or manuscripts, and
information on publication history. Presentation of works is
chronological, according to the date of first publication. First
two volumes cover titles to 1923. A long preface by Claude

Pichois and a detailed chronology by Jacques Frugier for the
pertinent years head up each of the first two volumes; both are
annotated separately. Notices on specific works by collaborators
are detailed but are not annotated separately. Long anticipated by
scholars, this prestigious edition will surely be deemed the
definitive one for research purposes. Contents of vol. 1:
*Claudine à l'école. Claudine à Paris. Claudine en ménage.
Claudine s'en va (journal d'Annie). L'Ingénue libertine. La
Retraite sentimentale. Les Vrilles de la vigne. La Vagabonde.*
Contents of vol. 2: *Douze dialogues de bêtes. La Paix chez les
bêtes. Autres bêtes. Notes de tournées. L'Envers du music-hall.
L'Entrave. Les Heures longues. Dans la foule. Mitsou. Chéri.
La Chambre éclairée. La Maison de Claudine. Le Voyage
égoïste. Le Blé en herbe.* «La Vérité sur *Chéri*», by Bertrand de
Jouvenel [annotated separately]. References to this edition in
other sections of the bibliography use the abbreviation *OP*
followed by the volume number.

Reviews:
Europe, no. 667-68 (Nov.-Dec. 1984): 189-94. Pierre Gamarra.
Express, no. 1714 (18 May 1984): 92-93. Jean-Didier Wolfromm.
Figaro, 18 May 1984, 32. André Brincourt.
Figaro, 18 May 1984, 32. Jean Chalon.
Figaro, 19 Oct. 1984, 28. Jean Chalon.
French Review 59 (March 1986): 623-24. Robert D. Cottrell.
French Studies 39 (July 1985): 363-65; and 41 (Oct. 1987): 473.
    David Coward.
Lettres romanes 38 (Nov. 1984): 331-32. Raymond Pouilliart.
Magazine littéraire, no. 208 (June 1984): 64-65. Jean-Louis Hue.
Nouvel Observateur, no. 1019 (18 May 1984): 74-75. Jean-
    François Josselin.
Nouvelles, 21 June 1984, 48-49. Jérôme Garcin.
Revue d'histoire littéraire de la France 86 (March-April 1986): 326-
    28. Michel Picard.
Revue d'histoire littéraire de la France 88 (Jan.-Feb. 1988): 148.
    Paul D'Hollander.
Revue des deux mondes, Dec. 1984, 671-72. André Bourin.

xxxx ŒUVRES COMPLETES. Geneva: Eds. de Crémille, 1968-72. 46
    vol. Pocket-size hard-cover edition, beautifully bound with page
    marker. Each volume has a front illustration. Includes texts of
    the Flammarion (Le Fleuron) edition, plus *Lettres de la*

vagabonde, Lettres à Hélène Picard, Lettres au petit corsaire, Lettres à Marguerite Moreno, Derniers écrits and *Paysages et portraits.* Three volumes, all bearing the title *Les Albums de Colette* (subtitled: Naissance d'un écrivain. Colette s'épanouit. La grande Colette), contain iconography. Volumes are unnumbered and are annotated separately.

0054 ŒUVRES COMPLETES DE COLETTE. Paris: Flammarion (Le Fleuron), 1948-1950. 15 vol. Edition published under Colette's own supervision and considered by her to be definitive. Some texts were amended for this edition, a few greatly so. Includes a bibliography of Colette's books and of the main studies on her to date, but no correspondence. Publication notes on each work are supplied by Maurice Goudeket. The first "complete" edition, found in many libraries and still in use by many scholars. Contents: 1. *Claudine à l'école. Claudine à Paris.* 2. *Claudine en ménage. Claudine s'en va. La Retraite sentimentale.* 3. *L'Ingénue libertine. Les Vrilles de la vigne. Douze dialogues de bêtes. Autres bêtes.* 4. *La Vagabonde. L'Entrave. Dans la foule.* 5. *L'Envers du music-hall. Mitsou. La Paix chez les bêtes. Les Heures longues. La Chambre éclairée.* 6. *Chéri. La Fin de Chéri. Le Voyage égoïste. Aventures quotidiennes.* 7. *La Maison de Claudine. Sido. Noces. Le Blé en herbe. La Femme cachée.* 8. *La Naissance du jour. La Seconde. Prisons et paradis. Nudité.* 9. *Le Pur et l'impur. La Chatte. Duo. Le Toutounier. Belles saisons.* 10. *La Jumelle noire.* 11. *Mes apprentissages. Bella-Vista. Chambre d'hôtel. Julie de Carneilhan.* 12. *Journal à rebours. Le Képi. De ma fenêtre. Trois... six... neuf...* 13. *Gigi. L'Etoile vesper. Mes cahiers. Discours de réception.* 14. *Le Fanal bleu. Pour un herbier. Trait pour trait. Journal intermittent. La Fleur de l'âge. En pays connu. A portée de la main.* 15. Théâtre [*Chéri. La Vagabonde. En camarades. La Décapitée. L'Enfant et les sortilèges*]. *Mélanges.* Bibliographie. References to this edition in other sections of the bibliography use the abbreviation *OCLF* followed by the volume number.

Reviews:
Portique, no. 7 (1950): 96. Jacques Guignard.
Times Literary Supplement, no. 2557 (2 Feb. 1951): 61-63.

0055 ŒUVRES COMPLETES DE COLETTE (Edition du Centenaire). Paris: Flammarion-Eds. du Club de l'honnête homme, 1973. 16

vol. Handsome, large edition containing all texts of the Flammarion (Le Fleuron) edition, as well as *Lettres de la vagabonde, Lettres à Hélène Picard, Lettres au petit corsaire, Lettres à Marguerite Moreno, Lettres à ses pairs, Derniers écrits, Paysages et portraits* and *Contes des mille et un matins.* Part of this edition was produced in volumes lavishly illustrated by Bardone, Boncompain, Cathelin, Cavaillès, Fontanarosa, Fusaro, Garcia-Fons, Genis, Brasilier, Guiramand, and Thévenet. Contents: 1. *Claudine à l'école. Claudine à Paris. Claudine en ménage.* 2. *Claudine s'en va. La Retraite sentimentale. L'Ingénue libertine.* 3. *Les Vrilles de la vigne. Douze dialogues de bêtes. Autres bêtes. La Vagabonde.* 4. *L'Entrave. L'Envers du music-hall. La Paix chez les bêtes. Les Heures longues. Mitsou.* 5. *La Chambre éclairée. Chéri. La Fin de Chéri. Le Voyage égoïste. Aventures quotidiennes.* 6. *La Maison de Claudine. Sido. Noces. Le Blé en herbe. La Femme cachée. La Naissance du jour.* 7. *La Seconde. Prisons et paradis. Le Pur et l'impur. La Chatte.* 8. *Duo. Le Toutounier. Mes apprentissages. Bella-Vista.* 9. *Chambre d'hôtel. Julie de Carneilhan. Journal à rebours. Le Képi.* 10. *De ma fenêtre. Trois... six... neuf... Gigi. L'Etoile vesper.* 11. *Belles saisons. Nudité. Le Fanal bleu. Pour un herbier. En pays connu. Trait pour trait. Journal intermittent. La Fleur de l'âge. A portée de la main.* 12. *La Jumelle noire.* 13. Théâtre [*Chéri. La Vagabonde. L'Enfant et les sortilèges. En camarades. La Décapitée*]. *Paysages et portraits. Contes des mille et un matins.* 14. *Mélanges. Derniers écrits. Discours de réception. Mes cahiers. Lettres à Marguerite Moreno.* 15. *Lettres de la vagabonde. Lettres à Hélène Picard.* 16. *Lettres au petit corsaire. Lettres à ses pairs.* References to this edition in other sections of the bibliography use the abbreviation *OCC* followed by the volume number.

Review:
Monde, 22 March 1974, 15. Ginette Guitard-Auviste.

0056   ŒUVRES DE COLETTE. Illus. Yves Brayer, Dignimont, Grau Sala, Roland Oudot, Dunoyer de Segonzac, Térechkovitch, Van Dongen, and Vertès. Paris: Flammarion, 1960. 3 vol. Useful edition of Colette's major fiction and best-known collections of short pieces. Handsome blue silk binding and colored illustrations by some of her favorite artists make these three

volumes a pleasure to use. Contents: 1. *Claudine à l'école.*
Claudine à Paris. Claudine en ménage. Claudine s'en va. La
Retraite sentimentale. L'Ingénue libertine. La Vagabonde.
L'Entrave. 2. *Mitsou. Chéri. La Fin de Chéri. Le Blé en herbe.*
La Naissance du jour. La Seconde. La Chatte. Duo. Le
Toutounier. Julie de Carneilhan. Douze dialogues de bêtes. La
Paix chez les bêtes. 3. *L'Envers du music-hall. La Femme*
cachée. La Maison de Claudine. Sido. Le Pur et l'impur. Mes
apprentissages. Bella-Vista. Chambre d'hôtel. Le Képi. Gigi.
L'Etoile vesper. Le Fanal bleu. References to this edition in
other sections of the bibliography use the abbreviation *OF*
followed by the volume number.

Review:
Figaro, 19 Oct. 1984, 28. Jean Chalon. Review of re-edition.

SINGLE-VOLUME COLLECTIONS OF TEXTS FROM SEVERAL WORKS: FRENCH

0057 AUTOBIOGRAPHIE TIRÉE DES ŒUVRES DE COLETTE PAR
ROBERT PHELPS. Pref. Maurice Goudeket. Paris: Fayard,
1966. iv-419p. Originally published in English. See *Earthly
Paradise* for annotation and reviews. Only the French editions
contain Goudeket's preface, in which he asserts that Phelps' plan
for the collection was so convincing that his own reservations
about the project disappeared.

0058 AUTOBIOGRAPHIE TIRÉE DES ŒUVRES DE COLETTE PAR
ROBERT PHELPS. Pref. Maurice Goudeket. Paris: Club
français du livre, 1968. iv-418p. Coll. Essais 23. Another
edition of the preceding.

0059 LES 'CLAUDINE.' [Willy and Colette]. Presentation Claude
Abastado. Paris: Bordas, 1969. 256p. Coll. Classiques
contemporains Bordas. Student edition containing extracts from
the four Claudine novels. Includes a biography, a good basic
discussion of the novels, notes on theme, structure, style and

meaning, study questions and composition topics. Interesting
presentation of Colette the person. The first annotated edition of
any of Colette's texts.

0060 COLETTE. Paris: Crès, 1921. iv-239p. Coll. Bibliothèque de
l'adolescence, Les Auteurs «vivants» lus par les jeunes. Extracts
from *Dialogues de bêtes. La Retraite sentimentale. Les Vrilles
de la vigne. La Vagabonde. La Paix chez les bêtes. Dans la
foule. Les Heures longues. L'Entrave. La Chambre éclairée.*
Also one text, "L'expédition Scott au cinématographe,"
published in book form for the first time and not republished
until its appearance in *Colette: au cinéma*. Excellent unsigned
preface.

0061 COLETTE PAR COLETTE: LA JEUNESSE DE 'CLAUDINE.'
Pref. Claude Mauriac. Paris: Hachette, 1976. 440p. Contents:
La Maison de Claudine [all 35 texts]. *Sido. Les Vrilles de la
vigne* [20 texts]. *Mes Apprentissages.* A brief note precedes
each work.

0062 MORCEAUX CHOISIS. Paris: Gallimard, 1936. 331p. Brief
passages from many works arranged according to themes that
correspond roughly to periods in Colette's life. Without
commentary or analysis, however, the arrangement evokes an
unsettling image of Colette's world. Headings are: Ma mère et
moi. Province. Solitude. Bêtes. Sauvagerie. Jardins et paysages.
Bel-Gazou. Adolescents. Couples. Jalousie. La femme mûre.

0063 PAGES CHOISIES. Presentation Pierre Clarac. Paris: Hachette,
1957. 96p. Coll. Classiques illustrés Vaubourdolle 86. Student
edition. Extracts from *Claudine à l'école. Dialogues de bêtes.
Les Vrilles de la vigne. La Maison de Claudine. Sido. La
Femme cachée. La Naissance du jour. Prisons et paradis.*
Includes a brief introduction by Clarac, illustrations, essay and
study topics, and a passage from Goudeket's *Près de Colette.*

0064 LES PLUS BELLES PAGES DE COLETTE. Paris: Flammarion,
1930. 286p. Extracts from Colette's works to 1929: the
Claudine novels. *Les Vrilles de la vigne. La Vagabonde.
L'Entrave. L'Envers du music-hall. Chéri. La Fin de Chéri. La
Maison de Claudine. Le Blé en herbe. La Femme cachée. La
Naissance du jour. La Seconde.*

Review:
Action française, 26 Feb. 1931, 4. P.C.

0065 TEXTES CHOISIS DE COLETTE. Presentation Pierre Clarac.
Paris: Grasset, 1936. 293p. Coll. des textes choisis d'auteurs
contemporains. Student edition. Passages assembled
thematically and with notes. Arranged under four headings
[Enfance. Au fil d'une vie. Figures de roman. Bêtes]. Works
represented are: *Ces plaisirs. Claudine à l'école. Dialogues de
bêtes. L'Envers du music-hall. La Femme cachée. Les Heures
longues. La Jumelle noire. La Maison de Claudine. La
Naissance du jour. La Paix chez les bêtes. Prisons et paradis. La
Retraite sentimentale. Sido. La Vagabonde. Le Voyage égoïste.
Les Vrilles de la vigne.* Also good long introduction by Clarac.

SINGLE-VOLUME COLLECTIONS OF TEXTS
FROM SEVERAL WORKS: ENGLISH

BELLES SAISONS: A COLETTE SCRAPBOOK...

Assembled and with commentary by Robert Phelps. Splendid
collection of about 300 photographs, along with anecdotes and
informative tid-bits of all kinds. Photographs are of people, places,
books, manuscripts, sketches and other memorable objects,
arranged in rough chronological order. Commentary is often taken
from Colette's own works and is documented.

Reviews:
French Review 54 (Oct. 1980): 173-74. Joan Hinde Stewart.
Time 113 (1 Jan. 1979): 68. James Atlas.
Times Literary Supplement, no. 3999 (24 Nov. 1978): 1358.

American edition

0066 BELLES SAISONS: A COLETTE SCRAPBOOK... New York:
Farrar, Straus & Giroux, 1978. 303p.

British editions

0067 BELLES SAISONS: A COLETTE SCRAPBOOK... London:
Secker & Warburg, 1978. 303p.

0068 BELLES SAISONS: A COLETTE SCRAPBOOK...
Harmondsworth: Penguin, 1980. 202p.

THE CLAUDINE NOVELS

See *The Complete Claudine.*

COLETTE OMNIBUS

0069 COLETTE OMNIBUS. London: Secker & Warburg, 1988. 864p.
Contains 6 novels: *The Vagabond. Chéri. The Last of Chéri.
The Ripening Seed. The Cat. Gigi.* Not seen.

Review:
Observer, no. 10256 (1 May 1988): 43. Anita Brookner.

THE COLETTE OMNIBUS

0070   THE COLETTE OMNIBUS. Introd. Erica Jong. Garden City,
N.Y.: Nelson Doubleday, 1974. ix-583p. Contains 5 novels:
Chéri. The Last of Chéri. Gigi. The Vagabond. The Shackle.
Not the same collection as the previous one.

THE COLLECTED STORIES OF COLETTE

Edited by Robert Phelps. Trans. Matthew Ward, Herma Briffault,
Anne-Marie Callimachi, Antonia White, Una Vincenzo Troubridge,
Enid McLeod. Introd. Robert Phelps. An extremely popular and
interesting collection of short pieces from a great variety of works,
grouped loosely according to theme. Some were newly translated
for this edition. Includes *L'Envers du music-hall. La Femme
cachée. La Lune de pluie. L'Enfant malade. La Dame du
photographe. Le Képi. Le Tendron. La Cire verte. Armande.
Gribiche. Le Sieur Binard. Le Rendez-vous. Bella-Vista.* Also
selections from: *Mes cahiers. Contes des mille et un matins.
Paysages et portraits. La Chambre éclairée. Les Vrilles de la vigne.
La Fleur de l'âge. Douze dialogues de bêtes. La Maison de
Claudine. La Paix chez les bêtes. Gigi.*

Reviews:
American Scholar 53 (Autumn 1984): 549-52. Donna Rifkind.
American Spectator 17 (June 1984): 43-44. Victoria Sackett.
Booklist 9 (1 Sept. 1983): 4.
Christian Science Monitor 76 (7 Dec. 1983): 39. Kathy Field
Stephen.
Kirkus Reviews 51 (1 Sept. 1983): 980.
Library Journal 109 (Jan. 1984): 109. Marilyn Gaddis Rose.
Nation 237 (24 Dec. 1983): 675. Gary Giddins.
National Review 36 (4 May 1984): 61. Terry Teachout.
New Republic 190 (4 June 1984): 38-42. Isa Kapp.
New Statesman 108 (6 July 1984): 27-28. Marion Glastonbury.

New York Review of Books 21 (26 April 1984): 12-16. Gabriele Annan.
New York Times, 3 Nov. 1983, C30. Anatole Broyard.
New York Times Book Review, 25 Dec. 1983, 3, 14. Phyllis Rose. Also in *Writing of Women*, 90-95. Middletown, Conn.: Wesleyan University Press, 1985.
New Yorker 59 (19 Dec. 1983): 137-40. V.S. Pritchett.
Newsweek 102 (21 Nov. 1983): 100. Walter Clemons.
Observer, no. 10061 (5 Aug. 1984): 21. Lorna Sage.
Observer, no. 10127 (10 Nov. 1985): 25.
Publishers' Weekly 224 (23 Sept. 1983): 62.
Punch 287 (18 July 1984): 68.
Spectator 253 (4 Aug. 1984): 20-21. Kay Dick.
Sunday Times [London], 8 July 1984, 40. Peter Kemp.
Time 123 (9 Jan. 1984): 70, 73. Patricia Blake.
Times Educational Supplement, no. 3625 (20 Dec. 1985): 17. Shena Mackay.
Times Literary Supplement no. 4257 (2 Nov. 1984): 1238. Anne Duchêne.

American editions

0071   THE COLLECTED STORIES OF COLETTE. New York: Farrar, Straus & Giroux, 1983. xvi-605p.

0072   THE COLLECTED STORIES OF COLETTE. New York: Farrar, Straus & Giroux, 1983. xvi-605p. Coll. Noonday.

British editions

0073   THE COLLECTED STORIES OF COLETTE. London: Secker & Warburg, 1984. xvi-605p.

0074   THE COLLECTED STORIES OF COLETTE. Harmondsworth: Penguin, 1985. xvi-605p.

THE COMPLETE CLAUDINE
THE CLAUDINE NOVELS

Trans. Antonia White. Contains 4 novels: *Claudine at School. Claudine in Paris. Claudine Married. Claudine and Annie.*

Review:
Observer, no. 10190 (25 Jan. 1987): 27.

American editions

0075 THE COMPLETE CLAUDINE. New York: Farrar, Straus & Giroux, 1976. 632p.

0076 THE COMPLETE CLAUDINE. New York: Farrar, Straus & Giroux, 1976. 632p. Coll. Noonday N543.

0077 THE COMPLETE CLAUDINE. New York: Avenel Books, 1984. 632p.

British edition

0078 THE PENGUIN CLAUDINE NOVELS. Harmondsworth: Penguin, 1985. 560p. Republished as *The Claudine Novels*.

CREATURES GREAT AND SMALL

Trans. Enid McLeod. Excellent collection of 64 animal pieces, arranged in three sections. "Creature Conversations" is a translation of the 12 texts of *Douze dialogues de bêtes*. "Other Creatures" is a translation of the 22 texts of *Autres Bêtes*. "Creature Comfort" includes Colette's foreword and 30 texts of *La Paix chez les bêtes*. See those titles for specific texts.

Reviews:
New Statesman & Nation 43 (9 Feb. 1952): 161. Margaret Lane.
Observer, no. 8379 (6 Jan. 1952): 7. Edwin Muir.
Times Literary Supplement, no. 2636 (8 Aug. 1952): 513.
Twentieth Century 151 (Feb. 1952): 180.

American editions

0079 CREATURES GREAT AND SMALL. New York: Farrar, Straus
      & Cudahy, 1951. 322p.

0080 CREATURES GREAT AND SMALL. New York: Farrar, Straus
      & Giroux, 1978. 292p. Coll. Noonday 591.

British edition

0081 CREATURES GREAT AND SMALL. London: Secker &
      Warburg, 1951. 322p. Coll. Uniform 2.

EARTHLY PARADISE:

**An Autobiography Drawn from her Lifetime Writings
by Robert Phelps**

Trans. Helen Beauclerk, Herma Briffault, Derek Coltman, Enid
McLeod, Una Vincenzo Troubridge, Antonia White, Roger
Senhouse. Not an autobiography, but a collection of extracts from
many of Colette's books, arranged thematically so as to follow the
highlights of her life. Some are merely fragments, while others are
complete texts. An extremely popular collection, especially useful
for those who want a broad sampling of Colette's work. Includes
editor's foreword and excellent detailed chronology. Texts from:
Aventures quotidiennes. Gribiche [under title *Bella-Vista*]. *En pays
connu. Flore et Pomone. Journal à rebours. L'Etoile vesper. La
Chambre éclairée. La Maison de Claudine. La Naissance du jour.*

Le Fanal bleu. La Cire verte [under heading *Le Képi*]. *Le Pur et l'impur. Les Heures longues. Les Vrilles de la vigne. La Vagabonde. Autres bêtes. A portée de la main. Mes cahiers. Nudité. Discours de réception. Trait pour trait. Lettres au petit corsaire. Lettres à Marguerite Moreno. Lettres de la vagabonde. Mes apprentissages. Noces. De ma fenêtre. Paysages et portraits. Prisons et paradis. Sido. Trois... six... neuf...* Those listed as from *Belles saisons* are from *Mes cahiers, Nudité* and *Discours de réception.* See items 0057-58 for French editions.

Reviews:
A la page, no. 35 (May 1967): 796. Christian Melchior-Bonnet.
Antiquarian Bookman 37 (18 April 1966): 1676.
Approach, no. 61 (Fall 1966): 37-39. Carol Murphy.
Arts-Loisirs, no. 71 (1 Feb. 1967): 12-14. Claude Bonnefoy.
Atlantic 217 (May 1966): 125-26. Oscar Handlin.
Booklist 63 (1 Sept. 1966): 25.
Books & Bookmen 12 (Dec. 1966): 28-30. Francis King.
Bulletin critique du livre français 22 (March 1967): 199.
Canadian Forum 46 (March 1967): 284-85. Laure Riese.
Chicago Tribune Books Today 3 (1 May 1966): 1-3. Elaine P. Halperin.
Choice 3 (Feb. 1967): 1131.
Christian Science Monitor, 2 June 1966, 9. Donald Heiney.
Comment 8 (14 March 1970): 171. Roy Johnson.
Commonweal 86 (14 July 1967): 452-54. Alice Mayhew.
Commonweal 87 (1 Dec. 1967): 313. Alice Mayhew.
Express, no. 813 (16 Jan. 1967): 52. Madeleine Chapsal.
Fiera Letteraria, 13 April 1967, 14-15. Luigi Bàccolo.
Horn Book Magazine 51 (Oct. 1975): 493-94. Mary Silva Cosgrave.
Kirkus Reviews 34 (1 March 1966): 292.
Lettres françaises, 2 Feb. 1967, 3-4. Claude-Michel Cluny [spelt Cuny). Also in *La Rage de lire*, 248-52. Paris: Denoël, 1978.
Library Journal 91 (15 April 1966): 2065. Mary E. Kelley.
Life 60 (13 May 1966): 8, 12. Janet Flanner.
Listener 76 (8 Dec. 1966): 863-64. Marigold Johnson.
Livres de France 35 (March 1967): 23. Armand Rio.
Magazine littéraire, no. 4 (Feb. 1967): 19.
Monde, 1 Feb. 1967, ii. Christine de Rivoyre.
Nation 202 (13 June 1966):720-21. Mary Ellmann.
National Review 18 (28 June 1966): 636-38. Guy Davenport.

Neue Deutsche Hefte 117 (1968): 195-99. Johann Siering.
New Leader 49 (4 July 1966): 21-22. Fanny Howe.
New Statesman 73 (28 Oct. 1966): 632. Brigid Brophy.
New York Review of Books 6 (9 June 1966): 8-10. John
      Weightman.
New York Times Book Review, 1 May 1966, 1, 52-53. Elizabeth
      Janeway.
Newsweek 67 (9 May 1966): 102.
Newsweek 68 (19 Dec. 1966): 117.
Nouvel Observateur, no. 114 (18 Jan. 1967): 34-35. Jean Freustié.
      Also in *Chroniques d'humeur*, 51-55. Paris: Mercure de France,
      1969.
Nouvelles littéraires, 19 Jan. 1967, 5. R.-M. Albérès.
Observer, no. 9147 (30 Oct. 1966): 27. Marghanita Laski.
Observer, no. 9154 (18 Dec. 1966): 23. Edna O'Brien.
Observer, no. 9573 (19 Jan. 1975): 27.
Publishers' Weekly 189 (2 May 1966): 57.
Punch 251 (21 Dec. 1966): 936. Venetia Pollock.
Quinzaine littéraire, no. 23 (1 March 1967): 11-12. Geneviève
      Bonnefoi.
Reporter 35 (20 Oct. 1966): 59-60. Justin O'Brien. Also in *The
      French Literary Horizon*, 267-70. New Brunswick, N.J.:
      Rutgers University Press, 1967.
Revue de Paris 74 (July-Aug. 1967): 169. Christian Dedet.
Saturday Night 82 (Jan. 1967): 34-35. Robert Weaver.
Saturday Review 49 (7 May 1966): 89-90. Anna Balakian.
Sewanee Review 75 (April-June 1967): 351-54. David McDowell.
Spectator, no. 7219 (4 Nov. 1966): 590-91. Martin Turnell.
Sunday Times [London], 23 Oct. 1966, 50. John Raymond.
Time 87 (20 May 1966): 92.
Times [London], 27 Oct. 1966, 17.
Times Literary Supplement, no. 3376 (10 Nov. 1966): 1021.
Tribune 30 (25 Nov. 1966): 13. Winifred Horrabin.
Vogue [U.S.] 147 (15 April 1966): 65. Elizabeth Hardwick.

American editions

0082 EARTHLY PARADISE, AN AUTOBIOGRAPHY DRAWN
      FROM HER LIFETIME WRITINGS by Robert Phelps. New
      York: Farrar, Straus & Giroux, 1966. xxxiv-505p.

0083 "Colette: the many facets of love." *McCall's* 93 (April 1966): 114-15, 151-58. Extracts and commentary.

0084 EARTHLY PARADISE, AN AUTOBIOGRAPHY DRAWN FROM HER LIFETIME WRITINGS by Robert Phelps. New York: Farrar, Straus & Giroux (Sunburst), 1971. Not seen.

0085 EARTHLY PARADISE, AN AUTOBIOGRAPHY DRAWN FROM HER LIFETIME WRITINGS by Robert Phelps. New York: Farrar, Straus & Giroux, 1975. 505p. Coll. Noonday 519.

0086 "Sido." In *Mothers: Memories, Dreams and Reflections by Literary Daughters*, edited by Susan Cahill, 83-108. New York: Mentor, 1988. Synthesis of extracts highlighting the importance of the mother. From *Sido*, *La Naissance du jour* and *La Maison de Claudine*.

British editions

0087 EARTHLY PARADISE, AN AUTOBIOGRAPHY DRAWN FROM HER LIFETIME WRITINGS by Robert Phelps. Editor's foreword. Chronology. London: Secker & Warburg, 1966. xxxv-505p.

0088 EARTHLY PARADISE, AN AUTOBIOGRAPHY DRAWN FROM HER LIFETIME WRITINGS by Robert Phelps. Editor's foreword. Chronology. London: Sphere, 1970. 444p.

0089 EARTHLY PARADISE, AN AUTOBIOGRAPHY DRAWN FROM HER LIFETIME WRITINGS by Robert Phelps. Editor's foreword. Chronology. Harmondsworth: Penguin, 1974. 512p.

FLOWERS AND FRUIT

Edited by Robert Phelps. Trans. Matthew Ward. An interesting selection of pieces on the title theme. Contains *Pour un herbier*, *Flore et Pomone* and essays from: *Belles saisons*. *Aventures quotidiennes*. *Paysages et portraits*. *Prisons et paradis*. *Mélanges*.

Reviews:
Books & Bookmen, no. 367 (May 1986): 10-11. Frances Spalding.
Horticulture 64 (Aug. 1986): 58-59. Jacqueline Whidden.
Los Angeles Times Book Review, 30 March 1986, 4. Barbara Saltzman.
New York Times Book Review 91 (1 June 1986): 31-33. Germaine Greer.
New Yorker 62 (21 July 1986): 95.
Publishers' Weekly 229 (17 Jan. 1986): 59.
Punch 290 (16 April 1986): 54. Sally Vincent.

American edition

0090 FLOWERS AND FRUIT. New York: Farrar, Straus & Giroux, 1986. xi-163p.

British edition

0091 FLOWERS AND FRUIT. London: Secker & Warburg, 1987. xi-163p.

JOURNEY FOR MYSELF

Trans. David Le Vay. Combines 18 texts from *Aventures quotidiennes* with 29 texts from *Le Voyage égoïste*. Titles from *Aventures quotidiennes* are: Yesterday's Age, Tomorrow's Youth.

Assassins. Animals. Flowers. Doubles. Cinema. Spells.
Pedagogy. Tits. Heat. Conflicts. Summer. Beauties. Offspring.
Mausoleums. Newspapers. Wings. Back to School. Titles from *Le
Voyage égoïste* are: Sunday. I'm Hot. Respite. Invalid. Christmas
Presents. Visits. Tomorrow's Springtime. Farewell to the Snow.
Models. Elegance, Economy. Excursions. Captive Gardens.
Holidays. Grape Harvesters. Fur and Feather. Jewellery in Peril.
Too Short. Underneath. Make-up. Hats. Breasts. Paperweights.
Novelties. Late Season. Furs. Amateurs. Empty Pockets. Silks.
Logic.

Reviews:
Commonweal 95 (3 Dec. 1971): 233-34. Alice Mayhew.
Kirkus Reviews 40 (1 July 1972): 761.
Library Journal 97 (Aug. 1972): 2603. Ann Grace Mojtabai.
New York Times Book Review 122 (1 Oct. 1972): 6-7. Nancy
    Hale.
New Yorker 48 (28 Oct. 1972): 160.
Times Literary Supplement, no. 3625 (20 Aug. 1971): 986.
Tribune, 3 Sept. 1971, 15. Dulan Barber.
Washington Post Book World, 17 Sept. 1972, 15.

American editions

0092 JOURNEY FOR MYSELF: SELFISH MEMORIES. Indianapolis:
      Bobbs-Merrill, 1972. 156p.

0093 "While you are away." *Ladies' Home Journal* 89 (Sept. 1972): 125.
      Same text as: Respite.

British edition

0094 JOURNEY FOR MYSELF: SELFISH MEMORIES. London:
      Owen, 1971. 156p.

LOOKING BACKWARDS

Trans. David Le Vay. Foreword Maurice Goudeket. Combines *De ma fenêtre* with 21 texts from *Journal à rebours*: Sido and I. The Foot-warmer. A Salon in 1900. Autumn. Oum-el-Hassen. The Heart of Animals. The Small Cat Found. Provence I-VI. June 1940. La Providence. The Poet. Swallows. Danger. Ruins. Fever. Gone...

Reviews:
Booklist 72 (1 Sept. 1975): 13.
Choice 13 (April 1976): 230.
French Review 50 (Oct. 1976): 194-95. Charles Krance.
Kirkus Reviews 43 (1 March 1975): 271-72.
Library Journal 100 (15 March 1975): 573-74. Anthony S. Caprio.
New Statesman 89 (2 May 1975): 592-93. Joanna Richardson.
New York Times, 7 June 1975, 25. Anatole Broyard.
New Yorker 51 (18 Aug. 1975): 83-84.
Observer, no. 10190 (25 Jan. 1987): 27.
Publishers' Weekly 207 (31 March 1975): 44.
Saturday Review 2 (26 July 1975): 29. Dorothy Rabinowitz.
Times Educational Supplement, no. 3708 (24 July 1987): 21.
    Robin Buss.
Times Literary Supplement, no. 3825 (4 July 1975): 741. Barbara
    Wright. Le Vay's reply in no. 3828 (25 July 1975): 840.

American edition

0095 LOOKING BACKWARDS: RECOLLECTIONS. Bloomington:
      Indiana University Press, 1975. 214p.

British editions

0096 LOOKING BACKWARDS: RECOLLECTIONS. London: Owen,
      1975. 214p.

0097 LOOKING BACKWARDS: RECOLLECTIONS. Introd. Alice
      Hennegan. London: Women's Press, 1987. viii-214p.

PLACES

Trans. David Le Vay. Foreword Margaret Crosland. Collection of texts on a theme. Combines reminiscences and invention. Includes *Trois... six... neuf...* plus selections from: *En pays connu. Prisons et paradis. Paysages et portraits. Mes cahiers. A portée de la main.* Texts indicated as from *Journal intermittent* actually belong to *En pays connu* and *A portée de la main.*

Reviews:
America 126 (22 Jan. 1972): 73. M. Whitcomb Hess.
Booklist 68 (15 Jan. 1972): 411.
Choice 9 (April 1972): 220.
Christian Science Monitor 64 (23 Dec. 1971): 9. V.H.
Library Journal 96 (Aug. 1971): 2487. Ann Grace Mojbati.
Listener 84 (9 July 1970): 55. Geoffrey Strickland.
New York Times Book Review 122 (1 Oct. 1972): 6-7. Nancy
    Hale.
New Yorker 47 (25 Dec. 1971): 68.
Publishers' Weekly 200 (9 Aug. 1971): 42.
Times Literary Supplement, no. 3561 (28 May 1970): 593.
Tribune, 14 Aug. 1970, 10. D.B.

American edition

0098 PLACES. Indianapolis, New York: Bobbs-Merrill, 1971. 157p.

British edition

0099 PLACES. London: Owen, 1970. 157p.

THE RAINY MOON AND OTHER STORIES

See *The Stories of Colette.*

RECOLLECTIONS

0100 RECOLLECTIONS. Trans. David LeVay. New York: Collier-
      Macmillan, 1986. 288p. Combines *Journey for Myself* with
      Evening Star [trans. of *L'Etoile vesper*].

Review:
New York Times Book Review, 12 Oct. 1986, 48. Patricia
O'Connor.

SEVEN BY COLETTE

0101 SEVEN BY COLETTE. Introd. Janet Flanner. New York: Farrar,
      Straus & Cudahy, 1955. xv-194p.-296p.-223p. Contains 7
      titles: *Gigi. The Cat. Chéri. The Last of Chéri. My Mother's
      House. Chance Acquaintances. The Vagabond.*

SHORT NOVELS OF COLETTE

0102 SHORT NOVELS OF COLETTE. Introd. Glenway Wescott. New
      York: Dial Press (Permanent Library), 1951. lvii-733p.
      Contents: *Chéri. The Last of Chéri. The Other One. Duo. The
      Cat. The Indulgent Husband.* The excellent 50-page introduction
      [annotated separately] helped make this collection an important
      one at a time when serious English language criticism on
      Colette was just beginning.

Reviews:
American Mercury 75 (Dec. 1952): 100-3. William Phillips.
Commonweal 56 (5 Sept. 1952): 536-38. Richard Hayes.

Nation 174 (12 Jan. 1952): 40-41. Ernest Jones.
New York Times Book Review, 18 Nov. 1951, 5 and 52.
    Katherine Anne Porter.
New Yorker 27 (5 Jan. 1952): 63-66. Maeve Brennan.
Partisan Review 20 (May-June 1953): 332-38. Sonya Rudikoff.
Perspectives U.S.A. 3 (Spring 1953): 133-36. W.H. Auden.
Time 58 (19 Nov. 1951): 90-92.

SIX NOVELS

0103 SIX NOVELS. London: Secker & Warburg; Toronto: Stoddard,
    1988. 867p. Contents: *The Vagabond. Chéri. The Last of
    Chéri. The Ripening Seed. The Cat. Gigi.* Not the same
    collection as the following one.

Reviews:
Punch 294 (15 April 1988): 41-42. Allan Massie.
Times Literary Supplement, no. 4445 (10 June 1988): 641. Anne
    Duchêne.

SIX NOVELS BY COLETTE

0104 SIX NOVELS BY COLETTE. New York: Random (Modern
    Library), 1960. 697p. Contents: *Claudine at School. Music-
    Hall Sidelights. Mitsou. Chéri. The Last of Chéri. Gigi.* Not
    the same collection as the preceding one.

STORIES

0105   STORIES. Illus. David McCall Johnston. Franklin Center, Pa.;
        Franklin Library, 1977. 438p. Contains 4 novels: *Gigi. Julie de
        Carneilhan. Chéri. The Last of Chéri.* Not seen.

THE STORIES OF COLETTE
THE RAINY MOON AND OTHER STORIES
THE TENDER SHOOT AND OTHER STORIES

Trans. Antonia White. Contains 11 novellas: *Bella-Vista.
Gribiche. The Rendezvous. The Patriarch. The Rainy Moon. The
Kepi. The Tender Shoot. Green Sealing-Wax. Armande. The Sick
Child. The Photographer's Missus.*

Reviews:
New Statesman 56 (20 Dec. 1958): 888-90. Walter Allen.
New York Review of Books 6 (9 June 1966): 8-10. John
        Weightman.
New York Times Book Review 108 (16 Aug. 1959): 27. Robert
        Phelps.
Observer, no. 8736 (7 Dec. 1958): 17. J.G. Weightman.
Times Literary Supplement, no. 2963 (12 Dec. 1958): 717.

American editions

0106   THE TENDER SHOOT AND OTHER STORIES. New York:
        Farrar, Straus & Cudahy, 1959. 404p.

0107   THE TENDER SHOOT AND OTHER STORIES. New York:
        New American Library (Signet), 1961. Not seen.

0108   THE TENDER SHOOT AND OTHER STORIES. New York:
        Farrar, Straus & Giroux, 1975. 404p. Coll. Noonday N504.

British editions

0109   THE STORIES OF COLETTE. London: Secker & Warburg,
         1958. 404p.

0110   THE STORIES OF COLETTE. London: Mercury Books, 1962.
         404p. Coll. Mercury Books 36.

0111   THE RAINY MOON AND OTHER STORIES. Harmondsworth:
         Penguin, 1975. 347p.

THE TENDER SHOOT AND OTHER STORIES

See *The Stories of Colette.*

MEMOIRS, CHRONICLES AND REMINISCENCES

CES PLAISIRS

See *Le Pur et l'impur*.

DE MA FENETRE
PARIS DE MA FENETRE

0112 DE MA FENETRE. Paris: Aux Armes de France, 1942. 151p.

0113 PARIS, DE MA FENETRE. Pref. Francis Carco. Geneva: Eds. du Milieu du monde, 1944. 240p. Contents of 1942 are modified and expanded.

0114 PARIS DE MA FENETRE. Illus. Clément Serveau. Paris: Ferenczi, 1948. 127p. Coll. Le Livre moderne illustré 385.

0115 PARIS DE MA FENETRE. Illus. Touchagues. Paris: Eds. littéraires de France, 1951. 143p. Limited luxury edition.

0116   "La France." [Extract]. *Nouvelles littéraires*, 12 Aug. 1954, 8.

0117   PARIS DE MA FENETRE. Pref. Francis Carco. Paris: Hachette, 1976. 160p. Coll. Livre de poche 4749.

0118   DE MA FENETRE. Paris: Fayard, 1987. 189p.

Also in:
OCLF 12 [item 0054]: under title *De ma fenêtre*.
OCC 10 [item 0055]: under title *De ma fenêtre*.
La Chambre éclairée. [*Mélanges. Derniers écrits. Discours.*] *De ma fenêtre. Le Fanal bleu.* Item 0710.
L'Etoile vesper. De ma fenêtre. Item 0125.
Le Képi. De ma fenêtre. Item 0555.

Extracts in:
Autobiographie... [items 0057-58].
Bêtes libres et prisonnières [item 0702]: L'oiseau et l'homme. Les abeilles. Papillons. Les rats. Le rossignol.
Chats de Colette [items 0714-15]: Pierrot et Mitsou.
Chiens de Colette [items 0716-17]: Chiens de ville. Nuits de Noël.
Colette: au cinéma [item 0980]: Films documentaires.

Content substantially increased and title changed for the second and subsequent editions. Original title, which means "Paris from my window," is apt, for Colette addresses Parisians directly, especially the women. Although subjects vary and collection includes reminiscences and anecdotes, focus is on every-day life in war-time Paris. Colette frequently gives advice on how to "make do," given the shortages and hardships under which civilians must live. One article contains a recipe. Often praises Parisians for their ingenuity, their generous acts, their talent and their efforts. Three texts on raising children show Colette establishing a balance between parents' rights and the need for children to investigate for themselves. Contains a few texts on nature, especially birds. Typical of Colette's mature essay style, which reveals her own mind at the same time as it asserts the outer reality she portrays. Texts in original edition are dated.

Review:
Bulletin critique du livre français 1:7 (1947): 7.

English translations: American

xxxx "Pre-war," "The Flight from Paris" and "Occupation." Trans. David Le Vay. In *Looking Backwards* [item 0095].

Extracts in *Earthly Paradise* [items 0082, 0084-85]. Trans. Derek Coltman.

English translations: British

xxxx "Pre-war," "The Flight from Paris" and "Occupation." Trans. David Le Vay. In *Looking Backwards* [items 0096-97].

Extracts in *Earthly Paradise* [items 0087-89]. Trans. Derek Coltman.

L'ETOILE VESPER

0119 L'ETOILE VESPER. Geneva, Paris, Montreal: Eds. du Milieu du monde, 1946. 221p.

0120 [Extract]. *Revue littéraire*, no. 11 (March-April 1954): 16-20.

0121 "Douleur." *Nouvelles littéraires*, 12 Aug. 1954, 8.

0122 L'ETOILE VESPER. Lausanne: Guilde du livre, 1955. 223p.

0123 L'ETOILE VESPER. Illus. Marquet. Lausanne: Mermod, 1956. 261p.

0124 L'ETOILE VESPER. MES CAHIERS. Geneva: Crémille, 1971. 264p.

0125 L'ETOILE VESPER. DE MA FENETRE. Paris: Hachette, 1979. 315p.

0126 L'ETOILE VESPER. Paris: Fayard, 1986. 183p.

Also in:
OCLF 13 [item 0054].
OCC 10 [item 0055].
OF 3 [item 0056].

Extracts in:
Autobiographie... [items 0057-58].
Bêtes libres et prisonnières [item 0702]: La lionne. Le rossignol.
Chats de Colette [items 0714-15]: La chatte dernière.
Chiens de Colette [items 0716-17]: Souci. La chienne beauceronne.

Series of reminiscences and meditations, as the reader accompanies Colette through her days and sleepless nights. Prominent theme is that of the outside world, which enters the room of the immobile writer via visits, letters and glances through the window. Contains long passages on Colette's years with *L'Eclair* and *Le Matin* in the early decades of the century, as well as on the difficulties of life in Paris during World War II. An often recurring topic is the traumatic incident of Maurice Goudeket's incarceration at Compiègne in 1941-1942. Of special interest are three passages dealing with specific topics: one on Colette's experience with clairvoyants, a second on her fictional male characters Renaud, Max, Chéri and Farou, and a third on the controversial ending of *L'Entrave*, which Colette considered unsatisfactory. Incorporated into the volume are *Pour Hélène Picard*, "Vieux papiers" from *Broderie ancienne*, and two texts previously published in collaborative patriotic works during the war: "Maquis en sourdine" and "Le jardin libéré." All are annotated separately.

Reviews:
Atlantic 234 (Sept. 1974): 102. Edward Weeks.
Booklist 71 (1 Dec. 1974): 362.
Books & Bookmen 18 (March 1973): 56-57. Oswell Blakeston.
Boston Globe, 16 Oct. 1974, 22. Margaret Manning.
Bulletin critique du livre français 2:9 (1947): 4-5.
Bulletin de la Guilde du Livre 22 (Oct. 1957): 387. Edith Thomas.
Figaro littéraire, 19 July 1947, 2. André Rousseaux.
Kirkus Reviews 42 (1 July 1974): 712.
Library Journal 99 (Aug. 1974): 1935. Bettina L. Knapp.
Monde illustré, 9 Aug. 1947, 931. Roger Lannes.

Nation 220 (8 March 1975): 280-81. Glynne Hiller.
New Statesman 85 (2 Feb. 1973): 163-64. Francis Wyndham.
New York Times, 18 Sept. 1974, 57. Anatole Broyard.
New Yorker 50 (11 Nov. 1974): 213.
Nouvelles littéraires, 3 Feb. 1949, 2. Robert Kemp.
Observer, no. 9470 (28 Jan. 1973): 34. John Weightman.
Observer, no. 10190 (25 Jan. 1987): 27.
Publishers' Weekly 205 (24 June 1974): 57.
Revue des hommes et mondes, no. 16 (Nov. 1947): 480-85.
Thierry Maulnier.
Spectator, no. 7559 (12 May 1973): 594. E.S.
Sunday Times, 11 Feb. 1973, 30. Philippa Pullar.
Synthèses 3:1 (1948): 104-6. Nelly Cormeau.
Times Educational Supplement, no. 3708 (24 July 1987): 21.
Robin Buss.
Times Literary Supplement, no. 3710 (13 April 1973): 413.

English translations: American

0127 THE EVENING STAR: RECOLLECTIONS. Trans. and pref.
David Le Vay. Indianapolis, New York: Bobbs-Merrill, 1973.
144p.

Also in *Recollections* [item 0100].

Extracts in *Earthly Paradise* [items 0082, 0084-85]. Trans. Herma
Briffault, Derek Coltman.

English translations: British

0128 THE EVENING STAR. Trans. and pref. David Le Vay. London:
Owen, 1973. 144p.

0129 THE EVENING STAR. Trans. David Le Vay. Introd. Alison
Hennegan. London: Women's Press, 1987. 144p.

Extracts in *Earthly Paradise* [0087-89]. Trans. Herma Briffault,
Derek Coltman.

LE FANAL BLEU

0130 LE FANAL BLEU. Paris: Ferenczi, 1949. 243p.

0131 LE FANAL BLEU. MÉLANGES. Geneva: Crémille, 1971. 251p.

0132 LE FANAL BLEU. Paris: Hachette, 1975. 160p. Coll. Livre de poche 4221.

0133 LE FANAL BLEU. EN PAYS CONNU. JOURNAL INTERMITTENT. Paris: Hachette, 1979. 253p.

0134 LE FANAL BLEU. Paris: Fayard, 1987. 157p.

Also in:
OCLF 14 [item 0054].
OCC 11 [item 0055].
OF 3 [item 0056].
La Chambre éclairée. [*Mélanges. Derniers écrits. Discours.*] *De ma fenêtre. Le Fanal bleu.* Item 0710.

Extracts in:
Autobiographie... [items 0057-58].
Bêtes libres et prisonnières [item 0702]: Le moineau. Les nids dans les troênes. Sur les étangs.
Chats de Colette [items 0714-15]: La chatte dernière. Chat suisse.
Chiens de Colette [items 0716-17]: Souci. Bellaude et Pati. Moulouk. Modes.
Colette: au cinéma [item 0980].

Reminiscences and reflections published when Colette was seventy-six years old and incapacitated with arthritis. Often written in the present tense, they draw the reader into her daily life and into her mind, by their subject matter as well as by their conversational tone. Visits from friends, many of them famous, meetings of the Goncourt Academy, the arrival of letters and gifts, glimpses of people and animals from her window over the courtyard of the Palais Royal, items within her own room: nothing is too minor to awaken Colette's interest. Passages describing visits to Geneva, where she underwent medical treatment, and a trip to the

Beaujolais, date from 1946. Includes a short passage on Léon-Paul Fargue and a chapter on Marguerite Moreno previously published in *Trait pour trait.*

Reviews:
Bulletin critique du livre français 4 (1949): 531.
Choice 4 (May 1967): 295.
Commonweal 86 (14 July 1967): 452-54. Alice Mayhew.
Devoir, 2 Aug. 1949, 6. Jean-Louis Bruch.
Europe 41-42 (May-June 1949): 162-64. Elsa Triolet.
Figaro littéraire, 2 July 1949, 2. André Rousseaux.
Gegenwart 5 (15 July 1950): 25. H.H.
Lettres françaises, 9 June 1949, 3. André Wurmser.
New Republic 176 (11 June 1977): 27-29. Joyce Carol Oates.
New Statesman 66 (9 Aug. 1963): 169. Brigid Brophy. Also in
   Don't Never Forget, 264-68. London: Cape; New York: Holt,
   Rinehart & Winston, 1966.
New York Review of Books 1 (12 Dec. 1963): 3-4. Frank
   Kermode. Also in *Continuities*, 152-57. London: Routledge &
   Kegan Paul; New York: Random House, 1968.
New York Review of Books 6 (9 June 1966): 8-10. John
   Weightman.
New York Times Book Review, 20 Oct. 1963, 5. Robert Phelps.
Notre Temps, 17 Sept. 1949, 3. Julia Richer.
Nouvelles littéraires, 16 June 1949, 3. René Lalou.
Nouvelles littéraires, 4 Aug. 1949, 4. Francis de Miomandre.
Observer, no. 8975 (7 July 1963): 23. Stevie Smith.
Publishers' Weekly 190 (3 Oct. 1966): 90. Alice Hackett.
Revue de la Méditerranée 8 (May-June 1950): 344-48. Claude
   Delaunay.
Saturday Review 49 (17 Dec. 1966): 36.
Sunday Herald Tribune Book Week 1 (24 Nov. 1963): 4. Glenway
   Wescott.
Temps modernes, no. 48 (Oct. 1949): 749-50. Monique Lange.
Time 82 (18 Oct. 1963): 100.
Times Literary Supplement, no. 3207 (16 Aug. 1963): 627.
Washington Post Book Week 4 (18 June 1967): 13. MIM.

English translations: American

0135 THE BLUE LANTERN. Trans. Roger Senhouse. New York:
      Farrar, Straus, 1963. 161p.

0136 THE BLUE LANTERN. Trans. Roger Senhouse. Westport,
      Conn.: Greenwood Press, 1972. 161p. Not seen.

0137 THE BLUE LANTERN. Trans. Roger Senhouse. New York:
      Farrar, Straus & Giroux, 1977. 161p. Coll. Noonday 547.

      Also in *Break of Day. The Blue Lantern*. Item 0596.

      Extracts in:
      Earthly Paradise [items 0082, 0084-85]. Trans. Roger Senhouse,
      Derek Coltman.
      Gigi and Selected Writings [item 0501]. Trans. Elaine Marks.

English translations: British

0138 THE BLUE LANTERN. Trans. Roger Senhouse. London: Secker
      & Warburg, 1963. 161p. Coll. Uniform 16.

      Extracts in *Earthly Paradise* [items 0087-89]. Trans. Roger
      Senhouse, Derek Coltman.

LA MAISON DE CLAUDINE

0139 LA MAISON DE CLAUDINE. [Colette (Colette Willy)]. Paris:
      Ferenczi, 1922. 252p. Contains 30 texts: Où sont les enfants?
      Le sauvage. Amour. La petite. L'enlèvement. Le curé sur le
      mur. Ma mère et les livres. Propagande. Papa et Mme Bruneau.
      Ma mère et les bêtes. Epitaphes. La fille de mon père. La noce.
      Ma sœur aux longs cheveux. Maternité. Mode de Paris. La
      petite Bouilloux. L'ami. Ybañez est mort. Ma mère et le curé.
      Ma mère et la morale. Le rire. Ma mère et la maladie. Ma mère

et le fruit défendu. La merveille. Bâ-tou. Bellaude. Les deux chattes. Chats. Le veilleur.

0140 LA MAISON DE CLAUDINE. Illus. Clément Serveau. Paris: Ferenczi, 1923. 191p. Coll. Le Livre moderne illustré 2. Contains 29 texts. Omits 6 texts [La merveille. Bâ-tou. Bellaude. Les deux chattes. Chats. Le veilleur]. Adds 5 texts [La Toutouque. Le manteau de spahi. Printemps passé. La couseuse. La noisette creuse].

0141 "Le curé sur le mur." *Conférencia* 17 (15 Jan. 1923): 127-28.

0142 "Ma mère et le fruit défendu." *Conférencia* 17 (15 Oct. 1923): 413-14.

0143 "L'enlèvement." *Le Quotidien*, 16 April 1925, 4.

0144 LA MAISON DE CLAUDINE. Paris: A la cité des livres, 1927. 221p. Coll. Le Roman français d'aujourd'hui 17. Same 29 texts as item 0140.

0145 LA MAISON DE CLAUDINE. Illus. Deslignères. Paris: Rouffé, 1927. 265p. Coll. L'Arabesque 3. Same 29 texts as item 0140.

0146 "Ma mère et les bêtes." In *La femme selon...*, 93-99. Paris: Baudinière, 1928.

0147 LA MAISON DE CLAUDINE. Paris: Flammarion, 1929. 64p. Coll. Select-collection 286. Same 29 texts as item 0140.

0148 LA MAISON DE CLAUDINE. Illus. Hélène Perdriat. Paris: Cent femmes amies des livres, 1929. 219p. Contains 26 texts, those of item 0140 less: Printemps passé. La couseuse. La noisette creuse.

0149 LA MAISON DE CLAUDINE. Paris: Ferenczi, 1930. 281p. Contains all 35 texts published in items 0139 and 0140.

0150 LA MAISON DE CLAUDINE. Illus. Clément Serveau. Paris: Ferenczi, 1932. 39p. Coll. Les Cahiers illustrés 5. Same 29 texts as item 0140.

0151 "La couseuse." *Lisez-moi*, no. 358 (25 March 1937): 437-38.

0152 "Epitaphes." In *Les Plus Jolies Histoires d'enfants*, edited by
      Marcel Berger, 79-85. Paris: Emile-Paul, 1938.

0153 "Les deux chattes." *Lisez-moi*, no. 378 (25 Jan. 1938): 121-22.

0154 LA MAISON DE CLAUDINE. Paris: Flammarion, 1938. 63p.
      Coll. Select-collection 144. Same 29 texts as item 0140.

0155 LA MAISON DE CLAUDINE. SIDO. Lausanne: La Guilde du
      Livre, 1939. 203p. Contains first 24 texts of original ed.

0156 "La Toutouque." *Lisez-moi*, no. 403 (10 Feb. 1939): 191-92.

0157 "L'ami." "Le sauvage." "Ma mère et le fruit défendu." "La
      couseuse." In *Contemporary French Fiction*, edited by Irene
      Cornwall, 13-27. New York: Holt, 1940.

0158 LA MAISON DE CLAUDINE. Illus. Armand Vallée. Paris:
      Colbert, 1946. 215p. Coll. Le Lys d'or. Contains all 35 texts.

0159 LA MAISON DE CLAUDINE. Paris: Ferenczi, 1946. 219p.
      Contains all 35 texts.

0160 "Le veilleur." [Extract]. *Le Point*, no. 39 (May 1951): 48.

0161 "Le grand duc." [Extract from "Le veilleur"]. *Nouvelles littéraires*,
      12 Aug. 1954, 8.

0162 LA MAISON DE CLAUDINE. Paris: Ferenczi, 1955. 192p. Coll.
      Pourpre. Contains all 35 texts.

0163 LA MAISON DE CLAUDINE. Introd. and notes K. Wisbar.
      Paderborn: Schöningh, 1956. 47p. German school edition,
      containing only six texts: Où sont les enfants? Le sauvage.
      Propagande. La petite Bouilloux. Le manteau de spahi. L'ami.
      Includes French-German glossary.

0164 LA MAISON DE CLAUDINE. Paris: Club des jeunes amis du
      livre, 1957. 347p. Contains all 35 texts.

0165 LA MAISON DE CLAUDINE. Illus. Jacques Taillefer. Paris: Eds.
      G.P., 1958. 256p. Coll. Super 27. Contains all 35 texts.

0166 LA MAISON DE CLAUDINE. Introd. Maurice Métral. Neuchâtel:
      Nouvelle Bibliothèque, 1959. 205p. Coll. Club "Aux quais de
      Paris." Not seen.

0167 LA MAISON DE CLAUDINE. Paris: Hachette, 1961. 192p. Coll.
      Livre de poche 763. Contains all 35 texts.

0168 LA MAISON DE CLAUDINE. Introd. and notes Hugh Shelley.
      London: Harrap, 1964. 176p. Study edition for British students.
      Excellent long general introduction in English. Contains all 35
      texts.

0169 "Les pas au plafond." [Extract from "Le veilleur"]. In *Trente-Six
      Histoires de bêtes*, directed by Maurice Rat, 121-22. Paris:
      Casterman, 1964.

0170 "Où sont les enfants?" and "Le curé sur le mur." In *52 nouvelles et
      récits pour elles*, edited by Micheline Denis, 160-65. Paris:
      Gründ, 1965.

0171 LA MAISON DE CLAUDINE. Geneva: Crémille, 1969. 253p.
      Contains all 35 texts.

0172 "La Toutouque." [Extract]. *L'Ecole libératrice*, no. 4 (4 Oct. 1974):
      166.

0173 "La passion de la lecture." [Extract from "Ma sœur aux longs
      cheveux"]. *L'Ecole libératrice*, no. 22 (8 March 1974): 1087.

0174 "Mystère au grenier." [Extract from "Le veilleur"]. In *Les Animaux
      et nous*, edited by Pierre Frémy, 14-16. Paris: Hachette, 1975.
      Children's edition, with study questions.

0175 DE CLAUDINE A COLETTE. Pref. Claude Mauriac. Paris:
      Hachette, 1980. 219p. Coll. Club pour vous Hachette.
      Contains all 35 texts of *La Maison de Claudine*, plus *Sido*.

0176 LA MAISON DE CLAUDINE. Paris: Librairie générale française,
      1983. 158p. Coll. Livre de poche 763. Contains all 35 texts.

0177   LA MAISON DE CLAUDINE. SIDO. LES VRILLES DE LA
       VIGNE. MES APPRENTISSAGES. Paris: Hachette, 1985.
       435p. Not seen.

0178   LA MAISON DE CLAUDINE. LA MAISONNÉE. Presentation
       and commentary Danièle Thibaut. Paris: Hatier, 1988. 128p.
       Coll. Les classiques illustrés Hatier, Œuvres et thèmes. Student
       edition. Second part consists of passages on the theme of
       houses by other authors. First part contains extracts from *La
       Maison de Claudine*, with study questions and commentary.
       Contains 15 texts: Où sont les enfants? Amour. La petite. Le
       curé sur le mur. Ma mère et les livres. Papa et Madame
       Bruneau. Ma mère et les bêtes. Epitaphes. Ma sœur aux longs
       cheveux. La Toutouque. Le manteau de spahi. Le rire. Ma mère
       et le fruit défendu. Le veilleur. La couseuse.

       Also in:
       OP 2 [item 0053]: contains all 35 texts.
       OCLF 7 [item 0054]: contains all 35 texts.
       OCC 6 [item 0055]: contains all 35 texts.
       OF 3 [item 0056]: contains all 35 texts.
       Colette par Colette [item 0061]: contains all 35 texts.
       Sido et souvenirs d'enfance [item 0218]: contains 26 texts. Lacks:
           Mode de Paris. La petite Bouilloux. Ybañez est mort. Bâ-tou.
           Bellaude. Le veilleur. Printemps passé. La couseuse. La noisette
           creuse.

       Extracts in:
       Autobiographie... [items 0057-58].
       Bêtes libres et prisonnières [item 0702]: Hirondelles. L'araignée. La
           chenille. Le rossignol. Rapaces.
       Chats de Colette [items 0714-15]: Idylles. Bâtou. Premiers chats.
       Chiens de Colette [items 0716-17]: Le chiot de Musette. La
           Toutouque. Domino. Bellaude. Pati.
       De la patte à l'aile [item 0723]: Araignée. Chénille.
       Histoires pour Bel-Gazou, all eds.: Ma mère et les bêtes. Où sont
           les enfants? Le curé sur le mur. Ma sœur aux longs cheveux. La
           Toutouque.
       Morceaux choisis [item 0062]: Ma mère et les bêtes. Le veilleur.
           Où sont les enfants? Maternité. Ma mère et la maladie. Ma mère
           et le fruit défendu.

Pages choisies [item 0063]: Ma mère et les bêtes. Le veilleur. Les deux chattes. Maternité. La Toutouque. La noisette creuse. La couseuse.

Les Plus Belles Pages de Colette [item 0064]: Ybañez est mort. La petite Bouilloux. Le curé sur le mur. La noce. Où sont les enfants? Les épitaphes.

Textes choisis de Colette [item 0065]: Ma mère et les bêtes. Ma mère et la maladie. Ma mère et les livres. Propagande. Le sauvage. Le veilleur. Où sont les enfants? Les deux chattes. L'ami. Maternité. Le rire. La Toutouque. Ma mère et le fruit défendu. La couseuse. La noisette creuse.

Beaumont and Parinaud [item 1063].

Jourlait [item 1098]: parts of: Où sont les enfants? Amour. La fille de mon père. Ma mère et le fruit défendu. Le veilleur. Printemps passé.

Lagarde and Michard [item 1764]: Jeux interdits.

Brief stories which, despite the title, do not deal with the fictional character, Claudine, but are based on Colette's own childhood. The main character is usually her mother, Sido, presented in a series of semi-autobiographical anecdotes arranged in roughly chronological order from the time of Colette's early youth to just before Sido's death. After the first edition, stories extraneous to the theme were culled and others were added, including some portraying Colette's own daughter. Later editions include both types. Selections from this book are sometimes used as illustrations of the art of the anecdote or short story. Excellent descriptive passages and characterization. One of Colette's most popular books, this work has played a large role in creating and perpetuating the Sido legend. "Amour" is titled "Jalousie" in many editions.

Reviews:
Books & Bookmen 12 (March 1967): 36. Judith Worthy.
Gaulois, 29 July 1922, 4. André Chaumeix.
Horn Book Magazine 51 (Oct. 1975): 493-94. Mary Silva Cosgrave.
Journal des débats, 9 Aug. 1922, 3. Jean de Pierrefeu.
Larousse mensuel illustré, no. 206 (April 1924): 433-34. Louis Coquelin.
Nation 177 (24 Oct. 1953): 335.
Nouvelles littéraires, 21 Oct. 1922, 1. Mireille Havet.

Saturday Review 36 (21 Nov. 1953): 27, 64. Rosemary Carr
    Benét.
Temps, 27 July 1922, 2. Paul Souday.
Times Literary Supplement, no. 1863 (16 Oct. 1937): 756.
Times Literary Supplement, no. 2683 (3 July 1953): 430.
Times Literary Supplement, no. 2960 (21 Nov. 1958): xxx.
Vinduet 2 (May-June 1948): 393-99. Asbjørn S. Aarnes.

English translations: American

0179 MY MOTHER'S HOUSE. SIDO. Introd. Roger Senhouse. New
      York: Farrar, Straus & Young, 1953. xix-219p. Trans. of *My
      Mother's House* by Una Vincenzo Troubridge and Enid McLeod.
      First title contains 29 texts: Where are the Children? The
      Savage. Jealousy. The Little One. The Abduction. The Priest
      on the Wall. My Mother and the Books. Propaganda. Father and
      Madame Bruneau. My Mother and the Animals. Epitaphs. My
      Father's Daughter. The Wedding. My Sister with the Long Hair.
      Maternity. The Rage of Paris. The Little Bouilloux Girl.
      Toutouque. The Spahi's Cloak. The Friend. Ybañez is Dead.
      My Mother and the Curé. My Mother and Morals. Laughter.
      My Mother and Illness. My Mother and the Forbidden Fruit.
      Bygone Spring. The Semptress. The Hollow Nut.

0180 MY MOTHER'S HOUSE. THE VAGABOND. Garden City,
      N.Y.: Doubleday (Anchor), 1955. 311p. Trans. of *My Mother's
      House* by Una Vincenzo Troubridge and Enid McLeod.
      Contains same 29 texts as item 0179.

0181 MY MOTHER'S HOUSE. SIDO. Introd. Roger Senhouse.
      Westport, Conn.: Greenwood Press, 1972. xviii-219p. Trans. of
      My Mother's House by Una Vincenzo Troubridge and Enid
      McLeod. Contains same 29 texts as item 0179.

0182 MY MOTHER'S HOUSE. SIDO. New York: Farrar, Straus &
      Giroux, 1975. 219p. Coll. Noonday 492. Trans. of *My
      Mother's House* by Una Vincenzo Troubridge and Enid McLeod.
      Contains same 29 texts as item 0179.

Also in *Seven by Colette* [item 0101]. Trans. of *My Mother's House* by Una Vincenzo Troubridge and Enid McLeod. Contains 28 texts, same as item 0179 but lacking "The Hollow Nut."

Extracts in:
The Collected Stories of Colette [items 0071-72]: Bygone Spring. The Seamstress. The Hollow Nut. The Watchman. Trans. Una Vincenzo Troubridge and Enid McLeod, Herma Briffault.
Earthly Paradise [items 0082, 0084-85]. Trans. Una Vincenzo Troubridge and Enid McLeod, Herma Briffault.
Gigi and Selected Writings [item 0501]: Where are the Children? Jealousy. The Priest on the Wall. My Mother and Illness. The Seamstress.

English translations: British

0183 THE MOTHER OF CLAUDINE. Trans. Charles King. London: T. Werner Laurie, 1937. 244p. Contains all 35 texts: Where are the Children? The Savages. Epitaphs. Boyhood's Fellowship. Mathieu. The Priest on the Wall. Forty Sous and a Packet of Tobacco. Propaganda. The Spahi's Cloak. Toutouque. Sido, Adrienne and I. Play is Over. The Lover of Yonne. The Meteorologist and her Flowers. My Mother and the Priest. My Long-haired Sister. The Boys and Juliette's Wedding. Motherhood. The Kidnapping. Paris Fashion. The Bouilloux Girl. The Boy-friend. The Maid's Wedding. My Mother and Morality. Ybañez is Dead. My Mother and the Books. My Father's Daughter. The Errand to the Butcher's. My Mother and her Animals. The Captain. The Links of Love. The Laugh. Ambition Unfulfilled. My Mother and the Forbidden Fruit. My Mother at the Gates of Death.

0184 MY MOTHER'S HOUSE. SIDO. Introd. Roger Senhouse. London: Secker & Warburg, 1953. xix-219p. Coll. Uniform 4. Trans. of *My Mother's House* by Una Vincenzo Troubridge and Enid McLeod. Contains same 29 texts as item 0179.

0185 MY MOTHER'S HOUSE. SIDO. Harmondsworth: Penguin, 1966. 208p. Trans. of *My Mother's House* by Una Vincenzo Troubridge and Enid McLeod. Contains same 29 texts as item 0179.

0186 MY MOTHER'S HOUSE. SIDO. RIPENING SEED. Illus.
      Rosemary Honeybourne. Front. Daniel Briffaud. London: Heron
      Books, 1968. 371p. Trans. of *My Mother's House* by Una
      Vincenzo Troubridge and Enid McLeod. Contains same 29 texts
      as item 0179.

0187 MY MOTHER'S HOUSE. SIDO. Introd. Roger Senhouse.
      London: Secker & Warburg, 1969. 219p. Trans. of *My
      Mother's House* by Una Vincenzo Troubridge and Enid McLeod.
      Contains same 29 texts as item 0179.

0188 MY MOTHER'S HOUSE. Trans. Una Vincenzo Troubridge and
      Enid McLeod. Introd. Ian Serraillier. London: Heinemann
      Educational Books, 1969. 141p. Coll. New Windmill 131.
      Contains same 29 texts as item 0179.

      Extracts in:
      The Collected Stories of Colette [items 0073-74]: same contents as
      American eds.
      Earthly Paradise [items 0087-89]. Trans. Herma Briffault, Una
      Vincenzo Troubridge and Enid McLeod.

      ## MES APPRENTISSAGES

0189 MES APPRENTISSAGES: CE QUE CLAUDINE N'A PAS DIT.
      Paris: Ferenczi, 1936. 223p. With photographs.

0190 MES APPRENTISSAGES: CE QUE CLAUDINE N'A PAS DIT.
      Paris: Hachette, 1954. 221p.

0191 MES APPRENTISSAGES. TROIS-SIX-NEUF. DISCOURS DE
      RÉCEPTION. Geneva: Crémille, 1970. 256p.

0192 MES APPRENTISSAGES: CE QUE CLAUDINE N'A PAS DIT.
      Paris: Livre de poche, 1972. 159p. Coll. Livre de poche 3288.

Also in:
OCLF 11 [item 0054].
OCC 8 [item 0055].
OF 3 [item 0056].
Autobiographie... [items 0057-58].
Colette par Colette [item 0061].
*La Maison de Claudine. Sido. Les Vrilles de la vigne. Mes
    apprentissages.* Item 0177.

Extracts in item 2103 Schifres.

The most autobiographical of all Colette's works. It recounts her
years with Willy, years in which his influence was paramount in
determining the direction of his wife's career. As Colette depicts the
Paris she knew between 1894 and 1910, cafés, fashions and
furnishings, and literary circles come alive for the reader. We are
offered a detailed portrait of Willy as seen through the eyes of his
young wife, as well as sketches of such famous persons as
Caroline Otero, Charlotte Kinceler, Marcel Schwob, Paul Masson,
Catulle Mendès, Léon Barthou, Polaire, Pierre Louÿs and Jean
Lorrain. Colette discusses her relations with Willy along with the
events leading up to their separation and divorce, the beneficial
effect of Willy's criticism on her early work, and the contributions,
both good and bad, that he made to the Claudine novels. The work
caused a furor when it was published in the weekly *Marianne*, 16
Oct.-18 Dec. 1935.

Reviews:
Annales 107 (25 Jan. 1936): 91-92. A. Lang.
Best Sellers 38 (Sept. 1978): 171-72. Njegos M. Petrovic.
Books & Bookmen 2 (July 1957): 27. Margaret Crosland.
Listener 58 (15 Aug. 1957): 247-48.
London Magazine 5 (Jan. 1958): 58-59. Anthony Quinton.
New Statesman 54 (6 July 1957): 28-29. Richard Mayne.
Nouvelle Revue française 46 (Feb. 1936): 273-76. E. Noulet. Also
    in *Alphabet critique*, vol. 1, 347-50. Brussels: Presses
    universitaires de Bruxelles, 1964.
Observer, no. 8661 (30 June 1957): 12. J.G. Weightman.
Sunday Times, 30 June 1957, 7. Cyril Connolly.
Times Literary Supplement, no. 2889 (12 July 1957): 429.
Washington Post Book World, 2 July 1978, F3. Stephen Koch.

English translations: American

0193 MY APPRENTICESHIPS. Trans. Helen Beauclerk. New York: Farrar, Straus & Giroux, 1978. 133p.

0194 MY APPRENTICESHIPS. Trans. Helen Beauclerk. New York: Farrar, Straus & Giroux, 1978. 133p. Coll. Noonday N587.

Extracts in *Earthly Paradise* [items 0082, 0084-85].

English translations: British

0195 MY APPRENTICESHIPS. MUSIC-HALL SIDELIGHTS. London: Secker & Warburg, 1957. 260p. Coll. Uniform 9. Trans. of *My Apprenticeships* by Helen Beauclerk.

0196 MY APPRENTICESHIPS. MUSIC-HALL SIDELIGHTS. Harmondsworth, Penguin, 1967. 219p. Trans. of *My Apprenticeships* by Helen Beauclerk.

Extracts in *Earthly Paradise* [items 0087-89].

NOCES

First published in 1944 in the original edition of *Gigi*, then dropped from that title. Also published as one of the texts of *Broderie ancienne* the same year. Finally moved to the *OCLF* under its own title, thereby gaining in importance. Recounts the day of Colette's wedding to Willy, the modest ceremony and dinner, the almost banal nature of the event, and her mother's distress. The dispassionate tone in which Colette describes what was actually a critical event in her life lends considerable poignancy to this otherwise minor essay. The portrait of her mother is very touching.

Also in:
OCLF 7 [item 0054].

OCC 6 [item 0055].
Autobiographie... [items 0057-58].
Broderie ancienne [item 0703].
Sido. Noces. La Femme cachée. Item 0219.

English translation: American

xxxx "Wedding Day." Trans. Herma Briffault. In *Earthly Paradise* [items 0082, 0084-85].

English translation: British

xxxx "Wedding Day." Trans. Herma Briffault. In *Earthly Paradise* [items 0087-89].

PARIS DE MA FENETRE

See *De ma fenêtre.*

LE PUR ET L'IMPUR

0197 CES PLAISIRS. Paris: Ferenczi, 1932. 251p.

0198 "Capteuse de sources..." [Extract]. *Lisez-moi*, no. 383 (10 April 1933): 520.

0199 CES PLAISIRS... Illus. Clément Serveau. Paris: Ferenczi, 1934. 159p. Coll. Le livre moderne illustré 189.

0200 LE PUR ET L'IMPUR. Paris: Aux Armes de France, 1941. 203p.

0201 "Jalousie." [Extract]. *Nouvelles littéraires*, 12 Aug. 1954, 8.

0202 LE PUR ET L'IMPUR. Geneva: Crémille, 1970. 251p.

0203 LE PUR ET L'IMPUR. Paris: Hachette, 1971. 191p. Coll. Livre de poche 3200.

0204 LE PUR ET L'IMPUR. Paris: Hachette, 1979. 135p.

0205 LE PUR ET L'IMPUR. Paris: Librairie générale française, 1988. 189p. Coll. Livre de poche 6479.

Also in:
OCLF 9 [item 0054].
OCC 7 [item 0055].
OF 3 [item 0056].

Extracts in:
Autobiographie... [items 0057-58]: Renée Vivien. Don Juan. La Chevalière. Amalia X. Sodome. Le pur et l'impur.
Morceaux choisis [item 0062].
Textes choisis de Colette [item 0065]: Capteuse de sources...
Beaumont and Parinaud [item 1063].

Completely different from any of Colette's other books, *Le Pur et l'impur* is as much a treatise as it is a connected series of essays on different types of love, especially "those that the commonalty condemns." It consists of eight distinct sections, wherein Colette refers to specific examples of the phenomenon under study. The book opens with two chapters comprising what may well be Colette's most compelling portrait: that of the unforgettable Charlotte, a mature woman in love with a young man and seeking solace and fulfillment in an opium den. Then, by contrast with Charlotte, Colette's Don Juan is a misogynist and a misanthropist, bitter and dissatisfied despite his conquests. Four chapters of the book are devoted to all-female attachments. Colette's portrait of the androgynous La Chevalière is sympathetic, as is her evocation of the world of the Sapphic poet, Renée Vivien, whom she knew well. Conversations with the knowledgeable Amalia X and a long reflective passage on "the two ladies of Llangollen," who, after a scandalous elopement during the eighteenth century, lived together for over fifty years, round out the series. Colette accords less space to male homosexuality, but after assessing its weaknesses and strengths, finds it to be on the whole more enduring than its female counterpart. A short chapter on jealousy, which includes passages on episodes in her own life, completes the book. This is an essential work for those who seek to know Colette's mind. Although she uses only initials and false names, many of the persons portrayed have been easily identified by researchers. The dispassionate style that Colette uses in presenting her difficult subject, and the restrained lyricism of several passages, make of this an extraordinary work. Originally published as *Ces Plaisirs* in 1932, it was substantially modified and enlarged before acquiring its final title in 1941. It incorporates two essays published earlier, *Renée Vivien* and *Supplément à Don Juan*.

Reviews:
Best Sellers 27 (15 Sept. 1967): 226. John P. McAleer.
Booklist 64 (1 Oct. 1967): 164.
Choice 5 (April 1968): 200-2.
Guardian, 10 May 1968, 9. Christopher Wordsworth.
Illustrated London News 252 (1 June 1968): 32. Maurice Prior.
Library Journal 92 (Aug. 1967): 2756. Dorothy Curley.
Listener 80 (12 Sept. 1968): 344. Mary Sullivan.
Mercure de France, 1 April 1932, 157-58. John Charpentier.
Monde, 25 Jan. 1973, 21. Gérard Bonal.
New Statesman 75 (17 May 1968): 658-59. Gillian Tindall.
Nueva Estafeta 50 (Jan. 1983): 86-87. Manuel Ríos Ruiz.
Observer, no. 9225 (5 May 1968): 26. Claire Tomalin.
Observer, no. 9385 (6 June 1971): 22.
Publishers' Weekly 191 (26 June 1967): 66.
Saturday Review 50 (9 Sept. 1967): 33. Laurent LeSage.
Saturday Review 2 (20 Sept. 1975): 30-32. Stephen Koch.
Spectator 220 (28 June 1968): 892-94. Bryan Robertson.
Sunday Times, 5 May 1968, 57. Cyril Connolly.
Times Literary Supplement, no. 3465 (25 July 1968): 805. Reply by Herma Briffault in no. 3469 (22 Aug. 1968): 905.

English translations: American

0206 THE PURE AND THE IMPURE: A CASE-BOOK OF LOVE. Trans. Edith Dally. Introd. Joseph Collins. On Murray Hill, N.Y.: Farrar & Rinehart, 1933. 229p. Translation of the earlier version, despite the title.

0207   THE PURE AND THE IMPURE. Trans. Herma Briffault. Introd.
       Janet Flanner. New York: Farrar, Straus & Giroux, 1967. 175p.

0208   THE PURE AND THE IMPURE. Trans. Herma Briffault. Introd.
       Janet Flanner. New York: Farrar, Straus & Giroux, 1975. 175p.
       Coll. Noonday N345.

       Extracts in *Earthly Paradise* [items 0082, 0084-85]: Renée Vivien.
       Don Juan. La Chevalière. Amalia X. Sodom. The Pure and the
       Impure. Trans. Herma Briffault.

English translations: British

0209   THESE PLEASURES. [Trans. Edith Dally]. Introd. J.C. [Joseph
       Collins]. London: White Owl Press, 1934. 232p. Translation of
       the early version.

0210   THE PURE AND THE IMPURE. THE INNOCENT LIBERTINE.
       Illus. André-Nicolas Suter. Front. Daniel Briffaud. London:
       Heron Books, 1968. 371p. Trans. of *The Pure and the Impure*
       by Herma Briffault.

0211   THE PURE AND THE IMPURE. Trans. Herma Briffault. Introd.
       Janet Flanner. London: Secker & Warburg, 1968. 172p.

0212   THE PURE AND THE IMPURE. Trans. Herma Briffault. Introd.
       Janet Flanner. Harmondsworth: Penguin, 1971. 138p.

       Extracts in *Earthly Paradise* [items 0087-89]: same contents as
       American eds.

RENÉE VIVIEN

0213   RENÉE VIVIEN. Abbeville: [F. Paillart], 1928. 24p. Coll. Les
       Amis d'Edouard 131. Small pamphlet, private edition. Born
       Pauline Tarn, Englishwoman Renée Vivien frequented the same

lesbian circles of Paris as Colette did during the first decade of
the century. Her reminiscences paint a delicate portrait of a
young woman who behind an effusive persona kept her own
secrets, before dying in 1909 at the age of 32. Incorporated into
Ces plaisirs and then into *Le Pur et l'impur*.

SIDO

0214   SIDO OU LES POINTS CARDINAUX. Paris: Kra, 1929. 79p.
       Coll. Femmes 5. The only edition to contain just two parts:
       Sido. Le capitaine.

0215   SIDO. Paris: Ferenczi, 1930. 183p. This and all subsequent
       editions contain three parts: Sido. Le capitaine. Les sauvages.

0216   SIDO. Illus. Clément Serveau. Paris: Ferenczi, 1935. 157p. Coll.
       Le Livre moderne illustré 216.

0217   SIDO. LES VRILLES DE LA VIGNE. Paris: Ferenczi, 1958.
       256p. Coll. Livre de poche 373.

0218   SIDO ET SOUVENIRS D'ENFANCE. Introd. Marcel Thiébaut.
       Paris: Hachette, 1961. 224p. Coll. du Flambeau. Includes *Sido*,
       26 texts from *La Maison de Claudine*, "Le pays que j'ai quitté"
       from *Les Vrilles de la vigne, Flore et Pomone*, and "Ma
       Bourgogne pauvre" from *En pays connu*.

0219   SIDO. NOCES. LA FEMME CACHÉE. Geneva: Crémille, 1970.
       249p.

0220   SIDO. LES VRILLES DE LA VIGNE. Paris: Eds. G.P., 1973.
       255p. Coll. Super 180.

Also in:
OCLF 7 [item 0054]: contains all 3 parts.
OCC 6 [item 0055]: contains all 3 parts.
OF 3 [item 0056]: contains all 3 parts.

Colette par Colette [item 0061]: contains all 3 parts.
De Claudine à Colette [item 0175]: contains all 3 parts.
La Maison de Claudine. Sido. Item 0155: contains all 3 parts.
*La Maison de Claudine. Sido. Les Vrilles de la vigne. Mes
    apprentissages.* Item 0177: contains all 3 parts.
Peytard [item 1971]: contains all 3 parts.

Extracts in:
Autobiographie... [items 0057-58].
Bêtes libres et prisonnières [item 0702]: Et ma mère parlait...
Chiens de Colette [items 0716-17]: Moffino.
Morceaux choisis [item 0062].
Pages choisies [item 0063].
Textes choisis de Colette [item 0065].
Beaumont and Parinaud [item 1063].
Collet [item 1424].
Lagarde and Michard [item 1764].
Schifres [item 2103].

The first edition of this very popular work contained only two
sections. In "Sido" Colette evokes the pivotal role played by that
legendary figure in her children's lives, as well as her relations with
the village people. In "Le Capitaine," her father's devotion to Sido
is sensitively described; the passages wherein Colette writes of his
secret sadness and broken dreams are especially touching. In all
subsequent editions, a third section, "Les Sauvages," rounds out the
family portrait. Colette's sister Juliette and her two brothers, Léo
and Achille, live again for the reader, as does this semi-fictional
version of the young Gabrielle Colette. Despite the three divisions,
the presence of Sido dominates the entire work. Next to *La Maison
de Claudine*, this book is a favorite of the young and, together with
that title, has been a major factor in the creation and perpetuation
of the Sido legend, whereby Colette's mother is immortalized as a
wise earth-mother who reigned over a village kingdom of children,
animals and plants.

Reviews:
Annales, 1 Aug. 1930, 103. Benjamin Crémieux.
Europe, no. 99 (15 March 1931): 428-29. J.R.
Figaro, 22 July 1930, 5. Henri de Régnier.
Horn Book Magazine 51 (Oct. 1975): 493-94. Mary Silva
    Cosgrave.

Mercure de France, 1 Aug. 1930, 678-79. John Charpentier.
Nation 177 (24 Oct. 1953): 335.
Nouvelle Revue française 35 (1 Aug. 1930): 284. B.Cr. [Benjamin Crémieux].
Nouvelles littéraires, 28 June 1930, 3. Edmond Jaloux.
Œuvre, 8 July 1930, 5. André Billy.
Petit Parisien, 8 July 1930, 4. Jean Vignaud.
Quinzaine critique 1 (25 Jan. 1930): 290-91. René Lalou.
Quinzaine critique 2 (25 July 1930): 447. René Lalou.
Saturday Review 36 (21 Nov. 1953): 27, 64. Rosemary Carr Benét.
Temps, 15 Aug. 1930, 3. André Thérive.
Times Literary Supplement, no. 2683 (3 July 1953): 430.
Vinduet 2 (May-June 1948): 393-99. Asbjørn S. Aarnes.

English translations: American

xxxx   SIDO. Trans. Enid McLeod. In *My Mother's House. Sido*. Items 0179, 0181-82.

Extracts in:
Earthly Paradise [items 0082, 0084-85].
Gigi and Selected Writings [item 0501]: The Savages.

English translations: British

xxxx   SIDO. Trans. Enid McLeod.

In:
My Mother's House. Sido. Items 0184-85, 0187.
My Mother's House. Sido. Ripening Seed. Item 0186.

Extracts in *Earthly Paradise* [items 0087-89].

SUPPLÉMENT A DON JUAN

0221 SUPPLÉMENT A DON JUAN. Illus. Gérard Cochet. Paris: Eds.
du Trianon, 1931. 73p. Coll. Suppléments à quelques œuvres
célèbres 15. Study of the Don Juan phenomenon. Colette later
incorporated it into her long study of diverse sexual patterns, *Le
Pur et l'impur*.

TROIS... SIX... NEUF...

0222 TROIS-SIX-NEUF. Illus. Dignimont. Paris: Corrêa, 1944. 111p.

0223 TROIS... SIX... NEUF... Paris: Corrêa, 1946. 109p.

0224 TROIS... SIX... NEUF... Pref. Maurice Goudeket. Paris:
Buchet/Chastel, 1970. 109p.

Also in:
OCLF 12 [item 0054].
OCC 10 [item 0055].
Bella-Vista. Trois... six... neuf. Item 0230.
Mes apprentissages. Trois, six, neuf. Discours de réception. Item
0191.

Extracts in *Autobiographie...* [items 0057-58].

In conversational style and in chronological order, Colette describes
the houses and apartments in which she lived in Paris, from the
time of her first marriage to that of her second installation in the
Palais Royal more than forty years later. Details of furniture and
furnishings, reactions of animals and friends, comments about her
own adaptability and her own likes and dislikes: all are mingled
with Colette's impressions of the dozen or so dwellings in
question. Even for those not familiar with Colette's biography this
book makes fascinating reading.

Reviews:
Bulletin critique du livre français 2:3 (1947): 6-7.
Bulletin critique du livre français 26:1 (1971): 11.
Figaro littéraire, 19 July 1947, 2. André Rousseaux.
Nouvelles littéraires, 13 Feb. 1947, 3. Intérim. [René Lalou].
Nouvelles littéraires, 3 Feb. 1949, 2. Robert Kemp. Also in *La Vie des livres*, vol. 2, 210-14. Paris: Albin Michel, 1962.

English translations: American

xxxx "Three... Six... Nine..." Trans. David Le Vay. In *Places* [item 0098].

Extracts in *Earthly Paradise* [items 0082, 0084-85]. Trans. Herma Briffault.

English translations: British

xxxx "Three... Six... Nine..." Trans. David Le Vay. In *Places* [item 0099].

Extracts in *Earthly Paradise* [items 0087-89]. Trans. Herma Briffault.

NOVELS AND NOVELLAS

ARMANDE

In *Le Képi*, all eds. See that title.

Light-hearted tale of Maxime, a young man in love with a girl he has known all his life but who intimidates him so much that he is afraid to confess his feelings. A sudden accident elicits from Armande a reaction destined to bring about a happy ending. Appealing characters finely drawn.

English translations: American

0225 "Armande." [Trans. Antonia White]. *Mademoiselle* 48 (Feb. 1959): 112, 155-61.

Also in:
The Collected Stories of Colette [items 0071-72].
Gigi and Selected Writings [item 0501].
The Tender Shoot and Other Stories [items 0106-8].

English translations: British

xxxx   ARMANDE. Trans. Antonia White.

In:
The Collected Stories of Colette [items 0073-74].
The Rainy Moon and Other Stories [item 0111].
The Stories of Colette [items 0109-10].

BELLA-VISTA

0226   BELLA-VISTA. Paris: Ferenczi, 1937. 251p. Contains 4 novellas: *Bella-Vista. Gribiche. Le Rendez-vous. Le Sieur Binard.*

0227   BELLA-VISTA. Illus. Jacques Thévenet. Paris: Eds. de la Galerie Charpentier, 1947. 113p. Contains only the title novella.

0228   BELLA-VISTA. Paris: Flammarion-Hachette, 1971. 219p. Same contents as item 0226.

0229   BELLA-VISTA. Geneva: Crémille, 1971. 245p. Same contents as item 0226.

0230   BELLA-VISTA. TROIS... SIX... NEUF... Paris: Hachette-Buchet/Chastel, 1974. 224p. Coll. Livre de poche 4004. First title has same contents as item 0226.

0231   BELLA-VISTA. Paris: Fayard, 1986. 171p. Same contents as item 0226.

Also in:
OCLF 11 [item 0054]: same contents as item 0226.
OCC 8 [item 0055]: same contents as item 0226.
OF 3 [item 0056]: same contents as item 0226.

Extracts in *Chiens de Colette* [items 0716-17]: Pati.

Marvellous demonstration of how to create an atmosphere of mystery from a series of trifles. Semi-autobiographical narrator Madame Colette is staying at a small hotel while workmen invade her villa at Saint Tropez. The novella explores the question of appearances as Madame Colette becomes more and more aware of mystery on two fronts. What is the secret of the guest, Monsieur Daste, a pleasant businessman given to night wanderings, skilled at climbing trees, feared by birds and held in aversion by the dog? And what is the secret of the inn's owners, the garrulous Madame Suzanne and the masculine Madame Ruby, as expert at embroidery as at provoking tears from the maid Lucie? Little by little, the surprising conclusion unfolds. An intriguing tale offering, as a bonus, splendid descriptive passages of the south of France.

Reviews:
Action française, 9 Dec. 1937, 5. Robert Brasillach. Also in
    Œuvres complètes de Robert Brasillach, vol. 12, 122-23. Paris:
    Club de l'honnête homme, 1964.
Mercure de France, 15 Feb. 1938, 133-34. John Charpentier.
Nouvelle Revue française 50 (Feb. 1938): 127-29. Jean Vaudal.
Times Literary Supplement, no. 1879 (5 Feb. 1938): 88.

English translations: American

xxxx BELLA-VISTA. Trans. Antonia White.

In:
The Collected Stories of Colette [items 0071-72]. Trans. of pref.
    Matthew Ward.
The Tender Shoot and Other Stories [items 0106-8].

English translations: British

xxxx BELLA-VISTA. Trans. Antonia White.

In:
The Collected Stories of Colette [items 0073-74]. Trans. of pref.
    Matthew Ward.
The Rainy Moon and Other Stories [item 0111].
The Stories of Colette [items 0109-10].

LE BLÉ EN HERBE

0232 LE BLÉ EN HERBE. Paris: Flammarion, 1923. 249p.

0233 LE BLÉ EN HERBE. Paris: Flammarion, 1924. 71p. Coll. Le Roman d'aujourd'hui 23.

0234 LE BLÉ EN HERBE. Illus. Clément Serveau, Renefer. Paris: Flammarion, 1927. 211p. Coll. Le Signet d'or.

0235 LE BLÉ EN HERBE. Illus. G. Bernard. Paris: Ferenczi, 1928. 157p. Coll. Le Livre moderne illustré 69.

0236 LE BLÉ EN HERBE. Paris: Flammarion, 1932. 211p.

0237 LE BLÉ EN HERBE. Paris: Flammarion, 1934. 64p. Coll. Select-collection 49 (new series).

0238 LE BLÉ EN HERBE. Illus. Jean Berque. Paris: Jean Berque, 1946. 189p. Private edition.

0239 LE BLÉ EN HERBE. Illus. Marianne Clouzot. Paris: Flammarion, 1947. 217p.

0240 AVRIL: UN CHAPITRE ANTICIPÉ DU 'BLÉ EN HERBE.' Paris: Pour les amis de Colette et de Daragnès, 1949. 23p. Private edition of only 50 copies. Rejected chapter in which Phil and Vinca stumble upon a couple making love. Also in some eds. of *La Fleur de l'âge*.

0241 LE BLÉ EN HERBE. Illus. Jacques Cura, Clément Serveau. Paris: Ferenczi, 1952. 127p. Coll. Le Livre moderne illustré 400.

0242 LE BLÉ EN HERBE. Paris: Flammarion, 1954. 203p.

0243 LE BLÉ EN HERBE. Paris: Club des Editeurs, 1956. 203p. Coll. Club des éditeurs 4. Not seen.

0244 LE BLÉ EN HERBE. Paris: Flammarion, 1958. 191p. Coll. J'ai lu 2.

0245 LE BLÉ EN HERBE. Paris: Eds. J'ai lu, 1969. 192p. Coll. J'ai lu 2.

0246 LE BLÉ EN HERBE. Chronology and pref. Claude Pichois. Paris: Garnier-Flammarion, 1969. 190p. Coll. Garnier-Flammarion 218.

0247 LE BLÉ EN HERBE. Geneva: Crémille, 1969. 241p.

0248 LE BLÉ EN HERBE. Paris: Flammarion, 1970. 221p.

0249 LE BLÉ EN HERBE. Illus. P. Debraine-Nemo. Paris: Club du Livre selectionné, [1970-1975]. 260p. Not seen.

0250 LE BLÉ EN HERBE. Illus. Brianchon. Paris: Les Francs-Bibliophiles, 1971. 139p. Coll. Société des Francs bibliophiles 21.

0251 LE BLÉ EN HERBE. Paris: Ediclub-Rombaldi, 1975. 255p.

0252 LE BLÉ EN HERBE. Pref. Emile Henriot. Front. Picasso. Geneva: Farnot, 1975. 253p. Coll. Classiques du XXe siècle. Not seen.

0253 LE BLÉ EN HERBE. Foreword Pierre Kyria. Paris: France Loisirs, 1977. 32-160p. Coll. un auteur, une œuvre 3. Includes chronology, press notices and comments by other writers.

0254 LE BLÉ EN HERBE. Paris: J'ai lu, 1979. 128p. Coll. J'ai lu 2.

0255 LE BLÉ EN HERBE. Introd. and notes Brian Stimpson. London: Hodder & Stoughton, 1980. 160p. Coll. Textes français classiques et modernes. British student edition. Excellent long introduction.

0256 LE BLÉ EN HERBE. Illus. Marianne Clouzot. Paris: Flammarion, 1982. 191p. Coll. Bibliothèque du chat perché.

Also in:
OP 2 [item 0053]: includes "Avril."
OCLF 7 [item 0054].

OCC 6 [item 0055].
OF 2 [item 0056].

Extracts in:
Morceaux choisis [item 0062].
Les Plus Belles Pages de Colette [item 0064].
Beaumont and Parinaud [item 1063].

The only one of Colette's novels set in the Breton landscape and
her only fictional portrayal of adolescent love. Since infancy, Phil's
family and Vinca's have spent the summers together at the seaside.
This year the two children are sixteen and fifteen respectively. Now
conscious of their own bodies and of their attraction to each other,
they are emotionally inexperienced in handling desire. The plot is
complicated by the presence of the mysterious "lady in white," who
seduces Phil. Initial publication in *Le Matin* was suspended before
the last chapter, in which the sexual act is discreetly depicted. In
her portrait of Vinca, Colette exploits one of her recurring minor
themes: the tenacity, wisdom and even inherent superiority of the
female.

Reviews:
Action française, 20 Nov. 1923, 4. Orion.
Annales politiques & littéraires, 7 Oct. 1923, 387-88. G. de
      Pawlowski.
Books & Bookmen 1 (Dec. 1955): 39-41. John Peene Harris.
Commonweal 64 (10 Aug. 1956): 473. Alice Saxon.
Estafeta Literaria, no. 480 (15 Nov. 1971): 755. Emilio Rey.
Europe 1 (15 Sept. 1923): 503-4. Paul Colin.
Europe nouvelle, 18 Aug. 1923, 1047-48. Dominique Braga.
Figaro, 7 Aug. 1923, 3. Henri de Régnier.
French Review 55 (Feb. 1982): 417-18. Joan Hinde Stewart.
French Studies 26 (July 1972): 359-60. Sheila M. Bell.
National & English Review 145 (Dec. 1955): 355. Milward
      Kennedy.
New Statesman & Nation 50 (12 Nov. 1955): 633-34. Richard
      Lister.
Nouvel Observateur, 10 Aug. 1970, 30-31. Jean Freustié.
Nouvelle Revue critique 7 (15 Sept. 1923): 492-95. André Keller-
      Lautier [Fernande Keller and André Lautier].
Nouvelle Revue française 21 (1 Sept. 1923): 361-62. Henri
      Pourrat.

Nouvelles littéraires, 25 Aug. 1923, 2. Benjamin Crémieux.
Revue mondiale 154 (15 Aug. 1923): 436. Nicolas Ségur.
Saturday Review 2 (20 Sept. 1975): 30-32. Stephen Koch.
Temps, 12 July 1923, 3. Paul Souday.
Times Educational Supplement, no. 3412 (20 Nov. 1981): 27.
   Robin Buss.
Times Literary Supplement, no. 1559 (17 Dec. 1931): 1029-30.
Times Literary Supplement, no. 2810 (6 Jan. 1956): 5.

English translations: American

0257 THE RIPENING. Trans. Ida Zeitlin. On Murray Hill, N.Y.: Farrar
      & Rinehart, 1932. 244p.

0258 THE RIPENING SEED. Trans. Roger Senhouse. New York: New
      American Library (Signet), 1955. Not seen.

0259 THE RIPENING SEED. Trans. Roger Senhouse. New York:
      Farrar, Straus & Cudahy, 1956. 186p.

0260 RIPENING SEED. Trans. Roger Senhouse. Westport, Conn.:
      Greenwood Press, 1972. 152p.

0261 THE RIPENING SEED. Trans. Roger Senhouse. New York:
      Farrar, Straus & Giroux, 1975. 186p. Coll. Noonday N506.

English translations: British

0262 THE RIPENING CORN. Trans. Phyllis Mégroz. London:
      Gollancz, 1931. 279p.

0263 RIPENING SEED. Trans. Roger Senhouse. London: Secker &
      Warburg, 1955. 152p. Coll. Uniform 7.

0264 RIPENING SEED. Trans. Roger Senhouse. Harmondsworth:
      Penguin, 1959. 122p.

0265 THE RIPENING SEED. Trans. Roger Senhouse. London: Secker
      & Warburg, 1969. 148p.

Also in:
Colette Omnibus [item 0069].
My Mother's House. Sido. Ripening Seed. Item 0186. Trans.
   Roger Senhouse.
Six Novels [item 0103]. Trans. Roger Senhouse.

CHAMBRE D'HOTEL

0266   CHAMBRE D'HOTEL. Paris: Fayard, 1939. 219p. Includes *La
       Lune de pluie.*

0267   CHAMBRE D'HOTEL. Illus. Clément Serveau. Paris: Ferenczi,
       1946. 127p. Coll. Le livre moderne illustré 368. Includes *La
       Lune de pluie.*

0268   CHAMBRE D'HOTEL. Paris: Fayard, 1954. 191p. Includes *La
       Lune de pluie.*

0269   CHAMBRE D'HOTEL. Paris: Fayard, 1964. 191p. Coll. Livre de
       poche 1312. Includes *La Lune de pluie.*

0270   CHAMBRE D'HOTEL. Geneva: Crémille, 1971. 245p. Includes
       La Lune de pluie.

0271   CHAMBRE D'HOTEL. Paris: Fayard, 1984. 192p. Includes *La
       Lune de pluie.*

Also in:
OCLF 11 [item 0054]: includes *La Lune de pluie.*
OCC 9 [item 0055]: includes *La Lune de pluie.*
OF 3 [item 0056]: includes *La Lune de pluie.*

Extracts in *Chats de Colette* [items 0714-15]: Chats des voyages.

Narrator Madame Colette sublets a country chalet from a music-
hall acquaintance, Lucette, but her disappointment with it causes
her to move to a nearby hotel, where she meets Antoinette and

Gérard Haume. Gérard's strange behaviour awakens her curiosity, draws her unwillingly into listening to his confession, and finally into making an enquiry on his behalf. Her discovery causes a rift between them. The main interest lies, not in the story, but in the characters themselves, and in Madame Colette's reactions to them. Subtle but remarkable are the contrasts that Colette establishes among the diverse characters: between Gérard and Antoinette, between Antoinette and Lucette, and even between Gérard and Lucette's humble lover, Luigi.

Reviews:
American Mercury 75 (Dec. 1952): 100-3. William Phillips.
Candide, 26 March 1941, 5. Jacques de Lacretelle. Also in *L'Heure qui change*, 139-45. Geneva: Eds. du Milieu du monde, 1941.
Hispano Americano 67 (25 Aug. 1975): 56. A.M.E. [Antonio Magaña Esquival].
New Statesman & Nation 44 (19 July 1952): 82-83. John Raymond.
Partisan Review 20 (May-June 1953): 332-38. Sonya Rudikoff.
Time & Tide 33 (26 July 1952): 857-58. Gerard Hopkins.
Times Literary Supplement, no. 2636 (8 Aug. 1952): 513.

English translations: American

xxxx CHANCE ACQUAINTANCES. Trans. Patrick Leigh Fermor.

In:
Gigi. Julie de Carneilhan. Chance Acquaintances. Items 0499 and 0502.
Seven by Colette [item 0101].

English translations: British

xxxx CHANCE ACQUAINTANCES. Trans. Patrick Leigh Fermor.

In *Julie de Carneilhan. Chance Acquaintances.* Items 0549-50.

LA CHATTE

0272 LA CHATTE. Paris: Grasset, 1933. 211p. Coll. Pour mon plaisir 3.

0273 LA CHATTE. Paris: Grasset, 1933. 211p. Coll. Œuvres de Colette 11.

0274 LA CHATTE. Illus. Guyot. Paris: Ferenczi, 1935. 160p. Coll. Le Livre moderne illustré 224.

0275 LA CHATTE. Illus. Jean A. Mercier. Paris: Fayard, 1945. 200p.

0276 LA CHATTE. Paris: Ferenczi, 1947. 211p.

0277 LA CHATTE. Paris: Ferenczi, 1948. 191p. Coll. du jour.

0278 LA CHATTE. Front. G. de Sainte-Croix. Paris: Compagnons du livre, 1952. 219p.

0279 LA CHATTE. Paris: Ferenczi, 1955. 191p. Coll. Pourpre.

0280 LA CHATTE. Paris: Ferenczi, 1955. 184p. Coll. Livre de poche 96.

0281 LA CHATTE. Paris: Grasset, 1957. 248p. Contains manuscript fac-simile of the "assassination" scene.

0282 LA CHATTE. BELLES SAISONS. Geneva: Crémille, 1970. 241p.

0283 LA CHATTE. Paris: Ediclub-Rombaldi, 1975. 239p.

0284 LA CHATTE. Paris: Librairie générale française, 1988. 160p. Coll. Livre de poche 96.

Also in:
OCLF 9 [item 0054].
OCC 7 [item 0055].
OF 2 [item 0056].

Extracts in:
Chats de Colette [items 0714-15].
Morceaux choisis [item 0062].
Beaumont and Parinaud [item 1063].
Lagarde and Michard [item 1764].

A marriage is arranged between Camille, a modern young woman who is fond of fast cars and the latest fashions, and Alain, a pampered but old-fashioned young man attached to his past. More and more jealous of Alain's beloved cat, Saha, Camille views it as a rival of whom she must rid herself. The result is dramatic and irrevocable. The surprise ending of this novel has made it one of Colette's most controversial. Her remarkable portrayal of the cat Saha, whose psychology is revealed without any recourse to anthropomorphic characterization, and the delicacy with which she awakens complex reactions on the part of the reader, make this unusual novel an artistic *tour de force*.

Reviews:
Annales, 14 July 1933, 47. André Lang.
Europe nouvelle, 8 July 1933, 646-47. Pierre Bost.
Illustration, no. 4716 (22 July 1933): 430-31. Albéric Cahuet.
Journal des débats 14 (7 July 1933): 69. Henry Bidou.
Mercure de France, 1 Sept. 1933, 413-15. John Charpentier.
Nouvelle Revue française 41 (Aug. 1933): 273-75. Marcel Arland.
Revue mondiale, 15 July 1933, 33-34. Louis-Jean Finot.
Time 28 (17 Aug. 1936): 69.
Times Literary Supplement, no. 1645 (10 Aug. 1933): 534.
Times Literary Supplement, no. 1833 (20 March 1937): 214.
Times Literary Supplement, no. 2698 (16 Oct. 1953): 657.

English translations: American

0285 THE CAT. Trans. Morris Bentinck. Decorations Susanne Suba. On Murray Hill, N.Y.: Farrar & Rinehart, 1936. 165p.

0286 THE CAT. Trans. Antonia White. New York: Popular Library, 1974. Not seen.

Also in:
Seven by Colette [item 0101]. Trans. Antonia White.
Short Novels of Colette [item 0102]. Trans. Morris Bentinck.

Extracts in *Gigi and Selected Writings* [item 0501]. Trans. Antonia White.

English translations: British

0287   SAHA, THE CAT. Trans. Morris Bentinck. London: T. Werner Laurie, 1936. 176p.

xxxx   THE CAT. Trans. Antonia White.

In:
Colette Omnibus [item 0069].
Gigi. The Cat. Items 0503-4.
Six Novels [item 0103].

CHÉRI

0288   CHÉRI. [Colette (Colette Willy)]. Paris: Fayard, 1920. 253p.

0289   CHÉRI. [Colette (Colette Willy)]. Illus. Georges Jeanniot. Paris: Fayard, 1924. 127p. Coll. Le Livre de demain 18.

0290   CHÉRI. [Colette (Colette Willy)]. Illus. Lobel-Riche. Paris: Blanchetière, 1925. 203p.

0291   CHÉRI. Paris: Grasset, 1928. 229p. Coll. Œuvres de Colette 1.

0292   CHÉRI. Paris: Flammarion, 1928. 64p. Coll. Select-collection 283.

0293   CHÉRI. Illus. Marcel Vertès. Paris: Ed. de la Roseraie, 1929. 173p.

0294 CHÉRI. Paris: Fayard, 1932. 40p. Coll. Les Feuillets littéraires 3.

0295 CHÉRI. Paris: Flammarion, 1936. 63p. Coll. Select-collection 91 (new series).

0296 "Chéri." *Lisez-moi*, no. 344 (25 Aug. 1936): 241-54; no. 345 (10 Sept. 1936): 365-78; no. 346 (25 Sept. 1936): 423-37; no. 347 (10 Oct. 1936): 481-95.

0297 CHÉRI. [Colette (Colette Willy)]. Paris: Calmann-Lévy, 1939. 192p. Coll. Pourpre.

0298 CHÉRI. Rio de Janeiro: Americ=Edit, 1940. 240p.

0299 CHÉRI. Illus. Courbouleix. Paris: A l'emblème du Secrétaire, 1941. 191p.

0300 CHÉRI. Illus. Jacques Cura. Paris: Athêna, 1947. 278p. Coll. Athêna-Luxe.

0301 CHÉRI. Introd. Jean Nicollier. Front. Paul Monnier. Geneva: A l'enseigne du Cheval ailé, 1947. 189p. Coll. Classiques français du XXe siècle 6.

0302 CHÉRI. Paris: Fayard, 1950. 223p. Coll. Romans et littérature.

0303 CHÉRI. Illus. Grau Sala. Paris: Vialetay, 1952. 191p.

0304 CHÉRI. Paris: Fayard, 1958. 192p. Coll. Livre de poche 307.

0305 CHÉRI. LA FIN DE CHÉRI. Illus. Grau Sala. Pref. Maurice Goudeket. Includes "Colette" by Gabrielle Blot. Paris: Club des amis du livre, 1961. 461p. Coll. Le Meilleur livre de la femme.

0306 CHÉRI. Geneva: Crémille, 1968. 247p.

0307 CHÉRI. Paris: Flammarion, 1970. 189p.

0308 CHÉRI. Pref. Maurice Goudeket. Paris: Tallandier, 1974. 191-46p. Coll. Ecrivains du siècle. Appendix includes photos and comments by others.

0309   CHÉRI. Paris: Ediclub-Rombaldi, 1975. 271p.

0310   CHÉRI. Paris: France Loisirs, 1982. 32-192p. Coll. un auteur,
       une œuvre 20. Includes press notices, appreciations by other
       writers, photographs and a chronology.

0311   CHÉRI. Paris: Grands Ecrivains, 1983. 189p. First in the series
       "Grands écrivains choisis par l'Académie Goncourt," and
       accompanied by a publicity piece [item 1075].

0312   CHÉRI. Paris: Fayard, 1984. 223p.

       Also in:
       OP 2 [item 0053].
       OCLF 6 [item 0054].
       OCC 5 [item 0055].
       OF 2 [item 0056].
       Claudine à l'école. L'Ingénue libertine. Chéri. Item 0350.

       Extracts in:
       Autobiographie... [items 0057-58]: Colette's pref. for *OCLF*.
       Morceaux choisis [item 0062].
       Les Plus Belles Pages de Colette [item 0064].
       Beaumont and Parinaud [item 1063].

       Colette's most famous novel and worthy of its fame. It aroused
       much controversy, particularly among anti-feminists, when it was
       published, but placed its author firmly in the first rank of French
       writers. Recalls, in flashbacks, the liaison between Léa, a beautiful
       and gracious middle-aged courtesan, and Chéri, a spoiled and
       strikingly handsome young man. When Chéri agrees to an arranged
       marriage with a young woman, the liaison ends, but not without
       much suffering to the major protagonists. The novel provides a
       penetrating analysis of the psychology of love, interesting
       caricatures of known persons in the secondary characters, and a fine
       evocation of the *demi-monde* of pre-World War I Paris. Should be
       read with its sequel, *La Fin de Chéri.*

       Reviews:
       Aspects de la France, 9 Feb. 1984, 9. François Léger.
       Contemporary Review 194 (Nov. 1958): 278. Beryl Gaster.

Ecrits nouveaux 9 (Jan. 1922): 72-76. André Germain. Also in *De Proust à Dada*, 47-54. Paris: Sagittaire, 1924.

Europe nouvelle, 8 Aug. 1920, 1117. R. de la Vaissière.

Eve, 10 Oct. 1920, 11. Raymond Clauzel.

Fine Print 9 (Oct. 1983): 154-56. Doris Grumbach.

Hudson Review 6 (Winter 1954): 626-33. Marvin Mudrick.

Journal des débats, 13 Oct. 1920, 2. Jean de Pierrefeu.

Listener 46 (16 Aug. 1951): 275. John Russell.

Literary Review 2 (Aug. 1981): 35. Alice Wooledge Salmon.

Marginales 25 (Aug. 1970): 58-59. Constant Burniaux.

Ms. 8 (July 1979): 28. Susan Brownmiller.

Nation 177 (8 Aug. 1953): 116-17.

National & English Review 137 (Sept. 1951): 178-80. Milward Kennedy.

New Statesman & Nation 42 (11 Aug. 1951): 158-60. V.S. Pritchett.

Nouvel Observateur, 10 Aug. 1970, 30. Jean Freustié.

Nouvelle Revue française 15 (1 Dec. 1920): 938-40. Benjamin Crémieux.

Nouvelles littéraires, 21 Oct. 1922, 1. Mireille Havet.

Observer, no. 8356 (29 July 1951): 7. Harold Nicolson.

Partisan Review 42 (Fall 1975): 475-76. Stephen Koch.

Quinzaine critique, no. 1 (10 Nov. 1929): 37. Jean Bruller.

Revue critique des idées et des livres 30 (10 Oct. 1920): 196-202. André Thérive. Also in item 2149 Thérive, 11-18.

Revue universelle 3 (1 Oct. 1920): 105-9. Pierre Lasserre.

Temps, 22 July 1920, 5. Paul Souday.

Times Literary Supplement, no. 1462 (6 Feb. 1930): 98.

Times Literary Supplement, no. 2584 (10 Aug. 1951): 497.

Twentieth Century 150 (Sept. 1951): 258.

Vinduet 2 (May-June 1948): 393-99. Asbjørn S. Aarnes.

Washington Post Book World 12 (5 Sept. 1982): 12.

English translations: American

0313   CHÉRI. Trans. Janet Flanner. Illus. Herman Post. New York: Boni, 1929. 227p.

0314   CHÉRI. Trans. Janet Flanner. New York: Boni (Bonibooks), 1930. 227p.

0315 CHÉRI. THE LAST OF CHÉRI. Trans. Roger Senhouse. New
      York: Farrar, Straus & Young, 1951. 296p.

0316 CHÉRI. THE LAST OF CHÉRI. Trans. Roger Senhouse. New
      York: New American Library (Signet), 1955. 221p.

0317 CHÉRI. THE LAST OF CHÉRI. Trans. Roger Senhouse. Farrar,
      Straus & Giroux, 1976. 304p. Coll. Noonday 521.

0318 CHÉRI. THE LAST OF CHÉRI. [Trans. Roger Senhouse]. New
      York: Ballantine, 1982. 264p.

0319 CHÉRI. Trans. Janet Flanner. Introd. Wallace Fowlie. San
      Francisco: George F. Ritchie, 1983. xiv-97p.

      Also in:
      The Colette Omnibus [item 0070]. Trans. Roger Senhouse.
      Seven by Colette [item 0101]. Trans. Roger Senhouse.
      Short Novels of Colette [item 0102]. Trans. Janet Flanner.
      Six Novels by Colette [item 0104]. Trans. Roger Senhouse.
      Stories [item 0105].

      Extract in *Earthly Paradise* [items 0082, 0084-85]: Colette's pref.
      for *OCLF*. Trans. Derek Coltman.

English translations: British

0320 CHÉRI. Trans. Janet Flanner. London: Gollancz, 1930. 286p.

0321 CHÉRI. Trans. Roger Senhouse. London: Secker & Warburg,
      1951. 154p.

0322 CHÉRI. THE LAST OF CHÉRI. Trans. Roger Senhouse. Introd.
      Raymond Mortimer. London: Secker & Warburg, 1951. xii-
      296p. Coll. Uniform 1.

0323 CHÉRI. THE LAST OF CHÉRI. Trans. Roger. Senhouse. Introd.
      Raymond Mortimer. Harmondsworth: Penguin, 1954. 256p.

0324 CHÉRI. Trans. Roger Senhouse. Illus. Philippe Jullian. London:
      Folio Society, 1963. 161p.

0325 CHÉRI. THE LAST OF CHÉRI. Trans. Roger Senhouse. Introd.
Raymond Mortimer. Harmondsworth: Penguin (Modern
Classics), 1984. 256p.

Also in:
Colette Omnibus [item 0069].
Six Novels [item 0103]. Trans. Roger Senhouse.

Extract in *Earthly Paradise* [items 0087-89]: Colette's pref. for
OCLF. Trans. Derek Coltman.

LA CIRE VERTE

In *Le Képi*, all eds. See that title.

Extracts in *Autobiographie...* [items 0057-58].

Village anecdote in which avarice and murder play leading roles,
and in which a semi-fictional fifteen-year-old Gabrielle Colette and
her mother are secondary figures. Of special interest are Sido's
comments on the psychology of crime, and Colette's depiction of
adolescent behaviour.

English translations: American

xxxx GREEN SEALING-WAX. Trans. Antonia White.

In:
The Collected Stories of Colette [items 0071-72].
The Tender Shoot and Other Stories [items 0106-8].

Extracts in:
Earthly Paradise [items 0082, 0084-85].

English translations: British

xxxx   GREEN SEALING-WAX. Trans. Antonia White.

In:
The Collected Stories of Colette [items 0073-74].
The Rainy Moon and Other Stories [item 0111].
The Stories of Colette [items 0109-10].

Extracts in:
Earthly Paradise [items 0087-89].

CLAUDINE A L'ÉCOLE

0326   CLAUDINE A L'ÉCOLE. [Willy]. Pref. Willy. Paris: Ollendorff,
       1900. 332p. In the preface, Willy describes how he discovered
       the "author" Claudine and why he decided to publish the book.

0327   CLAUDINE A L'ÉCOLE. [Willy and Colette Willy]. Pref. Willy.
       Illus. H. Mirande. Paris: Albin Michel, 1911. 309p.

0328   CLAUDINE A L'ÉCOLE. [Willy and Colette Willy]. Pref. Willy.
       Illus. Chas Laborde. Paris: Jonquières, 1925. 327p. Coll. Les
       Beaux Romans 12.

0329   CLAUDINE A L'ÉCOLE. [Willy and Colette Willy]. Pref. Willy.
       Paris: Albin Michel, 1930. 325p. Coll. Choix.

0330   CLAUDINE A L'ÉCOLE. [Willy and Colette Willy]. Pref. Willy.
       Paris: Albin Michel, 1931. 254p. Coll. Les Albin Michel à 6
       francs.

0331   CLAUDINE A L'ÉCOLE. [Willy and Colette Willy]. Illus.
       Mariette Lydis. Paris: Eds. de Cluny, 1939. 241p.

0332   CLAUDINE A L'ÉCOLE. [Willy and Colette Willy]. Pref. Willy.
       Illus. Henri Mirande. Paris: Albin Michel, 1939. 319p.

0333 CLAUDINE A L'ÉCOLE. [Willy and Colette Willy]. Illus. Jean Routier. Paris: Gründ, 1942. 274p. Coll. Gründ illustrée 18.

0334 CLAUDINE A L'ÉCOLE. [Willy and Colette Willy]. Pref. Willy. Illus. Christian Bérard. Monte-Carlo: Eds. du Livre; Lausanne: Eds. du Grand Chêne, 1946. 373p.

0335 CLAUDINE A L'ÉCOLE. [Willy and Colette Willy]. Pref. Willy. Illus. Grau Sala. Paris: La Bonne Compagnie, 1947. 237p. Coll. Les Quatre Claudine 1.

0336 CLAUDINE A L'ÉCOLE. [Willy and Colette Willy]. Pref. Willy. Illus. Suzanne Ballivet. Brussels: Eds. du Houblon, 1949. 245p.

0337 CLAUDINE A L'ÉCOLE. Paris: Albin Michel, 1949. 317p.

0338 CLAUDINE A L'ÉCOLE. Paris: Le Club du meilleur livre, 1953. 296p. Coll. Romans.

0339 CLAUDINE A L'ÉCOLE. Paris: Albin Michel, 1953. 248p. Coll. Pourpre.

0340 CLAUDINE A L'ÉCOLE. Paris: Club français du livre, 1954. 256p.

0341 CLAUDINE A L'ÉCOLE. Illus. Renée Ringel. Brussels: Terres latines, 1955. 208p. Coll. Leurs chefs-d'œuvre 18.

0342 CLAUDINE A L'ÉCOLE. [Willy and Colette]. Paris: Albin Michel, 1956. 248p. Coll. Livre de poche 193.

0343 CLAUDINE A L'ÉCOLE. [Willy and Colette]. Illus. Henri Mirande. Paris: Club des éditeurs, 1958. 267p. Coll. Club du livre des éditeurs 74.

0344 CLAUDINE A L'ÉCOLE. CLAUDINE A PARIS. [Willy and Colette]. Pref. Françoise Giroud. Illus. Grau Sala. Paris: Culture, art, loisirs, 1965. 463p. Coll. Le Meilleur livre de la femme 21. Includes notes on Colette, Grau Sala and Giroud.

0345   CLAUDINE A L'ÉCOLE. [Willy and Colette]. Geneva: Crémille, 1968. 247p.

0346   CLAUDINE A L'ÉCOLE. [Willy and Colette]. Illus. Pierre Lelong, Jean Cocteau. Paris: Pierre de Tartas, 1972. 237p. Coll. Les Quatre Claudine.

0347   CLAUDINE A L'ÉCOLE. [Willy and Colette]. Illus. Claude-Michel Grosjean. Brussels: Club international du livre, 1972. 276p.

0348   CLAUDINE A L'ÉCOLE. [Willy and Colette]. Paris: Albin Michel, 1975. 256p. Coll. Livre de poche 193.

0349   CLAUDINE A L'ÉCOLE. CLAUDINE A PARIS. CLAUDINE EN MÉNAGE. CLAUDINE S'EN VA. [Colette and Willy]. Pref. Gérard Bonal. Paris: Albin Michel, 1977. 599p.

0350   CLAUDINE A L'ÉCOLE. L'INGÉNUE LIBERTINE. CHÉRI. Pref. Marie Cardinal. Paris: Club français du livre, 1977. xvi-606p. Coll. Les Portiques.

0351   CLAUDINE A L'ÉCOLE. [Colette and Willy]. Paris: France Loisirs, 1977. 255p.

0352   CLAUDINE A L'ÉCOLE. [Willy and Colette]. Paris: Librairie générale française, 1979. 320p. Coll. Prestige du livre 58.

Also in:
OP 1 [item 0053].
OCLF 1 [item 0054].
OCC 1 [item 0055].
OF 1 [item 0056].

Extracts in:
Bêtes libres et prisonnières [item 0702]: Chers bois!
Chats de Colette [items 0714-15]: Chats des premières années.
Les 'Claudine' [item 0059].
Morceaux choisis [item 0062].
Pages choisies [item 0063].
Les Plus Belles Pages de Colette [item 0064].

Textes choisis de Colette [item 0065].
Beaumont and Parinaud [item 1063].

Colette's first novel, written in collaboration with her first husband
Henry Gauthier-Villars, better known as Willy. Written in journal
form, the novel recounts Claudine's day-to-day life during her final
year at the village school, her penchant for the assistant mistress
Aimée as well as for Aimée's sister Luce, and the complications of
the headmistress' relationship with both Aimée and the local deputy
minister. Many of the incidents recounted were judged scabrous by
the French reading public of 1900, but the modern reader is more
likely to be offended by the apparent intention to shock. Models for
most of the characters have been identified by researchers. Despite
the book's weaknesses, Colette already reveals a talent for
caricature, and a tendency towards lyricism in her depiction of
nature. In 1949 she began to publish the Claudine novels under her
own name but an action by Willy's son, Jacques Gauthier-Villars,
brought about re-establishment of the double authorship.

Reviews:
Commonweal 66 (5 April 1957): 22-23. Alice Saxon.
Mercure de France, May 1900, 472-75. Rachilde. Also in item
    1057 *Album Masques: Colette*, 58-59; and item 1104 La Hire,
    183-89.
New Statesman 66 (6 Dec. 1963): 842. Brigid Brophy.
Nouvel Observateur, no. 372 (30 Jan. 1978): 80. Jean Freustié.
Revue dorée, no. 33 (Nov. 1902): 145-48. Georges Casella. Also
    in item 1104 La Hire, 230-35.
Revue encyclopédique, 5 May 1900, 352-53. Charles Maurras.
    Also in item 1104 La Hire, 193-97.
Saturday Review 40 (2 March 1957): 16. Jean Campbell Jones.
Spectator, no. 6680 (20 July 1956): 105. Daniel George.
Temps, 1 April 1900, 2. Gaston Deschamps. Also in item 1104
    La Hire, 189-91.
Time 69 (18 Feb. 1957): 82.
Times Literary Supplement, no. 1506 (11 Dec. 1930): 1067.
Times Literary Supplement, no. 2838 (20 July 1956): 433.
Tribune 27 (1 Nov. 1963): 8. Robert Nye.

English translations: American

0353 CLAUDINE AT SCHOOL. [Colette and Willy]. Trans. Janet Flanner. Illus. H. Mirande. New York: Boni, 1930. 297p.

0354 CLAUDINE AT SCHOOL. Trans. Antonia White. New York: Farrar, Straus & Cudahy, 1957. 286p.

0355 CLAUDINE AT SCHOOL. Trans. Antonia White. New York: Berkley (Medallion), 1965. 202p. Not seen.

0356 CLAUDINE AT SCHOOL. Trans. Antonia White. New York: Ballantine, 1982. 224p.

Also in:
The Complete Claudine [items 0075-77]. Trans. Antonia White.
Six Novels by Colette [item 0104]. Trans. Antonia White.

English translations: British

0357 CLAUDINE AT SCHOOL. [Willy and Colette]. Trans. Janet Flanner. London: Gollancz, 1930. 286p.

0358 CLAUDINE AT SCHOOL. Trans. Antonia White. London: Seck< & Warburg, 1956. 286p. Coll. Uniform 8.

0359 CLAUDINE AT SCHOOL. Trans. Antonia White. Harmondsworth: Penguin, 1963. 271p.

Also in *The Penguin Claudine Novels* [item 0078]. Trans. Anton White.

CLAUDINE A PARIS

0360 CLAUDINE A PARIS. [Willy]. Paris: Ollendorff, 1901. 321p.

0361 CLAUDINE A PARIS. [Willy and Colette Willy]. Pref. Willy.
Illus. Auguste Roubille. Paris: Ollendorff, 1911. 279p.

0362 CLAUDINE A PARIS. [Willy and Colette Willy]. Pref. Willy.
Illus. Chas Laborde. Paris: Jonquières, 1925. 247p. Coll. Les
Beaux romans 16.

0363 CLAUDINE A PARIS. [Willy and Colette Willy]. Pref. Willy.
Paris: Albin Michel, 1931. 251p. Coll. Les Albin Michel à 6
francs.

0364 CLAUDINE A PARIS. [Willy and Colette Willy]. Pref. Willy.
Paris: Albin Michel, 1931. 286p. Coll. Choix.

0365 CLAUDINE A PARIS. [Willy and Colette Willy]. Pref. Willy.
Illus. A. Roubille. Paris: Albin Michel, 1931. 313p.

0366 CLAUDINE A PARIS. [Willy and Colette Willy]. Illus. Mariette
Lydis. Paris: Eds. de Cluny, 1939. 189p.

0367 CLAUDINE A PARIS. [Willy and Colette Willy]. Front.
Christian Bérard. Monte-Carlo: Aux Eds. du livre; Lausanne:
Aux Eds. du Grand Chêne, 1946. 291p.

0368 CLAUDINE A PARIS. [Willy and Colette Willy]. Illus. Grau
Sala. Paris: La Bonne Compagnie, 1947. 187p. Coll. Les
Quatre Claudine.

0369 CLAUDINE A PARIS. Paris: Albin Michel, 1950. 255p.

0370 CLAUDINE A PARIS. Paris: Albin Michel, 1953. 248p. Coll.
Pourpre.

0371 CLAUDINE A PARIS. Illus. Renée Ringel. Brussels: Terres
latines, 1955. 156p. Coll. Leurs chefs-d'œuvre 19.

0372   CLAUDINE A PARIS. [Willy and Colette]. Strasbourg: Sélection des amis du livre, 1956. 227p.

0373   CLAUDINE A PARIS. [Willy and Colette]. Paris: Albin Michel, 1956. 248p. Coll. Livre de poche 213.

0374   CLAUDINE A PARIS. [Willy and Colette]. Geneva: Crémille, 1968. 255p.

0375   CLAUDINE A PARIS. Illus. Claude-Michel Grosjean. Brussels: Club international du livre, 1972. 260p.

0376   CLAUDINE A PARIS. Illus. Gabriel Dauchot. Paris: Pierre de Tartas, 1973. 191p. Coll. Les Quatre Claudine.

0377   CLAUDINE A PARIS. [Colette and Willy]. Paris: France Loisirs, 1977. 223p.

Also in:
OP 1 [item 0053].
OCLF 1 [item 0054].
OCC 1 [item 0055].
OF 1 [item 0056].
Claudine à l'école. Claudine à Paris. Item 0344.
Claudine à l'école. Claudine à Paris. Claudine en ménage. Claudine s'en va. Item 0349.

Extracts in:
Chats de Colette [items 0714-15]: Chats des premières années.
Les 'Claudine' [item 0059].
Les Plus Belles Pages de Colette [item 0064].
Beaumont and Parinaud [item 1063].

Second of the Claudine novels, written in collaboration with Willy. At the end of her schooling, Claudine, her father, their servant Mélie and the cat Fanchette have moved to Paris. Claudine misses her old home immensely but through her aunt Cœur she is introduced to new social milieux, where she meets her "uncle" Renaud and his homosexual son, Marcel. It is through Claudine's conversations with the latter that most of the "spice" of the novel is injected. At the end of the book, Claudine has grown in self-awareness and has found love. Of particular interest is Colette's portrayal of Parisian life of the period. Many of the characters are modelled on real people.

Reviews:
Listener 59 (6 Feb. 1958): 252. Hilary Corke.
Mercure de France, April 1901, 188-89. Rachilde.
New Statesman 55 (18 Jan. 1958): 77-78. G.S. Fraser.
New Statesman 66 (6 Dec. 1963): 842. Brigid Brophy.
New York Times Book Review, 14 Sept. 1958, 4-5. Robert Phelps.
Nouvel Observateur, no. 372 (30 Jan. 1978): 80. Jean Freustié.
Revue dorée, no. 33 (Nov. 1902): 145-48. Georges Casella. Also in item 1104 La Hire, 230-35.
Revue universelle (1901): 397-98. B.-H. Gausseron.
Times Literary Supplement, no. 1541 (13 Aug. 1931): 622.
Times Literary Supplement, no. 2916 (17 Jan. 1958): 29.
Tribune 27 (1 Nov. 1963): 8. Robert Nye.

English translations: American

0378 YOUNG LADY OF PARIS. [Colette and Willy]. Trans. James Whitall. Illus. A. Roubille. New York: Boni, 1931. 292p.

0379 CLAUDINE IN PARIS. Trans. Antonia White. New York: Farrar, Straus & Cudahy, 1958. 204p.

0380 CLAUDINE IN PARIS. Trans. James Whitall. New York: Belmont Productions, 1964. 157p.

0381 CLAUDINE IN PARIS. New York: Ballantine, 1982. 192p. Not seen.

Also in *The Complete Claudine* [items 0075-77]. Trans. Antonia White.

English translations: British

0382 CLAUDINE IN PARIS. [Willy and Colette]. [Trans. James Whitall]. London: Gollancz, 1931. 287p.

0383 CLAUDINE IN PARIS. Trans. Antonia White. London: Secker & Warburg, 1958. 204p. Coll. Uniform 11.

0384 CLAUDINE IN PARIS. Trans. Antonia White. Harmondsworth: Penguin, 1963. 191p.

Also in *The Penguin Claudine Novels* [item 0078]. Trans. Antonia White.

CLAUDINE AMOUREUSE

See *Claudine en ménage*.

CLAUDINE EN MÉNAGE

0385 CLAUDINE AMOUREUSE. [Willy]. Paris: Ollendorff, 1902. 351p. Pre-original edition of *Claudine en ménage*. Because of a quarrel with the publisher the stock was burned, with only a few copies escaping the conflagration. After revisions and a change in title, the novel was moved to another publisher.

0386 CLAUDINE EN MÉNAGE. [Willy]. Paris: Mercure de France, 1902. 292p.

0387 "Lettre de Claudine à Renaud." *Le Damier* 1 (April 1905): 28-30. Also in *OP*1, 527-29. Of slightly doubtful authenticity, this letter affirms Claudine's love for Renaud, while emphasizing both the negative and the salutary effects of jealousy. It was never actually incorporated into the Claudine novels. D'Hollander suggests that it may have been published as publicity for the series.

0388 CLAUDINE EN MÉNAGE. [Willy and Colette Willy]. Pref. Willy. Paris: Mercure de France, 1911. 292p.

0389 CLAUDINE EN MÉNAGE. [Willy and Colette Willy]. Pref. Willy. Paris: Mercure de France, 1923. 268p.

0390 CLAUDINE EN MÉNAGE. [Willy and Colette Willy]. Pref. Willy. Illus. Chas Laborde. Paris: Jonquières, 1924. 265p. Coll. Les Beaux Romans 8.

0391 CLAUDINE EN MÉNAGE. [Willy and Colette Willy]. Pref. Willy. Paris: Albin Michel, 1931. 289p. Coll. Choix.

0392 CLAUDINE EN MÉNAGE. [Willy and Colette Willy]. Illus. Mariette Lydis. Paris: Eds. de Cluny, 1939. 177p.

0393 CLAUDINE EN MÉNAGE. [Willy and Colette Willy]. Pref. Willy. Front. Christian Bérard. Monte-Carlo: Eds. du Livre; Lausanne: Eds. du Grand Chêne, 1946. 289p.

0394 CLAUDINE EN MÉNAGE. [Willy and Colette Willy]. Illus. Grau Sala. Paris: La Bonne Compagnie, 1947. 195p. Coll. Les Quatre Claudine.

0395 CLAUDINE EN MÉNAGE. Paris: Mercure de France, 1948. 222p.

0396 CLAUDINE EN MÉNAGE. Illus. Renée Ringel. Brussels: Terres latines, 1955. 152p. Coll. Leurs chefs-d'œuvres 20.

0397 CLAUDINE EN MÉNAGE. [Willy and Colette]. Paris: Mercure de France, 1957. 242p. Coll. Livre de poche 219.

0398 CLAUDINE EN MÉNAGE. CLAUDINE S'EN VA. Notice on the author by Françoise Fabrice. Illus. Grau Sala. Paris: Culture, art, loisirs, 1966. 464p. Coll. Le Meilleur livre de la femme.

0399 CLAUDINE EN MÉNAGE. [Willy and Colette]. Geneva: Crémille, 1968. 245p.

0400 CLAUDINE EN MÉNAGE. Illus. Claude-Michel Grosjean. Brussels: Club international du livre, 1972. 248p.

0401 CLAUDINE EN MÉNAGE. [Willy and Colette]. Paris: Mercure de France, 1973. 243p. Coll. Folio 335.

0402 CLAUDINE EN MÉNAGE. Illus. Gaston Barret. Paris: Pierre de
      Tartas, 1973. 199p. Coll. Les Quatre Claudine.

0403 CLAUDINE EN MÉNAGE. [Colette and Willy]. Introd. and notes
      Paul D'Hollander. Paris: Klincksieck, 1975. 423p. Coll. Textes
      du XXe siècle 1. Excellent critical edition. D'Hollander's long
      introduction [annotated separately] provides details on Colette's
      and Willy's collaboration, and publication information about
      both the first edition and the pre-edition. Includes variants,
      correspondence relevant to the novel's two publications, press
      notices, a summary of provincialisms, a list of neologisms and
      popular expressions used in the novel, a map of Saint-Sauveur
      with notes comparing its topography with that of Montigny,
      site of the novel, and a bibliography.

0404 CLAUDINE EN MÉNAGE. [Colette and Willy]. Paris: France
      Loisirs, 1978. 192p.

0405 CLAUDINE EN MÉNAGE. [Willy]. Paris: Mercure, 1984. 208p.

      Also in:
      OP 1 [item 0053].
      OCLF 2 [item 0054].
      OCC 1 [item 0055].
      OF 1 [item 0056].
      *Claudine à l'école. Claudine à Paris. Claudine en ménage. Claudine
      s'en va.* Item 0349.

      Extracts in:
      Bêtes libres et prisonnières [item 0702]: Chers bois!
      Chats de Colette [items 0714-15]: Chats des premières années.
      Les 'Claudine' [item 0059].
      Les Plus Belles Pages de Colette [item 0064].
      Beaumont and Parinaud [item 1063].

      Third novel in the Claudine series. Claudine has married Renaud,
      through whom she becomes acquainted with the literary and artistic
      circles of Paris. The action of the book turns on her involvement
      with a young woman and Renaud's complicity in the liaison. As a
      result, the marriage founders. Although some passages are intended
      to titillate the reader, Colette's craft is much surer and her
      characterization more adept than in the earlier works. As with the

other novels in the series, models for many of the secondary characters have been identified by researchers.

Reviews:
Art moderne 22 (22 June 1902): 209-10. A. Gilbert de Voisins.
Bulletin critique du livre français 30 (1975): 1699.
Illustrated London News 237 (10 Sept. 1960): 448. E.D. O'Brien.
Journal, 29 May 1902, 1. Jean Lorrain.
Lettres romanes 33 (Feb. 1979): 121-22. Dominique Allard.
Listener 64 (1 Sept. 1960): 357. Elizabeth Jennings.
Mercure de France, June 1902, 750-53. Rachilde. Also in item
    1104 La Hire, 203-8.
New Statesman 66 (6 Dec. 1963): 842. Brigid Brophy.
Nouvel Observateur, no. 372 (30 Jan. 1978): 80. Jean Freustié.
Renaissance latine 1 (12 June 1902): 254-55. Marcel Boulenger.
Revue dorée, no. 33 (Nov. 1902): 145-48. Georges Casella. Also
    in item 1104 La Hire, 230-35.
Times Literary Supplement, no. 3052 (26 Aug. 1960): 549.
Tribune 27 (1 Nov. 1963): 8. Robert Nye.

English translations: American

0406 THE INDULGENT HUSBAND. Trans. Frederick A. Blossom.
      Illus. J. O'H. Cosgrave II. New York: Farrar & Rinehart, 1935.
      273p.

0407 CLAUDINE MARRIED. Trans. Antonia White. New York:
      Farrar, Straus & Cudahy, 1960. 192p.

0408 CLAUDINE MARRIED. CLAUDINE AND ANNIE. Trans.
      Antonia White. New York: Ballantine, 1983. 278p.

Also in:
The Complete Claudine [items 0075-77]. Trans. Antonia White.
Short Novels of Colette [item 0102]. Trans. Frederick A. Blossom.

English translations: British

0409 CLAUDINE MARRIED. Trans. Antonia White. London: Secker
      & Warburg, 1960. 192p. Coll. Uniform 13.

0410 CLAUDINE MARRIED. Trans. Antonia White. Harmondsworth: Penguin, 1963. 182p.

Also in *The Penguin Claudine Novels* [item 0078].

CLAUDINE S'EN VA

0411 CLAUDINE S'EN VA. [Willy]. Paris: Ollendorff, 1903. 320p.

0412 CLAUDINE S'EN VA. [Willy and Colette Willy]. Pref. Willy. Illus. Albert Jarach. Paris: Ollendorff, 1912. 311p.

0413 CLAUDINE S'EN VA. [Willy and Colette Willy]. Pref. Willy. Illus. Chas Laborde. Paris: Jonquières, 1925. 219p. Coll. Les Beaux romans 17.

0414 CLAUDINE S'EN VA. [Willy and Colette Willy]. Pref. Willy. Paris: Albin Michel, 1931. 251p. Coll. Choix.

0415 CLAUDINE S'EN VA. [Willy and Colette Willy]. Pref. Willy. Paris: Albin Michel, 1931. 254p. Coll. Les Albin Michel à 6 francs.

0416 UN CHAPITRE INÉDIT DE CLAUDINE S'EN VA: CLAUDINE ET LES CONTES DE FÉES. Introd. Dr. Lucien-Graux. Paris: Dr. Lucien-Graux, 1937. 27p. Coll. Pour les amis du Dr. Lucien-Graux 13. Private edition of an ostensibly rejected chapter, in which Claudine tells Annie of her long-time dislike for fairy tales but then relates one. Interesting because of her use of patois. Introduction claims that Colette willingly supplied missing fragments of the manuscript, discovered by Lucien-Graux after its many peregrinations. D'Hollander offers cogent reasons in favor of the probability that the chapter was never intended to be part of *Claudine s'en va* but was written later.

0417 CLAUDINE S'EN VA. [Willy and Colette Willy]. Illus. Mariette Lydis. Paris: Eds. de Cluny, 1939. 163p.

0418 CLAUDINE S'EN VA. [Willy and Colette Willy]. Pref. Willy.
       Front. Christian Bérard. Monte-Carlo: Eds. du livre; Lausanne:
       Eds. du Grand-Chêne, 1946. 263p.

0419 CLAUDINE S'EN VA. [Willy and Colette Willy]. Illus. Grau
       Sala. Paris: La Bonne Compagnie, 1947. 175p. Coll. Les
       Quatre Claudine.

0420 CLAUDINE S'EN VA. Paris: Albin Michel, 1950. 189p.

0421 CLAUDINE S'EN VA. Paris: Albin Michel, 1954. 183p. Coll.
       Pourpre.

0422 CLAUDINE S'EN VA. Illus. Renée Ringel. Brussels: Terres
       latines, 1955. 129p. Coll. Leurs chefs-d'œuvre.

0423 CLAUDINE S'EN VA. Presentation Jean Garcia. Paris: Club du
       livre du mois, 1955. 201p. Coll. Chefs-d'œuvre d'hier et
       d'aujourd'hui.

0424 CLAUDINE S'EN VA. [Willy and Colette]. Paris: Albin Michel,
       1957. 184p. Coll. Livre de poche 238.

0425 CLAUDINE S'EN VA. [Willy and Colette]. Geneva: Crémille,
       1969. 243p.

0426 CLAUDINE S'EN VA. Illus. Claude-Michel Grosjean. Brussels:
       Club international du livre, 1972. 199p.

0427 CLAUDINE S'EN VA. Illus. Grau Sala. Paris: Pierre de Tartas,
       1973. 165p. Coll. Les Quatre Claudine.

0428 CLAUDINE S'EN VA. Paris: France Loisirs, 1978. 189p.

Also in:
OP 1 [item 0053]: includes "Claudine et les contes de fées."
OCLF 2 [item 0054].
OCC 2 [item 0055].
OF 1 [item 0056].
*Claudine à l'école. Claudine à Paris. Claudine en ménage. Claudine
    s'en va.* Item 0349.
Claudine en ménage. Claudine s'en va. Item 0398.

Extracts in:
Chats de Colette [item 0714-15]: Chats des premières années.
Chiens de Colette [items 0716-17]: Toby.
Les 'Claudine' [item 0059].
Les Plus Belles Pages de Colette [item 0064].
Beaumont and Parinaud [item 1063].

Although this novel is the fourth in the Claudine series its central
character is Claudine's acquaintance Annie, a submissive wife who
writes the book as a diary. During her priggish husband's absence
in South America, Annie discovers his infidelity, develops her own
self-assertion, and ends up fleeing from marriage. Strength comes
from her growing friendship with Claudine during a sojourn at the
baths at Arriège and at the Wagner festival at Beyreuth. Throughout
the book, Annie's domestic situation is contrasted with the now
idealized relationship between Claudine and Renaud. Especially
interesting is Colette's evocation of the Bayreuth milieu, which she
knew well. Secondary characters of the two previous novels in the
series reappear. Autobiographical elements are easily traced.

Reviews:
New Statesman 66 (6 Dec. 1963): 842. Brigid Brophy.
Nouvel Observateur, no. 372 (30 Jan. 1978): 80. Jean Freustié.
Revue illustrée 18 (1 Oct. 1903): 56. Georges Casella.
Thyrse 28 (28 March 1926): 55. Renée Dunan.
Times Literary Supplement, no. 1694 (19 July 1934): 513.
Times Literary Supplement, no. 3131 (2 March 1962): 133.
Tribune 27 (1 Nov. 1963): 8. Robert Nye.

English   translations: American

0429   THE INNOCENT WIFE. [Colette and Willy]. Trans. Frederick A.
       Blossom. Illus. J.O'H. Cosgrave II. New York: Farrar &
       Rinehart, 1934. 272p.

xxxx   CLAUDINE AND ANNIE. Trans. Antonia White.

In:
Claudine married. Claudine and Annie. Item 0408.
The Complete Claudine. Items 0075-77.

English translations: British

0430 THE INNOCENT WIFE. [Colette, in collaboration with M. Willy]. Trans. Frederick A. Blossom. London: John Long, 1934. 288p.

0431 CLAUDINE AND ANNIE. Trans. Antonia White. London: Secker & Warburg, 1962. 190p. Coll. Uniform 15.

0432 CLAUDINE AND ANNIE. Trans. Antonia White. Harmondsworth: Penguin, 1963. 159p.

Also in *The Penguin Claudine Novels* [item 0078]. Trans. Antonia White.

LA DAME DU PHOTOGRAPHE

In *Gigi*, some eds. See that title.

The suicide attempt of Madame Armand, the photographer's wife, is foiled by her neighbour, Mademoiselle Devoidy. Her explanation for the attempt constitutes the main interest of this novella, which emphasizes the qualities of ordinary women. Just as appealing as Madame Armand is Mademoiselle Devoidy, whose profession as a pearl-stringer is analyzed in long fascinating passages on the beauty of pearls and the vogue they inspired early in the century.

English translations: American

xxxx THE PHOTOGRAPHER'S MISSUS. Trans. Antonia White.

In:
Gigi and Selected Writings [item 0501].
The Tender Shoot and Other Stories [items 0106-8].

Also in *The Collected Stories of Colette* [items 0071-72], under the title "The Photographer's Wife."

English translations: British

xxxx   THE PHOTOGRAPHER'S MISSUS. Trans. Antonia White.

In:
The Rainy Moon and Other Stories [item 0111].
The Stories of Colette [items 0109-10].

Also in *The Collected Stories of Colette* [items 0073-74], under the title "The Photographer's Wife."

DUO

0433   DUO. Paris: Ferenczi, 1934. 229p.

0434   DUO. Illus. Colette Pettier. Paris: Ferenczi, 1938. 159p. Coll. Le Livre moderne illustré 290.

0435   DUO. Paris: Flammarion, 1939. 63p. Coll. Select-collection 162 (new series).

0436   DUO. LE TOUTOUNIER. Paris: Le Club français du livre, 1947. 240p. Coll. Romans 15.

0437   DUO. LE TOUTOUNIER. Paris: Ferenczi, 1955. 192p. Coll. Livre de poche 123.

0438   DUO. LE TOUTOUNIER. Pref. Dominique Aury. Front. Dunoyer de Segonzac. Lausanne: La Guilde du livre, 1955. xvi-227p. Coll. La Guilde du livre 226.

0439   DUO. LE TOUTOUNIER. Geneva: Crémille, 1970. 245p.

0440 DUO. Paris: Hachette, 1985. 229p.

Also in:
OCLF 9 [item 0054].
OCC 8 [item 0055].
OF 2 [item 0056].
Beaumont and Parinaud [item 1063].

Extracts in *Morceaux choisis* [item 0062].

Alice is spending the summer with her husband Michel at Cransac,
his family property in the south of France. Beset by financial
problems and cheated by his manager, Michel is aware that he runs
the risk of losing his home. By chance he discovers that Alice has
been unfaithful to him, though the affair is long since over. The
novel's title evokes the interplay of discoveries, emotions and
conversations between the couple during the crisis, right up to the
death of one of the protagonists. Almost spartan in its simplicity,
this novel emphasizes the woman's power of endurance and her will
to survive in the face of attack, and it highlights the extent to
which misunderstanding and lack of communication can ruin the
lives of two individuals in love.

Reviews:
Action française, 6 Dec. 1934, 3. Robert Brasillach. Also in
    Œuvres complètes de Robert Brasillach, vol. 11, 483-85. Paris:
    Club de l'honnête homme, 1964.
Booklist 72 (1 Oct. 1975): 219-20.
Bulletin critique du livre français 10 (1955): 705.
Europe nouvelle, 12 Jan. 1935, 32-33. Gabriel Marcel.
Guardian Weekly 114 (1 Feb. 1976): 21. Norman Shrapnel.
Kirkus Reviews 43 (15 May 1975): 580.
Library Journal 100 (15 June 1975): 1238. Elizabeth Tingom.
Mercure de France, 15 Jan. 1935, 358-59. John Charpentier.
New Statesman 91 (23 Jan. 1976): 108. Susannah Clapp.
Nouvelle Revue française 44 (March 1935): 451-53. Marcel Arland.
Nuova Antologia 303 (1 Oct. 1935): 433-35. Diego Valeri.
Publishers' Weekly 207 (19 May 1975): 171.
Publishers' Weekly 211 (24 Jan. 1977): 332.
Sunday Times, 25 Jan. 1976, 41. Jill Neville.
Times Higher Education Supplement 248 (23 July 1976): 15.
    Anthony Kelly.

Times Literary Supplement, no. 1760 (24 Oct. 1935): 672.
Times Literary Supplement, no. 3854 (23 Jan. 1976): 76. Judith
Landry.

English translations: American

0441 DUO. Trans. Frederick A. Blossom. On Murray Hill, N.Y.: Farrar
      & Rinehart, 1935. 203p.

0442 DUO. LE TOUTOUNIER. Trans. and introd. Margaret Crosland.
      Indianapolis, New York: Bobbs-Merrill, 1975. 214p.

0443 DUO. LE TOUTOUNIER. Trans. and introd. Margaret Crosland.
      New York: Dell (Laurel), 1977. 203p.

      Also in *Short Novels of Colette* [item 0102]. Trans. Frederick A.
      Blossom.

English translations: British

0444 THE MARRIED LOVER. Trans. Marjorie Laurie. London: T.
      Werner Laurie, 1935. 254p.

0445 DUO. LE TOUTOUNIER. Trans. and introd. Margaret Crosland.
      London: Owen, 1976. vii-214p.

0446 DUO. LE TOUTOUNIER. Trans. Margaret Crosland. London:
      Women's Press, 1979. 214p.

LES EGAREMENTS DE MINNE

0447 LES EGAREMENTS DE MINNE. [Willy]. Paris: Ollendorff,
      1905. 300p. Abridged and revised version became the second
      part of *L'Ingénue libertine*, published in 1909. See that title.

L'ENFANT MALADE

In *Gigi*, some eds. See that title.

Impressive example of Colette's ability to evoke sensations by means of images. A child confined to bed and expected to die has nevertheless a rich inner life, which flourishes mostly at night or when he is alone. In his imagination, he flies through the skies, riding bits of cloud or wafts of perfume. Sounds take on a visual aspect, and every-day objects a life of their own. The story follows Jean into the imaginary world in which he dwells in dreams and fever, where the "real world" penetrates less and less often as he passes through the crisis that brings him, not to the beckoning door of death, but back into the banal world of life. A *tour de force* of imagery and evocations.

English translations: American

xxxx THE SICK CHILD. Trans. Antonia White.

In:
The Collected Stories of Colette [items 0071-72].
Gigi and Selected Writings [item 0501].
The Tender Shoot and Other Stories [items 0106-8].

English translations: British

xxxx THE SICK CHILD. Trans. Antonia White.

In:
The Collected Stories of Colette [items 0073-74].
The Rainy Moon and Other Stories [item 0111].
The Stories of Colette [items 0109-10].

L'ENTRAVE

0448 L'ENTRAVE. [Colette (Colette Willy)]. Paris: Librairie des lettres, 1913. 307p.

0449 *Poèmes intimes de Colette 2:* "Sommeil." Paris: Durand, 1927. 7p. Extract set to music for voice and piano by Albert Wolff.

0450 L'ENTRAVE. Illus. Dignimont. Paris: Mornay, 1929. 271p. Coll. Les Beaux livres 47.

0451 L'ENTRAVE. Paris: Grasset, 1929. 225p. Coll. Œuvres de Colette 4.

0452 L'ENTRAVE. Illus. Morin-Jean. Paris: Fayard, 1937. 110p. Coll. Le Livre de demain 176.

0453 L'ENTRAVE. Paris: Flammarion, 1947. 309p.

0454 L'ENTRAVE. Paris: Eds. J'ai lu, 1961. 256p. Coll. J'ai lu 106.

0455 L'ENTRAVE. Geneva: Crémille, 1969. 249p.

0456 L'ENTRAVE. Paris: Flammarion, 1970. 237p.

0457 L'ENTRAVE. Paris: Loisirs-livres, 1980. 214p.

Also in:
OP 2 [item 0053].
OCLF 4 [item 0054].
OCC 4 [item 0055].
OF 1 [item 0056].

Extracts in:
Bêtes libres et prisonnières [item 0702]: Mouettes, cygnes.
Colette [item 0060].
Morceaux choisis [item 0062].
Les Plus Belles Pages de Colette [item 0064].
Le Voyage égoïste [item 0898]: A l'aube. Griefs. Un soir. Sommeil.

Beaumont and Parinaud [item 1063].
Bouvier [item 1290].

Sequel to *La Vagabonde*. Now financially independent, Renée Néré confides to paper her loneliness and inability to abandon her travelling companions, May and Jean, in spite of her disapproval of May's blustery submission to Jean's authority. An unexpected glimpse of Max, the lover she rejected in *La Vagabonde*, seems to crystallize her problem. The plot turns upon Jean's attempts to become Renée's lover and her efforts to resist him. The ending is unconvincing, and a troublesome one for feminists. It was later repudiated by Colette. Much of the book's value lies in the passages of poetic nostalgia and meditation wherein Renée yearns for her childhood and a purity she feels she has lost.

Reviews:
Comœdia, 9 Nov. 1913, 3. G. de Pawlowski.
Matin, 24 Oct. 1913, 1. Maurice Donnay.
Mercure de France, 1 Dec. 1913, 587-88. Rachilde.
New Statesman 66 (6 Dec. 1963): 842. Brigid Brophy.
Nueva Estafeta 50 (Jan. 1983): 86-87. Manuel Ríos Ruiz.
Opinion, 8 Nov. 1913, 589-91. Jean de Pierrefeu.
Polybiblion 79 (1914): 27. [Armand Praviel].
Renaissance contemporaine 7 (10 Nov. 1913): 1200-3. Héra
    Mirtel.
Revue critique des idées et des livres 23 (10 Nov. 1913): 268-76.
    Henri Clouard.
Revue du mois 9 (10 Feb. 1914): 260-61. Jules Sagaret.
Temps, 25 Oct. 1913, 3-4. Raoul Aubry.
Times Literary Supplement, no. 1554 (12 Nov. 1931): 896.
Times Literary Supplement, no. 3235 (27 Feb. 1964): 161.
Washington Post Book World 12 (1 Aug. 1982): 12.

English translations: American

0458 RECAPTURED. Trans. Viola Garvin. New York: Cosmopolitan,
    1931. Not seen.

0459 RECAPTURED. Trans. Viola Garvin. Garden City, N.Y.:
    Doubleday, Doran, 1932. 304p.

0460   "The Shackle." [Trans. Antonia White]. Introd. Robert Phelps.
       Mademoiselle 69 (July 1969): 110-38. Includes most of the
       novel.

0461   THE SHACKLE. Trans. Antonia White. New York: Farrar, Straus
       & Giroux, 1976. 224p.

0462   THE SHACKLE. Trans. Antonia White. New York: Farrar, Straus
       & Giroux, 1976. 224p. Coll. Noonday N520.

0463   THE SHACKLE. Trans. Antonia White. New York: Ballantine,
       1982. 168p.

       Also in *The Colette Omnibus* [item 0070]. Trans. Antonia White.

       English translations: British

0464   RECAPTURED. Trans. Viola Gerard Garvin. London: Gollancz,
       1931. 287p.

0465   THE SHACKLE. Trans. Antonia White. London: Secker &
       Warburg, 1964. 224p. Coll. Uniform 17.

0466   THE CAPTIVE. Trans. Antonia White. Harmondsworth: Penguin,
       1970. 158p.

LA FIN DE CHÉRI

0467   LA FIN DE CHÉRI. Paris: Flammarion, 1926. 247p. or 279p.
       The first run was printed and distributed with a complete chapter
       missing, hence the two paginations.

0468   LA FIN DE CHÉRI. Paris: Grasset, 1928. 201p. Coll. Œuvres de
       Colette 2.

0469 LA FIN DE CHÉRI. Illus. Constant Le Breton and Paul Allier. Paris: Fayard, 1929. 110p. Coll. Le Livre de demain 80.

0470 LA FIN DE CHÉRI. Paris: Flammarion, 1931. 64p. Coll. Select-collection 333.

0471 LA FIN DE CHÉRI. Paris: Flammarion, 1936. 64p. Coll. Select-collection 95 (new series).

0472 LA FIN DE CHÉRI. Paris: Calmann-Lévy, 1939. 189p. Coll. pourpre.

0473 LA FIN DE CHÉRI. Rio de Janeiro: Americ=Edit, 1943. 232p.

0474 LA FIN DE CHÉRI. Paris: Eds. J'ai lu, 1960. 192p. Coll. J'ai lu 68.

0475 LA FIN DE CHÉRI. Geneva: Crémille, 1969. 241p.

0476 LA FIN DE CHÉRI. Paris: Flammarion, 1970. 217p.

0477 LA FIN DE CHÉRI. Paris: Ediclub-Rombaldi, 1975. 255p.

0478 LA FIN DE CHÉRI. Postface Albert Demazière. Geneva: Farnot, 1975. 272p. Coll. Les Grands romans contemporains. Not seen.

0479 LA FIN DE CHÉRI. Introd. Yannick Resch. Paris: Flammarion, 1983. 192p. Coll. Garnier-Flammarion 390. Also chronology and press notices.

Also in:
OCLF 6 [item 0054].
OCC 5 [item 0055].
OF 2 [item 0056].
Chéri. La Fin de Chéri. Item 0305.

Extracts in:
Morceaux choisis [item 0062].
Les Plus Belles Pages de Colette [item 0064].
Beaumont and Parinaud [item 1063].

Surprising sequel to *Chéri,* written six years before. Chéri has returned from the Great War to find that family and friends have changed. Haunted by the specter of age and yearning for past happiness, he seeks out Léa, whose years and solidity shock and disorient him. Still wealthy and extraordinarily handsome, he is nevertheless unable to cope with a loss whose nature he does not understand. He thus rejects the future, choosing instead the ultimate escape.

Reviews:
Divan 14 (April 1926): 187. H.M. [Henri Martineau].
Excelsior, 9 May 1926, 4. Maurice Lena.
Hudson Review 6 (Winter 1953): 626-33. Marvin Mudrick.
Listener 46 (16 Aug. 1951): 275. John Russell.
Marginales 25 (Aug. 1970): 58-59. Constant Burniaux.
Mercure de France, 15 May 1926, 151-52. John Charpentier.
Ms. 8 (July 1979): 28. Susan Brownmiller.
Nation 177 (8 Aug. 1953): 116-17.
National & English Review 137 (Sept. 1951): 178-80. Milward
    Kennedy.
New Statesman & Nation 42 (11 Aug. 1951): 158-60. V.S.
    Pritchett.
Nouvel Observateur, 10 Aug. 1970, 30. Jean Freustié.
Nouvelle Revue française 27 (Aug. 1926): 247-49. François de
    Roux.
Nouvelles littéraires, 3 April 1926, 5. Edmond Jaloux.
Observer, no. 8356 (29 July 1951): 7. Harold Nicolson.
Œuvre, 23 March 1926, 4. André Billy.
Opinion, 17 April 1926, 14-16. André Thérive. Also in item 2149
    Galerie de ce temps, 19-25. Long passages also in *Chronique
    des lettres françaises* 4 (1926): 369-70.
Partisan Review 42 (Fall 1975): 475-76. Stephen Koch.
Revue mondiale 170 (15 April 1926): 389-90. Louis-Jean Finot.
Revue universelle 25 (15 April 1926): 234-35. Robert Kemp.
Temps, 8 April 1926, 3. Paul Souday.
Times Literary Supplement, no. 2584 (10 Aug. 1951): 497.
Twentieth Century 150 (Sept. 1951): 258.
Washington Post Book World 12 (5 Sept. 1982): 12.

English translations: American

0480 THE LAST OF CHÉRI. [Trans. Viola Gerard Garvin]. New York: Putnam's, 1932. 250p.

0481 THE LAST OF CHÉRI. Trans. Roger Senhouse. New York: Berkley, 1966. 143p. Coll. Berkley Medallion. Not seen.

Also in:
Chéri. The Last of Chéri. Items 0315-18. Trans. Roger Senhouse.
The Colette Omnibus [item 0070]. Trans. Roger Senhouse.
Seven by Colette [item 0101]. Trans. Roger Senhouse.
Short Novels of Colette [item 0102]. Trans. Viola Garvin.
Six Novels by Colette [item 0104]. Trans. Roger Senhouse.
Stories [item 0105].

Extracts in *Gigi and Selected Writings* [item 0501]. Trans. Roger Senhouse.

English translations: British

0482 THE LAST OF CHÉRI. Trans. Viola Gerard Garvin. London: Gollancz, 1933. 287p.

0483 THE LAST OF CHÉRI. Trans. Roger Senhouse. London: Secker & Warburg, 1951. 144p.

Also in:
Chéri. The Last of Chéri. Items 0322-23, 0325. Trans. Roger Senhouse.
Colette Omnibus [item 0069].
Six Novels [item 0103]. Trans. Roger Senhouse.

GIGI

0484   GIGI ET AUTRES NOUVELLES. Lausanne: La Guilde du livre, 1944. 221p. Also contains: *La Dame du photographe. Flore et Pomone. Noces.*

0485   GIGI. Paris: Ferenczi, 1945. 255p. Also contains: *L'Enfant malade. La Dame du photographe. Flore et Pomone.*

0486   GIGI. Illus. Mariette Lydis. Paris: Georges Guillot, 1948. 95p. Handsome limited edition containing only title story.

0487   GIGI. Illus. Christian Bérard. Paris: n.p. [P. Dupont, Mourlot frères], 1950. 131p. Boxed luxury edition, containing only title story.

0488   GIGI. Illus. Grau Sala. Paris: Les Heures claires, 1950. 117p. Luxury edition containing only title story.

0489   GIGI. Illus. Jacques Cura. Paris: Ferenczi, 1952. 126p. Coll. Le Livre moderne illustré 399. Same contents as item 0485.

0490   GIGI. Paris: Ferenczi, 1954. 192p. Coll. Livre de poche 89. Same contents as item 0485.

0491   GIGI. Paris: Ferenczi, 1955. 192p. Coll. Pourpre. Same contents as item 0485.

0492   GIGI. Illus. Jacques Taillefer. Paris: Eds. G.P., 1959. 256p. Coll. Super 33. Same contents as item 0485.

0493   GIGI. LE TOUTOUNIER. Paris: Hachette, 1962. 255p. First title has same contents as item 0485.

0494   GIGI. Paris: Flammarion-Hachette, 1971. 213p. Same contents as item 0485.

0495   GIGI. Geneva: Crémille, 1971. 251p. Same contents as item 0485.

0496 GIGI. Paris: Ediclub-Rombaldi, 1975. 271p. Same contents as item 0485.

0497 GIGI. Paris: France Loisirs, 1985. 157p. Same contents as item 0485.

0498 GIGI. Paris: Hachette, 1988. 252p. Same contents as item 0485.

Also in:
OCLF 13 [item 0054]: same contents as item 0485.
OCC 10 [item 0055]: same contents as item 0485.
OF 3 [item 0056]: same contents as item 0485.

Extracts in item 1764 Lagarde and Michard.

Gigi is fifteen, the grand-daughter and grand-niece of once-famous *courtisanes*. Her own mother has rejected the family profession to become a second-rate opera singer but Gigi is being trained to follow in the footsteps of her older relatives, who wish to ensure for her a future of security and wealth. Their plans are focused on Gaston, a young man who, because of his social rank and liaisons with well-known women, is often mentioned in the gossip columns. In the end he offers Gigi the future envisaged by her relatives, but Gigi's reaction surprises everyone. The novel provides an often amusing picture of certain segments of French society at the turn of the century, but will not please feminists.

Reviews:
American Mercury 75 (Dec. 1952): 100-3. William Phillips.
Arche 2 (Oct. 1945): 168-71. Dominique Aury.
Fontaine 8 (Oct. 1945): 751-53. Gérard Jarlot.
Partisan Review 20 (May-June 1953): 332-38. Sonya Rudikoff.
Revue de Paris 52 (Oct. 1945): 94-97. Marcel Thiébaut.
Times Literary Supplement, no. 2698 (16 Oct. 1953): 657.

English translations: American

0499 GIGI. JULIE DE CARNEILHAN. CHANCE ACQUAIN-TANCES. Illus. Irma Selz. New York: Farrar, Straus & Young, 1952. 315p. Trans. of *Gigi* by Roger Senhouse.

0500   GIGI. JULIE DE CARNEILHAN. New York: New American
        Library (Signet), 1958. 159p. Trans. of *Gigi* by Roger
        Senhouse.

0501   GIGI AND SELECTED WRITINGS. Foreword Elaine Marks.
        New York: New American Library (Signet), 1963. 256p.
        Includes all *Gigi* and extracts from: *L'Envers du music-hall,
        Sido, La Fin de Chéri, La Maison de Claudine, La Naissance du
        jour,* "Regarde," *La Chatte, Le Fanal bleu, Dialogues de bêtes,
        La Dame du photographe, Armande, L'Enfant malade, Pour un
        herbier.* Trans. of *Gigi* by Roger Senhouse.

0502   GIGI. JULIE DE CARNEILHAN. CHANCE ACQUAIN-
        TANCES. New York: Farrar, Straus & Giroux, 1976. 315p.
        Coll. Noonday 522. Trans. of *Gigi* by Roger Senhouse.

        Also in:
        The Colette Omnibus [item 0070]. Trans. Roger Senhouse.
        Seven by Colette [item 0101]. Trans. Roger Senhouse.
        Six Novels by Colette [item 0104]. Trans. Roger Senhouse.
        Stories [item 0105]. Trans. Roger Senhouse.

        English translations: British

0503   GIGI. THE CAT. London: Secker & Warburg, 1953. 193p. Coll.
        Uniform 5. Trans. of *Gigi* by Roger Senhouse.

0504   GIGI. THE CAT. Harmondsworth: Penguin, 1958. 157p. Trans. of
        Gigi by Roger Senhouse.

0505   GIGI. Trans. Roger Senhouse. Oxford: Isis Large Print, 1986.
        208p. Not seen.

        Also in:
        Colette Omnibus [item 0069].
        Six Novels [item 0103]. Trans. Roger Senhouse.

GRIBICHE

In *Bella-Vista*, some eds. See that title.

Extracts in *Autobiographie...* [items 0057-58] under title *Bella-Vista*.

Set against a background of Colette's music-hall days and narrated in her own name, this is a somber story of misery and abortion, and a fine example of Colette's art of understatement. Gribiche is a young girl who plays minor roles in the chorus of the music-hall. The reader is never told the facts of the situation, nor its outcome, but is led to guess what happens from the reactions of the narrator and her companions. Offers splendid character portraits. The last sentence of the novella is one of Colette's finest.

English translations: American

xxxx GRIBICHE. Trans. Antonia White.

In:
The Collected Stories of Colette [items 0071-72].
Earthly Paradise [items 0082, 0084-85] under title *Bella-Vista*.
The Tender Shoot and Other Stories [items 0106-8].

English translations: British

xxxx GRIBICHE. Trans. Antonia White.

In:
The Collected Stories of Colette [items 0073-74].
Earthly Paradise [items 0087-89] under title *Bella-Vista*.
The Rainy Moon and Other Stories [item 0111].
The Stories of Colette [items 0109-10].

L'INGÉNUE LIBERTINE

0506 L'INGÉNUE LIBERTINE. [Colette Willy]. Prefs. Willy and
Colette Willy. Paris: Ollendorff, 1909. 323p.

0507 L'INGÉNUE LIBERTINE. [Colette (Colette Willy)]. Illus. Chas
Laborde. Paris: Jonquières, 1922. 253p. Coll. Les Beaux
Romans 3.

0508 L'INGÉNUE LIBERTINE. [Colette Willy]. Prefs. Willy and
Colette Willy. Paris: Albin Michel, 1925. 312p.

0509 L'INGÉNUE LIBERTINE. [Colette Willy]. Prefs. Willy and
Colette Willy. Illus. Louis Icart. Paris: Excelsior, 1926. 193p.

0510 L'INGÉNUE LIBERTINE. Illus. Dignimont. Paris: A la Cité des
livres, 1928. 239p.

0511 L'INGÉNUE LIBERTINE. Prefs. Willy and Colette Willy. Paris:
Grasset, 1932. 283p. Coll. Œuvres de Colette 10.

0512 L'INGÉNUE LIBERTINE. Prefs. Willy and Colette Willy. Paris:
Albin Michel, 1932. 255p. Coll. Les Albin Michel à 6 francs.

0513 L'INGÉNUE LIBERTINE. Prefs. Willy and Colette Willy. Illus.
Suzanne Ballivet. Monte-Carlo: Eds. du Livre; Lausanne: Eds.
du Grand Chêne, 1947. 269p.

0514 L'INGÉNUE LIBERTINE. Illus. Paul-Emile Bécat. Paris: Georges
Guillot, 1947. 219p.

0515 L'INGÉNUE LIBERTINE. Prefs. Willy and Colette Willy. Paris:
Albin Michel, 1947. 269p.

0516 L'INGÉNUE LIBERTINE. Illus. Marcelle Meunier. Brussels: de
Kogge, 1947. 292p. Coll. L'Hippocampe.

0517 L'INGÉNUE LIBERTINE. Brussels: Le Livre plastic, 1948. 249p.

0518 L'INGÉNUE LIBERTINE. Pref. Colette. Paris: Albin Michel, 1950. 253p.

0519 L'INGÉNUE LIBERTINE. Illus. Camille Berg. Annemasse: Eds. du Madrigal, 1951. 350p.

0520 [Extract]. In *L'Erotisme dans la littérature française*, edited by René Varin, 130-32. Lyon: Champs-Fleuris, 1951; Paris: Pensée moderne, 1969.

0521 L'INGÉNUE LIBERTINE. Pref. Colette. Illus. Maurice Pouzet. Paris: Eds. du Panthéon, 1952. 279p. Coll. Pastels.

0522 L'INGÉNUE LIBERTINE. Pref. Colette. Saverne: Sélection des amis du livre, 1953. 224p.

0523 L'INGÉNUE LIBERTINE. Pref. Colette. Paris: Albin Michel, 1953. 253p. Coll. Livre de poche 11.

0524 L'INGÉNUE LIBERTINE. Paris: Albin Michel, 1954. 256p. Coll. Pourpre.

0525 L'INGÉNUE LIBERTINE. Illus. Garcia. Paris: Club du livre du mois, 1954. Coll. Chefs-d'œuvre d'hier et d'aujourd'hui. Not seen.

0526 L'INGÉNUE LIBERTINE. Pref. Colette. Paris: Club français du livre, 1955. 263p. Coll. Romans 192.

0527 L'INGÉNUE LIBERTINE. Illus. Georges Braun. Paris: Le Livre Club du Libraire, 1957. 258p. Coll. Le Livre club du libraire 38.

0528 L'INGÉNUE LIBERTINE. Paris: Eds. du Panthéon, 1957. Coll. Club. Not seen.

0529 L'INGÉNUE LIBERTINE. Pref. Colette. Illus. Gaston Barret. Brussels: Terres latines, 1965. 174p. Coll. Leurs Chefs-d'œuvre 34.

0530 L'INGÉNUE LIBERTINE. Geneva: Crémille, 1969. 259p.

0531   L'INGÉNUE LIBERTINE. Pref. Colette. Paris: France Loisirs,
       1973. 253p. Coll. Sélection France Loisirs.

0532   L'INGÉNUE LIBERTINE. Pref. Colette. Paris: Ediclub-Rombaldi,
       1975. 301p.

0533   L'INGÉNUE LIBERTINE. Pref. Colette. Paris: Albin Michel,
       1977. 315p. Coll. Prestige du livre.

0534   L'INGÉNUE LIBERTINE. Pref. Colette. Paris: Albin Michel,
       1985. 223p.

       Also in:
       OP 1 [item 0053].
       OCLF 3 [item 0054].
       OCC 2 [item 0055].
       OF 1 [item 0056].
       Claudine à l'école. L'Ingénue libertine. Chéri. Item 0350.

       Extracts in:
       Morceaux choisis [item 0062].
       Beaumont and Parinaud [item 1063].

       In *Mes Apprentissages* Colette recounts how she drafted a novella
       of some 60 pages, which at Willy's request she stretched into a
       novel, *Minne*, published under Willy's name in 1904. Colette then
       wrote a sequel, *Les Egarements de Minne*, which Willy again
       published as his own, in 1905. After the couple's separation, the
       two novels, heavily revised, became the two parts of *L'Ingénue
       libertine*, published in 1909 under the signature Colette Willy. In
       the first part, Minne, a beautiful fourteen-year-old girl, pampered
       and protected by her mother, dreams of finding love and adventure
       among the Paris *apaches* of 1900. Nourished by an over-active
       imagination, her fantasies lead her to an all-night escapade, from
       which she returns unharmed though disillusioned. In the second
       part, Minne seeks with other men the sexual satisfaction she has
       been unable to find with her husband Antoine. A surprise ending,
       skillfully done, goes far towards redeeming this half of the book,
       already much purged of Willy's influence when Colette combined
       the two earlier works to make the whole.

Reviews:
Arts and Decoration 34 (March 1931): 62, 86. Burton Rascoe.
Best Sellers 38 (Sept. 1978): 171-72. Njegos M. Petrovic.
Eve, 11 Feb. 1923, 10. Raymond Clauzel.
Listener 80 (12 Sept. 1968): 344. Mary Sullivan.
Mercure de France, 1 Jan. 1910, 107. Rachilde.
Nouvelles littéraires, 13 July 1929, 10. Clément-Janin.
Observer, no. 9242 (1 Sept. 1968): 23. Stephen Wall.
Sunday Telegraph, 1 Sept. 1968, 10. Francis King.
Times Literary Supplement, no. 1512 (22 Jan. 1931): 58.
Times Literary Supplement, no. 3481 (14 Nov. 1968): 1269.
Washington Post Book World, 2 July 1978, F3. Stephen Koch.

English translations: American

0535 THE GENTLE LIBERTINE. Trans. R.C.B. [Rosemary Carr Benét]. On Murray Hill, N.Y.: Farrar & Rinehart, 1931. 274p.

0536 THE GENTLE LIBERTINE. Trans. R.C.B. [Rosemary Carr Benét]. New York: Grosset & Dunlap, 1941. 274p.

0537 THE INNOCENT LIBERTINE. Trans. Antonia White. New York: Farrar, Straus & Giroux, 1968. 214p.

0538 THE INNOCENT LIBERTINE. Trans. Antonia White. New York: Farrar, Straus & Giroux, 1978. 214p. Coll. Noonday N586.

English translations: British

0539 THE GENTLE LIBERTINE. Trans. R.C.B. [Rosemary Carr Benét]. London: Gollancz, 1931. 288p.

0540 THE INNOCENT LIBERTINE. Trans. Antonia White. London: Secker & Warburg, 1968. 214p.

0541 THE INNOCENT LIBERTINE. Trans. Antonia White. London: Heron Books, 1968. Not seen.

0542 THE INNOCENT LIBERTINE. Trans. Antonia White. Harmondsworth: Penguin, 1972. 190p.

Also in *The Pure and the Impure*. *The Innocent Libertine*. Item
0210. Trans. Antonia White.

JULIE DE CARNEILHAN

0543   JULIE DE CARNEILHAN. Paris: Fayard, 1941. 219p.

0544   JULIE DE CARNEILHAN. Paris: Fayard, 1950. 190p. Coll. Le
Livre de demain (new series).

0545   JULIE DE CARNEILHAN. Paris: Fayard, 1970. 160p. Coll. Livre
de poche 2825.

0546   JULIE DE CARNEILHAN. Geneva: Crémille, 1971. 241p.

0547   JULIE DE CARNEILHAN. Paris: Fayard, 1981. 188p. Coll.
Folio 1344.

0548   JULIE DE CARNEILHAN. Paris: Fayard, 1984. 191p.

Also in:
OCLF 11 [item 0054].
OCC 9 [item 0055].
OF 2 [item 0056].

Extracts in item 1063 Beaumont and Parinaud.

Remnant of an aristocratic but impoverished family, the middle-
aged Julie de Carneilhan answers the call of her ex-husband, Count
Herbert d'Espivant, now wed to a rich widow but rumored to be in
serious medical condition. Ever susceptible to Herbert's charm,
though full of scorn for his weaknesses, she agrees to help him get
money from his wife through a ruse. Subsequent events illustrate
the profound superiority of both women over the man, and a
strength of character in Julie de Carneilhan of which she herself has
not been aware. Julie ranks among Colette's most memorable
female characters.

Reviews:

American Mercury 75 (Dec. 1952): 100-3. William Phillips.
Figaro, 17 Jan. 1942, 4. André Rousseaux.
Life & Letters Today 36 (March 1943): 190-92. Monica Stirling.
New Statesman & Nation 44 (19 July 1952): 82-83. John
     Raymond.
Partisan Review 20 (May-June 1953): 332-38. Sonya Rudikoff.
Revue universelle, no. 27 (10 Feb. 1942): 235-37. Thierry
     Maulnier.
Temps, 7 Jan. 1942, 3. Emile Henriot. Also in item 1690 *Maîtres
     d'hier et contemporains.*
Time & Tide 33 (26 July 1952): 857-58. Gerard Hopkins.
Times Literary Supplement, no. 2636 (8 Aug. 1952): 513.

English translations: American

xxxx JULIE DE CARNEILHAN. Trans. Patrick Leigh Fermor.

In:
Gigi. Julie de Carneilhan. Item 0500.
Gigi. Julie de Carneilhan. Chance Acquaintances. Items 0499,
     0502.
Stories [item 0105].

English translations: British

0549 JULIE DE CARNEILHAN. CHANCE ACQUAINTANCES. [On
     dust-jacket: *Chance Acquaintances*]. Trans. Patrick Leigh
     Fermor. London: Secker & Warburg, 1952. 230p. Coll.
     Uniform 3.

0550 JULIE DE CARNEILHAN. CHANCE ACQUAINTANCES.
     Trans. Patrick Leigh Fermor. Harmondsworth: Penguin, 1957.
     188p.

LE KÉPI

0551   LE KÉPI. Paris: Fayard, 1943. 205p. Contains four novellas: *Le Képi. Le Tendron. La Cire verte. Armande.*

0552   LE KÉPI. Illus. Clément Serveau. Paris: Ferenczi, 1947. 127p. Coll. Le Livre moderne illustré 373. Same contents as item 0551.

0553   LE KÉPI. Paris: Fayard, 1955. 158p. Coll. Le Livre de demain 66. Same contents as item 0551.

0554   LE KÉPI. Paris: Livre de poche, 1968. 160p. Coll. Livre de poche 2388. Same contents as item 0551.

0555   LE KÉPI. DE MA FENETRE. Geneva: Crémille, 1971. 260p. First title has same contents as item 0551.

0556   LE KÉPI. Paris: Fayard, 1984. 207p. Same contents as item 0551.

Also in:
OCLF 12 [item 0054]: same contents as item 0551.
OCC 9 [item 0055]: same contents as item 0551.
OF 3 [item 0056]: same contents as item 0551.

Extracts in item 1063 Beaumont and Parinaud.

Story of the love affair between a poor but distinguished middle-aged woman and a young military man. All goes well until the woman, who has flourished under love's influence, dons the young man's kepi. The end comes quickly. Authenticity is lent to the tale by its framework. Paul Masson and Willy are secondary characters, while a semi-fictional Colette interprets events. Treatment of both feminine and masculine psychology during the Belle Epoque is very subtle. All editions contain three other novellas, annotated separately.

English translations: American

xxxx THE KEPI. Trans. Antonia White.

In:
The Collected Stories of Colette [items 0071-72].
The Tender Shoot and Other Stories [items 0106-8].

English translations: British

xxxx THE KEPI. Trans. Antonia White.

In:
The Collected Stories of Colette [items 0073-74].
The Rainy Moon and Other Stories [item 0111].
The Stories of Colette [items 0109-10].

LA LUNE DE PLUIE

In *Chambre d'hôtel*, all eds. See that title.

One of Colette's rare explorations of the supernatural. The narrator, a Madame Colette of the first decade of the 1900's, senses a mystery at the home of her typist, Rosita Barberet. Drawn towards Rosita's sister, Délia, because of the fact that Délia lives in a room in which she herself once lived and suffered, Madame Colette moves from sympathy to astonishment when she learns that Délia is engaged in casting a spell on her estranged husband, Eugène. Convinced that Eugène will die when seven moons have passed, Rosita begs for Madame Colette's aid. Colette's technique of suggestion--for little is stated openly here--as well as her use of a subtle network of symbols and the interplay of light and shadow, are admirable. The title refers to the rainbow made by light passing through a prism. Colette uses it as a motif to connect the narrator's past suffering to that of Délia in the present. Considered by some critics to be Colette's best-crafted novella.

English   translations: American

xxxx   THE RAINY MOON. Trans. Antonia White.

In:
The Collected Stories of Colette [items 0071-72].
The Tender Shoot and Other Stories [items 0106-8].

English   translations: British

xxxx   THE RAINY MOON. Trans. Antonia White.

In:
The Collected Stories of Colette [items 0073-74].
The Rainy Moon and Other Stories [item 0111].
The Stories of Colette [items 0109-10].

MINNE

0557   MINNE. [Willy]. Paris: Ollendorff, 1904. 295p. Abridged and
revised version became the first part of *L'Ingénue libertine*,
published in 1909. See that title.

MITSOU
OU COMMENT L'ESPRIT VIENT AUX FILLES

0558   MITSOU OU COMMENT L'ESPRIT VIENT AUX FILLES. EN
CAMARADES. [Colette (Colette Willy)]. Paris: Fayard, 1919.
253p.

0559 MITSOU OU COMMENT L'ESPRIT VIENT AUX FILLES.
[Colette (Colette Willy)]. Illus. Hermann-Paul. Paris: Fayard,
1923. 96p. Coll. Le Livre de demain 2.

0560 MITSOU OU COMMENT L'ESPRIT VIENT AUX FILLES.
Illus. Jean Oberlé. Paris: Jonquières, 1926. 185p. Coll. Les
Beaux Romans 18.

0561 MITSOU OU COMMENT L'ESPRIT VIENT AUX FILLES.
[Colette (Colette Willy)]. Illus. Dignimont. Paris: Crès, 1926.
197p. Coll. Maîtres et jeunes d'aujourd'hui 23 (second series).

0562 MITSOU OU COMMENT L'ESPRIT VIENT AUX FILLES.
Illus. Edgar Chahine. Paris: Devambez, 1930. 129p.

0563 "Mitsou." *Lisez-moi*, no. 364 (25 June 1937): 881-92; no. 365 (10
July 1937): 47-58; no. 366 (25 July 1937): 101-11.

0564 MITSOU OU COMMENT L'ESPRIT VIENT AUX FILLES. EN
CAMARADES. Paris: Fayard, 1956. 191p.

0565 MITSOU OU COMMENT L'ESPRIT VIENT AUX FILLES. EN
CAMARADES. Paris: Fayard, 1960. 181p. Coll. Livre de
poche 630.

0566 MITSOU. L'ENVERS DU MUSIC-HALL. DANS LA FOULE.
Geneva: Crémille, 1969. 251p.

0567 MITSOU OU COMMENT L'ESPRIT VIENT AUX FILLES.
Paris: Flammarion, 1970. 188p.

0568 MITSOU OU COMMENT L'ESPRIT VIENT AUX FILLES. EN
CAMARADES. Paris: Fayard, 1984. 191p.

Also in:
OP 2 [item 0053].
OCLF 5 [item 0054].
OCC 4 [item 0055].
OF 2 [item 0056].

Extracts in:
Morceaux choisis [item 0062].
Beaumont and Parinaud [item 1063].

Mitsou is a young music-hall performer, who, like many of her
kind, has found security under the protection of a wealthy patron.
Almost against her wishes, she falls in love with a World War I
soldier on leave from the front. The psychology of the very
appealing Mitsou is delicately and convincingly presented.
Consisting of a mixture of narrative, letters and theatrical dialogue,
this novel is experimental in form and contains some of Colette's
rare light comedy.

Reviews:
London Magazine 5 (Jan. 1958): 58-59. Anthony Quinton.
Marges 16 (15 June 1919): 371. Maurice Le Blond.
New York Review of Books 6 (9 June 1966): 8-10. John
    Weightman.
Nouvel Observateur, 10 Aug. 1970, 30. Jean Freustié.
Observer, no. 8668 (18 Aug. 1957): 12. John Davenport.
Quinzaine critique, 25 April 1930, 98-99. Jean Bruller.
Revue du mois 14 (10 Nov. 1919): 524. Camille Marbo.
Revue mondiale 131 (15 June 1919): 773-75. Nicolas Ségur.
Temps, 11 April 1919, 2. Paul Souday.
Temps, 22 March 1923, 3. Paul Souday.
Times Literary Supplement, no. 1491 (28 Aug. 1930): 686.
Times Literary Supplement, no. 2895 (23 Aug. 1957): 505.

English translations: American

0569 MITSOU OR HOW GIRLS GROW WISE. Trans. Jane Terry.
        Introd. Janet Flanner. Illus. Hermann Paul. New York: Boni,
        1930. 162p.

0570 MITSOU. MUSIC-HALL SIDELIGHTS. New York: Farrar,
        Straus & Cudahy, 1958. 260p. Trans. of *Mitsou* by Raymond
        Postgate.

0571 MITSOU. MUSIC-HALL SIDELIGHTS. New York: Farrar,
        Straus & Giroux, 1976. 242p. Coll. Noonday 542. Trans. of
        Mitsou by Raymond Postgate.

Also in *Six Novels by Colette* [item 0104]. Trans. Raymond
   Postgate.

English translations: British

0572   MITSOU OR HOW GIRLS GROW WISE. Trans. Jane Terry.
   London: Gollancz, 1930. 159p.

0573   MITSOU OR THE EDUCATION OF YOUNG WOMEN. Trans.
   Raymond Postgate. London: Secker & Warburg, 1957. 134p.
   Coll. Uniform 10.

0574   MITSOU. [Trans. Raymond Postgate]. London: Transworld
   (Corgi), 1967. 128p.

LA NAISSANCE DU JOUR

0575   LA NAISSANCE DU JOUR. Paris: Flammarion, 1928. 247p.

0576   LA NAISSANCE DU JOUR. Paris: Flammarion, 1930. 225p.

0577   LA NAISSANCE DU JOUR. Illus. Clément Serveau. Paris:
   Ferenczi, 1931. 167p. Coll. Le Livre moderne illustré 119.

0578   LA NAISSANCE DU JOUR. Illus. Luc-Albert Moreau. Paris: Les
   XXX de Lyon, 1932. 267p. Magnificent limited edition.

0579   LA NAISSANCE DU JOUR. Paris: Flammarion, 1933. 71p.
   Coll. Select-collection 7 (new series).

0580   [Extract]. *Lisez-moi*, no. 394 (25 Sept. 1938): 460.

0581   LA NAISSANCE DU JOUR. Illus. André Jacquemin. Paris:
   Flammarion, 1942. 170p. Deluxe edition.

0582 LA NAISSANCE DU JOUR. Paris: Flammarion, 1950. 71p. Coll. Select-collection 7.

0583 "Ma Maison." [Extract]. *France-Illustration* 394 (2 May 1953): 585.

0584 LA NAISSANCE DU JOUR. Paris: Flammarion, 1958. 248p. Coll. Les Flammes 1. Includes passages from Maurice Goudeket's *Près de Colette* as well as photographs of Saint Tropez, site of the novel.

0585 LA NAISSANCE DU JOUR. Pref. Gilbert Sigaux. Lausanne: Rencontre, 1961. 251p. Coll. Chefs-d'œuvre du vingtième siècle. Not seen.

0586 LA NAISSANCE DU JOUR. Paris: Ditis, 1962. 192p. Coll. J'ai lu 153.

0587 LA NAISSANCE DU JOUR. Paris: Club de la femme, 1965. 255p. Includes many photographs.

0588 LA NAISSANCE DU JOUR. Pref. and chronology Claude Pichois. Paris: Garnier-Flammarion, 1969. 189p.

0589 LA NAISSANCE DU JOUR. Paris: Flammarion, 1970. 221p.

0590 LA NAISSANCE DU JOUR. Geneva: Crémille, 1970. 241p.

0591 LA NAISSANCE DU JOUR. Paris: Ediclub-Rombaldi, 1975. 255p.

0592 LA NAISSANCE DU JOUR. Pref. and chronology Claude Pichois. Paris: Flammarion, 1984. 192p. Coll. G.-F. 430. Similar to item 0588, but with a fuller preface and a dossier consisting of three letters from Colette's mother as well as notes on real persons mentioned in the novel. The letters are those "quoted" in the novel, but comparison reveals that Colette changed the wording for her own purposes. An excellent study edition.

Also in:
OCLF 8 [item 0054].
OCC 6 [item 0055].
OF 2 [item 0056].

Extracts in:
Autobiographie... [items 0057-58].
Bêtes libres et prisonnières [item 0702]: Connivence. Papillons.
Chats de Colette [items 0714-15]: Chartreux. En livrée de nuit. Les
    deux matous.
Morceaux choisis [item 0062].
Pages choisies [item 0063].
Les Plus Belles Pages de Colette [item 0064].
Textes choisis de Colette [item 0065].
Beaumont and Parinaud [item 1063].
Brincourt [item 1313].
Chaillet [item 1365].
Lagarde and Michard [item 1764].

Remarkable for the diffuse complexity of its form, this novel
combines fact with fantasy, and autobiography with imagination.
The story is set on the French Côte d'Azur, where the heroine, a
middle-aged Madame Colette, rejects the overtures of a young man,
in order to concentrate more fully on her own spiritual development
and sense of self. The model for growth and renewal will be, as
always, her dead mother, "Sido." Narrated in the first person, the
tenuous plot is interlaced with numerous digressions, anecdotes and
personal reminiscences of the author. A successful experiment in
non-traditional form, and written at the peak of Colette's career,
this novel contains some of her finest lyrical writing.

Reviews:
Annales, 1 May 1928, 413-14. Benjamin Crémieux.
Choice 4 (May 1967): 295.
Chronique des lettres françaises 6 (July-Aug. 1928): 541-43. E.R.
Commonweal 86 (14 July 1967): 452-54. Alice Mayhew.
Comœdia (3 April 1928): 3. Eugène Marsan. Also in *Signes de
    notre temps*, 129-30. Paris: Libraire de France, 1930.
Divan 16 (June 1928): 274-75. P.L.
Europe nouvelle, 28 April 1928, 589-90. André Maurois.
Eve, 22 April 1928, 10. Raymond Clauzel.

Evening Standard, 2 Aug. 1928, 5. Arnold Bennett. Also in
  Evening Standard Years: Books and Persons, 181-83. London:
  Chatto & Windus, 1974.
Figaro, 10 April 1928, 3. Henri de Régnier.
Horn Book Magazine 51 (Oct. 1975): 493-94. Mary Silva
  Cosgrave.
Liberté (2 April 1928): 1. [Robert Kemp].
Mercure de France, 1 June 1928, 415-17. John Charpentier.
Monde, 25 Jan. 1973, 21. Gérard Bonal.
Ms. 6 (July 1977): 34. Sandy Dennis.
Nouvelle Revue française 31 (July 1928): 127-29. Marcel Arland.
  Also, under title "La vieillesse de Colette," in *Essais critiques*,
  140-43. Paris: Gallimard, 1931; and in *Essais et nouveaux
  essais critiques*, 90-92. Paris: Gallimard, 1952.
Nouvelles littéraires, 21 April 1928, 3. Edmond Jaloux.
Nueva Estafeta 50 (Jan. 1983): 86-87. Manuel Ríos Ruiz.
Point et virgule, June 1928, 12-15. Louise Martial.
Publishers' Weekly 190 (3 Oct. 1966): 90. Alice Hackett.
Revue de Paris 35 (1 June 1928): 685-88. Henry Bidou.
Revue des deux mondes 98 (1 June 1928): 697-98. André
  Chaumeix.
Revue mondiale 29 (15 April 1928): 422. Louis-Jean Finot.
Saturday Review 49 (17 Dec. 1966): 36.
Temps, 19 April 1928, 3. Paul Souday.
Times Literary Supplement, no. 1386 (23 Aug. 1928): 605.
Times Literary Supplement, no. 1575 (7 April 1932): 252.
Times Literary Supplement, no. 3081 (17 March 1961): 165.
Washington Post Book Week 4 (18 June 1967): 13. MIM.

English translations: American

0593 A LESSON IN LOVE. Trans. Rosemary Benét. On Murray Hill,
      N.Y.: Farrar & Rinehart, 1932. 239p.

0594 BREAK OF DAY. Trans. Enid McLeod. Introd. Glenway Wescott.
      New York: Farrar, Straus & Cudahy, 1961. 143p.

0595 BREAK OF DAY. Trans. Enid McLeod. Introd. Glenway Wescott.
      New York: Avon, 1963. Not seen.

0596 BREAK OF DAY. THE BLUE LANTERN. Introd. Glenway
Wescott. New York: Farrar, Straus & Giroux, 1966. xiv-143-
159p. Trans. of *Break of Day* by Enid McLeod.

0597 BREAK OF DAY. Trans. Enid McLeod. New York: Farrar, Straus
& Giroux, 1974. 143p. Coll. Noonday N493.

0598 BREAK OF DAY. Trans. Enid McLeod. New York: Ballantine,
1983. 128p.

0599 BREAK OF DAY. Trans. Enid McLeod. Introd. Robert Phelps.
Illus. Françoise Gilot. New York: Limited Editions Club,
1983. xiii-137p. Not seen.

Extracts in:
Earthly Paradise [items 0082, 0084-85]. Trans. Enid McLeod.
Gigi and Selected Writings [item 0501]. Trans. Enid McLeod.

English translations: British

0600 MORNING GLORY. [Trans. Rosemary Benét]. London: Gollancz,
1932. 254p.

0601 BREAK OF DAY. Trans. Enid McLeod. London: Secker &
Warburg, 1961. 143p. Coll. Uniform 14.

0602 BREAK OF DAY. Trans. Enid McLeod. London: Women's Press,
1979. 144p.

Extracts in *Earthly Paradise* [items 0087-89]. Trans. Enid McLeod.

LE RENDEZ-VOUS

In *Bella-Vista*, some eds. See that title.

Also in *Fleurs du désert* [item 0806].

Different from Colette's other fiction in both geography and perspective, this novella was inspired by a visit she made to North Africa in 1929. Bernard Bonnemains has come to Tangiers on a working holiday with the three Bessiers: his employer Cyril, Cyril's wife Odette, and Cyril's sister-in-law Rose, a young widow with whom Bernard has been having an affair and whom he wishes to marry. Despite the vigilance of the other Bessiers and Rose's fear of being discovered, the lovers arrange a tryst in the garden at night. What they find in the garden changes both their lives, and Bernard learns a great deal about himself and about what he truly wants. Narrated in the third person, from Bernard's perspective, this novella represents one of Colette's few studies of masculine psychology.

English translations: American

0603   "Journey's end." Trans. Antonia White. *Mademoiselle* 49 (June 1959): 48-50, 91-106.

xxxx   THE RENDEZVOUS. Trans. Antonia White.

In:
The Collected Stories of Colette [items 0071-72].
The Tender Shoot and Other Stories [items 0106-8].

English translations: British

xxxx   THE RENDEZVOUS. Trans. Antonia White.

In:
The Collected Stories of Colette [items 0073-74].
The Rainy Moon and Other Stories [item 0111].
The Stories of Colette [items 0109-10].

LA RETRAITE SENTIMENTALE

0604 LA RETRAITE SENTIMENTALE. [Colette Willy]. Pref. Colette Willy. Paris: Mercure de France, 1907. 266p.

0605 LA RETRAITE SENTIMENTALE. [Colette (Colette Willy)]. Paris: Flammarion, 1914. 292p.

0606 LA RETRAITE SENTIMENTALE. [Colette (Colette Willy)]. Paris: Flammarion, 1917. 78p. Coll. Select-collection 47.

0607 LA RETRAITE SENTIMENTALE. Illus. Robert Bonfils. Brussels: La Chimère, 1922. 187p.

0608 LA RETRAITE SENTIMENTALE. Illus. André Guillaume. Paris: Baudinière, 1926. 160p. Les Maîtres de la plume (Series B).

0609 LA RETRAITE SENTIMENTALE. Paris: Grasset, 1929. 239p. Coll. Œuvres de Colette 7.

0610 LA RETRAITE SENTIMENTALE. Illus. Georges Gobô. Paris: Les Bibliophiles comtois, 1932. 215p. Also brief preamble by Colette.

0611 LA RETRAITE SENTIMENTALE. Paris: Baudinière, 1934. 222p. Coll. Hebdo.

0612 LA RETRAITE SENTIMENTALE. Paris: Flammarion, 1937. 63p. Coll. Select-collection 129.

0613 LA RETRAITE SENTIMENTALE. Pref. Colette Willy. Paris: Mercure de France, 1945. 208p.

0614 LA RETRAITE SENTIMENTALE. Illus. Alice Delaye. Paris: Eds. du Panthéon, 1946. 242p. Coll. Le Panthéon des lettres.

0615 LA RETRAITE SENTIMENTALE. Pref. Colette. Paris: Union bibliophile de France, 1946. 279p. Coll. Vox. Includes bibliography with preamble of item 0610 and Rachilde's review of the novel.

0616 LA RETRAITE SENTIMENTALE. Pref. Colette. Paris: Les
      Fermiers généraux - Club du livre illustré, 1952. 210p. Includes
      note by André Parinaud.

0617 LA RETRAITE SENTIMENTALE. Paris: Plon, 1954. 255p.
      Coll. Bibliothèque Plon (red series) 46.

0618 LA RETRAITE SENTIMENTALE. Pref. Pierre Brisson. Front.
      André Dunoyer de Segonzac. Monte-Carlo: André Sauret, 1957.
      269p. Coll. Grand prix des meilleurs romans d'amour 2.

0619 LA RETRAITE SENTIMENTALE. Pref. Colette Willy. Paris:
      Mercure de France, 1958. 244p. Coll. Livre de poche 341.

0620 LA RETRAITE SENTIMENTALE. Pref. Colette Willy. Pref.
      Gilbert Sigaux. Lausanne: Rencontre, 1961. 327p. Coll. Prix
      Rencontre 5.

0621 LA RETRAITE SENTIMENTALE. Pref. Colette Willy. Illus.
      Forain. Paris: Cercle du bibliophile, 1968. 255p.

0622 LA RETRAITE SENTIMENTALE. Geneva: Crémille, 1969.
      256p.

0623 LA RETRAITE SENTIMENTALE. Pref. Colette. Paris: Mercure
      de France, 1972. 243p. Coll. Folio 135.

      Also in:
      OP 1 [item 0053].
      OCLF 2 [item 0054].
      OCC 2 [item 0055].
      OF 1 [item 0056].
      La Vagabonde. La Retraite sentimentale. Item 0679.

      Extracts in:
      Bêtes libres et prisonnières [item 0702]: Ecureuils. Chers bois!
      Chats de Colette [items 0714-15]: Péronnelle.
      Chiens de Colette [item 0716-17]: Toby.
      Colette [item 0060].
      De la patte à l'aile [item 0723]: Chauve-souris, hérisson, crapaud.
      Morceaux choisis [item 0062].
      Les Plus Belles Pages de Colette [item 0064].

Textes choisis de Colette [item 0065].
Beaumont and Parinaud [item 1063].

Fifth and last in the Claudine series, and the first of Colette's
novels to be written under her own name. With Renaud in hospital
in Switzerland, Claudine seeks solace with Annie at the latter's
country home in the Jura. At the end of the novel, Renaud dies.
Although vestiges of Willy's influence can still be seen in two
incidents--the sexual fiasco involving Annie and the visiting
Marcel, as well as Annie's confessions of her amorous adventures--
Colette's meditative style predominates. The novel has no real plot
and is written in journal form. It contains beautiful descriptive
passages and much reflection on some of Colette's favorite themes:
love, aging, the passing of time, and the salutary effects of nature.

Reviews:
Atlantic 234 (Sept. 1974): 102. Edward Weeks.
Booklist 71 (1 Sept. 1974): 21-22.
Books & Bookmen 20 (June 1975): 57-58. Jean Stubbs.
Contemporary Review 194 (Nov. 1958): 278. Beryl Gaster.
Library Journal 99 (1 May 1974): 1324. Lucy McCallum
    Schwartz.
Listener 92 (12 Dec. 1974): 786. Sara Maitland.
Mercure de France, 1 March 1907, 112-14. Rachilde.
New Statesman 88 (4 Oct. 1974): 477-78. Peter Straub.
New Yorker 50 (26 Aug. 1974): 90-91.
Observer, no. 9552 (25 Aug. 1974): 23. John Coleman.
Saturday Review/World 1 (13 July 1974): 20-21. Charles Lam
    Markmann.
Times Literary Supplement, no. 3797 (13 Dec. 1974): 1420.
Times Literary Supplement, no. 3825 (4 July 1975): 741. Barbara
    Wright.
Village Voice 19 (10 Oct. 1974): 33. Annette Kuhn.

English translations: American

0624 RETREAT FROM LOVE. Trans. and introd. Margaret Crosland.
      Indianapolis: Bobbs-Merrill, 1974. 226p.

0625   RETREAT FROM LOVE. Trans. and introd. Margaret Crosland.
       San Diego, New York, London: Harcourt Brace Jovanovich
       (Harvest/HBJ), 1980. 226p.

English translations: British

0626   RETREAT FROM LOVE. Trans. and introd. Margaret Crosland.
       London: Owen, 1974. 226p.

0627   RETREAT FROM LOVE. Trans. and introd. Margaret Crosland.
       London: Hamlyn Paperbacks, 1983. 158p.

LA SECONDE

0628   LA SECONDE. Paris: Ferenczi, 1929. 271p.

0629   LA SECONDE. Paris: Grasset, 1929. 273p. Coll. Œuvres de
       Colette 5.

0630   LA SECONDE. Illus. Clément Serveau. Paris: Ferenczi, 1931.
       165p. Coll. Le Livre moderne illustré 131.

0631   LA SECONDE. Paris: Flammarion, 1934. 71p. Coll. Select-
       collection 25 (new series).

0632   LA SECONDE. Paris: Ferenczi, 1946. 227p.

0633   LA SECONDE. Paris: Ferenczi, 1955. 186p. Coll. Livre de poche
       116.

0634   LA SECONDE. Paris: Ferenczi, 1956. 192p. Coll. Pourpre.

0635   LA SECONDE. Geneva: Crémille, 1970. 245p.

0636   LA SECONDE. Paris: Hachette-Flammarion, 1971. 205p.

0637 LA SECONDE. Paris: Stock, 1984. 226p.

Also in:
OCLF 8 [item 0054].
OCC 7 [item 0055].
OF 2 [item 0056].

Extracts in:
Morceaux choisis [item 0062].
Les Plus Belles Pages de Colette [item 0064].
Beaumont and Parinaud [item 1063].

Fanny discovers that her playwright husband Farou has again been
unfaithful, this time with Jane, his secretary but also Fanny's
companion and helper. Should Fanny dismiss her? The novel is
devoted to her consideration of this question. The conclusion has
shocked some readers, dismayed others, and given pleasant surprise
to those who equate Colette's picture of feminine solidarity with an
extraordinary courage. Her subtle analysis of Fanny's suffering and
emotional honesty is the book's most impressive feature.

Reviews:
Action française, 28 March 1929, non-pag. [3-4]. Robert Le
    Diable.
Annales, 15 April 1929, 353. Benjamin Crémieux.
Books & Bookmen 18 (Feb. 1973): 125.
Bulletin critique du livre français 10 (1955): 614.
Europe, no. 78 (15 June 1929): 308-10. Andrhée Huguier.
Figaro, 16 April 1929, 5. Henri de Régnier.
Illustrated London News 236 (20 Feb. 1960): 328. E.D. O'Brien.
Mercure de France, 1 May 1929, 654-57. John Charpentier.
New Republic 176 (11 June 1977): 27-29. Joyce Carol Oates.
New York Review of Books 6 (9 June 1966): 8-10. John
    Weightman.
New York Times Book Review, 3 April 1977, 53.
New York Times Book Review, 1 May 1977, 12. Anatole Broyard.
Nouvelle Revue française 33 (1 June 1929): 876-78. Roger Allard.
Nouvelles littéraires, 27 April 1929, 3. Edmond Jaloux.
Nueva Estafeta 50 (Jan. 1983): 86-87. Manuel Ríos Ruiz.
Observer, no. 8797 (7 Feb. 1960): 21. John Davenport.
Observer, no. 9461 (26 Nov. 1972): 33. Helen Dawson.

Opinion 22 (27 April 1929): 11-13. André Thérive. Also in item
2149 *Galerie de ce temps*, 26-33.
Revue de Paris 36 (1 May 1929) 203-7. Henri Bidou.
Revue mondiale 30 (15 April 1929): 416-18. Louis-Jean Finot.
Revue universelle 37 (1 June 1929): 626. Robert Kemp.
Spectator, no. 6868, (12 Feb. 1960): 228. John Coleman.
Temps, 4 April 1929, 3. Paul Souday.
Times Literary Supplement, no. 1536 (9 July 1931): 549.
Times Literary Supplement, no. 3024 (12 Feb. 1960): 101.

English translations: American

0638   THE OTHER ONE. Trans. Viola Gerard Garvin. New York:
       Cosmopolitan Book Corporation, 1931. 241p.

0639   THE OTHER ONE. Trans. Elizabeth Tait and Roger Senhouse.
       New York: Farrar, Straus & Cudahy, 1960. 160p.

0640   THE OTHER ONE. Trans. Elizabeth Tait and Roger Senhouse.
       New York: New American Library (Signet), 1962. 142p.

0641   THE OTHER ONE. Trans. Elizabeth Tait and Roger Senhouse.
       Westport, Conn.: Greenwood Press, 1972. 160p.

0642   THE OTHER ONE. Trans. Elizabeth Tait and Roger Senhouse.
       New York: Farrar, Straus & Giroux, 1977. 160p. Coll.
       Noonday N548.

       Also in *Short Novels of Colette* [item 0102]. Trans. Viola Gerard
       Garvin.

English translations: British

0643   FANNY AND JANE. Trans. Viola Gerard Garvin. London:
       Gollancz, 1931. 283p.

0644   THE OTHER ONE. Trans. Elizabeth Tait and Roger Senhouse.
       London: Secker & Warburg, 1960. 160p. Coll. Uniform 12.

0645   THE OTHER ONE. Trans. Elizabeth Tait and Roger Senhouse.
       Harmondsworth: Penguin, 1972. 157p.

LE SIEUR BINARD

In *Bella-Vista*, some eds. See that title.

0646   "Le sieur Binard." *Lisez-Moi*, no. 405 (10 March 1939): 320-22.

Too short to be termed a true novella but classified as such because
of its inclusion by Colette with others. The work has also inspired
criticism because the title character appears for the first time only
half-way through the story, the first part consisting of long
passages focusing on the work and adventures of Colette's
physician-brother Achille. Analysis shows, however, that the
preliminary anecdotes are not superfluous to the plot but are an
elaborate preparation for the Sieur Binard passages. Significant
because it paints a rare picture of the ugly side of Colette's
childhood paradise, and because it is a concise example of Colette's
genius at presenting a sordid subject--in this case, incest--
dispassionately yet with no attempt at whitewash or euphemism.

English translations: American

xxxx   THE PATRIARCH. Trans. Antonia White.

In:
The Collected Stories of Colette [items 0071-72].
The Tender Shoot and Other Stories [items 0106-8].

English translations: British

xxxx   THE PATRIARCH. Trans. Antonia White.

In:
The Collected Stories of Colette [items 0073-74].
The Rainy Moon and Other Stories [item 0111].
The Stories of Colette [items 0109-10].

LE TENDRON

0647   LE TENDRON. Illus. Ramah. Brussels: Lumière, 1944. 73p.
Coll. La Flèche d'or 2. Contains only the title novella.

0648   LE TENDRON. Illus. Jean Haramboure. Paris: Gründ, 1946. 71p.
Coll. Bagatelle 16. Contains only the title novella.

Also in *Le Képi*, all eds.

A reformed seductor recounts to the narrator an adventure which,
many years before, made him lose his previous taste for young
girls. Attracted by the young Louisette during a holiday in the
country, his conquest of the girl is successful until he is unmasked
for what he is by Louisette's mother. Long descriptive passages of
the Franche-Comté region complement the characterization of two
of Colette's most fascinating women characters. The dialogue
structure, whereby the male protagonist offers replies to the
narrator's own questions, provides a subtle commentary on the
hero's morality.

English translations: American

xxxx THE TENDER SHOOT. Trans. Antonia White.

In:
The Collected Stories of Colette [items 0071-72].
The Tender Shoot and Other Stories [items 0106-8].

English translations: British

xxxx THE TENDER SHOOT. Trans. Antonia White.

In:
The Collected Stories of Colette [items 0073-74].
The Rainy Moon and Other Stories [item 0111].
The Stories of Colette [items 0109-10].

LE TOUTOUNIER

0649 LE TOUTOUNIER. Paris: Ferenczi, 1939. 171p.

0650 LE TOUTOUNIER. Paris: Ferenczi, 1947. 165p.

0651 LE TOUTOUNIER. Paris: Stock, 1984. 167p.

Also in:
OCLF 9 [item 0054].
OCC 8 [item 0055].
OF 2 [item 0056].
Duo. Le Toutounier. Items 0436-39.
Gigi. Le Toutounier. Item 0493.

Sequel to *Duo*. After Michel's suicide, Alice returns to Paris where two of her three sisters still live in the family's shabby apartment. Feeling betrayed by Michel's suicide, she gains strength, optimism and self-assurance from her sisters' daily courage, and from her own

recognition of their feminine solidarity. The book takes its title
from the family term for an old couch, still used for a bed. The
family jargon is an illustration of Colette's interest in words for
their own sake.

Reviews:
Action française, 6 April 1939, 5. Robert Brasillach. Also in
     Œuvres complètes de Robert Brasillach, vol. 12, 278-79. Paris:
     Club de l'honnête homme, 1964.
Booklist 72 (1 Oct. 1975): 219-20.
Bulletin critique du livre français 10 (1955): 705.
Guardian Weekly 114 (1 Feb. 1976): 21. Norman Shrapnel.
Kirkus Reviews 43 (15 May 1975): 580.
Library Journal 100 (15 June 1975): 1238. Elizabeth Tingom.
Mercure de France, 1 March 1939, 390-91. John Charpentier.
New Statesman 91 (2 Jan. 1976): 108. Susannah Clapp.
Nouvelle Revue française 52 (March 1939): 510-12. Marcel Arland.
Publishers' Weekly 207 (19 May 1975): 171.
Publishers' Weekly 211 (24 Jan. 1977): 332.
Sunday Times, 25 Jan. 1976, 41. Jill Neville.
Times Higher Education Supplement 248 (23 July 1976): 15.
     Anthony Kelly.
Times Literary Supplement, no. 3854 (23 Jan. 1976): 76. Judith
     Landry.

English translations: American

xxxx   LE TOUTOUNIER. Trans. Margaret Crosland.

In *Duo. Le Toutounier*. Items 0442-43.

English translations: British

xxxx   LE TOUTOUNIER. Trans. Margaret Crosland.

In *Duo. Le Toutounier*. Items 0445-46.

LA VAGABONDE

0652 LA VAGABONDE. [Colette Willy]. Paris: Ollendorf, 1910. 336p.

0653 LA VAGABONDE. [Colette Willy]. Paris: Ollendorf, 1913. 344p.
Not seen.

0654 LA VAGABONDE. [Colette Willy]. Paris: Ollendorff, 1922.
191p. Coll. Les Grands Romans.

0655 LA VAGABONDE. [Colette Willy]. Paris: Crès, 1923. 269p.
Coll. Maîtres et jeunes d'aujourd'hui 3 (second series).

0656 LA VAGABONDE. Illus. Mich. Paris: Société du livre d'art, 1924.
235p.

0657 LA VAGABONDE. [Colette Willy]. Paris: Albin Michel, 1925.
320p.

0658 LA VAGABONDE. Illus. Dignimont. Paris: Mornay, 1926. 335p.
Coll. Les Beaux livres 33.

0659 LA VAGABONDE. Illus. Marcel Vertès. Paris: A la cité des
livres, 1927. 279p.

0660 LA VAGABONDE. Paris: Calmann-Lévy, 1927. 319p.

0661 LA VAGABONDE. Illus. Renefer. Paris: Hachette, 1928. 269p.
Coll. Les Grands Ecrivains 2.

0662 LA VAGABONDE. Paris: Grasset, 1929. 273p. Coll. Œuvres de
Colette 3.

0663 LA VAGABONDE. Illus. Jodelet. Paris: Les Bibliophiles du
Palais, 1930. 211p.

0664 LA VAGABONDE. Paris: Albin Michel, 1932. 256p. Coll. Les
Albin Michel à 6 francs.

0665   LA VAGABONDE. Illus. Morin-Jean. Paris: Fayard, 1936. 128p.
       Coll. Le Livre de demain 164.

0666   LA VAGABONDE. Paris: Sequana, 1936. 255p.

0667   LA VAGABONDE. Illus. Géol. Brussels: La Nouvelle Revue de
       Belgique, 1942. 244p.

0668   LA VAGABONDE. Illus. Albert Jarach. Paris: Colbert, 1945.
       277p. Coll. Le Lys d'or.

0669   LA VAGABONDE. Illus. Berthommé Saint-André. Paris: Eds.
       nationales, 1945. 236p. Coll. La Vie en France au début du
       XXe siècle.

0670   LA VAGABONDE. Paris: Albin Michel, 1946. 253p.

0671   LA VAGABONDE. Illus. Grau Sala. Monte-Carlo: Aux Eds. du
       livre, 1950. 301p.

0672   LA VAGABONDE. Front. Jacques Lechantre. Paris: Les
       Compagnons du livre, 1950. 299p.

0673   LA VAGABONDE. Paris: Fayard, 1951. 192p. Coll. Le Livre de
       demain 14 (new series).

0674   LA VAGABONDE. Front. Matisse. Paris: André Sauret, 1951.
       283p. Coll. Grand Prix des meilleurs romans du demi-siècle 13.

0675   [Extract]. *Revue littéraire*, no. 11 (March-April 1954): 4-8.

0676   LA VAGABONDE. Paris: Albin Michel, 1957. 249p. Coll. Livre
       de poche 283.

0677   LA VAGABONDE. Paris: Club de la femme, 1961. 255p. Includes
       interview with Maurice Goudeket.

0678   LA VAGABONDE. Illus. Paulette Debraine. Paris: Club du livre
       selectionné, 1964. 286p.

0679 LA VAGABONDE. LA RETRAITE SENTIMENTALE. Illus. Grau Sala. Paris: Culture, art, loisirs, 1967. 479p. Coll. Le Meilleur Livre de la femme.

0680 LA VAGABONDE. Geneva: Crémille, 1969. 255p.

0681 LA VAGABONDE. Paris: Flammarion-Albin Michel, 1970. 237p.

0682 LA VAGABONDE. Lausanne: La Guilde du livre, 1973. 271p. Coll. Romans-essais 893.

0683 LA VAGABONDE. Paris: Ediclub-Rombaldi, 1975. 319p.

0684 LA VAGABONDE. Caen: Laurence Olivier Four, 1983. 2 vol. Large print edition.

Also in:
OP 1 [item 0053].
OCLF 4 [item 0054].
OCC 3 [item 0055].
OF 1 [item 0056].

Extracts in:
Autobiographie... [items 0057-58].
Bêtes libres et prisonnières [item 0702]: La biche.
Chiens de Colette [items 0716-17]: Margot et les chiens. Fossette. Nelle.
Colette [item 0060].
Morceaux choisis [item 0062].
Les Plus Belles Pages de Colette [item 0064].
Textes choisis de Colette [item 0065].
Beaumont and Parinaud [item 1063].

Many of the characters and incidents in this book parallel those of Colette's own life as a music-hall performer. The heroine, Renée Néré, confides in the reader that, since the break-up of her disastrous marriage, she fears any permanent love relationship. Attracted towards a new admirer, who is much superior to her former husband, she is finally obliged to choose between a marriage of love and wealth and her own newly-established need for independence. A good evocation of music-hall life of the period. Often interpreted as an implicit manifesto of Colette's feminism.

Reviews:
Best Sellers 34 (1 Jan. 1975): 434. Robert V. Williams.
Horn Book Magazine 51 (Oct. 1975): 493-94. Mary Silva
    Cosgrave.
Larousse mensuel, no. 51 (May 1911): 123-24. J. Bompard.
Listener 52 (28 Oct. 1954): 731. George D. Painter.
Mercure de France, 16 Dec. 1910, 683. Rachilde.
Nation 180 (26 March 1955): 268. Joseph Wood Krutch.
New Statesman & Nation 48 (2 Oct. 1954): 414-16. John
    Raymond.
Nouvelle Revue française 5 (1 March 1911): 469-70. J.S. [Jean
    Schlumberger].
Opinion 3 (10 Dec. 1910): 757. M.C.
Ord och Bild 64 (1955): 159-65. Elisabeth Bergh.
Partisan Review 22 (Spring 1955): 275-82. William S. Poster.
Partisan Review 42 (Fall 1975): 475-76. Stephen Koch.
Revue hebdomadaire, 17 June 1911, 424-33. François Le Grix.
Saturday Review 2 (20 Sept. 1975): 30-32. Stephen Koch.
Times Literary Supplement, no. 1525 (23 April 1931): 328.
Times Literary Supplement, no. 2753 (5 Nov. 1954): 701.
Vient de paraître 7 (May 1927): 793. Raymond Escholier.

English translations: American

0685 RENÉE, LA VAGABONDE. Trans. Charlotte Remfry-Kidd.
      Garden City: Doubleday, Doran, 1931. 314p.

0686 THE VAGABOND. Trans. Enid McLeod. New York: Farrar,
      Straus & Young, 1955. 223p.

0687 THE VAGABOND. Trans. Enid McLeod. Westport, Conn.:
      Greenwood Press, 1972. 223p.

0688 THE VAGABOND. Trans. Enid McLeod. New York: Farrar,
      Straus & Giroux, 1975. 223p.

0689 THE VAGABOND. Trans. Enid McLeod. New York: Farrar,
      Straus & Giroux, 1976. 223p. Coll. Noonday N479.

0690 THE VAGABOND. Trans. Enid McLeod. New York: Ballantine,
      1982. 215p. Not seen.

Also in:
The Colette Omnibus [item 0070]. Trans. Enid McLeod.
My Mother's House. The Vagabond. Item 0180. Trans. Enid
   McLeod.
Seven by Colette [item 0101]. Trans. Enid McLeod.

Extracts in *Earthly Paradise* [items 0082, 0084-85]. Trans. Enid
McLeod.

English translations: British

0691 THE VAGRANT. [Colette Willy]. Trans. Charlotte Remfry-Kidd.
   London: Eveleigh Nash, 1912. 298p.

0692 RENÉE NÉRÉ (LA VAGABONDE). Trans. Charlotte Remfry-
   Kidd. London: Nash & Grayson, 1931. 316p.

0693 THE VAGABOND. Trans. Enid McLeod. London: Secker &
   Warburg, 1954. 223p. Coll. Uniform 6.

0694 THE VAGABOND. Trans. Enid McLeod. Harmondsworth:
   Penguin, 1960. 192p.

Also in:
Colette Omnibus [item 0069].
Six Novels [item 0103]. Trans. Enid McLeod.

Extracts in *Earthly Paradise* [items 0087-89]. Trans. Enid McLeod.

BOOKS OF ESSAYS, ARTICLES
AND SHORT STORIES

A PORTÉE DE LA MAIN

In:
OCLF 14 [item 0054].
OCC 11 [item 0055].
*En pays connu. Trait pour trait. Journal intermittent. La Fleur de
l'âge.* [*A portée de la main.*] Item 0757.
La Fleur de l'âge. En pays connu. A portée de la main. Item 0801.

Extracts in:
Autobiographie...[items 0057-58]: Tentations.
Découvertes [item 0724]: Moi, je suis gourmande. Tentations.
   Reliques. Province. Le miracle d'Auray. Nouvelles du pays.
   Alfred d'Orsay. Là-haut. Rien n'est loin.
En pays connu [items 0754-55]: Tentations. L'image parlante.
   Cavernes. Leurs petits et les nôtres. L'enfant caché. Le miracle
   d'Auray. Finistère [Province]. All are grouped with other texts
   under the heading "Journal Intermittent."

Although less well-known than many of Colette's essay
collections, these 17 texts, unpublished in book form until the

OCLF, reflect the immense variety of her interests. They are also more somber in tone, and with more direct social criticism and feminist moralizing than her early pieces. In one text, France's legal code and the members of its judiciary system elicit harsh criticism for permitting child abuse and wife-battering to go unpunished. In another, the trial of Valentine Nozière provokes biting commentary on family relations, while two texts express sympathy for unwed mothers and child prodigies. "Leurs petits et les nôtres" is a bitter diatribe on behalf of animals used and abused by human beings; this text reflects Colette's most active social crusade. "L'image parlante," which focuses on superstition, contains references to Colette's own alleged power as a water-diviner. A few pieces are lighter in tone but subjects remain varied. They include childhood, the temptation of theft in both animals and humans, the loneliness of single people, the education of deaf girls, perfume, and lottery-mania. Also memorable descriptions of Brittany and three texts recalling Colette's own experiences in flight. Individual titles: Moi, je suis gourmande. Tentations. L'image parlante. Le drame et le procès. Cavernes. Leurs petits et les nôtres. L'enfant caché. Solitaires. Enfants prodigieux. Reliques. Province. Le miracle d'Auray. Nouvelles du pays. Alfred d'Orsay. Là-haut. Rien n'est loin. Mes voyageurs.

English translations: American

Extracts in:
Earthly Paradise [items 0082, 0084-85]: Temptations. Trans. Derek
    Coltman.
Places [item 0098]: Finistère [Province].

English translations: British

Extracts in:
Earthly Paradise [items 0087-89]: Temptations. Trans. Derek
    Coltman.
Places [item 0099]: Finistère [Province].

AUTRES BETES

In:
OP 2 [item 0053].
OCLF 3 [item 0054].
OCC 3 [item 0055].
Les Vrilles de la vigne. Douze dialogues de bêtes. Autres Bêtes.
  Item 0938.

Extracts in:
Autobiographie... [items 0057-58].
Chats de Colette [items 0714-15]: Le siamois. Simplette. Le petit
  chat noir. Capucin et Adimah. Fastagette. La chatte du petit
  café. La fleur. Blanc. Noir. Ernesse. La chatte au miroir.
  L'honnête commerçant. Le trésor. Au lion noir. Le long-chat.
De la patte à l'aile [item 0723]: Crabe, crevettes.

Texts from several previous volumes were combined under this
title for the *OCLF*: the 5 texts of *Chats*, the 2 texts of *Regarde...*,
4 texts from *De la patte à l'aile* [Rouge-gorge. Perruche bleue.
Lézards, grenouille, sauterelle. Poisson rouge] and 2 from *Broderie
ancienne* [Domino. Le long chat]. Nine new texts were added under
the umbrella title "Chats de Paris." Most passages offer imaginary
conversations or monologues and fanciful situations. Generally
light and sometimes playful in tone. Contents: Le siamois.
Simplette. Le petit chat noir. Capucin et Adimah. Fastagette.
Domino. Le long-chat. La chatte du petit café. La fleur. Blanc.
Noir. Ernesse. La chatte au miroir. L'honnête commerçant. Le
trésor. Au lion noir. Rouge-gorge. Perruche bleue. Lézards,
grenouille, sauterelle. Poisson rouge. "Regarde..." La flaque.

English translations: American

xxxx "Other Creatures." In *Creatures Great and Small* [items 0079-80].
      Includes all 22 texts of the *OCLF*: The Siamese. Simpleton.
      The Little Black Cat. Capucin and Adimah. Fastagette.
      Domino. The Long-Cat. The She-Cat at the Little Café. The
      Flower. White. Black. Ernie. The She-Cat in the Mirror. The
      Honest Shopkeeper. The Treasure. Black Lion Brand. Robin.

Blue Parakeet. Lizards, Frog, and Grasshopper. Gold-Fish. "Look!" The Rock Pool.

0695   "The Long-cat." *Vogue* 130 (15 Aug. 1957): 102, 152-54.

Extracts in:
Earthly Paradise [items 0082, 0084-85]: At the sea [from: Look!].
Gigi and Selected Writings [item 0501]: "Look!"

English translations: British

xxxx   "Other Creatures." In *Creatures Great and Small* [item 0081]: same contents as American ed.

Extracts in *Earthly Paradise* [items 0087-89]: same contents as American eds.

AVENTURES QUOTIDIENNES

0696   AVENTURES QUOTIDIENNES. Paris: Flammarion, 1924. 249p. Contains 22 texts of a generally more substantial nature than most of Colette's collections of the 1920's. Subjects are diverse, as is the treatment. Aging, child-parent relations, education of children, child abuse and trafficking in children, all provoke Colette's comment. "Vieillesse d'hier, jeunesse de demain" offers portraits of celebrated actresses Eleonora Duse and Sarah Bernhardt, while "Mausolées" contrasts Marie Bashkirtseff's life-style with Renée Vivien's. "Bêtes" is a bitter attack on humanity's disregard for the welfare of animals, especially on our use of them for scientific experiments. Excellent descriptive passages of nature, especially birds, are found in several texts. And nowhere else is Colette's skill at evoking crowds and street scenes shown to greater advantage than in this collection. It is a pity that she removed "Accidents de printemps" from the collection when preparing the *OCLF*, for her description of people learning to drive in the early days of automobile traffic is

immensely entertaining. Texts in the first edition are: Vieillesse
d'hier, jeunesse de demain. Accidents de printemps. Assassins.
Foules. Bêtes. Fleurs. Doubles. Cinéma. Sortilèges. Pédagogie.
Mésanges. L'usurpateur. Chaleur. Combats. Beautés. Eté.
Progéniture. Fugue. Mausolées. Journaux. Ailes. Rentrée.

Also in:
OCLF 6 [item 0054]: 18 texts. Omits: Accidents de printemps.
    Foules. L'usurpateur. Fugue.
OCC 5 [item 0055]: same 18 texts as *OCLF*.
*Belles Saisons. Nudité. Mes cahiers. Paysages et portraits.
    Aventures quotidiennes.* Item 0701: same 18 texts as *OCLF*.
Le Voyage égoïste. Aventures quotidiennes. Item 0905: same 18
    texts as *OCLF*.

Extracts in:
Autobiographie... [items 0057-58]: La Duse.
Bêtes libres et prisonnières [item 0702]: Confiance des bêtes. Les
    mésanges. Tableaux marins. Deux cormorans.
Colette: au cinéma [item 0980]: Cinéma.
Histoires pour Bel-Gazou, all eds: Mésanges.
Lettres à Moune et au Toutounet [item 0008]: Sortilèges.
Morceaux choisis [item 0062]: Fleurs. Combats. Assassins.
    Mésanges.

Reviews:
Annales politiques et littéraires, 22 Feb. 1925, 196. G. de
    Pawlowski.
Figaro, 27 Jan. 1925, 3. Henri de Régnier.
Mercure de France, 1 April 1926, 146-47. Jean de Gourmont.
Œuvre, 10 Feb. 1925, 4. André Billy.

English translations: American

xxxx "Everyday Adventures."

In:
Journey for Myself [item 0092]: 18 texts of *OCLF*. See item 0092
    for specific texts.
Recollections [item 0100]: same contents as *Journey for Myself*.

Extracts in:
Colette at the movies [item 0984]: Cinema.
Earthly Paradise [items 0082, 0084-85]: Eleanora Duse. Trans.
    Derek Coltman.
Flowers and Fruit [item 0090]: Flower Shows.

English translations: British

xxxx   "Everyday Adventures." In *Journey for Myself* [item 0094]: same
        contents as American ed.

Extracts in:
Earthly Paradise [items 0087-89]: same contents as American ed.
Flowers and Fruit [item 0091]: same contents as American ed.

BELLES SAISONS

0697   BELLES SAISONS. Illus. Christian Caillard. Paris: Eds. de la
        Galerie Charpentier, 1945. 105p. Luxury edition. Contains only
        the section later designated as "Belles Saisons I." One passage
        beginning "Un tam-tam de guerre" had already been published in
        the *Quatrième cahier de Colette*.

0698   BELLES SAISONS. Illus. Pierre Bonnard. Lausanne: Mermod,
        1947. 113p. Coll. du Bouquet 39. Same contents as item 0697
        with only minor changes.

0699   BELLES SAISONS. Paris: Flammarion, 1955. 267p. Much
        enlarged edition includes other titles. Contains both Belles
        Saisons I and Belles Saisons II as well as *Nudité* and the
        following texts from *Mes cahiers*: Notes de tournées. Portraits
        [Proust. Balzac. Aristide Briand. Joseph Caillaux. Gaston
        Doumergue. Edouard Herriot. Anatole de Monzie]. Monstres
        [Marie Becker. Stavisky. Weidmann]. Also *Discours de
        réception* and *Derniers écrits*.

0700 BELLES SAISONS. Paris: Flammarion, 1975. 192p. Coll. Livre de poche 4192. Same contents as item 0699.

0701 BELLES SAISONS. NUDITÉ. MES CAHIERS. PAYSAGES ET PORTRAITS. AVENTURES QUOTIDIENNES. Paris: Flammarion, 1985. 416p. First title contains both Belles Saisons I and Belles Saisons II.

Also in:
OCLF 9 [item 0054]: contains only Belles Saisons I.
*OCC*11 [item 0055]: contains Belles Saisons I and II.
La Chatte. Belles Saisons. Item 0282: contains Belles Saisons I and II.

Extracts in:
Bêtes libres et prisonnières [item 0702]: Deux cormorans. Les fourmis.
Chats de Colette [items 0714-15]: Vacances.

Original edition containing "Belles Saisons I" is a collection of essays without individual titles but written at different times. Although subjects vary, the collection is cohesive because emphasis is on the seasons and the passage of time. In splendid passages evoking the seasons at Saint Tropez, where Colette had a summer home, one senses her growing disenchantment as tourists began to invade the area during the 1930's. A long text on the art of tapestry, which Colette practised during her later years, strikes an especially personal note. "Belles Saisons II" is a collection of seven articles [Les rois. Paris. Cheveux en quatre. Esthétiques. Silhouettes. Rentrons. Noël] directed especially to women readers, having no particular theme to tie them to the title but focusing mainly on fashion. Corresponding subjects are: Epiphany, clothes, hair-styles, women's figures, the life of a fashion model, the end of summer vacation, and Christmas gifts. Not among Colette's most important works.

Review:
Arts, 22 June 1945, 3. Max Aubry.

English translation: American

Extracts in *Flowers and Fruit* [item 0090]: From the Midi [from "Belles Saisons I"].

English translation: British

Extracts in *Flowers and Fruit* [item 0091]: same contents as American ed.

BETES LIBRES ET PRISONNIERES

0702 BETES LIBRES ET PRISONNIERES. Paris: Albin Michel, 1958. 221p. Collection of short passages from many of Colette's works and focusing on a great variety of animals, birds, reptiles, sea creatures and insects. Passages are organized according to theme or animal group. Chiefly descriptive with a few anecdotes. Contents: Et ma mère parlait. Confiance des bêtes. Connivence. La truie. Le lapin. La biche. La jument. Animaux de cirque. Jardin zoologique. La panthère noire et les lions. La lionne. Léopards. Serpents. Singes. Amertume. Ecureuils. Le hérisson et Toby-Chien. Les rats. L'oiseau et l'homme. Le moineau. Les oiseaux du jardin. Les nids dans les troènes. Le rouge-gorge. Les mésanges. Le rossignol. Le paon. Hirondelles. Mouettes, cygnes. Oiseaux de mer et de marais. Rapaces. Les cigales. Les fourmis. La guêpe. L'araignée. Les abeilles. La chenille. Papillons. Les couleuvres. Les lézards. Tableaux marins. Chers bois! Deux cormorans. Sur les étangs. Taken from: *Aventures quotidiennes. Belles saisons. Claudine à l'école. Claudine en ménage. De ma fenêtre. Dialogues de bêtes. En pays connu. L'Entrave. L'Envers du music-hall. L'Etoile vesper. Le Fanal bleu. Flore et Pomone. Les Heures longues. Journal à rebours. La Maison de Claudine. La Naissance du jour. La Paix chez les bêtes. Prisons et paradis. La Retraite sentimentale. Sido. La Vagabonde. Les Vrilles de la vigne.*

Reviews:
Bulletin critique du livre français 14 (1959): 5.
Figaro littéraire, 13 Dec. 1958, 2. André Rousseaux.

BRODERIE ANCIENNE

0703 BRODERIE ANCIENNE. Monaco: Eds. du Rocher, 1944. 73p.
Contains 4 texts. In "Vieux papiers," later incorporated into
L'Etoile vesper, Colette reminisces about the years just before
and after World War I, when she contributed to literary journals
or directed a literary column. Especially featured are her days at
Le Matin and the people with whom she came into contact
there. "Noces," previously published in book form under its
own title, offers a picture of her wedding day. "Le long chat"
and "Domino" are anecdotes about a cat and a dog belonging to
Sido's household; both were transferred to *Autres Bêtes* with
publication of the *OCLF*.

CAHIERS DE COLETTE

See *Mes cahiers*.

CELLE QUI EN REVIENT

0704 CELLE QUI EN REVIENT SUIVI DE QUELQUES AUTRES
DIALOGUES DE BETES. Paris: Flammarion, 1921. 65p.
Coll. Une heure d'oubli 60. Seven imaginary conversations
among animals, most of them starring Toby-Chien and the cat
Kiki-la-Doucette. Fanciful and usually amusing texts, although

the title story portrays a dog still suffering from the effects of World War I. Four texts [Sentimentalités. Le voyage. Le dîner est en retard. Le premier feu] are those of the original *Dialogues de bêtes*. A fifth [Elle est malade] is taken from *Sept dialogues de bêtes*. The remaining two [La chienne qui en revient. Les bêtes et la tortue] are new. All were incorporated into the 1930 *Douze dialogues de bêtes* and most subsequent editions.

LA CHAMBRE ECLAIRÉE

0705 LA CHAMBRE ECLAIRÉE. [Colette (Colette Willy)]. Illus. Picart le Doux. Paris: Edouard-Joseph, 1920. 201p. Coll. L'Edition originale illustrée 3. Contains 31 texts: La chambre éclairée. Fantômes. Conte de Bel-Gazou à sa poupée. Bel-Gazou et le cinéma. Les bêtes et l'absence. Le retour des bêtes. Présages. Une lettre. La nuit paisible. Une réponse. Les foins. Confidences sans signature. Nouveaux riches. «Un timbre à 0. fr. 60, s.v.p!» Le «Maître». Plomberie et gaz. La «transformiste». La barrière. Pages oubliées des Mémoires de Mme Vigée-Lebrun. Petit Manuel de l'aspirant-scénariste [La femme fatale. Le jeune premier. La femme-du-monde et la lettre. Le luxe au cinéma]. Rêverie de Nouvel An. Malade. Dimanche. Répit. J'ai chaud. Convalescence. Les «Petites Filles». Cinéma.

0706 "Ma première tournée Baret." *Figaro littéraire*, 22 June 1935, 5-6. Includes "La transformiste."

0707 "Conte de Bel-Gazou à sa poupée." In *Les plus jolis contes de Noël*, edited by Marcel Berger. Paris: Emile-Paul, 1938. Not seen.

0708 "Conte de Bel-Gazou à sa poupée." *Annales* 61 (Sept. 1954): 22-23.

0709 LA CHAMBRE ECLAIRÉE. [MÉLANGES. DERNIERS ECRITS. DISCOURS DE RÉCEPTION.] Paris: Fayard, 1987. 175p. First title contains only 14 texts: La chambre éclairée.

Fantômes. Conte de Bel-Gazou à sa poupée. Bel-Gazou et le cinéma. Le retour des bêtes. Présages. Une lettre. La nuit paisible. Une réponse. Confidences sans signature. Nouveaux riches. «Un timbre à 0 fr. 60, S.V.P!» Le maître. Plomberie et gaz.

0710 LA CHAMBRE ECLAIRÉE. [MÉLANGES. DERNIERS ECRITS. DISCOURS DE RÉCEPTION.] DE MA FENETRE. LE FANAL BLEU. Paris: Fayard, 1987. 172p.-186p.-158p. Contains same 14 texts as item 0709.

Also in:
OP 2 [item 0053]: original 31 texts.
OCLF 5 [item 0054]: same 14 texts as item 0709.
OCC 5 [item 0055]: same 14 texts as item 0709.
La Paix chez les bêtes. Les Heures longues. La Chambre éclairée. Item 0846: same 14 texts as item 0709.

Extracts in:
Album Masques: Colette [item 1057]: La femme du monde [et la lettre].
Autobiographie... [items 0057-58]: La chambre éclairée.
Colette [item 0060]: J'ai chaud. Malade... Le retour des bêtes. Conte de Bel-Gazou à sa poupée.
Colette: au cinéma [item 0980]: Petit manuel de l'aspirant scénariste [all 4 parts]. Bel-Gazou et le cinéma. Le cinéma français en 1918 [Cinéma].
Morceaux choisis [item 0062]: La chambre éclairée.
Troisième cahier [item 0831] and *Mes cahiers* [item 0833]: La transformiste.
Le Voyage égoïste [item 0898]: La nuit paisible. Retour des bêtes.
Le Voyage égoïste, all eds.: Répit. Dimanche. Malade. J'ai chaud.
Chauviere [item 1072], 41-44: Conte de Bel-Gazou à sa poupée.

Collection of 31 texts of different types, most of them previously published in newspapers and reviews from 1909 to 1918. Book takes its title from the first text: Colette's small daughter Bel-Gazou is the real source of light in the war-darkened bedroom. Typical of Colette's mature descriptive and anecdotal style. Several texts depict the hardships endured by civilians and the loneliness of soldiers during World War I. Others are personal, such as those dealing with an illness and the series recounting the reactions of

Bel-Gazou to war-time shortages. Several essays poke fun at silent films. Most are written in the first person and some are epistolary in form. Tone varies from the humorous to the lyric; a few passages are ironic. Dialogues in which the characters speak dialect or non-standard French are especially interesting. Only one of the original texts had previously been published in book form: "Les foins" appeared in the 1917 *Les Heures longues*, and was later restored to that title. Of the original 31 texts, only 14 were retained for the *OCLF*. The remaining ones were either transferred to other collections or dropped completely. The peregrinations of texts published under this title demonstrate the complexities facing anyone doing research in the publication history of Colette's short pieces.

English translations: American

Extracts in:
Colette at the Movies [item 0984]: A Short Manual for the Aspiring Scenario Writer. Bel-Gazou and the Cinema. The French Cinema in 1918.
The Collected Stories of Colette [items 0071-72]: The 'Master.' Trans. Matthew Ward.
Earthly Paradise [items 0082, 0084-85]: The Lighted Room. Trans. Herma Briffault.

0711   "Absence." No translator. *Atlantic Monthly* 166 (July 1940): 76-77. Trans. of "Les bêtes et l'absence."

English translations: British

Extracts in:
The Collected Stories of Colette [items 0073-74]: same contents as American eds.
Earthly Paradise [items 0087-89]: same contents as American eds.

CHATS

0712   CHATS. [Jacques Nam and Colette]. Paris: Jacques Nam, 1935.
       34p. Limited folio edition, unbound, each copy signed by Nam.
       Illustrations dominate Colette's contribution. Contains 5 light-
       hearted texts [Simplette. Le petit chat noir. Le siamois.
       Capucin et Adimah. Fastagette].

0713   CHATS. Lausanne: Jean Marguerat, 1945. 100p. Tiny book
       containing mostly photographs of cats, preceded by the texts of
       item 0712.

       Also in:
       Autres Bêtes, all eds.
       Chats de Colette [items 0714-15].

CHATS DE COLETTE

0714   CHATS DE COLETTE. Paris: Albin Michel, 1950. 205p. Coll.
       Scènes de la vie des bêtes.

0715   CHATS DE COLETTE. Paris: Albin Michel, 1984. 205p. Same
       texts as in earlier edition.

xxxx   "Le chat." [Preface to item 0714]. In *Mélanges*, all eds.

       Collection of 39 passages of different lengths taken from Colette's
       other works, including memoirs and fiction, and illustrated by
       photographs of cats. Touching preface stresses the favorable
       influence that cats have had in Colette's life. Texts are : Saha.
       Chats des dialogues de bêtes. Chats des voyages. Péronnelle.
       Idylles. Bâ-tou. Chat suisse. Chartreux. Nocturnes. En livrée de
       nuit. Les deux matous. Gris, gris et encore gris. Pierrot et Mitsou.
       La chatte dernière. Prrou. Le long chat. Chats de Paris [La chatte du
       petit café. La fleur. Blanc. Noir. Ernesse. La chatte au miroir.

L'honnête commerçant. Le trésor. Au lion noir]. Chats [Le
siamois. Simplette. Le petit chat noir. Capucin et Adimah.
Fastagette]. La mère chatte. Le matou. «La Shâh». Le naturaliste et
la chatte. Poum. Le tentateur. Vacances. Premiers chats. Chats des
premières années. Taken from: *Autres Bêtes. Belles saisons.
Broderie ancienne. Chambre d'hôtel. La Chatte. Chats. Claudine à
l'école. Claudine à Paris. Claudine en ménage. Claudine s'en va.
L'Etoile vesper. Le Fanal bleu. Les Heures longues. La Maison de
Claudine. La Naissance du jour. La Paix chez les bêtes. Paris de ma
fenêtre. Prisons et paradis. La Retraite sentimentale. Sept dialogues
de bêtes.*

Reviews:
Bulletin critique du livre français 5 (1950): 212.
Figaro, 19 Oct. 1984, 28. Jean Chalon.
Figaro littéraire, 13 Dec. 1958, 2. André Rousseaux.

CHIENS DE COLETTE

0716   CHIENS DE COLETTE. Paris: Albin Michel, 1957. 191p. Coll.
       Scènes de la vie des bêtes.

0717   CHIENS DE COLETTE. Paris: Albin Michel, 1984. 191p. Same
       texts as in item 0716.

Collection of 37 passages, some of them complete essays, articles
or stories, borrowed from a great variety of Colette's other books,
including memoirs and novels. Numerous photographs make this a
very appealing edition for dog lovers. Contents are: En guise
d'introduction. Celle qui en revient. Perruche bleue. Chiens
savants. La petite chienne à vendre. Exposition canine. Chiens
sanitaires. La chienne trop petite. Chienne bull. Le cœur des
chiens. Les chiens et la lune. Chiens de ville. La chienne
beauceronne. Modes. Médicinales. La peur. Courses de lévriers.
Toby. Poucette et la bergère flamande. Poucette. La chienne qui
mérita de revenir. Vorace. Fossette. Lola. Le chiot de Musette. La
Toutouque. Domino. Pati. Bellaude. Bellaude et Pati. Moffino.

Nuits de Noël. Moulouk. Diane. Margot et les chiens. Nelle.
Souci. Taken from: *Bella-Vista. Claudine s'en va. De la patte à
l'aile. De ma fenêtre. Douze dialogues de bêtes. En pays connu.
L'Envers du music-hall. L'Etoile vesper. Le Fanal bleu. Les Heures
longues. Journal à rebours. Journal intermittent. La Maison de
Claudine. La Paix chez les bêtes. Pour un herbier. Prisons et
paradis. La Retraite sentimentale. Sido. La Vagabonde. Les Vrilles
de la vigne.*

Reviews:
Bulletin critique du livre français 13 (1958): 341.
Figaro, 19 Oct. 1984, 28. Jean Chalon.
Figaro littéraire, 13 Dec. 1958, 2. André Rousseaux.

CONTES DES MILLE ET UN MATINS

0718 CONTES DES MILLE ET UN MATINS. Paris: Flammarion,
1970. 253p. Fifty articles dating from May 1911 to Aug. 1914,
most of them published in Colette's column of the same title in
Le Matin. Includes all 16 texts of *Dans la foule.* Although
many focus on events of public interest, the personal style
reflects the column's sub-title from 1913, "Journal de Colette."
Colette does not attempt to depict events objectively, but
instead offers her own impressions and often partisan view-
point. Several articles deal with women's aptitude (or inaptitude,
for Colette appears to waver on the question) for politics. Of
different lengths, the pieces are reflective, anecdotal, analytical
and descriptive. Some are in form of dialogue; others contain
portraits of well-known persons. "Réveillons" and "Les sabots"
reflect the nostalgia for childhood that characterizes many of
Colette's longer works. All texts demonstrate her already well-
developed powers of observation and her ability to evoke
sensations. The collection as a whole offers a bird's-eye
panorama of Parisian public life just before World War I. Texts
are organized into eight sections [Conquête de l'air. Faits divers.
Les modes et les mœurs. Sur la scène et autour. Salons et lieux
publics. La rue, la foule. Solennités et célébrations. Dialogues à

une voix]. Individual titles are: La bulle. Là-haut. Au salon de l'aviation. A Tours. Dans la foule. La bande. Les belles écouteuses. La musique au restaurant. Un couple. La culture physique et les femmes. Doit-on le dire? Dans le train. Le martyrologe. Sévices. Propos d'une Parisienne. A l'Université populaire. Mes impressions de chatte. La mode au théâtre. Ça manque de femmes! Le «ciné». Ecole de danse. Métiers de femmes. A la Chambre des Députés. Les femmes au Congrès. En visite. La Joconde. Un dîner le 17 mars. Spectacle mondain. La foule le soir des élections. La fin d'un Tour de France. Impressions de foule. Le cimetière Montmartre. A Gand, le marchand de cercueils. Les petites boutiques. Le vent. On détruit Passy. Autour des trous. La revue. Les voilà, les voilà! Réveillons. Les sabots. Jour de l'An. 14 Juillet. Littérature. Ma filleule. Un coiffeur. Une masseuse. Ma corsetière. La vendeuse. Une interview.

Also in *OCC* 13 [item 0055].

Extracts in:
OP 1 [item 0053]: Les sabots.
Colette: au cinéma [item 0980]: Le «ciné».

Reviews:
Books & Bookmen 18 (March 1973): 56-57. Oswell Blakeston.
Bulletin critique du livre français 25 (June 1970): 546.
Culture française 17 (Sept.-Oct. 1970): 317. E. de Domenico.
Express, no. 975 (16 March 1970): 118. Matthieu Galey.
Figaro littéraire, 2 March 1970, 24. J.C.
Figaro littéraire, 16 March 1970, 26. André Billy.
Kirkus Reviews 41 (1 May 1973): 539.
Lettres françaises, 22 April 1970, 10-11. Hubert Juin.
Library Journal 98 (July 1973): 2105-6. S. Lynn Fell.
Monde, 28 March 1970, ii. Gabrielle Rolin.
New Statesman 85 (2 Feb. 1973): 163-64. Francis Wyndham.
New York Review of Books 20 (24 Jan. 1974): 3-6. Rosemary Tonks.
New Yorker 49 (14 Jan. 1974): 99.
Nouvelles littéraires, 5 March 1970, 2. François Nourissier.
Observer, no. 9470 (28 Jan. 1973): 34. John Weightman.
Plaisir de France 377 (April 1970): 64. Yves Gandon.
Rapports-Het Franse Boek 41 (Jan. 1971): 34-35. Mieke Bal.

Spectator, no. 7559 (12 May 1973): 594. E.S.
Sunday Times, 11 Feb. 1973, 30. Philippa Pullar.
Times Literary Supplement, no. 3710 (13 April 1973): 413.
Village Voice 18 (13 Dec. 1973): 41, 45. Molly Haskell.
Washington Post Book World, 12 Aug. 1973, 15.

English translations: American

0719 THE THOUSAND AND ONE MORNINGS. Trans. Margaret
Crosland and David Le Vay. Introd. Margaret Crosland. New
York, Indianapolis: Bobbs-Merrill, 1973. 155p. Grouped under
eight headings [Conquest of the Air. News Items. Modes and
Manners. On and Around the Stage. Salons and Public Places.
Streets and Crowds. Solemnities and Celebrations. One-sided
Dialogues]. Individual texts are: The Bubble. Up There. At the
Air Show. At Tours. In the Crowd. The Gang. The Lovely
Listeners. Restaurant Music. A Couple. Physical Culture and
Women. Should one say it? In the Train. The Martyrologist.
Brutality. A Parisienne Speaks. At the Université populaire. On
being a Cat. Fashion in the Theatre. There's a Shortage of
Women. The Movies. Dancing School. Jobs for Women. In the
Chamber of Deputies. Women at the Congrès. Visiting. The
Gioconda. A Dinner on 17 March. Fashionable Entertainment.
The Crowd, Election Night. End of a Tour de France. Crowd
Impressions. The Cemetery of Montmartre. The Coffin-Seller
of Ghent. The Little Shops. The Wind. They're Destroying
Passy. Around the Holes. The Review. They're here, they're
here! New Year Party. The Clogs. New Year's Day. 14 July.
Literature. My Godchild. A Hairdresser. A Masseuse. My
Corset-maker. The Saleslady. An Interview.

Extracts in *The Collected Stories of Colette* [items 0071-72]:
Dialogues for One Voice [Literature. My Goddaughter. A
Hairdresser. A Masseuse. My Corset Maker. The Saleswoman.
An Interview]. Trans. Matthew Ward.

English translations: British

0720 THE THOUSAND AND ONE MORNINGS. Trans. Margaret
      Crosland and David Le Vay. Introd. Margaret Crosland. London:
      Owen, 1973. 155p.

      Extracts in *The Collected Stories of Colette* [items 0073-74]: same
      texts as American eds.

DANS LA FOULE

0721 DANS LA FOULE. [Colette (Colette Willy)]. Paris: Crès, 1918.
      159p.

0722 "La fin d'un Tour de France." In *L'Equipe de France*, edited by
      Gilbert Prouteau, 154-57. Paris: Plon, 1972. Under umbrella
      title "Les lutteurs du cirque."

      Also in:
      OP 2 [item 0053].
      OCLF 4 [item 0054].
      Mitsou. L'Envers du music-hall. Dans la foule. Item 0566.

      Extracts in:
      Colette [item 0060]: Impressions de foule. La bulle. La fin d'un
      Tour de France. La revue. Là-haut.
      Prisons et paradis [item 0871]: Le procès Guillotin [A Tours].
      Le Voyage égoïste [item 0898]: Réveillons.

      The title of the collection is apt, since these journalistic pieces
      express Colette's own impressions of a variety of pre-World War I
      events: a political congress, a parade, a boxing match, a bicycle
      marathon, a New Year's party, the state visit of England's king and
      queen, a famous trial, the capture of a notorious band of brigands,
      and Colette's own first flights in dirigible and balloon. Of special
      interest are her remarks on the peripheral political scene. Titles are:
      A la Chambre des Députés. La revue. Les femmes au Congrès. Les

voilà, les voilà! A Tours. Dans la foule. La bande. La foule le soir
des élections. La fin d'un Tour de France. Là-haut. La bulle.
Impressions de foule. A l'Université populaire. Le cimetière
Montmartre. Réveillons. Les belles écouteuses. Although the
collection was never re-published under its own title, all 16 texts
were incorporated into the 1970 *Contes des mille et un matins*.

Review:
Temps, 11 April 1919, 2. Paul Souday.

DE LA PATTE A L'AILE

0723 DE LA PATTE A L'AILE. Illus. Chastel. Paris: Corrêa, 1943.
103p. Handsomely illustrated volume containing 11 short
pieces, some previously published. Mostly anecdotal in form,
narrated in Colette's own voice, and rich in descriptive material.
Generally light in tone but in "Ecureuil" Colette declaims
bitterly against those who abuse animals. All texts witness her
deep interest in the life of other creatures. "Chauve-souris,
hérisson, crapaud," identified in the Table of Contents as a *fin
inédite* [unpublished ending] for *La Retraite sentimentale*, can
actually be found, nearly complete, at the beginning of the
novel's third chapter. Consists of four passages later collected in
Autres bêtes [Rouge-gorge. Perruche bleue. Lézards, grenouille,
sauterelle. Poisson rouge], two each from *La Maison de
Claudine* [Araignée. Chenille] and *Prisons et paradis* [Lézard.
Ecureuil], and one each from *Douze dialogues de bêtes* [Les
bêtes et la tortue], *La Retraite sentimentale* [Chauve-souris,
hérisson, crapaud] and *Regarde*: La flaque [Crabe, crevettes].

Extracts in *Chiens de Colette* [item 0716-17]: Perruche bleue.

DÉCOUVERTES

0724   DÉCOUVERTES. Illus. Berthe Morisot. Lausanne: Mermod, 1961. 146p. Twelve texts borrowed from other titles. The collection has no central theme, other than the idea announced in the title: discoveries. Subjects include the attractions of Paris, swallows, food, the temptation of theft, traditions, the teaching of the deaf, the charms of Brittany, the lottery, flight and perfumes. Usually descriptive, occasionally anecdotal, and always informal in tone. In fact, this is a typical Colette bouquet, with 9 texts from *A portée de la main* [Moi, je suis gourmande. Tentations. Reliques. Le miracle d'Auray. Province. Nouvelles du pays. Là-haut. Alfred d'Orsay. Rien n'est loin] and 3 from *En pays connu* [Découvertes. Provinces de Paris. Hirondelles]. The "Là-haut" of this collection is not the same "Là-haut" as the one in *Contes des mille et un matins*, nor is "Hirondelles" the same as the one in *Journal à rebours*.

DERNIERS ECRITS

In:
OCC 14 [item 0055].
Belles saisons [items 0699-700].
La Chambre éclairée. [*Mélanges. Derniers écrits. Discours de réception.*] Item 0709.
La Chambre éclairée. [*Mélanges. Derniers écrits. Discours de réception.*] *De ma fenêtre. Le Fanal bleu.* Item 0710.
Paysages et portraits. Derniers écrits. Item 0859.

Umbrella title used to designate Colette's last two texts: "Ces dames anciennes" [item 0993] and "Gîte d'écrivain" [item 1005].

DIALOGUES DE BETES
SEPT DIALOGUES DE BETES
DOUZE DIALOGUES DE BETES

0725   DIALOGUES DE BETES. [Colette Willy]. Paris: Mercure de France, 1904. 123p. Contains four texts: Sentimentalités. Le voyage. Le dîner est en retard. Le premier feu.

0726   "Le voyage." [Colette Willy]. *La Vie heureuse* 3 (15 May 1904): vii.

0727   SEPT DIALOGUES DE BETES. [Colette Willy]. Pref. Francis Jammes. Paris: Mercure de France, 1905. 187p. Contains seven texts, those of item 0725 plus: Elle est malade. L'orage. Une visite.

0728   SEPT DIALOGUES DE BETES. [Colette Willy]. Pref. Francis Jammes. Illus. Jacques Nam. Paris: Mercure de France, 1912. Same seven texts as item 0727.

0729   "Le dîner est en retard." In *Petite Anthologie des auteurs gais contemporains*, edited by Léon Treich. Paris: Flammarion, 1918. Not seen.

0730   "Le premier feu" [extracts]. In *Anthologie des écrivains français contemporains*, edited by Gauthier-Ferrières, 180-83. Paris: Larousse, 1923.

0731   DIALOGUES DE BETES. Pref. Francis Jammes. Illus. Valette. Paris: Baudinière, 1924. 185p. Coll. Les Maîtres de la plume. Same seven texts as item 0727.

0732   SEPT DIALOGUES DE BETES. Pref. Francis Jammes. Illus. Jean Pavie. Paris: Les Arts et le livre, 1927. ix-157p. Same seven texts as item 0727.

0733   DOUZE DIALOGUES DE BETES. Pref. Francis Jammes. Paris: Mercure de France, 1930. xiii-235p. Contains 12 texts: Celle qui en revient. La chienne. Les bêtes et la tortue.

Sentimentalités. Le voyage. Le dîner est en retard. Elle est malade. Le premier feu. L'orage. Une visite. Music-hall. Toby-chien parle.

0734 DIALOGUES DE BETES. Pref. Francis Jammes. Paris: Baudinière, 1936. 191p. Coll. Hebdo. Not seen.

0735 "Une visite." *Lisez-moi*, no. 408 (25 April 1939): 509-10.

0736 "L'orage." In *Contemporary French Fiction*, edited by Irene Cornwall, 30-36. New York: Holt, 1940.

0737 DOUZE DIALOGUES DE BETES. Illus. Maurice Mourlot. Paris: Eds. du Moulin de Pen-Mur, 1945. 195p. Same 12 texts as item 0733.

0738 DOUZE DIALOGUES DE BETES. Paris: Hartmann, 1952. 161p. Coll. Civilisation 10. Same 12 texts as item 0733.

0739 DOUZE DIALOGUES DE BETES. Pref. Francis Jammes. Postface Claude Pichois. Paris: Club des libraires de France, 1961. 235p. Coll. Livres de toujours 61. Same 12 texts as item 0733. Includes many photographs of Colette, Willy and animals.

0740 SEPT DIALOGUES DE BETES. Pref. Francis Jammes. Photographs Patrice Molinard. Paris: Club français du livre, 1962. viii-160p. Coll. Récits 40. Same 7 texts as item 0727.

0741 "Sentimentalités" and "Le premier feu." In *De la Poesía Moderna Francesa: Colette*, 4-23. Monterrey, Mexico: Instituto Tecnológico y de Estudios Superiores, 1962. Special issue of *Poesía en el Mundo* (36 [Feb. 1962]), sponsored by the Asociación de Estudiantes de Arquitectura. French text on left, Spanish text on right.

0742 DOUZE DIALOGUES DE BETES. Pref. Francis Jammes. Paris: Mercure de France, 1964. 197p. Same 12 texts as item 0733.

0743 DIALOGUES DE BETES. Pref. Francis Jammes. Paris: Mercure de France 1965. 192p. Coll. Livre de poche 1538. Same 12 texts as item 0733.

0744 "Le chat, le chien et le feu." [Extract from "Le premier feu"]. In *52 nouvelles et récits pour elles*, edited by Micheline Denis, 181-87. Paris: Gründ, 1965.

0745 DIALOGUES DE BETES. Pref. Francis Jammes. Illus. Nicole Claveloux. Paris: Gallimard, 1974. 153p. Coll. 1000 soleils. Contains 9 texts [Sentimentalités. Le voyage. Le dîner est en retard. Elle est malade. Le premier feu. L'orage. Une visite. Celle qui en revient. Les bêtes et la tortue] as well as "Kiki-la-Doucette et Toby-Chien dans leur univers," a series of cartoons with captions borrowed from the dialogues.

0746 DIALOGUES DE BETES. Pref. Francis Jammes. Paris: Gallimard, 1975. 189p. Coll. Folio 701. Same 12 texts as item 0733.

0747 "Chien et chat dialoguent." [Extract from "Le dîner est en retard"]. In *Les Animaux et nous*, edited by Pierre Frémy, 41-43. Paris: Hachette, 1975.

0748 "Le dîner est en retard." In *Contes et nouvelles*, vol. 1, edited by Jacques Gouttenoire, 41-55. Paris: Hachette, 1977.

0749 "Le voyage." In *15 Histoires de chiens*, 125-34. Illus. Jacques Pecnard. Paris: Gautier-Languereau, 1985.

Also in:
OP 2 [item 0053]: same 12 texts and preface as item 0733 plus a short text hitherto unpublished in book form: Le dessus et le dessous.
OCLF 3 [item 0054]: same 12 texts and preface as item 0733.
OCC 3 [item 0055]: same 12 texts and preface as item 0733.
OF 2 [item 0056]: same 12 texts and preface as item 0733.
Les Vrilles de la vigne. Douze dialogues de bêtes. Autres Bêtes.
Item 0938: same 12 texts and preface as item 0733.

Extracts in:
Bêtes libres et prisonnières [item 0702]: Le hérisson et Toby-chien.
Chats de Colette [items 0714-15]: Chats des 'Dialogues de bêtes.'
Chiens de Colette [items 0716-17]: Celle qui en revient. Toby.
Colette [item 0060]: Le premier feu. Sentimentalités. L'orage.
De la patte à l'aile [item 0723]: Les bêtes et la tortue.

Histoires pour Bel-Gazou, all eds.: Le voyage.
Morceaux choisis [item 0062]: Les bêtes et la tortue.
Pages choisies [item 0063]: L'orage. Une visite.
Textes choisis de Colette [item 0065]: Le premier feu. Une visite.
Gavoty [item 1607]: Les bêtes et la tortue.

The first work published by Colette under her own name. Original
Dialogues de bêtes contained only four stories [Sentimentalités. Le
voyage. Le dîner est en retard. Le premier feu]. The 1905 *Sept
dialogues de bêtes* added three more [Elle est malade. L'orage. Une
visite]. In 1930, under the title *Douze dialogues de bêtes*, 5 more
texts [Music-hall. Toby-Chien parle. La chienne. Celle qui en
revient. Les bêtes et la tortue] were borrowed from other book titles
to increase the number to twelve. Most though not all editions
after the first having the title *Dialogues de bêtes* contain 12 texts.
The first seven stories are charming and fanciful conversations
between animals, on the subject of their own lives and of those of
their human owners. Though frivolous in tone, they demonstrate
Colette's already keen insight into human motivations and the
ridiculous aspects of human activity. Later stories are sometimes
graver in tone and express an awareness of the human and animal
suffering that came to be one of Colette's preferred themes.
Principal characters are the dog Toby-Chien and the cat Kiki-la-
Doucette, modelled on Colette's own pets.

Reviews:
Bulletin critique du livre français 30 (1975): 1720.
Essais, April 1904, 60-61. J.-L.V. [Jean-LouisVaudoyer].
Informateur, 5 May 1904, 1. C.P. [Camille Pert]. Also in item
      1104 La Hire, 263-65.
Journal amusant, 3 Dec. 1904, 3.
Journal des débats, 17 April 1904, 2. André Chaumeix.
Mercure de France, April 1904, 181-82. Rachilde. Also in item
      1104 La Hire, 248-50.
Revue illustrée 19 (May 1904): non-pag. Georges Casella.
Vie parisienne, 30 April 1904, 260. X.Y.Z.

English translations: American

0750 BARKS AND PURRS. [Colette Willy]. Trans. Maire Kelly. Pref.
      Francis Jammes. Illus. Jacques Nam. New York: Desmond

FitzGerald, 1913. xiv-164. Contains the seven dialogues of *Sept dialogues de bêtes*. English titles are: Sentimentalities. On the Train. Dinner is Late. She is Ill. The First Fire. The Storm. A Caller.

xxxx "Creature conversations." In *Creatures Great and Small* [items 0079-80]. Contains 12 texts: Sentimentalities. The Journey. Dinner is Late. The First Fire. She is Ill. The Storm. A Visit. Music-Hall. Toby-Dog Speaks. The Bitch. The One who Came Back. The Creatures and the Tortoise.

Extracts in:
The Collected Stories of Colette [items 0071-72]: The Bitch.
Gigi and Selected Writings [item 0501]: The Journey.

English translations: British

xxxx "Creature conversations." In *Creatures Great and Small* [item 0081]: same contents as American eds.

Extract in *The Collected Stories of Colette* [items 0073-74]: The Bitch.

DISCOURS DE RÉCEPTION

0751 DISCOURS DE RÉCEPTION A l'ACADÉMIE ROYALE BELGE DE LANGUE ET DE LITTÉRATURE FRANÇAISES. Paris: Grasset, 1936. 59p.

0752 "Discours." In *L'Ombre des jours*, by Anna de Noailles, [i-xxxi]. Illus. J.E. Laboureur. Paris: Société du Livre d'art, 1938.

0752a "Discours de réception de Madame Colette successeur de la comtesse de Noailles à l'Académie royale de Belgique." In *La Comtesse de Noailles oui et non*, by Jean Cocteau, 195-209. Paris: Perrin, 1963.

Also in:
OCLF 13 [item 0054].
OCC 14 [item 0055].
Belles Saisons [items 0699-700].
La Chambre éclairée. [*Mélanges. Derniers écrits. Discours de réception.*] Item 0709.
La Chambre éclairée. [*Mélanges. Derniers écrits. Discours de réception.*] *De ma fenêtre. Le fanal bleu.* Item 0710.
Mes apprentissages. Trois, six, neuf. Discours de réception. Item 0191.

Extracts in:
Autobiographie... [items 0057-58].
Lettres à ses pairs, all eds.

Acceptance address of 4 April 1936, when Colette was formally welcomed into the Belgian Academy of French Language and Literature. This speech is remarkable in that Colette, who took over the chair of the late Countess Anna de Noailles, chose not to discuss her predecessor's work, but instead concentrated on her memories of their long acquaintanceship. After emphasizing her own Belgian roots through the family of her mother, Sido, Colette evokes Noailles' presence by describing physical characteristics, temperament, character and habits, both in the poet's youth and shortly before her death. Listeners and readers are left at the end with a portrait which is both sympathetic and admiring, but which scarcely mentions Noailles' intellectual achievements.

English translations: American

Extracts in *Earthly Paradise* [items 0082, 0084-85]: On Being Elected to the Belgian Academy. Trans. Derek Coltman.

English translations: British

Extracts in *Earthly Paradise* [items 0087-89]: On Being Elected to the Belgian Academy. Trans. Derek Coltman.

DOUZE DIALOGUES DE BETES

See *Dialogues de bêtes*.

EN PAYS CONNU

0753 EN PAYS CONNU. Illus. Luc-Albert Moreau. Paris: M. Bruker, 1949. 115p. Coll. Invitation aux voyages 2. Deluxe edition containing six pieces plus an "Avant-propos" in which Colette offers the volume in memory of Moreau, who had recently died. Texts are: La fôret proche. Au coin du feu. Ma Bourgogne pauvre. Province de Paris. Découvertes. Paradis terrestre.

0754 EN PAYS CONNU. Paris: Hachette, 1950. 239p. Augmented edition containing 13 texts under this title, as well as *Trait pour trait* and sections of *Journal intermittent, A Portée de la main* and *Mes cahiers*. Section bearing title "En pays connu" is comprised of 5 texts from item 0753 [lacking "Au coin du feu" and with "La forêt proche" retitled "La maison proche de la forêt"], plus 5 from *La Fleur de l'âge* [Des mères, des enfants... Le cirque. Œufs de Pâques. Trésors épars. Noël ancien] and 3 new ones [Le désert de Retz. Hirondelles... Amertume].

0755 EN PAYS CONNU. Paris: Hachette, 1975. 223p. Coll. Livre de poche 4112. Same contents as item 0754 but with selections from *Journal intermittent, A Portée de la main* and *Mes cahiers* all under the heading "Journal intermittent."

0756 EN PAYS CONNU. Pref. Yves Berger. Illus. Madeleine Paradis. Paris: M. Broutta, 1985. Not seen.

0757 EN PAYS CONNU. TRAIT POUR TRAIT. JOURNAL INTERMITTENT. LA FLEUR DE L'AGE. [A PORTÉE DE LA MAIN.] Paris: Fayard, 1986. 303p. First title contains 9 texts: 6 original texts of item 0753 with "La forêt proche" retitled "La maison proche de la forêt" and 3 more added [Hirondelles. Amertume. Le désert de Retz].

Also in:
OCLF 14 [item 0054]: same 9 texts as item 0757.
OCC 11 [item 0055]: same 9 texts as item 0757.
Le Fanal bleu. En pays connu. Journal intermittent. Item 0133:
same 9 texts as item 0757.
La Fleur de l'âge. En pays connu. A portée de la main. Item 0801:
same 9 texts as item 0757.

Extracts in:
Autobiographie... [items 0057-58].
Bêtes libres et prisonnières [item 0702]: Animaux de cirque.
Amertume. Les mésanges. Hirondelles. Les lézards. Deux
cormorans. Papillons.
Chiens de Colette [items 0716-17]: La peur.
Découvertes [item 0724]: Découvertes. Provinces de Paris.
Hirondelles.
Paradis terrestre [item 0854]: La maison proche de la forêt. Le
désert de Retz. Amertume. Paradis terrestre.
Sido et souvenirs d'enfance [item 0218]: Ma Bourgogne pauvre.

Reflective essays typical of Colette's style over several decades.
Mostly descriptive, with personal commentary. The original six
texts and the eight others added to various editions demonstrate
Colette's profound knowledge of animals and plants, and her ability
to portray each creature as individual and dynamic. "La maison
proche de la forêt," the title of which refers to one of her former
dwellings in the Paris suburbs, evokes a sense of mystery, while
the ruins in "Le désert de Retz" are portrayed as victims of the
onslaught of nature. "Hirondelles" expresses praise of swallows.
"Découvertes" summarizes the many small attractions of Colette's
Paris neighbourhood, as does "Province de Paris" of the city in
general. Most of "Paradis terrestre" recounts visits to the zoological
Parc de Clères but also offers interesting detail on Colette's
collaboration with Ravel. Its opening paragraphs, as well as the
entire essay "Amertume" [Bitterness], are the most serious passages
in the book, for their acerbic tone witnesses Colette's on-going
crusade to better the lot of animals whose lives touch those of
human beings. "Des mères, des enfants..." affords readers yet
another glimpse of her legendary childhood. Remaining texts,
while excellent of their type, are generally trivial in content. Some
texts included in the second edition were moved to *La Fleur de
l'âge.*

Reviews:
Bulletin critique du livre français 5 (1950): 605.
Montréal-Matin, 29 Sept. 1950, 2. Pierre Descaves.
Portique 7 (1950): 110. Jacques Guignard.

English translations: American

Extracts in:
Earthly Paradise [items 0082, 0084-85]. Trans. Herma Briffault,
    Derek Coltman.
Places [item 0098]: My poor Burgundy. The House by the Forest.
    Le Désert de Retz. An Earthly Paradise. Discoveries. Provincial
    Paris.

English translations: British

Extracts in:
Earthly Paradise [items 0087-89]: same contents as American ed.
Places [item 0099]: same contents as American ed.

LES ENFANTS DANS LES RUINES

0758 LES ENFANTS DANS LES RUINES. Paris: La Maison du livre,
      1917. 13p. Coll. Samothrace 2. Booklet containing only one
      text, first published in *Le Matin*, 6 June 1915. Colette then
      used it to make up the major part of "Jour de l'An en Argonne,"
      one of the texts of *Les Heures longues*, also published in 1917.
      Describes Christmas in a war-ravaged zone, and especially the
      children's reactions to small luxuries of which they have long
      been deprived.

L'ENVERS DU MUSIC-HALL

0759   L'ENVERS DU MUSIC-HALL. [Colette (Colette Willy)]. Paris: Flammarion, 1913. 248p.

0760   "Chiens savants." [Colette (Colette Willy)]. *Lisez-moi*, no. 193 (10 Sept. 1913): 27-29.

0761   "L'accompagnatrice." [Colette (Colette Willy)]. *Lisez-moi*, no. 196 (25 Oct. 1913): 319-20.

0762   "L'enfant de Bastienne." [Colette (Colette Willy)]. *Lisez-moi*, no. 200 (25 Dec. 1913): 635-39. Contains both parts.

0763   "L'enfant prodige." [Colette (Colette Willy)]. *Lisez-moi*, no. 202 (25 Jan. 1914): 105-7.

0764   "La caissière." [Colette (Colette Willy)]. *Lisez-moi*, no. 204 (25 Feb. 1914): 265-66.

0765   "La Fenice." [Colette (Colette Willy)]. *Lisez-moi*, no. 208 (25 April 1914): 639-40.

0766   "Le 'laissé-pour-compte'." [Colette (Colette Willy)]. *Lisez-moi*, no. 216 (25 May 1915): 561-66.

0767   "L'amour." [Colette Willy]. *Lisez-moi*, no. 223 (10 Sept. 1915): 425-26.

0768   L'ENVERS DU MUSIC-HALL. [Colette (Colette Willy)]. Paris: Flammarion, 1919. 70p. Coll. Select-collection 80.

0769   L'ENVERS DU MUSIC-HALL. Illus. J.-E. Laboureur. Paris: Au sans pareil, 1926. 171p. Coll. La Grande collection 1.

0770   L'ENVERS DU MUSIC-HALL. Illus. Henri Mirande. Paris: Ferenczi, 1929. 173p. Coll. Le Livre moderne illustré 90.

0771   MUSIC-HALL. Paris: Flammarion, 1934. 64p. Coll. Une heure d'oubli. Contains only the first 14 texts.

0772 L'ENVERS DU MUSIC-HALL. Letter-pref. Colette. Illus.
Edouard Chimot. Paris: Guillot, 1937. 201p.

0773 L'ENVERS DU MUSIC-HALL. Rio de Janeiro: Americ=Edit,
1938. 248p.

0774 L'ENVERS DU MUSIC-HALL. Paris: Flammarion, 1939. 63p.
Coll. Select-collection 179 (new series).

0775 L'ENVERS DU MUSIC-HALL. Paris: Flammarion, 1985. 104p.
Fac-simile of Centenaire edition.

Also in:
OP 2 [item 0053]: includes 3 previously uncollected texts [Music-
hall. Mes impressions de Chatte dans la «Revue de Ba-Ta-
Clan». Minuit six].
OCLF 5 [item 0054].
OCC 4 [item 0055].
OF 3 [item 0056].
Mitsou. L'Envers du Music-Hall. Dans la foule. Item 0566.

Extracts in:
Bêtes libres et prisonnières [item 0702]: Animaux de cirque.
Chiens de Colette [items 0716-17]: Chiens savants. Lola.
Morceaux choisis [item 0062]: Chiens savants. Lola. Malaise.
Les Plus Belles Pages de Colette [item 0064]: L'enfant prodige.
Amour. L'ouvroir.
Textes choisis de Colette [item 0065]: L'affamé.

Series of compelling chronicles based on Colette's own experience
of the music-hall from 1909 to 1913 and particularly the *tournées*
in the French provinces and nearby countries. Contains 26 texts:
La halte. On arrive, on répète. Le mauvais matin. Le cheval de
manège. L'ouvroir. Matinée. L'affamé. Amour. La travailleuse.
Après minuit. Lola. Malaise. Fin de route. «La grève, bon Dieu, la
grève...!» L'enfant de Bastienne I and II. L'accompagnatrice. La
caissière. L'habilleuse. Chiens savants. L'enfant prodige. Le laissé-
pour-compte I-III. La Fenice. Gitanette. All are short pieces,
chiefly in the form of short stories, anecdotes and word portraits.
Frequent use of present tense creates sense of immediacy and drama.
Critics have complained that Colette's sympathy for the performers
results in a white-washing of the milieu, for there is no doubt that,

despite the occasional portrayal of negative characters, she stresses their qualities of courage, perseverance and hard work. Many texts evince Colette's compassion for the hardships endured by theater animals. Models for some characters have been identified by researchers. Two texts, "Lola" and "Chiens savants," are in *Prrou, Poucette et quelques autres*, published the same year as the first edition, and in some editions of *La Paix chez les bêtes*. "L'habilleuse" is re-titled "Nostalgie" in most modern editions.

Reviews:
Books & Bookmen 2 (July 1957): 27. Margaret Crosland.
Cahiers d'aujourd'hui 4 (April 1913): 201-5. André Salmon.
Listener 58 (15 Aug. 1957): 247-48.
London Magazine 5 (Jan. 1958): 58-59. Anthony Quinton.
Mercure de France, 16 May 1913, 369-71. Rachilde.
New Statesman 54 (6 July 1957): 28-29. Richard Mayne.
New York Review of Books 6 (9 June 1966): 8-10. John
    Weightman.
Nouvelle Revue française 5 (1 July 1913): 155-58. Edouard
    Dolléans.
Nueva Estafeta 50 (Jan. 1983): 86-87. Manuel Ríos Ruiz.
Observer, no. 8661 (30 June 1957): 12. J.G. Weightman.
Sunday Times, 30 June 1957, 7. Cyril Connolly.
Times Literary Supplement, no. 2889 (12 July 1957): 429.

English translations: American

xxxx   MUSIC-HALL SIDELIGHTS. Trans. Anne-Marie Callimachi. In
       Mitsou. Music-Hall Sidelights. Items 0570-71. English titles
       are: The Halt. Arrival and Rehearsal. A Bad Morning. The
       Circus Horse. The Workroom. Matinée. The Starveling. Love.
       The Hard Worker. After Midnight. "Lola." Moments of Stress.
       Journey's End. "The Strike, Oh Lord, the Strike!" Bastienne's
       Child. The Accompanist. The Cashier. Nostalgia. Clever Dogs.
       The Child Prodigy. The Misfit. "La Fenice." "Gitanette."

Also in:
The Collected Stories of Colette [items 0071-72], under title
    "Backstage at the Music-Hall."
Six Novels by Colette [item 0104].

Extracts in *Gigi and Selected Writings* [item 0501]: The Halt. Arrival and Rehearsal. A Bad Morning.

English translations: British

xxxx MUSIC-HALL SIDELIGHTS. Trans. Anne-Marie Callimachi. In *My Apprenticeships. Music-Hall Sidelights.* Items 0195-96.

Also in *The Collected Stories of Colette* [items 0073-74], under title "Backstage at the Music-Hall."

LA FEMME CACHÉE

0776 LA FEMME CACHÉE. Paris: Flammarion, 1924. 249p.

0777 "Le juge." *Annales politiques et littéraires*, no. 2131 (27 April 1924): 469-70.

0778 "L'aube." In *Anthologie des conteurs d'aujourd'hui*, edited by André Fage, 109-14. Paris: Delagrave, 1924.

0779 LA FEMME CACHÉE. Paris: Flammarion, 1926. 62p. Coll. Select-collection 250.

0780 "Le bracelet." *Lisez-moi*, no. 355 (10 Feb. 1937): 175-76.

0781 "Châ." *Lisez-moi*, no. 400 (25 Dec. 1938): 959-60.

0782 "L'assassin." In *Les Plus Belles Histoires de peur*, edited by Marcel Berger, 59-64. Paris: Emile-Paul, 1942.

0783 LA FEMME CACHÉE. Paris: Flammarion, 1947. 62p. Coll. Select-collection 199 (new series).

0784 "La main." *Nouvelles littéraires*, 12 Aug. 1954, 8.

0785   "La main." *Médecine de France* 57 (1954): 39-40.

0786   LA FEMME CACHÉE. Paris: Gallimard, 1974. 194p. Coll. Folio
       612.

0787   "L'assassin." In *L'Affaire de la lapine blanche*, edited by Antoine
       Castaing, 185-89. Paris: Opta, 1977.

0788   "Le renard." In *Contes et nouvelles*, vol. 2, edited by Jacques
       Gouttenoire, 62-67. Paris: Hachette, 1979.

0789   LA FEMME CACHÉE. Paris: Flammarion, 1985. 96p. Not seen.

       Also in:
       OCLF 7 [item 0054].
       OCC 6 [item 0055].
       OF 3 [item 0056].
       Sido. Noces. La Femme cachée. Item 0219.

       Extracts in:
       Histoires pour Bel-Gazou, all eds.: Le renard.
       Morceaux choisis [item 0062]: L'assassin. L'autre femme. La
          main. L'impasse. Le conseil.
       Pages choisies [item 0063]: Le renard. Le bracelet.
       Les Plus Belles Pages de Colette [item 0064]: L'autre femme. La
          main. L'impasse.
       Textes choisis de Colette [item 0065]: Le renard. Le bracelet. Châ.

       22 short stories. Although subjects vary--love, family relations,
       crime, art and nostalgia are all explored--the title of the collection
       is apt, for the focus is on the hidden inner life of one or more
       characters. Colette also demonstrates how people inadvertently
       reveal themselves by a look, word or gesture, and how a minor
       event can destroy happiness. Most of the drama is psychological,
       and both male and female viewpoints are presented. Individual titles
       are: La femme cachée. L'aube. Un soir. La main. L'impasse. Le
       renard. Le juge. L'omelette. L'autre femme. Monsieur Maurice. Le
       cambrioleur. Le conseil. L'assassin. Le portrait. Le paysage. Demi-
       fous. Secrets. «Châ». Le bracelet. La trouvaille. Jeux de miroirs.
       L'habitude.

Reviews:

AB Bookman's Weekly 49 (17 April 1972): 1420. MAM [Mary Ann O'Brian Malkin].

Booklist 68 (15 May 1972): 795.

Choice 9 (Feb. 1973): 1595.

Eve, no. 213 (26 Oct. 1924): 11. Raymond Clauzel.

Library Journal 97 (1 Jan. 1972): 84. Ann Grace Mojtabai.

Listener 86 (22 July 1971): 120. Stewart Trotter.

New Statesman 82 (9 July 1971): 54-55. Lucy Cadogan.

New York Times Book Review 122 (1 Oct. 1972): 6-7. Nancy Hale.

Nouvelles littéraires, 21 June 1924, 3. Edmond Jaloux.

Publishers' Weekly 201 (31 Jan. 1972): 245.

Revue mondiale 158 (15 April 1924): 424. Nicolas Ségur.

Saturday Review 55 (1 April 1972): 74-75. Nancy Ryan.

Temps, 18 Sept. 1924, 3. Paul Souday.

Times Literary Supplement, no. 3625 (20 Aug. 1971): 986.

Tribune, 3 Sept. 1971, 15. Dulan Barber.

English translations: American

0790 "Monsieur Maurice." No translator. In *The Best French Short Stories of 1923-24*, edited by Richard Eaton, 88-91. Boston: Small, Maynard, 1924.

0791 "The Fox." No translator. *Harper's Bazaar*, May 1933, 52, 88.

0792 "Triumph." No translator. *Collier's* 91 (24 June 1933): 15. Trans. of "Jeux de miroirs."

0793 "Three unpublished stories" [The Hand. "Châ." The Fox]. Trans. Margaret Crosland. *Vogue* 159 (15 Jan. 1972): 70-73.

0794 THE OTHER WOMAN. Trans. Margaret Crosland. Indianapolis & New York: Bobbs-Merrill, 1972. 140p. Contains 20 texts: The Secret Woman. Dawn. One Evening. The Hand. The Dead End. The Fox. The Judge. The Other Wife. The Burglar. The Murderer. The Portrait. The Landscape. Secrets. "Châ." The Bracelet. The Find. Mirror-play. Habit. The Victim. My Friend Valentine. The first 18 are from *La Femme cachée* and the last two from *Paysages et portraits*.

0795   THE OTHER WOMAN. Trans. Margaret Crosland. Introd. Erica
       Jong. New York: New American Library (Signet), 1975. xiii-
       143p. Same 20 texts as item 0794.

       Also in *The Collected Stories of Colette* [items 0071-72].
       Contains all 22 stories. Trans. Matthew Ward. Titles are
       slightly different from Crosland translation: The Hidden
       Woman. Dawn. One Evening. The Hand. A Dead End. The
       Fox. The Judge. The Omelette. The Other Wife. Monsieur
       Maurice. The Burglar. The Advice. The Murderer. The Portrait.
       The Landscape. The Half-Crazy. Secrets. Châ. The Bracelet. The
       Find. Mirror-Games. Habit.

English translations: British

0796   "Three Stories" [The Hand. "Châ." The Fox]. [Trans. Margaret
       Crosland]. *Encounter* 37 (July 1971): 3-7.

0797   THE OTHER WOMAN. Trans. and introd. Margaret Crosland.
       London: Owen, 1971. 140p. Same 20 texts as item 0794.

0798   THE OTHER WOMAN. Trans. and introd. Margaret Crosland.
       Feltham: Hamlyn, 1983. 140p. Same 20 texts as item 0794.

       Also in *The Collected Stories of Colette* [items 0073-74]: same
       contents as American eds.

LA FLEUR DE L'AGE

0799   LA FLEUR DE L'AGE. Paris: Le Fleuron, 1949. 99p. Contains 8
       texts: La fleur de l'âge. La trêve. Des mères, des enfants... Au
       fil de l'eau. Le cirque. Œufs de Pâques. Trésors épars. Noël
       ancien.

0800 LA FLEUR DE L'AGE. Illus. Matisse. Geneva: Mermod, 1960. 145p. Contains 11 texts, same as item 0799 plus: Florie. Rivalité. Avril.

0801 LA FLEUR DE L'AGE. EN PAYS CONNU. A PORTÉE DE LA MAIN. Geneva: Crémille, 1971. 241p. First title contains same 11 texts as item 0800.

Also in:
OCLF 14 [item 0054]: same 11 texts as item 0800.
OCC 11 [item 0055]: same 11 texts as item 0800.
En pays connu. Trait pour trait. Journal intermittent. La Fleur de l'âge. [A portée de la main.] Item 0757: same 11 texts as item 0800.

Extracts in:
Autobiographie... [items 0057-58]: Des mères, des enfants...
En pays connu [items 0754-55]: Des mères, des enfants... Le cirque. Œufs de Pâques. Trésors épars. Noël ancien.

Mixture of short stories and articles. As is often the case with Colette, the four short stories [La fleur de l'âge. La trêve. Florie. Rivalité] highlight the psychological side of human relationships, usually love, and in particular the individual's hidden thoughts or unexpected reactions. Endings generally offer a surprise. "Avril" is an unused chapter of *Le Blé en herbe*. The other texts are first-person reminiscences or journalistic pieces, some of them nostalgic in tone. "Des mères, des enfants..." evokes once more the fecundity of Sido's domain, "Trésors épars" the agricultural abundance of yester-year, and "Noël ancien" Sido's attitude towards Christmas. "Le cirque" and "Œufs de Pâques" are similarly inspired by childhood memories, while "Au fil de l'eau" briefly enumerates the attractions of the running stream. As a collection, typical of Colette's variety, both in subject and in presentation. "Florie" and "Rivalité" had previously appeared in book form under the title *Florie*, and "Avril" separately under its own name [item 0240]. Several of the texts have also appeared in editions of *En pays connu*.

English translations: American

0802   "Her Young Husband." Trans. Denver Lindley. *Collier's* 101 (26
       March 1938): 19. Trans. of "La Fleur de l'âge."

0803   "Rivals." Trans. Denver Lindley. *Collier's* 101 (7 May 1938): 16.
       Trans. of "Rivalité."

0804   "Respite." Trans. Anna Rose. *Mademoiselle* 37 (July 1953): 46-
       47, 104. Trans. of "La Trêve."

       Extracts in:
       The Collected Stories of Colette [items 0071-72]: Florie. In the
       Flower of Age. The Rivals. The Respite. April. Trans.
       Matthew Ward.
       Earthly Paradise [items 0082, 0084-85]: Mothers and Children.
       Trans. Herma Briffault.

English translations: British

       Extracts in:
       The Collected Stories of Colette [items 0073-74]: same contents as
       American eds.
       Earthly Paradise [items 0087-89]: same contents as American eds.

LES FLEURS [LA FLEUR]

0805   LES FLEURS [title page: *La Fleur*]. Villefranche: J. Bonthoux,
       1937. 24p. Special issue of *Mieux Vivre* (no. 10, October
       1937). Focusing on the vegetation of Provence, Colette
       meditates on what she calls the friendship of flowers and the
       possibility of their having an emotional life. Her four-page text
       is accompanied and followed by photographs of flowers as well
       as related advertisements. Although the *OCLF* does not
       acknowledge it, this passage was incorporated into *Belles
       Saisons* in 1945.

FLEURS DU DÉSERT

0806 FLEURS DU DÉSERT. Letter-pref. Maurice Goudeket. Illus. Christian Caillard. Paris: Les Francs-bibliophiles, 1960. x-165p. Collection of passages inspired by three trips Colette made to North Africa: to Algeria in 1920, to Morocco in 1926, and to Spain, Morocco and Tangiers three years later. Goudeket's letter provides informative background on the voyages. Contains the entire novella *Le Rendez-vous* plus 12 texts from *Prisons et paradis*: Fleur du désert. Ahmed. Ouled-Naïl. Marrakech. Le muet. Rabat. Lyautey. Fez. Sefrou. Dar-El Jamaï. Déjeuner marocain. L'audience du pacha.

FLORE ET POMONE

0807 FLORE ET POMONE. Illus. Laprade. Paris: Eds. de la Galerie Charpentier, 1943. 163p.

0808 "La carrière des fleurs." [Extract]. *Nouvelles littéraires*, 12 Aug. 1954, 8.

Also in:
Gigi, many eds.
Sido et souvenirs d'enfance [item 0218].

Extracts in:
Autobiographie tirée des œuvres de Colette [items 0057-58].
Bêtes libres et prisonnières [item 0702]: Les mésanges.

Series of descriptive passages and reminiscences extolling the merits of diverse flowers and fruit, the attractions of gardens in France and elsewhere, and the perils and joys of botanical explorers. Liberally sprinkled with portraits and anecdotes. Despite Colette's extensive knowledge of the subject and her impressive botanical vocabulary, her easy conversational style makes the subject accessible to the average reader.

English translations: American

xxxx   "Flora and Pomona." In *Flowers and Fruit* [item 0090].

Extracts in *Earthly Paradise* [items 0082, 0084-85]. Trans. Derek Coltman.

English translations: British

xxxx   "Flora and Pomona." In *Flowers and Fruit* [item 0091].

Extracts in *Earthly Paradise* [items 0087-89]. Trans. Derek Coltman.

FLORIE

0809   FLORIE. Illus. Louis Touchagues. Cap d'Antibes: La Joie de vivre, 1946. 59p. Handsome, unbound edition containing only two stories, "Florie" and "Rivalité," both of which were transferred to *La Fleur de l'âge* for the *OCLF*.

LES HEURES LONGUES

0810   LES HEURES LONGUES (1914-1917). [Colette (Colette Willy)]. Paris: Fayard, 1917. 237p.

0811   "Sous les bombes de Verdun." [Extract from "A Verdun"]. *Annales politiques et littéraires*, 22 Dec. 1918, 561.

0812 "Notes prises à Rome en juillet 1915." [Extract from "Impressions d'Italie"]. *Annales politiques et littéraires*, 27 April 1919, 403-4.

0813 "Le vieux monsieur." *Annales politiques et littéraires*, 3 Oct. 1920, 265-66.

0814 "La marmaille romaine." [Extracts from "Impressions d'Italie"]. *Conférencia* 17 (1 Oct. 1923): 356.

0815 LES HEURES LONGUES (1914-1917). Paris: Fayard, 1984. 239p. Reproduction of original edition.

Also in:
OP 2 [item 0053]: same contents as 1917 edition.
OCLF 5 [item 0054]: abridged. See annotation for contents.
OCC 4 [item 0055]: abridged. See annotation for contents.
La Paix chez les bêtes. Les Heures longues. La Chambre éclairée.
Item 0846: abridged. See annotation for contents.

Extracts in:
Autobiographie tirée des œuvres de Colette [items 0057-58].
Bêtes libres et prisonnières [item 0702]: Hirondelles.
La Chambre éclairée, some eds.: Les foins.
Chats de Colette [items 0714-15]: Nocturnes.
Chiens de Colette [items 0716-17]: Vorace.
Colette [item 0060]: La nouvelle. Bel-Gazou et la vie chère. Bel-Gazou et la guerre. Un zouave.
Morceaux choisis [item 0062]: Bel-Gazou et la vie chère. La chienne.
Textes choisis de Colette [item 0065]: Citadins. Les foins.
Gavoty [item 1607]: Apollon, déménageur.

Fruit of Colette's reporting activities during World War I for a variety of journals and newspapers. She travelled in both France and Italy, often under air-raid, and sites visited include hospitals, farms and a dog-training station. Colette's descriptions provide a valuable document of the effect on civilians of the war and of their reactions to events. Hers is a very personal style of reporting, often using present tense, and these texts make little reference to military activities. Colette stresses merits of the common people and expresses admiration of Italians. Although a keen patriot, she frequently declares strong aversion to war. Original edition contained 42 texts. Titles are: La nouvelle. Le "réservoir." Blessés: l'aube. Blessés: la tête. Blessés: renouveau. Le premier café-concert. Le vieux monsieur. Les lettres. La chasse aux produits allemands. A Verdun. Jour de l'An en Argonne. Bel-Gazou et la guerre. Les retardataires. Femmes seules. En attendant le Zeppelin. Modes. L'enfant de l'ennemi. Les mêmes. Le refuge. Jouets. Répétition générale. Chiens sanitaires. Un camp anglais. Un zouave. Impressions d'Italie. Un taube sur Venise. Nocturnes. Un entretien avec un prince de Hohenlohe. Les foins. "Citadins." L'exilé. Devoirs de vacances. La résurrection des vieux. Lac de Côme (octobre 1916). Lac de Côme (novembre 1916). Le petit accident. Déménagement. Apollon, déménageur. Bel-Gazou et la vie chère. La chienne. Pieds. Ceux d'avant la guerre. One text [Jour de l'An en Argonne] had been published separately the same year under the title *Les Enfants dans les ruines*. "La chienne" was moved to *Douze dialogues de bêtes* in 1930. Only 12 texts were retained for the *OCLF* [La nouvelle. A Verdun. Jour de l'An en Argonne. Bel-Gazou et la guerre. Les mêmes. Un zouave. Impressions d'Italie. Un taube sur Venise. Nocturnes. Les foins. Apollon, déménageur. Bel-Gazou et la vie chère].

Review:
Mercure de France, 16 Feb 1918, 672-74. Rachilde.

English translations: American

0816   "Between friends." No translator. *Collier's* 91 (15 April 1933): 15. Trans. of "La chienne."

Extracts in *Earthly Paradise* [items 0082, 0084-85]. Trans. Herma Briffault.

English translations: British

Extracts in *Earthly Paradise* [items 0087-89]. Trans. Herma Briffault.

HISTOIRES POUR BEL-GAZOU

0817 HISTOIRES POUR BEL-GAZOU. Illus. A. Le Petit. Paris: Stock, 1930. 151p. Coll. Maïa 14 (series B).

0818 HISTOIRES POUR BEL-GAZOU. Illus. Jean Reschofsky. Paris: Hachette, 1958. 189p. Coll. Idéal-Bibliothèque 153.

0819 HISTOIRES POUR BEL-GAZOU. Introd. and notes Grazia Vitale. Rome: A. Signorelli, 1964. 101p. Coll. Scrittori francesi. Study edition for Italian students. Not seen.

0820 HISTOIRES POUR BEL-GAZOU. Illus. Annie-Claude Martin. Paris: Hachette, 1977. 156p. Coll. Vermeille.

0821 HISTOIRES POUR BEL-GAZOU. Illus. Véronique Cau. Paris: Hachette-Jeunesse, 1985. 156p. Coll. Idéal-bibliothèque.

"Bel-Gazou" was Colette's pet name for her daughter, Colette de Jouvenel, born in 1913. As the title suggests, this book contains 17 stories suitable for children. All are borrowed from previously published works: 8 from *La Paix chez les bêtes* [Bel-Gazou et Buck. Le naturaliste et la chatte. La petite truie de M. Rouzade. La chienne bull. Ricotte. La chienne trop petite. Conte pour les petits enfants des poilus. Les papillons], 5 from *La Maison de Claudine* [Ma mère et les bêtes. Où sont les enfants? Le curé sur le mur. Ma sœur aux longs cheveux. La Toutouque], and one each from *Aventures quotidiennes* [Mésanges], *Dialogues de bêtes* [Le voyage], *La Femme cachée* [Le renard], and *Les Vrilles de la vigne* [Le dernier feu].

Reviews:
Nouvelles littéraires, 20 Dec. 1930, 3. Yves Gandon.
Quinzaine critique, no. 27 (10 Feb. 1931): non-pag. Lili P. Landowski.

JOURNAL A REBOURS

0822 JOURNAL A REBOURS. Paris: Fayard, 1941. 219p.

0823 "Automne." In *La Guirlande des années: images d'hier et pages d'aujourd'hui*, 47-68. Paris: Flammarion, 1941. Colette's essay on autumn is complemented by passages on the other seasons by François Mauriac, Jules Romains and André Gide. With splendid illustrations taken from medieval manuscripts.

0824 "Automne." In *La Guirlande des années: images d'hier et d'aujourd'hui*. Geneva: Cercle du bibliophile, n.d. [1971-1975]. Miniature book containing same texts as item 0823 but illustrations are eighteenth-century engravings.

0825 JOURNAL A REBOURS. Geneva: Crémille, 1971. 253p.

0826 JOURNAL A REBOURS. Paris: Fayard, 1974. 192p. Coll. Livre de poche 3841.

0827 JOURNAL A REBOURS. Paris: Fayard, 1984. 221p. Reproduction of original edition.

Also in:
OCLF 12 [item 0054].
OCC 9 [item 0055].

Extracts in:
Autobiographie... [items 0057-58]: La chaufferette. Maurice Ravel. Le cœur des bêtes. Fin juin 1940. Ruines. Automne. Sido et moi.
Bêtes libres et prisonnières [item 0702]: Le lapin. La jument. Les oiseaux du jardin. Hirondelles. Les cigales. Papillons. Les couleuvres. Deux cormorans. Sur les étangs. Connivence.
Chiens de Colette [items 0716-17]: Souci. Le cœur des chiens. Les chiens et la lune. Bellaude.
Schifres [item 2103]: Le cœur des bêtes [complete].

Mixed collection of 23 texts, including several on animals and nature. The first few vividly describe Colette's experiences during

World War II, just after the invasion, when she sought safety at her daughter's chateau in the south of France; they dwell heavily on the difficulties of life there. Other texts date from before the war, as Colette moves *à rebours* [backwards] in time. "Oum-el-Hassen," the report of a trial Colette covered in Fez in 1938, is remarkable for the way in which she stresses the horror of the crimes at the same time as she manages to express a certain sympathy, and even admiration, for their perpetrator. "Un salon en 1900" provides a valuable picture of Colette's contacts with the world of music at the turn of the century and her subsequent relations with Ravel. "La chaufferette" paints an interesting picture of her early school-days and includes an oft-cited passage on her lack of writing vocation. The six texts comprising "Provence" depict various aspects of her summer life at Saint Tropez during the twenties and thirties. In "Automne," Colette declares her preference for autumn and uses her own and Sido's lives as points of reference, as she richly evokes the beauty and plenitude of nature at that season. The over-all theme is a celebration of the cyclical nature of life. Taken as a group, the collection provides a good sample of the variety of subject and treatment generally found in Colette's personal essays. Individual titles are: Fin juin 1940. La Providence. Le poète. Hirondelles. Danger. Ruines. Fièvre. Partis. Oum-el-Hassen. Automne. Un salon en 1900. Sido et moi. La chaufferette. Le cœur des bêtes. Le petit chat retrouvé. Papillons. Plein air. Provence I-VI. Several texts had been published previously in collaborative works with other authors. "Papillons" served as the text for *Splendeur des papillons* and "Provence III-VI" had already appeared in the *Quatrième cahier*.

Review:
Nouvelle Revue française 55 (1 July 1941): 118-19. Jean-Pierre Maxence.

English translations: American

Extracts in:
Earthly Paradise [items 0082, 0084-85]: The Footwarmer. Maurice Ravel. The Heart of Animals. Sido and I. Late June 1940. Ruins. Autumn. Trans. Herma Briffault, Derek Coltman.
Looking Backwards [item 0095]: contains 21 texts. See that title for specific contents.

English translations: British

Extracts in:
Earthly Paradise [items 0087-89]: same contents as American eds.
Looking Backwards [items 0096-97]: same contents as American
   eds.

JOURNAL INTERMITTENT

0828   JOURNAL INTERMITTENT. Paris: Le Fleuron, 1949. 93p.
       Texts cover four different years: 1915 [Notes d'Italie]. 1923
       [L'acquittée. La manière. Le tombeau rouvert. Les lunettes.
       Papillons]. 1934. 1941.

Also in:
OCLF 14 [item 0054]: same texts as item 0828 plus 4 texts of
   1939-40 [Lumières bleues. Paris de guerre et de paix. Trois
   heures du matin rue de Grenelle. Printemps de guerre].
OCC 11 [item 0055]: same texts as in *OCLF*.
*En pays connu. Trait pour trait. Journal intermittent. La Fleur de
   l'âge.* [*A Portée de la main.*] Item 0757. Third title contains
   same texts as *OCLF*.
Le Fanal bleu. En pays connu. Journal intermittent. Item 0133.
   Third title contains same texts as *OCLF*.
Pour un herbier. Trait pour trait. Journal intermittent. Item 0867.
   Third title contains same texts as *OCLF*.

Extracts in:
OP 2 [item 0053]: Notes d'Italie, 1915. Text of original
   manuscript.
Chiens de Colette [items 0716-17]: Courses de lévriers. Diane.
En pays connu [items 0754-55]: from "1923" and "1934."

Miscellaneous collection of notes and pieces written at different
times. Segments dated 1915 are written in cryptic and partial
sentences and record impressions received during Colette's visits to
Rome and Venice during World War I; a comparison of these with

finished passages on the same subject under other titles would make an interesting study, for sounds, sights, odours, movement and forms of life are already evoked in the "journal." Pieces dated 1923 and 1934 contain reports of trials, including that of Valentine Nozière. In them, Colette presents some of her own theories about the causes of crime. Other passages focus on butterflies, noise, the opening of King Tutankhamen's tomb, the disadvantages of eyeglasses for children, the problems of crossing the border to Spain, and the Loch Ness monster. With the *OCLF*, a group of essays bearing the heading "1939-1940" was added to this title. In them, Colette recalls the previous war and dwells on some of the problems of the new one. Particularly poignant is a passage in which she expresses the hope that the spring of 1940 will be the only spring of the war: the reader knows that, for Colette, long difficult years are ahead. Many of the texts published under the sub-title "Journal intermittent" in the 1950 *En pays connu* are borrowed from other collections.

MÉLANGES

In:
OCLF 15 [item 0054].
OCC 14 [item 0055].
La Chambre éclairée. [*Mélanges. Derniers écrits. Discours de réception.*] Item 0709.
La Chambre éclairée. [*Mélanges. Derniers écrits. Discours de réception.*] *De ma fenêtre. Le Fanal bleu.* Item 0710.
Le Fanal bleu. Mélanges. Item 0131.

Umbrella title given by Colette to a miscellaneous collection of 18 pieces published in the *OCLF*. Includes five prefaces, a few texts for collaborative works and a number of publicity texts. Their inclusion reminds one that Colette earned her living by her pen and that many of her short pieces were written because she needed money. Titles are: Fleurs. Perce-neige. Peindre... Lectures. Le chat. Palais-Royal. A la maison. La captive. Préface pour 28 compositions de Michel Dubost. La femme et son décor sous le

Consulat et l'Empire. Nez fin. Vins de France. Fragrance. Préface à *La Maison dans l'œil du chat* par Mireille Havet. Préface à *Sabat* par Hélène Picard. Préface à *Aux Iles de la lumière* par Renée Hamon. Préface à *Ravel et nous* par Hélène Jourdan-Morhange. Préface à *Souvenirs de ma vie* par Marguerite Moreno. Texts readily accessible in original format are annotated separately in "Miscellaneous."

English translations: American

xxxx   "Snowdrop" [trans. of "Perce-neige"] and "Redouté's Roses" [trans. of "Fleurs"]. In *Flowers and Fruit* [item 0090].

English translations: British

xxxx   "Snowdrop" [trans. of "Perce-neige"] and "Redouté's Roses" [trans. of "Fleurs"]. In *Flowers and Fruit* [item 0091].

MES CAHIERS

0829   PREMIER CAHIER DE COLETTE. Illus. Dignimont. Paris: Les Amis de Colette, 1935. 101p. Contents: Clouk [Introd. L'autre table. L'écran. Clouk tout seul. Clouk et la noce. La petite classe]. Chéri [Chéri. Le retour. Les perles].

0830   DEUXIEME CAHIER DE COLETTE. Illus. Daragnès. Paris: Les Amis de Colette, 1935. 89p. Contents: Notes marocaines [Notes marocaines. Marrakech. Rabat. Fez]. La Décapitée.

0831   TROISIEME CAHIER DE COLETTE. Illus. Luc-Albert Moreau. Paris: Les Amis de Colette, 1935. 92p. Contents: En tournée. Music-hall [La transformiste. Le ténor. Un faune].

0832   QUATRIEME CAHIER DE COLETTE. Illus. Dunoyer de Segonzac. Paris: Les Amis de Colette, 1936. 97p. Contents:

Portraits: Leur beau physique [Aristide Briand. M.J. Caillaux.
M. Gaston Doumergue. M. Edouard Herriot. Anatole de
Monzie]. Paysages [Provence. Camping! Un serpent dans la
cuisine. Beau langage. Fin de saison en Provence. Chez nous].

0833   MES CAHIERS. Paris: Aux Armes de France, 1941. 201p.
Contents: Notes de tournées. Music-hall [La transformiste. Le
ténor]. Clouk [L'autre table. L'écran. Clouk tout seul. Clouk et
la noce. La petite classe. Chéri. Le retour. Les perles]. Notes de
voyage [Algérie, 1920. Séville, Jours saints. Soleil de minuit.
Entre Bergen et Trondhjem. New York et la «Normandie»].
Monstres [Marie Becker, empoisonneuse. Stavisky. Weidmann].
La Décapitée.

Also in:
OCLF 13 [item 0054]: Notes de tournées. «Clouk» et «Chéri» [7
texts, same as in the *Premier cahier* less "La petite classe"].
Leur beau physique [same 5 texts as in the *Quatrième cahier*].
Notes de voyage [same 5 texts as in item 0833 plus "Chez
nous"]. Monstres [same 3 texts as in item 0833].
OCC 14 [item 0055]: same contents as *OCLF* except that "Leur
beau physique" contains two extra texts: Proust. Balzac.
L'Etoile vesper. Mes cahiers. Item 0124: same contents as *OCLF*.

Extracts in:
OP 2 [item 0053]: Texts of item 0829. "Un faune" of item 0831.
"Le tenor" of items 0831 and 0833. "Notes de tournées" [En
tournée] of items 0831 and 0833.
Autobiographie... [items 0057-58].
Belles Saisons [items 0699-700]: Notes de tournées. Monstres.
Leur beau physique [all 7 portraits].
Belles Saisons. Nudité. Mes cahiers. Paysages et portraits.
Aventures quotidiennes. Item 0701: same texts as *OCC*.
En pays connu [items 0754-55]: Notes de voyage, with texts from
other works under heading "Journal intermittent."
En tournée [item 0002]: Notes de tournées.
Journal à rebours, all eds.: see annotation.
Notes marocaines [item 0835]: Algérie 1920.
Prisons et paradis, all eds.: see annotation.

Mixed collections of mainly unpublished items and material from
Colette's notebooks. Selections from the four *Cahiers de Colette*

make up the 1941 *Mes cahiers*, but with changes, additions and cuts. Contents were again changed for the *Mes cahiers* of the *OCLF*.

The *Premier cahier* and the 1941 *Mes cahiers* contain five chapters of a rejected version of *Chéri*, wherein the hero was the unattractive Clouk, and three early versions of recognizable chapters of the novel as it was finally published. These are of documentary interest, especially to those wishing to study the development of Colette's techniques. Later publications omit "La petite classe."

The *Deuxième cahier* contains "Notes marocaines" [Notes marocaines. Marrakech. Rabat. Fez] as well as the theater piece *La Décapitée*. The former section disappears from subsequent editions of *Mes cahiers*, only to reappear, with changes, as the seven texts added to *Prisons et paradis* in 1935. *La Décapitée* appeared in the 1941 *Mes cahiers* but for the *OCLF* and most subsequent collections it is grouped with Colette's other theater works.

The *Troisième cahier* contains two major sections, "En tournée" and "Music-hall." The first section represents notes that Colette made while on the music-hall; they became "Notes de tournées" for *Mes cahiers* and were shortened further for inclusion in the *OCLF*. In the second section, one text, "La transformiste," first appeared in *La Chambre éclairée*. It was also included in the 1941 *Mes cahiers* but dropped from subsequent editions. It is nevertheless an interesting text for the modern reader because it depicts a phenomenon no longer seen on the stage: a woman whose performance consists of dressing up as different people or as different human types one after the other. The humorous "Un faune" was dropped after its initial book publication.

The *Quatrième cahier* contains five portraits of French politicians, under the umbrella title "Leur beau physique." These were omitted from the 1941 *Mes cahiers* for political reasons, then restored to the title for the *OCLF*. The six texts with the umbrella title "Paysages" were dropped from the 1941 edition, but the first four became "Provence III-VI" in *Journal à rebours*, while the fifth-- beginning "Un tam-tam de guerre"--was incorporated into *Belles saisons*. The sixth, "Chez nous," was restored to *Mes cahiers* with the *OCLF*.

For the 1941 *Mes cahiers*, Colette used selections from the four previous *cahiers*, sometimes with changes, and added new material. Although she did not travel extensively, she made several trips out of France and her powers of observation are nowhere so keenly exhibited as in the "Notes de voyage." In the three fascinating texts of "Monstres" Colette ponders the psychology of mass murderers and re-affirms ideas that she reiterates in almost every other passage in which she treats the subject: that the murderer is burdened with an overwhelming urge to confess, that murder is not an end but a beginning, that it is an act which irrevocably separates the murderer from the rest of society, and that the "monster" or mass murderer bears the physical stamp of his or her moral deformity.

Review:
Nouvelle Revue française 16 (1 Feb. 1942): 239-40. Henri de
    Portelaine.

English translations: American

Extracts in:
The Collected Stories of Colette [items 0071-72]: Clouk/Chéri
    [The Other Table. The Screen. Clouk Alone. Clouk's Fling.
    Chéri. The Return. The Pearls]. The Quick-change Artist. The
    Tenor. Trans. Matthew Ward.
Earthly Paradise [items 0082, 0084-85]. Trans. Herma Briffault.
Places [item 0098]: Maiden Voyage of the Normandie. Midnight
    Sun. Seville: Holy Days.

English translations: British

Extracts in:
The Collected Stories of Colette [items 0073-74]: same contents as
    American ed.
Earthly Paradise [items 0087-0089]: same contents as American ed.
Places [item 0099]: same contents as American ed.

NOTES ALGÉRIENNES ET MAROCAINES

0834 NOTES ALGÉRIENNES ET MAROCAINES. Paris: Lidis, 1960.
Not seen [contents unknown].

NOTES MAROCAINES

0835 NOTES MAROCAINES. Illus. Raoul Dufy. Geneva: Mermod,
1958. 123p. Selections from *Mes cahiers* and *Prisons et paradis*.
Contents: Notes marocaines [Marrakech. Le muet. Rabat.
Lyautey. Fez. Sefrou. Dar-El Jamaï. Déjeuner marocain.
L'audience du Pacha]. Algérie 1920. En Algérie [Fleur du désert.
Ahmed. Ouled-Naïl].

NUDITÉ

0836 NUDITÉ. Illus. Carlègle. Brussels: Eds. de la Mappemonde, 1943.
85p. Single long essay inspired by a performance of the Revue
des Folies-Bergère in 1940. Remarkable for its dispassionate
commentary. Colette finds nothing scabrous in the performance,
and contents herself with drawing parallels between the
motionless women of the Revue and the classical statuary of
antiquity. Digressions on peripheral topics, such as nude
performers Colette used to know, changes in the fashionable
female form over the decades, dolls and wax figures, and an
incident demonstrating when nudity is and is not suitable in
marriage, fill out the essay.

Also in:
OCLF 8 [item 0054].
OCC 11 [item 0055].
Belles Saisons [items 0699-700].
Belles Saisons. Nudité. Mes cahiers. Paysages et portraits. Aventures quotidiennes. Item 0701.
Prisons et paradis. Nudité. Item 0879.

Extracts in *Autobiographie...* [items 0057-58].

English translations: American

Extracts in *Earthly Paradise* [items 0082, 0084-85]. Trans. Derek Coltman.

English translations: British

Extracts in *Earthly Paradise* [items 0087-89]. Trans. Derek Coltman.

LA PAIX CHEZ LES BETES

0837 LA PAIX CHEZ LES BETES. [Colette (Colette Willy)]. Paris: Crès, 1916. vii-242p. Coll. les Proses. Contains Colette's foreword and 33 texts. The first 12 texts are from *Prrou, Poucette et quelques autres* [Poum. La chienne jalouse. «Prrou». Poucette. «La Shâh». Le matou. La petite chienne à vendre. La chienne trop petite. «Lola». Chiens savants. La mère chatte. Le tentateur]. The remaining 21 texts are new [Nonoche. La chienne bull. Automne. Le naturaliste et la chatte. Jardin zoologique. Ricotte. Les couleuvres. L'homme aux poissons. Les chats-huants. La petite truie de M. Rouzade. Les papillons. Exposition canine. L'ours et la vieille dame. Insectes et oiseaux vivants. Salon d'automne. La salivation psychique. Les lutteurs au cirque. Bel-Gazou et Buck. Conte pour les petits enfants des poilus. Chiens sanitaires. La paix des bêtes].

0838   "La chienne trop petite." In *Petite Anthologie des Auteurs gais contemporains*, edited by Léon Treich. Paris: Flammarion, 1918. Not seen.

0839   "Poum." *Conférencia* 17 (1 Dec. 1923): 560-61.

0840   "La chienne jalouse." *Conférencia* 17 (1 Dec. 1923): 561-62.

0841   "La chienne trop petite." *Conférencia* 17 (1 Dec. 1923): 563-64.

0842   LA PAIX CHEZ LES BETES. Illus. A. Roubille. Paris: Eds. du Capitole, 1926. 149p. Same 33 texts as item 0837.

0843   LA PAIX CHEZ LES BETES. Paris: Grasset, 1929. 249p. Coll. Œuvres de Colette 6. Same 33 texts as item 0837.

0844   LA PAIX CHEZ LES BETES. Illus. S. Lecoanet. Paris: Fayard, 1933. 111p. Coll. Le livre de demain 122. Same 33 texts as item 0837.

0845   LA PAIX CHEZ LES BETES. Illus. Jean Reschofsky. Paris: Hachette, 1961. 191p. Coll. Idéal-bibliothèque. Contains no foreword and only 18 texts: Poum. La chienne jalouse. «Prrou». Poucette. «La Shah». La petite chienne à vendre. «Lola». Chiens savants. La mère chatte. Jardin zoologique. Les couleuvres. L'homme aux poissons. Les chats-huants. Exposition canine. L'ours et la vieille dame. Insectes et oiseaux vivants. Chiens sanitaires. La paix des bêtes.

0846   LA PAIX CHEZ LES BETES. LES HEURES LONGUES. LA CHAMBRE ECLAIRÉE. Geneva: Crémille, 1969. 253p. Contains only 30 texts. Omits: Lola. Chiens savants. Nonoche.

0847   "Les lutteurs au cirque." In *L'Equipe de France*, edited by Gilbert Prouteau, 157-58. Paris: Plon, 1972.

0848   "Conte de Noël pour les petits enfants des poilus." In *Découvrir les animaux fabuleux*, edited by Michel Cosem, 119-26. Paris: Seghers, 1980.

0849   LA PAIX CHEZ LES BETES. Paris: Fayard, 1984. 255p. Same
       33 texts as item 0837.

0850   LA PAIX CHEZ LES BETES. Illus. Véronique Cau. Paris:
       Hachette, 1985. 156p. Coll. Idéal-bibliothèque. Same 18 texts
       as item 0845.

Also in:
OP 2 [item 0053]: same 33 texts as item 0837.
OCLF 5 [item 0054]: same 30 texts as item 0846.
OCC 4 [item 0055]: same 30 texts as item 0846.
OF 2 [item 0056]: same 30 texts as item 0846.

Extracts in:
Bêtes libres et prisonnières [item 0702]: Rapaces. Papillons. Les
   couleuvres. Chers bois! Deux cormorans. La truie. Jardin
   zoologique. Ecureuils.
Chats de Colette [items 0714-15]: Prrou. La mère chatte. Le
   matou. La Shah. Le naturaliste et la chatte. Poum. Le tentateur.
Chiens de Colette [items 0716-17]: La petite chienne à vendre.
   Exposition canine. Chiens sanitaires. La chienne trop petite.
   Poucette.
Colette [item 0060]: La petite chienne à vendre. La chienne bull
   [Poucette]. Poum. La mère chatte. Les chats-huants. La chienne
   trop petite. La petite truie de M. Rouzade. Bel-Gazou et Buck.
   Jardin zoologique. Les couleuvres. Ricotte. Conte pour les
   petits enfants des poilus. Les papillons.
Histoires pour Bel-Gazou, all eds.: Bel-Gazou et Buck. Le
   naturaliste et la chatte. La petite truie de M. Rouzade. La
   chienne bull. Ricotte. La chienne trop petite. Conte pour les
   petits enfants des poilus. Les papillons.
Morceaux choisis [item 0062]: La chienne jalouse. Le matou. Les
   chats-huants. Le tentateur.
Textes choisis de Colette [item 0065]: La petite truie de M.
   Rouzade. Le tentateur. Bel-Gazou et Buck.
Le Voyage égoïste [item 0898]: Automne.

Collection whose focus is announced in Colette's foreword to the
original edition and in her final essay, "La paix des bêtes": she
dreams that humans will soon cease to make war on animals.
Original edition includes all 12 texts of *Prrou, Poucette et quelques
autres*. Three texts borrowed from other works for the original

edition were dropped from this title for the *OCLF*: "Nonoche" [*Les Vrilles de la vigne*], "Chiens savants" and "Lola" [*L'Envers du music-hall*]. Tone varies from the playful to the poignant, and many different types of animals are portrayed. Colette's trend towards a more serious approach to the life and the plight of animals is evident when this collection is compared with the *Dialogues de bêtes*, published twelve years earlier. "Salivation psychique," in particular, is an early expression of her bitterness towards those who abuse animals, for she subtly calls for vengeance against scientists engaged in pavlovian experimentation. Colette's celebrated skill at reading the heart of animals is at its peak in this much-loved volume. "Automne" is re-titled "Octobre" in some editions.

Reviews:
Bulletin critique du livre français 16 (1961): 374.
Current Opinion 61 (Aug. 1916): 121-22.
Egoist 3 (1 May 1916): 68-69. Ciolkowski [Muriel Cialkowska].
Mercure de France, 1 June 1916, 501-2. Rachilde.
Revue 117 (15 Oct. 1916): 103-4. Nicolas Ségur.
Temps, 6 May 1916, 3. Paul Souday.
Times Literary Supplement, no. 756 (13 July 1916): 330.
Vogue 65 (15 Jan. 1925): 102. Rev. of *Cats, Dogs and I*.

English translations: American

0851 CATS, DOGS AND I: STORIES FROM 'LA PAIX CHEZ LES BETES.' Trans. Princess Alexandre Gagarine. New York: Henry Holt, 1924. 154p. Contains 21 texts: "Poum"--The Devil Cat. The Jealous Dog. Prrou--The Cat who had such a Sad Life. The Shah--The Persian Cat. The Tomcat. For Sale: A Little Dog. Too Small for a Dog. "Lola"--The White Bonjoi. Performing Dogs. Nonoche--A Cat and a Kitten. The Mother Cat. The Little Bulldog. Autumn. The Taxidermist and the Cat. The Zoological Garden. Ricotte--The Brazilian Squirrel. Snakes. The Man with the Fishes. Monsieur Rouzade's Little Pig. Politicians on the Old Lady and the Bear. Ambulance Dogs.

0852 "The Naturalist and the Cat." No translator. *Atlantic Monthly* 162 (Nov. 1938): 688-89.

xxxx "Creature Comfort." In *Creatures Great and Small* [items 0079-80]. Contains Colette's foreword and the 30 texts of item 0846: "Poum." The Jealous Bitch. "Prrou." Poucette." The She-Shah." The Tom-Cat. The Little Dog for Sale. The Dog who was Too Small. The Mother Cat. The Tempter. The French Bull-dog. October. The Cat and the Taxidermist. Zoological Garden. Ricotte. The Snakes. The Fish Man. The Tawny Owls. Monsieur Rouzade's Little Sow. The Butterflies. Dog Show. The Old Lady and the Bear. Live Birds and Insects. Autumn Salon. Salivation by Suggestion. The Circus Wrestlers. Bel-Gazou and Buck. Tale for the Soldiers' Little Ones. The Ambulance Dogs. A Truce for the Creatures.

Extracts in:
The Collected Stories of Colette [items 0071-72]: October.
Gigi and Selected Writings [item 0502]: The Old Lady and the Bear.

English translations: British

0853 "Mirette, the Story of a 'Too Little' Dog." [Collette (sic) Willy]. No translator. *Living Age* 300 (25 Jan. 1919): 235-36.

xxxx "Creature Comfort." In *Creatures Great and Small* [item 0081]: Same contents as American ed.

Extracts in *The Collected Stories of Colette* [items 0073-74]: October.

PARADIS TERRESTRE

0854 PARADIS TERRESTRE. [Colette and Izis]. Photographs Izis-Bidermanas. Lausanne: Clairefontaine, 1953. 130p. Contains four complete texts [La maison proche de la forêt. Le désert de Retz. Amertume. Paradis terrestre]. Quotations from the four texts are also used as captions for the many photographs; eight captions were specially written by Colette for this edition. All four texts are from *En pays connu*.

PARADIS TERRESTRES

0855 PARADIS TERRESTRES. Illus. Jouve. Lausanne: Gonin, 1932. 139p. Limited edition with magnificent full-page illustrations.

0856 PARADIS TERRESTRES. Postface Maurice Goudeket. Illus. Barye, Seurat, Bonnard, Picasso, Auberjonois. Lausanne: Mermod, 1961. 142p. The postface is of particular interest because it contains Colette's notes for these texts and others.

The 10 texts, which also appear in *Prisons et paradis* published the same year, depict as many types of animals: serpents, peacocks, squirrels, bulldogs, lizards, wild felines, owls, birds of prey, leopards and monkeys. Rarely frivolous in tone, they contain some of Colette's finest descriptive passages and demonstrate the high esteem in which she held all forms of animal life. This is a small collection of very high quality. Titles are: Serpents. Les paons. La panthère noire et les lions. Chats-huants. Léopards. Lézard. Chienne bull. Ecureuil. Singes. Rapaces.

PAYSAGES ET PORTRAITS

0857 PAYSAGES ET PORTRAITS. Paris: Flammarion, 1958. 275p.

0858 "Gastronomie." *A la page*, no. 2 (Aug. 1964): 196-200.

0859 PAYSAGES ET PORTRAITS. DERNIERS ECRITS. Geneva: Crémille, 1971. 243p. First title has same contents as item 0857.

Also in *OCC* 13 [item 0055].

Extracts in:
Album Masques: Colette [item 1057]: L'envers du cinéma.
Autobiographie... [items 0057-58].
Belles Saisons. Nudité. Mes cahiers. Paysages et portraits.
    Aventures quotidiennes. Item 0701: same texts as item 0857.
Colette: au cinéma [item 0980]: Films documentaires. L'envers du
    cinéma.
Cazals [item 1359]: 4 paragraphs from "L'envers du cinéma."
Mallet [item 1821]: Pour Francis Jammes.

Posthumous collection of pieces dating from 1909 to 1953, not
previously published in book form, and varying in importance.
Although portraits, anecdotes, speeches, radio talks, thematic
essays and notes from different years are presented with little regard
to chronology, they are grouped in a natural way according to type
or subject. "Le passé" is a good example of the restrained lyricism
with which Colette often expresses the favorite theme of her own
past. "L'envers du cinéma," written when she was making a film in
Rome in 1917, gives the reader an insight into the life of actors
and others involved in the making of silent movies. It has been re-
published several times [see section "Film Writing and Film
Criticism" for details]. The fact that Colette considered her
olfactory sense to be the most discerning of the five renders the
three passages comprising "Parfums" doubly interesting. "Colette
vous parle" is a series of talks made to French and American radio
listeners at the beginning of World War II. "Vie et mort du
phyllocactus," on the other hand, contains references to the *cactus
rose* so beloved by Sido in *La Naissance du jour*. Contents:
Préface. Le passé. Maternité. Mon amie Valentine [Mon amie
Valentine. La victime. Renoncement d'Alix]. Paysages [Dans la
dune. Printemps. France, le plus beau pays du monde. Flore et
faune de Paris et d'ailleurs. Décembre aux champs. L'hiver à
Rome]. Portraits [Pour Francis Jammes. Yvonne de Bray. Anglais
que j'ai connus. Un suicidé]. Danseuses [Isadora Duncan. Ida
Rubinstein. Matisse et ses danseuses]. Gastronomie. Parfums.
L'envers du cinéma. La poésie que j'aime. Colette vous parle.
Dernières pages [Dans le cyprès. Vie et mort du phyllocactus].
Notes.

Reviews:
Figaro littéraire, 13 Dec. 1958, 2. André Rousseaux.
Nouvelle Nouvelle Revue française 7 (1 Jan. 1959): 130-31. Roger Judrin.

English translations: American

Extracts in:
Colette at the Movies [item 0984]: Backstage at the Studio.
The Collected Stories of Colette [items 0071-72]: A Letter. The Sémiramis Bar. If I had a Daughter... Rites. Newly Shorn. Grape Harvest. In the Boudoir. Alix's Refusal. The Victim. Trans. Herma Briffault, Matthew Ward.
Earthly Paradise [items 0082, 0084-85]. Trans. Herma Briffault, Derek Coltman.
Flowers and Fruit [item 0090]: Flora and Fauna of Paris and Environs. December in the Fields. The Life and Death of the Phyllocactus.
The Other Woman [items 0794-95]: The Victim. My Friend Valentine.
Places [item 0098]: Rome in Winter. France, the Most Beautiful Country in the World.

English translations: British

Extracts in:
The Collected Stories of Colette [items 0073-74]: same contents as American ed.
Earthly Paradise [items 0087-89]: same contents as American ed.
Flowers and Fruit [item 0091]: same contents as American ed.
The Other Woman [items 0797-98]: same contents as American eds.
Places [item 0099]: same contents as American ed.

POUR MISSY

0860 POUR MISSY. [Madame Colette Willy]. Illus. Gustave Fraipont. Tours: n.p. [Deslis frères], 1908. 25p. Contents: Nuit blanche. Jour gris. Le dernier feu. Only one copy is known to have been printed, by Colette for the Marquise de Morny. The contents, which Colette published almost simultaneously in *Les Vrilles de la vigne*, are assumed to have been written for the Marquise, known as Missy. Not seen [source: *OP* 1, 1675].

POUR UN HERBIER

0861 POUR UN HERBIER. Lausanne: Mermod, 1948. 127p. Coll. du Bouquet 43.

0862 POUR UN HERBIER. Illus. Raoul Dufy. Lausanne: Mermod, 1951. 94p.

0863 "L'Orchidée." *Le Point*, no. 39 (May 1951): 46-48.

0864 POUR UN HERBIER: LES FLEURS ET LES SAISONS. Illus. Pia Roshardt. Lausanne: Clairefontaine, 1953. 108p. Not seen.

0865 POUR UN HERBIER. Illus. Manet. Lausanne: Mermod, 1955. 127p.

0866 POUR UN HERBIER. Illus. Manet. Lausanne: Mermod, 1955. 127p. Distr. Cercle du Bibliophile. Almost a miniature book, this is not the same edition as item 0865.

0867 POUR UN HERBIER. TRAIT POUR TRAIT. JOURNAL INTERMITTENT. Geneva: Crémille, 1971. 251p.

0868   POUR UN HERBIER. Presentation Pierre de Tartas. Illus. Jean
       Commère. Bièvres: Pierre de Tartas, 1972. 155p. Limited
       edition, each copy signed by Commère and Tartas.

       Also in:
       OCLF 14 [item 0054].
       OCC 11 [item 0055].

       Extracts in *Chiens de Colette* [items 0716-17]: Souci. Médicinales.

       All editions contain the same 22 essays on flowers. Treatment is
       varied, although style is conversational and even rambling. Often
       Colette describes the flower carefully, detailling nuances of form,
       colour, odour, movement and even taste. Sometimes she comments
       on its origins, its varieties, its traditions or her own experience of
       it. Her profound knowledge of and love for the subject are so
       apparent that the reader cannot help but become more informed.
       Illustrations are a great boon to most readers of this collection.
       Titles of essays are: La rose. Lys. Monologue du gardénia.
       Orchidée. Mœurs de la glycine. Tulipe. «Faust». Fétidité. Souci.
       Bleu. Le lackee et le pothos. Muguet. Camélia rouge. Jacinthe
       cultivée. Anémone. Broutilles. L'adonide chez la concierge.
       Jeannettes. Médicinales. L'arum pied-de-veau. Pavot. Ellébore.

       Reviews:
       Nouvelles littéraires, 3 Feb. 1949, 2. Robert Kemp.
       Times Literary Supplement, no. 3017 (25 Dec. 1959): 756.

       English   translations: American

0869   FOR A FLOWER ALBUM. Trans. Roger Senhouse. Illus. Manet.
       New York: David McKay, 1959. 70p. Contains same 22 essays
       as French editions. English titles are: Rose. Lily. The
       Gardenia's Monologue. Orchid. Habits of the Wistaria. Tulip.
       "Faust." Rankness. "Souci," or Marigold. Blue. *Lackee* and
       Pothos. Lily of the Valley. Red Camellia. Hyacinths.
       Anemone. Nibblings. *L'Adonide chez la Concierge*. Narcissi.
       Medicinal Herbs. Calfs'-foot Arum. Poppy. Hellebore.

       Also in *Flowers and Fruit* [item 0090] under title "For an
       Herbarium."

Extracts in *Gigi and Selected Writings* [item 0501]: Orchid.

English translations: British

0870 FOR A FLOWER ALBUM. Trans. Roger Senhouse. Illus. Manet.
London: Weidenfeld & Nicolson, 1959. 70p. Same contents as
American ed.

Also in *Flowers and Fruit* [item 0091] under title "For an
Herbarium."

PRISONS ET PARADIS

0871 PRISONS ET PARADIS. Paris: Ferenczi, 1932. 271p. Contains
39 texts: Serpents. Les paons. Ecureuil. Chienne bull. Lézard.
La panthère noire et les lions. Chats-huants. Rapaces. Léopards.
Singes. Première Treille muscate. Voyages. Le poisson au coup
de pied. Midi sévère. Treille muscate 1930. Vins. En
Bourgogne. Récriminations. Le feu sous la cendre. Trente-huit,
cinq. Puériculture. Rites. Déjeuner marocain. Sur l'«Eros».
Philippe Berthelot. Mistinguett. Chanel. Le procès Guillotin.
Landru. Pierre Faget, sorcier. Fleur du désert. Ahmed. Ouled-
Naïl. Le pionnier. L'audience du pacha. Fleurs. A une jeune
femme [5 passages]. Le coin du voile. Luxe [6 passages].

0872 [Extracts from "Le feu sous la cendre"]. In *L'Oustal*, by Jules
Malrieu, 169-71. Cahors: Les Amis du Vieux Figeac, 1932. In
the poems and commentary that make up the rest of his book
Malrieu occasionally addresses or mentions Colette. Reference
on title page to "Cahier de Colette" is misleading.

0873 "Le vin de Bourgogne." In *La Bourgogne vue par les artistes*. Paris:
Galerie d'Art du Bûcheron, 1933. [6p.]. Preface to a program
folder for an exhibition of art-work, photographs and household
articles, 16 May-30 June 1933. Final paragraphs of "En

Bourgogne" evoke an interesting picture of wine-making in Burgundy.

0874   PRISONS ET PARADIS. Paris: Ferenczi, 1935. 217p. Contains 41 texts, same as item 0871 but omitting 5 texts [Le procès Guillotin. Le pionnier. A une jeune femme. Le coin du voile. Luxe] and adding 7 texts from the *Deuxième cahier* [Marrakech. Le muet. Rabat. Lyautey. Fez. Sefrou. Dar-El Jamaï]. Also minor changes.

0875   "Le 'bas' de la France." [Voyages]. *Lisez-moi*, no. 391 (10 Aug. 1938): 176.

0876   PRISONS ET PARADIS. Illus. Clément Serveau. Paris: Ferenczi, 1939. 159p. Coll. Le Livre moderne illustré 310. Contains same 41 texts as item 0874.

0877   PRISONS ET PARADIS. Paris: Ferenczi, 1950. 223p. Contains same 41 texts as item 0874.

0878   "Pitiriki." [most of: Ecureuil]. In *Trente-six histoires de bêtes*, edited by Pierre Frémy, 123-27. Paris: Casterman, 1964.

0879   PRISONS ET PARADIS. NUDITÉ. Geneva: Crémille, 1970. 251p. First title contains same 41 texts as item 0874.

0880   PRISONS ET PARADIS. Paris: Hachette, 1973. 159p. Coll. Livre de poche 3499. Contains same 41 texts as item 0874.

0881   PRISONS ET PARADIS. Paris: Fayard, 1986. 159p. Contains same 41 texts as item 0874.

Also in:
OCLF 8 [item 0054]: same 41 texts as item 0874.
OCC 7 [item 0055]: same 41 texts as item 0874.

Extracts in:
Autobiographie... [items 0057-58]: Première Treille muscate. Vins. Récriminations. Landru. Fleur du désert. Lézard. Serpents. Léopards. Fleurs. Truffes.

Bêtes libres et prisonnières [item 0702]: Le paon. Rapaces. Les lézards. Léopards. Serpents. Singes. La panthère noire et les lions. Ecureuil.

Chats de Colette [items 0714-15]: Gris, gris et encore gris [from: Seconde Treille muscate].

Chiens de Colette [items 0716-17]: Chienne bull.

De la patte à l'aile [item 0723]: Lézard. Ecureuil.

Fleurs du désert [item 0806]: Marrakech. Le muet. Rabat. Lyautey. Fez. Sefrou. Dar-El Jamaï. Déjeuner marocain. L'audience du Pacha. Fleur du désert. Ahmed. Ouled-Naïl.

Morceaux choisis [item 0062]: Serpents. Les paons. Lézard. Léopards. Fleurs. Première Treille muscate [untitled extract].

Notes marocaines [item 0835]: Marrakech. Le muet. Rabat. Lyautey. Fez. Sefrou. Dar-El Jamaï. Déjeuner marocain. L'audience du Pacha. Fleur du désert. Ahmed. Ouled-Naïl.

Pages choisies [item 0063]: Midi sévère. Le poisson au coup de pied. Vins. Les paons. Rapaces. Lézard. Singes. Serpents.

Textes choisis de Colette [item 0065]: Fleur du désert. Rapaces. Les paons. Lézard. Serpents. Midi sévère. Le poisson au coup de pied. Le bas de la France.

Cardinal [item 1353]: Serpents [almost complete].

Articles written at different times and collected according to theme. Includes the 10 texts of *Paradis terrestres* and the 7 of *La Treille muscate*. "Le procès Guillotin" had been published earlier in *Dans la foule* under the title "A Tours," and 7 others [Marrakech. Le muet. Rabat. Lyautey. Fez. Sefrou. Dar-El Jamaï] had appeared in the *Deuxième cahier* before being added to this collection. Title refers to the first ten essays in which Colette depicts animals she has known, including some in zoos, and describes places she has loved, such as her summer home at Saint Tropez as well as areas visited in North Africa. Includes wonderful portraits of animals, and cutting remarks about humanity's deficient behaviour towards them. Texts on wine, cooking, flowers, illness and yachts fill out the volume, along with reports of trials and portraits of celebrities. Contains some lyrical passages and much description, replete with imagery that dramatically evokes Colette's own sensory experience. "Treille muscate 1930" is titled "Seconde Treille muscate" in some editions.

Reviews:
Action française, 25 Aug. 1932, 3. Robert Brasillach. Also in
　　Œuvres complètes de Robert Brasillach, vol. 11, 302-3. Paris:
　　Club de l'honnête homme, 1964.
Journal des débats 39 (9 Sept. 1932): 436-38. Henry Bidou.
Mercure de France, 1 Dec. 1932, 414-15. John Charpentier.

English translations: American

Extracts in:
Earthly Paradise [items 0082, 0084-85]: La Treille muscate.
　　Recriminations. Wines. Truffles. Landru. Desert Flower. A
　　Lizard. Leopards. Snakes. Flowers. Trans. Derek Coltman.
Flowers and Fruit [item 0090]: Secrets [Le procès Guillotin].
Places [item 0098]: In Burgundy. La Treille Muscate I. La Treille
　　Muscate 1930. Algeria [Desert Flower. Ahmed. Ouled-Naïl].
　　Morocco [Moroccan Notebook: Marrakesh. The Mute. Rabat.
　　Lyautey. Fez. Sefrou. A Moroccan Luncheon. Dar-el-Jamaï.
　　The Pasha's Audience].

English translations: British

Extracts in:
Earthly Paradise [items 0087-89]: same contents as American ed.
Flowers and Fruit [item 0091]: same contents as American ed.
Places [item 0099]: same contents as American ed.

PRROU, POUCETTE ET QUELQUES AUTRES

0882　PRROU, POUCETTE ET QUELQUES AUTRES. [Colette
　　　　Willy]. Paris: Librairie des lettres, 1913. 105p. These 12 short
　　　　pieces about cats and dogs demonstrate that Colette's approach
　　　　to the portrayal of animals had begun to change well before the
　　　　beginning of World War I. Often playful or light in tone,
　　　　sometimes in form of dialogue or monologue in which the

animals speak, they demonstrate Colette's growing concern for animal welfare and her capacity to adopt their point of view. Two serious essays, "Chiens savants" and "Lola," depict the often unhappy lot of music-hall animals and were incorporated into *L'Envers du music-hall*, published the same year. Contents: Prrou. Poum. Poucette. La chienne jalouse. La Shâh. La petite chienne à vendre. Le matou. La chienne trop petite. Lola. Chiens savants. La mère chatte. Le tentateur. The entire collection was transferred to *La Paix chez les bêtes* in 1916.

Review:
Nouvelle Revue française 5 (1 July 1913): 155-58. Edouard Dolléans.

QUATRE SAISONS

0883 QUATRE SAISONS [On cover: *Quatre-Saisons*]. Paris: Philippe Ortiz, 1925. 49p. Private edition containing 12 articles first published in *Vogue* from Dec. 1924 to Dec. 1925. Represents journalism at its finest. Texts are personal in tone, yet elegantly written. Many contain fine descriptive passages. Subjects vary, but recurring theme is Paris fashion. Colette sometimes expresses disapproval of the fashions of 1925. In "Mannequins" she displays an interest in the psychology of models, while "Poil et plume" is a bitter invective against hunters and others who make animals suffer. Entire contents were transferred to *Le Voyage égoïste* in 1928. Texts are: Cadeaux de Noël. Visites. Printemps de demain. Adieu à la neige. Mannequins. Elégance, économie? Voyages. Jardins prisonniers. Vacances... Vendangeuses. Poil et plume. Les joyaux menacés.

REGARDE

0884   REGARDE. [Colette and Méheut]. Illus. Méheut. Paris: J.-G. Deschamps, 1929. Non-pag. [19 pages of text]. Contains two essays, "Regarde..." and "La flaque." The first focuses on Colette's famous invocation to look at the world, since "To look is to learn." Difference between the child's way of seeing and the adult's way is also analyzed. Second essay portrays vividly the myriad forms of life in pools made by the sea. Also in *Autres Bêtes*, all eds.

REVERIE DE NOUVEL AN

0885   REVERIE DE NOUVEL AN. Introd. Marcel Sauvage. Illus. Creixams. Paris: Stock, 1923. 64p. Coll. Les Contemporains 8.

0886   "Rêverie de Nouvel An." [Extract]. *Lisez-moi*, no. 352 (25 Dec. 1936): 902.

0887   REVERIE DE NOUVEL AN. Illus. Michel Terrasse. Paris: Les Centraux bibliophiles, 1963. 95p.

Six pieces dating from as early as 1911. Individual titles are: Rêverie de Nouvel An. Malade. Dimanche. Répit. J'ai chaud. Convalescence. Title essay is a poetic evocation of the snow, of a New Year spent in solitude in nature; includes meditative passages on childhood and the passing of time. The other five follow the course of a fever to its cure. Good example of Colette's early meditative and descriptive style. All six pieces had appeared in *La Chambre éclairée* in 1920, and four of them [Malade. Dimanche. Répit. J'ai chaud] had also been published in *Le Voyage égoïste* in 1922. The title essay was eventually moved to *Les Vrilles de la vigne*.

SEPT DIALOGUES DE BETES

See *Dialogues de bêtes.*

SPLENDEUR DES PAPILLONS

0888 SPLENDEUR DES PAPILLONS. Selection and composition of illustrations Dr. Hans Zbinden. Paris: Plon, 1936. 36p. Coll. Iris. Reminiscences about the butterfly collection of Colette's two brothers, liberally sprinkled with erudite references to the several species of the order *lepidoptera*, especially their unique features and their beauty, and ending with a short passage on the butterflies of Provence. The text has no direct connection with the magnificent full-page illustrations, which show exotic butterflies so splendid that they actually upstage Colette's fascinating text. Also in *Journal à rebours*, under the text's title "Papillons."

TRAIT POUR TRAIT

0889 TRAIT POUR TRAIT. Paris: Le Fleuron, 1949. 131p. Collection of 15 word portraits. Individual titles in original edition: Claude Debussy. Marcel Proust. La comtesse de Noailles. Léon-Paul Fargue: le nocturne. Léon-Paul Fargue: la dernière soirée. Courteline. Sarah Bernhardt. Emma Calvé. Marguerite Moreno. Luc-Albert Moreau. Daragnès. Dignimont. Vertès. Camoin. A propos de Madame Marneffe. The last essay is less a portrait than it is a comment on the characters and fashions of Balzac's world. For the *OCLF*, the essay on Moreno and the second one on Fargue were deleted, for incorporation into *Le Fanal bleu*, and five more portraits added [André Maginot. Prélude pour Mondor. Polaire. Nigg. Christian Bérard]. The portraits of Nigg and Mondor had previously served as prefaces to publications by others. Some of the subjects portrayed were well-known to Colette personally, others only through their art. Colette excels at the portrait, and tends to evoke the presence of the subject, rather than to describe it fully. She often seizes on a physical feature, a gesture, a way of speaking or a behavioral characteristic to express the personality. Sometimes she interprets the person through his or her work. Because of the large number of artists portrayed, some idea of Colette's views on art can be gleaned here.

0890   "Marcel Proust." *Le Point*, no. 39 (May 1951): 43.

0891   "Marcel Proust." *Livres de France* 5 (Oct. 1954): 9.

0892   [Luc-Albert Moreau: extract]. In *Luc-Albert Moreau*, 2-3. Paris: Maison de la Pensée française, 1954. Publicity piece for exhibition of Moreau's work.

0893   [Two untitled prefaces]. In *Rencontres*, by Léon-Paul Fargue, 3-4, 5-7. Illus. Daragnès and Dunoyer de Segonzac. Paris: Mme Daragnès, 1954. Book of reminiscences by Fargue, reserved for friends of Daragnès. Colette's contribution consists of a passage from "Léon-Paul Fargue: le nocturne" followed by "Daragnès."

Also in:
OCLF 14 [item 0054]: see annotation for contents.
OCC 11 [item 0055]: same contents as in *OCLF*.
En pays connu [items 0754-55]: same contents as in *OCLF*.
En pays connu. Trait pour trait. Journal intermittent. La Fleur de l'âge. [*A portée de la main.*] Item 0757: same contents as in *OCLF*.
Pour un herbier. Trait pour trait. Journal intermittent. Item 0867: same contents as in *OCLF*.

Extracts in:
Autobiographie... [items 0057-58]: Sarah Bernhardt. Claude Debussy. André Maginot.
Lettres à ses pairs, all eds.: La comtesse de Noailles. Prélude pour Mondor. Léon-Paul Fargue: le nocturne. Léon-Paul Fargue: la dernière soirée.

English translations: American

Extracts in *Earthly Paradise* [items 0082, 0084-85]: Sarah Bernhardt. Claude Debussy. André Maginot. Trans. Derek Coltman.

English translations: British

Extracts in *Earthly Paradise* [items 0087-89]: same contents as American eds.

LA TREILLE MUSCATE

0894 LA TREILLE MUSCATE. Illus. Dunoyer de Segonzac. Paris: Aimé Jourde, 1932. 92p. Limited luxury edition. Contents: Première Treille muscate. Vins. Voyages. Le poisson au coup de pied. Fleurs. Seconde Treille muscate.

0895 LA TREILLE MUSCATE. Illus. Marianne Clouzot. Paris: Marcel Lubineau, 1955. 67p. Contents: Première Treille muscate. Voyages. Midi sévère. Seconde Treille muscate.

0896 LA TREILLE MUSCATE. Illus. Dunoyer de Segonzac. Lausanne: Mermod, 1956. 109p. Contents: Première Treille muscate. Voyages. Vins. Le poisson au coup de pied. Fleurs. Seconde Treille muscate. Midi sévère.

0897 LA TREILLE MUSCATE. Illus. Constantin Térechkovitch. Paris: R. Léger, 1961. 95p. Contents: Première Treille muscate. Voyages. Vins. Le poisson au coup de pied. Fleurs. Seconde Treille muscate. Also contains a short passage by Dunoyer de Segonzac, "Une journée de Colette à 'La Treille muscate'," recalling Colette's activities during the time he knew her at Saint Tropez. A brief "Lettre à Colette" by Jean Cocteau reminisces about his friendship with her at Saint Tropez and at the Palais Royal.

Volumes bearing this title vary in content. However, the four core essays portray Colette at her summer home at Saint Tropez, which she acquired in 1926 and which she named after the climbing vine on the premises. "Première Treille muscate" evokes, for all the senses, the area around her new property and the plant life there. "Voyages" enumerates the charms of Provence, which Colette had come to know only during her music-hall days. In "Midi sévère" she mentally wanders through the area away from the port, a region still unknown to the many tourists who had by 1930 begun to invade the coast. And in "Seconde Treille muscate" she summarizes the changes that the climate has wrought to her property in the years since she first purchased it. This essay concludes with a marvellous portrait of Colette's last cat, model for the novel of the same name, *La Chatte*. Together, the four essays constitute a worth-while document on an important period of Colette's life and witness her extraordinary ability to conjure up, in the imagination of her readers, a landscape or milieu that she herself knows well. Additional texts are peripheral to the theme. All 7 texts of item 0896 were incorporated into *Prisons et paradis*.

LE VOYAGE EGOÏSTE

0898   LE VOYAGE EGOÏSTE. [Colette (Colette Willy)]. Illus. Charles Guérin. Paris: Edouart Pelletan-Helleu & Sergent, 1922. 115p. Contains 12 texts: Répit. Dimanche. A l'aube. Le retour des bêtes. Malade. Griefs. J'ai chaud. Un soir. Automne. Sommeil. Réveillons. La nuit paisible.

0899   *Poèmes intimes de Colette* 1: "J'ai chaud." Paris: Durand, 1927. 7p. Passage set to music for voice and piano by Albert Wolff.

0900   *Poèmes intimes de Colette* 3: "Répit." Paris: Durand, 1927. 7p. Passage set to music for voice and piano by Albert Wolff.

0901   LE VOYAGE EGOÏSTE. QUATRE SAISONS. Paris: Ferenczi, 1928. 219p. Contains 29 texts: Dimanche. J'ai chaud. Répit. Malade. Cadeaux de Noël. Visites. Printemps de demain. Adieu

0934   "Les vrilles de la vigne." [Extracts]. In *Contemporary French Fiction*, edited by Irene Cornwall, 28-29. New York: Holt, 1940.

0935   LES VRILLES DE LA VIGNE. Illus. Hervé Baille. Paris: La Nouvelle France, 1949. Contains same 20 texts as item 0930. Not seen.

0936   "Belles-de-jour." In *Les Vingt meilleures nouvelles françaises*, edited by Alain Bosquet, 349-56. Paris: Seghers, 1956.

0937   "Belles-de-jour." *Jours de France*, no. 406 (Aug. 1962): 26-31.

0938   LES VRILLES DE LA VIGNE. DOUZE DIALOGUES DE BETES. AUTRES BETES. Geneva: Crémille, 1969. 247p. Contains 17 texts, same as item 0930 less: Toby-Chien parle. Dialogue de bêtes. Le miroir.

0939   "La dame qui chante." In *Choix de nouvelles modernes*. Munich: Deutscher Taschenbuch, 1978. Not seen.

Also in:
OP 1 [item 0053]: same 20 texts as item 0930 plus: Toby-chien et la musique. Printemps de la Riviera.
OCLF 3 [item 0054]: same 17 texts as item 0939.
OCC 3 [item 0055]: same 17 texts as item 0939.
Colette par Colette [item 0061]: same 20 texts as item 0930.
Sido. Les Vrilles de la vigne. Item 0217: same 20 texts as item 0930.
Sido. Les Vrilles de la vigne. Item 0220: same 20 texts as item 0930.

Extracts in:
Autobiographie... [items 0057-58]: Les vrilles de la vigne. Nuit blanche. Revêrie de nouvel an. Also fragments.
Bêtes libres et prisonnières [item 0702]: Le rouge-gorge. Le rossignol. Oiseaux de mer et de marais. La guêpe. Papillons.
Chiens de Colette [items 0716-17]: En guise d'introduction. Poucette et la bergère flamande. Poucette. La chienne qui mérita de revenir.
Colette [item 0060]: Jour gris. En marge d'une plage blanche [En baie de Somme]. Le dernier feu.

Histoires pour Bel-Gazou, all eds: Le dernier feu.
Morceaux choisis [item 0062]: Le dernier feu. Jour gris [extract].
 Rêverie de nouvel an [extract].
Pages choisies [item 0063]: En baie de Somme. Le rossignol. Le
 pays que j'ai quitté. Le dernier feu.
Les Plus Belles Pages de Colette [item 0064]: Nonoche. Jour gris.
 La guérison.
Sido et souvenirs d'enfance [item 0218]: Le pays que j'ai quitté.
Textes choisis de Colette [item 0065]: Les vrilles de la vigne. Jour
 gris. Le dernier feu. La guérison. Rêverie de nouvel an. Le
 miroir.
Beaumont and Parinaud [item 1063].
Castex and Surer [item 1358], 101-11: Forêt de Crécy [extract from
 "En baie de Somme"].
Collet [item 1424]: Les vrilles de la vigne. Jour gris. En baie de
 Somme. [All extracts].
Thoraval [item 2156]: Le dernier feu [extracts].

A total of 22 texts have appeared in collections bearing this title,
but never more than 20 in a volume. Title is taken from the
leading essay in which the story of a nightingale struggling to
escape from a vine in which it has became enmeshed while
sleeping becomes an allegory for Colette's own life. Especially rich
in the painting of sensations are "Chanson de la danseuse," "Nuit
blanche" and "Jour gris," which deal with love and with nostalgia,
and "La dame qui chante," which offers a magnificent description of
the psychological effects of auditory sensations. "Le dernier feu"
contains passages often studied in courses on style. "Belles-de-
jour," "De quoi est-ce qu'on a l'air" and "La guérison" star Colette's
fictional friend, Valentine, and lightly mock the follies of the life
of an upper-class woman. Other pieces feature descriptions of
landscapes and animals. "Rêverie de Nouvel An," added to the
collection only in 1934, had been published previously in book
form under its own title as well as in *La Chambre éclairée* in 1920.
"Nonoche" has appeared in many editions of *La Paix chez les bêtes*.
"Dialogue de bêtes" and "Toby-Chien parle" were transferred to
Douze dialogues de bêtes in 1930. The collection is a favorite
source for the selection of brief passages to be used in anthologies
and style manuals.

Reviews:
Marges, March 1909, 126-32. Louise Lalanne [Guillaume
Apollinaire].
Times Literary Supplement, no. 364 (31 Dec. 1908): 498.

English translations: American

Extracts in:
The Collected Stories of Colette [items 0071-72]: Morning
Glories. What Must We Look Like? The Cure. Sleepless
Nights. Gray Days. The Last Fire. A Fable: The Tendrils of the
Vine. Trans. Herma Briffault, Matthew Ward.
Earthly Paradise [items 0082, 0084-85]: The Tendrils of the Vine.
Night Without Sleep. A New Year Reverie. Also fragments.
Trans. Herma Briffault, Derek Coltman.

English translations: British

Extracts in:
The Collected Stories of Colette [0073-74]: same contents as
American eds.
Earthly Paradise [items 0087-89]: same contents as American eds.

THEATER AND SPECTACLE

CHÉRI

0940 CHÉRI. [Colette and Léopold Marchand]. Paris: Librairie théâtrale, 1922. 217p.

0941 CHÉRI. [Colette and Léopold Marchand]. *Paris-Théâtre*, no. 49 (1951): 1-40. Revised version. Includes some press notices.

0942 CHÉRI. [Colette and Léopold Marchand]. *Avant-Scène théâtre*, no. 708 (15 April 1982): 13-41. Special issue also includes press notices, appreciations, and other documentation.

Also in:
OCLF 15 [item 0054]: revised version.
OCC 13 [item 0055]: revised version.
Théâtre: En camarades. Chéri. Item 0948: revised version.

Extracts in *OP* 2 [item 0053].

Original four-act play was first performed in Paris at the Théâtre Michel, 13 Dec. 1921. Its framework diverges from the novel of the same name in several important ways. In Act I, Léa learns from

Charlotte that Chéri and Edmée are to be married, whereas in the opening scene of the novel she is already aware of it. Secondly, Edmée plays a more visible and dramatic role in the play than she does in the novel. Thirdly, a completely new character, Masseau, appears in several scenes. Finally, as one might expect, the conversation contains a good deal more verbal thrust than in the novel. The effect of the loss of the novel's descriptive passages is immediately noted, for neither Léa's nor Chéri's character is as fully delineated as in the novel, their psychology being less complex and less subtle. Indeed, the two lovers seem much more banal than in the original work. Despite these apparent weaknesses, the play has remained popular in both the French and the English versions, and even with international audiences. Colette herself took the role of Léa for many performances from 1922 to 1926. A revised version was first performed at the Théâtre de la Madeleine, 30 Oct. 1949.

Reviews:
Arts & Decoration 23 (July 1925): 47, 66. Allan Ross MacDougall.
Cahiers d'occident 2 (July 1928): 112-14. François Mauriac.
Figaro magazine, no. 151 (6 March 1982): 44. Jean-Jacques Gautier.
France-Illustration, no. 214 (19 Nov. 1949): 567-68. Yves Gandon.
Hispano Americano 55 (19 May 1969): 58. A.M.E. [Antonio Magaña Esquival].
Journal des débats, 19 Dec. 1921, 1-2. Henry Bidou.
Lettres françaises, 3 Nov. 1949, 7. Elsa Triolet. Also in *Chroniques théâtrales: Les Lettres françaises 1948-1951*, 122-23. Paris: Gallimard, 1981.
Marges, 15 Jan. 1922, 57-61. Claude Berton.
Mercure de France, 1 June 1926, 427-30. André Rouveyre.
Monde, 25 March 1969, 19. B. Poirot-Delpech.
Monde, 27 June 1973, 15. Colette Godard.
Monde, 2 Feb. 1982, 13. Michel Cournot.
Mondo, 3 June 1950, 10. Bergotte.
Mondo, 8 Dec. 1951, 11. Corrado Alvaro.
Nation 189 (7 Nov. 1959): 339. Harold Clurman.
New Republic 141 (26 Oct. 1959): 19-20. Robert Brustein.
Nouvelle Revue des deux mondes, no. 3 (March 1982): 691-95. Philippe Sénart.
Nouvelles littéraires, 27 Oct. 1949, 8. Claude Cézan.

Nouvelles littéraires, 10 Nov. 1949, 8. René Lalou.

Observer, no. 8276 (15 Jan. 1950): 6. Janet Flanner.

Ord och Bild 60:3 (1951): 148-50. Holger Ahlenius.

Revue de Paris 32 (15 April 1925): 897-99. Gérard d'Houville.

Revue de Paris 33 (1 April 1926): 691-92. Albert Flament.

Revue des hommes et mondes, no. 41 (Dec. 1949): 604. Bernard Simiot.

Sabato, 24 Nov. 1951. Silvio d'Amico. Also in *Palcoscenico del Dopoguerra*, vol. 2, 268-71. Turin: Edizioni Radio Italiana, 1953.

Vie des peuples, no. 62 (June 1925): 343-47. Maurice Courtois-Suffit.

English version: American

0943 CHÉRI. [Colette and Anita Loos]. Based on the novels *Chéri* and *The Last of Chéri*. New York: David McKay, 1959. 75p. Not seen.

LE CIEL DE LIT

0944 LE CIEL DE LIT. *France-Illustration (supplément théâtral et littéraire)*, no. 144 (Dec. 1953): 1-26. Includes sample of press notices.

0945 LE CIEL DE LIT. *Œuvres libres*, no. 318 (Jan. 1954): 257-308.

Adaptation in French by Colette of Jan de Hartog's *The Four Poster*. Dated but amusing sentimental three-act comedy, the story of a happy marriage. The French version was first performed in Paris at the Théâtre de la Michodière, 14 April 1953.

Review:
Revue française de l'élite européenne, no. 243 (June 1971): 49. Yves Florenne.

LA DÉCAPITÉE

First published in *Deuxième cahier de Colette* [item 0830], then in
Mes Cahiers [item 0833], before being grouped with Colette's
other theater writing in the *OCLF*.

Also in:
OCLF 15 [item 0054].
OCC 13 [item 0055].
La Vagabonde. La Décapitée. L'Enfant et les sortilèges. Item 0968.

Described as a *féerie-ballet* by Colette, this one-act melodramatic
fantasy was written in 1908 but never had a public performance.
The sultan's wife seeks diversion while awaiting her lord's return
from the hunt. Hearing a flute, she commands her slaves to bring
the musician to her. Finding him a handsome young man and
succumbing to the spell his music casts, she embraces him. When
the sultan arrives, the musician hides, but his audacity leads to
discovery and both he and the wife are quickly slain. To the sultan's
horror, the woman's dead body arises and dances. Overcome with
grief, he laments the loss of the woman he still loves.

EN CAMARADES

0946   EN CAMARADES. *Le Monde illustré, théâtral et littéraire*, no. 13
       (15 Nov. 1947): 1-15.

0947   THÉATRE: EN CAMARADES. CHÉRI. Geneva: Crémille,
       1971. 237p.

Also in:
OCLF 15 [item 0054].
OCC 13 [item 0055].
Mitsou, some eds.

Light two-act comedy first performed at the Théâtre des Arts in Paris on 22 Jan. 1909, with Colette in the principal role. A young couple committed to an open marriage discover that they prefer fidelity. The names of the characters--Max, Marthe, Fanchette--as well as Fanchette's *petite fille* relationship with Max echo elements of Colette's earliest novels, especially *Claudine en ménage*.

Reviews:
Figaro magazine, 6 July 1985, 30. Jacques Nerson.
Mercure de France, 16 Feb. 1909, 725. André Fontainas.

L'ENFANT ET LES SORTILEGES

0948 L'ENFANT ET LES SORTILEGES. Paris: Durand, 1925. 26p. Text only.

0949 L'ENFANT ET LES SORTILEGES. Paris: Durand, 1925. 212p. Text and music.

0950 L'ENFANT ET LES SORTILEGES. Paris: Durand, 1925. 101p. Text and music.

0951 L'ENFANT ET LES SORTILEGES. Paris: Durand, 1932. 49p. Includes both French and English texts. English translation [*The Bewitched Child*] by Kathleen Wolff.

0952 L'ENFANT ET LES SORTILEGES. Illus. Michel Terrasse. Paris: Ed. d'Aude, 1949. Not seen.

0953 L'ENFANT ET LES SORTILEGES. Illus. Adrienne Ségur. Paris: Flammarion, 1967. 38p. Children's picture book.

Also in:
OCLF 15 [item 0054].
OCC 13 [item 0055].
La Vagabonde. La Décapitée. L'Enfant et les sortilèges. Item 0968.

Celebrated fantasy set to music by Maurice Ravel, performed for the first time at the Théâtre de Monte-Carlo in March 1925, then at the Opéra-Comique in Paris. A badly-behaved child, given to acts of destruction and cruelty, falls asleep and dreams that his victims, both animals and inanimate objects, speak. When he assists an injured squirrel, they recognize that he is not completely wicked, and he becomes aware of the benefits that kindness can bring.

Reviews:
Bulletin of the Center for Children's Books 19 (April 1966): 128.
Childhood Education 43 (Sept. 1966): 44. S.H. [Selah Horner].
Courrier musical et théâtral 27 (15 April 1925): 217-18. Ch. Tenroc.
Eclaireur de Nice, 23 March 1925, 7. Henri Madel.
Journal de Monaco, 24 March 1925, 4. A.C. [André Corneau].
Library Journal 91 (1 Jan. 1966): 418.
Listener 74 (28 Oct. 1965): 680. Rollo Myers.
Ménéstral 87 (3 April 1925): 166-67. Xavier Lion.
Mercure de France, 15 March 1926, 701-4. Jean Marnold.
Mercure de France, 15 July 1939, 461-65. René Dumesnil.
Musique et théâtre, 15 April 1925, 5. Arthur Honegger.
Revue des deux mondes 52 (1 Aug. 1939): 701-3. Louis Laloy.
Revue musicale, 1 April 1925, 105-9. Henry Prunières.
Saturday Review 48 (11 Dec. 1965): 45. Alice Dalgliesh.
Times Literary Supplement, no. 3274 (26 Nov. 1964): 1080.
Virginia Kirkus Service 33 (15 Nov. 1965): 1155.
Washington Post Book Week 3 (22 May 1966): 10. Maurice Sendak.

English translation: American

0954 THE BOY AND THE MAGIC. Trans. Christopher Fry. Illus. Gerald Hoffnung. New York: Putnam's, 1965. [32p.].

English translation: British

0955 THE BOY AND THE MAGIC. Trans. Christopher Fry. Illus. Gerald Hoffnung. London: Dennis Dobson, 1964. [32p.].

See also item 0951.

GIGI

0956 GIGI. [Adaptation Pierre Laroche]. Paris: Opéra, 1949. 30p. Not seen.

0957 GIGI. [Colette and Anita Loos]. *France-Illustration (supplément théâtral et littéraire)*, no. 158 (1954): 1-29.

0958 GIGI. [Colette and Anita Loos]. *Œuvres libres* 325 (Aug. 1954): 239-308.

0959 GIGI. [Colette and Anita Loos]. *Avant-Scène Théâtre*, no. 759-60 (1 Dec. 1984): 30-64. Includes notes by Claude Pichois and by Jean Meyer.

First performance of the French version took place in Paris at the Théâtre des Arts, 22 Feb. 1954, with Evelyne Ker in the title role. This two-act version, the product of Colette's collaboration with Anita Loos, follows Colette's novel closely, except that the ambiguous ending of the novel is made specific: in the stage play, Gaston asks for Gigi's hand in marriage and she accepts. The philosophy and life-style of the major characters may displease some modern spectators, as is the case with the novel. However, Gigi herself is charming, and it is probably for this reason that the play has for so long been a great favorite with the general public on both sides of the Atlantic. First U.S. performance of the English adaptation by Anita Loos was at New York's Fulton Theatre, 24 Nov. 1950, with Audrey Hepburn in the title role. First British performance was at the Theatre Royal in Brighton, 9 April 1956.

Reviews:
Figaro littéraire, 27 Feb. 1954, 12. Jacques Lemarchand.
Figaro magazine, 13 April 1985, 26. Pierre Marcabru.
Figaro magazine, 11 May 1985, 62. Jean-Jacques Gautier.
Hispano Americano 65 (19 Aug. 1974): 60. A.M.E. [Antonio Magaña Esquival].
Illustrated London News 228 (9 June 1956): 704. J.C. Trewin.
Life 28 (3 April 1950): 71-76.
Life 31 (10 Dec. 1951): 103-7.

Mondo, 3 June 1950, 10. Bergotte.
Mondo, 10 May 1955, 15. Nicola Chiaromonte.
Nation 173 (15 Dec. 1951): 530-31. Joseph Wood Krutch.
Ord och Bild 61:7 (1952): 431. Holger Ahlenius.
Punch, 12 May 1976, 866. Sheridan Morley.
Revue des deux mondes 17 (July 1985): 203-5. Philippe Sénart.

English versions: American

0960 GIGI. [Anita Loos from the novel by Colette]. New York: Random House, 1952. 169p.

0961 GIGI. [Anita Loos from the novel by Colette]. *Théâtre Arts* 36 (July 1952): 41-69. Includes background article by Gilbert Miller.

0962 GIGI. [Anita Loos from the novel by Collette (sic)]. New York: Samuel French, 1953. 104p. Acting edition.

English version: British

0963 GIGI. [Colette and Anita Loos]. London: Samuel French [1953]. 75p. French's Acting Edition 260.

LA SECONDE

0964 LA SECONDE. [Colette and Léopold Marchand]. *Paris-Théâtre*, no. 49 (1951): 41-80. Four-act play first performed in Paris at the Théâtre de la Madeleine, 23 Jan. 1951. Follows the novel fairly closely but the long passages in which Fanny ponders the crisis in her life are necessarily externalized, with the result that her character is less delicately portrayed and less appealing.

0965 LA SECONDE. [Renaud de Jouvenel, based on the version by Colette and Léopold Marchand]. Cannes: Renaud de Jouvenel,

1982. 83p. Diverges considerably from both the novel and the previous dramatic version. For instance, Jane is now called Jeanne, Fanny is interested in money, and Jean is old enough to be completely independent. In fact, Colette's original work can scarcely be detected in Jouvenel's version. In his introduction, where he states that the changes are intended to up-date the play, Renaud de Jouvenel identifies himself with Jean, and his father, Henry de Jouvenel, with Farou. Never performed.

Reviews:
Lettres françaises, 25 Jan. 1951, 7. Elsa Triolet. Also in *Chroniques théâtrales: Les Lettres françaises 1948-1951*, 229-33. Paris: Gallimard, 1981.
Fiera letteraria, 4 Nov. 1951, 8. Roberto Rebora.

LA VAGABONDE

0966 LA VAGABONDE. [Mme Colette and Léopold Marchand]. *La Petite Illustration*, no. 141 (14 April 1923): 1-38.

0967 LA VAGABONDE. [Colette and Léopold Marchand]. Paris: Flammarion, 1923. 248p.

0968 THEATRE: LA VAGABONDE. LA DÉCAPITÉE. L'ENFANT ET LES SORTILEGES. Geneva: Crémille, 1971. 247p. Revised version containing prologue and three acts.

Also in:
OCLF 15 [item 0054]: revised version of prologue and 3 acts.
OCC 13 [item 0055]: same version as in *OCLF*.

First performed at the Théâtre de la Renaissance in Paris, 20 Feb. 1923. Because the long meditations and soul-searching of this novel do not lend themselves well to the theater, this play departs significantly from its original. The first act, which Colette reduced to a prologue in the later version, dramatically portrays the rupture between Renée and her first husband, Adolphe Taillandy; the rupture has already taken place when the novel opens. In both the first and second acts, Margot is the recipient of confidences that in the novel Renée expresses mostly to herself. In the final scene, Max arrives in Marseilles and decides to follow Renée's tour, since he sees that she has become attached to her new profession; on stage, he is thus portrayed as much more liberal-minded than in the novel. For the later version, which underwent much revision, Colette changed the ending to reflect the novel's, so that the rupture between the lovers seems final.

Reviews:
Vie des peuples, no. 62 (June 1925): 343-47. Maurice Courtois-
    Suffit.

THEATER CRITICISM

0969 LA JUMELLE NOIRE: une année de critique dramatique. Paris: Ferenczi, 1934. 285p. Criticism from Oct. 1933 to June 1934.

0970 LA JUMELLE NOIRE: deuxième année de critique dramatique. Paris: Ferenczi, 1935. 265p. Criticism from Oct. 1934 to May 1935.

0971 LA JUMELLE NOIRE: troisième année de critique dramatique. Paris: Ferenczi, 1937. 217p. Criticism from Sept. 1935 to July 1936.

0972 LA JUMELLE NOIRE: quatrième année de critique dramatique. Paris: Ferenczi, 1938. 223p. Criticism from Oct. 1936 to July 1937.

0973 LA JUMELLE NOIRE. 3 vols. Geneva: Crémille, 1970. Consists of items 0969-72 plus criticism to June 1938.

0974 "Inédit: critique dramatique." *Cahiers Colette*, no. 1 (1977): 19-25. Review of *L'Accroche-cœur* by Sacha Guitry, which opened at the Théâtre de l'Etoile in Paris, 6 May 1924. Includes fac-simile of the article in manuscript.

0975 "Maurice Chevalier." *Cahiers Colette*, no. 2 (1980): 45-48. Colette declares her admiration for Chevalier's stage presence and for his self-discipline.

0976 "Le second article de Colette sur 'Les Cenci': 'Le spectacle à voir'." In *Artaud vivant*, by Odette Virmaux and Alain Virmaux, 203-6. Paris: Nouvelles Eds. Oswald, 1980. Presents review first published in 1935 but deemed lost or non-existent until recently discovered among Colette's papers. Artaud referred to it in an article of his own, citing Colette's enthusiasm for his play in the face of general hostility. The first article to which the title indirectly alludes was collected in *La Jumelle noire* and is less partisan.

0977 "Critiques pour 'Sélection de la vie artistique'." *Europe*, no. 631-32 (Nov.-Dec. 1981): 146-86. Nineteen newly-discovered reviews, written during the first half of 1935 for the short-lived *Sélection de la vie artistique*. Each one urges the reader to see a play, in a "pick-of-the-week" approach. Plays reviewed are of many kinds. Some were also reviewed for other newspapers, and comparison with those subsequently published in *La Jumelle noire* reveals that Colette was not repetitive, even when writing of the same performance.

Also in:
OCLF 10 [item 0054]: same contents as item 0973.
OCC 12 [item 0055]: same contents as item 0973.

Extracts in:
Colette: au cinéma [item 0980]: Les cinéacteurs, 1934. Noir et blanc, 1935. Une comédienne de l'écran, Maë West, 1938.
Textes choisis de Colette [item 0065]: extracts from *La Jumelle noire*.

Although not generally ranked among Colette's most important works, *La Jumelle noire*, which consists of theater criticism dating from October 1933 to June 1938, represents a major long-term project and contains some of her finest and most memorable passages. Her own experience in both acting and writing for the stage endowed her with legitimate authority for the post. In the preface to the *OCLF*, where the unpublished criticism of 1937-1938 was combined with that of the four earlier volumes, she

writes that she considers herself to be an indulgent critic. It is true
that her reproaches--whether made to performers, to dramatists or to
others involved--are often delicately phrased, but she is by no
means always complimentary and here, as always, she proves
herself a keen observer of detail. She reviews many kinds of
theater: experimental plays, French farces, translations of
Shakespeare and Gœthe, music-hall, revues of the Folies Bergère.
Her style in these pages is personal: the reader has the impression
of watching the play with Colette. Many of her opinions have been
justified with time. Thus, 1933 finds her giving short shrift to *La
Dame aux camélias*, which she deems out-dated, while the
following year Cocteau's new *La Machine infernale* receives her
unqualified approval, as does Anouilh's *Le Voyageur sans bagages*
in 1937. Comments on performers now internationally acclaimed,
such as Jean-Louis Barrault, Madeleine Renaud, Jean-Pierre
Aumont, and even Mickey Rooney, prove that Colette also had a
sharp eye for new talent. Many reviews remain uncollected.

ENGLISH TRANSLATIONS

Extracts in *Colette at the Movies* [item 0984]: Mae West. Black
and White.

0978   [Review of Artaud's *Les Cenci* of 12 May 1935]. Trans. Victoria
       Nes Kirby. In "Antonin Artaud's 'Les Cenci'." *Drama Review*
       16 (June 1972): 134-35. Translated from *La Jumelle noire*, this
       is the "first" article on Artaud's play, as opposed to that of item
       0976.

FILM WRITING
and
FILM CRITICISM

0979 "L'envers du cinéma." In *Soixante-dix beaux métiers: du laboureur au cosmonaute*, edited by Jules Carrez, 330-40. Paris: Gründ, 1962. Previously published in *Paysages et portraits*. Also in item 1057 *Album Masques: Colette*, 177-80. First published in *Le Film* in 1917, this article consists of a fine series of portraits of those working on the film of *La Vagabonde* in Italy. It is also a valuable document, revealing the difficulties of the life of the silent film star. Colette speculates on the motives, both pecuniary and psychological, driving the actors and actresses, and she weighs the attractions of film over stage acting.

0980 COLETTE: AU CINÉMA: critiques et chroniques, dialogues des films. Presentation Alain Virmaux and Odette Virmaux. Paris: Flammarion, 1974. 325p. An immensely valuable collection of material, with an excellent general introduction and a specific introduction to each section. Reviews and partial reviews dating from 1914 to 1938 show Colette enthusiastic about all aspects of film work. Her early reviews are considered by some critics to have influenced the direction of future French film activity. Particularly interesting are her remarks on characteristics of

French films and on the growing American mass film industry.
Later reviews discover her still attached to the silent film. Some
of Colette's film writing has been lost, but this collection
includes sub-titles for the German film *Jeunes filles en
uniforme* (1932), the dialogue for *Lac-aux-dames* (1933), and the
scenario for *Divine* (1935). Rounding out the picture are
interviews, excerpts from some of Colette's other publications,
and miscellaneous related passages. Some of the reviews were
previously published in other Colette collections. See also item
2184 Virmaux, item 1188 Barrot, and item 1359 Cazals.

Reviews:
Figaro littéraire, 1 Feb. 1975, 13-14. André Brincourt.
Film Quarterly 34 (Summer 1981): 60. John Fell.
Nouvelle Revue des deux mondes 9 (Sept. 1975): 737-38. Pierre
    Audinet.

0981   "M. Charles Boyer, d'Hollywood..." *Cahiers Colette*, no. 2 (1980):
       49-53. Colette meditates on the demands that the American film
       public makes on its stars, saying that French stars who go to
       America sometimes cannot or will not adapt to those demands
       and so return to France. Not so, Boyer. Text of 1939.

0982   "Commentaire pour Yannick Bellon." *Europe*, no. 631-32 (Nov.-
       Dec. 1981): 133-37. Colette's notes for short documentary
       Bellon made on Colette in 1950. Includes fac-similes of
       handwritten passages on the Monts-Boucons.

0983   "Lac-aux-dames." *Avant-Scène Cinéma*, no. 284 (15 March 1982):
       3-47. Text of Marc Allégret's 1933 film for which Colette
       wrote the dialogue. Fanciful and poetic, it starred the young
       Jean-Pierre Aumont and Simone Simon, and is one of Colette's
       few ventures into adolescent psychology. Preceded by an extract
       from the Virmaux commentary of *Colette: au cinéma*, as well
       as notes on Simon and Allégret, and followed by a selection of
       press notices.

ENGLISH TRANSLATIONS

0984 COLETTE AT THE MOVIES: CRITICISM AND SCREEN
PLAYS. Trans. Sarah W.R. Smith. New York: Frederick
Ungar, 1980. viii-213p. Abridged version of item 0980. In
particular, the Virmaux's informative introduction is shortened
and the section on the German film, *Jeunes Filles en uniforme*
(1932), for which Colette wrote the French sub-titles, is
omitted. Several film reviews and supporting passages have also
been cut. Despite these differences, the English edition still
gives the reader a fascinating insight into a little-known facet of
Colette's work and a glimpse into the film world of yesteryear.
Major works are the dialogue for *Lac-aux-dames* (1933) and the
reconstructed script of *Divine* (1935). Titles included are: Film.
The Scott Expedition on Film. The Cheat. Civilization. The
Despoiler. Mater Dolorosa. Women of France. The Stranger.
Maciste the Alpinist. Film and Fashion. Should Woman
Forgive? How Are You? Her Hero. The Friend of Film. They're
All Going to the Cinema. Civilization's Child. The Shadow.
The French Cinema in 1918. A Short Manual for the Aspiring
Scenario Writer. Bel-Gazou and the Cinema. Cinema. Mae
West. Black and White. Backstage at the Studio. Also: M.
Charles Boyer, of Hollywood [trans. of item 0981, not included
in *Colette: au cinema*].

MISCELLANEOUS PUBLICATIONS
[items not listed elsewhere]

FRENCH

0985 "A la maison." In *Réflexions sur l'hiver*, by Princesse Lucien
Murat, Colette, Gérard Bauër, Eugène Marsan, Germaine
Beaumont, 2-4. Illus. Van Dongen. Paris: La Grande Maison
de Blanc, 1926. In this publicity brochure Colette evokes joy;
of her childhood, especially early morning and the meals of th
day. Rejecting the fashion for slimness, she extolls the deligh
of good French cooking presented on a beautifully-laid table.
Also in *Mélanges*.

0986 "Avant-propos." In *Jean Cocteau, ou L'Illustre inconnu*, by
Georges Sion, 7. Liège: Dynamo, 1964. Coll. Brimborions
123. Brief message to Cocteau, written in 1950 and stressing
their friendship.

0987 "Avertissement à Bel-Gazou et aux autres lecteurs." [Colette
Willy]. In *La Maison dans l'œil du chat*, by Mireille Havet, v
ix. Paris: Crès, 1917. Preface in which Colette recommends
this book of children's stories to her young daughter, then age
four. She emphasizes the gap between the perception of adults
and that of children. Also in *Mélanges*.

0988   "Balzac." In *De Jeanne d'Arc à Philippe Pétain*, by Sacha Guitry et al., 217-20. Paris: Sant'Andrea et Lafuma, 1944. Colette reminisces about the books she read in childhood and in particular those of Balzac, always her favorite author. She reflects on Balzac's wealth of characters and on his relationship to them. Also in *Mélanges*, under title "Lectures."

0989   "Bêtes que j'ai connues." In *Le Mystère animal*, by Colette, Edmond Jaloux et al., v-ix. Paris: Plon, 1939. Introduction to a volume exploring the intelligence of animals as compared with that of humans. Colette relates how a mother cat mysteriously located her missing kitten after its absence of 30 hours. Incorporated into *Journal à rebours* under the title "Le petit chat retrouvé."

0990   "Le bois, le lac et les Français." *Cahiers Colette*, no. 2 (1980): 15-16. Colette deplores the public's tendency to litter and despoil public parks, especially the Bois de Boulogne.

0991   "Bricoleurs." *Cahiers Colette*, no. 2 (1980): 33-36. Light-hearted evocation of Colette's and others' expertise in secondary activities. The title means "handymen." Provisionally dated at 1934-1935 by editors of the journal.

0992   "Carnaval brabançon." *Cahiers Colette*, no. 2 (1980): 61-64. Written in Brussels while on tour about 1910. Colette evokes the performers' discouragement at playing to a half-empty house during the good weather, and the ways in which they try to raise their own spirits.

0993   CES DAMES ANCIENNES. Paris: Estienne, 1954. 26ff. Coll. Les Inédits d'Estienne. Limited non-commercial publication by students at the Ecole Estienne. Amusing account of old women in Colette's childhood village. Written in 1951, it became one of the two texts of the posthumous *Derniers écrits*.

0994   "Le Cœur des bêtes." In *Affaires de cœur*, by Abel Hermant, Abel Bonnard, Colette, and Paul Morand, 53-65. Paris: Nativelle, 1934. Published for the fiftieth anniversary of Laboratoire Nativelle and reserved for the Corps Médical. Wonderful descriptions of animals whose sterling qualities Colette has found admirable. Incorporated into *Journal à rebours*.

0995 "Colette à New York." *Lire*, no. 130-31 (Summer 1986): 46-50.
Text of one of Colette's radio broadcasts to America in 1939, in
which she recalls her visit to New York in 1935. Contains
colorful passages evoking her reactions to the onslaught of
reporters, the non-arrival of baggage in time for the evening
banquet, and the spectacle of lights from the thirty-fifth floor of
their hotel. Colette confesses that, abandoning all official
functions, she and Maurice Goudeket visited and fell in love
with the city itself--its shops, its cinemas, its parks and its
people. Includes fac-simile of the first part of the radio script
with corrections in Colette's handwriting.

0996 "Colette devant la mort: 'Je me serai toujours bien amusée en
chemin...'" *Lettres françaises*, 12 Aug. 1954, 3. Also extract in
item 1592. Fragment of text recorded by Colette in 1951
affirms her commitment to writing, in spite of pain. Consists
partly of brief passages from her last works.

0997 "Colette parle aux Américains." *Cahiers Colette*, no. 9 (1987): 5-
11. One of a series of talks Colette gave during World War II on
radio Paris-Mondial to foreign listeners, especially Americans.
This text dated night of 21-22 Jan. 1940. Its authenticity is not
verified but judged probable by its editors. Colette comments on
letters she has received from soldiers and civilians, letters which
demonstrate to her the essential lyricism and sensitivity of the
French.

0998 "Dans un cyprès." *Le Point*, no. 39 (May 1951): 11. Fanciful text
evoking impressions received while in a room dominated by an
immense cypress tree just outside the window. Later published
in the posthumous *Paysages et portraits* under the title "Dans le
cyprès."

0999 [Dedication]. In *Les Jardins de Paris*, by André Daguesseau. Paris:
Eds. de la Revue moderne, 1956. A short dedication, in fac-
simile of Colette's own handwriting, for a book of poems about
the public gardens of Paris. Colette had encouraged Daguesseau
in his desire to make the gardens better known.

1000 "Ephémérides." In *Almanach de Paris, an 2000*. Paris: Gescofi,
1949. In this publication in honor of the two thousandth
anniversary of the city of Paris, Colette writes a few lines for

every day of the year 1950. Included are quotations, scraps of advice, reminiscences, comments on Paris landmarks, and passing thoughts of every kind.

1001   "Faits divers." *Cahiers Colette*, no. 2 (1980): 29-31. Newspaper report of a suicide pact made between two young people brings to Colette's mind memories of Charlotte Kinceler, who also took her own life.

1002   [Film presentation]. In item 1095 *Hommage à Colette*, non. pag. Also in *OP* 2, 1275-76. Passage recorded by Colette as introduction to the first public showing, to students, of *Le Blé en herbe*, 19 Jan. 1954. The actual recording was reported as an unforgettable event by those who were present. Terming it her own favorite, Colette speaks of *Le Blé en herbe* as a novel of beginnings and unfolding, of a troubling experience that the students themselves will undergo. She stresses that all life is a never-ending process of learning and development, and once more emphasizes the perennial miracle of life itself.

1003   "Fleurs." In *Choix des plus belles fleurs par P.-J. Redouté*. Paris: Denis, 1939. Foreword in which Colette compares the art of painting flowers with the art of the writer. She praises the loving exactitude with which Redouté portrayed flowers and the careful craftsmanship of the illustrations in the volume. Also in *Mélanges*.

1004   "Florilèges: Luc-Albert Moreau vu par ses amis (1950)." In item 0008 *Lettres à Moune et au Toutounet*, 383-85. Touching tribute to artist friend Moreau recalls 15 years of summers with him as neighbor at Saint Tropez.

1005   "Gîte d'écrivain." *Figaro littéraire*, 24 Jan. 1953, 1, 6. As part of special issue for Colette's eightieth birthday. She declares that the need to write is still with her. Evokes objects near and dear to her, as well as visitors to her Palais Royal apartment. Trivial content, but interesting. With item 0993, this text became *Derniers écrits*.

1006   "Graphismes." *Cahiers Colette*, no. 2 (1980): 5-9. Of pens and letters, both written and received. Colette states that character is betrayed in the signature.

1007 "Il fait froid." *Cahiers Colette*, no. 2 (1980): 17-19. Text of 1923 in which Colette deplores the rigours of unaccustomed cold weather, in particular the distress of children obliged to endure outdoor exercise under such conditions.

1008 [Introduction]. In *Vingt-cinq ans d'élégance à Paris, 1925-1950*, 9-11. Paris: Tisné, 1951. Colette passes in review fashion highlights for women of the previous twenty-five years.

1009 "Le jardin libéré." In *Palmes: hommage à la Résistance*, 13-16. Paris: n.p., 1945. Brief text later incorporated into *L'Etoile vesper*. Colette describes the silent resistance of the Palais Royal to occupation by German armies during World War II.

1010 "Je vous ai regardé grand visage." *Combat*, 22 Feb. 1951, 6. Brief homage to Gide upon his death. Colette emphasizes the authority of Gide's physical presence but confesses to having little in common with him.

1011 [Letter-preface]. In *Croisière autour de mes souvenirs*, by André Pascal [pseud. of Henri de Rothschild], i-iii. Paris: Emile-Paul, 1933. In this book of memoirs, Colette refers to her own voyage on Rothschild's yacht as a fairy-tale experience.

1012 [Letter-preface]. In *Dignimont*, by André Warnod, 1-3. Paris: Henry Babou, 1929. Coll. Les artistes du livre 9. Letter in fac-simile, praising Dignimont's illustrations for *L'Ingénue libertine* and *La Vagabonde*.

1013 [Letter-preface]. In *Une Dynastie millénaire*, edited by Gabriel Ollivier, vol. 2, non-pag. [25]. Monaco: Imprimerie nationale de Monaco, 1950. Greetings from Colette to Prince Rainier III on the occasion of his accession to the throne of Monaco, after the death of Prince Louis II in 1949.

1014 [Letter-preface]. In *Le Pain au lièvre*, by Joseph Cressot, 5-6. Metz: "le Républicain lorrain," 1952; Metz: Serpenoise, 1980. Fac-simile of hand-written letter, in which Colette affirms her liking for the rural pleasures described in the book.

1015 "Lettre à l'éditeur." In *Souffler n'est pas jouer (Dress Rehearsal)*, by Monica Stirling, 3-4. Paris: Laffont, 1952. Coll. Pavillons.

Letter-preface in which Colette disclaims knowledge of
Stirling's work but affirms her admiration and friendship for
Stirling herself, whom she had met at the end of World War II.

1016 [Luc-Albert Moreau]. In *La Naissance du jour* [invitation-catalogue
      for an exhibition of Moreau's work at the Galerie Cardo, 16
      March-4 April 1933], 5-9. With the addition of an extra
      paragraph, this passage became the essay "Luc-Albert Moreau"
      later published in *Trait pour Trait*.

1017 "Les mamans." In item 1057 *Album Masques: Colette*, 111-13.
      This very moving text of 1914 analyzes the attitudes of mothers
      and wives of World War I soldiers from whom they are parted. It
      is a good example of Colette's patriotic writing, in which she
      declares her partisanship, and an illustration of the type of
      writing which demonstrates that, contrary to popular opinion,
      she was neither unaware of nor silent on the great events of
      history. It also shows, however, that the human aspects of
      those events interested her far more than the political.

1018 "Maquis en sourdine." In *Jours de gloire: histoire de la libération de
      Paris*, 37-48. Paris: S.I.P.E., n.d. [1945]. Short text later
      incorporated into *L'Etoile vesper*. Colette evokes the long wait
      during the German occupation of Paris, the silent resistance of
      "the man with the canaries," the first news of the Allies'
      approach and their final entry into Paris.

1019 "Marseille." *Cahiers Colette*, no. 2 (1980): 55-60. Also in
      Marseille, no. 120 (1980): 60-61. Amusing portrait of
      Baptistin, a man from Marseilles, who visited Colette's dressing
      room while she was on tour. Text of 1909.

1020 "Message de Colette à l'occasion de l'Avènement au Trône de
      S.A.S. le Prince Souverain Rainier III de Monaco, le 11 avril
      1950." In item 1095 *Hommàge à Colette*, non-pag. Colette
      expresses regret that poor health prevents her from being present
      on the happy occasion of Rainier's coronation. She recalls
      previous meetings with Rainier and emphasizes their continuing
      friendship.

1021 *Minet: fantaisie féline*. [Madame Willy]. Geneva: J.C. Müller-
      Darier, n.d. [dated by *OP* 1 at about 1904]. 3p. Song, with

music, about a cat on a roof. Cat replies to questions asking what it is doing and what it sees. Contains what is possibly Colette's first attempt at onomatopeic animal expression. Title above music is *Minet!* with description "Chansonnette."

1022 "Modes." In *Falbalas et fanfreluches (Almanach des modes présentes, passées et futures pour 1923)*, 3-7. Paris: Meynial, 1923. Colette compares the slim fashionable female figure of 1923 unfavorably with the more rounded one of fifteen years earlier.

1023 "Music-Hall." In item 1057 *Album Masques: Colette*, 79-81. Impressions of Colette the music-hall performer on tour with Georges Wague and Christine Kerf. Includes several cameo descriptions, not all favorable, of performers and theater officials, and an interesting passage in which Colette deplores the audience's lack of warmth. Text of 1909.

1024 [Notice]. In *Bérard*, edited by Gabrielle Vienne, 9-11. Paris: Eds. des Musées nationaux, 1950. Colette's contribution to the catalogue for an exhibition of Christian Bérard's work at the Musée national d'Art moderne, 23 Feb.-23 April 1950, is one of several. In an untitled passage, she expresses admiration for the artist's work and reminisces about her acquaintance with him personally.

1025 "Onze pannes sur mille kilomètres..." In item 1239 Berriau, 172-74. Amusing account of an incident-filled automobile trip from Paris to the south of France.

1026 "Paresse." *Cahiers Colette*, no. 2 (1980): 37-40. Of Colette's desire to do nothing in the hot weather, and of what she sees while strolling in her Paris neighbourhood. Text of 1937.

1027 *Paris*. Illus. Reine Cimière. Paris: Eds. du Club de France, 1938. [90p.]. In text accompanying pictures of Paris, Colette affirms her love of the city that has been her home for over forty years.

1028 "Paris vacances." *Cahiers Colette*, no. 2 (1980): 41-43. Colette is reminded that Paris has many private gardens, which are veritable oases in the summer heat. She would prefer to see more liberty accorded to children playing in the gardens of the Palais Royal. Text of 1941.

1029   "Un peu plus..." *Cahiers Colette*, no. 2 (1980): 11-13. Of the role that chance has played in her life. Text of 1933.

1030   [Poems]: "Mon âne." "La perle égarée." "Le rouge-gorge." In item 1607 Gavoty, 61-62. Three poems set to music by Jean-Michel Damase. Sung by Lyliane Guitton, 17 Nov. 1970, at the Colette evening of "Rencontres du Palais-Royal." Although Colette occasionally wrote verse, only a few of these charming pieces are known today. First pages, including music, of "Le rouge-gorge" [Paris: Lemoine, 1939] and "La perle égarée" [Paris: Lemoine, 1948] are also in item 1056 *Album Colette*, 206-7.

1031   "Le Portrait." In item 1236 Bernac. Charming poem, which was set to music by Francis Poulenc. Both French and English versions are given in the English edition.

1032   POUR HELENE PICARD. Paris: Revue de Paris, 1945. 8p. In memoriam for Hélène Picard, who died in February 1945. Colette reviews events of their long friendship and pays homage to Picard's poetic talent. Includes Picard's poem "Délivrance." First printed in the *Revue de Paris*, 1 May 1945, then revised for incorporation into *L'Etoile vesper*. Also in *Lettres à Hélène Picard*.

1033   [Preface]. In *Commerce et qualité*, non-pag. [1-8]. Lyons: Consortium Général de Publicité, 1947. Untitled preface to a publicity piece for a consortium of merchants. Colette evokes fashions of 1847, and in particular those portrayed in Balzac's novels. She declares that ugly trends in home furnishings are soon rejected in France. Also in *Trait pour trait*, under title "A propos de Madame Marneffe."

1034   [Preface]. In *Les Fleurs et les fruits depuis le Romantisme*, non-pag. [2-3]. Paris: Galerie Charpentier, 1942. In catalogue for the Galerie Charpentier, Colette likens the painting of flowers to the portrayal of ephemeral objects such as rainbows or butterflies, and praises painters of past and present who have succeeded in the task. Also in *Mélanges* as "Peindre."

1035 [Preface]. In *Ravel et nous*, by Hélène Jourdan-Morhange, 9-11.
Geneva: Eds. du Milieu du monde, 1945. Hélène Jourdan-
Morhange, violin prodigy who had to abandon a promising
musical career because of illness, was friend to both Colette and
Ravel. Here Colette evokes both Morhange's presence and the
drama of Ravel's decline. Also in *Mélanges*; and in *Lettres à
Moune et au Toutounet*.

1036 "Préface." In *Sabbat*, by Hélène Picard, 5-7. Paris: Ferenczi, 1923.
Colette was a close friend of Picard, whose early renown
suffered decline well before World War II. As so often when she
wrote of her, she praises Picard's wealth of imagination. Also in
Mélanges.

1037 "Préface." In *Souvenirs de ma vie*, by Marguerite Moreno, ix-xi.
Paris: Flore, 1948. Colette and actress Moreno were friends
from the time of Colette's first marriage. The autobiography to
which this passage is preface was under publication when
Moreno died suddenly, so that Colette's preface is, in fact, a
brief eulogy for her friend. Also in *Mélanges* and in *Lettres à
Marguerite Moreno*.

1038 [Preface]. In *Vingt-huit compositions de Michel Dubost*, non-pag.
Lyon: Chez Marius Audin, 1930. In this publicity piece for silk
fabrics by the Soieries Ducharne, Colette praises the ability of
artist Dubost to capture nature visually by painting on silk and
other fashion materials. Also in *Mélanges*.

1039 "Prélude: lettre à une dame." In *Trio pour Henri Mondor*, by Alain,
Georges Duhamel, and Paul Valéry, non-pag. [1-6]. Paris:
Imprimerie Gauthier-Villars, 1939. In this tribute to writer-
surgeon Henri Mondor, Colette gives readers a graphic portrait
of both Mondor's physical appearance and his character. Later
incorporated into *Trait pour trait*.

1040 [Presentation]. In *Le "Six à huit" des vins de France*, 1-3. Paris:
Nicolas, 1934. In this publicity folder for wine dealers Nicolas,
Colette sings the praises of wine as a beverage that will always
be in fashion. Also in *Mélanges*, under title "Vins de France."

1041 "Présentation de Renée Hamon." In *Aux Iles de la lumière*, by
Renée Hamon, 5-9. Paris: Flammarion, 1940. Hamon was a

young Breton who thirsted for travel to far-off places. Colette encouraged her to write the book to which this passage is preface. It gives an account of Hamon's travels to the South Seas. Also in *Mélanges* and in *Lettres au petit corsaire*.

1042 [Program note]. In *A toutes les gloires de la France*, 2. Paris: Secrétaire d'État aux Beaux-Arts et le Comité National pour la Sauvegarde du Château de Versailles, 1955. Souvenir program for a *son et lumière* promoting conservation of the Château de Versailles. Colette's contribution draws parallels between her own Palais Royal and the royal palace of Louis XIV.

1043 QUELQUES TOILES DE CHARMY, QUELQUES PAGES DE COLETTE. Paris: Galerie d'Art ancien et moderne, [1921]. [24p.]. Publicity piece for an exhibition of paintings, some of which are reproduced in the book. Colette praises Emily Charmy's portrayal of women and of flowers.

1044 [Raoul Dufy]. In *Raoul Dufy*, 12-17. Paris: L'Amour de l'art, 1953. Special number of the review *L'Amour de l'art* [fasc. 76-78], devoted to the art of Raoul Dufy. Colette praises Dufy's illustrations to the Mermod edition of her *Pour un herbier*.

1045 "Un Salon de musique en 1900." In *Maurice Ravel par quelques-uns de ses familiers*, by Colette, Maurice Delage et al., 115-24. Paris: Tambourinaire, 1939. Fascinating evocation of meetings with Ravel, Fauré and other celebrities of the Belle Epoque. Relates her collaboration with Ravel on *L'Enfant et les sortilèges* and his subsequent decline. Incorporated into *Journal à rebours* as "Un salon en 1900."

1046 "'Saviez-vous, madame?...'" *Cahiers Colette*, no. 2 (1980): 25-27. Colette ponders the psychology of those who, aware of domestic violence in someone's home, do nothing to stop it.

1047 "Le silence des enfants." *Cahiers Colette* no. 2 (1980): 21-24. Colette affirms her admiration of infant children. Text of 1939.

1048 "Souvenirs." *Poésie I*, nos. 112-14 (Nov.-Dec. 1983): 175. From a publicity piece of 1936 or 1937 for Source Perrier. Colette evokes the pleasures of drinking water and of drinking Perrier in particular.

1049 "Textes inédits: neuf conférences prononcées à Radio-Mondial en 1939-1940." In item 1109 Malige, 135-88. Text of nine overseas radio talks broadcast from 18 Nov. 1939 to 2 May 1940. Colette's declared intention is to interest American listeners in France and in the French. Talks are rambling and topics are many, but nearly all focus on the merits of Parisians in wartime and all are superficial. One can easily detect therein echos of passages from *Paris de ma fenêtre*, which addresses many of the same subjects: Colette's trip to America in 1935, the fashion industry, wartime shortages, children, the people of Paris, animals, love, and familiar objects. Other broadcasts from the same series can be found in *Paysages et portraits*.

1050 TOI. Illus. Jean Dupas. Paris: Fourrures Max, 1926. [20p.]. During the same decade in which she wrote this free-verse text promoting furs for women, Colette was publishing other passages expressing severe judgments against hunters. Curiously enough, analysis of these lines reveals that nowhere here does she urge women to buy furs. Instead, she addresses "woman" directly, suggesting poetically that the wearing of furs is an expression of her primordial instincts.

1051 "Les vendanges en Beaujolais." In item 1703 Hill-Marchand. Three paragraphs from a recording by Colette on the Beaujolais wine harvest of 1947.

xxxx See also item 1171 Dr. P.B..

ENGLISH TRANSLATIONS
of uncollected works

1052 "Paris! City of Love." No translator. *Holiday* 13 (April 1953): 108-9, 122-24. Apparently a synthesis or restatement of passages from various works, focusing on the attractions of Paris.

1053 "Paris from my Window." Trans. Janet Flanner. *Harper's Bazaar* 78 (Nov. 1944): 74-75, 144. Colette's correspondence indicates that this article was written specially for this publication, but many passages bear a close resemblance to parts of *Paris de ma fenêtre*. Emphasizes merits of fellow-residents of the Palais Royal during World War II.

1054   "Pirate's blood." Trans. Denver Lindley. *Collier's* 101 (28 May 1938): 18. Short story never published in book form in French. A bank official feels the pirate blood of his ancestor surging in his veins, with surprising results.

xxxx   "Portrait." Poem set to music by Poulenc. See item 1031.

1055   "Young wife." Trans. Edward L. McKenna. *Collier's* 103 (25 Feb. 1939): 58. Short story never published in book form in French. Loss of her necklace reveals to a young woman the truth about herself and her husband.

CRITICISM ON COLETTE

BOOKS, MONOGRAPHS
and PAMPHLETS ON COLETTE

1056 *Album Colette*. Iconography selected and commented by Claude
and Vincenette Pichois, with the collaboration of Alain Brunet.
Paris: Gallimard, 1984. 325p. Bibliothèque de la Pléiade, Coll.
Album 23. Excellent pictorial biography. Includes pictures of
people, places, posters, manuscripts, book-jackets, book
illustrations, and many other objects related to Colette's work
and personal life. Biographical detail is objectively presented.
See item 1991 Pichois/Brunet for corrections and addenda.

Reviews:
French Studies 39 (July 1985): 363-65. David Coward.
Lettres romanes 38 (Nov. 1984): 331-32. Raymond Pouilliart.
Revue d'histoire littéraire de la France 86 (Mar.-April 1986): 326-
28. Michel Picard.

1057 *Album Masques: Colette*. Edited by Katy Barasc and Jean-Pierre
Jœcker. Paris: Masques, 1984. 192p. Suppl. no. 23 of the
journal *Masques*. An interesting rag-bag of photographs,
documents, short articles, press notices, comments by Colette's
contemporaries, and excerpts from both Colette's and Willy's
works. Of special interest is the polemic related to the question
of a religious burial for Colette, excerpts from the press relative
to the 1907 scandal of the Moulin Rouge, public letters

witnessing the quarrel in the media carried on by Willy and Colette in 1909, and a passage from Willy's *Lélie, fumeuse d'opium*, in which he satirizes Colette. Annotated separately are articles by Katy Barasc, Jean-Pierre Jœcker, Maïté Carrère, Philippe Carteron, Jean-Luc Barré, Milorad, Daniel Arsand, Jacques Dupont, Françoise d'Eaubonne, Bruno Villien, and Yannick Resch. Excellent photographs.

1058   *Les Albums de Colette*. Pref. Maurice Goudeket. Geneva: Eds. de Crémille, 1972. 3 vols. Iconography arranged roughly according to periods in Colette's life. Sub-titles of the three volumes are: *Naissance d'un écrivain*, *Colette s'épanouit*, and *La «Grande» Colette*. Includes excellent photographs of Colette, her family, friends, colleagues, posters, manuscripts, book-covers, letters, book dedications, and similar material. Passages from her writing or from Goudeket's *Près de Colette* are interspersed with the illustrations and are sometimes used as captions. The resulting presentation is somewhat slanted in perspective but is nevertheless extremely interesting.

1059   Andry, Marc. *Chère Colette*. Paris: Presses de la Cité, 1983. 221p. Also Paris: France Loisirs, 1985. 218p. Also as *Colette*. Pref. Paul Guth. Paris: Presses de la Cité, 1984. 255p. Coll. Presses Pocket 2283. Account of Colette's life written in novel form, complete with dialogue and presumed motivations of characters. Readers very familiar with Colette's works will be able to recognize most of the sources that have served as inspiration for the various passages. Despite occasional inaccuracies, the book provides a fascinating picture of Paris during the Belle Epoque. Many details are supplied and many names mentioned. The later years are less richly presented. References to Colette's works are generally limited to brief plot summaries and speculation about parallels in the writer's own life, although interesting details surrounding publication are often recounted.

1060   *Autour de Colette à Saint-Tropez* [on front cover: *Colette 1926-1936*]. Saint Tropez: Eds. de l'Académie du Bailly, 1987. [188p.]. Text of papers delivered at the Colloque Universitaire International, held at Saint Tropez, 13-14 Sept. 1986. Includes texts by: Bernard Bray, Pierre Brunel, Etienne Brunet, Mireille Gouaux, Odette Joyeux, Michel Lebrun, Georges Sion, Pierre-Olivier Walzer, and correspondence with Paule Tondut. Also illustrations for *Pour un herbier* by artist Simone Carrat, and correspondence from Colette to François Fracchia, who was in charge of renovations to her summer home at Saint Tropez. Although interesting, the collection offers little in the way of new ideas or material, except for the correspondence. Papers vary a good deal both in topic and in length, and are generally undocumented. All are annotated separately.

1061 Bal, Mieke. *La Complexité d'un roman populaire: ambiguité dans 'La Chatte.'* Paris: La Pensée universelle, 1974. 95p. Asserts that, despite their apparent clarity, Colette's novels reveal a profound ambiguity, and that *La Chatte* demonstrates this fact. Readers of this novel tend to blame one of the three major characters--Alain, Camille or the cat Saha--for the failure of the marriage. In order to determine why each has both supporters and detractors, Bal analyzes the narrative perspective, the psychology of the characters, the space-time structure, and the symbolic motifs and themes. The final chapter, in which an attempt is made to explain that Colette's tendency to portray characters who cannot live an adult life was caused by elements in her own and her mother's psychology, is somewhat peripheral to the declared intention of the book, but the analysis itself is perceptive.

1062 Barjavel, René. *Colette à la recherche de l'amour.* Moulins: La Nouvelle Province littéraire, 1934. 47p. Declared intention is to define the role played by love in Colette's life. Treating her novels as personal confessions, Barjavel concludes that secretly she wants to be dominated. A superficial and often fanciful essay, occasionally patronizing of Colette's work.

1063 Beaumont, Germaine, and André Parinaud. *Colette.* Paris: Seuil, 1951. 192p. Coll. Ecrivains de toujours 5. Photographs and excerpts from Colette's work are arranged chronologically and commented by Parinaud, who states that the purpose of the whole is to present a picture of Colette as she appeared physically over the years, and to capture her inner essence. The reader thus acquires an impression of Colette as she portrays herself in her books. Many of her characters are also made to speak on her behalf. Necessarily superficial in content, this book is nevertheless an interesting general introduction to Colette's life and work, so much so that it has been updated and continues to be popular. It is introduced by a long, personal essay by novelist-critic Germaine Beaumont, one of Colette's long-time friends. Consisting mostly of memoirs and references to lessons learned from Colette, it evokes her in her daily round and in her attitude to life. Beaumont insists on Colette's role as a moralist. Also chronology and brief bibliography.

Reviews:
Bulletin critique du livre français 7 (1952): 80-81.
Critique, no. 61 (June 1952): 491-97. Gabriel Venaissin.
Fiera letteraria, 18 May 1952, 2. Fiorenza Verona.
French Studies 7 (July 1953): 281-82. Enid Starkie.
Pensée, no. 44 (Sept.-Oct. 1952): 135. Georges Cogniot and René Maublanc.

1064 Biolley-Godino, Marcelle. *L'Homme-objet chez Colette*. Paris: Klincksieck, 1972. 172p. Colette's claim to originality owes much to the fact that in her novels the principal female character perceives the man as a love-object, and implicitly acquires thereby an inherent superiority which external events, however unfavorable to her, do little to dissipate. Such a reversal of traditional male-female roles, even in literature, was the source of much critical comment, especially in the early years of Colette's career. This book offers an analysis of the ways in which Colette demythifies man at the same time as she accords him a significant role in the life of the woman. It also attempts to identify elements in Colette's life related to the development of such a perspective, as well as conflicts and contradictions accompanying it.

Reviews:
Bulletin critique du livre français 27 (April 1973): 536.
Figaro littéraire, 18 Aug. 1973, 2. Claudine Jardin.
French Review 47 (Oct. 1973): 203-5. Alba Amoia.
French Studies 30 (April 1976): 235-36. Henri Godin.
Journal de Genève, 29 Sept. 1973, non-pag. [17]. P.-O. Walzer.
Monde, 25 Jan. 1973, 21. Gérard Bonal.
Nouvel Observateur, no. 432 (19 Feb. 1973): 66. Catherine David.
Rapports-Het Franse Boek 43 (Nov. 1973): 110-17. Mieke Bal.
Revue belge de philologie et d'histoire 55 (1977): 302-3. Marc Quaghebeur.

1065 Boivin, Marguerite. *«Sur les pas de Colette à Saint-Sauveur en Puisaye»*. Charny: Association du Château de Saint-Sauveur, 1986. 98p. Fund-raising book for the Colette museum in the village in which she was born. Contains photographs of the village and countryside, focusing on places described in Colette's books. Each photo is accompanied by a pertinent quotation from her work or by descriptive details. All are identified on a map. Also includes photographs of some of the local people whom Colette used as models. A fascinating publication for readers interested in Colette's life and in the way in which she transformed experience into literature.

1066 Bonal, Gérard. *Colette par moi-même*. Paris: Ramsay, 1982. 184p. Coll. Affinités électives. The first director of the *Cahiers Colette* explains what Colette's books have meant to him at different stages of his life, then provides a subjective evaluation of some of her publications. Contains interesting sections on Colette de Jouvenel and other persons close to Colette.

Review:
Nouvelles littéraires, 4 Feb. 1982, 44-45. Gérard Spiteri.

1067 Boncompain, Claude. *Colette*. Lyons: Confluences, 1945. 119p. General thematic and stylistic study of Colette's work up to World War II. Asserts that her originality lies partly in her portrayal of animals as individuals whose lives interact with those of human beings, and that one of her most valuable contributions is her painting of worlds that have disappeared: the Paris of 1900 and the music-hall of pre-World War I. Despite some rather dated preconceptions about what the ideal relationship between men and women should be, passages on the novels contain many perceptive remarks. Excellent short chapter on Colette's "art," in which is stressed the role of the characters' psychology in determining events.

Review:
Confluences 4 (1944): 87-88. Paul Ribes.

1068 Bonmariage, Sylvain. *Willy, Colette et moi*. Paris: Charles Frémanger, 1954. 317p. Rambling account of the author's relations with Willy and with Colette during the period up to about 1930. Chiefly anecdotal in form but offering personal opinions that create subtle innuendo. Complimentary towards Willy but replete with offensive remarks, not only about Colette, but about many other well-known people. Several passages contain direct personal attacks on Colette, accusing her of being tactless, lacking in manners, hypocritical, envious, untruthful, vindictive, and fond of intrigue and domination. Bonmariage also mocks her accent, origins and appearance and claims knowledge of letters from Colette to Willy asking for reconciliation.

1069   Brésillon, Jean-Pierre. *La Bourgogne de Colette*. Aix-en-Chapelle: Edisud, 1983. 104p. Coll. Les Chemins de l'œuvre. Extremely interesting book offering many photographs of places in Burgundy that Colette knew and wrote about, as well as details about her relationship with them and with the region in general. Compares what she says about places with their reality then and now.

1070   Caradec, François. *Feu Willy, avec et sans Colette*. Paris: Carrère-J.-J. Pauvert, 1984. 335p. Literary biography of Colette's first husband. Crammed with names and anecdotes, this book follows Willy's rise and decline as a celebrity in Paris' literary world. Several chapters provide interesting details about the relationship between Colette and Willy both before and after the separation. The tableau of recriminations and petty acts of vengeance is not an edifying one, despite the author's insistence on the fact that the Colette-Willy collaboration continued long after their separation, but Caradec attempts to give a fair account of events and has good things to say about both spouses. His surprising conclusion is that Colette's "hate" for Willy in later years proves that she never stopped wanting him back. The passages dealing with Willy's *atelier* of writers are especially valuable.

Reviews:
Magazine littéraire, no. 216-17 (March 1985): 108-9. Pierre Kyria.
Nouvelle Revue française 71 (July-Aug. 1985): 157-59. Janine Aeply.
Quinzaine littéraire, no. 432 (16 Jan. 1985): 15-16. Hubert Juin.

1071   Carco, Francis [pseud. of François Marie Alexandre Carcopino-Tusoli). *Colette «mon ami»*. Illus. Ch.-M. Echard. Paris: Rive-

Gauche, 1955. 125p. Carco and Colette were close friends over
several decades. Contains many interesting, often well-known
anecdotes about her, though little in the way of new
information.

1072 Chauvière, Claude. *Colette.* Paris: Firmin-Didot, 1931. 302p.
Coll. Visages contemporains. Written by a close acquaintance
and one-time secretary of Colette, this fascinating book offers
not only a picture of Colette's day-to-day activities during her
most prolific period, but impressions of literary Paris during
those years as well. Anecdotes, portraits, personal opinions,
quotations, extracts from correspondence, press notices, excerpts
from articles, evaluations by foreign critics, and reported
conversations all juggle for space. Quotes copiously from the
works and words of others. Although divided into chapters, the
material is only roughly organized and is seldom documented.
Among the most interesting items are a letter from Olympe
Terrain, Colette's former school-mistress at Saint-Sauveur, and
three letters from Colette to her daughter at school. Ends with
an "Essai de bibliographie" by Francis Ambrière. Some items
are annotated separately.

Reviews:
Action française, 8 Oct. 1931, 3. Robert Brasillach.
Annales, 1 Nov. 1931, 389-90. Benjamin Crémieux.

1073 Cocteau, Jean. *Colette: discours de réception à l'Académie royale de
langue et de littérature françaises.* Paris: Grasset, 1955. 122p.
Also in *Bulletin de l'Académie royale de langue et de littérature
françaises* 33:3 (1955): 179-99; and in *Poésie critique*, vol. 2,
107-36. Paris: Gallimard, 1960. Abridged version in *Figaro
littéraire*, 8 Oct. 1955, 1, 5-6. Extract in item 1057 *Album
Masques: Colette*, 136. Acceptance speech of 1 Oct. 1955,
when Cocteau took Colette's place in the Belgian Academy.
Contrasts her with her predecessor, Anna de Noailles, in both
personality and output. Attributes the origin of her greatness to
the fact that she did not appear to differentiate between good and
evil. Praises her as pioneer in the true depiction of female
psychology. Often reminisces about his long friendship with
Colette. Original edition includes response by Fernand Desonay,
which makes passing references to Colette.

English translations [abridged]: "A speech on Colette." Trans.
Margaret Crosland. *London Magazine* 3 (May 1956): 16-24.
Also, under title "Colette," in *My Contemporaries*, edited by
Margaret Crosland, 128-39. London: Owen, 1967. Also
excerpts, under title "Colette," trans. Richard Howard, in
Professional Secrets: An Autobiography [drawn from his
lifetime writings by Robert Phelps], 280-83. New York: Farrar,
Straus & Giroux, 1972.

1074 *Colette*. Edited by Monique Cornand and Madeleine Barbin. Pref.
Etienne Dennery. Paris: Bibliothèque Nationale, 1973. xvi-
216p. Catalog for exhibition at the Bibliothèque Nationale,
May-Sept. 1973. Includes entries for 745 items: manuscripts,
editions, photographs, posters, portraits, correspondence,
dedications and personal items, arranged in roughly
chronological order. All are carefully described, and many of the
documents are quoted.

Review:
Bulletin critique du livre français 28 (Nov. 1973): 1303.

1075 *Colette*. Paris: Académie Goncourt, 1984. 20p. Publicity piece to
accompany the novel *Chéri*, chosen by the Goncourt Academy
for its collection Les Grands Ecrivains. Provides a concise
summary of Colette's life and career, brief unsigned articles
about different aspects of her work and ideas, and a suggested
list of other books by her to read. Includes many photographs.
For the general public.

1076 *Colette: The Woman, The Writer*. Edited by Erica Eisinger and
Mari McCarty. Foreword Elaine Marks. University Park, Penn.
and London: Pennsylvania State University Press, 1981. xi-
200p. Compendium of scholarly articles on diverse topics and
using a variety of methodologies. Generally feminist oriented.
Comprised of three sections: Genesis, Gender and Genre, and
Generation. Texts by: Françoise Mallet-Joris, Michèle Blin
Sarde, Anne Duhamel Ketchum, Janet Whatley, Joan Hinde
Stewart, Donna Norell, Sylvie Romanowski, Jacob Stockinger,
Erica Eisinger, Claire Dehon, Margaret Crosland, Mari
McCarty,Yannick Resch, Suzanne Relyea, Nancy K. Miller,
Ann Cothran and Diane Crowder, and Christiane Makward. All
are annotated separately.

Reviews:
French Studies 39 (July 1985): 363-65. David Coward.
Library Journal 107 (1 Feb. 1982): 260. Myrna J. McCallister.

1077 *Colette, Nouvelles Approches critiques: Actes du Colloque de
Sarrebruck (22-23 Juin 1984)*. Edited by Bernard Bray. Paris:
Nizet, 1986. 208p. Text of welcoming address and 17 papers
presented at the colloquium on Colette at Sarrebrücken in June
1984. Classified under four headings: Problèmes d'identité et
d'identification, Critique génétique, Etudes formelles, and
Réception. Articles by: Peter Robert Franke, Mieke Bal,
Jacques Dupont, Paul D'Hollander, Christiane Milner, Claude
Pichois, Michel Mercier, Maurice Delcroix, Bernard Bray,
Hermann Hofer, Michel Baude, R. Kloepfer and V. Borsô-
Borgarello and J. Mecke and S. Kleinert and E. Stern, Danielle
Bouverot and Chantal Schaefer, Marie-Françoise Berthu-
Courtivron, Danielle Deltel, Yannick Resch, Hartmut Köhler,
and Horst Wagner. Summary of discussion follows each paper.
All are annotated separately.

1078 Cosentino-La Rocca, Licia. *Colette: les animaux dans son œuvre*.
Caltanissetta [Italy]: Lipani & Granata, 1939. 123p. Traces
Colette's presentation of animals through her different
publications. Recognizes her skill in depicting them, but insists
that her understanding of them is at the level of instinct.
Maintains that for Colette the animal becomes both ally and
consolation. Asserts that her human characters are often inferior
animals and that *La Chatte* in particular provides proof of her
preference of animals over people, this preference having its
roots in Colette's childhood. Does make some attempt to rank
Colette among other animal writers such as La Fontaine and
Buffon.

1079 Cottrell, Robert D. *Colette*. New York: Ungar, 1974. ix-150p.
Coll. Modern Literature Monographs. Excellent introductory
study for students and general readers. Treats each major work
separately, noting that Colette's works, especially the early
ones, have affinities with *art nouveau*. Unlike most critics,
Cottrell treats the *Dialogues des bêtes* as a significant work.
Does not consider Colette a feminist in the modern sense of the
word, but notes the preponderance of heroines who are superior
to their male counterparts. Attributes this to the notion of Sido

as ideal. Emphasizes the polarity of influence of Colette's mother and first husband in her life as well as in her themes and style. Terms Colette's world "Janus-faced," because of the separation of the characters' lives from the ideal. Bibliography and index.

Reviews:
Books Abroad 49 (Spring 1975): 280. Gretchen R. Besser.
French Review 48 (Feb. 1975): 638-39. Elaine Marks.

1080   Covert, Christopher, and Barbara Spence Potter. *Colette: The Colours of Love.* Toronto: Playwrights Union of Canada, 1983. 63p. Text of a play very loosely based on Colette's life and work. First performed at the Phœnix Theatre in Toronto, Jan.-April 1980.

1081   Crosland, Margaret. *Colette: The Difficulty of Loving.* London: Owen, 1973. 200p. Also: Introd. Janet Flanner. Indianapolis: Bobbs-Merrill, 1973. xxx-289p.; New York: Dell (Laurel), 1975. 203p. General presentation of Colette and her works, especially in their relationship to the events of her life, and suitable for readers with little knowledge of either Colette or her writing. Details provided are not always accurate in the light of current information, and the frequent use of suppositional expressions such as "she must have been" and "perhaps she felt" used in describing Colette's motivations tend to erode the reader's confidence. Despite these weaknesses, the short passages in which individual novels are analyzed sometimes contain perceptive comments. Written in a familiar style that is easy to read.

Reviews:
Books Abroad 48 (Autumn 1974): 731. Gretchen R. Besser.
Books & Bookmen 18 (March 1973): 56-57. Oswell Blakeston.
Bulletin critique du livre français 28 (1973): 1306.
Culture française 20 (Nov.-Dec. 1973): 363-64. Luigi Losito.
Figaro littéraire, 18 Aug. 1973, 2. Claudine Jardin.
Horn Book Magazine 51 (Oct. 1975): 493-94. Mary Silva Cosgrave.
Journal de Genève, 29 Sept. 1973, non-pag. [17]. P.-O. Walzer.
Ms. 2 (April 1974): 31-33. Erica Jong.
New Statesman 85 (2 Feb. 1973): 163-64. Francis Wyndham.

New York Review of Books 20 (24 Jan. 1974): 3-6. Rosemary
   Tonks.
New York Times Book Review, 9 Dec. 1973, 3, 26-27. Mavis
   Gallant.
Observer, no. 9470 (28 Jan. 1973): 34. John Weightman.
Saturday Evening Post 246 (June-July 1974): 89-90. Paul Engle.
Spectator, no. 7559 (12 May 1973): 594. E.S.
Sunday Times, 11 Feb. 1973, 30. Philippa Pullar.
Times Literary Supplement, no. 3710 (13 April 1973): 413.
Village Voice 18 (13 Dec. 1973): 41, 45. Molly Haskell.
Washington Post Book World, 6 Jan. 1974, 1-2. Ann Birstein.

French translation: *Colette ou la difficulté d'aimer*. Trans. Marie
   Matignon. Paris: Albin Michel, 1973. 264p.

1082   Crosland, Margaret. *Madame Colette: A Provincial in Paris*.
       London: Owen, 1953; New York: British Book Centre, 1954.
       222p. Colette herself provided some of the material for this
       book. Some of the "facts" provided are now known to be
       inaccurate, and the clichés about masculinity and femininity are
       irritating, as are some of the other generalizations ("A passion
       for gardening is usually a sign of middle age"), but the book
       reads easily and contains useful passages on the reception of
       Colette's work in England. In the last chapter Crosland attempts
       to compare Colette with writers of other centuries. She also
       praises her as a natural and consistent writer, who ignored
       fashions in literature but was aware of change.

       Reviews:
       Nation 179 (25 Sept. 1954): 264.
       New Republic 331 (6 Sept. 1954): 16-17. Robert Phelps.
       New Statesman & Nation 45 (25 April 1953): 494. Enid McLeod.
       Romanic Review 46 (Feb. 1955): 70-71. Alvin Labat.
       Saturday Review 37 (28 Aug. 1954): 21. Rosemary C. Benet.
       Time 64 (23 Aug. 1954): 74-75.
       Times Literary Supplement, no. 2680 (12 June 1953): 383.

1083   Daguesseau, André. *A l'ombre de Colette*. Paris: Eds. de la Revue
       moderne, 1959. 80p. Poems inspired by Colette and by the
       Palais Royal, dating from Feb. 1946 to Dec. 1958. "Pour les
       quatre-vingt ans de Colette" pays homage to her eightieth
       birthday. "Adieu Colette" evokes the days just after her death,

when the crowds lined up in the courtyard of the Palais Royal to pay their respects. Not an important book but one that witnesses Colette's immense popularity.

1084   Davies, Margaret. *Colette*. Edinburgh & London: Oliver & Boyd, 1961. 120p. Coll. Writers and Critics. Also New York: Grove Press, 1961. 120p. Coll. Evergreen Pilot. Excellent early general study. Warns against identifying Colette completely with her characters. Attempts to compare aspects of Colette's early novels with literary and social trends then current. Remarks on Chéri as a representative of post-World War I *angst* are interesting, as are the parallels drawn between Chéri and Alain of *La Chatte*. Insists on the importance of rhythm in Colette's style. Comments about symbolic elements in the novels invite thought. The final chapter provides an over-all assessment of Colette's reception by critics.

Reviews:
Durham University Journal 55 (Dec. 1962): 43-45. H.T. Mason.
Studi francese, no. 25 (1965): 188. S. Haig.
Times Literary Supplement, no. 3126 (26 Jan. 1962): 52.

1085   De Ridder, André. *Colette Willy*. Brussels: Le Thyrse, 1914. 20p. Also in *Le Thyrse* 15 (1913-14): 178-83. One of the earliest detailed evaluations of Colette's fiction, especially interesting because many of its judgments anticipate those of later critics. Considers Colette already the greatest female novelist in France, and one of the three or four greatest prose writers of the age. Praises her for being the first writer to portray the interior life of women but also for not being a feminist. Detects in Claudine and Minne a reflection of youth of the time, their faults redeemed in part by their regret and the lessons they have learned, and in *La Vagabonde* and *L'Entrave* an expression of passion mixed with humanity.

1086   D'Hollander, Paul. *Colette, ses apprentissages*. Montreal: Presses de l'Université de Montréal; Paris: Klincksieck, 1978. 424p. Fine effort to shed light on the nature and extent of Colette's literary debt to Willy. To this end, D'Hollander examines manuscripts, biographical sources and internal features of her first seven novels. Concludes that not all of the negative elements in her early work are due to Willy's influence alone.

The biographical section of the book is of much value to scholars. Extensively documented.

Reviews:
Esprit créateur 20 (Summer 1980): 79-80. Janet M. Paterson.
French Forum 4 (Sept. 1979): 284-86. Robert D. Cottrell.
Lettres romanes 36 (Feb. 1982): 92-93. Dominique Allard.
Modern Language Journal 64 (Spring 1980): 153-54. Susan Keane.
Romanic Review 74 (Jan. 1983): 114-16. Adrian C. Ritchie.
University of Toronto Quarterly 49 (Summer 1980): 442-43. Paulette Collet.
World Literature Today 54 (Winter 1980): 74-75. D. McDowell.

1087 Dormann, Geneviève. *Amoureuse Colette.* Lausanne and Paris: Herscher, 1984. 319p. Also Paris: Albin Michel, 1985. 251p. Also Paris: Libraire générale française, 1987. 248p. Coll. Livre de poche 6296. Because of its size and numerous photographs, one is tempted to term the original edition of this impressive publication a coffee-table book, especially as it is evidently designed for the general reader. On the other hand, extensive quotations from unpublished correspondence and the inclusion of hundreds of photographs, many of them unknown to Colette readers, attest to its biographical value even for scholars. Material is arranged roughly chronologically. Interpretation of Colette's work focuses mostly on its relation to her life and especially her loves.

Reviews:
Bulletin critique du livre français 41 (1986): 167.
Figaro, 19 Oct. 1984, 28. Jean Chalon.
French Review 59 (May 1986): 984-85. Catherine Slawy-Sutton.
Library Journal 111 (15 Feb. 1986): 177. Grover Kroger.
Magazine littéraire, no. 212 (Nov. 1984): 54-55. Jean-Louis Hue.
Modern Fiction Studies 33 (Summer 1987): 384-85. Mary Beth Pringle.
New Yorker 62 (21 July 1986): 95.
Observer, no. 10120 (22 Sept. 1985): 26. John Weightman.

English translation: *Colette: A Passion for Life.* Trans. David Macey and Jane Brenton. New York: Abbeville Press; London: Thames & Hudson, 1985. 320p.

1088   Duquette, Jean-Pierre. *Colette: l'amour de l'amour.* Ville LaSalle
       [Canada]: Hurtubise, 1984. 228p. Coll. Constantes. Adheres to
       stated intention to concentrate on the presentation of love in
       Colette's work, but focuses almost exclusively on her novels.
       Finds her mature heroines to be stronger than the younger, more
       submissive ones, and considers them to be a new element in
       French novel writing. Speculates about, and draws conclusions
       on, the effects of Colette's own experience on her fictional
       portrayal of love. Detects in her a disgust of the physical
       aspects of love, connecting it with the themes of lost innocence
       and lost paradise. Often quotes other critics, especially Biolley-
       Godino. Half the book is devoted to a summary examination of
       Colette's novel structures, as well as settings, chapter divisions
       and the different types of communication used by her fictional
       lovers. Incorporates item 1523 as chapter 2.

       Reviews:
       Ecrits du Canada français, no. 51 (1984): 157-59. Simone
       Beaulieu.
       Revue d'histoire littéraire de la France 86 (June-July 1986): 787-88.
       Yannick Resch.

1089   Fillon, Amélie. *Colette.* Paris: Eds de la Caravelle, 1933. 143p.
       Coll. Aujourd'hui 5. Consists of two main parts: a biography
       and an assessment of Colette's writing to date. The biography
       betrays a tendency to view Colette as the innocent victim of the
       machinations of others, and it deplores the effect that her life
       had on the public's acceptance and interpretation of her work.
       The second part contains one of the first serious attempts to
       trace an evolution in Colette's novel technique, with *La
       Naissance du jour* identified as the richest and most complex
       work to date. Unlike most critics of the time, Fillon considers
       Colette's masculine characters to be as varied and alive as the
       feminine ones. Stresses the autobiographical element in all her
       work, and her search for excellence.

1090   Forestier, Louis. *Chemins vers 'La Maison de Claudine' et 'Sido':
       notes pour une étude.* Paris: Société d'édition d'enseignement
       supérieur, 1968. 75p. Begins with a rare attempt to place
       Colette within the context of literary movements, by showing
       their parallels with some of her themes and stylistic features.
       Much of the book tries to demonstrate that the definitive edition

of *La Maison de Claudine* is not unstructured, but represents a descent from childhood to adulthood, a subsequent exploration of possible avenues of ascent, and a final merger with the Sido image. Using *La Maison de Claudine* and *Sido*, defined here as Colette's masterpieces, Forestier finally establishes a definition of Colette's code of morality, based on her mother's, and extrapolates moral lessons from it.

Reviews:
Carrefour, 18 Dec. 1968, 22-23. Pascal Pia.
Information littéraire 20 (May-June 1968): 135. M.D. [Michel Décaudin].

1091 Giry, Jacqueline. *Colette et l'art du discours intérieur*. Paris: Pensée universelle, 1980. 224p. Attempts to study Colette's dialogue with her inner self through her writing, but tends to be descriptive and interpretive rather than analytical, and does not make a firm distinction between the real Colette and her fictional creations. Sometimes focuses on Colette's "art" and sometimes on the idea of dialogue. Locates the source of Colette's strength in her early solitude, noting the geographic imprecision of her childhood world, despite its preponderance of specific detail. Although there is a certain vagueness in the movement of the over-all argument, this book offers some valuable ideas, particularly with respect to Colette's use of mirrors as a device for dialogue, the use of the hand as symbol of the Sido-Willy polarity, Colette's meaning of "purity," and the dialogue aspects of *La Naissance du jour*. Contains extracts from an unpublished letter to Pierre Moreno and a long bibliography arranged chronologically.

1092 Goudeket, Maurice. *La Douceur de vieillir*. Paris: Flammarion, 1965. 227p. Memoirs of Colette's third husband, beginning with his childhood and sometimes divulging details of his personal life that some readers might wish had remained unwritten. The center section is devoted to his years with Colette and contains many passages from her letters to him from Saint Tropez. These demonstrate Colette's skill at spontaneous description, especially of animals and nature. Some passages deal with the genesis of *La Naissance du jour*.

Reviews:
Chicago Tribune Books Today, 1 May 1966, 1-3. Elaine P.
   Halperin.
Commonweal 86 (14 July 1967): 452-54. Alice Mayhew.
Guardian, 3 Feb. 1967, 7. Francis Fytton.
New York Review of Books 6 (9 June 1966): 8-10. John
   Weightman.
New York Times Book Review, 1 May 1966, 1, 52-53. Elizabeth
   Janeway.
Rapports-Het Franse Boek 36 (April 1966): 70. G.J. van Putten.
Reporter 35 (20 Oct. 1966): 59-60. Justin O'Brien. Also in *The
   French Literary Horizon*, 267-70. New Brunswick, N.J.:
   Rutgers University Press, 1967.
Times Literary Supplement, no. 3393 (9 March 1967): 194.
Yorkshire Post, 27 July 1967, 6. George Taylor.

English translation: *The Delights of Growing Old*. Trans. Patrick
   O'Brian. New York: Farrar, Straus & Giroux, 1966. 214p. Also
   London: Michael Joseph, 1967. 175p.

1093   Goudeket, Maurice. *Près de Colette*. Paris: Flammarion, 1956.
   285p. Also Paris: Club de la femme, 1966. 253p. Also extracts
   in item 0063 *Pages choisies* and item 0584 *La Naissance du
   jour*. By evoking their life together over some thirty years,
   Colette's third and last husband reveals his great admiration and
   affection for his wife. A generally disjointed but roughly
   chronological presentation of anecdotes, reminiscences and
   commentary, providing valuable insights into Colette's method
   of writing, as well as details of her daily life, her habits and
   preferences, and her relationships with others.

Reviews:
Antares 6 (1958): 75-76. Hildegard Gerbert.
Books & Bookmen 2 (July 1957): 27. Margaret Crosland.
Figaro littéraire, 13 Dec. 1958, 2. André Rousseaux.
Listener 58 (15 Aug. 1957): 247-48.
Marginales 11 (Dec. 1956): 69-70. Constant Burniaux.
New Republic 137 (30 Sept. 1957): 17-18. Hayden Carruth.
New Statesman 54 (6 July 1957): 28-29. Richard Mayne.
New York Times Book Review 106 (30 June 1957): 4. Henri
   Peyre.
New Yorker 32 (29 Sept. 1956): 110-12. Janet Flanner [Genêt].

New Yorker 33 (June 1957): 104-13. William Maxwell.
Observer, no. 8661 (30 June. 1957): 12. John Weightman.
Patrie, 2 Sept. 1956, 72. Roger Duhamel.
Reporter 16 (13 June 1957): 40-42. Hortense Calisher.
Saturday Review 40 (25 May 1957): 30. Frances Keene.
Spectator, no. 6700 (23 Nov. 1956): 733-34. Peter Quennell.
Sunday Times, 30 June 1957, 7. Cyril Connolly.
Table ronde 106 (Oct. 1956): 123-25. Jacques Robichon.
Time 70 (22 July 1957): 64-66.
Times Literary Supplement, no. 2848 (28 Sept. 1956): 570.
Times Literary Supplement, no. 2889 (12 July 1957): 429.

English translation: *Close to Colette: An Intimate Portrait of a Woman of Genius*. Trans. Enid McLeod. Introd. Harold Nicolson. New York: Farrar, Straus & Cudahy, 1957. 245p. Also London: Secker & Warburg, 1957. 218p.; Westport, Conn.: Greenwood Press, 1972. 245p.

1094 Harris, Elaine. *L'Approfondissement de la sensualité dans l'œuvre romanesque de Colette*. Paris: Nizet, 1973. 254p. Attempts to deduce from *Le Pur et l'impur* Colette's ideas on sensuality in love, then studies her presentation of them in the novels and major novellas. The first book to treat the subject at length, but disappointing in that it offers little in the way of new ideas. Refutes the notion advanced by many old-guard critics that in Colette's books love is strictly of the senses. The most interesting section is a too-sketchy inquiry into Colette's esthetic treatment of the subject.

1095 *Hommage à Colette*. Monaco: Imprimerie Nationale de Monaco, 1955. Non-pag. [32p.] Published under the aegis of the Conseil Littéraire de la Principauté de Monaco, of which Colette had been Honorary President. Texts by: Prince Rainier III, Roland Dorgelès, Gérard Bauer, Jacques Chenevière, André Billy, Jean Giono, Georges Duhamel, Maurice Genevoix, Pierre Gaxotte, Paul Géraldy, Julien Green, Franz Hellens, Emile Henriot, Jules Roy, Philippe Hériat, André Maurois, Gabriel Ollivier, Marcel Pagnol, Léonce Peillard, Jules Supervielle, and Henri Troyat. Also two texts by Colette: one for Prince Rainier's accession to the throne in 1950, and one for the first film showing of *Le Blé en herbe* to a student audience. All are annotated separately but none are significant. Interesting photographs.

1096   Houssa, Nicole. *Le Souci de l'expression chez Colette*. Brussels:
       Palais des Académies, 1958. 235p. The first long systematic
       analysis of components of Colette's style. Compares stylistic
       features of *Les Vrilles de la vigne*, *La Naissance du jour* and
       L'Etoile vesper. Studies every kind of sensation--taste, sound,
       smell, hearing, sight and movement--as well as combinations
       appearing in images, and establishes a hierarchy of them
       according to Colette's preferences. The section in which Houssa
       concludes that, not only are rhythm, meaning and sound factors
       in Colette's choice of words, but spelling is as well, is novel
       and intriguing. The book is rich in examples from the works
       studied.

       Reviews:
       Flambeau 42 (1959): 272-75. Marianne Stoumon.
       Lettres romanes 14 (Aug. 1960): 289-92. Henri Simons.
       Modern Language Notes 75 (March 1960): 279-80. Micheline
          Herz.
       Vie wallonne, no. 285 (Jan.-March 1959): 63. A. Soreil.

1097   Joubert, André. *Colette et 'Chéri.'* Paris: Nizet, 1972. 221p. The
       only thorough study of *Chéri* so far published. Explores all
       aspects of the work, including genesis. Convincingly questions
       Colette's own statement, or at least the common interpretation
       of it, that the creation of Clouk preceded that of Chéri. Points
       out inconsistencies in the chronology of the novel, but finds
       them insignificant. Provides a lengthy analysis of the novel's
       dramatic, temporal and spatial structures, and assesses the role
       of the novelist's own presence. Studies the role of images
       appertaining to each of the major characters. Asserts that the
       novel's dramatic tension is partly due to the tension inherent in
       the contrast in the levels of language used by the author and her
       characters. Offers a reasoned opinion on the stage version of the
       novel. The final chapter compares different aspects of the novel
       with those of other literary works, and concludes that it is
       indeed original. An excellent aid to in-depth study of *Chéri*.

       Reviews:
       Rapports-Het Franse Boek 43 (Nov. 1973): 110-17. Mieke Bal.
       Revue belge de philologie et d'histoire 55 (1977): 300-2. J.P. van
          der Linden.

1098   Jourlait, Daniel. *'La Maison de Claudine' de Colette*. Paris:
       Hachette, 1972. 80p. Coll. Lire aujourd'hui. Designed for
       students, this slim volume provides a brief biography of Colette
       as well as short sections on *La Maison de Claudine*'s genesis,
       themes and content, meaning, structure and style, and reception
       by critics. Seven passages of the work are then subjected to a
       brief *explication de textes*, to which a glossary of difficult and
       important words is appended. Final section had also appeared in
       Le français dans le monde 68 (Oct.-Nov. 1969): 19-26.

1099   Jouve, Nicole Ward. *Colette: A Rose of the Winds*. Bloomington:
       Indiana University Press; Brighton: Harvester, 1987. xvi-232p.
       Coll. Key Women Writers. Written in a very informal style,
       this unusual book proposes to analyze Colette's psychology and
       achievements as a *woman* writer. To this end, its perspective is
       refreshing, in that it often causes the reader to reconsider the
       standard interpretation of what Colette says, but its frequent
       assumptions without logical demonstration are sometimes
       disturbing as well. Arguments outlining the specific nature and
       source of Colette's ideas are therefore not always persuasive,
       though the conclusions are not unreasonable.

       Reviews:
       Choice 25 (Feb. 1988): 913. A.M. Rea.
       Modern Fiction Studies 35 (Summer 1989): 359-60. Hela Michot-
           Dietrich.
       Modern Language Review 84 (Oct. 1989): 998-99. Sandra
           Freeman.
       World Literature Today 62 (Autumn 1988): 630. Lucille F. Becker.

1100   Keller, Fernand, and André Lautier. *Colette (Colette Willy): son
       œuvre*. Paris: Eds. de la Nouvelle Revue Critique, 1923. 63p.
       Coll. Critique (Célébrités d'aujourd'hui) 10. Written during
       Colette's most productive years, this book is particularly
       interesting for the insight it provides into her relations with
       critics at that time. It ranks her novels according to their
       apparent sincerity and their fidelity to Colette's own experience.
       Also compares her with other writers, especially Kipling and
       Bataille. Occasionally digresses into peripheral comment on the
       music-hall's gradual replacement by cinema and legitimate
       theater and on the relative merits of these different entertainment
       media. Some topical allusions will escape today's reader.

Review:
Mercure de France, 1 May 1924, 746-47. Jean de Gourmont.

1101   Ketchum, Anne A. *Colette ou 'La Naissance du jour': étude d'un malentendu*. Paris: Minard, 1968. 305p. Coll. Bibliothèque des Lettres modernes 12. Adopting the premise that Colette has not been well understood to date, Ketchum attempts to trace Colette's dialectics as they are revealed chronologically in her major works. Offers few new conclusions, but provides a sympathetic portrayal of the subject.

Reviews:
Bulletin critique du livre français 24 (May 1969): 438.
Carrefour, 18 Dec. 1968, 22-23. Pascal Pia.
Modern Language Journal 54 (March 1970): 210-11. Micheline W. Herz.
Romanic Review 62 (April 1971): 154-55. Elaine Marks.

1102   Köberle, Martin. *Moderne Tendenzen in Colette's Sprache*. Munich: Hohenhaus, 1930. 135p. Published dissertation, whose declared purpose is to identify stylistic tendencies in modern French by examining work published by one modern writer, namely Colette, with emphasis on her output of the previous fifteen years. Köberle adopts the premise that the richness of Colette's language is due partly to the diversity of her experience and partly to social changes. That Colette might not be the best choice for the study of stylistic currents does not lessen the importance of this book, since for decades it was one of the few long analytical studies written on her style and it is still useful. Köberle compares passages of different periods in an effort to detect prevailing characteristics as well as changes in Colette's use of language, and was one of the first to remark on impressionist elements in her work.

1103   Lachgar, Lina. *Colette*. Paris: Henri Veyrier, 1983. 160p. Coll. Albums. Mostly photographs of Colette or of persons and places figuring in her life, but rich in representations of other visual material such as book covers and illustrations, posters, drawings, letters and postcards. Some of the photographs are well known; others will be new to most readers. Many of the captions are quotations from Colette's work. The long foreword stresses Colette's originality and her special aptitude for evoking sensations and the movements of the heart. Concludes by affirming that Colette's boldness in portraying the reality of love did a great service to French literature by opening the way for others to do the same. Also chronology and bibliography.

1104   La Hire, Jean de. *Ménages d'artistes: Willy et Colette.* Paris: Bibliothèque indépendante d'édition, 1905. 287p. Although the title indicates that the book is about both Willy and Colette, the latter receives much less space than her husband. This accurately reflects the relative importance of the two authors in 1905, before their separation and when Colette was known only as a collaborator on the Claudine novels and as the author of the first *Dialogues de bêtes.* Most of the passages on the Claudine novels are in the sections devoted to Willy. Ironically, the four Claudine novels published before this book appeared receive more praise than do Willy's own. Contains photographs and cartoons, a not-always-accurate bibliography of reviews and critical articles to date, and a bouquet of opinions and excerpts of articles, chiefly on Willy.

Review:
Informateur, no. 11-12 (July-Aug. 1905): 570-74.

1105   Larfod, Claude. *Etude préliminaire sur Colette académicienne.* Buenos Aires: Moly & Lassere, 1936. 47p. The initial essay is followed by an article translated and published in the evening newspaper *El Diario* in 1931. Effusive summary of the general characteristics of Colette's work to date terms her a colossus of letters, insisting that her work will survive because it deals with human problems. Dwells on the "Frenchness" of Colette's writing, and attempts to distinguish between what "young girls' literature" is and what "modern young girls" can safely read, then places Colette's books in the latter category. Identifies Willy with the masculine protagonist of "La Main" in *La Femme cachée.*

1106   Larnac, Jean. *Colette: sa vie, son œuvre.* Paris: Kra, 1927. 233p. Coll. Les Documentaires. A fairly superficial and now dated general study, in which Colette's life and publications are reviewed chronologically, but a land-mark publication in that it was the first book-length study of Colette's work. Glosses over her lesbian relationships. Notes the anticipatory elements in her novels. Recognizes the moral perspective inherent in her essays, and views the stories of *La Femme cachée* as studies of the subconscious mind. The chapters on Colette's style and technique are the least valuable in the light of modern criticism, whereas sections on Colette as actress and dramatic author contain the most interesting passages.

Reviews:
Revue hebdomadaire 36 (3 Dec. 1927): 102-4. Jean Balde.
Temps, 19 April 1928, 3. Paul Souday.
Times Literary Supplement, no. 1362 (8 March 1928): 164.

1107   Le Hardouin, Maria. *Colette*. Paris: Eds. universitaires, 1956. 136p. Coll. Classiques du XXe siècle 24. Also in *Femmes et Littérature*, edited by Jean-Pierre Delarge, 49-132. Romorantin: Martinsart, 1980. Chapter 8, "Savoir vieillir," and chapter 9, "Colette et la postérité," under umbrella title "Images de Colette," also in *Revue des deux mondes* 2 (15 Jan. 1956): 328-41. Expressed purpose of the book is to penetrate to the essence of Colette's mind. However, biographical information is limited to generally well-known facts or details borrowed from her books. Minimizes the autobiographical element in the Claudine novels, and stresses the lack of psychological unity in the early fictional characters. Judges Colette's women characters as much like each other. Chapter 9, which attempts to present Colette's art of growing old, is actually a sympathetic commentary on an admired author.

Reviews.
Listener 59 (1 May 1958): 743.
Synthèses 11 (July 1956): 513-16. Pierre Lesdain.
Times Literary Supplement, no. 2952 (26 Sept. 1958): 542.

English translation: *Colette: A Biographical Study*. Trans. Erik de Mauny. London: Staples Press, 1958. 186p.

1108   Lextrait, François Gaston. *Les Animaux dans l'œuvre de Colette*. Toulouse: [Imprimerie parisienne], 1959. 55p. Published doctoral thesis in veterinary medicine. Expressed purpose is to discover if Colette observes animals justly and impartially without yielding to anthropomorphism, and to determine whether or not she makes a contribution to our knowledge of

them. Compares her to Kipling and Jules Renard in her
knowledge and love of animals. Concludes that Colette's
portrayals are rarely anthropomorphic, but that she over-rates
animals' capacity for feeling. Considers her work to have value
in providing balance to society's too-human preoccupations.

1109 Malige, Jeannie. *Colette: qui êtes-vous?* Lyons: La Manufacture,
1987. 216p. Mostly popular biography interspersed with
general comments about Colette's work. Chiefly anecdotal,
often titillating or speculative, with frequent allusions to well-
known persons and many brief quotations. Does attempt to
portray both negative and positive aspects of Colette's character.
Includes text of nine unpublished radio talks by Colette dating
from the beginning of World War II [annotated separately].

1110 Marks, Elaine. *Colette.* New Brunswick, N.J.: Rutgers University
Press, 1960; London: Secker & Warburg, 1961. 265p. Also
Westport, Conn.: Greenwood Press, 1981. 265p. The first
complete study of Colette by an American and still a sound,
easy-to-read introduction to her life and works. Biographical
details included are those relevant to Colette's work, rather than
those of piquant interest. Marks immediately posits the
difficulty of separating fact from fiction in the first-person
works and is one of the first critics to note that much of the
early shock value of Colette's novels lay in the fact that her
female characters view men in the same way that many men
have viewed women, that is, as objects of pleasure. She divides
Colette's female characters into two groups, the Colette-
Claudine and the Colette-Sido, remarking that the male
characters tend to depict characteristics of Colette's first
husbands. Marks finds much humor in *Chéri* and notes that the
short stories provide good study of some of Colette's
techniques. This is one of the first books to deal with Colette's
plays and theater criticism. Defines her meaning of the word
purity as a privileged state, in which the person is committed to
a ruling passion, and declares Colette's main problem to be the
loss of this purity. Ranks *Pour un herbier*, not usually
considered an important work, as the highest expression of
Colette's descriptive powers.

Reviews:
American Scholar 30 (Winter 1960-1961): 142. Cornelia Schæffer.
Criticism 4 (Winter 1962): 84-85. David Hayman.
Esprit créateur 3 (Summer 1963): 90-91. John Hyde.
Illustrated London News 239 (23 Sept. 1961): 510. E.D. O'Brien.
Modern Fiction Studies 6 (Winter 1960-1961): 368-69.
Modern Language Notes 76 (Dec. 1961): 923-25. Micheline W.
    Herz.
New Statesman 62 (18 Aug. 1961): 215-18. Penelope Gilliatt.
New York Times Book Review 110 (25 Sept. 1960): 6. Robert
    Phelps.
Observer, no. 8876 (13 Aug. 1961): 20. John Weightman.
Prairie Schooner 34 (1960): 382. George Ross Ridge.
Romanic Review 53 (Dec. 1962): 309-10. Alvin Labat.
Saturday Review 43 (3 Sept. 1960): 25. Otis Fellows.
Spectator 207 (18 Aug. 1961): 237. John Mortimer.
Studi francese, no. 29 (May-Aug. 1966): 391. L.L. Pardini.
Time & Tide 42 (24 Aug. 1961): 1401. Margaret Davies.
Times Literary Supplement, no. 3126 (26 Jan. 1962): 52.

1111   Massie, Allan. *Colette.* Harmondsworth: Penguin, 1986. 152p.
        Coll. Lives of Modern Women. Not a perceptive book, this is
        essentially a popular biography on which discussion of a few of
        Colette's books has been grafted. It does make an effort to set
        her early works and experience within the context of French
        society of the Third Republic. Massie insists that the dominant
        role of Colette's mother in the family may have been a
        disturbing factor in Colette's other love-relations, and he
        speculates at length on her relationship with Bertrand de
        Jouvenel, without offering evidence for his suppositions.
        Although an index of names and titles is included, quotations
        are not identified.

        Reviews:
        Books & Bookmen, no. 367 (May 1986): 10-11. Frances Spalding.
        Modern Fiction Studies 33 (Summer 1987): 384-85. Mary Beth
            Pringle.

1112   Maulnier, Thierry [pseud. of Jacques Talagrand]. *Introduction à
        Colette.* Paris: La Palme, 1954. 71p. Long essay, in which
        Maulnier identifies Colette's major theme as the double
        movement of loss and enrichment, with the first being

paradoxically the source of the second. Emphasizes the idea that her works reveal a search for equilibrium through an oscillation of the two sides of her personality, represented in part by her two distinguishable styles, the lyrical and the succinct. Rejects the view that Colette's male characters are insignificant, insisting that the recognized novelty of their depiction lies in the fact that they are described only from outside. Refutes view of many earlier critics that the use of a feminine perspective is equivalent to subjectivity. Praises Colette's theater criticism as an enduring chronicle of the theater of the time, written by one who was familiar with all its facets. Still a useful study.

Review:
Figaro littéraire, 29 Jan. 1955, 2. André Billy.

1113 Mignon, Maurice. *Autour de Colette*. Nevers: [Imprimerie de Cloix], 1958. 14p. Pamphlet sketching origins of the Colette family and the influence on Colette's attitude to life of other family members, especially her mother.

1114 Mignon, Maurice. *Notes sur Colette*. Clamecy: n.p., 1959. 12p. Pamphlet written on the fifth anniversary of Colette's death. Incorporates material from item 1113 *Autour de Colette*.

1115 Mignon, Maurice. *Souvenirs sur Colette*. Milan: Nicolà, 1957. 6p. Pamphlet evoking Mignon's last meeting with Colette in the spring of 1954, and expressing personal ideas about her talent, her death and her childhood. Previously published in *Lingue e Cultura* 3 (Jan.-March 1957).

1116 Mitchell, Yvonne. *Colette: A Taste for Life*. London: Weidenfeld & Nicolson; New York: Harcourt Brace Jovanovich, 1975. 240p. Popular biography with many photographs. Comments on Colette's publications are mostly general, the emphasis of the book being, as its title indicates, on Colette herself and especially her attitude towards life. The numerous quotations from her books and letters are not identified and are often presented in such a way as to give the impression that her fictional characters are speaking for her. Definitely an unscholarly work, but an interesting one offering a warm picture of Colette the person.

Reviews:
Choice 13 (May 1976): 374.
Daily Telegraph Magazine, no. 563 (12 Sept. 1975): 32. Selina
   Hastings.
Economist 256 (20 Sept. 1975): 125.
New Statesman 90 (3 Oct. 1975): 412-13. Victoria Glendinning.

1117   Moberg, Eva. *Karlek och kon: En Studie i Colettes Diktning.*
       Stockholm: Bonniers, 1963. 168p. General study of Colette's
       work, with focus on her characters. Analyzes both male and
       female characters by type, as well as the relations between men
       and women according to physical or emotional tie. Includes a
       short biography, and often links ideas to details of Colette's
       own experience.

1118   Mühr, Alfred. *Sanftes alter Colette*. [Cologne-Ehrenfeld:
       Natterman, 1969]. [40p.]. Reviews the highlights of Colette's
       life, especially those of her later years: her election to the
       Goncourt Academy, her suffering from arthritis, and Maurice
       Goudeket's devotion. A sympathetic essay, which emphasizes
       Colette's continuing development and her inner strength.

1119   Pavlovic, Mihaïlo B. *Sidonie-Gabrielle Colette: le monde animal
       dans sa vie et dans sa création littéraire.* Bordeaux: Bière;
       Belgrade: Faculty of Philology of the University of Belgrade,
       1970. 192p. Published dissertation completed some fifteen years
       earlier. In the first of the two main sections, Pavlovic attempts
       to identify biographical reasons for Colette's fondness for
       animals, to determine the extent to which she was "animalistic"
       (the term is not defined) and to identify the role that animals
       actually played in her life. The second section focuses on the
       portrayal of animals in her books, and is largely descriptive and
       compilatory. Now very out-dated in both ideas and approach,
       this potentially useful book provides no table of contents and
       was not updated for publication.

1120   Perche, Louis. *Colette*. Paris: Seghers, 1976. 158p. Coll.
       Ecrivains d'hier et d'aujourd'hui 48. Fairly superficial mixture of
       biography and general literary interpretation. Assumes a close
       connection between Colette and her literary heroines. Praises
       Colette's generosity in not overtly blaming her father and sister
       for the family's financial reverses. Most novels are only briefly

discussed, except for *Chéri, La Fin de Chéri* and *Le Blé en herbe*, for which some of Colette's techniques are identified. Includes a long and interesting chronological table, paralleling events of Colette's life with literary, artistic and historic incidents of the same years.

Reviews:
Bulletin critique du livre français 31 (1976): 958.
Figaro, 16 April 1976, 16. Claude Mauriac.

1121 *Pour le centenaire de Colette*. Brussels: Palais des Académies, 1973. 57p. Also in *Bulletin de l'Académie royale de langue et de littérature françaises* 51:3-4 (1973): 140-94. Collection of addresses celebrating the one hundredth anniversary of Colette's birth. Texts by Georges Sion, Françoise Mallet-Joris, Pierre Falize, Lucienne Desnoues and Carlo Bronne. All are annotated separately.

1122 Raaphorst-Rousseau, Madeleine. *Colette: sa vie et son art*. Paris: Nizet, 1964. 319p. Useful all-round study, published just when Colette was beginning to be taken seriously by scholars. Excellent summary biography, despite frequent speculation about Colette's own motives and a tendency to identify her with her heroines. Considers Colette's three main themes to be love, nature and animals, and attempts to situate her use of them within currents in French literature. Recognizes Colette's intelligence and the superiority of her style, but stresses the role of sensuality and instinct. Contains a valuable summary of many of Colette's basic techniques, with specific illustrations from her work.

Reviews:
French Review 40 (Nov. 1966): 307-8. Elaine Marks.
Revue belge de philologie et d'histoire 44:3 (1966): 1039-40. G. Gillain.
Studi francesi, no. 30 (Sept.-Dec. 1966): 592-93. S. Robiolio.

1123 Reboux, Paul. *Colette ou le génie du style*. Paris: Vald. Rasmussen, 1925. 63p. Coll. Critique. One of the first long studies of Colette's style. Expresses unreserved admiration for her style, and offers many quotations in illustration. No real stylistic analysis is attempted, however, and passages from

Colette's works are not identified. Compares her style to that of painters, especially the Impressionists, and praises her precision of language. Despite its shortcomings, this book helped to focus attention on the elements making up Colette's already famous style. Incorporates item 2035.

Review:
Œuvre, 1 July 1925, 6. André Billy.

1124   Resch, Yannick. *Corps féminin, corps textuel: essai sur le personnage féminin dans l'œuvre de Colette*. Pref. Raymond Jean. Paris: Klincksieck, 1973. 207p. Applies critical theories on lexical space to five novels: *Duo*, *La Seconde*, *La Chatte*, *Julie de Carneilhan* and *Chéri*. Using the computer, Resch analyzes Colette's use of terms relating to parts of the female body for each main character, explores implications of these terms, then presents them statistically to reconstitute a composite or archetypal woman. One does not always agree with Resch's conclusions, but this is a fascinating and enlightening study which has generated further work in the field. Her ideas on Colette's views on why communication breaks down between men and women are especially interesting.

Reviews:
Figaro littéraire, 18 Aug. 1973, 2. Claudine Jardin.
French Review 48 (Oct. 1974): 228-29. Eugenia V. Osgood.
French Studies 32 (July 1978): 357-58. Henri Godin.
Journal de Genève, 29 Sept. 1973, non-pag. [17]. P.O. Walzer.
Revue d'histoire littéraire de la France 74 (Sept.-Oct. 1974): 931-32. Claire Quilliot.

1125   Reymond, Evelyne. *Colette et la Côte d'Azur*. Pref. Brigitte Bardot. Aix-en-Provence: Edisud, 1988. 128p. An account of the time Colette spent in the south of France as music-hall performer, summer resident and finally arthritis patient. Most of the book pertains to her life at La Treille Muscate, the summer home she owned at Saint Tropez from 1926 to 1938. Not only is the daily round described in detail, but Colette's animals, servants, habits and cooking secrets are all accorded a chapter. Many names are mentioned and many anecdotes related, some of them quotations from Colette's own work. Very little of the material included is new, but this is the first book-length publication to treat solely of Colette's affection for the region, and the many drawings and photographs, some published for the first time, render it extremely interesting.

1126   Reymond, Evelyne. *Le Rire de Colette*. Paris: Nizet, 1988. 99p. The only book-length publication to study Colette's humor. It is unfortunate that few of the unnumbered chapters go beyond identifying and classifying humorous passages in her work. A few chapters attempt to identify the types of subjects that Colette makes humorous. Despite its limitations, the book contains valuable remarks on the nuances of language in *Mitsou* and it does insist on Colette's use of humor as a mask for suffering, both in her own life and in those of her fictional characters.

1127   Richardson, Joanna. *Colette*. New York: Franklin Watts; London: Methuen, 1983. 276p. Popular biography, which divides Colette's life into six periods, each of them reflecting a phase of her emotional life. A certain patchiness in the depth to which the book portrays those periods, as well as a tendency to quote opinions of Colette's relatives, friends and critics as if they were proven, lessen the book's value, and Colette the person does not really come alive for the reader. Nevertheless, in its presentation of facts, the biography is sound. Many names are mentioned. Those sections which comment on Colette's writing are the least satisfactory parts.

Reviews:
London Review of Books 5 (6 Oct. 1983): 14-15. Brigid Brophy.
New Republic 190 (4 June 1984): 38-42. Isa Kapp.
New York Review of Books 21 (26 April 1984): 12-16. Gabriele Annan.
New Yorker 60 (19 March 1984): 147-48.
Times Literary Supplement, no. 4194 (19 Aug. 1983): 879. Anne Duchêne.

1128   Sarde, Michèle. *Colette, libre et entravée*. Paris: Stock, 1978. 487p. Coll. Femmes dans leur temps. Also Paris: Seuil, 1984. 487p. Coll. Points. Immensely popular feminist biography. An obvious partisanship and a tendency to toss out generalizations as if they explained specific events in Colette's life will trouble readers seeking only facts and objectivity, but the liveliness and enthusiasm of this presentation compensate in part for these weaknesses. Quotes freely from Colette's books and letters, without discriminating between author and fictional character. Passages discussing Colette's marriage with Willy within its historical framework of social and financial considerations are probably the book's most valuable contribution to criticism.

Reviews:
Atlantic 245 (March 1980): 98-101. Benjamin DeMott.
Bulletin critique du livre français 39 (1984): 1410.
Cahiers de sémiotique textuelle 8-9 (1986): 153-75. Danielle Deltel. Detailed critique.
Christian Science Monitor 72 (14 April 1980): B10. Carolyn Hall.
Devoir, 21 Oct. 1978, 22. Monique Roy.
Esprit 22 (Oct. 1978): 144-45. Fernande Schulmann.
Express, no. 1414 (14 Aug. 1978): 70-72. Rosa Laisné.
Figaro littéraire, 1 July 1978, 21. Geneviève Dormann.
French Review 52 (May 1979): 937. Joan Hinde Stewart.
Library Journal 105 (15 March 1980): 726. Sally Mitchell.
Literary Review 2 (Sept. 1981): 29-30. Jennifer Birkett.
London Review of Books 2 (2 Oct. 1980): 15-17. Angela Carter.
Magazine littéraire, no. 40 (Sept. 1978): 58. Pierre Kyria.
Modern Language Journal 64 (1980): 386-87. Anne Ketchum.
Monde, 22 June 1978, 1, 26. Gabrielle Rolin.
New York Times Book Review 129 (30 March 1980): 12. Doris Grumbach.
New Yorker 56 (21 April 1980): 146.
Nouvelles littéraires, 13 July 1978, 8. Gérard Spiteri.
Observer, no. 9916 (13 Sept. 1981): 25. A.N. Wilson.
Quinzaine littéraire 283 (15 July 1978): 9-10. Hubert Juin.
Signs 5 (Winter 1979): 350-51. Irene Finel-Honigman.
Spectator 247 (19 Sept. 1981): 19. Anita Brookner.
Sunday Times, 6 Sept. 1981, 41. Emma Tennant.
Times Literary Supplement, no. 4113 (29 Jan. 1982): 112. Phyllis Grosskurth.
Washington Post Book World 10 (30 March 1980): 4. Stephen Koch.

English translation: *Colette: Free and Fettered*. Trans. Richard Miller. New York: Morrow, 1980; London: Michael Joseph, 1981. 479p.

1129 Sigl, Robert. *Colette*. Paris: Belles Lettres, 1924. 55p. Coll.
Bibliothèque critique des belles lettres. One of the earliest
serious assessments of Colette's work. Traces her sensibility
and naturalness, not just to her early life, but also to the literary
traditions of the nineteenth century, especially symbolism. Sigl
admires Colette's imagery and powers of description, which, he
maintains, help to identify her as an anti-romantic. Deems
Colette's sense of humor to be rare among women writers and
says that her irony comprises the intellectual aspect of her
work. Concludes that Colette's writing is durable and that some
of her books will one day serve as a source of study of the
social evolution of women.

Review:
Mercure de France, 1 April 1926, 145-48. Jean de Gourmont.

1130 Stewart, Joan Hinde. *Colette*. Boston: Twayne, 1983. 158p. Coll.
Twayne's World Authors Series 679. Exceptionally well-written
assessment of Colette's major and minor works. Views
Colette's achievement in the Claudine novels as an embodiment
of her refusal of conventional values in family, school, marriage
and fidelity. Sees in *La Maison de Claudine* the "negative" of
Claudine à l'école as *La Vagabonde* is to *L'Entrave*. Offers many
perceptive remarks about the significance of names and words in
several of the novels, especially *L'Ingénue libertine*, *La
Vagabonde*, *L'Entrave* and *Gigi*. Offers a valuable analysis of
Colette's use of mirrors and letters. This is one of the few
critical books to assess novellas such as *Bella-Vista* and *Le
Képi*. It identifies the tension in these as the result of Colette's
multiple role as participant, observer, narrator and writer. It also
notes the importance of her function as *confidante*. Preceded by
a useful chronology, this is a very fine scholarly study, written
from a fresh perspective and free of the clichés to which Colette
criticism is still subject. Incorporates items 2129-2133.

Reviews:
Esprit créateur 24 (Fall 1984): 83-84. Elaine Marks.
French Review 58 (March 1985): 585-86. Robert D. Cottrell.

1131 Tegyey, Gabriella. *Analyse structurelle du récit chez Colette*.
Debrecen: Kossuth Lajos Tudományegyetem, 1988. 98p.
Romance Studies of the University of Debrecen, Literary series

no. 13. Structuralist analysis of some seventeen of Colette's major fictional works. Deduces from them a system of underlying constants consisting of archimodel with variants. Examines narrative discourse, duration and perspective in these works, to produce sometimes surprising conclusions. The least satisfactory section is that in which Tegyey attempts to deduce a chronological pattern from the data, whereas those in which she deals with Colette's use of places and space are especially fine.

1132   Tinter, Sylvie. *Colette et le temps surmonté*. Geneva: Slatkine, 1980. 93p. Traces the problem of aging as it is depicted in Colette's books. Concludes that Colette's mother was her ideal in this respect, but an ideal to which Colette only gradually adhered. Also considers that the act of writing was for Colette a partial solution to the aging problem. Analyzes relationships of several of Colette's fictional couples in which one partner is much older than the other, discovering in these relationships echoes of Œdipal structures. Makes little distinction between Colette and her fictional characters, and does not treat all of her novels. Although few of the ideas offered in this small book are completely new, it is the only major publication to focus on the aging theme.

1133   Trahard, Pierre. *L'Art de Colette*. Paris: Jean-Renard, 1941. 239p. Coll. Sainte-Beuve. Also Geneva: Slatkine Reprints, 1971. xxxiii-248p. [reprint of the 1941 edition augmented by a new introduction and an up-to-date bibliography]. One of the best early general studies, despite its tendency towards obliqueness and over-quotation of Colette's work. Attempts to distinguish between the "sense of nature" and the "sentiment of nature," saying that it is the former that makes Colette's work original. Insists that *La Fin de Chéri*, *La Chatte*, *Duo* and *La Seconde* prove that Colette is interested in both morality and psychology. Rejecting the early view that Colette's art is instinctive, Trahard emphasizes her dedication to precision and hard work, giving short shrift to several named critics and their views. The chapter in which he attempts to characterize Colette's style contains much new and valuable commentary. Holding that Colette's work demonstrates that French is not just clear, logic and formal, but also plastic, colorful and musical, Trahard considers her to have renewed the French language. Occasional inaccuracies do not significantly detract from the over-all value of Trahard's book. In the 1970 introduction he insists that his opinion of Colette remains unchanged, but the tenor of these later remarks is less laudatory than those of the book itself.

Review:
Nouvelle Revue française 56 (April 1942): 493-94. G. Jean-Aubry.

1134 Truc, Gonzague. *Madame Colette*. Paris: Corrêa, 1941. 191p. This book's declared purpose is to arrive at the essential Colette through her works. Truc finds Colette's novels to be the result of a process of personal study of herself through doubles and mirrors. He makes an interesting analysis of the Claudine-Annie-Colette relationship. Modern readers may be offended by Truc's reiteration of the once-popular notion that Colette's skill at evoking sensation is particularly suitable for portraying children, women or characters like Chéri, who live only by the senses. Despite the occasional remark of this type, Truc admires Colette's work and finds in it evidence of a coherent moral perspective. He was also one of the first critics to publicly recognize the role of Colette's conscious intellect in developing her art to a high standard. Incorporates items 2168-70.

1135 Viel, Marie-Jeanne. *Colette au temps des Claudine*. Paris: Publications essentielles, 1978. 176p. Synthesis of interview material, reminiscences and passages from Colette's work. Acknowledgment of sources is capricious, often incomplete or even missing. Contains some errors of fact, a few of which are corrected in a post-face. Despite these deficiencies, the book is lively and intriguing in the picture it paints of the Paris that Colette knew at the turn of the century. Contains long sections on Willy's public activities, as well as on controversial events of the time, such as the Dreyfus affair. Recognizes Colette's uniqueness. Maintains that her work was little marked by influences particular to the period in which she was writing.

Review:
Contrepoint 28 (Oct.-Dec. 1978): 171-72. J.B. [Janine Bouissounouse].

1136 Voigt, Waltraut. *Colette: Leben und Werk*. Jena: Otto Jensen, 1935. 102p. Published dissertation. General discussion of

Colette's life and works to about 1933. Attempts to correct
some of the misinterpretations caused by the difficulty that early
male critics had of understanding or accepting her perspective,
but insists that one cannot consider her work without reference
to her life.

1137   Willy [pseud. of Henry Gauthier-Villars]. *Indiscrétions et
commentaires sur les 'Claudine.'* Foreword Pierre Varenne and
Alfred Diard. Paris: Pro Amicis, 1962. 38p. Long foreword by
two of Willy's friends gives background to the controversy
surrounding the authorship of the Claudine novels, and defends
Willy's actions and reactions. Advances the premise that Colette
re-wrote the manuscripts now generally held to be the originals,
so as to minimize her husband's role in their creation.
Maintains that *Mes Apprentissages* contains errors and
contradictions and that Colette purposely calumniated Willy.
Concludes that Willy and Colette are indebted to each other and
that both are admirable. Followed by a series of letters written
by Willy to Jules Marchand, first published in the review *Sur la
Riviera*, 25 Jan. and 1 Feb. 1931. In them, Willy gives names
to the originals of many of the characters of the four novels,
describes the problems surrounding the publication of each
novel, and asserts that he has been the victim of many
ignominies. Despite, or perhaps because of, the book's obvious
bias in favor of Willy, it provides an extremely interesting and
useful counterpoint to Colette's own accounts of the subject.

Review:
Journal de Genève, 15 Dec. 1962, 20. P.-O. Walzer.

1138   Willy [pseud. of Henry Gauthier-Villars]. *Souvenirs littéraires... et
autres*. Paris: Montaigne, 1925. 147p. Forgettable book of
"memoirs," actually anecdotes and commentary, by Colette's
first husband, roughly covering the period 1880-1910 and
originally intended to be followed by a second volume, never
completed. An index of more than 200 names is provided but is
rendered almost useless by the absence of corresponding page
numbers. In any case, many of the persons mentioned have long
been forgotten. References to Colette or to the Claudine novels
are not numerous [pages 6, 12, 56-59, 67, 82 and 140]. The
most interesting chapter is the final one, in which Willy defends
his use of ghost writers, including Colette.

ARTICLES ON COLETTE
[alphabetically by author, anonymous articles at end]

1139　A., A. "Autant-Lara ou le moraliste en herbe." *Esprit* 220 (Nov. 1954): 614-18. Review of Autant-Lara's film version of *Le Blé en herbe*. Praises Colette's art but insists that her universe is non-moral and non-thinking, and has little in common with masculine intellectuality. Reproaches Autant-Lara for having gratuitously accorded a didactic dimension to the novel and for having thereby diminished the esthetic and poetic appeal of Colette's adolescent world.

1140　Accaputo, Nino. "Leggendo 'Le Kepi' di Colette." In *Di Alcuni contemporanei della letteratura francese*, 5-12. Naples: Pellerano-Del Gaudio, 1955. Analyzes the classical features of *Le Képi* and the role of the witnesses in establishing the objectivity of the first-person narration.

1141　Adam, Jean-Michel, and Jean-Pierre Goldenstein. "Une poétique du signe: 'les choses par leur nom'?..." In *Linguistique et discours littéraire*, 28-41. Paris: Larousse, 1976. Linguistic study of the role and importance of the word *presbytère* in the text "Le curé sur le mur" in *La Maison de Claudine*. Traces use of the word as the child attempts to give it meaning, and the invasion or destruction of the child's world by conventions imposed by adults as they dispel her illusions. Asserts that the child's

refusal to accept the adult meaning of the word demonstrates her
need to poeticize her universe and offers Colette's text as
evidence that meaning imposed upon children is done by
conflict rather than by more innocent means. A fascinating
article which sheds new light on the portrayal of Colette's
childhood paradise.

1142   Aghion, Max. "En mémoire de trois rencontres." *Journal de
Genève*, 28 Dec. 1963, 12. Brief reminiscences of three
meetings with Colette--in 1907 during the scandal of the
Moulin Rouge, in 1911 at the offices of *Le Matin*, and in 1951
at Monte-Carlo.

1143   Ahlenius, [Karl Sven] Holger. "Om Colette." *Ord och Bild* 57
(Nov. 1948): 411-18. Also in *Svenskt och Franskt: Studier och
inlägg*, 272-92. Stockholm: Bonniers, 1950. General survey of
Colette's work. Emphasizes her "Frenchness" but traces her
feeling for nature to her claimed black ancestry. Judges her over-
all output as intellectually insignificant but stylistically
impressive.

1144   Alain [pseud. of Emile Chartier]. In *Cahiers de Lorient*, vol. 2, 18-
19. Paris: Gallimard, 1964. Notebook paragraph positing the
view that educated women prefer the Claudine novels to "great
literature" because they associate the latter with school texts,
which by definition are unconnected with "real life."

1145   Albersmeier, Franz-Josef. "Colettes Filmwerk oder das Kino an der
Peripherie von Roman und Theater." In *Die Epoche des
Stummfilms (1895-1930)*, 299-308 and 449-54. Vol. 1 of *Die
Herausforderung des Films an die französische Literatur*.
Heidelberg: Winter, 1985. Coll. Reihe Siegen 49,
Romanistische Abteilung. Contends that, although Colette
purposely omitted her film work from the *OCLF*, her scenarios
and other film writing should not be under-estimated. Considers
Colette to have played a significant role in the film industry,
particularly towards the end of the silent film era. Demonstrates
that she viewed film-making as an important artistic medium,
and emphasizes the wide range of her film activities. Includes
extensive documentation and bibliography.

1146 Albert, Henri [pseud. of Henri-Albert Haug]. In *Willy*. Paris: Sansot, 1904. 48p. Coll. Les Célébrités d'aujourd'hui. Brief biography and appreciation of Colette's first husband, written when Willy was at the peak of his popularity and before the true authorship of the Claudine novels was generally known, contains many favorable comments about the novels and their presumed author. Includes a selection of excerpts from critics.

1147 Alonzo, Anne-Marie. "Des œuvres de joaillière." *La Vie en rose*, no. 18 (July 1984): 51. Terms Colette's versatility amazing and reading her books like savoring a whole era. Lists favorite titles.

1148 Amblard, Emile. "Les Elections au Conseil Général de Saint-Sauveur en 1880 (Pierre Merlou, Jules Colette et Paul Hérold)." *Bulletin de la Société des Sciences historiques et naturelles de l'Yonne* 97 (1957-1958): 191-210. Recounts Captain Colette's campaign for the Republican nomination as representative to the Conseil Général de l'Yonne in 1880, including his skirmish with Dr. Merlou, whom Colette caricatured in *Claudine à l'école*. Includes candidates' letters to the newspapers, three of them by Colette's father. Passages written by Captain Colette demonstrate Colette's contention that he handled language well, despite his failure to write anything of significant length. A valuable biographical article.

1149 Ambrière, Francis. "Chez Colette." *Nouvelles littéraires*, 16 Nov. 1929, 2. Interview-conversation in which Colette refuses to comment on the possibility of her being elected to the Goncourt Academy. In fact, she was elected only in 1945.

1150 Anglès, Auguste. "Claudine à l'école." *Action*, 11 May 1945, 8. Insists on Colette's originality and the superiority of her style, especially her precision of vocabulary. Maintains that even Colette's short pieces are treated like an exercise done in the classroom, in that she never neglects to invoke the writing principles that she had learned at school.

1151 Anouilh, Jean. [No title]. *Figaro littéraire*, 24 Jan. 1953, 5. Lauds Colette as a rebel against convention.

1152   Anselmi, Luciano. "Ricordo di Colette." *Fiera Letteraria*, 26 April 1964, 3, 5. Brief sketch of Colette's life and major works available in Italian.

1153   Aragon, Louis. "Madame Colette." *Lettres françaises*, 12 Aug. 1954, 1, 5. Long elegiac poem--185 lines--on the occasion of Colette's death. Stresses her suffering, her love for nature, her regret for the past. Recalls her theatrical career and bids her a personal farewell.

1154   Aragonés, Juan Emilio. "Exposición-Homenaje a Colette." *Estafeta Literaria* 531 (Jan. 1974): 40-41. Account of the opening of a Colette exhibition sponsored by Los Amigos de Colette en España, at which the president of the group quoted Colette as saying that the models for the characters in *Gigi* had been owners of a hotel on the Costa Azul.

1155   Arese, Simone [signed: S.A.]. "La deuxième mort de Colette." *Esprit* 2 (July-Aug. 1978): 109. Deplores the effect on Colette's reputation of television programs that give viewers an inferior idea of her written work, and of publicity stunts that have a negative effect on her public image.

1156   Arland, Marcel. "Sous 'Le Fanal bleu' de Madame Colette." In *Lettres de France*, 54-61. Paris: Albin Michel, 1951. Admires Colette's enthusiasm for life in the face of infirmity and old age, but judges that her writing has in consequence become focused on herself, instead of opening out onto the world as it once did.

1157   Arland, Marcel. "La vieillesse de Colette." In *Essais critiques*, 140-43. Paris: Gallimard, 1931. Also in *Essais et nouveaux essais critiques*, 90-92. Paris: Gallimard, 1952. Terms *La Naissance du jour* Colette's most durable work to date, but judges it too long, too personal, too much centered on love, and with too much stylistic ornamentation.

1158   Arnault, Kitty. "Notre Colette'." *Avant-Scene Théâtre*, no. 708 (15 April 1982): 48. Poem of homage to Colette.

1159   Arnoux, Alexandre. "'L'infaillibilité sensuelle...'" *Figaro littéraire*, 24 Jan. 1953, 3. Colette's fellow member of the Goncourt

Academy reiterates the once-common view of Colette as a great writer whose "instinctive profundity, peasant tranquillity and sensual infallibility," unaccompanied by any system of morality or metaphysics, amaze and enchant her readers. Does recognize Colette's originality.

1160 Arsand, Daniel. "Quelques personnages masculins-ambiguïté." In item 1057 *Album Masques: Colette*, 151-63. Fanciful evocation of five of Colette's fictional works: *Chéri*, *La Fin de Chéri*, *Bella-Vista*, *La Chatte* and *Duo*. Despite its impressionistic and subjective nature, this article offers some perceptive remarks, especially in the section on *Bella-Vista*. Views Colette's men characters as symbols of a crumbling world with which they do not even try to cope.

1161 Astaldi, Maria Luisa. "La scrittrice." *Il Giornale d'Italia*, 5 Aug. 1954, 3. Summary of Colette's life and work. Argues that *La Naissance du jour* represents a critical stage in her development.

1162 Auclair, Marcelle, and Françoise Prévost. "Marie Laurencin, Champrosay et Colette." In *Mémoires à deux voix*, 243-50. Paris: Seuil, 1978. In dialogue form the two writers recall Colette's giving advice to Prévost about her appearance, then describe a visit to her in the Palais Royal. They conclude that Colette's fame will increase even more as public esteem grows for books by women.

1163 Audinet, Pierre. "Colette par Colette." *Nouvelles littéraires*, 8 Nov. 1962, 7. Interview with Roberte Forbin, who at the time was assisting Claude Pichois in preparing Colette's correspondence for publication. Attempts to assess the stage at which public dissemination of her correspondence has arrived.

1164 Augué, Fernand. "La jeunesse de Colette." *Nouvelles littéraires*, 4 July 1925, 1. Sketches the genesis of the Claudine novels and their reception by the press. Concludes that even though the ensuing scandal was caused in part by Colette's negative portrayal of people she knew at Saint-Sauveur, these novels represent a pilgrimage on her part to the village of her youth.

1165   Aumont, Jean-Pierre. In *Le Soleil et les ombres*, 56. Paris:
       Laffont, 1976. Brief anecdote recalling a visit paid by actor
       Aumont to Colette at Saint Tropez just before World War II.

1166   Aury, Dominique. "Colette." *Nouvelle Nouvelle Revue française* 4
       (1 Sept. 1954): 508-9. Declares that Colette's universe is that of
       women, since it is composed of small things and has no use for
       abstract principles. Says that Colette became more moralistic
       over time.

1167   Aury, Dominique. "Colette ou le gynécée." *Nouvelle Nouvelle
       Revue française* 1 (March 1953): 505-11. Also in *Lecture pour
       tous*, 63-76. Paris: Gallimard, 1958. Also, as preface to item
       0438 *Duo et Le Toutounier*. Generalizes about the female
       characters in Colette's novels, comparing them to inhabitants of
       a gynæceum or women's enclosure. Notes that all are healthy,
       sensual and preoccupied with love but that, although all adapt
       readily to the wishes of the male, they invariably hold him in
       contempt. Contains negative remarks about Colette's style in
       her mature novels.

       English translation: "Colette." Trans. Denise Folliot. *London
       Magazine* 7 (Aug. 1960): 56-61. Also, under title "The
       Gynæceum," in *Literary Landfalls*, 50-58. London: Chatto &
       Windus, 1960.

1168   Autant-Lara, Claude. "'Colette de France'." *Lettres françaises*, 12
       Aug. 1954, 5. Blames Roman Catholic prelates for not agreeing
       to a religious burial for Colette, arguing that the admiration and
       sympathy of so many French people more than compensate for
       Colette's lapses from Catholic practice.

1169   Autran, André. "Colette en Provence: en pays connu..." *Marseille*,
       no. 120 (Jan.-March, 1980): 57-59. Account of Colette's long
       relationship with the south of France, first while touring as a
       music-hall performer, then as owner of a summer home at Saint
       Tropez, and finally as a visitor to Monte Carlo in old age.

1170   B., J. "Pas assez grands..." *Bulletin de la Société scientifique et
       artistique de Clamecy*, no. 47 (1973): 55-57. Identifies Colette
       as a witness to the lack of power or rights of women at the turn

of the century. Suggests that she married Willy to get away from her village. Reproaches her for concentrating on the everyday and the concrete in her books rather than furthering the cause of women's emancipation, as she might have done when she became known. Concludes that her work is therefore trivial. Reprinted from *La Montagne* (28 Jan. 1973).

1171 B., Dr. P. "Colette par Colette." *Le Fureteur* 14 (15 Feb. 1955): 47-48. Offers details about the relations between Colette and Willy in 1910. Includes an autobiographical sketch signed Colette Willy and presumed to be publicity for pantomime performances in Nice the same year.

1172 Bàccolo, Luigi. "Un decennio di Colette." *Il Mondo*, 29 Dec. 1964, 8. Notes that Colette's letters to Marguerite Moreno and to Renée Hamon [*le petit corsaire*] contain a veritable thesis on how to write. Insists that Colette became gradually more aware of a world beyond the physical, and that her friendship with Hamon was important in this development.

1173 Bal, Mieke. "Colette devant la critique." *Rapports-Het Franse Boek* 41 (1971): 56-63. Critical overview of major studies on Colette. Deplores the general paucity of systematic textual analysis as well as an excessive curiosity about Colette's life. Brief but sound critique of books by Larnac, Truc, Goudeket, Beaumont, Chauvière, Le Hardouin, Houssa, Lextrait, Marks, Ketchum and Davies.

1174 Bal, Mieke. "Figures narratologiques." In *Narratologie: essais sur la signification narrative dans quatre romans modernes*, 21-58. Paris: Klincksieck, 1977; Utrecht: H.E.S. Publishers, 1984. Incorporates item 1176, then sets forth and examines eight "rules" of narrative observed in *La Chatte*. A fine analysis of Colette's narrative techniques.

English translation: "The Narrating and the Focalizing: A Theory of the Agents in Narrative." Trans. Jane Lewin. *Style* 17 (Spring 1983): 234-69.

1175 Bal, Mieke. "Inconsciences de 'Chéri'--Chéri existe-t-il?" In item 1077 *Colette, Nouvelles Approches critiques*, 15-25. Adopts the hypothesis that Colette's mother came to represent a psychological weight on her daughter and that Léa reflects, not Colette as many critics assume, but her mother. Analyzes *Chéri* in the light of this idea. Also posits the view that Colette spreads the maternal negativity over several characters in the novel, and that Chéri's psychology is fixed at the childhood level. A penetrating interpretation of Colette's creative process.

1176 Bal, Mieke. "Narration et focalisation: pour une théorie des instances du récit." *Poétique*, no. 29 (Feb. 1977): 107-27. Critique of Genette's theories on narrative discourse, and in particular of his ideas on focalization. Presents a modified theory, with illustrations drawn from Colette's novel, *La Chatte*, especially the opening scene and the dream. Attempts to prove that responsibility for both moral and narratological misunderstandings on the part of readers can be traced to Colette's narrative techniques, which favor Alain. This study offers a challenging technical analysis, and significantly advances our understanding of one of Colette's most difficult and most controversial novels.

1177 Banier, François-Marie. "Jacques Grange chez Colette." *Elle*, no. 2081 (25 Nov. 1985): 112-17. Pictorial article about Colette's former apartment in the Palais Royal, now inhabited by decorator Grange. Most of the photographs show the rooms as they presently are. See also item 1801.

1178 Banti, Anna. "Le 'moralités' di Colette." *Paragone* 27 (April 1976): 79-91. Also, under title "Una piccola mano impura," in *Scritti in onore di Giovanni Macchia*, 183-94. Milan: Mondadori, 1983. Attempts to assess the extent to which Colette's work can be termed moral or immoral, by extrapolating from *Le Pur et l'impur*, and to a lesser extent *La Retraite sentimentale* and *La Naissance du jour*, the characteristics which Colette would consider pure. Analysis of passages is often limited to summary or paraphrase, but this article contains many perceptive remarks.

1179 Banti, Anna. "Saluto a Colette." *Paragone* 5 (Aug. 1954): 3-5. Obituary. Terms Colette a descendant of the eighteenth-century naturist movement but emphasizes her originality, especially in comparison with earlier nature writers.

1180 Barasc, Katy. "Colette, les saveurs du texte." In item 1057 *Album Masques: Colette*, 25-31. Asserts that Colette's reluctance to write gradually changed to sensual satisfaction, even pleasure. Considers that the novel *Chéri*, as well as the importance Colette accords to metaphors in general, demonstrates this idea. An interesting article, not always convincingly argued. The use of bold-face type for isolated words without apparent reason is disconcerting.

1181 Barasc, Katy. "Le monde des amies: Marguerite Moreno, Hélène Picard, Renée Hamon." In item 1057 *Album Masques: Colette*, 119-26. Emphasizes Colette's sense of Moreno's physical presence, the contribution she made to Picard's renown, and her mentor relationship with Hamon. Insists that Colette's relationships with women friends represent a renewal of the dialogue with the mother, but offers no firm evidence for this hypothesis. Quotes heavily from published correspondence.

1182 Barasc, Katy, and Jean-Pierre Jœcker. "Colette, une vie..." In item 1057 *Album Masques: Colette*, 5. Introduction to issue justifies the method of presentation of material, and stresses the diversity and enthusiasm characterizing Colette's life.

1183 Bardot, Brigitte. "Préface." In item 1125 Reymond, 5-7. Actress Bardot, a modern resident of Saint Tropez, recalls meeting Colette as a teenager. Declares that she now befriends the descendants of Colette's own cats but deplores the present state of Colette's former summer home.

1184 Barney, Natalie Clifford. "Colette." In *Aventures de l'esprit*, 201-3. Paris: Emile-Paul, 1929. Also extract in item 1057 *Album Masques: Colette*, 43. Brief and fanciful portrait by one who with Colette frequented lesbian circles in Paris during the first few years of the century.

1185 Barney, Natalie Clifford. "La Colette que j'ai connue." In *Souvenirs indiscrets*, 187-209. Paris: Flammarion, 1960. Also extract in item 1057 *Album Masques: Colette*, 131; another in *Magazine littéraire*, no. 42 (July 1970): 14. Rambling anecdotal reminiscences, interspersed with largely unsubstantiated statements about Colette's marriages, friendships and business acumen. Insists that Colette did not understand Renée Vivien despite the sympathetic portrait of her in *Le Pur et l'impur*. Defends what some critics consider the limits of Colette's work. Of biographical interest because Barney is usually considered to have been the model for the Miss Flossie of the Claudine novels. Includes two post-World War II letters from Colette, both trivial in content.

1186 Barokas, Bernard. "Colette: une leçon de vie." *Nouvelles littéraires*, 29 Jan. 1973, 4. Barokas describes pleasure he received from reading Colette's nature descriptions when at school, then later his discovery of new riches with *Le Pur et l'impur*.

1187 Barré, Jean-Luc. "Colette, Henry de Jouvenel et le Seigneur Chat." In item 1057 *Album Masques: Colette*, 103-8. Outlines Colette's early relationship with Henry de Jouvenel, their marital problems and their rupture. Identifies Philippe Berthelot, whom Colette called "Seigneur Chat," as one to whom she turned for advice and assistance.

1188 Barrot, Olivier. In *L'Ecran français 1943-1953*. Paris: Les Editeurs français réunis, 1979. Reminiscences include several references to Colette's film work, as well as two letters from Colette to Musidora [annotated separately].

1189 Barry, Joseph A. "La grande Colette--Aging, Ailing, Adored." *New York Times Magazine* 99 (22 Jan. 1950): 18, 44. Also, with minor changes and the title "Colette," in *Left Bank, Right Bank: Paris and Parisians*, 110-18. New York: Norton, 1951. Anecdotal overview of Colette's life. Deplores the fact that she is deemed great in France but little known so far in the United States.

1190 Barry, Naomi. "Colette." *Gourmet* 42 (Oct. 1982): 36-37, 96-98. Fascinating article about Colette's well-known but seldom studied interest in food and cooking, but disappointing in that it relies heavily on Colette de Jouvenel's reminiscences and on recipes scattered throughout Colette's works, without identifying the sources specifically.

1191 Baude, Michel. "La distance dans 'La Vagabonde', techniques et
thèmes romanesques." In item 1077 *Colette, Nouvelles
Approches critiques*, 109-16. Analyzes Colette's techniques for
distancing Renée from Max as she seeks her own identity.
Examines techniques used for distancing in time, space,
personal relations, and even reader response. An extremely
interesting article, which reveals the subtle complexities of
Colette's early work.

1192 Bauër, Gérard. "Chez Colette." *Le Point*, no. 39 (May 1951): 5-8.
Excellent description of Colette receiving visitors at the Palais
Royal. Insists on the striking quality of Colette's gaze,
unchanged in forty years, on her perennial interest in people and
objects around her, and on her fascination with the present
despite a predilection for writing of the past. Detects in the aged
Colette a profound dignity and an acceptance of whatever life
has to offer.

1193 Bauër, Gérard. "Colette." In *Chroniques*, vol. 3, 222-25. Paris:
Gallimard, 1967. Text of address of 19 March 1966 at the
ceremony dedicating the Place Colette in Paris, and marking a
significant event in the flowering of Colette's renown. Also
summarizes the history of the site over several centuries.

1194 Bauër, Gérard. "Deux mois que Colette est morte..." *Éducation
nationale*, 10 (14 Oct. 1954): 3-4. Two months after Colette's
death, emphasizes her naturalness and lucidity. Considers her
style a universal model, which reaches all levels of society.

1195 Bauër, Gérard. "Place Colette." In *Chroniques*, vol. 3, 91-93. Paris:
Gallimard, 1967. Meditation on the aptness of the Paris square
chosen to commemorate Colette. Reviews the obstacles she
overcame during her long climb to fame and popularity after
obscure beginnings and an early notoriety.

1196 Bauër, Gérard. "Un reportage de génie..." *Figaro littéraire*, 24 Jan.
1953, 3. Emphasizes Colette's ability to capture on paper the
events of the moment, especially in *Dans la foule* and *L'Envers
du music-hall*.

1197   Bauër, Gérard. "Le souvenir de Colette." *Livres de France* 5 (Oct. 1954): 3-4. Judges Colette a wonderful chronicler, but without much invention or imagination. Praises her natural style. Terms her work a picture of society filtered through experience.

1198   Bauër, Gérard [signed: Guermantes]. "Sur fond d'azur." In *Chroniques*, vol. 1, 248-50. Paris: Gallimard, 1964. Memories of a meal with Colette in Monte Carlo.

1199   Bauër, Gérard. "Visages de Colette." *Figaro littéraire*, 7 Aug. 1954, 1, 4. Defines Colette's genius as feminine. Asserts that, in spite of her out-going personality and the confessional nature of much of her work, Colette maintained a certain reserve. Praises her exactitude of description and powers of penetration.

1200   Bauër, Gérard. "La vivante prose de Mme Colette." *Le Capitole*, 22 Dec. 1924, non-pag. [10-11]. Attempts to define Colette's genius as rooted in her habit of objective observation. Asserts that the subjective aspect of her work derives only from her reaction to reality, that both reality and reaction are objectively communicated to readers.

1201   Bauër, Gérard. [No title]. In item 1095 *Hommage à Colette*, non-pag. Lauds Colette's personal qualities and relates her "discovery" of Audrey Hepburn.

1202   Baumès, Arlette. "A la recherche de la 'libération': Colette et ses poèmes en prose." *Quaderno* 17 (1983): 5-24. Not seen.

1203   Bazin, André. "Les incertitudes de la fidelité." *Cahiers du cinéma* 32 (Feb. 1954): 37-42. Long, generally favorable, review of Claude Autant-Lara's film of Colette's novel *Le Blé en herbe*. Reproaches Autant-Lara for portraying Madame Dalleray as a possible lesbian and for the film's apparent neglect of the parents. Recognizes that olfactory and tactile sensations important in the book cannot be transferred to the screen, especially in black and white.

1204   Bazin, Hervé. "Colette." *Cahiers Colette*, no. 6 (1984): 3-7. Assesses the extent to which Colette's work will last and which of her genres later generations will not find dated. Divides her work into four types: the *enfances* with roots in her life, the nature works, those focusing on love, and the drama criticism. Considers her greatest work to be her poetry of every-day life and the evocation of sensations and reality, and her greatest accomplishment the polish of her prose.

1205 Beaton, Cecil. "Paris re-visited." *Vogue* [London] 101 (Nov. 1945): 44-45. Brief report of visit to Paris a year after its liberation, during which Beaton visited several French writers, including Colette. Interesting because he alludes to Colette writing *L'Etoile vesper* and agreeing to contribute to *Jours de gloire*.

1206 Beaton, Cecil. In *The Wandering Years: Diaries 1922-1939*, 275. London: Weidenfeld & Nicolson; Boston: Little, Brown, 1961. Very brief note, classifying Colette as typically Parisian in that she always seems to have time for visitors.

1207 Beaton, Cecil, and Kenneth Tynan. In *Persona Grata*, 29-30. London: Wingate, 1953. Brief assessment of Colette as a writer. Emphasizes her skill and moral neutrality.

1208 Beaumont, Germaine. "Colette--de l'Académie Goncourt." *Nouvelles littéraires*, 3 May 1945, 1. Lavish praise of Colette's talent and accomplishments upon her election to the Goncourt Academy.

1209 Beaumont, Germaine. "Colette et la Bretagne." *Le Goéland* 113 (July-Sept. 1954): non-pag. Reminiscences, by one of Colette's long-time friends, of vacations at Rozven. Stresses Colette's pleasure in small things.

1210 Beaumont, Germaine. "Les demeures de Colette." *Vogue* [Paris], June 1948, 33-35, 106. Appealing evocation of some of Colette's residences, especially Rozven, where Beaumont spent many summers with Colette. Excellent photographs.

1211 Beaumont, Germaine. "Esquisse pour un portrait de Colette." *Nouvelles littéraires*, 12 Aug. 1954, 1, 4. Reminiscences and anecdotes. Beaumont dwells on Colette's kindness, and on her capacity to distinguish quality in people as well as in writing.

1212   Beaumont, Germaine. "Fantasmagories." *Table ronde*, no. 29 (May
       1950): 169-72. Subjective but evocative account of visits to the
       filming of *Chéri* and of *Minne*. Declares that Colette created
       several character types.

1213   Beaumont, Germaine. "La leçon de Colette." *Table ronde*, no. 82
       (Oct. 1954): 126-30. Declares that Colette's influence on her as
       a child was a favorable one, because she gave her lessons in
       living. Detects parallels between Colette and George Sand.
       Effusively written.

1214   Beaumont, Germaine. "Neuilly et l'Etoile." *Table ronde*, no. 38
       (Feb. 1951): 180-84. Report of a New Year's visit to Colette as
       well as one to Natalie Clifford Barney. Expresses admiration of
       Colette's equanimity in the face of suffering.

1215   Beaumont, Germaine. "Wenceslas à la manière de Colette
       (modestement)." *Le Capitole*, May 1923, non-pag. [13].
       Fanciful pastiche of Colette's lyrical writing and portrayal of
       animals.

1216   Beaunier, André. "La nouvelle Marianne." In *Les Idées et les
       hommes*, vol. 2, 61-76. Paris: Plon, 1915. Detects parallels
       between Renée Néré and Marivaux's Marianne, but considers
       Colette's heroine more cynical. Praises her style and concision.
       Contains a good deal of plot summary but significant because it
       is a very early serious attempt to place Colette's writing within
       a framework of recognized literary achievement.

1217   Beauvoir, Simone de. In *Le Deuxième sexe*, 2 vol. Paris:
       Gallimard, 1949. In this famous work on women in the western
       world, Beauvoir frequently uses passages from Colette's work to
       illustrate her ideas. References are wide-ranging, and include
       passages relating to childhood, love, adolescence, sensuality,
       sexuality, marriage, childbirth, the mother, role-playing, and
       social oppression.

       English translation: *The Second Sex*, translated and edited by H.M.
       Parshley. New York: Knopf, 1964.

1218 Beauvoir, Simone de. In *La Force des choses*, 255-56, 673. Paris: Gallimard, 1963. Account of a visit to Colette and a dinner in her company at Simone Berriau's. Unalike both psychologically and intellectually, Beauvoir and Colette had little in common, and Beauvoir's comments on the latter are rarely flattering.

English translation: *Force of Circumstance*, 247-48. Trans. Richard Howard. New York: Putnam's, 1964; London: André Deutsch, and Weidenfeld & Nicolson, 1965; Harmondsworth: Penguin, 1968.

1219 Beauvoir, Simone de. In *La Vieillesse*, 322-23. Paris: Gallimard, 1970. Judges that, despite her courage, Colette had difficulty coping with old age.

English translation: *Old Age*, 304. Trans. Patrick O'Brian. London: André Deutsch, and Weidenfeld & Nicolson, 1972.

1220 Bellon, Yannick. "Le souvenir que je garde de Colette." *Europe*, no. 631-32 (Nov.-Dec. 1981): 132. Reminiscences of 1950, when Bellon's short film "Colette" was released. Reported by Odette and Alain Virmaux.

1221 Belloy, Danièle. "Colette et l'amour des bêtes." *Bêtes & Nature*, no. 68 (Sept. 1969): 56-58. Article in popular nature magazine expresses admiration for Colette's portraits of animals and finds in *La Chatte* evidence of a preference for them over people.

1222 Belloy, Danièle. "Colette fille de Sido et interprète des plantes." *Betes & Nature*, no. 107 (March 1973): 30-32. Popular article drawing heavily on fragments of Goudeket's *Près de Colette* and of Colette's own work to illustrate her well-known knowledge of and love for plants. Credits "Sido" with engendering this trait but confuses Colette's mother with her fictional creation.

1223 Benda, Julien. In *Belphégor*, 173-77, 215-19. Paris: Emile-Paul, 1947. Attack on modern writing frequently mentions Colette. Benda terms women writers skilled at expressing elementary states of the soul, and characterized by the cult of the concrete, the absence of ideas, and an obsession with the self. Opinion remains unchanged from the 1929 edition of same book.

English translation: *Belphégor*, 77-85. Trans. S.J.I. Lawson. New York: Payson & Clarke, 1929.

1224   Benedick, Claude. "Colette faisait partie de l'univers de chacun." *La Presse*, 4 Aug. 1954, 14. In memoriam, stressing importance accorded to Colette by humble people, and her courage in the face of physical suffering.

1225   Benet, Mary Kathleen. "Colette." In *Writers in Love*, 185-251. New York: Macmillan, 1977; Boston: Hall, 1984. Detailed study of Colette's major love relationships. Suggests that Jouvenel represented an escape from touring, that Colette used people then jettisoned them in her climb to fame, and that her pregnancy and Sido's death were connected. Judges Colette's apparent ignorance about some things to be a facade. Interesting and provocative, but a bit slick in that no evidence is given for sometimes surprising statements, such as that to Colette's mother literature was not real. An attempt to psycho-analyze both Colette and her mother is based on the premise that the mother was a smothering influence on her daughter. Wrongly asserts that Colette's brother Achille never married. Draws parallels between Colette and the other writers studied, Katherine Mansfield and George Eliot. Also occasional references to Colette in other sections of the book.

1226   Benisti, Edmond. "Colette." *Revue hebdomadaire* 8 (3 June 1939): 44-51. Also in *La Main de l'écrivain*, 62-71. Paris: Stock, 1939. Describes Colette's character, based on a reading of her hand. Finds her authoritarian, independent, wilful, clairvoyant, fond of both company and the solitary life. Discerns in her a certain duality, expressed in her love of sensual pleasures combined with self-control. Includes handprint and sample of handwriting.

1227   Benoit, Pierre. "Anticipations en compagnie de Colette." *Le Capitole*, 22 Dec. 1924, non-pag. [8]. Title refers to a voyage to Canada that Benoit hoped to make with Colette and to another that he expected Colette to undertake to Egypt within a few weeks. Neither voyage materialized.

1228 Benstock, Shari. In *Women of the Left Bank: Paris, 1900-1940*, 54-59, 79-98. Austin: University of Texas Press, 1986. Attempts to place Colette's lesbian experiences and long-term relationships with known lesbians within the context of the whole lesbian movement. Emphasizes her ambivalence towards lesbianism, insisting that she functioned within the framework of male-female stereotypes. Draws parallels between Colette, Gertrude Stein and Edith Wharton in their common move towards independence through writing but portrays Colette as the "poor sister" of the group because of her pecuniary difficulties. Insists on the importance of Paris as the necessary milieu for the group's intellectual and psychological growth. An impressive analysis of some of Colette's most controversial relationships. Colette casually mentioned in other sections of the book.

French translation: *Femmes de la Rive Gauche: Paris, 1900-1940*, 67-71, 90-107. Trans. Jacqueline Carnaud, Anne-Marie Casu, Marie-Françoise Desmeuzes, Jacqueline Lahana, Martine Laroche, Claire Malroux, Sabine Porte and Les Editions des Femmes. Paris: Eds. des Femmes, 1987.

1229 Béraud, Henri. "Colette gastronome." *Le Capitole*, 22 Dec. 1924, non-pag. [9-10]. Confirms, from personal experience, Colette's reputed expertise in food and wine.

1230 Beregi, Theodore. "Le génie romanesque dans l'œuvre de Colette." In *Sur le chemin de l'immortalité*, 229-32. Vol. 1 of *Littérature et art en France*. Cosme-sur-Loire: Art et Poésie, 1986. Brief assessment of Colette's work. Considers her female protagonists to demonstrate the thesis that women's lives center on love of a man. Lauds her skill at portraying their psychology. High praise also for *Prisons et paradis* and for *Lettres à Hélène Picard*.

1231 Berger, Marcel [signed: Criticus]. "Le style au microscope: Colette." *Revue mondiale* 30 (15 Aug. 1929): 409-18. Early attempt to analyze Colette's style, by studying the opening paragraphs of *Chéri*. Defines Colette's art as a combination of the visual and the plastic arts. Judges her a better stylist than Flaubert.

1232   Bergner, Georges. "Colette." *Alsace française*, 20 Jan. 1923, 59.
        Lists Colette's creative assets as intuition, observation,
        sensuality and curiosity, but judges her without imagination.

1233   Berl, Emmanuel. "Une fée bienfaisante." *Le Monde*, 25 Jan. 1973,
        20. Bouquets on the one-hundredth anniversary of Colette's
        birth. Praises her skill as a descriptive writer.

1234   Berl, Emmanuel. In *Présence des morts*, 37, 46, 102. Paris:
        Gallimard, 1982. Brief reminiscences and impressions of
        Colette's apartment bereft of her living presence.

1235   Berman, Nils. "Nya tillskott till samlingen." *Bokvännen* 23 (Nov.
        1963): 187-93. Includes paragraphs on some of Colette's early
        books and journalistic activities.

1236   Bernac, Pierre. "Colette." In *Francis Poulenc et ses mélodies*, 177-
        78. Paris: Buchet/Chastel, 1978. Relates origins of Poulenc's
        song, "Le Portrait," based on an unpublished prose poem by
        Colette, whom Poulenc admired. Insists that only a woman
        could have written the poem.

        English translation: "Colette--Laurence de Beylié--Jean Anouilh."
        In *Francis Poulenc: The Man and his Songs*, 193-97. Trans.
        Winifred Radford. London: Gollancz; New York: Norton, 1977.
        Includes both English and French versions of the prose poem.

1237   Bernard, Harry [signed: L'Illettré]. "Colette n'est plus." *Le Courrier
        de Saint-Hyacinthe*, 17 Sept. 1954, 2. Effusively ranks Colette
        as the greatest stylist of modern France and the greatest master
        ever of the French language. Considers her work easy to read
        because she conveys sensation to the reader. Selects five titles
        as her best.

1238   Bernstein, Henry. "Colette." *Le Capitole*, 22 Dec. 1924, non-pag.
        [6-7]. Describes "glorious" Colette as versatile and essentially
        maternal in her approach to the world.

1239   Berriau, Simone. In *Simone est comme ça*, 49-57, 75-78, 172-74.
        Paris: Laffont, 1973. Extracts in item 0980 *Colette: au cinéma*,
        288-89. Memoirs of Berriau, singer, long-time theater director,

and Colette's personal friend, contain colorful accounts of
meetings with her over the years, as well as casual references
throughout the book. Some inaccuracies in the details. Passages
dealing with Albert Wolff, who launched *L'Enfant et les
sortilèges,* are especially interesting.

English translation: extracts in item 0984 *Colette at the movies,*
206-7.

1240   Bertaut, Jules. "Le roman féminin de George Sand à Colette."
Causeries françaises, 28 March 1924, 57-72. Condescending
evaluation, typical of the era, of major female French authors,
especially George Sand, Colette, Gérard d'Houville, Anna de
Noailles and Marcelle Tinayre. Recognizes that Claudine is an
original creation and judges her an enduring character. Considers
Colette's nature descriptions to be the expression of a pantheist
attitude with roots in romanticism.

1241   Berthu-Courtivron, Marie-Françoise. "Le retour au pays natal dans
l'œuvre de Colette." In item 1077 *Colette, Nouvelles Approches
critiques,* 139-50. Traces the development of the theme of the
return to the nest in Colette's work as a whole. An interesting
treatment of the long-recognized *paradis perdu* theme.

1242   Berton, Jean-Claude. "'La Naissance du jour' 1928." In *50 romans
clés de la littérature française,* 110-11. Paris: Hatier, 1983. Coll.
Profil Formation 359-360. Short summary and assessment of
the title novel.

1243   Bichonnier, H. "Le come back des Claudine." *F. Magazine,* no. 4
(April 1978): 67. Enthusiastic review of Edouard Molinaro's
film series based on the Claudine novels. Declares that there has
been a resurgence of interest in Colette after many years of
neglect following her death in 1954.

1244   Bienvenu, Reine. "Chiens et chats de Colette, ou le portrait
médiateur." In *Le Portrait,* edited by Joseph-Marc Bailbé, 137-
51. Rouen: Université de Rouen, 1987. Analyzes twelve
portraits in the 1913 edition of *Prrou, Poucette et quelques
autres,* considered here to be Colette's first true animal portraits.
Summarizes her portrait techniques. Stresses the importance of

precision, nuance, individuality and role of images. Concludes that the reader reacts to the portrait because of the relation portrayed between the animal and human beings. Suggests that Colette evokes the existence of an animal dimension that is beyond our understanding. Calls Colette a mediator between people and animals because of this greater existence she assigns to them and because she rejects the limited role customarily accorded to them.

1245   Bienvenu, Reine. "'La Treille muscate' de Colette et son illustration par Dunoyer de Segonzac." In *Iconographie et Littérature: d'un art à l'autre*, 161-81. Paris: Presses universitaires de France, 1983. Traces artist Segonzac's collaboration with Colette on the 1932 edition of *La Treille muscate*. Asserts that illustrations of the vine of the title are actually of a sister vine, the original having fallen victim to Colette's landscaping reforms since her purchase of the Saint Tropez property. Reveals how carefully Colette chose her illustrators and how closely she worked with them. Identifies objects in original illustrations, analyzes their artistic characteristics and explains their significance. Concludes that Colette's and Segonzac's conceptions of the world are fundamentally different. Compares and contrasts texts and illustrations to demonstrate their different types of lyricism. Peripherally offers an extremely interesting analysis of Colette's lyrical style. Because of the many details relating to Saint Tropez and to Colette's friendship with Segonzac there, this article sheds light on aspects of *La Naissance du jour* as well. Carefully documented article with illustrations.

1246   Billy, André [signed: A.B.]. "A propos de la tombe de 'Sido'." *Figaro littéraire*, 25 Sept. 1954, 2. Apology for unintentional offence to the Robineau-Duclos family caused by item 1255.

1247   Billy, André. "Le brevet de Colette." *Figaro littéraire*, 10 Aug. 1957, 2. Insists that the importance that Colette accords to Claudine's brevet examinations proves their significance in her own life. Quotes details of Colette's results, as summarized in Dubreuil's article of July 1957 in *Le Cerf-volant*. Results show that Colette was indeed a fine all-round student who excelled in French composition.

1248   Billy, André. "Colette." *Annales politiques et littéraires* 93 (1 Nov.
       1929): 408. Also in *Intimités littéraires*, 149-54. Paris:
       Flammarion, 1932. Recalls visits to Colette in her different
       residences, especially her summer home at Saint Tropez.

1249   Billy, André. "Colette." In *L'Epoque contemporaine: 1905-1930*,
       265-68. Paris: Jules Tallandier, 1956. Gossipy though
       interesting overview of Colette's life and work. Contains
       anecdote of 1923, when rumor had it that Colette was being
       asked to seek membership in the French Academy. Quotes
       reminiscences by Georges Wague from the same period.

1250   Billy, André. "Colette artiste en prose." *Gavroche*, no. 37 (10 May
       1945): 5. Outlines incidents surrounding Colette's election to
       the Academy Goncourt, her election to the Belgian Academy,
       and her failure to become the first woman elected to the French
       Academy. Recognizes her as one of several naturists writing
       about 1907 and attempts to place her within the movement.
       Attributes her durability to the fact that she wrote only of what
       she knew and was free from ideology, which quickly becomes
       dated. Last part of this article repeated in item 1251.

1251   Billy, André. "Colette, de l'Académie Goncourt: une grande figure
       de la littérature française." *Litterair Paspoort* 5 (Sept. 1946): 8-
       9. Brief overview of Colette's work. Stresses her independence
       of other literary movements, as well as her lack of imitators.
       Includes passage from item 1250.

1252   Billy, André. "Colette journaliste." In *La Muse aux bésicles*, 21-
       26. Paris: Renaissance du livre, 1924. Written after reading *Les
       Heures longues* in January of 1918. Anecdote witnessing
       Colette's powers of observation and sensual memory. Lauds her
       patriotism and her professionalism, likening all her work to
       journalism.

1253   Billy, André. "Les femmes de lettres." In *L'Epoque 1900: 1885-
       1905*, 214-33. Paris: Jules Tallandier, 1951. Calls 1900 a
       banner opening year for French women writers, noting that
       Colette published her first novel that year under Willy's name.
       Sketches her life with Willy and praises her *Mes apprentissages*
       as a precious document of those years. Useful because it places

Colette within a literary context and attempts to draw parallels
between her work and that of others, especially in importance
accorded to nature.

1254   Billy, André. "La gloire posthume de Colette." *Figaro littéraire*, 12
       Feb. 1955, 2. Brief passage refuting the suggestion that interest
       in Colette by critics and researchers has declined.

1255   Billy, André. "Histoire d'un paroissien. Sur la tombe de Sido. De la
       neige en juillet." *Figaro littéraire*, 28 Aug. 1954, 2. Speculates
       on Colette's reputed indifference to religion. Describes the
       family burial plot at Châtillon-Coligny and expresses surprise
       to find only a general family marker. Ponders the veracity of the
       passage in *Sido* in which Colette's mother recalls snow in July.
       See item 1246 for reader reaction.

1256   Billy, André. "Le mouvement littéraire contemporain." *Causeries
       françaises*, 22 June 1923, 323-44. In this long article on
       contemporary French literature, Billy comments on the work of
       many writers but highlights that of Barrès, Loti, France, Gide
       and, to a lesser extent, Colette. Considers Colette to be the real
       originator of the confession novel, of which Billy has a poor
       opinion in general, but avers that she has favorably influenced
       the feminine novel of the whole era, especially because of her
       portrayal of sensations.

1257   Billy, André. "Si le Bon Dieu l'avait voulu." *Figaro littéraire*, 4
       May 1970, 29. Defends Colette against opinion expressed in
       Gide's journal that Colette had been "contaminated" by the
       milieux she frequented with Willy. Reminds readers that Gide
       frequented many of the same people and places, but was wealthy
       enough to be able to choose his work.

1258   Billy, André. "Une sorte de dandysme féminin..." *Figaro littéraire*,
       24 Jan. 1953, 3. Compares Colette to a breath of fresh air after
       the turgidity of the symbolist movement.

1259   Billy, André. "Vraiment pas de rue Willy?" *Figaro littéraire*, 22
       Aug. 1959, 2. Questions why there has never been a street
       named after Willy, since a committee had been formed some 25
       years earlier to promote one. Quotes an old letter from Ernest

Gaubert to Belval-Delahaye, defending Willy against the charge
that he never wrote anything himself and paid his writers badly,
and claiming that he, Gaubert, was the real author of Henri
Albert's book on Willy. Provocative in that it seems to refute
some of the statements made by Colette about her first husband.

1260 Billy, André. "Willy, nègre des nègres. Colette, Proust et Mme
Arman." *Figaro littéraire*, 5 Sept. 1959, 2. Comments and
anecdotes, some of them taken from Willy's *Souvenirs
littéraires et autres*... Provides details on Colette's and Willy's
relations with Anatole France and Madame Arman de Caillavet,
the latter caricatured as Madame Barmann in the Claudine
novels. It was at her place that Colette first met Proust, of
whom she left several word portraits.

1261 Billy, André. [No title]. In item 1095 *Hommage à Colette*, non-
pag. Brief passage praising Colette's femininity and her high
level of "feminine intelligence."

1262 Billy, André. In *La Littérature française contemporaine*, 119-22,
145-46. Paris: Colin, 1932. Cites Colette as one of the top five
female writers in France, the others being Anna de Noailles,
Marcelle Tinayre, Lucie Delarue-Mardrus and Gérard d'Houville.
Stresses the originality of her *Dialogues de bêtes*. While
recognizing her assiduity, Billy terms her sensuality animal and
her genius instinctive. Interesting as a typical example of the
condescending praise often accorded to Colette by male critics
during her lifetime.

1263 Blanchart, Paul. "Colette ou le poète ingénu." *Le Capitole*, May
1923, non-pag. [8-9]. Generous praise of Colette's gifts, with
emphasis on her sincerity and apparent spontaneity. Terms her
work completely subjective but considers her subjectivity an
asset. Admires her sense of measure in treating delicate subjects.

1264 Blin, Michèle. "Une pédagogie pour jeunes filles pauvres: de
'Claudine à l'école' à 'Mes apprentissages'." *Romantisme* 13-14
(1976): 215-27. Terms *Claudine à l'école* a valuable socio-
economic document on rural girls' schools, which were less
numerous than boys' schools during the 1880's in France and
received fewer privileges. Declares that teachers in such schools

were extremely vulnerable because the accepted model for their behaviour was that of nuns, their predecessors in the church schools, and that such a standard of conduct was impossible in a lay setting. Notes that the teachers were dependent on the good will of sometimes conflicting forces: their superiors, the community, and individual local officials. Analyzes Colette's portrayal of the life of schoolmistresses in the light of this idea, offering evidence for the view that they were exploited politically, socially and financially, despite their apparent independence. Confirms Colette's picture of the probable future of girls leaving the village school. Calls *Mes apprentissages* a continuation of *Claudine à l'école* in that it portrays the obstacles facing girls leaving village schools at that time and emphasizes social obstacles confronting Colette during the first fifty years of her life. A valuable article, which looks at Colette's work from an unusual perspective and which suggests that Colette was from the beginning more aware of currents of public opinion than she seemed to be.

1265   Blinkenberg, Andreas. In *L'Ordre des mots en français moderne*, vol. 1, 55, 187, 194; vol. 2, 106, 115. Copenhagen: Andr. Fred. Høst, 1928-1933. Notes passages in which Colette uses chiasmus. Significant mostly because of the early date of this publication in which Colette's work appears as a model along with that of other important writers.

1266   Bloomberg, Edward. "Colette et la glycine." *Archiv für das Studium der Neueren Sprachen und Literaturen* 210 (1973): 140-43. Analyzes four different passages in which Colette describes the wistaria vine. Concludes that for Colette nature is not always seen as a positive force, that the wistaria represents for her its negative aspect, which she commonly ignores in favor of its beauty. An unusual but convincing argument.

1267   Blot, Gabrielle. "Colette." In item 0305 *Chéri. La fin de Chéri*, 446-55. Random comments on Colette's life and fiction, with no specific reference to the two novels in the volume.

1268   Bo, Carlo. "Chéri." In *In Margine a un vecchio libre*, 37-41. Milan: Bompiani, 1945. Emphasizes difficulty of classifying Colette or even of drawing parallels between her and other writers of her era. Analyzes her poetic expression in *Chéri* as a good example of her mature work.

1269 Bo, Carlo. "Colette et l'idolatria delle cose." *Paragone* 1 (Feb. 1950): 22-27. Also under the title "Colette" in *Della Lettura e Altri Saggi*, 227-33. Florence: Vallecchi, 1953. Also as "L'ultima Colette" in *Da Voltaire a Drieu La Rochelle*, 107-13. Milan: La Goliardica, 1965. Effusive and impressionistic evaluation of Colette's work, stressing her originality, her independence and the importance she accords to physical objects.

1270 Bogan, Louise. "Colette." In *Selected Criticism*, 28-32. New York: Noonday, 1955; London: Owen, 1958. Also in *A Poet's Alphabet*, edited by Robert Phelps and Ruth Limmer, 75-78. New York: McGraw-Hill, 1971. From a 1930 review of English editions of *Chéri* and *Mitsou*. Holds that Katherine Mansfield was influenced by Colette but that Colette is superior to Mansfield and "goes further."

1271 Boisdeffre, Pierre de. "Heureuse Colette." In *Une histoire vivante de la littérature d'aujourd'hui: 1938-1958*, 201-2. Paris: Le livre contemporain, 1958. Considers the Claudine novels to be in step with the current women's liberation movement, but concludes that the love portrayed therein is mostly physical attraction.

1272 Boisdeffre, Pierre de. "Heureuse Colette..." *Nouvelles littéraires*, 29 Jan. 1973, 3. Also, with only editorial changes, in *L'Ile aux livres: littérature et critique*, 53-56. Paris: Seghers, 1980. Also, with minor changes, in *Historia*, no. 453 (Aug.-Sept. 1984): 78-80. Ambivalent appreciation of Colette's life and work, praising her freedom, naturalness and spontaneity, but expressing doubts as to the durability of her style. Detects sadness associated with sexuality in many of her novels. Not the same article as item 1271 but contains sentences from it.

1273 Boivin, Marguerite (with the collaboration of Vincenette Pichois). "Sido à Châtillon." *Cahiers Colette*, no. 8 (1986): 117-44; and no. 9 (1987): 95-113. Two-part index to item 0013 *Sido: Lettres à sa fille*. Boivin, whose family is from the region of Châtillon-Coligny to which the Colette family moved after the

loss of their home in Saint-Sauveur, provides information on
many local people mentioned by Colette's mother in her letters.
Comments on inconsistencies and contradictions, Sido's mis-
spelling of names and places, and small errors of fact. She also
corrects some wrong datings assigned to the letters by editors of
the volume, noting errors in dating of as much as two years.
This is an essential article for any researcher working on the
Sido letters. Includes a map of the region.

1274   Boivin, Marguerite, and Jacques Lodier. "Le musée Colette à Saint-
Sauveur-en-Puisaye." *Monuments historiques*, no. 156 (April-
May 1988): 98-99. Summarizes planning and negotiations for a
Colette museum, beginning with 1974 plans to establish it in
Colette's old apartment in the Palais Royal, through obstacles
placed in its way by the Goudeket family, to the project's final
realization in Colette's native village. Explains why the chateau
was chosen rather than the Colette family home.

1275   Bonal, Gérard. "Pourquoi les 'Cahiers Colette'." *Cahiers Colette*,
no. 1 (1977): 5-6. Announces purpose of the *Cahiers*, which is
to respond to a growing interest in Colette's works on the part
of both researchers and general readers.

1276   Bordillon, Henri. "Colette et Willy en ménage." *Europe*, no. 631-
32 (Nov.-Dec. 1981): 56-60. Defends Willy as a victim, from
neglect, of Colette's admirers. Argues that Willy's novels from
1895 to 1910 form a coherent universe centered on Henry
Maugis and that they are unified by form, tone and theme.
Insists that the Claudine novels are of the same ilk. Maintains
that Willy was never able to forget Claudine and Colette and
that he was a link between Mallarmé and Jarry.

1277   Borgese, Guiseppe Antonio. "'La Vagabonde'." Trans. Anne-Marie
Pizzorusso. *Cahiers Colette*, no. 7 (1985): 37-44. Borgese was
an influential Italian critic of his day and this article was
instrumental in bringing Colette's work to Italian readers. He
equates women's literature with autobiography and says that
only a woman could have written *La Vagabonde* because men
have less finesse, are more systematic and more used to
reasoning. Praises Colette for not trying to deny her femininity
by writing like a man, nor trying to please men by writing as a

man expects a woman to write. Terms her an authentic woman
writer. A perceptive article for the time. First published in
Italian: *La Stampa*, 15 May 1911, 3; and *La Vita e il Libro*,
vol. 3, 249-57. Turin: Bocca, 1913.

1278 Boulestin, X.-M. [Marcel]. In *A Londres, naguère...*, 21-25, 34-45.
Paris: Fayard, 1946. Memoirs and anecdotes refer to Boulestin's
first meeting with Colette, his job as secretary to Willy, and
later communication with them both. Though not rich in new
facts on Colette, these anecdotes evoke the flavor of Colette's
first decades in Paris.

English translation: *Ease and Endurance*, 8-21. Trans. Robin Adair.
London: Home & Van Thal, 1948.

1279 Bourdil, Pierre-Yves. "Le temps retrouvé dans l'espace." In *Les
Miroirs du moi: les héros et les fous*, 67-83. Paris: L'Ecole,
1987. Attempts to identify the significance of Colette's choice
of the past as subject through an analysis of *Journal à rebours*.
Concludes that for her the past signifies an escape from, and
even the refusal of, an intolerable present. Declares that the past
also offers her a way of clarifying the future, in that writing the
text provides her with a mirror of her life. Draws parallels with
Proust and comments on Colette's interest in words themselves.
Also brief allusions to her in other sections of the book. An
excellent article.

1280 Bourgoyne, Beverly. "'La Chatte' par Colette: 'un pas de trois'." In
*Proceedings: Pacific Northwest Conference on Foreign
Languages* 21 (1970): 24-26. Brief attempt to analyze the drama
of *La Chatte* in terms of its triangular structure.

1281 Bourin, André. "A Saint-Sauveur-en-Puisaye où il y a 80 ans
naissait Colette." *Nouvelles littéraires*, 22 Jan. 1953, 1, 4.
Also, with photographs and under title "La Puisaye de Colette,"
in *La France littéraire en zigzag*, 209-16. Brussels: Meddens,
1965. Recounts visit to Colette's childhood village. Mentally
evokes her young presence in the house and countryside around.

1282 Bourin, André. "Colette." *Larousse mensuel*, no. 482 (Oct. 1954):
533-35. Brief biography and overview of Colette's work. Notes

a movement from autobiographically inspired works to more
objective ones, as well as a later penchant for the meditative
essay. Lauds specific aspects of her output.

1283   Bourin, André. "De Claudine à Mme Colette." *Preuves* 24 (Feb.
1953): 85-87. Praises Colette's diversity, harmonious style,
sense of humor, and serenity as evinced in *Le Fanal bleu*.

1284   Bourin, André. "Le Palais-Royal et ses hôtes." *Nouvelles
littéraires*, 25 Aug. 1949, 1, 7. In article devoted to the Palais
Royal and its residents, both past and present, Bourin describes
Colette's apartment and relates an insubstantial conversation
with her there.

1285   Boustani, Carmen. "Autrement écrit." *Phares* [Lebanon], no. 3
(1986): 81-90. Not seen.

1286   Boustani, Carmen. "Colette ou le corps/texte." *Public* [Lebanon],
no. 8 (1988): 38-40. Not seen.

1287   Boustani, Carmen. "Le roman féminin français: Renée Néré,
l'héroïne de 'La Vagabonde'." *Elfeker-El Arali-El Marrasser*
[Lebanon], no. 34 (1985). In Arabic. Not seen.

1288   Boutterin, Maria-Catherine. "Colette à Besançon ou 'La Retraite
sentimentale'." *Le Jura français*, no. 139 (July-Sept. 1973): 57-
61. Native of the region where Colette wrote some of her early
works evokes her presence at the Monts-Boucons, on which
Casamène of *La Retraite sentimentale* is modelled. Boutterin
alludes to her grandparents' reminiscences of that time and to a
letter that Colette wrote to them on the death of her great-
grandfather. Quotes freely from Colette's books.

1289   Bouverot, Danielle, and Chantal Schaefer. "De la lexicologie à la
sémiotique: le vocabulaire de la végétation dans 'Sido'." In item
1077 *Colette, Nouvelles Approches critiques*, 131-38.
Computer-based analysis of the frequency and contexts of
vocabulary referring to the garden. Finds the vocabulary
remarkable only by its context and notes that "Sido's" use of it
differs from Colette's own.

1290 Bouvier, Emile. In *Initiation à la littérature d'aujourd'hui*, 141-44.
Paris: Renaissance du livre, 1928. Studies passage from
L'Entrave as an example of the interior monologue used by
novelists of the early twentieth century to express the
complexity of a protagonist's feelings as well as his or her
tendency towards self-analysis. Considers Colette less skilled at
the technique than Duhamel or Larbaud.

1291 Bouvier-Ajam, Maurice. "Colette et Ravel." *Europe*, no. 631-32
(Nov.-Dec. 1981): 116-18. Outlines the genesis and history of
L'Enfant et les sortilèges.

1292 Bouvier-Ajam, Maurice. "Willy et Colette Willy." *Europe*, no.
631-32 (Nov.-Dec. 1981): 52-54. Brief defence of Willy,
especially of his *La Maitresse du Prince Jean*, for which the
article offers evidence of Colette's collaboration.

1293 Brasillach, Robert. "Colette ou la sagesse de Sido." *Revue française*
26:11 (1931): 250-51 and 26:12 (1931): 272-74. Also in
Portraits, 3-27. Paris: Plon, 1935. Also, under title "Colette et
son univers," in *Revue universelle* 63 (1 Oct. 1935): 38-53. All
developed from shorter early version entitled "La sagesse de
Colette." *Action française*, 14 Aug. 1930, 3. Poetic essay
focusing on the autobiographical aspects of Colette's work and
on the influence of her mother. Notes that she never preaches
but portrays joy and suffering in the material world. Identifies
nature, family and memories of childhood as Colette's avenues
of escape from unpleasant reality. Deems her the greatest of the
feminine romantics flourishing about 1900, for whom nature
replaced God. Argues that Colette was not the hedonist many
consider her to be, and that she was conscious of forces beyond
individual existence. Insists that her rediscovery of the lessons
of childhood, which permitted her to draw closer to her dead
mother, also demonstrates her awareness of a broader dimension
of being.

1294 Brasillach, Robert. "En marge de Daphnis et Chloé: sonnets." *La
Tramontane*, no. 111 (March 1926): 45-47. Four sonnets
inspired by Colette, and especially by her *Le Blé en herbe*.
Interesting as evidence of Brasillach's fervent admiration for
Colette even as an adolescent.

1295 Brasillach, Robert. "Pour compléter le miracle de Colette." In *Les Quatre Jeudis*, 364-75. Paris: Balzac, 1944. Two passages written during the mid-1930's: "Colette critique" and "Passage de Willy." Brasillach judges that Colette's theater reviews reveal that she looks at theater as she looks at life and that *Mes apprentissages* is an outstanding document of pre-World War I Paris. Praises Colette's restraint in the latter book, claiming that her portrait of Willy will be his passage to fame.

1296 Brasillach, Robert. In *Notre avant-guerre*, 75-76. Paris: Plon, 1941. Also in *Une Géneration dans l'orage*, 74. Paris: Plon, 1968. Briefly recounts visit to Colette in the spring of 1929.

1297 Braunschvig, Marcel. "La littérature féminine: le roman." In *La Littérature française contemporaine étudiée dans les textes*, 278-84. Paris: Colin, 1958. Restates views offered by others. Asserts that Colette dominated all feminine literature of the early twentieth century. Praises her keen observation and analysis of sentiment, terming her original and sincere. These passages demonstrate with what tenacity critics clung to fixed ideas about Colette, for they remained unmodified by their author over several revised editions and more than two decades of new Colette publications.

1298 Bray, Bernard. "La manière épistolaire de Colette: réalité et inventions." *Cahiers Colette*, no. 3-4 (1981): 100-18. Praises new currents in Colette criticism, which focus on the text instead of trying to relate it to her life. Notes that Colette herself mixed reality and fiction and that her correspondence offers insights into her ideas about death and suffering. Summarizes characteristics of her epistolary habits, especially that of adapting her style to her correspondent and the protective attitude often detectable in her letters. Identifies five main styles of her letter-writing. Notes the importance to her of the type of paper and pen used and her consciousness of the letter as an art form. A valuable and extremely interesting article on a subject that so far has received little serious critical attention.

1299 Bray, Bernard. "Note sur le Colloque universitaire international 'Autour de Colette' à Saint-Tropez (13-14 septembre 1986)." *Cahiers Colette*, no. 9 (1987): 41-44. The colloquium at Saint

Tropez celebrated the sixtieth anniversary of Colette's buying
her summer home there. Suggests that a suitable repository
might be established in Colette's honor at Saint Tropez, since
Colette belonged as much to that region as to Saint-Sauveur,
which will be able to claim a museum devoted to her memory.

1300 Bray, Bernard. "La réécriture de 'Mitsou'." In item 1077 *Colette,
Nouvelles Approches critiques*, 85-94. Compares the book
version of *Mitsou* with the shorter pre-original published in *La
Vie parisienne* in 1917. Insists that, although the manuscript is
missing, comparison suggests that the longer book version
represents mostly a desire to develop nuances already expressed
in the novel. Also offers reasons for changes in vocabulary and
style, characterization, and use of irony.

1301 Bray, Bernard. "Saint-Tropez se souvient de Colette." In item 1060
Autour de Colette à Saint-Tropez, non.-pag. [41-46]. Welcome
to the Colloque Universitaire International, 13-14 Sept. 1986 at
Saint Tropez. Emphasizes Colette's love for the region and its
importance to both her personal life and her literary output.

1302 Bray, Bernard. "1984: les études sur Colette prennent leur vrai
départ." *Romanistische Zeitschrift für Literaturgeschichte* 9:1-2
(1985): 233-39. Brief assessment of latest Colette criticism.
Expresses hope that a recent flurry of publications and colloquia
will encourage significant critical activity.

1303 Brechon, Robert. "Deux centenaires: Colette et Péguy." *Colóquio*
13 (May 1973): 77-80. Establishes superficial contrasts between
Colette and Péguy, both of whom were born in 1873. Ranges
Colette among the "moderns" with Gide and Proust because
suffering is an important theme in her books and because her
outlook is sensual, whereas Péguy's roots lie in the Christian
mystique of the Middle Ages. Brechon's preference for Péguy
over Colette is manifest.

1304 Brée, Germaine. "The Divided Image: Seductions and Deductions."
In *Women Writers in France: Variations on a Theme*, 46-54,
74-75. New Brunswick, N.J.: Rutgers University Press, 1973.
Excellent article in which Colette's work is studied in the
context of French women's writing in general. Sees *Le Pur et*

l'impur as a landmark publication and Colette's greatest
contribution to literature, especially in its portrayal of the
power of the senses. Terms Colette and Beauvoir the major
French women writers of the century to date and the two who
most typically illustrate the contrasting periods of French
culture during the same years.

1305 Brée, Germaine. "Le mythe des origines et l'autoportrait chez
George Sand et Colette." In *Symbolism and Modern Literature:
Studies in Honor of Wallace Fowlie*, edited by Marcel Tetel,
103-12. Durham: Duke University Press, 1978. Compares and
contrasts Colette's and Sand's personal situations and their
presentation of the mother. Concludes that, whereas Sand
intellectualizes her childhood conflict and sense of loss in order
to resolve a personal identity crisis in the present, Colette seeks
through writing to recreate the lost childhood of which her
mother is a crucial element, in order to reconcile the present
self, seen as inferior, with her former purer self. Thus the
autoportrait means a return to the mother for both authors, but
for different reasons. An excellent article, which sheds new light
on the role of Colette's childhood in her work, and one whose
premises and conclusions have been adopted by later critics.

1306 Brejaart, Marjo, and Marja van Buuren. "Amour et lesbianisme
chez Colette." In *Analyses de textes*, edited by Jacques Plessen
and A. van Zoest, 86-108. Groningen: Instituut voor Romanse
Talen, 1982. Cahiers de recherches des instituts néerlandais de
langue et littérature françaises 4-5. Analyzes the importance of
non-verbal communication in Colette's work. Adopts as
premise the idea that her novels express the search for an answer
to a personal question: in love, should one dominate or serve?
Insists that Willy's domination of her was a reversal of what her
parents' example had taught her and that not until her third
marriage was the original pattern re-established in real life, the
novels in the interim years reflecting the vacillations of her own
mind. Asserts that "the look" is an important means of
establishing one's position with respect to "the other," because
it is by "the look" that one dominates, judges or submits.
Insists that Colette's on-going need to view and judge herself is
not narcissism but introspection expressing her search for a
psychosexual identity. Acknowledges that she is not a

theoretical feminist, writing to change existing ideas and patterns of behaviour, but that her approach is practical in that it touches on specific problems. An important article with a fresh perspective.

1307 Brenner, Jacques. "Colette." In *Les Critiques dramatiques*, 158-62. Paris: Flammarion, 1970. Brief assessment of Colette's importance as drama critic. Terms her an indulgent critic who offers an opinion on the plot, that is on the reality of the situation, rather than on the merit of the play itself. Finds many of her opinions surprising. Judges that she is better acquainted with the *théâtre du boulevard* than with more literary plays, but notes that she early approved of Cocteau, Anouilh and Giraudoux and so might be termed an avant-garde critic.

1308 Brenner, Jacques. "Colette." In *Mon histoire de la littérature française contemporaine*, 71-73. Paris: Grasset, 1987. Identifies Colette's true mark of originality as her habit of never attempting to convince readers of her views. Calls her a great *moraliste*, whose works objectively portray the manners of an age. Colette also casually mentioned in other passages of the book.

1309 Bresard, Suzanne. "Colette." In *Empreintes*, 15-19. Neuchâtel: Delachaux & Niestlé, 1968. Fascinating analysis of Colette's handwriting. Insists that it reveals her double nature, which combines lucid intelligence with simple animality, and that this duality expressed itself in Colette's life by alternate phases rather than by conflict.

1310 Brésillon, Jean-Pierre. "Aimer Colette aujourd'hui." In *Avec la muse des vins de Chablis: anthologie des lauréats du prix 79 et leurs amis*, non. pag. [1-30]. Chablis: Odette Magarian, [1979]. Text of an address for the fourth annual prize-giving of the Muse de Chablis. Confirms Colette's claim to being an authentic Burgundian, more through her loyalty to the region than because of ancestry or long-term residence. Detects in the public's tendency to be scandalized by her post-Claudine novels an expression of masculine fears that sensuality in literature by women signals their assertion of independence. Considers Colette a pioneer in opening the way for other women by writing about previously taboo subjects. Speculates on whether her tendency to portray only weak male protagonists reflects her father's infirmity, and wonders whether she attributes to the fictional Sido some of her own judgments. Terms her fifty years ahead of her time. Offers no new ideas but makes perceptive remarks. Quotes Colette freely, as well as her critics.

1311   Briant, Théophile. "Colette à Rozven." *Le Goéland*, no. 113 (July-Sept. 1954): non-pag. Detailed account of Briant's first meeting with Colette in 1922. Nostalgically recalls the many summers she spent in Brittany. Speculates on reasons for her apparent abandonment of Brittany when she purchased a cottage in the south of France. Refers to passages in her books, in which she speaks of Brittany. Remarks on her attraction to the occult, and on her relationship with the sea. Claims to have suggested the title of *L'Etoile vesper*.

1312   Briant, Théophile. "La dame de Rozven, Colette." *Cahiers d'histoire et de folklore* 2 (Jan.-March 1956): 49-53. Reminiscences of Colette in Brittany. Terms her Celtic in her loyalty to the seas of the north, her love of fire and of freedom, and her fondness for the magic of numbers and signs. Some overlap with item 1311.

1313   Brincourt, André. "Colette." In *Les Ecrivains du XXe siècle: un musée imaginaire de la littérature mondiale*, 197-201. Paris: Retz, 1979. Over-all assessment of some of the highlights of Colette's work. Insists on the essential unity of her diverse production and on its femininity. Doubts that her naturalism can be compared to recognized movements. Judges that *L'Etoile vesper* and *Le Fanal bleu* reflect her vision best because they express a perspective without agitation. Quotes a passage from *La Naissance du jour*.

1314   Brisson, Pierre. "Colette et l'amour." *Figaro littéraire*, 10 Aug. 1957, 1, 5. Also, under the title "Préface," in item 0618 *La Retraite sentimentale*, 11-18. Emphasizes Claudine's growing masculinity in *La Retraite sentimentale*, a masculinity defined here as the strength which she develops as Renaud weakens. Lauds the novel's lyrical ending.

1315   Brisson, Pierre. "Les quatre-vingts ans de Colette." *Le Figaro*, 22
        Jan. 1953, 1. Also in *Vingt ans de 'Figaro' 1938-1958*, 236-39.
        Paris: Gallimard, 1959. Effusive homage by *Figaro*'s director on
        the occasion of Colette's eightieth birthday.

1316   Brisson, Pierre. In *Autre temps*, 210-14. Paris: Gallimard, 1949.
        Brisson confesses that, with the publication of *Chéri*, he came
        to view Colette as one of the most important writers of her
        time because she struck a new note in literature, a note that was
        primitive, realistic and pagan. Once he got to know her, he saw
        her as a solitary anti-conformist, separated even from groups and
        individuals whose causes she championed. A perceptive article,
        despite its brevity and clichés.

1317   Brochard, Yvonne. "3 février 1933-28 novembre 1983." *Cahiers
        Colette*, no. 6 (1984): 15-19. Text of introduction to the
        exhibition "Hommage à Colette" at Nantes, 28 Nov.-21 Dec.
        1983. Includes fac-similes of the poster as well of the one used
        for Colette's own *conférence* at Nantes some fifty years earlier.
        Also brief reminiscences by Brochard, one of the two *petites
        fermières* who sent Colette food from the country during World
        War II.

1318   Brodin, Pierre. "Colette." In *Les Ecrivains français de l'entre-deux
        guerres*, 123-43. Montreal: Valiquette, 1942. Sympathetic
        biographical portrait and over-all assessment of Colette's work.
        Considers her interested only in love. Praises her style and her
        animal works, saying that her renown will endure because of
        them. Draws parallels between her and D.H. Lawrence.

1319   Brodin, Pierre. "Colette." In *Présences contemporaines*, vol. 2,
        195-211. Paris: Debresse, 1955. Apparently based on item 1318
        but sufficiently re-worked as to change the over-all evaluation of
        Colette's output. Recognizes that her work matured, even during
        the final ten years of her life, but is more critical and less prone
        to offer plaudits than in the earlier article. Identifies Colette
        with her heroines and stresses the role of instinct in her literary
        activity. Ranks her below Proust, Mauriac and Gide, insisting
        that she published no great work and created no unforgettable
        characters.

1320   Bromfield, Louis. "Colette vue par l'étranger: aux Etats-Unis
       d'Amérique." Trans. Suzanne Pidoux. In item 1072 Chauvière,
       274-76. Compares French and Anglo-Saxon perspectives on
       life, declaring that only the French can express a love of life in
       their books. Considers Colette a prime representative of this
       ability. Emphasizes the importance of her charm in her rise to
       fame and popularity.

1321   Bronne, Carlo. "Communication." *Bulletin de l'Académie royale de
       langue et de littérature françaises* 51 (1973): 177-80. Also in
       item 1121 *Pour le centenaire de Colette*, 40-43. Evokes
       Colette's ties with Belgium through her mother's family, as
       well as through visits there as a girl, as a performer, and as a
       member of the Academy. Reminds the public that Queen
       Elisabeth of Belgium was friend to Colette and had visited her at
       the Palais Royal.

1322   Brophy, Brigid. "Saint Colette." *Sunday Times Magazine*, 16 April
       1967, 18-24. Illustrated general article. Claims to identify
       Œdipal tensions in Colette's childhood and relates this idea to
       her marriage with Willy and her choice of names. Concentrates
       mostly on Colette's biography and personality but offers some
       analysis of *Chéri* and *La Fin de Chéri*. Vaguely stresses the
       importance of Colette's alleged black ancestry. Although
       extremely interesting, this is a frustrating article because the
       intermittent insertion of unsubstantiated hypotheses about
       Colette's psychology and the occasional inaccurate detail irritate
       the serious reader, and because the generally appealing lively
       style sometimes deteriorates into acerbity. Asserts that Colette
       sought her mother all her life.

1323   Broqueville, Huguette de. "Analyses mathématiques: 'Chéri' de
       Colette." In *L'Etrange Volupté de la mathématique littéraire*, 52-
       61. Brussels: Jacques Antoine, 1983. Attempts to show that
       Colette instinctively developed a geometrical sub-structure for
       the novel *Chéri* and that this plan preceded the actual writing.
       Illustrated by diagrams and equations. The sub-structure thus
       deduced is centered on Edmée.

1324   Bruézière, Maurice. "Colette." In *Histoire descriptive de la
       littérature contemporaine*, vol. 1, 81-87. Paris: Berger-Levrault,

1975. Consists mostly of summaries of Colette's principal novels. Ascribes her greatness to the fact that she accepted her destiny as a woman. Considers her a nature poet but asserts that her animal books demonstrate the weaknesses of human beings.

1325 Bruhl, Etienne. "Récit de Colette." In *Variantes: nouvelles et pastiches*, 233-40. Paris: Arthaud, 1951. Coll. Sempervivum. A not-very-successful pastiche featuring Colette and a cat.

1326 Brunel, Pierre. "'L'Enfance et les sortilèges'." In item 1060 *Autour de Colette à Saint-Tropez*, non-pag. [47-60]. Emphasizes the relationship between Colette's *L'Enfant et les sortilèges* and her other works, especially those inspired by her daughter or by her own childhood. Explores the meaning of the word *sortilège* and its different manifestations in her work. Interesting comments about Colette's use of the princess motif and its relationship to her concept of the mother.

1327 Brunet, Alain. "La Bibliographie de 'la Pléiade'." *Cahiers Colette*, no. 7 (1985): 133-36. Stresses the difficulty of establishing a bibliography of Colette's texts printed in newspapers and journals because information about her collaboration with many of them is lacking or not susceptible of verification. Moreover, some periodicals cannot be located, either at the Bibliothèque Nationale in Paris or in any other large collection. Followed by additions to the Pléiade bibliography for 1910.

1328 Brunet, Alain. "Editions originales ('Les Vrilles de la vigne')." *Cahiers Colette*, no. 9 (1987): 33-40. Several different editions of *Les Vrilles de la vigne* appeared in 1908. Article provides details such as color of cover, dedications and publisher's address, to help scholars distinguish one edition from the other.

1329 Brunet, Alain. "Une visite à Nantes: la collection de Léon Delanoë." *Cahiers Colette*, no. 5 (1983): 5-19. Delanoë, who collaborated on the first volume of the Pléiade edition of Colette's works and who died while this article was in press, had devoted an entire room to Colette material, including editions, manuscripts, portraits, letters, theses, recordings, photographs, and even files on Colette's husbands, friends and acquaintances. He had classified the material and established a substantial bibliography. This article records impressions of the vastness of the material collected and of the methodology underlying its ordering. It also calls for material still lacking.

1330   Brunet, Etienne. "Le Bestiaire de Colette: étude statistique et comparative." In item 1060 *Autour de Colette à Saint-Tropez*, non-pag. [154-83]. Computer-based analysis using concordances of *La Naissance du jour, Dialogues de bêtes, Claudine à l'école, La Maison de Claudine* and *Sido*. Conclusions of this statistical study on the frequency and type of references to animals offer no surprises, and the article admits that the statistics are crude in any case, but the details are interesting and include comparisons with other authors. Numerous statistical tables.

1331   Bruttin-De Preux, Françoise. "Des animaux dans l'œuvre de Colette." *Etudes de lettres* 5 (Oct.-Dec. 1962): 259-74. Uneven analysis of the role of animals in Colette's work. Establishes a hierarchy of species according to Colette's presumed preferences. Accepts the idea that animals represent for her an image of purity. The most interesting section highlights the techniques Colette uses to individualize animals, but many of these remarks could apply to Colette's general descriptive technique.

1332   Bryher [pseud. of Annie Winifred Ellerman]. In *The Heart to Artemis: A Writer's Memoirs*, 33-34. London: Collins, 1963. Brief reminiscences of an encounter with Colette.

1333   Buchet, Edmond. In *Les Auteurs de ma vie ou ma vie d'éditeur*, 114-15, 124-25, 241-42. Paris: Buchet/Chastel, 1969. Buchet's publishing house produced several books by Colette. Scattered remarks in his journal reveal her financial shrewdness. Also comments on Maurice Goudeket's business acumen. Suggests that petty motives lay behind the protests against the Catholic Church's refusal to permit a religious funeral for Colette.

1334   Buenzod, Emmanuel. "Colette, jeune femme." In *Une Epoque littéraire 1890-1910*, 147-53. Neuchâtel: La Baconnière, 1941. Fanciful interpretation of early works, particularly *La Retraite sentimentale*, as a portrayal of their author facing old age. States that Claudine's monologue after Renaud's death expresses the essential Colette.

1335 Bullough, Geoffrey. "Literary Relations of Shaw's Mrs. Warren."
Philological Quarterly 41 (Jan. 1962): 339-58. Compares *Gigi*
with Shaw's *Mrs. Warren's Profession* and Maupassant's *Yvette*,
considered by some scholars to be the source of Shaw's play.
Argues that Colette lacks Maupassant's amoral convictions, that
she evades the moral dilemma implicit in the novel by
accepting the morality of the characters' way of life and at the
same time ending the book with a marriage proposal. Concludes
that *Gigi*'s popularity means that the modern public likes mild
sexual titillation.

1336 Butureaunu, Silvia. "Colette en Roumanie." *Analele stintifice ale
Universitatii Iasi* 25 (1979): 99-105. Provides new information
on Colette's trip to Rumania in 1931, offering an account of
places visited, people met and public events. Also illuminates
Colette's creative process, by indicating that Colette never
actually attended a reception that she describes in an essay. An
article of potentially great documentary value.

1337 Butureaunu, Silvia. "Colette si lumea animalelor." *Analele
stintifice ale Universitatii Iasi* 15 (1969): 131-36. Assesses
Colette's success as an animal writer. Draws parallels between
her approach to animals and that of Jules Renard, Kipling ,
Buffon and La Fontaine.

1338 Butureaunu, Silvia. "Colette si natura." *Studii de Literatura
universala* 15 (1970): 109-17. Asserts that Colette's
presentation of nature has a moral dimension, allied to her stoic
courage, her lucidity and her psychological equilibrium.

1339 Butureaunu, Silvia. "La métaphore filée chez Colette." *Analele
stintifice ale Universitatii Iasi* 28 (1982): 39-42. Analyzes
chain metaphors and metaphor clusters in two passages from
Les Vrilles de la vigne and *Le Fanal bleu*, in order to assess
their function and effects. Concludes that Colette's metaphor
technique is a product of her original vision of the world and an
essential tool in her successful evocation of the material
universe. A brief but perceptive study of a phenomenon that has
long been noted in Colette's work but which has so far received
little detailled analysis.

1340 Butureaunu, Silvia. "Psihologie si morala la Colette." *Analele stintifice ale Universitatii Iasi* 16 (1970): 83-97. Insists that Colette was morally a non-conformist but was not immoral, that her work demonstrates the feminine soul in all its richness, sexuality and desire being but steps in its unfolding as love becomes more and more spiritualized. Characterizes the feminine soul by its search for happiness, its fear of solitude, its taste for independence, its self-discipline and its lucidity.

1341 C., L. "Peut-on prolonger la vie? Une conférence de Colette." *Le Journal*, 26 Oct. 1924, 2. Amusing account of Colette's alleged collaboration in a public experiment on blood transfusions for the purpose of rejuvenation.

1342 C., M. "Mauriac chez Colette." *Figaro littéraire*, 15 Nov. 1952, 1, 12. Brief account of visit to Colette by François Mauriac after he received the Nobel Prize for Literature. Despite differences in their ideas, Colette and Mauriac held one another in esteem.

1343 Cadieu, Martine. "'La Naissance du jour,' ou le consentement." In *Elles: héroïnes de romans, miroir de leur temps*, 41-59. Paris: Les Editeurs français réunis, 1975. Rambling, lyrical meditation in which Colette's presence is evoked. Especially significant to the evocation are passages of *La Naissance du jour*, preferred here for its dawn imagery and the wisdom expressed by its narrator. Compares the blues of Colette's imagery to those of Bonnard. One of a collection of nine reveries by women writers, on women who have written about women and with whom the author feels an affinity.

1344 Caillet, Gérard. "Images de Colette." *France-Illustration*, no. 368 (1 Nov. 1952): 479. Account of a visit to Colette, during which she re-affirms her interest in both the old and the new.

1345 Caillet, Gérard. "Sido, Claudine et Colette ne sont plus." *France-Illustration*, no. 414 (Sept. 1954): 78-80. Report of Colette's state funeral, stressing her importance in the life of both humble and mighty. Terms her life perfect, in that her work and her way of life were in total equilibrium. Also photographs of her life.

1346 Cain, Julien. "Ma voisine." *Lettres françaises*, 12 Aug. 1954, 1, 5.
One of Colette's neighbors at the Palais Royal avers that her
judgment of people and things was impeccable.

1347 Calvet, Jean, and Marcel Cruppi. "L'homme en société avec les
animaux." In *Le Bestiaire de la littérature française*, 225-34.
Paris: Lanore, 1954. Reproaches several animal writers,
including Colette, for neglecting the soul of man in order to
create one for animals. Judges Colette already dated but still at
the forefront of French animal writers, and the one who least
plays favorites. Considers that the scabrous nature of some of
her work is compensated for by her feeling for nature. Terms her
work impressionist.

1348 Campana, Madeleine. "Colette au bout du fil." *Figaro littéraire*, 18
Aug. 1973, 1-2. Reminiscences of a telephone operator and her
two meetings with Colette.

1349 Capote, Truman. "The White Rose." *Ladies' Home Journal* 88
(July 1971): 96-97, 127-28. Account of a visit made to Colette
some 23 years earlier, her remarks about her collection of paperweights, and the effect the experience had on Capote: he, too,
became a collector. Title refers to one of Colette's paperweights.

1350 Caprio, Frank S. In *Female Homosexuality: A Psychodynamic
Study of Lesbianism*, 87, 136. New York: Grove (Black Cat),
1962. Uses Colette's statement in *Le Pur et l'impur* that she
was more at ease with young male homosexuals than with other
men as support for the argument that lesbians prefer the
company of male homosexuals to that of male heterosexuals
because they fear being seduced by the latter. Uses passage from
La Vagabonde to support the idea that lesbianism represents a
flight from heterosexual difficulties.

1351 Carco, Francis [pseud. of François Marie Alexandre Carcopino-
Tusoli]. "Préface." In *Paris de ma fenêtre*, some eds. Insists on
the talent of women, and of Colette in particular, to detect
poetry in small things. Paints a picture of occupied Paris, many
details of which are echoed in Colette's text. Suggests that some
of Colette's anecdotes have been falsified so as to protect the

identity of those involved. Praises her courage. Carco was friend to Colette over several decades.

1352   Carco, Francis [pseud. of François Marie Alexandre Carcopino-Tusoli]. "Rien sans la douleur." *Figaro littéraire*, 24 Jan. 1953, 3. Calls Colette a great moralist whose stoicism and dignity in suffering offer a lesson to all.

1353   Cardinal, Marie. [Introduction]. In item 0350, i-xvi. Novelist Cardinal does not deal specifically with the three novels in the volume introduced--*Claudine à l'école*, *L'Ingénue libertine* and *Chéri*--but offers a solid, if subjective, assessment of Colette's qualities as a writer and as an individualist whose behaviour represented a certain feminist ideal. Quotes from an early letter from Colette to Marcel Schwob.

1354   Carrascal Sánchez, J. "Les personnages et l'élément comparatif dans une œuvre de Colette: 'La Chatte'." *Revue du Pacifique* 2 (Spring 1976): 50-60. Analyzes the effect of comparisons on the perspective of each of the protagonists of Colette's novel, *La Chatte*, as well as on that of the reader. Concludes that those attached to Camille announce a disintegration of personality, those attached to Alain reflect his dream-world, and those used to describe Saha accord her a mythical status. Includes several diagrams. An extremely interesting and thought-provoking article but too sketchy an analysis to be truly valuable.

1355   Carrère, Maïté. "L'amour, ce n'est pas un sentiment honorable." In item 1057 *Album Masques: Colette*, 34-39. Considers Colette to be a victim of misogyny even now. Emphasizes importance of love in her work, and the teaching of her mother. Quotes Colette's works freely.

1356   Carter, Angela. "Colette." *London Review of Books* 2 (2 Oct. 1980): 15-17. Impertinent but entertaining assessment of Colette's novels, as well as of the latest criticism. Shows little evidence of a real understanding of Colette's work or of biographical data concerning her. States that she used her own name in most of her novellas because she could not bear not to be on stage. Considers *La Vagabonde* still one of the most truthful expositions of the dilemma of a free woman in a male-dominated society, but terms Colette an ambivalent ally of the women's movement. Includes scathing attack on Simone de Beauvoir. Ends with a useful list of recent English editions.

1357 Carteron, Philippe. "Colette et Willy." In item 1057 *Album Masques: Colette*, 49-56. Traces Colette's relationship with Willy from before their marriage to after their divorce. Speculates on the reasons for Willy's offer of marriage and Colette's acceptance, on the effects of the ill-assorted couple on the circles they frequented in Paris, on the profound physical and psychological effect on Colette of her new existence, and on the genesis of the first Claudine novel. Depicts Colette as Willy's willing servant, and stresses the legal and financial obstacles discouraging her from leaving him. Very interesting article, despite its lack of new information and its minor inaccuracies.

1358 Castex, Pierre-Georges, and Paul Surer. "L'âme féminine: Colette." In *Manuel des études littéraires françaises: XXe siècle*, 102, 110-11. Paris: Hachette, 1953. Brief profile for students, and short analysis of a passage from *Les Vrilles de la vigne*.

1359 Cazals, Patrick. In *Musidora: la dixième muse*, 69-75, 109-16, 181-99. Paris: Veyrier, 1978. This biography of actress-writer Musidora refers to Colette many times in connection with their long friendship and their collaboration on silent films. Quotes Musidora's remarks about Colette, seen as an influential and impartial critic of her writing. Includes some correspondence, an article by Musidora about Colette and silent film, and part of the text of an address she gave on Colette in October 1945.

1360 Cenerini, Lucia. "La poetica dell'artista." In *Il Mestiere di scrivere: Colette, Simone de Beauvoir, Marguerite Duras*, 35-42. Foggia: Bastogi di A. Manuali, 1983. Sketches the development of Colette's pride in her workmanship and her interest in words themselves. Declares that principles deduced from her advice for writers are as valid as the theories of the Russian formalists.

1361 Cesbron, Gilbert. "A propos de l'enterrement civil de Colette: une réponse à Graham Greene." *Carrefour*, 18 Aug. 1954, 1, 5. Defends the Roman Catholic Church's decision not to permit a religious burial for Colette.

1362   Chabanis, Christian. "Colette aujourd'hui." *Nouvelles littéraires*,
       29 Jan. 1973, 4. Homage on the hundredth anniversary of
       Colette's birth. Insists that what is often termed Colette's
       sensualism was actually the love of love in all its forms.
       Mistakenly refers to Graham Greene as Julien Green.

1363   Chabrol, Brigitte. "Colette." *Médecine de France*, no. 248 (Jan.
       1973): 43-50. General article tracing milestones in Colette's
       private life and career, and attempting to place her activities in
       the context of the over-all artistic activity of the Belle Epoque.
       Praises all aspects of Colette's work. Emphasizes the solitary
       nature of her principal characters. Speculates on why she treats
       her childhood and her marriages in her work but rarely mentions
       her adolescence. Equates Colette's mother with the Sido of her
       books. Often quotes Colette's writing.

1364   Chaigne, Louis. In *Itinéraires d'une espérance: pages de journal*,
       305-6. Paris: Beauchesne; Fontenay-Le Comte: Lussaud, 1970.
       Brief reminiscences present Colette as a great journalist and a
       warm-hearted person.

1365   Chaillet, Jean. "Colette: 'La Naissance du jour'." In *Etudes de
       grammaire et de style*, vol. 2, 355-69. Paris: Bordas, 1969. For
       students. Detailed analysis of a page of text. Focuses on syntax,
       images, vocabulary, movement, and musical elements.

1366   Chalon, Jean. "Colette centenaire et révolutionnaire." *Figaro
       littéraire*, 20 Jan. 1973, 13. Terms Colette very modern and her
       work not at all out-dated. Considers her a liberated and modern
       woman, not only because of her life style but also because of
       such works as *Gribiche*, which deals with back-room abortions.
       Judges her novels hostile to men.

1367   Chalon, Jean. "Une Colette méconnue." *Magazine littéraire* 73
       (Feb. 1973): 42. Chalon deplores the fact that *La Jumelle noire*
       is not one of the titles noted among the critical works and new
       editions celebrating the hundredth anniversary of Colette's birth.

1368   Chalon, Jean. "Le monde de Colette." *Magazine littéraire* 42 (July
       1970): 15-16. Classifies Colette's characters into four
       "archetypes"--the mother, the fifty-year-old woman, the teen-age

girl and the handsome young man--and describes the features
shared by all four categories. Notes the almost total absence in
Colette's work of robust, masculine men.

1369 Chamine. "Des souvenirs de Colette... en attendant ses souvenirs."
Bulletin de Paris, no. 45 (20 Aug. 1954): 6. Terms Colette a
treasure of our time. Also reminiscences of 1930 and anecdotes
about her short-lived career as beautician.

1370 Chaney, Marc. "Colette, amoureuse de la nature." *Mémoires de
l'Académie des Sciences, Belles-Lettres et Arts de Lyon*, 3rd
series, no. 41 (1986): 165-74. Text of an address of 9 Dec.
1986, presenting Colette's life and work, and emphasizing her
love of nature and her skill at evoking sensation. Quotes freely
from her novels as if they were autobiographies. Condescending
at times but enthusiastic.

1371 Chapelan, Maurice. "Colette sera-t-elle aussi la Sévigné du XXe
siècle?" *Figaro littéraire*, 27 July 1957, 4. Remarks about the
forthcoming publication of the first volumes of Colette's
correspondence, still at the stage of being collected.

1372 Chaponnière, Paul. "Colette n'est plus..." *Journal de Genève*, 8
Aug. 1954, 3. Praises Colette's work highly, but expresses
reservations concerning the moral stature of her characters.

1373 Chaput-Rolland, Solande. "La grande Colette de France." *Le
Canada*, 9 Dec. 1952, 6. Warns against trying to identify
Colette with her fictional characters. Praises her psychological
insight. Lauds her as one of the few writers who depict the
whole of life, including its charnel aspects.

1374 Charasson, Henriette. "La littérature féminine." In *Vingt-cinq ans
de littérature française de 1895 à 1920*, vol. 2, edited by Eugène
Montfort, 52, 74-76, 91-92. Paris: Librairie de France, 1926.
This assessment of books by women attributes to Colette an
influential role in current literary activity by women, but ranks
Anna de Noailles as Colette's equal. Deplores Colette's subject
matter and expresses doubts about the durability of her renown.
Despite these areas of divergence from today's ideas about
Colette, Charasson's remarks are often astute and she is one of

the few critics of the time to see beyond Colette's popular
reputation as an "instinctive" writer.

1375   Charasson, Henriette. "Madame Colette." *Les Lettres* 3 (1 March
1921): 331-51. Significant because it is one of the few long
articles on Colette dating from the first half of her career and
because it offers both negative and positive comments, most of
them penetrating, about specific works. Disclaims the idea that
Colette's characters portray "woman," and deplores the scandal
surrounding her private life and publication of the Claudine
novels. Considers the latter as nature works containing passages
of great beauty, but prophesizes that their content will make
them out-moded. Foresees that Colette's style will guarantee her
long-term reputation. Contains a long section on *Chéri*, which
had just been published, but Charasson does not consider the
novel convincing despite the high quality of the writing. Praises
the portrayal of Léa as representative of a new class of women
in society.

1376   Charensol, Georges. In *D'une rive à l'autre*, 142-45. Paris: Mercure
de France, 1973. Curious mixture of expressions of admiration
for Colette and disobliging personal remarks. Very sympathetic
to Willy.

1377   Charles-Roux, Edmonde. "Madame Colette." *Cahiers Colette*, no.
7 (1985): 3-9. Text of short speech given at Père-Lachaise
cemetery on the thirtieth anniversary of Colette's death. Declares
that Colette's real greatness is demonstrated by her continuing
popularity.

1378   Charleux-Leroux, Elisabeth. "De Saint-Sauveur à 'Montigny'."
Cahiers Colette, no. 9 (1987): 13-28. Remarks and conclusions
as addenda to item 1384. In it, Charleux-Leroux and Boivin
identified about three-quarters of the approximately 200 local
people mentioned by Colette in the Claudine novels and *La
Maison de Claudine*, with several other identifications classified
as probable. Detects a movement towards greater sympathy for
her compatriots in Colette's later portraits, and a tendency to use
fictitious names when depicting influential people. Also notes
the frequent use of real names in *La Maison de Claudine*, even
for characters previously bearing fictitious ones. Attempts to

identify the reasons for these developments. Highlights Colette's penchant for eccentric or colorful figures.

1379   Charleux-Leroux, Elisabeth. "Le départ de Saint-Sauveur." *Cahiers Colette*, no. 5 (1983): 21-38. A very fine, well-documented article on the loss of the Colette family home in 1890-91, an event referred to several times in Colette's work but never actually described. Many critics believe it to be the traumatic incident at the root of her nostalgia for childhood and the garden. This article attempts to separate fact from fiction and corrects some misconceptions about the event. Includes important new information on the family's financial crisis during that time, on events leading up to the crisis, on the role of Juliette's in-laws and on Colette's later neglect of the house, which was placed at her disposal by well-meaning persons in 1926.

1380   Charleux-Leroux, Elisabeth. "L'Enfant perdu(e) de Claudine." *Cahiers Colette*, no. 10 (1988): 41-42. Report of research into the sources of a song of which Colette quotes a fragment in *Claudine s'en va*. Results turn up no author but other quotations and a possible source date.

1381   Charleux-Leroux, Elisabeth. "Gabrielle Colette à l'école élémentaire." *Bulletin de la Société des sciences historiques et naturelles de l'Yonne* 114 (1983): 87-97. Important biographical article. Presents results of research into the facts underlying some of Colette's references to her early school years. Contains many details of study programs, teaching conditions, prize-givings, and examinations. Carefully documented. A valuable article, not just for Colette scholars, but for anyone concerned with the educational history of the region. Also includes amendments to item 1382, of which it can be considered the continuation.

1382   Charleux-Leroux, Elisabeth. "Réalité et fiction dans 'Claudine à l'école'." *Bulletin de la Société des sciences historiques et naturelles de l'Yonne* 113 (1981): 121-64. Essential article for anyone interested in Colette's childhood, in her early novels and writing techniques or in the Willy-Colette collaboration. Presents results of research on the relationship of fact to fiction in Colette's first novel. Studies all aspects of the subject, such

as setting, dates, names of characters, details of houses and
schools, education, local events, and family relationships.
Concludes that some of the negative portraits were done at
Willy's instigation and that, despite liberties taken with the
truth, *Claudine à l'école* offers a good picture of conditions in
French education towards the end of the nineteenth century.
Heavily footnoted. A magnificent contribution to our
knowledge of Colette's life and to our understanding of her
creative process. See also item 1381.

1383   Charleux-Leroux, Elisabeth. "Sur une page de 'Journal à rebours'."
       Cahiers Colette, no. 10 (1988): 35-40. Refers to documents
       which cast doubt on Colette's presentation of her mother's
       remarks about the 1870 war in the Yonne. Also documentation
       about Juliette's schooling.

1384   Charleux-Leroux, Elisabeth, and Marguerite Boivin. "Personnages
       de Montigny et habitants de Saint-Sauveur." *Cahiers Colette*,
       no. 6 (1984): 33-60; no. 7 (1985): 45-97; no. 8 (1986): 29-79;
       no. 9 (1987): 45-67. Identifies the originals of characters
       modeled on people Colette knew in her home village of Saint-
       Sauveur and the surrounding region. Based on painstaking
       research in local archives, this is an immensely valuable
       biographical article and one that sheds considerable light on
       Colette's creative process, especially on the transformation of
       experience into fiction in the five Claudine novels, as well as in
       La Maison de Claudine and *Sido*. Gives the background and
       history of the model, noting similarities and differences between
       the real and the fictional persons. Some identifications have
       been verified by the authors, while others are speculative; all are
       supported by reasons. Also indicates where research has failed to
       unearth any real-life model. Includes corrections and
       contradictions to ideas previously advanced by others. Rich in
       details about Colette's family connections, but does not include
       her immediate family. A map of the town is included in the first
       part. Names are arranged alphabetically by fictional character,
       with additions and corrections at the end. Some photographs.

1385   Charpentier, Charlotte. "Colette, la petite compagnarde." *Revue des
       temps modernes*, no. 2 (10 Feb. 1936): 156-58. General article
       praising Colette, making little distinction between her life and

her fiction, in an attempt to describe the "image" of her emanating from the two. Details not always accurate.

1386 Charpentier, John. "Colette." *Mercure de France*, 1 Feb. 1931, 590-93. Generally favorable assessment of Colette's work, with emphasis on her early semi-autobiographical books, but consisting mostly of clichés about her instinct and her alleged animal nature.

1387 Charras, Marie-Claude. "Colette à travers 'La Lune de pluie'." *Rivista di letterature moderne e comparate* 39 (Oct.-Dec. 1986): 327-37. Speculates on the genesis of the novella *La Lune de pluie* and its sources of inspiration in Colette's own life. Adopting as premise the hypothesis that Délia Essendier is a consciously created double of Colette, Charras suggests parallels between the couple Colette-Claudine and the couple Madame Colette-Délia Essendier, as well as between the trios Sido-Willy-Colette and Rosita-Eugène-Délia. Analyzes the novella's structure in the light of this idea, particularly in so far as their relationships can be described as love-hate ones. Not convincing in every detail, but a thoughtful and provocative study. Remarks on coincidences in the chronology of events are intriguing.

1388 Charras, Marie-Claude. "Colette et 'Gigi': un miroir à quatre faces." *Saggi et ricerche di letterature francese* 19 (1980): 55-86. Analysis of *Gigi*, as example of Colette's impressionism, and particularly of her techniques of double focalization or narration with both an external and an internal perspective and at more than one level. Includes subtle analysis of the way she creates a psychological dimension as well as a narrative interplay between past and present. The four-way mirror of the title refers to the four women in the story, all of whom, claims Charras, reflect elements in Colette's own life and psychology. This article represents an important contribution to our understanding of what is often deemed one of Colette's less substantial works.

1389 Charras, Marie-Claude. "Si la vie m'était contée... Colette: 'La Femme cachée'." *Rivista di letterature moderne e comparate* 34 (June 1981): 127-51. Rightly terms *La Femme cachée* neglected by scholars, despite its popularity with readers. Identifies the book's central themes as the essential unity of life and the

solitude of the individual. Probes these features in the collection
of 22 short stories, by recounting each story briefly then
commenting on Colette's techniques of unity and differentiation.
Draws conclusions about Colette's over-all view of humanity.
A very fine article.

1390   Chassé, Charles. "L'œuvre de Colette, ou la femme aux mains
sentimentales." *Le Capitole*, 22 Dec. 1924, non-pag. [24-27].
The longest article in this special issue. Rich in inaccurate
assumptions but also in praise. Chassé reviews most of
Colette's early major works, finding therein a reflection of the
development of the writer's own life and in particular of her
sensibility. Notes the importance of touch in her presentation of
sensations.

1391   Chauvet, Louis. "Colette contre Bresson." *Le Figaro*, 17 March
1975, 21. Imaginary dialogue between Colette, film reviewer
Chauvet, and writer Robert Bresson.

1392   Chauvière, Claude. "Une Colette ignorée." *Le Capitole*, 22 Dec.
1924, non-pag. [35]. Draws on personal anecdote to confirm
Colette's talent and accomplishments as a musician. Name
incorrectly spelled "Chauvières" in this issue.

1393   Chavanon, André. In *Des souvenirs... ...de théâtre*, 30-35. Paris:
Pensée universelle, 1974. Account of three meetings with
Colette during the early decades of the century.

1394   Chenevière, Jacques. [No title]. In item 1095 *Hommage à Colette*,
non-pag. Emphasizes Colette's ability to capture life on paper.

1395   Chevalier, Maurice. "Colette chérie." *Gazette des lettres*, 29 Oct.
1949, 8. Famed entertainer Chevalier expresses his personal
esteem for Colette, whom he first met when a young man.
Recalls her when she was touring with Georges Wague and
Christine Kerf in the pantomime *La Chair*.

1396   Choisy, Maryse. "Colette." In *Sur la route de Dieu on rencontre
d'abord le diable: mémoires 1925-1939*, 294-98. Paris: Emile-
Paul, 1978. Colette's one-time neighbor at the Claridge Hotel
offers minor anecdotes and expressions of admiration.

1397 Chonez, Claudine. "Hier, aujourd'hui, demain." *Table ronde* 99 (March 1956): 60-64. Chonez sees Colette as an important link between female writers of pre- and post-World War II.

1398 Ciolkowska, Muriel [signed: Ciolkowski]. "A Master-Writer." *The Egoist* 3 (1 May 1916): 68-69. Actually a long review of *La Paix chez les bêtes*, but important because it shows that Colette's work was appreciated at an early date by English readers, even though very little of it was yet available in translation. Makes interesting distinctions between what women readers want and what men readers want. Calls Colette "the most perfect example in prose we possess in France today."

1399 Clarac, Pierre. "Introduction." In item 0065 *Textes choisis de Colette*, 7-28. Discerns three styles in Colette's work: the simplicity of *La Maison de Claudine*, the lyricism of passages in *Claudine à l'école*, and the mature style characterized by its plenitude and its purity. Attempts to relate each type of style to elements in her life. Regrets that she did not produce a major work in which World War I is an important factor. Insists that much of Colette's work is admirably suited to children's reading.

1400 Clarac, Pierre. "La vie et l'œuvre de Colette." In item 0063 *Pages choisies*, 3-6. Brief summary of Colette's life and work. Notes her preference for the shorter genres. Judges her work alien to post-World War II preoccupations and revelatory of the emptiness of lives not lived for a greater purpose. Sees in Colette and Proust the last great impressionist writers of French prose.

1401 Claudel, Paul. "Se réveiller chaque matin tout neuf..." *Figaro littéraire*, 24 Jan. 1953, 1. Also in *Figaro littéraire*, 7 Aug. 1954, 4. Fac-simile of hand-written note dated 18 Jan. 1953, affirming that life and the enjoyment of life have been a long privilege for Colette.

1402 Claudel, Paul. In *Positions et propositions*, 77-78. Paris: Gallimard, 1928. Brief note asserting that Colette and her mother exemplify the idea that style is a natural phenomenon nourished in the family.

1403 Clément, Frantz. "Colette." *Das Tage-buch* 7 (5 June 1926): 799-
      802. General evaluation of Colette, considered here to be
      unrivaled among French women writers. Avers that her works
      offer a precious compensation to world views posited by male
      writers. Praises her capacity to evoke sensations. Draws
      parallels between Colette and French women novelists of earlier
      centuries.

1404 Cleynen-Serghiev, Ecaterina. "Centenarul Colette." *Steaua* 24 (1-
      15 Oct. 1973): 26-27. Not seen.

1405 Clouard, Henri. "Descente dans le monde charnel: Colette." In
      Histoire de la littérature française du symbolisme à nos jours,
      vol. 2, 88-96. Paris: Albin Michel, 1949. Praises Colette as
      rival to both Gide and Proust in psychological insight. Views
      her as a chronicler of the human condition, but at the level of
      the charnel. Reproaches her for occasional preciosity and over-
      use of metaphors, but acknowledges her greatness as a prose
      writer.

1406 Cluny, Claude Michel. "Une romancière du bonheur raisonnable."
      Magazine littéraire, no. 42 (July 1970): 8-10. Also, combined
      with review of item 0057 *Autobiographie...* and under title
      "Colette," in *La Rage de lire*, 243-52. Paris: Denoël, 1978.
      Considers Colette's novels to be faithful paintings of the
      fashions and manners of an era. Stresses her preoccupation with
      aging. Insists that her women protagonists are characterized by
      their preference for truth over ideas.

1407 Cobb, Richard. "The World of Childhood." *Listener* 99 (20 April
      1978): 514-16. Also in *Promenades: A Historian's Appreciation
      of Modern French Literature*, 8. Oxford: Oxford University
      Press, 1980. In this text of the second of the radio series
      "Fiction, Fact and France," Cobb devotes one paragraph to
      Colette, to show that the sensations of childhood are more
      easily remembered than those of later times.

1408 Cocteau, Jean. "Colette parle." *Livres de France* 5 (Oct. 1954): 7-8.
      Handwritten text. Describes Colette sitting and walking while
      talking to him. Very interesting intimate passage.

1409   Cocteau, Jean. In *Entretiens avec André Fraigneau*, 67. Paris:
       Union générale d'éditions, 1965. In interview by Fraigneau,
       Cocteau recalls making documentary with Colette, during which
       both of them were intimidated by the microphone.

1410   Cocteau, Jean. In *Le Passé défini: journal 1951-1952*, 167, 172,
       279, 364, 375, 401. Paris: Gallimard, 1983. Scattered allusions
       throughout the book give a picture of Colette's physical decline
       in the last years of her life. At that time Cocteau, who lived
       near her in the Palais Royal, saw her frequently. Presents her as
       living a cocoon-like existence, protected from the outside world
       by Maurice Goudeket. Says that either Colette or Sartre should
       get the Nobel Prize for literature.

1411   Cocteau, Jean. In *Poésie de journalisme: 1935-1938*, 31-34, 39-42.
       Paris: Belfond, 1973. Recounts visit to the south of France and
       dinner with Colette, Hélène Jourdan-Morhange, Luc-Albert
       Moreau and others. Dated 1935.

1412   Cocteau, Jean. In item 1072 Chauvière, 171-72. Letter of March
       1929 to Colette, expressing friendship and praise for her latest
       novel, *La Seconde*.

1413   Coe, Richard N. In *When the Grass was Taller: Autobiography and
       the Experience of Childhood*, 31-32, 117-18, 145. New Haven
       & London: Yale University Press, 1984. Approaches the
       childhood theme in Colette's work from a psychological
       perspective. Considers that in *La Maison de Claudine* Colette
       uses the familiar technique of reconstruction of the writer's
       child-self, but that, since in her case it is the mother that is re-
       created rather than the child, the creation is indirect. Also
       interprets Colette's portrayal of her father as a depiction of the
       "collapsed father figure," the recognition of whose failure was
       one of the traumatic shocks of her childhood.

1414   Cœuroy, André. "Colette et Ravel." *Ecrits de Paris* 326 (June
       1973): 112-18. Brief resume of the genesis and plot of *L'Enfant
       et les sortilèges*. Disappointing article in that most of it deals
       with Ravel's music, and little attention is paid to Colette's
       contribution.

1415 Cœuroy, André. "Colette musicienne." *Ecrits de Paris* 323 (March
      1973): 109-17. Recalls first meeting Colette about 1920, when
      Cœuroy was chief editor of *Revue musicale*. Quotes passages
      from her books to demonstrate her discerning ear and musical
      sense, and her ability to evoke the exact quality of a sound.
      Includes several anecdotes.

1416 Cœuroy, André. "Claudine musicographe." *Ecrits de Paris* 324
      (April 1973): 111-18; 325 (May 1973): 110-18. Speculates on
      whether Colette wrote the music reviews published in *Gil Blas*
      under the pen name Claudine. Researchers are not in agreement
      on the question. Analyzes preferences and dislikes evident in the
      reviews, to demonstrate that opinions expressed therein about
      music, performers and composers must be those of Colette.
      Exact sources are, regrettably, not given for passages quoted in
      this extremely interesting and potentially useful article.

1417 Cogniat, Raymond. "Chez Mme Colette." *Comœdia*, 20 Oct.
      1923, 3. Interview in which Colette discusses the upcoming
      "Collection Colette" series of novels, which she will choose for
      Ferenczi.

1418 Cohen, Susan D. "An Onomastic Double Bind: Colette's 'Gigi' and
      the Politics of Naming." *PMLA* 100 (Oct. 1985): 793-809.
      Excellent analysis of the problems of feminine discourse as
      illustrated in *Gigi*. Presents Madame Alvarez as one who, in
      adopting a patronym, has accepted an entire phallogocentric
      sociolinguistic system, which permits exploitation of her own
      social sub-class but of which she is now a spokesperson. Insists
      that Gigi's first refusal of Gaston's offer represents the
      conscious rejection of a patriarchal code which suppresses
      women's identity and women's power through verbal and sexual
      occultation. The double bind of the title refers to Gigi's skirts,
      which express the idea of her choice between childhood
      asexuality and social non-existence or a female sexuality that
      must be repressed and is controlled by men. Concludes that
      interpretations of her acceptance of Gaston's offer as a happy
      ending mistake Colette's intention. Contrasts Gigi's choice with
      Colette's own at the time of her separation from Willy. The
      best article written on *Gigi*.

1419　Coiplet, Robert. "Colette dans les paysages de son enfance." In
　　　Demeures inspirées et sites romanesques, vol. 3, edited by Paul-
　　　Emile Cadhilac and Robert Coiplet, 347-55. Paris: Eds. de
　　　l'Illustration/Baschet, 1958. Detailed description of Colette's
　　　childhood homes. Focuses on features mentioned in her books:
　　　the house at Saint-Sauveur, the farms owned by the family
　　　before its financial ruin, and Achille's house at Châtillon-
　　　Coligny where the family found refuge. Excellent photographs.

1420　Coiplet, Robert. "La maison de 'L'Etoile vesper'." In *Demeures
　　　inspirées et sites romanesques*, vol. 3, edited by Paul-Emile
　　　Cadhilac and Robert Coiplet, 356-60. Paris: Eds. de
　　　l'Illustration/Baschet, 1958. Description and photographs of
　　　Colette's apartment in the Palais Royal and the view from her
　　　windows. Includes material on her earlier apartment there and
　　　relates how she finally acquired the apartment she wanted.

1421　Colette, Captain Jules. "Un poème du Capitaine Colette: 'Les
　　　Monts-Boucons'." *Figaro littéraire*, 24 Jan. 1953, 6. Also in
　　　item 1056 *Album Colette*, 55. Poem dated October 1901,
　　　written by Colette's father and dedicated to her. Expresses the
　　　wish to be with Colette and Willy at their summer home, the
　　　Monts-Boucons.

1422　Colette, Sidonie Landoy. "Lettres de Sido à sa fille Gabrielle."
　　　Figaro Littéraire, 24 Jan. 1953, 1, 6. Thirteen letters and
　　　extracts from 1904 to 1911, to Colette from her mother. In an
　　　intimate informal style Sido touches on many subjects, among
　　　them the other villagers, her new residence, her distaste for
　　　Juliette's in-laws, her esteem for Kipling's books, and Colette's
　　　pets. Her love for her daughter, her concern for the welfare of
　　　animals, and her perennial need for the presence of nature are
　　　manifest in every letter. Of particular interest are passages
　　　wherein she offers advice on Colette's budding theatrical career.
　　　An undated letter to Henry de Jouvenel accepting his invitation
　　　to visit, despite concern for her pet and her plants, echos the
　　　opening passage of *La Naissance du jour*. Most of the letters are
　　　also in item 0013 *Sido: lettres à sa fille*, also passages in item
　　　2107 Senhouse.

1423   Colin d'Amiens, Jean. In *Journal*, 140. Paris: Seuil, 1968. Brief
       paragraph praising Colette for drawing psychological profit
       from her own suffering.

1424   Collet, Francis. "Colette: 'Sido', 'Les Vrilles de la vigne'." *Ecole
       des lettres II* 78:9 (1987): 3-19 and 78:10 (1987): 3-16. Model
       for the French baccalaureat oral examination. Treats three
       extracts from each book, with analysis of their degree of
       adherence to a recognized genre, textual analysis of the language
       and movement of ideas, identification of themes, and general
       conclusion. A useful study of Colette's techniques at the student
       level.

1425   Collins, Joseph [signed: J.C.]. "Introduction." In *These pleasures*
       [trans. of *Le Pur et l'impur*], several eds. General presentation of
       Colette's work. States admiration for her reluctance to explain
       or justify homosexuality, and praises her portrayal of Charlotte.

1426   Contou, Jeanne. "Thèses sur Colette et son œuvre." *Cahiers
       Colette*, no. 1 (1977): 77-79; no. 2 (1980): 65-67; no. 3-4
       (1981): 141-44; no. 5 (1983): 89-91; no. 6 (1984): 85-87; no. 7
       (1985): 137-39; no. 8 (1986): 145-48; no. 9 (1987): 114-16;
       no. 10 (1988): 103-5. Lists theses on Colette, both completed
       and in progress.

1427   Cordié, Carlo. "Colette." *Cultura e Scuola* 25 (Oct.-Dec. 1986):
       94-104. Fine detailed summary of recent publications by or
       about Colette, as well as of colloquia and exhibitions in France
       and abroad. Comments at length on the new Pléiade edition of
       Colette's work, as well as on critical books and articles.

1428   Cormeau, Nelly [signed: N.C.]. "In memoriam Colette."
       Synthèses, no. 100 (Sept. 1954): 259-61. Emphasizes Colette's
       vitality and affinity for animals. Asserts that since she knew
       how to live well she knew how to face death.

1429   Cornwall, Irene. "Colette." In *Contemporary French Fiction*, edited
       by Irene Cornwall, 3-12. New York: Holt, 1940. Brief analysis
       of Colette's life and work as introduction to the first English-
       language student anthology with a large section on Colette.
       Despite the general title, Colette is actually the principal author

included in the anthology, which contains four texts from *La Maison de Claudine*, one from *Les Vrilles de la vigne*, and one from *Sept dialogues de bêtes*. Anthology also contains list of suggested readings and a long French-English glossary.

1430 Cothran, Ann. "'The Pure and the Impure': Codes and Constructs." *Women's Studies* 8:3 (1981): 335-58. Analyzes the semantics of *Le Pur et l'impur*. Argues that the apparently opposite types depicted by Colette, such as the lesbian and the Don Juan, share significant characteristics, and that Colette finds human sensuality to be essentially feminine in nature. Analyzes four "codes"--darkness, light, land, water--and four "thematic constructs"--illusion, excess, inner space and exchange--to demonstrate that Colette uses images of darkness and water to reshape our perception of woman. An excellent article shedding new light on Colette's most controversial book. Considerable overlap with item 1431.

1431 Cothran, Ann, and Diane Griffin Crowder. "Image Structure, Codes, and Recoding in 'The Pure and the Impure'." In item 1076 *Colette: The Woman, The Writer*, 176-84. Analyzes the codes of water and darkness in *Le Pur et l'impur*. Maintains that Colette recodes these traditional images so that darkness becomes, not danger, but refuge and recognition of identity, while water no longer represents the mother but autonomy, freedom and sensuality. Overlaps with item 1430, which is also more complete.

1432 Cottrell, Robert D. "Colette's Literary Reputation." In *Women, the Arts, and the 1920s in Paris and New York*, edited by Kenneth W. Wheeler and Virginia Lee Lussier, 8-13. New Brunswick, N.J.: Transaction Books, 1982. Analyzes early critics' reception of Colette, as well as the reasons for their sometimes equivocal opinions, and notes their desire to classify her with other female writers of the time. Points out that Colette's name has been the only one of the latter to endure, despite a slight decline in glory between 1954 and 1973. Suggests that her strong femininity is the main reason for her lack of influence on male writers. Considers the links established by the Art Nouveau movement between nature and the female form to be reflected in Colette's work. A fine assessment of Colette's place in French literature.

1433   Courant, Paul. "Une figure française: Willy inconnu." *Ecrits de Paris*, no. 118 (Feb. 1956): 56-60. Protests the severity of Colette's portrayal of her first husband. Defends Willy's commercialism. Stresses positive features of his talents, general culture, musicality, patriotism, and adherence to some of the bourgeois values in which he had been raised.

1434   Courcay, Jean. "A propos du jardin du Palais-Royal." *Le Cerf - volant*, July 1957, 13-15. Evokes history of the garden of the Palais Royal. Includes brief paragraph on the sight of Colette at her window.

1435   Couvreur, Dr. Jacques. "Colette et sa famille à Châtillon-Coligny." *Journal de Gien*, 22 Nov. 1973, non.-pag. Resident of the area traces incidents in the move of the Colette family from Saint-Sauveur to Châtillon-Coligny. Offers no new facts, but evokes a warm picture of the life there of both parents and children.

1436   Crémieux, Francis. "'Non' m'a dit la Présidente des Goncourt Madame Colette." *Lettres françaises*, 1 Dec. 1949, 1, 3. Light-hearted account of an interview in which Colette refuses to discuss literary criticism or general ideas.

1437   Cressanges, Jeanne. "Colette ou l'univers féminin." In *Vingt ans d'action littéraire*, presented by Jean Huguet, 77-82. Les Sables-d'Olonne: Le Cercle d'or, 1976. Interesting because written by a young person expressing what Colette means to her. Focuses on the motifs of earth, fire, mirror and lost paradise. Views Colette's life as a series of waves that can be interpreted in terms of voyage and haven, present and past, or as a movement in which the mirror plays a positive role in determining Colette's attitude to life. Concludes that Colette's writing explores completely the life of a woman.

1438   Croce, Elena Craveri. "Colette." *Aretusa* 4 (Sept.-Oct. 1944): 69-75. Over-all evaluation of Colette's work with main focus on the novels. Deplores the apparent limits of her world, but waxes enthusiastic about her insight into psychology, especially as demonstrated by her treatment of solitude in *Chéri*, *La Fin de Chéri* and *La Chatte*. Contrasts Colette's evocation of a happy past with Proust's more melancholy depiction.

1439 Crosland, Margaret. "Colette and Ravel: The Enchantress and the Illusionist." In item 1076 *Colette: The Woman, The Writer*, 116-24. Traces Colette's relations with Ravel from the time of their first meeting up to the first performance of *L'Enfant et les sortilèges*.

1440 Crosland, Margaret. In *Women of Iron and Velvet: and the Books They Wrote in France*, 92-96. London: Constable, 1976. Also, under the title *Women of Iron and Velvet: French Women Writers after George Sand*. New York: Taplinger, 1976. In this general survey of French women writers Crosland attempts to assess Colette's place within the entire twentieth-century French literary scene. Very interesting to read, although Crosland's remarks are often subjective and speculative. Considers *Mitsou* an unsatisfactory novel even though it represents an important step in Colette's movement away from autobiographical characterization. Also casual allusions to her throughout the book.

1441 Crozet, Vincent. "Les esclaves en littérature." *Magazine littéraire* 4 (Feb. 1967): 45-47. Colette's name figures prominently in this survey of cases where books written by one author were published under the name of another, without the real author receiving due credit for the work. The true authorship of the Claudine novels was not public knowledge until after the fourth one had been published.

1442 Curnonsky [pseud. of Maurice-Edmond Sailland]. "Colette à table." In *Souvenirs littéraires et gastronomiques*, 295-302. Paris: Albin Michel, 1958. Reminiscences of Colette's first marriage, when the celebrated gastronome worked for Willy. Also praises Colette's knowledge of wine and food.

1443 Dagenais-Lord, Monique. "Colette gourmette, gourmande, gloutonne." *Châtelaine* 22 (Aug. 1981): 62-74. Popular article for homemakers' magazine focuses on Colette's interest in gastronomy. Emphasizes her wide experience of regional cooking and her knowledge of wines. Signals passages in which she or her fictional characters discuss specific foods. Provides recipes for several of her favorite dishes.

1444   Dagey, Jean. "L'enfance de Colette. " *Le Progrès de la Côte d'or*, 4
        Feb. 1936, 4. Dijon newspaper claims Colette as one of its
        own upon her promotion to commander of the Legion of
        Honor. General biography emphasizing her ties with the region,
        with extensive references to *Sido*, *La Maison de Claudine*, and
        Larnac's book on Colette.

1445   Dalby, Henri [signed: Henry Dalby]. "Au pays de Colette."
        Nouvelles littéraires, 5 Nov. 1927, 7. Sentimental account of a
        walk in Saint-Sauveur and area by a writer from the region.

1446   Dalby, Henri. "Au pays de Colette." *Nouvelles littéraires*, 1 Sept.
        1928, 7. Evocation of Saint-Sauveur, and especially of Colette
        at school there. Notes that the family house has been put at
        Colette's disposition but is now empty. In fact, Colette never
        did return permanently to her childhood home. Not the same
        article as the preceding.

1447   Dalby, Henri. "On s'arrache Mme Colette..." *Figaro littéraire*, 6
        March 1948, 3. Argues that Colette is not truly Burgundian for
        several reasons: Saint-Sauveur belongs to the Auxerre district
        only for administrative purposes, her family origins are not of
        the region, and her accent reveals diverse influences.

1448   D'Angeli, Dina. "L'univers de Colette." *Culture française* 13
        (Sept.-Oct. 1966): 295-300. Asserts that Colette's world is
        limited, subjective and feminine, and derived from her own
        experience. Identifies usual three main themes in her work:
        love, nature and animals. Judges her masculine characters as
        inferior to the feminine ones. Terms Colette's attitude towards
        nature anti-romantic and ranks her presentation of animals with
        Kipling's. Recognizes the influence of Colette's mother in
        establishing the broad lines of her universe.

1449   Davanture, Maurice. "La notion de transfert dans la métaphore." In
        Mélanges littéraires François Germain, 313-27. Dijon: La
        Section de Littérature française de la Faculté de Lettres et
        Philosophie de Dijon, 1979. This article on the idea of transfer
        in metaphors chooses many of its examples from Colette's
        work. Analyzes differences between the function of Colette's
        metaphors and use of them by symbolist poets. Asserts that
        Colette's metaphors are successful because they are surprisingly

true, rather than because they are based on sensations.
Concludes that her achievement can be defined as an intelligent
co-ordinating of the real. A highly specialized but fascinating
study, offering valuable remarks on one of the major features of
Colette's famous style.

1450 Davray, Jean. In *Le Reflet et la réflexion*, 19-26, 93. Paris: Fayard,
1974. Relates unsavory anecdotes about Colette, all the while
acknowledging her greatness as a writer. Unedifying remarks, on
the whole.

1451 Debray, Pierre. "Colette, une eau claire qui charrie des monstres."
Aspects de la France, 6 Aug. 1954, 5. Terms Colette a great
writer, but views her subject matter negatively.

1452 Décaudin, Michel. "Colette et les 'Bacchantes' de 1900." *Cahiers
Colette*, no. 3-4 (1981): 136-40. Title refers to the group of
women poets that Colette frequented at the turn of the century.
Declares that they re-introduced sincerity and the natural into
poetry but no technical innovation, and that Colette differed
from them in her technical originality.

1453 Décaudin, Michel, and Daniel Leuwers. "Colette." In *De Zola à
Guillaume Apollinaire*, 300-6. Vol. 8 of *Littérature française*.
Paris: Arthaud, 1986. Good concise biography and over-all
assessment of Colette's achievements. Compares her work with
that of other women writers of the early decades of the century.
Attempts to define her notion of sensual pleasure.

1454 Declerck, Richard. "Colette en het probleem de vrouw." In
Gestalten en Gedachten, 167-68. Antwerp: Uitgeverij
Ontwikkeling, 1957. Terms Colette non-feminist, talented and
having a simple approach to life. Considers her the interpreter
of primary feminine feelings, indifferent to most other things,
but healthy psychologically. Repeats many of the clichés once
used about women and about Colette in particular.

1455 Defoix, Jean. "Dernières nouvelles." *Europe*, no. 631-32 (Nov.-
Dec. 1981): 20-29. Considers Colette's novellas to be written
according to a formula, the details of which Defoix enumerates.
Analyzes the role of the background and decor, the relationship
between the romantic and the banal aspects, the functions of the

narrator, and the revelatory techniques. An excellent study, which demonstrates that Colette's novella technique is far more complex than is usually acknowledged.

1456   Dehon, Claire. "Colette and Art Nouveau." In item 1076 *Colette: The Woman, The Writer*, 104-15. A fascinating article, which explores the extent to which Colette embraced the Art Nouveau style in her early works and remained faithful to it long after it had gone out of fashion. Analyzes the phenomenon in terms of Colette's style, choice of subjects, reference to dreams, use of ornamentation and irony, and dominance of the feminine. Notes her well-known preference for the curve. Suggests that the works of Proust and Gide could profitably be examined in the same light.

1457   Dehon, Claire L. "'La Dame du photographe': sa structure, son sens." *Revue du Pacifique* 4 (Spring 1978): 59-67. Interprets the title novella as an expression of *l'héroïsme banal*, the struggle of the humble person to cope with the demands of society. Analyzes the structure, characters and significant objects in the light of this idea. Except for the surprising conclusion--that Colette has a permissive attitude towards suicide--the analysis is convincing.

1458   Delaquys, Georges. "Colette." *Le Capitole*, May 1923, non.-pag. [6-7]. Lauds Colette's humility, vivacity, humanity and psychological insight.

1459   Delarue-Mardrus, Lucie. "Colette et les bêtes." *Le Capitole*, 22 Dec. 1924, non-pag. [13-14]. Identifies Colette's originality as rooted in her respect for animals and her refusal to present them in anthropomorphic terms.

1460   Delavenage, Frédéric. "Dans le ciel... ...du Palais Royal." *Bulletin de la Guilde du Livre* 20 (Dec. 1955): 485-87. Reiterates the idea, often expressed by Colette herself, that she worked constantly and that her goal was always the task well done.

1461   del Castillo, Michel. "De Jouvenel à Colette." *Cahiers Colette*, no. 10 (1988): 5-14. Impressions of a meeting with Colette's daughter, Colette de Jouvenel, some 25 years previously and an attempt to trace her various metamorphoses throughout the

different periods of her life. Concludes that she tried to
whitewash her father in an effort to attract his favor, but that
she was neglected by both parents. Also insists that Colette's
fame and achievements gave her daughter an inferiority complex
which prevented her from accomplishing much in life, and that
she was further intimidated by the portrait of her as "Bel-Gazou"
in Colette's books. Concludes that she was really happy only in
Italy. An interesting article about a controversial figure in
Colette's life, one who, the article asserts, seemed in her last
years to imitate her famous mother in both attitude and speech.

1462 del Castillo, Michel. "Un dévot littéraire." *Arts-Loisirs*, no. 72 (8
Feb. 1967): 4-5. Response to Claude Bonnefoy's review of
Earthly Paradise in the Feb. 1 issue. Accuses Goudeket of
exploiting Colette's memory. Depicts him as a hypocrite and a
parasite, who gives himself too much credit for his role in
Colette's life and work and who does her a disservice in writing
prefaces for new editions of her work.

1463 Delcroix, Maurice. "'La Petite' (1921), 'Les Petites' (1912): analyse
textuelle et genèse." In item 1077 *Colette, Nouvelles
Approches critiques*, 67-83. Based on a study of the different
editions of *La Maison de Claudine*. Attempts to identify the
reasons for the several arrangements, cuts and additions.
Concludes that a comparison of the two texts named in the title
shows that the change in focus from the childhood of Bel-Gazou
to the role of Sido in Colette's own life reflects the pattern of
the author's psychological development.

1464 Delluc, Louis. "La maison des danseuses (La vérandah)." In item
1057 *Album Masques: Colette*, 81-82. Judges Colette to be the
most original of all mimes. Article of 1913.

1465 Deltel, Danielle. "Colette: acceptation et refus de la féminité: notes
pour une étude de l'éthique de Colette." *Annales de la Faculté
des Lettres et Sciences humaines de Yaoundé* 8 (1977): 95-107.
Fine article developing the premise that all Colette's work is a
confrontation with her femininity. Asserts that the double
themes of nature and love reflect an effort to reconcile her adult
femininity with her childhood androgyny, and that her ethic has
its roots in this struggle. Draws parallels with George Sand and
Montaigne.

1466   Deltel, Danielle. "Journal manqué, autobiographie masquée:
       'Claudine à l'école' de Colette." *Revue des sciences humaines* 63
       (Oct.-Dec. 1983): 47-71. Detailled study of grammatical and
       syntactical elements in Colette's first novel, in an attempt to
       demonstrate that the novel is not a journal, as its narrator
       asserts, but an oral *récit*. Defines the narratee or listener as a
       Parisian unacquainted with the subject matter. Analyzes
       Colette's use of verb tense, direct and indirect speech, syntax,
       and parentheses. Identifies three levels of narration. Concludes
       that after this novel Colette moved away from the oral *récit* and
       towards the interior meditation. A penetrating analysis, which
       incidentally reveals how much in command of her art Colette
       was even at this stage of her career.

1467   Deltel, Danielle. "Le meccano du souvenir: les doublets
       autobiographiques chez Colette." *Cahiers de sémiotique
       textuelle* 12 (1988): 137-51. Analyzes Colette's creative process
       in presenting incidents related more than once in her semi-
       autobiographical works. Notes that she modified them for
       esthetic purposes. Likens her souvenirs to palimpsests, texts
       written over previous texts, true to the original but evolving.
       Concludes that Colette's presentation of her childhood is a
       collection of personal myths, which led her to a final
       construction of the self. A subtle and fascinating article which
       casts bright light on Colette's artistic evolution.

1468   Deltel, Danielle. "Une mise en scène [du sens]: la rhétorique du
       portrait dans 'Le Blé en herbe' de Colette." *Cahiers de
       sémiotique textuelle* 10 (1987): 37-53. Analyzes Colette's art of
       portraiture in *Le Blé en herbe* in order to demonstrate that her
       purpose is not just to observe and describe, but also to direct the
       reader to a moral significance. Explores the function and
       importance of the "look" in this novel as part of the character
       portrayal. Insists on Colette's dislike of the non-focalized
       portrait. Notes her fondness for synecdoche, antithesis and
       paradox. Although some of the ideas are old ones dressed up in
       modern terminological garb, this article offers fresh viewpoints
       and is one of the most important ones written on this novel to
       date.

1469   Deltel, Danielle. "Le scandale soufflé: le paradoxe dans l'écriture de
       Colette." In item 1077 *Colette, Nouvelles Approches critiques*,

151-65. Explores Colette's complex use of paradox in both situation and character. Analyzes two chapters of *Le Blé en herbe* and some passages of *La Maison de Claudine* as typical examples. Asserts that Colette seeks originality for its own sake and that her use of paradox is the result of an esthetic choice. A very interesting and worth-while article.

1470 Demy, Jacques. "Jacques Demy et 'La Naissance du jour'." *Europe*, no. 631-32 (Nov.-Dec. 1981): 138-39. Details and commentary about the film Demy made of Colette's novel in 1980. Insists that the film followed the book closely. Demy's remarks reported by Odette and Alain Virmaux.

1471 Derain, Lucie. "En parlant beauté avec Colette." *Les Annales* 95 (15 June 1932): 515. Effusive paragraphs about Colette's newly-established beauty products business, an enterprise that was to last only a year.

1472 Desanges, Paul. "Colette." *La Forge*, Feb. 1919, 81-99. Also long extract in *Mercure de France*, 1 April 1919, 516-17. Compendium of clichés common to the age. Terms Colette exceptional among women writers, defined here as void of original thought, but denies her an intellectual dimension. Praises her sincerity and her portrayal of animals but rejects her portraits of men as not true to reality.

1473 Deschamps, H.G. "D'un village bourguignon aux arcades du Palais Royal." *Revue dominicaine* 60 (Oct. 1954): 137-44. Defends the Roman Catholic Church's decision not to allow Colette religious burial rites. Draws on aspects of her life and books to support argument. Criticizes Graham Greene for his role in the controversy, but refers to him as an American. An interesting article because of the thoroughness and fervor of the arguments.

1474 Desnos, Robert. "Colette." In *Nouvelles Hébrides et autres textes 1922-1930*, 142-43. Paris: Gallimard, 1978. Asserts that for the youth of 1900 Colette's name evoked the erotic activities of her works brought to life, but that when she married Henry de Jouvenel the young were disillusioned since they preferred her previous image.

1475   Desnoues, Lucienne. "Colette aurait cent ans." *Bulletin de l'Académie royale de langue et de littérature françaises* 51: 3-4 (1973): 181-94. Also in item 1121 *Pour le centenaire de Colette*, 44-57. Text of an address commemorating the one-hundredth anniversary of Colette's birth. Insists that her stories take a position on social issues and that she would have deplored many aspects of modern life.

1476   Desnues, R.-M. "Colette." *Educatrices paroissiales* 46 (Nov. 1954): 67-75. Analyzes the suitability of Colette's work for students, especially Catholic girls. Ranks her as the greatest contemporary French writer with Mauriac. Includes detailed chronology of her life and works. Deplores Colette's conduct, but attributes causes partly to her upbringing and to Willy's influence and praises her personal character. Notes that she had many Catholic friends. Defends the Church's decision not to permit her religious burial. Praises many aspects of her work, especially those in books deemed suitable for young people. An interesting article presenting views widely held at the time of Colette's death, but rarely expressed with such finesse and detail and with such an evident attempt to be objective.

1477   Desonay, Fernand. "Notice sur Colette." *Annuaire de l'Académie royale de langue et de littérature françaises 1968*, 111-207. Brussels: Palais des Académies, 1968. Also in *Galerie des portraits: recueil des notices publiées de 1928-1972 sur les membres de l'Académie*, vol. 1, 305-401. Brussels: Palais des Académies, 1972. Major overview of Colette's life and work, including the correspondence and the plays. Depicts her affectionately in various sites. Acknowledges with gratitude Maurice Goudeket's friendship. Terms *La Naissance du jour* Colette's best work. Includes interesting remarks on the political maneuvering behind Colette's reception into the Academy, terming her acceptance speech a masterpiece of verbal agility. Considers her a poet rather than a novelist. A good broad assessment by an influential critic.

1478   Desonay, Fernand. "Quelques thèmes d'inspiration chez Colette." *Bulletin de l'Académie royale de langue et de littérature françaises* 32 (Oct. 1954): 125-40. Comments on five colettian themes: childhood, nature, animals, love, and Sido. Accepts Colette's semi-autobiographical texts as factual. Lauds her

originality as an animal writer. Attempts to determine the
extent to which she can be called a romantic. Considers her so-
called amorality a problem.

1479 Dessarre, Eve. "Les mots, jouets royaux." *Bulletin de la Guilde du
livre* 26 (Feb. 1961): 68-70. Likens Colette to Giraudoux, since
both loved books, round crystals and words for themselves.

1480 D'Hollander, Paul. "Colette et la femme de trente ans." *Revue
d'histoire littéraire de la France* 82 (May-June 1982): 424-30.
Studies thirty-year-old heroines in Colette's early novels.
Identifies *Claudine en ménage* as the point in Colette's career
where her attitude to love changed; after that she would portray
woman as superior to man, the unworthy adversary. Argues that
Colette created Annie in *Claudine s'en va* because Claudine
could no longer speak for her completely, and that she
eliminated Renaud because he was no longer a suitable
protagonist for her heroines. A subtle and convincing article,
whose arguments are based on psychological hypotheses drawn
from a close study of Colette's relations with Willy.

1481 D'Hollander, Paul. "Colette et les nostalgies de Claudine." *French
Review* 55 (Oct. 1981): 60-68. Attempts to determine whether
or not Colette's nostalgia for her native Puisaye would have
been as strong if she had remained there. Examines the decors of
the early novels in the light of this idea; notes that they are
always suited to the action. Suggests that Colette moved away
from the Claudine inspiration because she wanted to protect her
memories by turning them into myth. Although many of the
ideas presented in this article are only hypotheses based on
known facts, the arguments are persuasive and the conclusions
plausible.

1482 D'Hollander, Paul. "Introduction." In item 0403 *Claudine en
ménage*, 11-57. This carefully researched introduction to the
critical edition of the novel gives details about its publication
history, and about that of the pre-edition, *Claudine amoureuse*.
Attempts to establish relationship between the plot and events
in Colette's own life as well as identification of models used for
characters. After examination of manuscripts, D'Hollander draws
conclusions on the extent to which Willy collaborated on the
manuscript and editing. Relates this third novel in the Claudine

series to the two preceding ones; sees it as representing a
turning-point in Colette's artistic development. Includes an
excellent analysis of the phenomenon of lesbian relations in
Parisian life of the era. An important article.

1483   D'Hollander, Paul. "'La Naissance du jour' et 'Mes apprentissages',
ou la recherche d'un temps perdu." In item 1077 *Colette,
Nouvelles Approches critiques*, 37-44. Insists that in *La
Naissance du jour* Colette confronts her own guilt feelings
about her negative attitude towards her mother, a negativity
manifested in the early works by the absence of positive mother
figures. Analyzes the transformation of the mother image in
Colette's work after the death of her mother. Notes a double
movement as hate for her mother is transformed into love, and
love for Willy transformed into a hate that finds its ultimate
expression in *Mes apprentissages*.

1484   Dhouailly, Jeanne. "Etude d'une page de Colette." *Information
littéraire* 39 (Sept.-Oct. 1987): 159-65. Analyzes a short
passage from "Les sauvages" in *Sido*. Studies techniques used to
give an enigmatic, idealized and poetic character to portraits of
Colette's two brothers. Particularly interesting are remarks on
how Colette attempts to raise the portrait of Léo, whose lack of
ambition and attachment to the past made him a pathetic failure
by most people's standards, to the level of misunderstood poet.

1485   Diamond, Josephine. "L'impasse du demi-monde féminin dans
'Chéri' et 'La Fin de Chéri'." *Bulletin de la Société des
professeurs français en Amérique* (1986-1987): 115-30. Not
seen.

1486   Dick, Kay. "Colette." *Saturday Book* 12 (1952): 209-15. General
outline of Colette's life and works. Considers her primarily a
writer of love, and a true Parisian.

1487   Didier, Béatrice. "'La Retraite sentimentale' ou la représentation
romanesque de la libération." In *L'Ecriture-femme*, 211-21.
Paris: Presses universitaires de France, 1981. Attempts to
demonstrate that the "non-presence" of the male characters,
through sickness, death or a negative lifestyle, determines the
thematic structure of *La Retraite sentimentale*, by their
opposition to the presence, freedom and vitality of the women

characters. Insists that the superiority of both Claudine's and Annie's situations can be defined in terms of power, usually wielded by the male. Identifies Annie as the stronger of the two women and one whose slavery, which will never control her completely, has merely changed form. An unusual reading of a difficult novel.

1488 Dietschy, Marcel. In *Le Cas André Suarès*, 234. Neuchâtel: La Baconnière, 1967. Extract from a letter from Suarès to René Fauchois. Expresses intense dislike for Colette both as person and as writer. Dietschy points out that she is only one of a large number of writers for whom Suarès expressed such sentiments.

1489 Dignimont, André. "Quelques fleurs de Dignimont." *Figaro littéraire*, 24 Jan. 1953, 5. Artist's sketch of flowers for Colette's eightieth birthday, with a caption offering 80 kisses.

1490 Dilhan, Monique. "Das Roman-Werk der Colette." In *Frankreichs Zeitgenössische Literatur: Geist und Gestalt*, edited by Emile Callot, 89-123. Stuttgart: Dr. Roland Schmiedel, 1949. General study of Colette's novels. Emphasizes the notion of Colette's own presence in her works, even in the fiction, identifying her heroines with their author at different stages of her life. Praises especially her portrayal of transition periods in human life.

1491 Dorgelès, Roland. "Adieu à Colette." *Figaro littéraire*, 14 Aug. 1954, 3. Also in item 1095 *Hommage à Colette*, non-pag. Also, with modifications and under title "Colette," in *Images*, 202-6. Paris: Albin Michel, 1975. Text of peroration delivered at Colette's funeral. Contains no new ideas but touches on well-known features of her work and public life. Insists on Colette's intelligence, hard work, courage and fidelity to what is natural. Values her as the chronicler of a past age.

1492 Dorgelès, Roland. "Toute pareille à vos livres." *Figaro littéraire*, 24 Jan. 1953, 3. Fellow member of the Goncourt Academy cryptically declares that Colette's secrets are all on paper.

1493 Dorian, Jean-Pierre. "Colette perd son manuscrit." In *Ecoute le temps: feux d'artifice des années 1925-1950*, 190-91. Paris: Albin Michel, 1980. Banal anecdote about Colette relating how she lost a manuscript and began rewriting immediately.

1494   Dorian, Jean-Pierre. "Les jours et les plaisirs." *Matulu*, no.16
       (July-Aug. 1972): 2. Mostly trivial anecdotes about Colette in
       1952, portraying her as feisty and committed to music.

1495   Dormann, Geneviève. "Le dernier havre de Colette sera-t-il vendu?"
       Figaro littéraire, 7 Jan. 1978, 12. Speculates on the fate of
       Colette's Palais Royal apartment. At her death Colette had
       willed the apartment to her third husband Maurice Goudeket,
       who upon remarriage willed it to his second wife for the benefit
       of their young son and the exclusion of Colette's daughter,
       Colette de Jouvenel. At the time this article was written, the
       latter was trying to persuade monument officials to turn the
       apartment into a museum. She was not successful, and the
       Colette museum went to Saint-Sauveur.

1496   Doumergue, Gaston. In item 1072 Chauvière, 171. Letter of 15
       March 1929 to Colette, alluding to an interview-visit that she
       had made to him when he was president of France, and to a copy
       of *La Seconde* which she had just sent him.

1497   Doyon, René-Louis [signed: Le Mandarin]. "Lettre à Colette..." *La
       Connaissance* 3 (April 1922): 1167-68. Tongue-in-cheek plea to
       Colette to disregard attacks by Fortunat Strowski and to
       continue living and writing as at present.

1498   Dranch, Sherry A. "Reading Through the Veiled Text: Colette's
       'The Pure and the Impure'." *Contemporary Literature* 24
       (Summer 1983): 176-89. Argues evidence of a "censored style"
       in Colette's use of metaphor and ellipsis in *Le Pur et l'impur*,
       behind which can be glimpsed a sub-text, defined as the "clearly
       stated unsaid." Asserts that the book demonstrates Colette's
       awareness of the censorship that society imposes on women,
       and interprets it as the expression of a forbidden obsession, a
       sublimated desire for sexual satisfaction, especially lesbian.
       Identifies Colette with both the narrator and Charlotte. An
       interesting and provocative article.

1499   Drapier-Cadec, Mme L. "En suivant l'étoile... ou Colette en
       Bretagne." *Cahiers de l'Iroise* 17 (Jan.-March 1970): 15-18.
       Traces references to Brittany in Colette's work.

1500 Druilhe, Paule. "Les grandes créations de l'Opéra de Monte-Carlo: 'L'Enfant et les sortilèges' de Maurice Ravel." *Annales monégasques*, no. 9 (1985): 7-26. The best and most complete account of the genesis and peripetias of *L'Enfant et les sortilèges*, up to its first performance in 1925. Focus is on Ravel and on the quarrels between the administration and Sergei Diaghilev, then director of the Ballets Russes de Monte-Carlo, but Colette's role in events is also outlined. Includes extracts from Ravel-Colette correspondence and from critics' reviews.

1501 Druon, Maurice. "'Un destin parfait'." *Lettres françaises*, 12 Aug. 1954, 1, 4. Reproaches Catholic officials for refusing Colette religious rites but concludes that the Palais Royal is a more suitable place for her funeral in any case. Compares her with Saint Francis of Assisi. Terms her life an abundant and favored one.

1502 Dubois, Jacques. "Entretien avec Colette." *Lettres françaises*, 27 Nov. 1952, 1, 3. Very moving report of an interview with Colette. Although Dubois confines his remarks to expressions of admiration for Colette, the interview reveals her physical decline.

1503 Dubreuil, Léon. "Le brevet de Colette." *Le Cerf-volant*, no. 18 (July 1957): 16-17. An account of Colette's experience of the *brevet élémentaire* examination, which she took in 1889 and which served as a model for situations in *Claudine à l'école*. Although this was an informative article for 1957, recent research has furnished many more details on the event. Dubreuil was *inspecteur d'Académie* at Auxerre.

1504 Duclaux, Madame Mary. "Madame Colette." In *Twentieth Century French Writers: Reviews and Reminiscences*, 193-98. New York: Scribner's, 1920. Written not long after publication of *L'Entrave* (1913) this article is important because it expresses the views of many anti-feminist women of the time, few of whom committed their opinions to print. Admiration for Colette's ability is mingled with dismay at the scabrous aspects of her early novels, optimism that parting from Willy for a life in the music-hall will bring Colette into contact with purer influences, and satisfaction that the ending of *L'Entrave*, which finds the heroine committed to an unequal partnership with the

man she loves, has restored to Renée a place in organized
society.

1505   Dufour, Hortense. "Cruauté et gourmandise." *Le Monde*, 25 Jan.
1973, 21. Remarks on the tendency of Colette's protagonists to
enjoy their food in the midst of crisis.

1506   Dugast, Francine. "L'Image de l'enfance et ses fonctions dans
l'œuvre de Colette. Entre tradition et modernité." *Cahiers
Colette*, no. 3-4 (1981): 7-20. Inventories childhood images in
Colette's work. Declares that Colette created an entire fictional
universe, rooted in her own childhood but not identical with it.
Posits the view that by writing of childhood Colette renewed
her inspiration and that in later years the Palais Royal became a
substitute for the childhood home. Associates Colette with the
images of both Demeter and her daughter Persephone.

1507   Dugast-Portes, Francine. "'Cette forme décrétale de l'observation.'"
Europe, no. 631-32 (Nov.-Dec. 1981): 29-40. Identifies Sido's
peremptory as a factor of unity in Colette's work. Evaluates the
importance of observation, memory, the possession of
knowledge or truth, the moral aspects of Sido's teaching, and
the techniques that Colette uses to persuade her readers, in the
light of this idea. Terms all Colette's work an imperative, of
which the famous "Look!" is but a sample.

1508   Duhamel, Georges. "Le souvenir de Colette." *Mercure de France*, 1
Oct. 1954, 289-91. High praise for Colette as exemplifying
French writers, whose mission is declared here to be that of
upholding the French language by example.

1509   Duhamel, Georges. In item 1072 Chauvière, 169. Short letter of
1928 praising *La Naissance du jour*.

1510   Duhamel, Georges. In item 1095 *Hommage à Colette*, non-pag.
Briefly emphasizes the value of suffering in Colette's life.

1511   Duhamel, Roger. "La femme dans les lettres françaises: II. Du
XVIIIe siècle à nos jours." *Canada français* 29 (April 1942):
624-35. In this survey of French women writers, Duhamel
ranks Colette's style as the richest of all her contemporaries but
he does not rank her high among novelists generally.

1512   Dumani, Georges. "Colette." *Revue du Caire* 9 (April 1943): 534-
        63. Text of an address before Les Amis de la Culture française
        en Egypte, seventh of a series on the work of great women.
        Terms Christianity's lack of influence on Colette as both a
        strength and a weakness. Stresses her originality, intelligence,
        discipline and extraordinary sense of measure. Remarks on her
        style are limited to effusive generalizations and quotations.

1513   Dumay, Raymond. "Colette." *Médecine de France* 57 (1954): 33-
        38. General evaluation of Colette's life and work, drawing freely
        on quotations from her books. Paints a dismal picture of her
        years with Willy. Considers her presentation of male-female
        relations and of a world in which failure and defeat play a strong
        role to be a pessimistic one, but finds that her sincerity and her
        presentation of nature compensate for negative factors. Judges
        her attitude to life exemplary. Draws parallels with Montaigne's
        skepticism, balance, mental health and piquancy of expression.
        Followed by text of "La Main" [p. 39-40].

1514   Dumay, Raymond. "La Maison de Colette." *Le Point*, no. 39 (May
        1951): 38-40. Claims that interviews with one of Colette's
        former schoolmates at Saint-Sauveur confirm the general
        veracity of the Claudine novels. Discerns a positive influence,
        on her work, of the Colette family home.

1515   Dumay, Raymond. "Paradoxes de Colette." *Preuves* 4 (Sept. 1954):
        77-79. Considers that Colette represents France better than any
        other writer because she appeals to both educated and uneducated
        minds. Reproaches past critics for being reluctant or afraid to
        accord her the glory she so long deserved, and lauds Colette for
        her persistence despite apparent setbacks.

1516   Dunoyer de Segonzac, André. [No title]. *Figaro littéraire*, 24 Jan.
        1953, 5. Also in *Lettres à ses pairs*, all eds., and in item 1353
        Cardinal. One of Colette's favorite illustrators reminisces about
        summers at Saint Tropez. Offers interesting sidelights on
        Colette's work habits of those years.

1517   Dupont, Jacques. "Actualité, mode et modernité chez Colette."
        Cahiers Colette, no. 3-4 (1981): 89-99. Comments on Colette's
        penchant for the spectacle, especially in the domains of fashion,
        novelty and *faits divers*. Notes her fondness for spectacle

involving levitation, such as dancing and skating. Quotes heavily from her work. An unusual article.

1518   Dupont, Jacques. "Colette et l'université: trente ans d'études." *Cahiers Colette*, no. 6 (1984): 9-14. Summary assessment of university studies on Colette from 1954 to 1984. Identifies a new wave of interest in the prehistory of her novels, beginning about 1968. Applauds use of computers in recent studies, as well as in-depth analysis of her narrative technique. Signals many lacunæ in topics studied.

1519   Dupont, Jacques. "Colette, ou la voyageuse de nuit." *Le Journal de voyage et Stendhal: Actes du Colloque de Grenoble*, edited by V. Del Litto and E. Kanceff, 381-90. Geneva: Slatkine, 1986. Studies the much-neglected topic of Colette's travels, the descriptions of which are scattered throughout her books, often in the form of notes that have been re-arranged or are difficult to date. Attempts to identify the types of things she noticed, to define her perspective of other lands, and to analyze what liberties she took with the truth. Terms her travel writing subjective, yet psychologically empty, which fact supports the thesis that her travels had little influence on her. Uses many examples from her work. A perceptive and illuminating article which has created a new dimension in Colette criticism.

1520   Dupont, Jacques. "Les déserts de l'amour: remarques sur 'Le Pur et l'impur'." In item 1057 *Album Masques: Colette*, 165-67. Refutes Colette's own statement that she has no general ideas. Argues that she portrays her characters in *Le Pur et l'impur* as captives, despite their seemingly liberated life-style. Quotes Colette freely.

1521   Dupont, Jacques. "Identité et identifications dans l'œuvre de Colette." In item 1077 *Colette, Nouvelles Approches critiques*, 27-36. Analyzes Colette's often expressed desire for change and renewal. Identifies in her a life-long anguish born of a constant struggle to maintain her sense of identity. Assesses, in the light of this idea, the way in which she deals with the maternal image and the function of the paternal act of writing.

1522   Dupont, Jacques. "Sur l'Orient de Colette." *Cahiers Colette*, no. 5 (1983): 61-69. Attempts to assess the extent of Colette's knowledge of the Orient (actually North Africa), and to define her vision of the blend of misery and beauty discovered during travels in Tunisia and Algeria. Argues that the harem image plays an important role in her works, and quotes freely from them.

1523 Duquette, Jean. "La fatalité de l'amour chez Colette." *Ecrits du Canada français*, no. 47 (1983): 37-60. Argues that Colette depicts love as a tyrant and that her presentation of homosexuality is based on stereotypes. Also, under the title "L'amour comme fatalité," as chapter 2 of his book *Colette: l'amour de l'amour*.

1524 Duranteau, Josane. "Art de vivre, art d'écrire." *Education*, 18 Jan. 1973, 22-23. Assessment of Colette the person. Considers her a more courageous feminist than those of today, because she was alone in making decisions. Terms her tendency not to separate literature and personal life a feminine trait.

1525 Dutoit, Ernest. In *Domaines: les idées et les mots*, 30, 118-19. Fribourg: Eds. universitaires, 1960. Brief remarks noting the frequency of mirrors in Colette's work and judging her manner of perception to be the secret of her style.

1526 Duvernois, Henri. "Colette, conteur." In item 1072 Chauvière, 96-99. Effusive praise for Colette's achievement as a short story writer. Includes some analysis of "Le veilleur" from *La Maison de Claudine*.

1527 Duvernois, Henri. "L'œuvre de Colette." *Le Capitole*, May 1923, non.-pag. [3]. Effusive praise for Colette's writing skill. Terms it inimitable and youthful in expression.

1528 Eaubonne, Françoise d'. "'L'ennemie des femmes': souvenir de Colette." In item 1057 *Album Masques: Colette*, 169-72. Begins with personal anecdotes, then refutes Beauvoir's accusation that Colette had contempt for women because she seemed unconcerned about morality or justice. Detects in Colette a never-satisfied aspiration towards spirituality and a revolt against a love that imprisons and degrades women, but never men, a love of which she had personal experience and which she portrayed in her women characters. Speculates on the likelihood that Colette married Willy because she had fallen into social disgrace. An interesting article, despite minor inaccuracies and a rambling style.

1529   Ehrhard, Jean E. In *Le Roman français depuis Marcel Proust*, 68-73. Paris: Nouvelle Revue critique, 1932. General assessment of Colette's work in terms typical of the time. Ranks her style as a fine example of naturist expressionism, equated here with turn-of-the century feminine literature of sensation and desire, with no abstract preoccupations. Makes little attempt to compare her work with that of other writers.

1530   Eisinger, Erica. "'The Vagabond': A Vision of Androgyny." In item 1076 *Colette: The Woman, The Writer*, 95-103. Interprets the novel as a search for psychic androgyny on the part of Renée. Emphasizes Colette's persistent concern with the question of psychosexual identity. Views Renée's rejection of Max not as a renunciation but as an affirmation of self.

1531   Eisinger, Erica, and Mari McCarty. "Charting Colette." *Women's Studies* 8:3 (1981): 255-56. Introduction to special issue on Colette. Hails new critical techniques for opening the way to a deeper understanding of Colette. Identifies Colette as a bridge to French feminist writing through her inauguration of a gynocentric optic.

1532   Eisinger, Erica, and Mari McCarty. "Introduction." In item 1076 *Colette: The Woman, The Writer*, 1-4. Emphasizes Colette's importance in opening up new avenues for women's writing by speaking in a woman's voice and refusing to be defined by men. Declares the aim of this volume of feminist criticism to be the exploration of Colette's two vocations as writer and woman, of the relation between her life and her work, and of the connection between women and language.

1533   Engle, Paul. "Colette." *Poetry* 88 (Aug. 1956): 321-23. Series of five free-form sonnets, inspired by Colette's life and books.

1534   Engle, Paul. "Three sonnets for Colette." *Sewanee Review* 64 (Winter 1956): 128-29. Three poems inspired by Colette focus on the contrast between Paris and the countryside, on Colette's exploitation of the theme of love, and on her femininity.

1535 Ernest-Charles, J. "Le cas Willy." In *La Revue bleue* 42 (7 Oct.
1905): 473-77. Also in *Les Samedis littéraires*, vol. 5, 114-32.
Paris: Sansot, 1907. A fair assessment of both sides of the
scandal emanating from exposure of Willy's stable of ghost
writers, written soon after the facts became common currency.
Points out that Willy is not the only person to publish the
work of others under his own name but terms him a writer of
pornography. Judges him a victim of his own thirst for
publicity. Evaluates the roles of Henri Albert and Jean de la
Hire in the situation.

1536 Escholier, Raymond. "Du nouveau sur l'adolescence de Colette."
Figaro littéraire, 17 Nov. 1956, 1, 9-10; and 24 Nov. 1956, 1,
5, 7. Offers not always accurate details of events leading up to
the marriage of Colette's mother with her first husband, Jules
Robineau-Duclos. Emphasizes the intrigues among members of
the latter's family and others concerned. Source of information
is mostly interviews with inhabitants of the region, but no
documentation is provided. See items 1603 Gauthier-Villars,
1652 Goudeket and 2199 Wague for replies of 8 and 15 Dec.

1537 Espil, Pierre. "Colette à Biarritz." *Revue régionaliste des Pyrénées*,
no. 205-206 (Jan.-June 1975): 20-23. Relates two meetings
with Colette, neither of them of special interest.

1538 Ethier-Blais, Jean. "Colette: rêver à ses créatures." In *Signets*, vol.
1, 91-96. Ottawa: Le Cercle du livre de France, 1967. Brief
assessment of Colette's work praises her genius but deplores her
apparent lack of interest in morality. Detects in her letters
evidence of both her humanity and her limitations.

1539 Evans, Martha Noel. "Colette: 'The Vagabond'." In *Masks of
Tradition: Women and the Politics of Writing in Twentieth-
Century France*, 36-74. Ithaca, London: Cornell University
Press, 1987. Interpretation of *La Vagabonde* as the expression
of a turning point in Colette's career, when she recognized the
obstacles confronting her both as a writer and as a person.
Examines Renée's masks of protection against the advantaged
male, to whom alone tradition has accorded the power of
language. Traces Renée's path towards self-discovery and self-
possession, with the power to speak in her own voice and the
right to possession of the world's goods in her own name.

1540   Fabre, Eugène. "Madame Colette n'est plus." *Journal de Genève*, 4
       Aug. 1954, 8. In memoriam, including overview of Colette's
       achievements. Terms some of her characters tragic figures.
       Credits her with furthering the careers of many young writers
       while at *Le Matin*.

1541   Fabrègues, Jean de [signed: J.F.]. "[L'univers de Colette] ...ses
       mérites et ses limites." *La France catholique*, 13 Aug. 1954, 2.
       Warns Catholic readers not to confuse literary value with moral
       value when approaching Colette's work.

1542   Fabureau, Hubert. "Robineau-Desvoidy, le père de Claudine à
       l'école." *Mercure de France*, 1 Jan. 1950, 188-90. Traces life of
       Dr. Robineau-Desvoidy, who spent years studying the flies of
       the Saint-Sauveur region, and who, Fabureau suggests, was the
       model for Claudine's father in Colette's first novels.

1543   Fabureau, Hubert. "Le terroir de Colette." *Mercure de France*, 1
       Feb. 1950, 381-84. Continuation of item 1542. Furnishes data
       on geography and climate of Colette's native region, as well as
       details on the researches of Dr. Robineau-Desvoidy, who sought
       there traces of the former Celtic inhabitants.

1544   Falcão, Luiz Annibal. "Colette." *Colloquios Transatlanticos e
       outros*, 41-46. Rio de Janeiro: Atlantica, 1941. Memories of
       Colette at *Le Matin*. Text of 1933.

1545   Falize, René. "Discours." *Bulletin de l'Académie royale de langue
       et de littérature françaises* 51 (1973): 174-76. Also in item 1121
       Pour le centenaire de Colette, 37-39. Compendium of effusive
       compliments by the Belgian Minister of French Culture on the
       one hundredth anniversary of Colette's birth.

1546   Fallet, René. "Je connais Chéri." *Gazette des lettres*, 29 Oct. 1949,
       9. Recounts a 1943 meeting with a young man whom Fallet
       terms a modern Chéri.

1547   Fantasio. "Ce mois qui court." *Revue générale belge* 90 (15 Aug.
       1954): 1765-71. Includes stop-press announcement of Colette's
       death earlier in the month.

1548 Fantasio. "Ce mois qui court." *Revue générale belge* 91 (15 Dec. 1954): 341-43. Speculates on who will succeed Colette at the Belgian Academy, Cocteau's name being the one most frequently mentioned. Alludes to politics complicating the selection, and insists on the esteem in which Colette was held by her colleagues. Includes an unflattering account of a "Hommage à Colette" evening held the preceding month.

1549 Fantasio. "Ce mois qui court." *Revue générale belge* 91 (15 Oct. 1955): 2125-30. Includes account of a glittering reception for Cocteau, and his acceptance speech at the Belgian Academy.

1550 Fargue, Léon-Paul. "Colette et la sensibilité féminine française." *Revue du Caire* 9 (Nov. 1946): 389-92. Also in *Adam* 14 (Nov.-Dec. 1946): 4-5; *Erasme* 13 (Jan. 1947): 27-29; *Montréal-Matin*, 20 Sept. 1947, 11. Also, with changes, in *Portraits de famille*, 17-19. Paris: Janin, 1947; and *Lettres à ses pairs*, all eds. Extract in item 1057 *Album Masques: Colette*, 42. Terms Colette the voice of French women, different from them only by her degree of talent. Identifies the feminine world as one limited to the experience of the senses. Representative of much Colette criticism of the middle decades.

1551 Faure-Favier, Louise. "La muse aux violettes." *Mercure de France*, 1 Dec. 1953, 633-54. Title refers to Renée Vivien, who is the main subject of the article. The second part, "Un soir chez Vivien avec Colette," which contains an account of Colette dancing the "Danse du sphinx" at Renée's place is especially interesting because it evokes the atmosphere of the social gatherings of at least one lesbian circle to which Colette belonged during the first decade of the century. Also alludes to further brief meetings with Colette between 1910 and 1923.

1552 Feltin, Maurice Card., Archbishop of Paris. Letter concerning the Roman Catholic Church's refusal to permit religious burial for Colette. For annotation see item 1662 Greene.

1553 Fernandez, Ramon. "Colette." *Nouvelle Revue française* 30 (1 March 1942): 348-53. Also in *Messages*, 282-87. Paris: Grasset, 1981. Attempts to identify Colette's style by comparing it with "feminine" style, defined as either precious or impressionistic, but recognizes her originality and her skill at portraying the concrete. Deplores her lack of interest in the "great problems" of life, and the apparent animality of her fictional characters. Not an enlightening study, even for its day.

1554   Ferrand, Brigitte. "Dialogue soliloque." *Europe*, no. 631-32 (Nov.-Dec. 1981): 96-106. Inquiry into the *non-dit* of the *Sept dialogues de bêtes*. Seeks to identify Colette's reason for writing the seven dialogues, described here as disguised confessions. Concludes that, in spite of its humor, the book is a lament that received no response from those to whom it was addressed.

1555   Ferrier, Nicole. "L'angoisse de Colette." *Cahiers Colette*, no. 3-4 (1981): 21-35. Attempts to define the meaning of *angoisse* as Colette uses the term, and considers her modern because of it. Identifies its sources in Colette's awareness of the limits of the physical world, the lack of communication among beings, and the human condition. Concludes that against this sentiment Colette erected a powerful philosophy of life rooted in discipline and courage.

1556   Filippi, Elena Belloni. "Colette musicale." *La Scala*, no. 80 (July 1956): 30-31. Selects passages demonstrating the finesse of Colette's auditory discrimination and her inherent musicality. Stresses the importance of the auditory in both her writing and her other activities, such as dancing.

1557   Fiorioli, Elena. "Souvenir de Colette." *Culture française* 11 (Sept.-Oct. 1964): 283-86. Overview of Colette's work. Identifies her as a painter of sensations. Finds her characters of little interest to moderns, judging her autobiographical works to have the best chance for immortality.

1558   Fischler, Alexander. "Unity in Colette's 'Le Blé en herbe'." *Modern Language Quarterly* 30 (June 1969): 248-64. Studies Colette's use of dialectic and structure in the title novel, in order to demonstrate the idea of unity, then that of the duality leading to its breakdown. Interprets this unity in terms of theme, classical drama, myths and archetypes.

1559   Fisher, Claudine Guégan. "Solitude et liberté: dilemme de Colette dans 'La Vagabonde'." *Proceedings of the Pacific Northwest Conference on Foreign Languages* 25:1 (1974): 212-16. Short interpretation of *La Vagabonde*, containing much paraphrase. Sees in Renée a model for modern women. Surprisingly compares her to Sisyphus.

1560 Flament, Albert. "Colette ou l'écrivain-protée." *Revue de Paris* 30 (1 March 1923): 202-6. Evokes rehearsals of the stage adaptation of *La Vagabonde*, with Colette in the lead role.

1561 Flanner, Janet. "Introduction." In *The Pure and the Impure*, some eds. Also, under title "Colette," in *Janet Flanner's World: Uncollected Writings 1932-1975*, edited by Irving Drutman, 314-19. New York: Harcourt Brace Jovanovich, 1979. Relates background to publication of *Le Pur et l'impur*, including its abrupt cancellation by *Gringoire* before all instalments were published. Gives credit to Maurice Goudeket for development in Colette's work during the mid-1920's. Views *Le Pur et l'impur* as a serious analysis of sex and sexual relations, in all their variety and ambiguity. Terms Colette's understanding of men and women hermaphroditic. Summarizes main passages of the book, and attempts to relate Colette's life to the characters mentioned. Notes that it is one of Colette's few works in which nature does not play a dominant role.

1562 Flanner, Janet. "Introduction." In item 0101 *Seven by Colette*, v-xv. Good short introduction to Colette's work. Considers her relationship to nature to be unique in French literature, and her work a cohesive whole because of her presence in every book. Compares her technique in *La Fin de Chéri* to Proust's mnemonic process.

1563 Flanner, Janet [signed: Genêt]. "Letter from Paris." *New Yorker* 25 (12 Nov. 1949): 88-91. Also in *Paris Journal 1944-1965*, edited by William Shawn, 110. New York: Atheneum, 1965; London: Gollancz, 1966. Includes announcement of Colette's elevation to president of the Goncourt Academy as well as a description of the public acclaim she received at the opening night of the latest production of *Chéri*.

1564 Flanner, Janet [signed: Genêt]. "Letter from Paris." *New Yorker* 26 (29 July 1950): 50-53. Review of Jacqueline Audry's film *Minne, l'ingénue libertine*, starring Danièle Delorme.

1565   Flanner, Janet [signed: Genêt]. "Letter from Paris." *New Yorker* 28
       (7 Feb. 1953): 59-63. Also in *Paris Journal 1944-1965*, edited
       by William Shawn, 193-94. New York: Atheneum, 1965;
       London: Gollancz, 1966. Includes report of Colette's eightieth
       birthday honors. Quotes passages from letters printed in the
       public press by Gide and Proust.

1566   Flanner, Janet [signed: Genêt]. "Letter from Paris." *New Yorker* 30
       (21 Aug. 1954): 70-76. Also in *Paris Journal 1944-1965*, edited
       by William Shawn, 236-40. New York: Atheneum, 1965;
       London: Gollancz, 1966. The most comprehensive and probably
       the most objective account published of Colette's state funeral
       and the decision of the Roman Catholic church not to accord her
       religious burial. Describes the ceremony at the Palais Royal,
       the flowers and the arrangement of persons present. Terms the
       event a demonstration of the abyss existing between church and
       state in France. Comments briefly on Colette's work and life,
       and reports on eulogies appearing in the press.

1567   Flanner, Janet [signed: Genêt]. "Paris Letter." *New Yorker* 6 (9
       Aug. 1930): 57-58. Also, under title "'Sido'," in *Paris was
       Yesterday 1925-1939*, edited by Irving Drutman, 70-71. New
       York: Viking, 1972. Comments on France's reception of *Sido*.
       Notes that nature enjoys but a small role in French literature,
       thus making Colette's work somewhat exotic to French readers.

1568   Flanner, Janet. "The Story of Colette." *New Yorker* 31 (2 April
       1955): 125-29. Summary of Colette's life and work, inspired by
       the publication of *La Vagabonde* in English. Considers *Chéri*
       her masterpiece. Emphasizes her amorality and her affinity for
       nature and animals.

1569   Flers, Robert de. "Préface." *Le Capitole*, 22 Dec. 1924, non-pag.
       [5]. Effusive praise expressed in many of the clichés used by
       critics of the period when discussing Colette's work. Insists that
       her writing is splendid and original but, as a product of instinct,
       beyond analysis.

1570   Fletcher, John. "Colette." In *Great Foreign Language Writers*,
       edited by James Vinson and Daniel Kirkpatrick, 138-41. New
       York: St. Martin's Press, 1984. Encyclopædia-type summary of
       biographical dates, honors received, brief bibliography and over-

view of Colette's writing achievement. Ranks her higher as a giant figure for feminism than for her literary talent.

1571 Fleurent, Maurice. "Paris, de 'sa' fenêtre: un entretien avec Colette." *Paru* 22 (Sept. 1946): 10-12. Interview-conversation, consisting mostly of trivialities. Expresses admiration of Colette's courage during the war.

1572 Folliet, Joseph. "Inventaire après décès: Mme Colette." *Chronique sociale de France* 2 (April 1956): 177-82. Analyzes the Catholic church's decision not to accord Colette religious burial, terming Graham Greene naive and later regretful of his protest. Contrasts Willy's death with Colette's. Considers Colette and her work to have been forever tainted by the Claudine novels, and makes snide comments about Colette's morals. Praises her style but criticizes the content of her work as feminine, hence insignificant.

1573 Fonteneau, Jean-Marie. "Colette et Chéri." *Avant-Scene Théâtre*, no. 708 (15 April 1982): 4-7. General article on the stage play *Chéri*. Traces the history of the novel and its sequel *La Fin de Chéri*, as well as that of the play's first performance in 1921 and later performances by various companies, including the revised version of 1949 and the 1950 film. Comments on differences between the novels and the play, and on the merits of the performers. Speculates on the relative contributions of Colette and Marchand to the play, and assesses the play's importance to Colette's career.

1574 Fonteneau, Jean-Marie. "Colette et Léopold Marchand." *Avant-Scene Théâtre*, no. 708 (15 April 1982): 8. Sketches Colette's collaboration with playwright Marchand on the stage adaptation of *Chéri* in 1921, that of *La Vagabonde* in 1922 and finally that of *La Seconde* in 1950. Quotes passages by Colette concerning Marchand. Followed by a summary of theater based on her work [p. 9-10].

1575 Forde, Marianna. "Spatial structures in 'La Chatte'." *French Review* 58 (Feb. 1985): 360-67. Interesting analysis of *La Chatte*, using the system of binary oppositions developed by Jean Weisgerber and Michael Issacharoff, with emphasis on the search for and defence of space. Oppositions studied are those of down-up, old-modern, noble-common, animate-inanimate, dynamic-static, past-future, and closed-open. Also draws on botanical symbols and on framing and focalizing techniques for the argument. Concludes that Colette does not favor Alain, as many critics claim, but sympathizes with both him and Camille. Excludes Saha from the analysis, as not possessing her own space. Some of the ideas have been presented by other critics in less analytical terms, but this is a valuable article for a deeper understanding of the novel.

1576   Forestier, Louis. "Critique dramatique et création littéraire." *Cahiers Colette*, no. 3-4 (1981): 119-35. One of the few serious articles on Colette's theater criticism. Insists that each review follows the same plan and that Colette's personal experience of all aspects of theater makes her criticism original. Attempts to relate the drama criticism to her other work, to identify the principles on which it is based and to assess Colette's influence on the public and on the genre. Concludes that *La Jumelle noire* holds a key position in Colette's work.

1577   Fortuna, Horia. "Colette vue par l'étranger: en Romanie." In item 1072 Chauvière, 279-82. Text of address given at a banquet in Colette's honor in Bucharest in 1931. Consists mostly of an elegant expression of pleasure at Colette's visit to Rumania.

1578   Fouchereaux, Jean. "Feminine archetypes in Colette and Marie-Claire Blais." *Journal of the Midwest Modern Language Association* 19 (Spring 1986): 43-49. Interesting comparison between Colette's Chéri and Marie-Claire Blais' Patrice of *La Belle Bête*. Asserts that both have an archetypal dimension centered on the Narcissus figure. Not a thorough study of the subject, but includes some evidence for the argument, and is one of the few articles comparing Colette's techniques with those of other writers.

French version: "Archétypes féminins chez Colette et Marie-Claire Blais." *Québec français*, no. 64 (Dec. 1986): 57-59.

1579   Fowlie, Wallace. "Introduction." In item 0319 *Chéri*, vii-xiv. Terms boldness a characteristic of great French women writers, including Colette. Considers her a master of litote. Discusses *Chéri* only briefly and in general terms.

1580 Foyard, Jean. "Pour un jardin imaginaire de Colette." *Cahiers Colette*, no. 5 (1983): 39-59. Attempts to place Colette within a system of classification of the attitudes of writers about gardens, and to define the extent and limits of her childhood garden as she presents it to readers. Maintains that the essential garden for her was not the real one, but the imaginary one, which she used to mirror her universe. Terms Colette surrealist in that the garden was for her the site of initiations and relations with the unknown. A thought-provoking article using a new approach to an oft-treated subject.

1581 Fraiman, Susan D. "Shadow in the Garden: The Double Aspect of Motherhood in Colette." *Perspectives on Contemporary Literature* 11 (1985): 46-53. Well-argued article which examines the family house of *La Maison de Claudine* and *Sido* as the architectural analogue of the mother. Interprets the space of house and garden as being divided into that imposed by man and representing the institution of motherhood, and that belonging to the woman and consisting of the experience of motherhood persisting behind the masculine facade. Presents Sido as partly complicitous with the patriarchal system or shadow, whereas the daughter, Colette, escapes from it towards a freer perspective. Through the latter movement a re-definition of the daughter-mother relationship becomes possible.

1582 Franceschetti, Giancarlo. "Colette, Sidonie-Gabrielle." In *Dizionario critico della letteratura francese*, vol. 1, 279-82. Turin: Unione Tipografico-Editrice Torinese, 1972. Detailed resume of critics' reception of Colette's principal works to date. Includes brief comments about many well-known books and articles.

1583 Franc-Nohain [pseud. of Maurice Le Grand]. "Colette: 'La Maison de Claudine'." In *Le Cabinet de lecture*, 242-48. Paris: Renaissance du livre, 1922. Praises the mimetic force of Colette's style, using clichés popular at the time among her critics. Often paraphrases the title work and assumes it is autobiographical.

1584 Frank, Nino. "Colette, retour de Saint-Tropez." *Nouvelles littéraires*, 13 Oct. 1928, 8. Interview with Colette about her summer at Saint Tropez and other trivialities. Colette talks

about her need to visit the sea, her future travels to North
Africa, and her gift of water-divining.

1585   Franke, Peter Robert. "Allocution." In item 1077 *Colette,
       Nouvelles Approches critiques*, 9-11. Welcoming address to the
       Colloque de Sarrebruck, June 1984. Includes outline of the way
       German encyclopædias presented Colette from 1929 to 1976.

1586   Fresnay, Pierre. [No title]. *Figaro littéraire*, 24 Jan. 1953, 5.
       Anecdote of the 1920's, when Fresnay played Chéri to Colette's
       Lea on the stage. Says that her loyalty to the music-hall and her
       drama criticism prove her enduring attachment to the theater.

1587   Fresnois, André du. "Colette Willy." *Akademos* 1 (15 Feb. 1909):
       178-84. Significant because it discusses all the early works
       published by Colette and because it was written during what
       was probably the most difficult period of her life. Welcomes the
       liberation announced by the metaphor of the "tendrils of the
       vine" and hails her as a superior writer to other *bacchantes* of
       the previous twenty years, who confuse sensibility with
       disorder. Considers her novels to be morally neutral.

1588   Frugier, Jacques. "Chronologie." In item 0053 *OP* 1, cxxiii-clxix;
       and *OP* 2, lix-xcv. The finest and most complete published
       chronology of events and incidents relating to Colette's life and
       work. Begins with the birth of her parents, and includes
       incidents leading up to their marriage. Places these within a
       chronology of social, political and literary events. Especially
       useful are precise dates of voyages Colette made, sentimental
       upheavals, performances given and works published. First two
       volumes include chronologies of 1829-1910 and 1911-1924. An
       invaluable aid to scholars.

1589   Frugier, Jacques. "La 'Collection Colette'." *Cahiers Colette*, no. 5
       (1983): 71-85. History of Ferenczi's "Collection Colette" series,
       published between Oct. 1923 and March 1925. Lists all 20
       novels, some of which are now inaccessible, and describes the
       most important ones. Only a few of the authors are still known,
       but even those names witness Colette's skill at selecting good
       work. Includes a few letters and unpublished paragraphs that
       Colette wrote as insertions. A valuable article dealing with a
       poorly researched facet of Colette's literary activity.

1590 Fuglsang, Irene Frisch. "Colette." In *Fremmede digtere i det 20. århundrede*, vol. 1, 253-67. Copenhagen: G.E.C. Gads, 1967. Long general resume of Colette's life and works. Discussion of the latter is limited to descriptive summary, with little critical evaluation.

1591 Fuglsang, Irene Frisch. "Le style de Colette." *Orbis litterarum* 3 (1945): 1-28, 261-81; and 4 (1946): 95-123, 229-52. One of the best long studies written during Colette's lifetime, and still a sound basic analysis of her style. Analyzes a wide variety of works. Contains four sections: the sensations and their poetic significance; the poetic images; the choice of words and their placement in the sentence; the harmonic effects. Draws conclusions on the use of sensations in different works written at different periods of Colette's life, on her predilections and aversions, and on her use of *audition colorée*. Many of the ideas presented in this very rich article have been confirmed by more modern analytic techniques.

1592 G. "De Saint-Sauveur-en-Puisaye à Castel-Novel sur les pas de l'auteur de 'Claudine'..." *Bulletin de la Société scientifique et artistique de Clamecy*, no. 47 (1973): 51-54. Brief biography followed by extract from item 0996. Reprinted from *La Montagne* (28 Jan. 1973).

1593 Gandon, Yves. "Le cœur et les bêtes: Colette conférencière." *Nouvelles littéraires*, 15 May 1937, 2. Impressions from a member of the audience listening to Colette talking about animals. Cites several of her animal anecdotes.

1594 Gandon, Yves. "Colette." In *Trésors du pastiche*, edited by François Caradec, 211-13. Paris: Horay, 1971. Pastiche of the ending of *La Chatte*, in which Alain makes Camille jump off the balcony.

1595 Gandon, Yves. "Colette ou la sainteté du style." In *Le Démon du style*, 203-24. Paris: Plon, 1938. One of the first serious attempts to analyze Colette's style and still a valid research tool. Detects two distinct types of style in Colette's work, one manifest in her presentation of childhood, the other connected with adult experience, and summarizes the characteristics of each.

1596   Gandon, Yves. "Critique romancée: au jardin de Colette."
        Nouvelles littéraires, 31 Aug. 1929, 4. Also in *Mascarades
        littéraires*, 45-55. Paris: Trémois, 1930. Playful imaginary
        conversation between Colette and Cupid, in the garden with pets
        Toby-Chien and Kiki-la-Doucette. Colette confesses preferences
        for *Le Blé en herbe*, *La Naissance du jour* and *La Maison de
        Claudine* as true to the spirit of the "real Claudine."

1597   Garcia, Irma. In *Promenade femmilière*, 2 vols. Paris: Eds. des
        femmes, 1981. Colette is one of several female authors whose
        works are frequently quoted as illustrations of ideas presented in
        this study of female discourse. Not every example is convincing
        but one finds interesting remarks on Colette's need to write as
        an assertion of identity, her relationship to words, her fondness
        for the journal form, and her use of ellipsis and silence.

1598   García Calderón, Ventura. "Colette en sandales." *Figaro littéraire*,
        16 Aug. 1958, 1, 7. Anecdotes and reminiscences dating from
        García Calderón's first meeting with Colette soon after the
        scandal of the Moulin-Rouge. Despite negative comments
        presenting her as an unhappy and excitable woman who bore
        unjust rancor against many, especially Willy, García Calderón
        declares admiration and friendship for Colette.

1599   Gascar, Pierre. "Colette ou la littérature du don." *Gazette de
        Lausanne*, 14 Aug. 1954, 7. Attempts to assess the whole of
        Colette's work in the light of its immortality. Considers her
        novels to be sexually polarized, with usual male and female
        characterization reversed. Insists that her works are completely
        divorced from all spirituality. Terms her unique in French
        literature.

1600   Gass, William H. "Three Photos of Colette." *New York Review of
        Books* 24 (14 April 1977): 11-19. Also in *The World within
        the World*, 124-46. New York: Knopf, 1978. Article inspired by
        three pictures of Colette at different periods of her life, but
        dwelling especially on the years with Willy and on the content
        of the Claudine novels. Portrays Willy in a very negative light.
        Suggests that the Claudine novels are a social document in that
        they offer a realistic picture of the oppressed conditions under
        which many young women lived in rural France at that time.

1601 Gaudard, Alain. "Histoires de 15 mai." *Cahiers Colette*, no. 8
      (1986): 25-28. Speculates on the possible significance of May
      15 in Colette's early work, noting that it is the date of her first
      marriage, Max's first communion and Renée's renouncement of
      him [*La Vagabonde*]. Cautiously suggests that the coincidence
      may be intentional.

1602 Gauthier-Villars, Jacques. "Un couple parisien de la Belle Epoque,
      ou Willy vu par son fils." *Œuvres libres*, no. 161 (Oct. 1959):
      175-96. Reminiscences of Willy and Colette by Willy's son.
      Relates visits, holidays, small and large events, personal
      characteristics, and details of relationships. Confesses to not
      fully understanding why the couple broke up. Although the
      article's stated purpose is to redress the balance of public
      opinion after publication of Colette's memoirs, which Gauthier-
      Villars considers too severe on Willy, he does not really take
      sides here and has good things to say about both.

1603 Gauthier-Villars, J.-H. [Jacques]. "Sur Colette et Sido." *Figaro
      littéraire*, 8 Dec. 1956, 4. Includes letter from Willy's son
      objecting to comments made about both Colette's and Willy's
      families in item 1536. Suggests that Escholier's motives in
      making them were less than laudable.

1604 Gautier, Félix. "Henry Gauthier-Villars (Willy)." *Revue illustrée*,
      no. 15 (15 July 1902): 23-27. Assesses all Willy's output but
      contains long paragraphs praising the first two Claudine novels.
      Terms *Claudine à l'école* a moral work, because of the heroine's
      character. An interesting example of the purple prose typical of
      some writers of the day, and because of its patronizing attitude.

1605 Gauwin, Marcelle. "La grande Colette." In *Colette*, 83-104. Paris:
      Horay, 1959. Chapter devoted to the history and meaning of the
      name 'Colette,' of which the writer Colette is the most
      illustrious bearer. Asserts that the name presupposes a strong
      person who wants to win and to achieve greatness. Traces the
      biography of Colette's father and speculates about her motives
      and secret thoughts during her early years. Connects the name
      with amiability, graciousness and coquetry, but is generally
      unsympathetic towards Colette as an individual. Likens her to
      the female praying mantis, which is reputed to rid itself of its
      mate once the male is no longer useful.

1606   Gavoty, Bernard. "Les femmes ont-elles du génie?" *Les Annales* 76
       (Jan. 1969): 41-54. Sometimes patronizing, sometimes tongue-
       in-cheek, Gavoty reviews famous names in music and literature.
       Concludes that Colette is the only woman genius in the history
       of French literature, partly because she had a "masculine
       component." Discounts the importance of social conditioning.
       Draws heavily from Colette's work and conversations to
       illustrate ideas.

1607   Gavoty, Bernard. "Notre Colette." Transcribed by Jean-Marie
       Fonteneau. *Avant-Scène Théâtre*, no. 708 (15 April 1982): 45-
       69. Text of an evening devoted to Colette and her work, in the
       Rencontres du Palais-Royal series, 17 Nov. 1970. Chief
       narrator is Gavoty, whose remarks bear on the main events of
       Colette's life, her personality, her achievements, and salient
       characteristics of her work. Guest performers enter into dialogue
       with Gavoty and with each other, reading extracts from Colette's
       books as if in her own voice. Includes "Hommage à Bernard
       Gavoty" and ends with a partial performance of the stage version
       of *Chéri*.

1608   Gavoty, Bernard. "Près de Colette." *Figaro*, 15 Feb. 1977, 30. In
       memoriam Maurice Goudeket. Gavoty emphasizes Goudeket's
       long devotion to Colette.

1609   Gaxotte, Pierre. In item 1095 *Hommage à Colette*, non-pag.
       Reminisces about meetings with Colette when he was chief
       editor of *Candide* and later.

1610   Genevoix, Maurice. In item 1095 *Hommage à Colette*, non-pag.
       Brief passage lauding Colette's skill at interpreting nature.

1611   Gennari, Geneviève. "Colette ou le retour aux sources." *Table
       ronde* 99 (March 1956): 75-77. Part of an inquiry into the
       sources of the literary vocation among women. Explains
       Colette's success by her perfect acceptance of herself and of the
       real. Says that her work presents female sensuality at all ages
       and without overt feminism.

1612   Gennari, Geneviève. "Comment les romancières voient les
       hommes." *Revue des deux mondes* 12 (15 June 1959): 655-71.
       Article on how female novelists see men contains passage

reproaching Colette for remaining inactive in the face of social inequality of the sexes, but credits her with being a major force in destroying the myth of romantic love, which puts man on a pedestal.

1613 Georgin, René. "Colette." In *La Prose d'aujourd'hui*, 313-15. Paris: Bonne, 1956. Concise appraisal of Colette's style, enumerating its characteristics. Considers that Colette's other gifts would be lost without her style, paradoxical because its spontaneity has been achieved with care.

1614 Georgin, René. "Comment elle écrivait." In *Jeux de mots*, 194-96. Paris: Bonne, 1957. Short commentary on the posthumous collection *Belles Saisons*. Terms its short pieces exercises in virtuosity. Offers illustrations of a few of Colette's techniques.

1615 Georgin, René. "En lisant Colette." *La Parisienne* 5 (May 1953): 649-57. Notes characteristics of Colette's style, and gives examples. Praises her syntax and her animal pieces. Not a profound study but a good concise one for its time.

1616 Géraldy, Paul. In item 1095 *Hommage à Colette*, non-pag. Brief imaginary conversation with Colette on trivial matters.

1617 Gibbard, Eleanor Reid. "A Chronology of Colette in Translation." *Philological Papers* 23 (1977): 75-93. The only complete bibliography to date of Colette's works in English. Lists both American and British editions, with translator. Also comments on editions. Notes the two surges of publication of Colette in English, the first around 1930 and the second soon after World War II.

1618 Gibbard, Eleanor Reid. "Rectification of an Image in Colette's 'Le dernier feu' and of the Publication History of 'Les Vrilles de la vigne'." *Philological Papers* 17 (June 1970): 72-75. Argues that a line of type was inadvertently left out of "Le dernier feu" when the *OCLF* were published and that it has never been restored. Traces the publication history of the collection to which it belongs, *Les Vrilles de la vigne*, and argues that, although the volume's contents as well as their order changed several times, omission of the line of type cannot be intended because it is the only undesirable change.

1619   Gibbard, Eleanor Reid. "Répertoire de 'La Jumelle noire'." *Cahiers Colette*, no. 6 (1984): 61-81; no. 7 (1985): 99-131; no. 8 (1986): 81-116; no. 9 (1987): 69-94. Alphabetical index of Colette's *La Jumelle noire*. Includes titles of plays, names of authors, actors, directors, costume designers, in fact any person mentioned. A useful aid for scholars working on Colette's theater criticism.

1620   Gide, André. "Hommage à Colette." *Le Point*, no. 39 (May 1951): 4. Also in *Livres de France* 5 (Oct. 1954): 6. Two paragraphs praising Colette's gifts, especially her self-discipline, rare among women writers in Gide's opinion.

1621   Gide, André. "'Tout étonné du si grand plaisir...'" *Figaro littéraire*, 24 Jan. 1953, 1. Also in item 1978 Pichois, 193-94; and item 1072 Chauvière, 148-49. Letter written 11 Dec. 1920, after reading *Chéri*. Gide praises Colette's intelligence, the simplicity and concision of the novel and the over-all perfection of her writing. Likens *Chéri* to *Adolphe* in reverse.

1622   Gide, André. In *Journal*, vol. 1, 1245; vol. 2, 69-70, 298. Paris: Pléiade, 1959-60. In well-known entry of 19 Feb. 1936, Gide expresses great admiration for Colette's gifts, but considers her contaminated by the time she spent in Willy's world. Although Gide admits that he, too, frequented that world, he declares that he escaped contamination. Also in item 1978 Pichois. Other entries reiterate his enthusiasm for her work but Gide admits to having nothing to say to her when they meet. Colette herself wrote that they could find no common ground for conversation.

1623   Gignoux, Régis. "Colette." *Cahiers d'aujourd'hui*, no. 8 (1914): 412-13. Coy description of Colette. Expresses apprehension about meeting her, because of the force of her gaze.

1624   Gille, Valère. "Discours." *Bulletin de l'Académie royale de langue et de littérature françaises* 15 (1936): 53-64. Also extract, under title "Madame Colette," in *Le Flambeau* 19:1 (1936): 453-57. Speech welcoming Colette to the Belgian Academy, 4 April 1936. Evokes her ties with Belgium through her mother. Attempts to define Colette's mind through references to her books. Terms her both romantic and classic. A polished address without significant content.

1625   Gillois, André. In *Ce siècle avait deux ans*, 201. Paris: Belfond,
       1980. Brief anecdote relating that Gillois once reminded Colette
       of the debt she owed to Willy for initiating her writing career.

1626   Gillouin, René. "Le charme de Colette." *Le Capitole*, 22 Dec.
       1924, non-pag. [17-18]. Defines Colette's work as anti-romantic
       because of its intellectual honesty, its discretion and its sense of
       measure. Terms its poetic aspects original.

1627   Gillouin, René. "Madame Colette Willy." In *Essais de critique
       littéraire et philosophique*, 87-95. Paris: Grasset, 1913. General
       remarks with few specific references. Deems Colette's talent
       worthy of more noble subjects than those so far treated in her
       novels but terms her without objective imagination. It is
       interesting that long before publication of *La Maison de
       Claudine* and *Sido* Gillouin compares Colette with Barrès
       because of the importance of childhood in their works.

1628   Giono, Jean. In item 1095 *Hommage à Colette*, non-pag. Recalls
       conversation with Colette at dinner.

1629   Giroud, Françoise. "Préface." In item 0344 *Claudine à l'école*, 19-
       26. Attempts to place Colette's novel in the context of the
       period in which it was written. Refers to her work as
       completely autobiographical and confessional.

1630   Giry, Jacqueline A. "Colette et le thème du paradis." *Bulletin of the
       Rocky Mountain Modern Language Association* 27 (March
       1973): 23-30. Argues that the source of the theme of paradise
       can be traced to the trauma of Colette's marriage with Willy,
       which destroyed the unity of her childish self. Interprets Willy's
       collaboration on the Claudine novels as a violation of Colette's
       childhood, and the creation of a public Claudine as a destruction
       of her unified self. Analyzes the double of the mirror, which
       reassures yet frightens, and the role of memory in the re-creation
       of the paradisiac garden. Concludes that Colette's imagistic
       writing is an attempt to rediscover and to communicate the
       completely terrestrial paradise and its extension throughout all
       of nature.

1631   Giry, Jacqueline A. "Le pouvoir du mot chez Colette: de la mère à
       la fleur." *L'Age nouveau*, no. 1 (Feb. 1987): 127-31. Brief but

perceptive article which attempts to define the role of writing in Colette's ongoing relationship to her past and to the world. Does so by analyzing the semantic presentation of the garden and the mother.

1632   Godard, Colette. "Colette et Sido: José Bersoza au Palais-Royal." *Le Monde*, 13 May 1973, 27. Favorable review of a television program on Colette, directed by Bersoza and in which Colette's ties with her mother are emphasized.

1633   Gold, Arthur, and Robert Fizdale. "The passions of Colette." *House & Garden* 157 (Oct. 1985): 70-92. Most of the article deals with Colette's public activities during the first decade of the century. Includes much speculation and frequently quotes Dormann and Richardson. Also relates a meeting with Colette in 1948. Superficial but entertaining.

1634   Gold, Arthur, and Robert Fizdale. In *Misia: The Life of Misia Sert*, 126-28, 272-74. New York: Knopf, 1980. Duo-pianists Gold and Fizdale offer brief anecdotes and frequent passing allusions to Colette in this popular biography of one of her long-time friends. Very readable, despite minor inaccuracies.

1635   Gómez de la Serna, Ramón. "Colette." In *Retratos contemporáneos*, 429-47. Buenos Aires: Sudamericana, 1941. Also in *Retratos completos*, 567-83. Madrid: Aguilar, 1961. Profile of Colette's life and career, with special reference to Willy's role in it.

1636   Gontier, Fernande. "La femme en chemin." In *La Femme et le couple dans le roman 1919-1939*, 87-99. Paris: Klincksieck, 1976. Discerns in Colette's early novels a consciousness of social and economic inequality between men and women, here defined as the first stages of the feminist revolution. Locates Colette at a historic turning point where women began to assert themselves economically in France, but insists that, although Colette early asserted her sexual liberty and although her novels usually portray men as inferior creatures, she did not fully reject male domination and establishment values in her own life.

1637   Goodhand, Robert. "Apollo and Dionysus: Bedfellows of Colette's 'Vagabond'." *Contemporary Literature* 24 (Summer 1983): 190-

203. Attempts to place *La Vagabonde* within the tradition of writers whose perception of the modern human predicament were sharpened and enriched by Nietzsche's views. Compares Colette's Renée with Camus' Janine and likens Renée's growing awareness of her relationship with the world to Nietzsche's articulation of the tragic sense of life. Insists that her writing incarnates Nietzsche's ideal fusion of the æsthetic principles of Dionysus and Apollo.

1638   Gouaux, Mireille. "La Provence dans l'œuvre de Colette." In item 1060 *Autour de Colette à Saint-Tropez*, non-pag. [61-68]. Attempts to delineate the main characteristics of Colette's Provence by drawing on her work, especially *La Naissance du jour*, for indications. Argues that Provence belongs to Colette's concept of paradise, implying refuge, creation, spiritual purity and a lost ideal. Draws parallels between Colette's ideal world and the vision of the Cathar sect during the Middle Ages.

1639   Gouaux-Coutrix, Mireille. "'Delight to Reason Joined' ou 'La naissance du jour'." In *Annales de la Faculté des Lettres et Sciences humaines de Nice*, no. 38 (1979): 193-200. Examines the theme of paradise in the novel, using an analogy that is both sexual and biblical. Insists that in the garden Sido's teachings equate touching with sexuality and both of them with loss or banishment and that the novel is an attempt to explore this idea at its source, and to heal the wound created at the time of expulsion. Borrows analogies from Milton's *Paradise Lost*.

1640   Gouaux-Coutrix, Mireille. "Des sens aux sens." *Cahiers Colette*, no. 3-4 (1981): 45-55. Attempts to define the focus of Colette's esthetics in terms of her mother's lessons. Notes that sexuality, related to death, is banned from Sido's garden. Detects in Colette's work a tension on the sexual plane between development and death, as she seeks an equilibrium, finally found in a focusing of the senses on a balance between culture and nature. Interesting remarks, tied to Freudian concepts, on *La Naissance du jour*.

1641   Gouaux-Coutrix, Mireille. "Fiction et autobiographie: le 'mentir-vrai' chez Colette." *Europe*, no. 631-32 (Nov.-Dec. 1981): 13-20. Briefly analyzes the relationship between fiction and autobiography in Colette's work. Asserts that, although she

apparently deals with her past, she assimilates and transforms
that past in order to work out hypothetical models for her
future. Sees *La Naissance du jour* as the culmination of this
habit. Argues that Colette's intent is not to reveal herself but to
explore herself with a view to self-protection against the world,
and that occasionally she reveals her intention and her vision. A
persuasive article, even though it assumes that the narrator of
the novel speaks in Colette's own voice.

1642   Goubault, Christian. "Colette et Debussy, 'compagnons de chaîne'
       au 'Gil Blas' en 1903." *Revue internationale de musique
       française*, no. 17 (June 1985): 75-86. In February 1895 six
       music reviews appeared in *La Cocarde* under Willy's name.
       Some critics believe Colette to have been their principal, if not
       their sole, author. In an effort to prove Colette's authorship,
       Goubault compares the six reviews with others generally
       accepted as her work, especially the 23 signed "Claudine au
       concert," and the 10 signed "Claudine au Conservatoire"
       published in *Gil Blas* in 1903. Article title refers to the fact
       that, during the longer of the two *Gil Blas* series, a column by
       Debussy often accompanied that signed "Claudine au concert,"
       sometimes treating the same music or performers. By analyzing
       both subject matter and style, and by comparing them with
       Debussy's and Willy's own, the article establishes a list of
       stylistic features and one of each author's likes and dislikes, and
       presents them as evidence for attributing the reviews to Colette.

1643   Goubault, Christian. "Henri Gauthier-Villars (1859-1931): le
       prince des critiques et la reine des ouvreuses." In *La Critique
       musicale dans la presse française de 1870 à 1914*, 122-32.
       Geneva, Paris: Slatkine, 1984. Discussion on Willy as music
       critic includes several references to Colette. Attributes to her the
       authorship of the "Claudine au concert" music reviews.

1644   Goudeket, Maurice. "Adieu à Hélène Jourdan-Morhange." *Lettres
       françaises*, 18 May 1961, 5. In memoriam for musician
       Morhange, long-time friend to both Colette and Goudeket.

1645   Goudeket, Maurice. "Colette et l'art d'écrire." *Annales de la Faculté
       des lettres et sciences humaines d'Aix* 33 (1959): 21-39. Text of
       an address to students. Only marginally a study of Colette's art
       of writing. Instead, Goudeket attempts to identify the qualities

that made Colette a great writer. Lists them as a profound curiosity, a special vision coupled with a desire to communicate it, the pursuit of perfection, a special kind of memory, hard work, and a tenderness for life. Contains a close analysis of the essay "Serpents" from *Prisons et paradis*, comparing it with the experience that inspired it. Insists that Colette's fictional characters are the product of a long germination process in her mind.

1646 Goudeket, Maurice. "Colette et le Palais-Royal." *Figaro*, 26 Jan. 1973, 1. Affirmation of Colette's love for the Palais Royal, where she lived, and the neighboring Bibliothèque Nationale.

1647 Goudeket, Maurice. "Colette son amie." *Figaro littéraire*, 19 Oct. 1963, 7. Homage on the death of Colette's friend, writer Jean Cocteau. Insists that he was the only person considered for Colette's place in the Belgian Academy.

1648 Goudeket, Maurice. "Les métamorphoses de Chéri." In item 0305 *Chéri. La Fin de Chéri*, 19-28. Introduction to the two novels, stressing the necessity of reading the sequel in order to understand the first novel. Traces genesis and development of Chéri from his earlier manifestation as Clouk some nine years before the novel actually appeared. Interpretation highlights Chéri's solitude, purity and desire for warmth.

1649 Goudeket, Maurice. "L'œil du témoin." *Cahiers Colette*, no. 1 (1977): 27-38. Long passages from an address before the Annales, 7 Dec. 1973. Consists mostly of anecdotes and reminiscences. Offers details about the publication in 1929 of *La Seconde* by *Les Annales* and discusses Colette's relations with that journal. Insists on the universal appeal of her work.

1650 Goudeket, Maurice. "Préface." In *Lettres au petit corsaire*, all eds. Interesting account of the development of Colette's friendship with the young Breton, Renée Hamon, and of the latter's cult for Colette. Includes remarks on the suicide, discovered by Hamon, of Erna Redtenbacher, Colette's German translator. Emphasizes Colette's mobility of mind, desire to help others and respect for their beliefs.

1651   Goudeket, Maurice. "Préface." In item 0224 *Trois... six... neuf...*,
        non-pag. [3-5]. Entertaining account of the curious mixture in
        Colette's character of vagabondage and home-making.

1652   Goudeket, Maurice. "Sur Sido et Colette." *Figaro littéraire*, 15
        Dec. 1956, 7. Open letter protesting item 1536. Quotes from
        the as-yet-unpublished letters to Colette from her mother, to
        refute or correct statements made by Escholier.

1653   Goudeket, Maurice. In *Ce que je ne crois pas*, 57-60, 86, 99-103,
        166-67. Paris: Flammarion, 1977. In rambling memoirs,
        published shortly before his death, Colette's third husband
        declares that his second marriage has not diminished his cult for
        her. The many allusions to her throughout demonstrate that he
        continued to nourish her image. Interesting remarks on Colette
        and criminals Landru, Weidmann and Staviski.

1654   Gougy-François, Marie. "La fin des salons littéraires." In *Les
        Grands Salons féminins*, 187-90. Paris: Nouvelles Eds.
        Debresse, 1965. Contrasts Colette and what is termed her
        primitive naturalness with the hostesses of the famous salons of
        the late nineteenth century. Stresses her attractiveness to people
        of all ranks, despite her lack of sophistication. Alludes to many
        rich or famous people who were friends to Colette.

1655   Goujerval, Jean. [No title]. *Réforme*, 14 Aug. 1954, 7. Supports
        the Roman Catholic Church's decision not to allow Colette
        religious rites. Argues that she had no notion of sin or of grace.

1656   Graczyk, Annette, and Eva-Marie Vering. "Le 2ème Colloque
        Colette--Ein Aufstieg in Die République des Lettres."
        Lendemains 35 (1984): 93-95. Account of Colette colloquium
        at Saarbrücken in June 1984. Lists the speakers and touches on
        their main points. Stresses the notion that until very recently
        Colette was read by few and accorded no serious study in
        Germany.

1657   Gramont, Elisabeth de. In *Souvenirs du monde de 1890 à 1940*,
        250-52. Paris: Grasset, 1966. Effusive, fanciful and subjective
        assessment of Colette. Credits her with an almost magical
        comprehension of creatures. Terms *Chéri* the greatest love novel
        of the age.

1658 Grau, Lucien. "Introduction." In item 0416 "Claudine et les contes de fées," 6-11. Relates that the manuscript of the rejected chapter of *Claudine s'en va* was acquired after many adventures and that Colette willingly filled in parts that were missing or had been damaged.

1659 Gray, Francine du Plessix. "The New 'Older Woman'." *New York Times Book Review,* 15 Jan. 1978, 3. Compares Colette with Doris Lessing in her presentation of the older woman-younger man relationship. Surprisingly terms France a deeply feminized society and Colette so profoundly rooted in it that only she could achieve such a successful portrayal. Terms the elasticity of sexual roles in Colette's work a great legacy for the feminist movement.

1660 Green, Julien. In item 1095 *Hommage à Colette,* non-pag. Green briefly states that Colette's gaze announces her to be a poet.

1661 Green, Julien. In *Journal,* vol. 1, 18-19; vol. 5, 295; vol. 6, 132-33, 273-74. Paris: Plon, 1938-1955. Brief anecdotal entries of 25 May 1929, 1 Oct. 1949 and 4 Dec. 1951, as well as entry of 7 Aug. 1954 commenting on Colette's death. Last two entries also in *Dans la gueule du temps,* 154, 161. Paris: Plon, 1978.

   English translation [abridged and signed: Julian Green]. In *Diary 1928-1957,* 248-49, 263. Trans. Anne Green. London: Collins & Harville; New York: Harcourt, Brace & World, 1964. Includes 1929, 1951 and 1954 entries.

1662 Greene, Graham. "Lettre à son Eminence le Cardinal-Archevêque de Paris." *Figaro littéraire,* 14 Aug. 1954, 1. Public letter vigorously protesting the Roman Catholic Church's decision not to permit the religious burial requested by Colette's family. Greene's letter aroused a storm of controversy, even in North America. In a public reply a week later [*Figaro littéraire,* 21 Aug. 1954, 1], Cardinal Feltin, Archbishop of Paris, defended the Church's decision. Readers' comments were published in issues of 21 Aug. [p. 5, 8] and 28 Aug. [p. 9]. Greene's letter also in *Gazette de Lausanne,* 14 Aug. 1954, 11. Also, as "La polémique dans 'Le Figaro' à la mort de Colette," in item 1057 *Album Masques: Colette,* 137-42.

1663   Gregory, Claude. "La leçon d'interview chez Mme Colette." *Arts*,
        17 April 1952, 1, 11. Interviewer reports that Colette insists on
        talking only about the trivial and the every-day.

1664   Grigson, Geoffrey, and Charles Harvard Gibbs-Smith. "A fiery
        particle." In *People: A Volume of the Good, Bad, Great &
        Eccentric who illustrate the Admirable Diversity of Man*, vol.
        1, 95-96. New York: Hawthorn; London: Grosvenor, 1954.
        Concise encyclopædic entry sketching highlights of Colette's
        life and work. Asserts that after her second marriage she became
        a moralist and a novelist of manners.

1665   Gripari, Pierre. "Couples et triangles." *Ecrits de Paris*, no. 468
        (May 1986): 79-84. Mixed review of "Chats et Chiens," a stage
        spectacle based on Colette's various animal works.

1666   Gripari, Pierre. "Félins et fauves." *Ecrits de Paris*, no. 455 (May
        1985): 82-87. Favorable review of "Colette, dame seule," a
        theater production in which passages from Colette's works were
        read to the audience.

1667   Groult, Benoîte. "Grâce aux 'Claudine' Colette superstar." *F.
        Magazine*, no. 4 (April 1978): 62-67. Terms Colette an
        admirable moralist and psychologist, even though many studies
        published since her death still depict her as scandal-prone and
        preoccupied with pleasure. Detects a longing for purity from the
        very first works. Considers her to have been harshly judged, if
        not ignored, by masculine critics and readers, hostile to non-
        traditional women. Groult was one of four women who adapted
        the Claudine novels for Edouard Molinaro's film series.

1668   Grunenberg, Angelika. "Genie als erhabenes Laster: Colette oder
        die Welt der Sinne unter dem Vergrösserungsglas des strengen
        Beobachters." *Frankfurter Allgemeine*, 8 Sept. 1984, 41.
        Extolls qualities of Colette's work for German readers, declaring
        that they have not treated it seriously enough. Summarizes her
        honors.

1669   Guérin, Raoul. "Colette." In *Souvenirs d'un dessinateur de presse*,
        165-66. Paris: Pensée universelle, 1979. Brief anecdotes by one
        who performed with Colette at Ba-ta-Clan.

1670 Guillot, Gérard. "Colette, loin du purgatoire." *Le Figaro*, 20 July 1979, 20. Insists that Colette's work has suffered no decline in popularity since her death. Argues that she was ahead of her time and that her books reflect modern preoccupations. Terms her attitude to men paradoxical in that she treats them badly in her books, but was often subservient to them in life.

1671 Guirec, Jean. "Madame Colette." *Le Cerf-volant*, no. 68 (Oct. 1969): 7-10. Also, under title "La leçon de Claudine," in *Inter Muses*, no. 1 (1978): 16-20. Reminiscences of a long conversation with Colette at *Le Matin*, during which she showed Guirec the manuscript of one of the Claudine novels and gave him advice on his own career.

1672 Guitard-Auviste, Ginette. "Le chemin d'une sagesse." *Le Monde*, 25 Jan. 1973, 20. Homage on the hundredth anniversary of Colette's birth. States that Colette's *sagesse* or wisdom lay in her positive approach to life. Quotes her work freely.

1673 Guitard-Auviste, Ginette. "Colette militante du M.L.F.?" *Matulu*, no. 23 (March 1973): 3. Disagrees with statements made in recent articles by others, particularly Jean Chalon. Asserts that Colette was never a militant feminist, but just a survivor.

1674 Guitard-Auviste, Ginette. "Etude: Colette vivante-centenaire." *Le Monde*, 25 Jan. 1973, 20. Complement to item 1672. Denies that Colette is a feminist, even by example. Considers that her wisdom can be traced to her ancestral roots, that its complete reflection is in her works.

1675 Guitton, Jean. "Mort de Colette." In *Journal: études et rencontres 1952-1955*, 259-61. Paris: Plon, 1959. Colette's passing inspires reflections on death, which have little to do here with either her or her work.

1676 Guth, Paul. "Colette le grand." In *Quarante contre un*, 71-76. Paris: Corrêa, 1947. Interesting mixture of reminiscences about Colette at different periods of her life.

1677 H., A. "La mort de Colette." *Le Fribourgeois*, 7 Aug. 1954, non-pag. In memoriam. Asserts that Colette has survived her literary generation, that her modern reputation derives largely from

films of her work, and that the esteem in which she is held
results in large part from publicity. Terms her a poet of the
ephemeral, but a minor author who, however agreeable to read,
offers little of substance.

1678   Hagen, Friedrich. "...la plus grande Dame de France..." *Das Buch*
3:10 (1951): 5-11. Assesses Colette as a writer in a society
dominated by men. Does not consider her feminist, but rather a
superior spokesperson for true femininity. States that all her
books are about herself.

1679   Haloche, Maurice. "Colette n'est plus." *Le Thyrse* 56 (1954): 359-
63. In memoriam, recalling Colette's reception to the Belgian
Academy. Includes brief summary and description of her later
works.

1680   Haloche, Maurice. "Madame Colette." *Le Thyrse* 37 (1935): 107-
12. Acclaims Colette's election to the Belgian Academy but
over-all praise is mixed with references to her limitations.
Considers her themes vague and her work without philosophical
subtlety. Attempts to define her talent.

1681   Hamadou, Bernard. "Colette ou comment faire pour être heureux."
Revue du Caire 33 (Nov. 1954): 251-60. Questions the wisdom
of the French government's decision to accord Colette a state
funeral, given the absence of reference to "great events" in her
work. Contrasts the search for happiness, considered here to be
the major theme in her books, with Stendhal's *chasse au
bonheur*. Expresses admiration for her animal portraits and her
portrayal of love, but terms women close to the forces of nature
in any case.

1682   Hanoteau, Guillaume. In *La Fabuleuse Aventure de 'Paris-Match,'*
123-25. Paris: Plon, 1976. Two anecdotes about the aged
Colette. In one she displays a sense of mischief, in the other her
escaping wheelchair puts her life in danger. She is also casually
mentioned elsewhere in the book.

1683   Hatzfeld, Helmut. In *Trends and Styles in Twentieth Century
French Literature*, rev. ed., 58-62, 281-83. Washington:
Catholic University of America Press, 1966. Colette's inclusion
in the chapter entitled "The Forces of the Earth" indicates the

perspective adopted for this simplistic interpretation of her life and work. Defines women by definition closer to nature than men, and likens all Colette's women characters to cats. Also casual references to Colette throughout the book.

1684 Hauser, Fernand. "L'ex-marquise de Belbeuf joue la pantomime en l'hôtel de la marquise, un rédacteur du 'Journal' assiste à une répétition de 'La Romanichelle'." In *Lettres de la vagabonde*, all eds. Account of a rehearsal where Colette and the Marquise perform in pantomime and at which Willy is also present. Text of 1906.

1685 Heilbrun, Carolyn G. In *Toward a Recognition of Androgyny*, 87. New York: Knopf, 1973. Briefly names Colette as the chief modern French figure, after Proust, to be "marvelously androgynous."

1686 Heiman, Monica. "Maupassant and Others: The Artinian Collection." *Library Chronicle of the University of Texas* 8 (Spring 1968): 56-57. Indicates the presence in the collection at the University of Texas of a large number of letters from Willy, dated 1890-1917, and some unspecified correspondence from Colette.

1687 Hellens, Franz [pseud. of Frédéric van Ermengem]. "Colette vue par l'étranger: en Belgique." In item 1072 Chauvière, 277-79. General praise for Colette's work, especially *Sido*.

1688 Hellens, Franz [pseud. of Frédéric van Ermengem]. "Sur Colette." In *Style et caractère*, 53-54. Brussels: Renaissance du livre, 1956. General commendation of Colette's style. Terms excellence in style unusual among women writers.

1689 Hellens, Franz [pseud. of Frédéric van Ermengem]. In item 1095 *Hommage à Colette*, non-pag. Imagines Colette in the south of France.

1690 Henri-Giraud, Madeleine. "Colette." *Journal littéraire*, no. 27 (25 Oct. 1924): 8. Interview in which Colette is reported as saying that feminine literature is always autobiographical.

1691   Henriot, Emile. "Colette." In *Maîtres d'hier et contemporains*, vol.
       2, 317-43. Paris: Albin Michel, 1956. Collection of four
       journalistic pieces dating from 1942 to 1954. Consists of
       reviews of *Julie de Carneilhan* and *L'Etoile vesper*, some first
       thoughts after her death, and a brief evaluation of her
       achievement. Insists that the Claudine novels are Colette's
       alone.

1692   Henriot, Emile. In item 1095 *Hommage à Colette*, non-pag. Brief
       passage stressing Colette's powers of observation.

1693   Hériat, Philippe. "'Cette clé de métal inaltérable...'" *Figaro
       littéraire*, 24 Jan. 1953, 3. Decides that much of Colette's
       appeal lies in the fact that she seems to speak personally to her
       readers.

1694   Hériat, Philippe. "Colette et ses secrets." *Figaro littéraire*, 11
       March 1965, 1. Text of an address given at the Comédie
       Française. Title alludes to the assertion here that, despite the
       autobiographical aspects of her books, Colette was actually a
       very private person. Accuses past critics of being hostile to her
       because they could not fit her into recognized categories. Terms
       the work of all women writers rooted in love of family.

1695   Hériat, Philippe. "Colette, la femme cachée." *Revue de Paris* 61
       (Sept. 1954): 9-15. Accepts as evidence of Colette's consistency
       the fact that her handwriting had not changed since her youth.
       Refutes the notion that she is amoral. Insists that *La Fin de
       Chéri* depicts the post-World War I syndrome common among
       European youth. Evokes the atmosphere of Colette's funeral.

1696   Hériat, Philippe. "Rien n'aura manqué à cette vie exemplaire."
       Lettres françaises, 12 Aug. 1954, 1. Ranks Colette as the
       greatest writer of the half-century and as one who, despite her
       fame, remained faithful to her instincts. Also includes a jab at
       the Roman Catholic authorities' decision on her burial.

1697   Hériat, Philippe. In item 1095 *Hommage à Colette*, non-pag. Brief
       expression of pride at being Colette's friend.

1698   Hérisson, Charles. "A propos de 'Gigi': littérature et sociologie."
       French Review 35 (Oct. 1961): 42-49. Offers historical and

sociological arguments to support the thesis that *Gigi* is a novel of manners. Includes interesting summary of the rise and decline of the *demi-monde* in France.

1699 Herman, Abel. "'Mitsou, ou comment l'esprit vient aux filles', de Mme Colette." In *La Vie littéraire*, vol. 2, 225-31. Paris: Flammarion, 1928. Declares dubious the then-current division of literature into masculine and feminine, but does agree with contemporary critics that sensibility governs books by women. Remarks on *Mitsou* are limited to a summary of the plot and a character portrait of the heroine. Text of 1919.

1700 Herriot, Edouard. "La femme française." *Les Annales* 57 (Dec. 1950): 3-11. In article on the late Yvonne Sarcey, Herriot likens Colette's richness of vocabulary to that of Anna de Noailles. Terms her the best prose writer since Chateaubriand.

1701 Herriot, Edouard. "Le plus grand poète français." *Figaro*, 12 Aug. 1954, 2. Also in *Lettres à ses pairs*, all eds. In memoriam by one who had known Colette from her music-hall days. Herriot emphasizes Colette's Frenchness, her interest in nature, her sincerity and her self-discipline.

1702 Highet, Gilbert. "Madam Cat." In *Talents and Geniuses: The Pleasures of Appreciation*, 75-83. New York: Oxford University Press, 1957. Superficial impressions of Colette and her work, not well grounded in fact but enthusiastically and entertainingly related.

1703 Hill-Marchand, Jacqueline. "Une explication de textes au laboratoire de langues." *Le français dans le monde* 106 (July-Aug. 1974): 38-44. Passage titled here "Les vendanges en Beaujolais," extracted from a radio talk by Colette, is used as illustration for an *explication* technique designed for language laboratory use at the first-year university level.

1704 Hirsch, Charles-Henry. "De Mademoiselle de Maupin à Claudine." *Mercure de France*, 6 June 1902, 577-88. Essentially descriptive of the first three Claudine novels. Terms Claudine a singular character when compared with young girls of the literature of the preceding century.

1705   Hirsch, Michèle. "Philomène de Watteville ou livre et créativité
       dans 'La Maison de Claudine'." *Roman 20-50*, no. 2 (Dec.
       1986): 147-64. Analyzes the significance and importance of *La
       Maison de Claudine* in Colette's psychological development.
       Declares that it explores the extent of her mother's influence on
       the formation of her creativity, both moral and literary. Adopts
       the premise that Colette found it necessary to confront guilt
       feelings towards both herself and others, and that she had to
       reconcile the conflicting desires of honoring her mother and of
       wishing to leave her. An interesting article, which takes its title
       from a repeated reference in Colette's works to a Balzac heroine.

1706   Hocquette, Hélène. "Colette et les noms de fleurs." *Vie et langage*,
       no. 268 (July 1974): 371-78. Mostly a compendium of
       quotations in which Colette mentions flowers. Apparent
       purpose is to make a list of those she mentions and to deduce
       from it a preference for violets and for pink and blue flowers.
       Mentions her several gardens. Concludes that study of those
       passages proves that Colette's detailed knowledge of flower
       characteristics and habits is impressive. Not a profound
       treatment of the subject but a significant article because,
       although Colette's love of flowers is well known and frequently
       mentioned, no real analysis of the content of her remarks about
       them has been published to date.

1707   Hofer, Hermann. "Colette critique musicale." In item 1077 *Colette,
       Nouvelles Approches critiques*, 95-106. Argues that Colette
       wrote, not only the series of 33 articles of music criticism
       appearing in *Gil Blas* from 12 Jan. to 29 June 1903 and signed
       "Claudine au concert," but also the ten articles signed "Claudine
       au conservatoire," appearing 17-29 July of the same year.
       Convincingly examines the evidence for this idea.

1708   Holmes, Diana. "The Hidden Woman: Disguise and Paradox in
       Colette's 'La Femme cachée'." *Essays in French Literature*, no.
       23 (Nov. 1986): 29-37. Declares that the notion of disguise is
       central to Colette's depiction of women because it permits self-
       expression, a paradox occurring thereby because in real life
       women must disguise their real selves in order to conform to
       male society's image of them. Terms the title story of *La
       Femme cachée* the most concentrated expression of this idea. An
       excellent article, clearly and convincingly argued.

1709 Hommel, Luc. "Hommage à Colette." *Audace*, no. 4 (Oct. 1954): 202-4. Also in *Bulletin de l'Académie royale de langue et de littérature françaises* 32:3 (1954): 206-9. Address given at Colette's funeral by Hommel as representative of the Belgian Academy. Emphasizes the connection between her life and her books. Detects in her work echos of the Song of Solomon.

1710 Hope-Wallace, Philip. "Paris, tout fleuri." *Time & Tide* 31 (6 May 1950): 443. Brief reference to the revival of the stage version of *Chéri*, with Valentine Tessier and Jean Marais. Avers that the play can never equal the novel.

1711 Houssa, Nicole. "Analyse d'un extrait du 'Fanal bleu' de Colette." *Revue des langues vivantes* 26:1 (1960): 4-12. General but systematic analysis of the vocabulary, syntax and sonority of a passage on death. Concludes that it is not death itself that Colette abhors but whatever is in opposition to life and mobility. Posthumous article preceded by "In memoriam Nicole Houssa" by Fernand Desonay [p. 3-4], who suggests that it contains auguries of Houssa's own death.

1712 Houssa, Nicole. "Au pays de Colette." *Marginales*, no. 69 (Dec. 1959): 2-15. Very personal and melancholy evocation of Colette's village and surrounding region after a pilgrimage there. Attempts to relate her impressions of their features to what Colette says about them, and remarks on the abyss between present reality and Colette's memories. A touching tribute by one of Colette's greatest admirers.

1713 Houssa, Nicole. "Balzac et Colette." *Revue d'histoire littéraire de la France* 60 (Jan.-March 1960): 18-46. Balzac was Colette's favorite writer and one of the few literary greats mentioned in her work. He is the only one on whom she wrote three major pieces. This study itemizes Colette's allusions to Balzac's *Comédie humaine*, noting that her preferences are shared by both Claudine and Sido. It offers statistics proving Colette's interest in Balzac (she mentions 55 of Balzac's characters and alludes to sometimes complex relationships) and confirms her memory of several passages. Published posthumously by Fernand Desonay.

1714   Houssa, Nicole. "Citations, références et allusions littéraires chez
       Colette." *Marche romane* 8 (Jan.-July 1958): 23-51.
       Compendium of literary quotations, references and allusions in
       Colette's work, using the *OCLF*, but excluding the theater
       criticism. Presented by Fernand Desonay.

1715   Houville, Gérard d' [pseud. of Maria de Heredia]. "Adieu Colette."
       Revue des deux mondes, no. 16 (15 Aug. 1954): 738-40.
       Argues that Colette's work ensures her immortality, since her
       life is so much reflected in that of her fictional characters.

1716   Howarth, W.D., and C.L. Walton. "Colette: 'Ma mère et les
       bêtes'." In *Explications: The Techniques of French Literary
       Appreciation*, 251-56. London: Oxford University Press, 1971.
       Model *explication de texte* of two paragraphs from "Ma mère et
       les bêtes" in *La Maison de Claudine*. Somewhat too brief and
       paraphrastic to be a useful stylistic analysis, but contains some
       study of ternary rhythms. Equates Colette with Claudine.

1717   Hubbard, George R. "Louisville and Colette: A Life for Love."
       Dance Magazine 62 (March 1988): 72-77. Report of the
       American première of Domy Reiter-Soffer's ballet *Paradise
       Gained*, on 19 Nov. 1987 by the Louisville Ballet. Its world
       première was by the Irish National Ballet at the 1980 Dublin
       Festival. Comments on the ballet itself mingle here with tidbits
       about Colette's life, on which it was based. Despite minor
       inaccuracies, this article is important in that it illustrates how
       well known Colette has become in America during the past
       decade, and in what diverse fields of artistic activity her
       influence has been felt.

1718   Husson, Henri. "Le palais des merveilles inconnues." *Le Figaro*,
       23 Sept. 1985, 25. Profile of Richard Anacréon, bookseller and
       collector, and owner of a hand-written copy of the chapter
       missing from the first edition of *La Fin de Chéri*. Includes
       anecdote of how he acquired it. See also item 2004.

1719   Jacques, Jean-Pierre. In *Les Malheurs de Sapho*, 22-39, 126-28,
       191-94, 215-17. Paris: Grasset, 1981. This study of the lesbian
       movement in French literature from 1830 to 1914 includes
       many allusions to Colette. Presents her as an authority on the
       subject and quotes statements in *Le Pur et l'impur*.

1720 Jammes, Francis. "Une préface aux *Dialogues de bêtes.*" *Mercure de France*, 15 March 1905, 200-3. Also in most subsequent editions of Colette's *Dialogues de bêtes*, *Sept dialogues de bêtes* and *Douze dialogues de bêtes*. Also in item 1104 La Hire, 242-48. Famous preface to the first book published under Colette's own name, the small collection of animal dialogues that established her as an animal writer. Colette and Jammes never met but she considered him her friend, bound to her by their common love of animals, and the two writers carried on an intermittent correspondence for several years. Colette was always grateful to Jammes for this preface, in which his acuity of judgment is much in evidence. Nearly two decades before publication of *La Maison de Claudine* or *Sido*, he terms her a *bourgeoise* like her mother, interested in every-day things, a natural person rather than the perverse literary figure she was deemed to be by some.

1721 Jammes, Francis. In item 1072 Chauvière, 142-43. Letter to Colette dated 29 May 1905. Although Jammes writes of trivial matters, the kinship he feels for Colette is evident. Praises her *Dialogues de bêtes*.

1722 Jean-Lameere, Nelly. "Colette." *Le Thyrse* 39 (1 May 1937): 189-99. Effusive but sound general evaluation of Colette's work, emphasizing the autobiographical aspects and her treatment of nature. Like most critics of the time, Jean-Lameere assumes that the fictional Sido is identical with Colette's real mother. Offers perceptive remarks about her technique in the short stories, particularly those of *La Femme cachée*.

1723 Jeanne, René. "Colette femme de théâtre." *Le Capitole*, May 1923, non-pag. [10-12]. Double-edged compliment praising Colette for the versatility demonstrated by her career but asserting that she is not nearly as good a dancer or mime as she is a writer.

1724 Jeanne, René. "Colette und der Film." *Antares* 2 (Dec. 1954): 50-52. Summarizes Colette's relationship with the film industry over the years. Suggests that her novels became good film material only when the industry's attentions turned to psychology or characterization. Concludes that, on the whole, casting for her films has not been well done.

1725   Jeanson, Henri. "Reportage sentimental...: un soir... en écoutant
       Colette..." *Le Capitole*, 22 Dec. 1924, non-pag. [30].
       Impressions of audience and speaker during a talk by Colette.

1726   Jeoffroy, Pierrette. "Colette et le music-hall." *Information littéraire*
       13 (May-June 1961): 97-103. Detects the same qualities serving
       Colette the writer as Colette the music-hall artist. Summarizes
       her music-hall career and includes excerpts of press notices.

1727   Jeune, Simon. "A propos de 'La Maison de Claudine'." *Information
       littéraire* 20 (March-April 1968): 84-85. Refutes statement in
       the *OCLF* that the 1930 *La Maison de Claudine* was re-edited
       from the 1922 edition. Gives reasons for choosing the 1923
       edition as a more harmonious collection of texts than either of
       the others.

1728   Jœcker, Jean-Pierre. "Colette ou la conquête d'un nom." In item
       1057 *Album Masques: Colette*, 7-10. Brief overview of
       Colette's career, stressing her indifference towards public
       opinion, the opposition or neglect she suffered at the hands of
       establishment groups, and her rise to popularity in the face of
       immense obstacles.

1729   Jœcker, Jean-Pierre. "La Vagabonde au Music-Hall." In item 1057
       Album Masques: Colette, 71-78. Continues item 1357
       Carteron, by tracing Colette's life from the time of her
       separation from Willy to about 1912. Judges those years rich in
       experience and invaluable to Colette's career, despite her frequent
       unhappiness. Dwells at length on her relations with Missy and
       other women, stressing that lesbianism was fashionable at the
       time.

1730   Jong, Erica. "Dear Colette." In *Loveroot*, 11-13. New York: Holt,
       Rinehart & Winston, 1975. Free verse poem in which writer
       Jong addresses Colette, whose life and writing, she says, have
       been a source of strength to her.

1731   Jong, Erica. "Intoxicating freedom." In item 0795 Colette, *The
       Other Woman*, vii-xiii. Introduction to translation of *La Femme
       cachée*. Declares freedom to be the principal theme of this
       collection of short stories, and the protagonist of "My friend
       Valentine" to be Colette's *alter ego*.

1732 Jong, Erica. "Reading 'The Vagabond'." *Mademoiselle* 79 (May 1974): 108. Terms Renée Néré one of the first feminist heroines of the modern novel and one of its first female artists. Rejects the notion that *La Vagabonde* is autobiographical, because Renée's choice at the end does not reflect Colette's own.

1733 Joseph, Jean R. "'Marcel Proust,' ou les métamorphoses du portrait." *Romanic Review* 75 (Nov. 1984): 492-503. Attempts to show that the figure in Colette's portrait of Proust in *Trait pour trait* consists of a network of symbols, and that the central paragraph works as a pivot. Insists that it also reflects the pattern of Proust's relationship to his own work from his early doubts to his anticipation of death. The final section, which establishes a schema of phrases from Proust's works that find an echo in Colette's, is unconvincing.

1734 Joudrain, Isabelle. "Les mets et les mots dans 'La Maison de Claudine'." *Littérature*, no. 47 (Oct. 1982): 68-82. Analyzes references to food in *La Maison de Claudine*. Uses as premise the notion that the desire for food expresses a broader desire for the material world. Equates eating with sexuality, to some extent. Not a convincing article, in that quotations used in illustration are identified only by title and not examined in context, nor is the book's place among Colette's works taken into consideration.

1735 Jouhandeau, Marcel. "L'art d'écrire tient du dessin, de la sculpture et de la peinture." *Arts*, 9 Jan. 1957, 5. Includes paragraph recalling Colette's voice.

1736 Jouhandeau, Marcel. "Colette." In *Carnets de l'écrivain*, 3rd ed., 346-48. Paris: Gallimard, 1957. Fragments from writer's notebook include anecdote about Colette's mischievousness in or about 1924, and report of a conversation in which she mentions that she still wants to write to her mother, even after the latter's death. Both are developed in item 1739.

1737 Jouhandeau, Marcel. "Colette." *Nouvelle Revue des deux mondes* 5 (May 1979): 388. Also in *Portraits*, 91-92. Brussels: Jacques Antoine, 1988. Brief note, stressing the youthfulness of Colette in old age, and recalling the quality of her voice.

1738   Jouhandeau, Marcel. [No title]. *Figaro littéraire*, 24 Jan. 1953, 5.
       Memories of a visit to Colette during which she taught
       Jouhandeau much about pigeons. Recalls the extraordinary
       quality of her voice.

1739   Jouhandeau, Marcel. In *Que la vie est une fête: journaliers 8
       (1961)*, 215-17. Paris: Gallimard, 1966. Develops themes from
       item 1736 and adds an anecdote as evidence that Colette was
       hard-hearted towards animals.

1740   Jourdan-Morhange, Hélène. "Il y a trois jours Colette m'a dit..."
       Lettres françaises, 15 Jan. 1953, 1, 4. Violinist Morhange
       portrays Colette giving advice to conductor Charles Münch,
       relates anecdotes illustrating Colette's musical aptitude and
       achievements, and outlines her collaboration with Ravel.

1741   Jourdan-Morhange, Hélène. "La regarder vivre était plus beau que
       tout." *Lettres françaises*, 12 Aug. 1954, 1, 5. Memories of
       Colette at Nice and at Saint Tropez. Expresses gratitude for
       Colette's teaching so many to savor the present moment.

1742   Jourdan-Morhange, Hélène. "Ravel et Colette ou la collaboration
       inattendue." *Revue de Paris* 64 (Dec. 1957): 134-38. An account
       of Colette's relations with Ravel, by one who knew both of
       them personally. Quotes freely from Colette's work and her
       correspondence with Ravel, but without indicating dates or
       chronology. Reminds readers that Ravel, too, loved animals and
       adored his mother.

1743   Jouvenel, Bertrand de. "Colette." *Time & Tide* 35 (14 Aug. 1954):
       1075-76. Also in *Time & Tide Anthology*, edited by Anthony
       Lejeune, 275-78. London: André Deutsch, 1956. Touching
       white-wash article by Colette's step-son written just after her
       death. Insists that no writer has been more persistently
       misunderstood than Colette. Asserts that she was without
       ambition or interest in political events, and that one of her great
       joys was communicating her vision to others.

1744   Jouvenel, Bertrand de. "Colette." In *Un Voyageur dans le siècle
       1903-1945*, 54-58. Paris: Laffont, 1980. Recounts his first
       meeting with Colette, his impressions then and later, their
       vacations together, and the good influence that Colette had on

him. Refers cautiously to their relationship just before Colette's divorce from his father, depicting it as innocent but misinterpreted by others. Important biographical article, less because of what it says than because of what it neglects to say. Also casual allusions to Colette throughout the book.

1745 Jouvenel, Bertrand de. "Il y a trente ans..." In item 0013 *Sido: Lettres à sa fille*, i-ii. Brief homage, stressing the importance of Colette's mother in her life.

1746 Jouvenel, Bertrand de. "La vérité sur 'Chéri'." In item 0053 *OP* 2, lv-lviii. Muted account of his liaison with Colette. Rejects the popular notion that it was the inspiration for the Chéri novels. Insists that *Le Blé en herbe* is based on an innocent relationship between him and Pamela Paramythioti, and that Colette de Jouvenel's memories of the English governess so affectionately depicted in the Bel-Gazou stories were less than fond.

1747 Jouvenel, Colette de. In *Colette de Jouvenel*. Paris: Société des Amis de Colette, 1982. 41p. Special issue of the *Cahiers Colette* consists entirely of material written by Colette's daughter. Much of it reveals Colette de Jouvenel as a melancholy person. "Notes et réflexions" is a very personal compendium of meditations on the disturbing effect on her of statements made by her mother, such as her comments on Léo's apparent inability to recover from the family's financial ruin, and Captain Colette's inaptitude for business. Also includes reminiscences of her childhood. "Bêtes familières" consists of short descriptive passages about animals, occasionally echoing her mother's work. "Colette" is a series of brief but interesting notes about her mother. Colette de Jouvenel offers the opinion that in writing about her heroines, Colette was able to expel the part of herself that they represented. "Lettres" are to Bernard Gavoty, Léon Delanoë and Jenny Bellay. In the single letter to Gavoty, dated 7 Sept. 1973, Colette de Jouvenel expresses admiration for her mother and recalls her tenderness and warmth. This letter contains interesting portraits of both parents, Colette and her second husband, Henry de Jouvenel. The six letters to Delanoë date from April 1978 to Oct. 1979 and touch on a variety of subjects, most of them trivial. They do, however, contain often negative comments about books on Colette. The two letters to Jenny Bellay are of 1980 and are inconsequential.

Although this collection of short pieces contains no major material, it is extremely evocative in the over-all picture it offers, not just of Colette de Jouvenel herself, but of Colette's relationships with her family.

1748   Joyeux, Odette. "Colette que j'ai connue." In item 1060 *Autour de Colette à Saint-Tropez*, non-pag. [69-78]. Reminiscences by actress-writer Joyeux, from Colette's first years at Saint Tropez to her old age. Describes how early negative impressions of Colette's brusqueness were finally transformed into appreciation of her understanding and penetrating mind.

1749   Jubécourt, Gérard Sthème de. In *Robert Brasillach, critique littéraire*, 31-32, 119-21. Lausanne: Les Amis de Robert Brasillach, 1972. This assessment of Brasillach as literary critic frequently alludes to the great admiration that he felt for Colette from his early years and the influence that she had on his style. Studies two articles that Brasillach published on Colette in the *Revue française* in 1931, and concludes that he was indulgent towards her.

1750   Jurt, Joseph. "Colette." *Neue Zürcher Zeitung*, 18 July 1973, 23. Impressions of a visit to the Bibliothèque Nationale's exhibition of Colette material. Emphasizes her originality and love of life.

1751   Kasterska, Maria. "Sophie Nalkowska: une Colette polonaise." *Revue mondiale* 3 (March 1933): 56-58. This early study of the foremost Polish female novelist of the time compares her with Colette because of her subtle analysis of the feelings of women, and her sympathy for the humble and for animals. However, Nalkowska is judged to be deeper intellectually and to have less charm and passion.

1752   Kemp, Peter. "Roguish reminders." *Times Literary Supplement*, no. 4320 (17 Jan. 1986): 62. Negative review of British television film on Colette. Terms it an inaccurate and titivating portrayal of her life. Reproaches its makers for omitting all mention of Maurice Goudeket, Colette's third husband.

1753   Kemp, Robert. "Colette, un sage." *Revue littéraire*, no. 11 (March-April 1954): 1-2. General effusion of compliments to accompany extracts of *La Vagabonde*, *Le Blé en herbe* and

L'Etoile vesper in this special issue devoted to Colette. Terms her a philosopher in her attitude towards old age.

1754 Ketchum, Anne Duhamel. "Colette and the Enterprise of Writing: A Reappraisal." In item 1076 *Colette: The Woman, The Writer*, 22-31. Refutes the popular notion that Colette was politically unaware, insisting instead that her work is an expression of her experience of the social order. Maintains that her illness soon after her marriage was a political act. Discusses several novels in the light of these ideas, asserting that in them Colette was denouncing the totalitarianism of men and thereby that of the state.

1755 Ketchum, Anne Duhamel. "Defining an Ethics from a Later Short Story by Colette." *Continental, Latin-American and Francophone Women Writers: Selected Papers from the Wichita State University Conference on Foreign Literature 1984-1985*, edited by Eunice Myers and Ginette Adamson, 71-77. Lanham, Md.: University Press of America, 1987. Interprets *Le Tendron* [*The Tender Shoot*] as a feminist statement of revolt against men's use of women as objects of ego-satisfaction, with Louisette's mother as the incarnation of an attitude affirming the dignity and self-respect of women. Views her as one of Colette's last fictional expressions of an ideal which had taken her decades to develop.

1756 Kies, Albert, and Claude Pichois. "Un oncle de Colette, Eugène Landoy, journaliste franco-belge." *Bulletin de l'Académie royale de langue et de littérature françaises* 34:1 (1956): 260-70. Biography of Colette's maternal uncle, Belgian journalist Eugène Landoy. Establishes parallels between Colette's gift for writing and love of life and similar characteristics displayed by members of her mother's family.

1757 Kloepfer, R., V. Borsò-Borgarello, J. Mecke, S. Kleinert and E. Stern. "La production du sens dans 'Chéri' de Colette (1920)." In item 1077 *Colette, Nouvelles Approches critiques*, 117-29. Analysis of *Chéri* from a narratological perspective. Stresses importance of the opening scene and analyzes its techniques. Especially interesting are remarks on the tension between the perceptual and the emotional levels, and on the use of flashbacks.

1758 Kogan, P.S. "Colette vue par l'étranger: en U.R.S.S." Trans.
Wladimir Pozner. In item 1072 Chauvière, 271-73. Attempts to
detect traces of communist aspirations in Colette's work. Insists
that in particular *La Fin de Chéri* reveals her distaste for the
decadence of bourgeois life, because of the humiliating role that
it assigns to women and the small value it accords to labor.

1759 Köhler, Hartmut. "Traduire en allemand l'œuvre de Colette." In
item 1077 *Colette, Nouvelles Approches Critiques*, 177-88.
Notes a paucity of German translations of Colette's work and
the difficulties of translating it satisfactorily, then compares
Erna Redtenbacher's translation of a passage from *La Naissance
du jour* with the original, passing judgment on its strengths and
weaknesses.

1760 Kresh, Paul. "These Women Can Speak for Themselves." *New
York Times*, 28 Nov. 1976, 32. Brief summary of recordings of
women reading their own works. Recommends a reading in
French by Colette herself, and one of passages in translation
read by others.

1761 Lacher, Walter. "De Colette à Giraudoux ou de la limite du
réalisme descriptif." In *Le Réalisme dans le roman
contemporain*, 250-56. Geneva: Imprimerie centrale, 1940.
Attempts to assess the quality and characteristics of Colette's
portrayal of the real by comparing it with that of writers current
at the time. Concludes that it is precise but superficial in that
she does not seek to portray great psychological depth.
Recognizes the importance of her images but considers that she
sometimes indulges in fantasy.

1762 Lacretelle, Jacques de. In item 1072 Chauvière, 172. Undated letter
from Lacretelle to Colette thanking her for a dedication and
expressing admiration for her work.

1763 Lacretelle, Jacques de. [No title]. *Figaro littéraire*, 24 Jan. 1953, 5.
Briefly declares preference for Colette's word portraits.

1764 Lagarde, André, and Laurent Michard. "Colette." In *XXe siècle*,
523-31. Paris: Bordas, 1969. Coll. Textes et littérature. Short
summary of Colette's life and work for students precedes
extracts from *La Maison de Claudine*, *Gigi*, *La Chatte*, *La*

Naissance du jour and *Sido*. Emphasizes her ability to evoke sensations and her enthusiasm for life. Signals a natural morality and a nobility of vision, especially in the later years.

1765 Lake, Carlton. In *Baudelaire to Beckett: A Century of French Art & Literature (A Catalogue of Books, Manuscripts and Related Material Drawn from the Collection of the Humanities Research Center)*, 60-63. Austin: University of Texas at Austin, 1976. Catalogued material includes first editions, manuscript pages, and letters from and about Colette.

1766 Lalanne, Louise [Guillaume Apollinaire]. "Littérature féminine." *Les Marges*, March 1909, 8-13. In this overview of women literary figures of the first decade, Apollinaire judges Colette to have as much talent as the more famous Anna de Noailles, but confesses that she intimidates him because of her original personality and her independence.

1767 Lalanne, Louise [Guillaume Apollinaire]. "Littérature féminine: Colette Willy. Lucie Delarue-Mardrus." *Les Marges*, March 1909, 126-32. Although Apollinaire devotes twice as much space to a review of Lucie Delarue-Mardrus' latest novel as he does to Colette's *Les Vrilles de la vigne*, he expresses confidence in Colette's writing future. He specifically praises her talent, the naturalness and beauty of her language, and her lack of intellectual pretention. It is to the credit of Apollinaire, who was to become one of the great lights of French poetry, that he had so many good things to say about Colette at this early stage of her career.

1768 Lalou, René. "Chère et grande Colette..." *Revue des hommes et mondes*, no. 98 (Sept. 1954): 161-66. Also, under the title "Qui était Colette?" in *A la page*, no. 2 (Aug. 1964): 190-96. In memoriam, including sketch of Colette's life, works and honors. Recognizes Colette's debt to both parents, especially her mother. Compares her with Lucretius.

1769 Lalou, René. In *Histoire de la littérature française contemporaine: 1870 à nos jours*, 640-43. Paris: Crès, 1924. Although Lalou follows then-current opinion in declaring that Colette's work is inspired solely by sensation, he asserts that the subtlety and depth with which she portrays it makes her one of the most

original writers of the time. He also lauds her for portraying
sexual relations openly and naturally. Considers her secondary
male characters to be more interesting than the principal ones,
which he says serve only as pretexts for ideas. A more
perceptive article than most written during the same decade.

1770   Lanco, Yvonne. "Colette à Belle-Ile-en-Mer." *Mercure de France*, 1
March 1955, 556-57. Anecdote about Colette in the early days
of her marriage, vacationing with Willy.

1771   Lanoux, Armand. "Colette, la bonne sorcière..." *Revue des lettres*
108 (Oct.-Dec. 1973): 15-29. Abridged version in *Cahiers
Colette*, no. 1 (1977): 63-72. Address of 17 Oct. 1973 to the
Société des Gens de Lettres. Views Colette as our contemporary
because of her concern for the environment, for nature and for
the quality of life; because of her feminist-oriented attitude to
male-female relationships; and because her preoccupation with
observation shows parallels with that of the *école du regard*
stream of the new novelists. Compares and contrasts her
fictional love situations with Maupassant's. Considers her
feminism to be very complex. Title refers to an ancient wisdom
and the possession of old truths assumed to have been passed on
to Colette by her mother. A rambling but worth-while article.

1772   Laplane, M. "La femme dans les lettres français[es] d'aujourd'hui:
de Colette à Simone de Beauvoir." *Bulletin des bibliothèques de
l'Institut français en Espagne* 37 (Nov. 1949): 9-15. Ranks
Colette above all other French women writers, but insists that
she is a creature of instinct with a marvellous literary vision.
Alleges that her work expresses a polarity between her
aspiration towards an impossible purity and her resigned
acceptance of the impure. Emphasizes her vital energy and ties
with nature, in effect portrays her as a primitive genius.

1773   Laporte, René. "Il n'y a plus de Chéri." *Gazette des Lettres*, 29 Oct.
1949, 9. Claims to detect in Chéri vestiges of the romantic
hero. Declares that the novel of which he is the hero can be
viewed as an historic document, portraying a way of life that is
history.

1774   Laprade, Jacques de. "Colette chez les Goncourt." *Arts*, no. 15 (11
May 1945): 3. Views as extraordinary Francis Jammes' insight

into Colette's mind, as expressed in his preface to the 1905 *Sept dialogues de bêtes*, because Jammes' strict moral and religious standards were so different from Colette's. Terms Colette's world limited but judges that her limits will serve her immortality.

1775 Larguier, Léo. "Colette chez Drouant." *Carrefour*, 19 May 1945, 5. Account of a conversation between Colette and fellow member of the Goncourt Academy. Colette assures Larguier that her writing owes much to hard work.

1776 Larnac, Jean. "Le règne de Mme de Noailles et de Mme Colette." In *Histoire de la littérature féminine en France*, 219-43. Paris: Kra, 1929. Attempts to place Colette's work in the context of then-known feminine literature. Accuses Colette and her female literary colleagues of confessional self-indulgence, thereby relegating men to second rank, and of attempting to elevate sensation above morality and intelligence. Considers that Colette's style and her love of nature redeem these negative features in her work. Larnac expresses many out-moded ideas about men and women--for instance, he deems it natural that women should write about love and sensibility, on the grounds that life limits women's perspective on all other matters--but he does offer some acute observations on other aspects of her work, and his criticism ranks among the most enlightened of the decade.

1777 Larnac, Jean. "...Sans avoir vu Colette." *Vient de paraître*, no. 72 (Feb. 1928): 79-80. Interesting details about how Larnac prepared his book on Colette. Refers to his correspondence with Colette's former schoolteacher, as well as to conversations with her former schoolmates and others. Says that the essence of the person can be found in her books.

1778 Larnac, Jean. "Le style de Colette." *Revue du siècle*, 5 (15 Dec. 1926): 7-13. Early essay on Colette's already famous style, emphasizing the plasticity of her language and her ability to evoke sensations. Includes some analysis of her use of verbs, adjectives and images. A modified form of much of this article was incorporated into Larnac's book on Colette, most of it into chapter nine.

1779   Lastinger, Valérie C. "'La Naissance du jour': la désintégration du 'moi' dans un roman de Colette." *French Review* 61 (March 1988): 542-51. Excellent article refuting the modern notion that Colette's work as a whole represents a search for psychological integrity. Draws on the entire corpus of her work, but especially *La Maison de Claudine, Sido* and *La Naissance du jour*, to support her thesis. Argues that *La Naissance du jour* is entirely fiction, and the mother figure in it likewise. Analyzes the interplay between real and fictional identities to suggest that the novel may represent the application of Proust's theories as presented in *Contre Sainte-Beuve*. Altogether, a subtle and unusual interpretation, which offers a valuable counter-weight to the many articles adopting as premise the opposite view.

1780   Laurent, Jacques. "Voici la gloire." *La Parisienne*, no. 21 (Oct. 1954): 1083-92. Meditates on the reason for Colette's being given a state funeral, the only two other writers receiving one in the preceding thirty years being Paul Valéry and Anatole France. Concludes that the state does not accord its honors, even by street names, on a logical basis. Asserts that Colette has been so honored because of her sex, her age and her personal renown, rather than because of her work.

1781   Léautaud, Paul. In *Journal littéraire*, edited by Pascal Pia and Maurice Guyot, 221, 305-7, 564-65. Paris: Mercure de France, 1968. Contains several passages mentioning Colette, dating from 1907 to 1951. Anecdotes and conversations reported are interesting but gossipy. Earlier ones show Léautaud attracted to Colette and at ease with her. Later he considers her work "commercial" and is scandalized at *Mes apprentissages*. Also casual references to Colette throughout the book.

1782   Lebrun, Michel. "Les films dans l'œuvre de Colette." In item 1060 *Autour de Colette à Saint-Tropez*, non.-pag. [79-106]. Offers a summary of Colette's film activity and of films made from her books. Cites names of many persons involved in their production. Evaluates each film, giving brief information on its reception by the public. Of special interest are quotations of publicity paragraphs written for some films. Expresses amazement that her work could still evoke scandal in 1950, and speculates on Hollywood's role in the inclusion of a moral at the end of the film version of *Gigi*.

1783 Lecarme-Tabone, Eliane. "Colette et Zola: l'hypothèse d'une réécriture dans 'La Maison de Claudine'." *Roman 20-50*, no. 2 (Dec. 1986): 137-46. Interesting article which attempts to shed light on Colette's creative process by tracing the relationship between several of the short pieces in *La Maison de Claudine* and specific works by Zola. Analyzes the effects of the difference in focalization and other modifications of place or voice in an effort to show how Colette transforms or "re-writes" Zola into her own creations.

1784 Leclercq, Pierre-Robert. "Le moi-je de Colette, ou l'affirmation d'une écriture-femme." *Etudes* 364 (June 1986): 785-92. Offers salient remarks about the assertion of the feminine presence of the writer in Colette's books. Adopts as premise that her books represent a long process of discovery, of herself and others. Considers *La Retraite sentimentale* a landmark publication in that its absence of significant male characters makes it an expression of integral feminine writing, that is, of women writing *as women* rather than as an adjunct or counterpoise to the masculine.

1785 Leclere, Marie-Françoise. "La belle saison de Colette." *Le Point*, no. 405 (23 June 1980): 109-10. Provides background information about the television film *La Naissance du jour*, starring Danielle Delorme in the role of the narrator, Madame Colette. Delorme had already played other Colette roles, notably Gigi, Minne and Mitsou.

1786 Le Clézio, J.-M. G. "Voici que nous nous sentons pris comme dans un piège." *Le Monde*, 25 Jan. 1973, 21. Also in *Cahiers Colette*, no. 1 (1977): 73-76. Offered as representative of what young writers think about Colette upon her centennial. Identifies Colette's genius as the ability to transform the mundane into the marvellous. Detects in her traces of wisdom coupled with sadness. Assumes Colette speaks through her heroines.

1787 Lefèvre, Frédéric. "Une heure avec Colette." *Nouvelles littéraires*, 27 March 1926, 1-2. Also, under title "Colette," in *Une heure avec...*, vol. 4, 129-42. Paris: Gallimard, 1927. Long light-hearted report of an interview during which, Lefèvre claims, Colette showed him 28 student exercise books of manuscript, including those of *Minne* and its sequel, with notes in Willy's handwriting in the margins. She also admitted to observing the post-World War I *angst* considered by some critics to characterize the hero of *La Fin de Chéri*, but denied feeling it herself. It is tempting to compare Colette's description of Proust as she is shown here depicting him at Madame de Caillavet's with written portraits of him in her later works.

1788   Lefèvre, Frédéric. "An Hour with Colette." *The Living Age* 347 (Feb. 1935): 533-37. Much more serious but less interesting interview than item 1787. Colette emphasizes the value of all experience, even negative, and her need to strive for perfection in her writing.

1789   Legrand-Chabrier. "Colette vagabonde de music-hall." *Le Capitole*, 22 Dec. 1924, non-pag. [35-36]. Attempts to define Colette's presentation of the music-hall in *L'Envers du music-hall*. Praises her abilities as both performer and critic.

1790   Le Hardouin, Maria. "Le sens de l'universel dans la littérature féminine." *Table ronde* 99 (March 1956): 102-3. Adopts traditional premises on the domains of men and women writers. Uses Colette as an example of women's attachment to love, nature and the real, and their lack of interest in general or abstract matters. Insists that, despite this difference, both sexes retain a perspective on the universal.

1791   Lehmann, Rosamond. [No title]. *Figaro littéraire*, 24 Jan. 1953, 5. Brief congratulations on the occasion of Colette's eightieth birthday. Cites Shakespeare's "Age cannot wither her..."

1792   Lejeune, Philippe. In *Je est un autre: l'autobiographie de la littérature aux médias*, 122-24, 135-37. Paris: Seuil, 1980. Informative passages on Colette's radio and television broadcasts, which were very popular with her readers but which have been generally neglected by researchers. Gives details of the 1950 series of interviews by André Parinaud, many of which have been lost. Includes descriptive analysis of Colette's voice, terming her adversarial and suspicious towards interviewers, even mischievous or malicious at times. A fascinating article. Also brief allusions to Colette throughout the book.

1793 Le Pavec, Michèle. "L'écriture de Colette: son évolution, ses supports." *Cahiers Colette*, no. 10 (1988): 87-100. Argues that the difficulties of dating manuscripts of Colette's articles can be eased by studying Colette's handwriting and the paper used. Notes that Colette herself found handwriting revealing; quotes passages in which she discusses the subject. Uses fac-similes of Colette's handwriting to illustrate its evolution from 1896. Stresses the value of handwriting analysis to identify passages inserted into a manuscript long after the original was written. Since such passages are numerous in Colette's case, Le Pavec recommends great caution to scholars studying them.

1794 Le Pavec, Michèle. "Les manuscrits de Colette à la Bibliothèque Nationale." *Cahiers Colette*, no. 10 (1988): 43-85. Repertoire of the manuscripts, letters and other documents in possession of the Bibliothèque Nationale in Paris. Also notes major lacunæ. Includes descriptions, catalogue numbers and sources. An essential article for researchers working on manuscript material.

1795 Le Rider, Georges. "Les acquisitions de la Bibliothèque Nationale: manuscrits de Barrès et de Colette." *Le Monde*, 19 July 1979, 1, 16. Details of manuscripts and documents acquired by the Bibliothèque Nationale in 1977 and 1979.

1796 Le Roux, B. "Le mal du siècle (1920-1940) dans 'La Fin de Chéri' de Colette." *Ecole III* 64 (21 Oct. 1972): 3-6. Model for a student analysis, focusing on the last pages of *La Fin de Chéri* and presenting Chéri's psychology as that of a mediocre but typical person of his age. Insists that Colette wished to portray in him the effects of World War I.

1797 Leroy, Gilbert. "Colette chez elle." *Gavroche*, 10 May 1945, 5. Account of an interview with Colette just after her election to the Goncourt Academy. Contains only trivial material.

1798 Leroy, Paul. "Colette." In *Femmes d'aujourd'hui: Colette, Lucie Delarue-Mardrus*, 17-110. Rouen: Imprimerie H. Maugard, 1936. Trifling series of anecdotes, impressions, reminiscences and general comment on Colette's life and career, arranged more or less chronologically. The most useful section argues that Colette rather than Willy wrote music criticism published under Claudine's name. Quotes Colette's own works freely.

1799   Lesser, Simon O. "The Wages of Adjustment: 'Chéri' and 'The Last of Chéri'." *Minnesota Review* 4 (Winter 1964): 212-25. Asserts that the suffering of the two principal characters of the two Chéri novels redeems them, in the readers' eyes, for their moral defects. Loosely interprets their relationship in Œdipean terms, but does not push the analysis very far.

1800   Lherbier, Marcel. "En souvenir..." *Lettres françaises*, 12 Aug. 1954, 5. Ranks Colette higher as poet than Anna de Noailles.

1801   Liagre, Christina de. "Homage to Colette." *House & Garden* 158 (Feb. 1986): 108-17, 215-16. Interesting pictorial article on the re-decoration of Colette's former apartment in the Palais Royal. Reports an interview with its decorator and present resident Jacques Grange. See also item 1177.

1802   Liebrecht, Henri. [No title]. *Figaro littéraire*, 24 Jan. 1953, 5. Expresses pride that the Belgian Academy elected Colette to its membership before any French academy did. Insists that she deserves to be a member of the Académie Française.

1803   Lignières, H.-L.de. "Les trois lauréates de 1966: 'Nous admirons Colette'." *Arts-Loisirs*, no. 71 (1 Feb. 1967): 14-15. Interviews by Lignières with Edmonde Charles-Roux, Irène Monesi and Marie-Claire Blais, winners of the 1966 Prix Goncourt, Prix Femina and Prix Médicis respectively. Charles-Roux declares that Colette's immortal creations are her mature heroines such as Léa, Julie de Carneilhan and Madame Dalleray. Monesi confesses to being unable to identify with Colette's world but admires her skill of portrayal. Blais expresses general admiration for Colette's work.

1804   Ligot, Marie-Thérèse. "La description chez Colette." In *Le Renouvellement des techniques romanesques dans la littérature française 1920-1940*, 137-44. Katowice: University of Silesia, 1983. Interprets the totality of Colette's work as the expression of a personal search, her writing activity as an attempt to return to her origins, and her choice of the family name as both a gesture to redeem her father's failed career and an affirmation of her own femininity.

1805 Lilar, Suzanne. In *Le Malentendu du deuxième sexe*, 152-54. Paris: Presses universitaires de France, 1970. Simone de Beauvoir's contempt of Colette as a non-feminist and non-activist is well known. Feminist studies often refer to the two women as representative of two different generations or polarized points of view. This study on Beauvoir contrasts the attitudes of the two women on maternity and sexuality, and chooses Colette's as the healthier.

1806 Lilienfeld, Jane. "The Magic Spinning Wheel: Straw to Gold-- Colette, Willy, and Sido." In *Mothering the Mind: Twelve Studies of Writers and their Silent Partners*, edited by Ruth Perry and Martine Watson Brownley, 164-78. New York: Holmes & Meier, 1984. Although not the same article as item 1807, the ideas presented on Colette are similar. Title alludes to the Rumpelstiltskin myth, with Willy cast in the role of Rumpelstiltskin, and Colette's schooldays seen as the straw to be spun into the gold of the Claudine novels.

1807 Lilienfeld, Jane. "Reentering Paradise: Cather, Colette, Woolf and their Mothers." In *The Lost Tradition: Mothers and Daughters in Literature*, edited by Cathy N. Davidson and E.M. Brouer, 160-75. New York: Ungar, 1979. Examines Colette's relationship to her mother, to Willy and to the Marquise de Morny. Draws parallels with the situations of Willa Cather and Virginia Woolf. Not always completely accurate in its premises or details.

1808 Lipatti, Valentin. "Colette." *Secolul XX*, no. 156 (1974): 121-24. Brief overview of Colette's life and works. Accompanied by Rumanian translation of extracts from her writing.

1809 Livermore, Ann. "Colette's Chopin." *Music Review* 33 (Nov. 1972): 275-84. Argues that Colette drew her inspiration for the relationship between Chéri and Léa from the one between George Sand and Chopin. Draws parallels between characters, events, situations, physical characteristics, conversations, habits, psychologies, tastes, preferences and even vocabulary in the light of this hypothesis. A fascinating and provocative article, even without source references.

1810   Louria, Yvette. In *La Convergence stylistique chez Proust*, rev. ed.,
       179-80. Paris: Nizet, 1971. The book analyzes Proust's use of
       the rhetorical device of *convergences*, then compares it with use
       by other writers, among them Colette.

1811   Louÿs, Pierre. "Un jugement de Colette Willy." *Cahiers Colette*,
       no. 10 (1988): 101-2. Anecdote once related by writer Louÿs to
       Colette, his account of her verdict on his behavior, and his
       expression of self-doubt as a consequence.

1812   Louÿs, Pierre. In item 1072 Chauvière, 162-63. Undated letter to
       Colette, expressing admiration of her style.

1813   Luz, Pierre de. "Colette et la langue française." *Neuphilologische
       Mitteilungen* 37 (1936): 226-44. Discusses Colette's use of
       language over the years. Terms Willy a pernicious influence, of
       which Colette had to break free in order to achieve her most
       successful use of language with *La Naissance du jour*.

1814   Lydon, Mary. "Myself and M/others." *Sub-Stance*, no. 32 (1981):
       6-14. Explores Colette's relationships with members of her
       family, including Willy, and with the Colette family home, in
       an attempt to identify psychological reasons for the writing of
       La Maison de Claudine and *Sido* in particular, and for her
       adoption of her father's surname. Suggests that her books can
       all be interpreted as inscription of the family names.

1815   Maack, Annigret. In *Die Rezeption Französischer Literatur in
       England nach dem Zweiten Weltkrieg*, 93-98. Bonn: Bouvier,
       1978. Traces English reception of French writers between the
       two World Wars. Classifies Colette, not with novelists and
       prose writers, but among the "Entertainers," along with
       Cocteau, Queneau, Aymé and Simenon. Considers that her
       vision of human nature is deeper than Somerset Maugham's.
       Notes the absence of all mention of her in some major histories
       of French literature. Concludes that a national puritanical strain
       causes many English critics to feel insecure about assessing
       Colette's books, or indeed those of any French writers. Quotes
       opinions of many English critics.

1816   Mac Orlan, Pierre. "Un prodigieux instinct vital..." *Figaro
       littéraire*, 24 Jan. 1953, 3. Humorously claims to prove the

extent of his homage to Colette on the occasion of her eightieth birthday by describing how her influence has caused him to try to understand what goes on in the mind of his own bulldog.

1817　Magny, Claude-Edmonde. In *Littérature et critique*, 398. Paris: Payot, 1971. Questions whether Colette's work is substantial enough to be ranked as literature.

1818　Maillard, Lucien. "Colette." *Comédie-Française* 17 (March 1973): 8-10. Publicity for a "Soirée littéraire: Colette," 16-17 April 1973, consists of summary of Colette's life and early career. Highlights her self-discipline and search for perfection, also the influence of her mother. Points out the rarity of her suffering no eclipse in renown, either during her lifetime or after her death. Considers her one of France's ambassadors to the world.

1819　Makward, Christiane. "Colette and Signs: A Partial Reading of a Writer 'Born *Not* to Write'." In item 1076 *Colette: The Woman, The Writer*, 185-92. Considers Bellon's 1950 film as the final jewel in the crown of Colette's mythology. Terms "Le poète" in *Journal à Rebours* her most serious statement on art. Notes her fascination with non-verbal graphic forms.

1820　Malige, Jeannie. "Préface." In item 0013 *Sido: lettres à sa fille*, iii-x. Brief general summary of Colette's relations with her mother, as background to the letters.

1821　Mallet, Robert. "Introduction." In item 0001 *Une Amitié inattendue*, 9-21. Good detailed account of Colette's friendship with Francis Jammes. Attributes their tie to common traits: a love of nature, a sense of poetry, and the importance of the mother in both their lives. Includes the text of one of Colette's earliest pen-portraits, an impressive evocation of Jammes himself, whom she never met; it was later incorporated into *Paysages et portraits* as "Pour Francis Jammes."

1822　Mallet-Joris, Françoise. "Discours." *Bulletin de l'Académie royale de langue et de littérature françaises* 51:3-4 (1973): 157-73. Also in item 1121 *Pour le centenaire de Colette*, 20-36, and in *Cahiers Colette*, no. 1 (1977): 41-60, under the title "Une vocation féminine?" Text of an address given before the Belgian Academy, 15 Dec. 1973. Sees Colette's career as a fulfilment of the failed destiny of both her father and her first husband. Terms her not a feminist, despite the strength and dignity of her female protagonists.

English translation [abridged]: "A Womanly Vocation." Trans. Eleanor Reid Gibbard. In item 1076 *Colette: The Woman, The Writer*, 7-15.

1823   Mallet-Joris, Françoise. "Rendez-vous avec Colette." *Le Point*, no. 19 (29 Jan. 1973): 64-65. Brief but interesting article, wherein Mallet-Joris recalls her feeling of intimidation on meeting Colette. Terms her more poet than novelist and identifies the secret of her genius as her ability to endow her characters with a sense of mystery at the same time as she seems to portray them fully.

1824   Malraux, Clara. "Travaux de dames." In *Visages et perspectives de l'art moderne*, edited by Jean Jacquot, 155-61. Paris: Eds. du Centre national de la recherche scientifique, 1956. Attempts to determine Colette's place among twentieth century French women writers. Concludes that she is non-modern because her female characters are interested mostly in every-day things.

1825   Mantéga, Anne de la. "La grande Colette." *Quo Vadis*, no. 74-76 (Oct-Dec. 1954): 49-52. Scathing overview of Colette's work and person. Terms her without talent and a corrupting influence on others. Says that she will be forgotten within ten years.

1826   Marcenac, Jean. "Le cristal de Colette." *Lettres françaises*, 12 Aug. 1954, 4. Uses the metaphor of a crystal to suggest how Colette filters sensations through her intellect and onto the printed page.

1827   Marchal, Lucie. "Une femme ne peut pas écrire 'Le Salaire de la peur'." *Table ronde* 99 (March 1956): 106-7. Brief but cogent assessment of the capacity of male writers to present convincing female characters, and the converse. Marchal concludes that the Claudine novels could never have been written by a man.

1828   Marchand, Léopold. "Colette auteur dramatique." *Le Capitole*, May 1923, non-pag. [7]. Playwright Marchand describes Colette concentrating on her writing even when surrounded by activity but does not actually assess her dramatic works.

1829 Marchessault, Jovette. "L'épicière de la littérature." *La Vie en rose*, no. 18 (July 1984): 50-51. Concise praise of Colette's ability to evoke sensations. Notes that she is but the fourth woman to be published in the Pléiade edition, after George Sand, Madame de Sévigné and Marguerite de Yourcenar.

1830 Marcoin, Francis. "'La Maison de Claudine': ne pas partir ou ne pas rester?" *Roman 20-50*, no. 3 (June 1987): 99-105. Comments on factors contributing to thematic unity of *La Maison de Claudine*. Points out that the house of the title is actually more than one house. Speculates on the relationship of Sido to the themes of liberty and exile.

1831 Margueritte, Eve Paul and Lucie Paul. In *Deux frères, deux sœurs, deux époques littéraires*, 113-14. Paris: [J. Peyronnet], 1951. Brief recollections of Colette as a young woman.

1832 Marie, André. "Madame Colette, Grand Officier de la Légion d'honneur." *Education nationale*, no. 15 (30 April 1953): 10. Partial text of address given during the ceremony awarding Colette the rank of grand officer of the Legion of Honor. Invokes a litany of frequent criticisms against her, then absolves her of all such complaints. Emphasizes her interest in education, especially in the school system, as exhibited in some of her non-fictional works.

1833 Marks, Elaine. "Foreword." In item 0501 *Gigi and Selected Writings*, vii-xvi. Excellent general introduction to Colette's work, with specific comments on every selection in the volume. Insists that the reasons for Colette's non-intellectualism and disinterest in metaphysics can be traced to her upbringing. Emphasizes her absence of sentimentality. Detects in the early works a conflict between lessons learned from her mother and those imposed by Willy. Includes an interesting explanation on the meaning of the pink cactus in *La Naissance du jour*.

1834 Marks, Elaine. "Foreword: Celebrating Colette." In item 1076 *Colette: The Woman, The Writer*, ix-xi. Emphasizes importance of the ambiguity inherent in Colette's mixing of gender, social classes, cultures and even literary genres. Identifies her use of the Madame Colette narrator as one of the main sources of the illusion of reality and the creation of a fiction surrounding her person. Acclaims the "new Colette" recognized by recent critics.

1835   Marks, Elaine. "Lesbian intertextuality." In *Homosexualities and French Literature: Cultural Contexts/Critical Texts*, edited by George Stambolian and Elaine Marks, 353-77. Ithaca: Cornell University Press, 1979. Fine effort to place Colette within the context of writers treating sexual relations between women. Considers *Le Pur et l'impur* to be one of those works which have radically disrupted the western world's view of homosexuality. Includes an excellent analysis of this little-understood work, especially of the section on the two Ladies of Llangollen. An important article for the understanding of Colette's ideas on female homosexuality.

1836   Marti, Anik. "Colette en scène." *Le Figaro*, 29 Oct. 1985, 34. Review of French television programme "Colette, dame seule," based on Colette's own texts and with Dominique Paquet playing Colette during her music-hall days.

1837   Martin, Georges. "Collette [sic] Willy, mime." *Renaissance contemporaine* 5 (10 Feb. 1911): 117-19. Sympathetic review of Colette dancing in "La Chair." Contrasts it favorably with public appearance by the Willy-Polaire-Colette trio some years earlier. Terms Willy's publicity tricks long out-dated.

1838   Martin, Georges. "Une interview de Colette Willy." *Renaissance contemporaine* 7 (10 Jan. 1913): 36-39. Interesting article because of its early date. Written just after publicity about Colette's retirement from the music-hall after her marriage with Henry de Jouvenel. Generally favorable to Colette but, like many critics of a later date, Martin suggests that she whitewashed life in the music-hall, transferring to its performers much of her own sensibility and sense of solitude.

1839   Martin du Gard, Maurice. "Colette." *Nouvelles littéraires*, 26 Jan. 1924, 1. Also in *Impertinences*, 59-65. Paris: Bloch, 1924. Pen-portrait of Colette during her time at *Le Matin*. Some description of the physical environment and activity. Contrasts her sensuality with Stendhal's, terming her novels evidence of the subjection of women to instinct.

1840 Martin du Gard, Maurice. "Colette à l'Académie belge de langue et
de littérature françaises." *Nouvelles littéraires*, 11 April 1936, 1.
Also in *Harmonies critiques*, 27-33. Paris: Sagittaire, 1936.
Report of Colette's reception at the Belgian Academy. Terms it
one of the most important events of the year in Europe's literary
world. Gives long description of the room, the order of events,
Valère Gilles' welcoming speech, Colette's own address, the
ovation, and Colette's clothes. Contrasts Colette with her
predecessor, Anna de Noailles. In short, a vivid picture of this
milestone in Colette's career.

1841 Martin du Gard, Maurice. "Colette à l'Académie belge de langue et
de littérature françaises." *Ecrits de Paris* 224 (March 1964): 102-
5. Also, under the title "Colette académicienne," in *Revue des
deux mondes* 3 (1 June 1968): 334-37. Interesting portrayal of
Colette in 1936, as she accepts her place in the Belgian
Academy. Not always complimentary towards her, Martin du
Gard contrasts her with Anna de Noailles, and presents Colette
as simple yet secretive, claiming that she is difficult to
understand, like all women. Although actually a modified
version of item 1840, this article is intriguing because the
changes made are such that Colette is presented much less
sympathetically than in the earlier version.

1842 Martin du Gard, Maurice. "Colette au 'Matin'." *La Parisienne* 22
(Nov. 1954): 1216-22. Also in *Les Mémorables (1918-1923)*,
135-42. Paris: Flammarion, 1957. Dated 28 Aug. 1921, this
article is a mixture of unsympathetic remarks about the person
Colette and of expressions of admiration for her work. Quotes
unflattering comments about her by several other persons.
Taken with items 1840 and 1841, it illustrates how wavering an
opinion some critics had of Colette during her life-time.

1843 Martine, Claude. "Colette, amie intime." *Arts*, 11 Aug. 1954, 7.
Memories of writer whose discovery of *La Maison de Claudine*
when a schoolgirl led to Colette's having a great influence upon
her in later years.

1844 Martineau, Henri. "Paul-Jean Toulet 'collaborateur' de Willy."
Mercure de France, 1 Oct. 1956, 225-47. Also as *P.-J. Toulet
'collaborateur' de Willy*. Paris: Le Divan, 1957. 91p. Although
the purpose of this article is to assess the extent of Toulet's

collaboration with Willy, it often refers to Colette, both writers having belonged to Willy's stable of writers. Declares that Colette's subsequent treatment of her first husband was unjust, and insists that Willy's methods were not so unusual for the time as they are commonly thought to be.

1845   Mauduit, Jean. "Vous n'êtes pas morte, Colette." *Témoignage chrétien*, 13 Aug. 1954, 5. Supports the Roman Catholic Church's decision not to accord religious burial to Colette but touchingly attempts to justify the promise of a paradisiacal after-life for her on the grounds that she must have been conscious of the lack of a religious dimension in her work.

1846   Mauriac, Claude. "Colette." *Figaro littéraire*, 1 Nov. 1952, 10. Review of Yannick Bellon's much-acclaimed documentary film on Colette. Expresses disappointment at its neglect of Colette's childhood home, but praises its presentation of her in old age. Notes that both she and Jean Cocteau, who also appeared in the film, are ill at ease before the camera.

1847   Mauriac, Claude. "Préface." In item 0061 *Colette par Colette*, 9-16. Also, under the title "Colette méconnue," in *Cahiers Colette*, no. 1 (1977): 9-18. Defines the four works *Les Vrilles de la vigne*, *La Maison de Claudine*, *Sido* and *Mes apprentissages* as memoirs of Colette's early years. Attempts to bring an objective perspective to bear on the question of Colette's ability to distinguish between good and evil. Identifies two directions in her memoirs: one towards a timeless world of childhood with its concomitant loves, the second towards the world of the Belle Epoque.

1848   Mauriac, François. "Eros." In *Journal 1932-1939*, vol. 1, 106-10. Paris: Table ronde, 1947. Echos opinion expressed in item 1849, that Colette's skill purifies the most sordid subject.

1849   Mauriac, François. In "Le roman d'aujourd'hui." *Revue hebdomadaire* 36 (19 Feb. 1927): 265-66. Also, under the title "Le roman," in *Le Roman*, 26-28. Paris: Artisan du livre, 1928. Renowned Catholic writer Mauriac praises Colette's sensitive portrayal of Chéri and Léa, the tragedy of whose lives, he insists, lies in the fact that they are devoted to the joys of the flesh without God.

1850 Mauriac, François. "Votre quatrième jeunesse, chère Colette..." *Figaro littéraire*, 24 Jan. 1953, 1. Finds Colette unchanged from youth to age, and still seeking happiness at age eighty, even though she has abandoned "pleasure."

1851 Mauriac, François. In *Le Nouveau bloc-notes*, vol. 1, 119-22; vol. 2, 266-67; vol. 3, 255-56; vol. 4, 130, 334. Paris: Flammarion, 1961-1970. Notebook entries from 1954 to 1967 include several short passages on Colette. Most refer to her spiritual state but some comment on her personal qualities or her writing. In all, they provide a useful indication of Mauriac's apparently paradoxical attitude towards Colette, whom he liked and admired but whose neglect of Catholic spirituality he deplored. Mauriac attributes to Colette his greater understanding of animals and birds.

1852 Maurice-Amour, L. "Colette et ses musiciens." *France-Illustration*, no. 414 (Sept. 1954): 81. Brief synopsis of Colette's relations with Poulenc, Ravel and Jean-Michel Damase, all of whom set her words to music.

1853 Maurin, Margaret Simpson. "Du mouvement et de l'immobilité dans 'La Chatte' de Colette." *Dalhousie French Studies* 6 (Spring-Summer 1984): 72-83. Reading of *La Chatte*, which explores the significance of motion and immobility with respect to the main characters. Makes some comparison with similar features in *Chéri*. Comments on but does not analyze the novel's triadic features.

1854 Maurois, André. In item 1095 *Hommage à Colette*, non-pag. Brief passage declaring that at recent meetings Colette seemed to be already hovering in spirit between life and death.

1855 Maurois, Michelle. In *Les Cendres brûlantes*, 9, 23, 33-34, 98-105, 473-74. Paris: Flammarion, 1986. Extremely interesting biography of Jeanne Pouquet, daughter-in-law of Madame Arman de Caillavet at the time Colette and Willy frequented the latter's salon, contains long passages on the couple's relations with their hostess and with Anatole France. Gives reasons for their falling-out with Madame Arman and describes their futile efforts to heal the breach. Contains fragments of correspondence between Colette and Jeanne Pouquet.

1856   May, Georges. In *L'Autobiographie*, 50-51. Paris: Presses
       universitaires de France, 1979. Attempts to find parallels
       between the childhood paradise portrayed in Colette's works and
       those presented by other writers. Compares her ability to
       recapture the past with Proust's.

1857   Mazars, Pierre. "Colette ou la fraîcheur." *Revue de la pensée
       française* 13 (Oct. 1954): 5-9. Unusual perspective on Colette's
       work leads Mazars to assert that she personified Parisian women
       of all ages, in both her person and her experience of life, and
       that even her celebrated style was the result of standards echoed
       in the work of Paris dressmakers.

1858   Mazars, Pierre. "Les derniers moments de Colette." *Figaro
       littéraire*, 7 Aug. 1954, 1. Presents a tableau of Colette's room
       just after her death, quoting remarks of her grieving servant
       Pauline, as well as those of the nurse in attendance.

1859   McCarty, Mari. "Possessing Female Space: 'The Tender Shoot'."
       Women's Studies 8:3 (1981): 367-74. Defines the world of
       Colette's fictional women as infinitely expanding, because they
       refuse to remain in the limited space assigned to "the other."
       They achieve this by moving to the fringes of society, and the
       mirror is the tool for self-knowledge needed to pursue positive
       action or to escape from phallic confines. Considers Albin of *Le
       Tendron* a case in point, a patriarchal power figure who must be
       kept out of the female dwelling. A convincing interpretation of
       one of Colette's most direct fictional expressions of feminism.

1860   McCarty, Mari. "The Theatre as Literary Model: Role-Playing in
       'Chéri' and 'The Last of Chéri'." In item 1076 *Colette: The
       Woman, The Writer*, 125-34. Insists that the theater dominates
       Colette's work, even the novels, and explores *Chéri* and its
       sequel in the light of this idea. Analyzes the major characters as
       both performer and spectator. Adopts as premise Julia Kristeva's
       thesis that the theater provides the key to all written work.

1861   Mégret, Christian. "Paul Géraldy qui a réussi ses tâches et ses
       jours." *Carrefour*, 14 Sept. 1960, 23. Includes interesting
       passage describing relations between Colette and Géraldy, who
       adapted *Duo* for the stage.

1862 Mercier, Michel. "Chronologie de Colette." *Europe*, no. 631-32 (Nov.-Dec. 1981): 187-99. Actually more a biography than it is a chronology. Facts are sketchy and interspersed with quotations from Colette's work as well as with Mercier's own judgments.

1863 Mercier, Michel. "De 'La Vagabonde' à 'L'Entrave': le soliloque et le conte." In *Le Récit amoureux*, edited by Didier Coste and Michel Zéraffa, 86-98. Seyssel: Champ Vallon, 1984. Defines *La Vagabonde* as a soliloquy rather than a love novel, and considers Max's function in it to be that of mirror substitute. In the light of this idea, Mercier defines Renée's rejection of Max as a rite of passage, equivalent to a final rejection of her first husband along with the negative self-image resulting from that marriage. Contrasts the novel with its sequel *L'Entrave*, which is defined as a real love novel, for which the mirror technique is no longer necessary. A perceptive article, which illuminates Colette's use of genre and narrative technique.

1864 Mercier, Michel. "'Homme, mon ami...' 'La Naissance du jour': l'analyse du texte et les apports de l'histoire du texte." In item 1077 *Colette, Nouvelles Approches critiques*, 59-65. Offers the hypothesis that the rejection of Vial reflects an attempt at exorcism on the part of Colette, that in *La Naissance du jour* Vial represents what Maurice Goudeket must not be, that in this way Colette dedicates the work to Goudeket. Concludes that their happy marriage proves that the attempt was successful.

1865 Mercier, Michel. "'La solitude, inexpugnable innocence'." *Europe*, no. 631-32 (Nov.-Dec. 1981): 3-12. Posits the view that Colette's childhood and her mother, re-created in her mind, furnished her with an art of living and of writing which endured into her old age. Sees in *La Naissance du jour* the culmination of this influence. Ideas are obliquely presented, but provocative of thought.

1866 Mercier, Michel. In *Le Roman féminin*, 101-5, 157-60. Paris: Presses universitaires de France, 1976. Considers Colette's portrayal of the tie between mother and daughter central to an understanding of her entire output, and three works, *La Maison de Claudine*, *Sido* and *La Naissance du jour*, to offer a complete picture of her world vision. Contrasts her picture of differences between men's and women's values with Virginia Woolf's.

1867   Merviel, Jean. "Colette et Judith Gautier." *Lettres françaises*, 5
       May 1945, 3. Questions whether Colette was fully aware of
       current scandals surrounding members of the Goncourt
       Academy, to which she had just been elected, because during a
       recent visit made to her by Merviel she wished only to
       reminisce about Judith Gautier, whom she had known at the
       turn of the century. Colette's true feelings about French literary
       figures accused of collaboration with the enemy during World
       War II have never been made totally clear.

1868   Miccinesi, Mario. "Le quattro 'Claudine' di Colette." *Uomini e
       Libri*, no. 107 (Jan.-Feb. 1986): 34. Brief resume of Colette's
       fictional publications, with special reference to those works
       translated into Italian.

1869   Michel, Jacqueline. "Montherlant et Colette... réflexions sur un
       'éloge'..." *Revue d'histoire littéraire de la France* 76 (May-June
       1976): 412-27. Thought-provoking article inspired by passage
       generally considered to be Montherlant's expression of
       admiration for Colette [item 1896] but interpreted by Michel as
       a recognition of the two writers' affiliation. Identifies common
       elements in their work and thought: a nostalgia for childhood,
       the longing for an impossible purity, and the idea of nature as a
       channel of communication with the real. Signals their essential
       divergence: in the face of adversity Colette opted for life,
       Montherlant did not.

1870   Mignon, Maurice. "Willy, Colette et Polaire." *Bulletin de la
       Société scientifique et artistique de Clamecy*, no. 35 (1960): 25-
       29. Also as *Willy, Colette et Polaire*. Clamecy: Imprimerie
       générale de la Nièvre, 1960. 7p. General summary of the Willy-
       Colette-Polaire publicity campaign. Draws a severe picture of
       Willy. Written by a resident of the Yonne, where Colette was
       born and where Polaire had relatives.

1871   Mignon, Maurice. [No title]. *Bulletin de la Société scientifique et
       artistique de Clamecy*, no. 47 (1973): 57. Brief extract of a talk
       given before the Société, 22 Sept. 1957. Mignon emphasizes
       Colette's love for the Puisaye region.

1872   Mignot-Ogliastri, Claude. In *Anna de Noailles: une amie de la
       Princesse Edmond de Polignac*, 368-82, 420-26. Paris:

Méridiens Klincksieck, 1987. Frequently quotes Colette's
expressions of friendship and admiration for Noailles, as well as
the latter's compliments to Colette, usually gleaned from
correspondence and personal book dedications. Also touches on
their relations over the years. Many passing allusions to Colette
in other parts of the book.

1873   Milhaud, Darius. "Souvenirs." *Le Point*, no. 39 (May 1951): 12.
Brief impressions of the few but memorable occasions on which
Milhaud has met Colette.

1874   Miller, Lee. "Colette, France's Greatest Living Woman Writer."
Vogue [U.S.] 105 (March 1945): 140-41, 171-76. Superficial
but sympathetic account of an informal interview just after
World War II, during which Colette talks of inconsequential
matters.

1875   Miller, Nancy K. "The Anamnesis of a Female 'I': In the Margins
of Self-Portrayal." In item 1076 *Colette: The Woman, The
Writer*, 164-75. A reading of *La Naissance du jour* against the
rhetorical strategies of the "auto-portrait," with the intention of
assessing to what extent Colette's "I" replicates the features of
the autoportrait it seems to mime and to what extent the gender
of that self-inscription inflects or deflects from the genre.
Reproaches Michel Beaujour's theories of the autoportrait for
never considering the gender and concludes that until now the
self-portrait has been a phallogocentric genre. Considers
Colette's text, however, to be coded by a culture that is
feminine, para-literary and matrilinear. An interesting and
discerning article.

1876   Miller, Nancy K. "D'une solitude à l'autre: vers un intertexte
féminin." *French Review* 54 (May 1981): 797-803. Important
analysis of the significance of the epigraph in *La Naissance du
jour* and of the relationship to it of different levels of text.
Identifies Colette's use of the Sido intratext as representative of
a recognizable feature in feminine literature since *La Princesse
de Clèves*.

1877   Miller, Nancy K. "Woman of Letters: The Return to Writing in
Colette's 'The Vagabond'." In *Subject to Change: Reading
Feminist Writing*, 229-64. New York: Columbia University

Press, 1988. Argues that *La Vagabonde* is essentially the story of a return to writing, coupled with a rejection of role-playing. Analyzes Colette's presentation of the sense of dichotomy instilled in female writers and artists by society, and draws parallels between this problem as presented in the novel and that experienced by Colette in her own life. Contrasts Colette's views with Balzac's. Traces Renée's journey towards psychological integrity and identity. A close analysis of the effects of the epistolary techniques used in the third part of the novel is especially interesting. Colette also mentioned briefly in other parts of the book.

1878   Miller, Nancy K. "Women's Autobiography in France: For a Dialectics of Identification." In *Women and Language in Literature and Society*, edited by Sally McConnell-Ginet, Ruth Borker and Nelly Furman, 258-73. New York: Praeger, 1980. Uses *La Naissance du jour* to illustrate the dangers of interpreting a novel as autobiography, and to demonstrate that Colette resembles many other writers in fictionalizing her own life.

1879   Millet, Raymond. "Colette chez elle." *Gringoire*, 30 Nov. 1928, 8. Banal report of an interview with Colette in her first Palais Royal apartment.

1880   Millot, Catherine. "La vocation de Colette." *L'Infini* 21 (Spring 1988): 60-75. Attempts to define Colette's pursuit of love and of writing in psychological terms. Adopts as premise the idea that her fictional characters speak for her. Judges *La Femme cachée* to be the central expression of one of Colette's main ideas: that in our society the feminine self reveals its true nature only through a mask.

1881   Milner, Christiane. "Le corps de Sido." *Europe*, no. 631-32 (Nov.-Dec. 1981): 71-84. Analyzes the importance of Sido's body in Colette's life and work. Insists that, metaphorically speaking, Colette never abandoned her own child-body clinging to her mother, and that she finally transformed it into text. Notes that the mother's body is always presented as a force, rather than as an object, and that she is revealed rather than explained by Colette. An interesting and important article for understanding Colette's writing process.

1882 Milner, Christiane. "Mélanie Klein et les sortilèges de Colette."
     Cahiers Colette, no. 3-4 (1981): 36-44. Outlines Klein's ideas
     on the psychology inherent in *L'Enfant et les sortilèges*, as
     presented in an address before the British Society of
     Psychoanalysis on 15 May 1929. Analyzes the child's actions
     as an expression of aggression against the mother and having
     roots in old, unresolved anguish. Insists on the importance of
     the music and other sounds for the child's psychological cure.

1883 Milner, Christiane. "L'oralité de Colette, une image inversée de
     l'anorexie." In item 1077 *Colette, Nouvelles Approches
     critiques*, 45-52. Freudian interpretation which asserts that
     Colette never lost the childhood habit of oral experimentation
     and that it is this response that she awakens in her readers.
     Applies this idea to her process of recovering the past. An
     unusual interpretation of Colette's celebrated ability to evoke all
     kinds of sensual experience.

1884 Milorad. "La Toute-Femme." In item 1057 *Album Masques:
     Colette*, 147-49. Offers the view that Colette is actually more
     greatly admired than critics assume. Considers the absence of
     general ideas in her work a sign of genius, rather than a
     limitation, and identifies her world as a truly feminine one.
     Terms her an antidote to Kafka.

1885 Miomandre, Francis de. "Le départ de Claudine." In *Figures d'hier
     et d'aujourd'hui*, 207-15. Paris: Dorbon aîné, 1911. Early
     assessment of the significance of Minne, Claudine and Annie in
     Colette's fiction to date. Argues that all three heroines
     demonstrate that Colette has diverged from the pattern of most
     women writers, who imitate men writers by portraying women
     as men wish them to be, rather than as they are.

1886 Mitford, Nancy. "The Unknown Paris." *Sunday Times*, 9 April
     1950, 2. Report of radio interviews quotes Colette as saying
     that Willy was a valuable part of her education and that she has
     long since forgiven him everything.

1887 Mitgang, Herbert. "Publishing: Kohout and Colette." *New York
     Times*, 18 Feb. 1977, C23. Summary of forthcoming and
     recent editions of Colette's works in English.

1888   Mockel, Albert. "Un romancier impressionniste: M. Willy et les
       trois Claudine." *Revue de Belgique* 34 (Oct. 1902): 110-25.
       Significant article because written before the true authorship of
       the Claudine novels was known. Declares it impossible that
       Willy could have written the first three novels himself. Offers
       opinions on their good and bad features. It is interesting to note
       that aspects most admired by Mockel are undoubtedly Colette's
       contribution.

1889   Mœrs, Ellen. "Educating Heroinism: Governess to Governor." In
       Literary Women, 211-42. Garden City: Doubleday, 1976.
       Incorporates material from item 1890 into study dealing with
       Virginia Woolf, Gertrude Stein and Colette, but presents no
       new ideas.

1890   Mœrs, Ellen. "Willa Cather and Colette: Mothers of us all."
       World, 27 March 1973, 51-53. Compares and contrasts Colette
       with Cather, both of whom were born in 1873. Summarizes
       centennial events and new publications in English. Notes that
       both were obsessed with the mother and that both influenced
       their nation's literature through their choice of subject matter
       and their use of language. Also draws parallels between Virginia
       Woolf's Mrs. Ramsay and Colette's Sido.

1891   Mondor, Henri. [No title]. *Figaro littéraire*, 24 Jan. 1953, 5.
       Recalls several pithy remarks that Colette made to him over the
       years. Terms her the glory of women writers of all time and one
       of the greatest classic prose writers ever.

1892   Mondrone, D. "Da Colette a Sagan." *La Civiltà Cattolica* 105 (20
       Nov. 1954): 436-44. Although the emphasis of this article is
       on recent publications by Françoise Sagan, Colette's entire
       output, as representative of an earlier current embracing work by
       Gide, Radiguet and Moravia, comes under scathing attack by
       reason of its subject matter.

1893   Monférier, Jacques. In *Le Suicide*, 151-52, 167-68. Paris: Bordas,
       1970. Student text on the theme of suicide in literature, in
       which Chéri's suicide is presented as the final act of a person
       incapable of any other.

1894 Monnier, Adrienne. "Un déjeuner avec Colette." In *Les Gazettes d'Adrienne Monnier (1925-1945)*, 289-93. Paris: Julliard, 1953. Detailled account of a private luncheon with Colette and two of her friends. Among the conversational topics are food, haunted houses, and clairvoyants, especially the Elise mentioned in Colette's books. Monnier reads Colette's palm, detecting a repressed mysticism, a rich sensuality, and a taste for violence that is safely channelled into her work. An intriguing if insubstantial article.

1895 Monnier, Philippe M. "En marge d'un centenaire: le souvenir de Colette à Genève." *Revue mensuelle des Musées de Genève*, May 1973, 6-10. Relates details of seven visits Colette made to Geneva between 1908 and 1947, and quotes passages of her work in which they are recorded. Also includes three letters to Swiss poet Elie Moroy, none of them significant.

1896 Montherlant, Henry de. "En relisant Colette." *Arts*, 22 Feb. 1952, 1. Also in *Carnets (1930-1944)*, 165-66. Paris: Gallimard, 1957. Terms Colette authentic because of the naturalness of her style. Briskly defends her against attacks on her intelligence, and points out that Gide and Valéry offer an equally limited metaphysical vision. Terms her a genius, along with Marie Noël.

1897 Montherlant, Henry de. In item 1072 Chauvière, 166-67. Undated passage praising *La Maison de Claudine*.

1898 Moreau, Abel. "Colette au brevet." *Nouvelles littéraires*, 4 Jan. 1930, 9. Offers details on the identity of persons on whom Colette modeled the school examiners in *Claudine à l'école*, on Colette's own examinations and on marks obtained. Bantering in tone, this article nevertheless represents one of the earliest serious efforts at discovering the reality behind the myth of Colette's childhood.

1899 Moreau, Luc-Albert. "Visages et maisons de Colette." *Lettres françaises*, 12 Aug. 1954, 1, 6. Portrait dated 1931 and illustrations from *La Naissance du jour*. Artist Moreau was a close friend of Colette's but pre-deceased her in 1948.

1900   Moreno, Marguerite. "Journal (août 1914)." In *Souvenirs de ma vie*, 217-41. Paris: Flore, 1948. Reminiscences of the early days of World War I contain several allusions to Colette. At that time Colette, Moreno, Annie de Pène and Musidora were living in common, sharing daily chores.

1901   Mornand, Pierre. "Dunoyer de Segonzac." *Courrier graphique* 15 (Jan.-Feb. 1950): 3-10. Concise appreciation of the work of Segonzac, who illustrated Colette's *La Treille muscate*. Her friend and neighbor at Saint Tropez, he vividly and accurately evoked life there.

1902   Mornand, Pierre. "Luc-Albert Moreau." *Courrier graphique* 13 (March-April 1948): 3-10. Both Moreau and his wife, musician Hélène Jourdan-Morhange, were Colette's long-time friends. His illustrations for *La Naissance du jour* were among her favorites. Renowned as a painter of light, Moreau died just before this article was printed.

1903   Mornand, Pierre. "Paul Jouve." *Courrier graphique* 18 (July-Aug. 1953): 5-12. A celebrated animal artist, Jouve illustrated Colette's *Paradis terrestres*. Mornand outlines the genesis of the book, which was a joint project of author and artist.

1904   Mornet, Daniel. "Colette (Colette Willy)." In *Histoire de la littérature et de la pensée françaises contemporaines (1870-1925)*: 176-77. Paris: Larousse, 1927. Early effort to place Colette's work within a framework of recognizable literary currents. Attempts to identify the extent to which she is romantic or realist. Terms her a poet of instinctive forms of life, defined here as those of animals and women. Extremely dated criticism but typical of many of the survey evaluations made of her work during the years just before and after World War I.

1905   Mortimor, Raymond. "Introduction." In *Chéri. The Last of Chéri*, some eds. Influential introduction to two of Colette's major novels. Attempts to define the moral principles implicit therein. Considers the two novels to present a classic analysis of the love relationship between a young man and an older woman. One of the few critics to recognize Colette's sense of comedy.

1906 Moser, Ruth. In *L'Impressionnisme français: peinture-littérature-
musique*, 108-10, 138-40. Geneva: Droz; Lille: Giard, 1952.
Concise outline of some of the techniques that have caused
many critics to term Colette's style impressionist without
actually identifying its specific features. Analyzes the opening
passage of *Chéri*, as well as lesser passages, highlighting
Colette's technique of presenting an exterior then "exploding" it
into color and life. Stresses the importance of the verb. Brief
but perceptive comments on her style. Draws parallels between
Colette, Loti and the Goncourt brothers. An important
contribution to our understanding of Colette's techniques and her
kinship with one of the major artistic currents of her life-time.

1907 Mouligneau, Michel. "Proust et Colette." *Bulletin de la Société des
amis de Marcel Proust et des amis de Combray*, no. 23 (1973):
1683-85. Also in *L'Apport de Proust*, 71-76. Paris: Nizet,
1976. Brief but interesting article comparing and contrasting the
two authors' poetic orientation towards life. Identifies their
common need for poetic expression of both sensibility and
sensuality as well as their desire to understand their own world,
but terms Colette a poet of the finite and physical and Proust a
poet of the metaphysical. Contrasts their treatment of time.

1908 Mounier, Monique. "Colette à New York." *Informations et
documents*, no. 78 (25 Dec. 1957): 32-36. Account of Colette's
visit to New York, 3-7 June 1935, after crossing the Atlantic
on the maiden voyage of the *Normandie*. Quotes heavily from
Colette's and Goudeket's own descriptions. Contains no new
material but does make a synthesis of details not generally
found together. With photographs.

1909 Mourão-Ferreira, David. "No centenário de Colette." *Diário de
Notícias*, 22 March 1973, 17-18. Extract from an address to
students. Emphasizes biographical details and the influence of
Colette's mother on her life and work.

1910 Mourlot, Fernand. "Colette." In *Souvenirs & portraits d'artistes*,
66-73. Paris: Mazo, 1974. Recounts meetings with Colette, her
visits to lithographers and her keen understanding of printing
processes used for illustration of flowers. Also contains
references to her relations with Vertès and Matisse.

1911   Mourlot, Fernand. "Colette et les 'Danseuses' de Matisse." In
       Gravés dans ma mémoire, 219-25. Paris: Laffont, 1979.
       Develops anecdote from item 1910, saying that, as Colette was
       never truly fond of Matisse's work, the collaboration in
       question, by which she was to write texts for his illustrations,
       never materialized.

1912   Mourousy, Prince Paul. "Le cœur innombrable d'Anna de
       Noailles." *Les Annales* 76 (Aug. 1969): 5-18. Contains short
       passage referring to Colette's long-time friendship with
       Noailles, and the fact that their contacts were frequently by
       telephone.

1913   Mudrick, Malcolm. "Colette and Minne." *Spectrum* 6 (Winter-
       Spring 1963): 136-50. Attempts to justify a preference for
       Minne as a superior creation to Claudine, and considers
       L'Ingénue libertine a durable work of art. Refutes Marks' and Le
       Hardouin's statements that Minne resembles Colette's first
       heroine. Sometimes dogmatic and abrasive in tone, this article
       nevertheless offers some sound observations.

1914   Mudrick, Malcolm. "Colette and Strether." *Hudson Review* 15
       (Spring 1962): 110-13. Rejects Marks' comparison between
       Colette's imperative "Look!" and the "Live!" of Henry James'
       Strether, offering in its place one between James' Chad and
       Colette's Chéri. Also draws parallels between Colette and D.H.
       Lawrence, and between her and Chaucer.

1915   Mudrick, Malcolm. "Colette, Claudine, and Willy." *Hudson
       Review* 16 (Winter 1963-64): 559-72. Criticizes the Claudine
       novels as dated and without charm for the modern reader,
       asserting that Colette included them in the *OCLF* only to
       reclaim them from Willy. Includes considerable plot summary
       and an interesting but unflattering description of Colette herself.

1916   Mulder, Elisabeth. "Adios a Colette y saludo a Claudina." *Insula*,
       no. 108 (15 Dec. 1954): 3. A warm tribute to Colette, but
       stressing the autobiographical aspects of her work.

1917   Musidora [pseud. of Jeanne Roques]. "Les beaux visages de France:
       Colette." In item 1359 Cazals, 181-93. Incomplete text of a
       talk given 20 Oct. 1945. Includes reminiscences and many

anecdotes about Musidora's friendship with Colette. Quotes
long passages from her work and letters. Very personal in
subject matter and informal in tone.

1918 Musidora [pseud. of Jeanne Roques]. "Colette scénariste." *Lettres
françaises*, 12 Aug. 1954, 3. Asserts that Colette was the
greatest writer of her time, and a fine film writer who
understood the cinema. For actress Musidora, Colette had
written *La Flamme cachée*, a film now lost. Also quotes two
letters from Colette on trivial matters.

1919 Nast-Verguet, Claudine. "Trois aspects de la gourmandise chez
Colette." *Europe*, no. 631-32 (Nov.-Dec. 1981): 107-15.
Identifies Colette's attitude to food as representative of her
attitude to all sensual pleasures and at the root of her ethic.
Insists that a study of Colette's style shows it to be the
necessary expression of an equilibrium underlying her
fundamental way of living and being.

1920 Neddermann, Emmy. "Ein besonders weibliches Genie: Frankreich
feiert die Colette." *Frankfurter Allgemeine*, 25 Aug. 1973, 42.
General appreciation of Colette's life and work on the one
hundredth anniversary of her birth.

1921 Nicollier, Jean. "Introduction." In item 0301 *Chéri*, 11-20. Views
Colette's novel writing, especially the creation of her heroines,
as acts of deliverance. Praises her insight into feminine
psychology. Judges that Léa dominates the novel *Chéri*, and
that the latter work is superior to its sequel.

1922 Nicollier, Jean. "La palette d'une grande artiste." *Gazette de
Lausanne*, 14 Aug. 1954, 7-8. In memoriam. Generally
favorable judgment of Colette's output, of which many titles are
mentioned. Mistakenly refers to her second husband by the
name of his brother, Robert de Jouvenel.

1923 Ninane de Martinoir, Francine. "Colette: 'La Naissance du jour'."
Ecole des lettres III, no. 15 (15 June 1984): 33-38. An
interesting and perceptive analysis, at the student level, of the
beginning of the second chapter of the novel. Likens Colette's
use of language to a tapestry, which redistributes reality
according to a pattern more important than the idea itself.

1924   Noailles, Anna de. "Colette." *Le Capitole*, 22 Dec. 1924, non-pag.
       [6]. Also in *Lettres à ses pairs*, all eds. Three paragraphs of
       hyperbole praising Colette's gifts of observation, understanding
       and communication.

1925   Noailles, Anna de. In *Le Livre de ma vie*, 111-13. Paris: Hachette,
       1932. Also excerpts in item 1057 *Album Masques*, 41; and in
       Lettres à ses pairs, all eds. The florid style typical of Noailles
       reveals better than any commentary the difference between
       Colette's descriptive style and that of her predecessor at the
       Belgian Academy. Still at the height of her fame, Noailles
       offers lavish praise but no analysis either of Colette's work or
       of Gérard d'Houville's, whose merit is extolled in the same
       passage, but she expresses gratitude for their friendship.

1926   Noailles, Anna de. In item 1072 Chauvière, 165. Undated letter
       praising *Le Blé en herbe*.

1927   Noguères, Henri. "Gérard Vée." *Cahiers Colette*, no. 8 (1986): 4.
       Homage on the death of Vée, honorary president of the Société
       des Amis de Colette.

1928   Nohain, Jean. In *La Main chaude*, 26-31. Paris: Julliard, 1980.
       Anecdote about Colette coming to dinner and announcing her
       separation from Willy.

1929   Norell, Donna. "Belief and Disbelief: Structure as Meaning in
       Colette's 'La Lune de pluie'." *Esprit créateur* 18 (Summer
       1978): 62-75. Also, under the title "The Relationship between
       Meaning and Structure in Colette's 'Rain-Moon'," in item 1076
       Colette: The Woman, The Writer, 54-65. Explores Colette's
       presentation of the occult, especially in the novella *La Lune de
       pluie*. Analyzes the network of elements designed to force the
       reader to face the possibility that the occult is real. Argues that
       the novella actually expresses one of Colette's major themes:
       the secret life of people. Demonstrates the careful structuring of
       the text. [P.A.F.]

1930   Norell, Donna. "Colette and the Burden of a Legend." *Journal of
       Women's Studies in Literature* 1 (Autumn 1979): 301-18.
       Trenchant analysis of the reception of Colette's work and the
       reasons for some misconceptions that persisted from the 1920's

to the 1970's. Includes an assessment of her position as an early feminist. [P.A.F.]

1931   Norell, Donna. "The Novel as Mandala: Colette's 'Break of Day'." *Women's Studies* 8:3 (1981): 313-34. Analyzes the structure and symbols of *La Naissance du jour* according to Jungian theories of the mandala, in order to demonstrate that the novel's form is a projection of Colette's psyche at the time of writing. Argues that it may represent a process of individuation on the part of the narrator, if not of Colette herself. Insists that the apparent digressions and descriptive passages are all necessary to the form. [P.A.F.]

1932   Normand, Suzanne. "Die Frau in der Kunst, Literatur und Wissenschaft." *Antares* 2 (July 1954): 38-44. Assesses Colette's role in the influence on society of women writers and artists. Suggests that self-expression for French women is more readily accessible through literature than through the other arts.

1933   Offord, Malcolm. "Colours in Colette's 'Le Blé en herbe'." *Nottingham French Studies* 22 (Oct. 1983): 32-52. Fascinating development of some of the ideas presented in item 1935 Olken. Terming *Le Blé en herbe* an excellent example of pictorial pathetic fallacy, Offord explores the thematic role that color plays in that novel, arguing that references to color form such an extensive and cohesive system that they create a sub-text.

1934   Offord, Malcolm. "Imagery in Colette's 'Le Blé en herbe'." *Nottingham French Studies* 25 (May 1986): 34-62. Compendium of color images by classification, to support arguments made in item 1933. Indicates the significance of each image with relation to the different characters, especially the three principal protagonists.

1935   Olken, Ilene Tova. "Aspects of Imagery in Colette: Color and Light." *PMLA* 77 (March 1962): 140-48. First of three excellent articles attempting to define principles and techniques inherent in the use of Colette's color and light imagery in *Chéri* and *La Fin de Chéri*. Emphasizes the importance of such imagery in all her writing. Notes her use of it to identify, indicate relationships, and suggest emotion or ideas. Mentions, but does not develop, parallels with the impressionist movement. Offers an interesting justification, on psychological and artistic grounds, for the importance of Chéri's portrayal as sex object and exile.

1936   Olken, Ilene Tova. "Imagery in 'Chéri' and 'La Fin de Chéri': Taste and Smell." *French Studies* 16 (July 1962): 245-61. Colette frequently referred to her sense of smell as the superior one of the five, and the presence of olfactory images in her work had long been recognized, though not much analyzed, when Olken published this article, which explores their significance in the two novels.

1937   Olken, Ilene Tova. "Imagery in 'Chéri' and 'La Fin de Chéri'." *Studies in Philology* 60 (Jan. 1963): 96-115. Completes studies in items 1935 and 1936 by analyzing Colette's use of sound and touch imagery in the title novels. Refers to some of her techniques as *pointillistes*. Together with Houssa's study, Olken's three articles provided an important point of departure for much later research on Colette's use of imagery.

1938   Ollivier, Gabriel. In item 1095 *Hommage à Colette*, non-pag. Brief anecdote about Colette's memory and powers of observation.

1939   Ottavi, Anne. "La figure maternelle chez Colette et Virginia Woolf." *Annales de la Faculté des Lettres et Sciences humaines de Nice*, no. 22 (1974): 181-91. Relates Colette's Sido, in *La Maison de Claudine* and *Sido*, to Virginia Woolf's Mrs. Ramsay in *To the Lighthouse*. Claims to detect in both women characters the poeticization of a protective symbol and an archetypal mother figure that is not always positive, and analyzes them in the light of these ideas. Considers *La Naissance du jour* to represent a confrontation with Colette's own reaction to these negative aspects. An excellent study which brings balance to a topic on which much one-sided criticism existed at the time it was published.

1940   Oulmont, Charles. In *Noces d'or avec mon passé*, 178-80. Paris: Crépin-Leblond, 1964. Brief reminiscences about Colette and Willy visiting Oulmont's mother, and about Colette and Lily Pons during Colette's old age. Insists that Colette never stopped esteeming masculine intelligence.

1941   Pagès, Gaston. "Colette ou le miracle." *La Grande Revue* 33
       (1 March 1929): 64-81. Early analysis of Colette's style,
       descriptive in its approach and elementary in comparison with
       modern studies, but perceptive for its time. Attempts to identify
       early influences on Colette's writing and to measure its
       objectivity, but the article's value is diminished by Pagès' effort
       to attribute to Colette's subconscious the operation of what
       many critics called her instinct. It is to this operation that the
       title of the article refers. Mistakenly accords to Colette's mother
       authorship of children's stories that are not hers. Occasionally
       tongue-in-cheek.

1942   Pagnol, Marcel. In item 1095 *Hommage à Colette*, non-pag. Short
       passage evoking the brilliance of Colette's presence.

1943   Pagot-Monnin, Simone. "Voyage au pays de Colette." *Mémoires
       de l'Académie des sciences, arts et belles-lettres de Dijon* 122
       (1973-1975): 457-59. Account of a visit to Saint-Sauveur.
       Describes features of the house, village and surrounding
       countryside. Generously strewn with brief quotations from
       Colette's work to evoke impressions received.

1944   Paillet, Léo. "Dialogue sur les bêtes avec Madame Colette."
       Maîtres de la plume 1 (15 May 1924): 8-11. Also, with minor
       changes and under the title "Dialogue sur les bêtes avec
       Colette," in *Dans la ménagerie littéraire: histoires buffones*, 41-
       52. Paris: Baudinière, 1925. Excerpts in *La Liberté*, 14 Oct.
       1925, 5. Report of an interview in which Colette reminds
       readers of their responsibility to animals and corrects some
       common misconceptions about them. At a time when the
       question of female membership in the French Academy was first
       being broached publicly, she also declares that she will never be
       a candidate.

1945   Paisant, Chantal. "La lice amoureuse." *Europe*, no. 631-32 (Nov.-
       Dec. 1981): 41-51. Attempts to define Colette's personal
       mythology through her demystification of myths about women
       and love. Freely quotes fragments of her work, not only in
       illustration of this idea but also to express it. Investigation
       limited to four novels: *La Vagabonde, Mitsou, L'Entrave,* and
       La Naissance du jour.

1946   Palante, Alain. "L'univers de Colette..." *La France catholique*, 13
       Aug. 1954, 2. Mixture of praise for Colette's achievements and
       regret for her apparent lack of moral preoccupation. Terms her
       an authentic writer, one whose art is greater than its subject.

1947   Palewski, Gaston. "Propos." *Nouvelle Revue des deux mondes*, no.
       2 (Feb. 1977): 388-401. Reminiscences of Proust include
       references to and quotations from Colette's portraits of him.

1948   Palin, Ronald. "They three." *Times Literary Supplement*, no. 3130
       (23 Feb. 1962): 73. Letter to the editor, consisting of a poem
       which lightly makes fun of John Henry Newman, Kenneth
       Tynan and Colette.

1949   Palmiery, René. "Sagesse de Colette." *Adam*, no. 376-78 (1973):
       40-42. Also in *Culture française* 20 (July-Aug. 1973): 197-200.
       General appraisal of Colette's work, terming it non-romantic,
       non-intellectual and pagan. Considers the problem of identifying
       Willy's contribution to the Claudine novels to be an easy one.

1950   Pancrazi, Pietro. "Colette in Italia." In *Italiani e stranieri*, 387-92.
       Milan: Mondadori, 1957. General evaluation of works to 1933.
       Praises all aspects of Colette's writing but detects a tendency
       towards more warmth and depth in the mature novels. Title is
       misleading.

1951   Parinaud, André. "Colette: ma vie est une belle aventure." *Arts*, 24
       July 1952, 1, 12. Report of conversation with Colette on many
       minor topics, but in which she elaborates on the creative role of
       memory in her work. Includes her mother's letter describing the
       burning barn.

1952   Parinaud, André. "Colette a rejoint Sido." *Arts*, 11 Aug. 1954, 1,
       7. Recounts discussions with Colette on the subject of death
       and on the reasons for the deaths of Renaud in *La Retraite
       sentimentale* and Chéri in *La Fin de Chéri*. Includes passages
       from items 1951 and 1953.

1953   Parinaud, André. "Dialogue avec... Colette." *Revue des hommes et
       mondes*, no. 79 (Feb. 1953): 240-47. Ostensibly the report of a
       conversation with Colette on the occasion of her eightieth
       birthday, but includes passages from item 1951.

1954 Partnow, Elaine. "Colette." In *The Quotable Woman: 1800-1975*, edited by Elaine Partnow, 142-46. Los Angeles: Corwin, 1977. Presents 109 quotations from Colette's work, but the criteria for their choice are not self-evident since few of them are either memorable or significant in context.

1955 Pascale. "Colette sous la Coupole ou un nouvel apprentissage." *Vendémiaire*, 1 Dec. 1937, 5. Speculates on whether Colette will be the first woman to be accepted into the Académie Française. Suggests that her lack of formal education will be a deterring factor.

1956 Passeron, Roger. In *Les Gravures de Dunoyer de Segonzac*. Paris: Bibliothèque des Arts, 1970. Artist Segonzac was one of Colette's favorite illustrators and a neighbor at Saint Tropez. His engravings for *La Treille muscate* are among his most admired work. This handsome book reproduces and provides background information about several of them.

1957 Pavlovic, Mihailo. "Colette et l'animalité." In *Recueil des travaux de la Faculté de philosophie*, 201-44. Belgrade: University of Belgrade, 1959. Attempts to identify reasons for Colette's love of animals and to enumerate its principal characteristics. Terms her a primitive and animalistic person. Considers her entire work to be essentially autobiographical. Many of the ideas presented in this article are also expressed in Pavlovic's book on Colette.

1958 Pavlovitch [Pavlovic], Mihailo. "Colette peintre." *Mercure de France*, 1 April 1959, 745-46. Briefly draws parallels between Colette's visual talent and that of painters.

1959 Peillard, Léonce. [No title]. *Revue littéraire*, no. 11 (March-April 1954): 3, 9, 15. Brief introductions to extracts from *La Vagabonde*, *Le Blé en herbe*, and *L'Etoile vesper*.

1960 Peillard, Léonce. [No title]. In item 1095 *Hommage à Colette*, non-pag. Recalls two meetings with Colette, one in 1935 on the *Normandie*, the other shortly before her death.

1961   Pellerin, Jean. "Colette: 'Puériculture'." In *Le Copiste indiscret*,
       19-25. Paris: Albin Michel, 1919. Parody of a passage from
       "Mon amie Valentine."

1962   Péret, Benjamin. "Pendant que Colette se maquille." *Journal
       littéraire*, no. 57 (23 May 1925): 2. Reports a brief interview in
       Colette's dressing room. She refuses to talk about her books,
       but surprisingly suggests that Daudet influenced her.

1963   Perroud, Robert. "Madame Colette." *Vita e pensiero* 33 (May
       1950): 262-69. Also in *Tra Baudelaire e Sartre*, 113-31. Milan:
       Vita e pensiero, 1952. Wide-ranging assessment of the current
       state of Colette criticism, the writer's literary and personal
       reputation, and the negative and positive aspects of her work.
       Defends her against the charge of immorality or spiritual
       poverty so often brought against her by critics in the middle
       years of the century. Perroud's argument, which focuses on the
       novels of which Claudine, Renée and Chéri are the central
       figures, is original and convincingly presented. Still a worth-
       while article.

1964   Perruchot, Henri. "Littérature féminine française contemporaine."
       Larousse mensuel, no. 514 (June 1957): 281-83. Accords
       Colette an important role in the evolution of the French novel,
       but finds her universe and that of many women writers to be a
       limited one.

1965   Peuteuil, Suzanne. "Madame Colette, de Casamène-Les Monts-
       Boucons, au Palais Royal." *Académie des sciences, belles-lettres
       et arts de Besançon: procès-verbaux et mémoires* 180 (1972-73):
       281-97. Text of an address given 22 June 1973. Provides
       extremely interesting details about Colette's activities at the
       Monts-Boucons, a property in the Franche-Comté region, where
       she spent considerable time both alone and with Willy. There
       she wrote *La Retraite sentimentale*, in which Annie's home,
       Casamène, is modelled on the Monts-Boucons. Article reports
       conversations with local people who remembered Colette's
       visits there or her later stops while touring with the music-hall.
       Includes many references to passages in which Colette refers to
       the area. Refers to unpublished personal letters from Colette.
       Followed by text published by the A.F.P. the evening after
       Colette's death.

1966 Pevel, Henri. "Colette." *Ecole libératrice*, 17 Sept. 1954, 19.
Homage upon Colette's death. Compares her to Rabelais and
Montaigne. Terms her perceptive of self as well as of the
exterior world. Reproaches her for her two divorces.

1967 Peyre, Henri. "Contemporary Feminine Literature in France." *Yale
French Studies*, no. 27 (Spring-Summer 1961): 47-65. Also
comprises much of the chapter "Feminine Literature in France"
in *French Novelists of Today*, 39, 276-78. New York: Oxford
University Press, 1967. Includes oft-quoted passages in which
eminent critic Peyre dismisses Colette as antediluvian and
grossly overrated, the chief reason for "the sad plight of
feminine writing in France up to the fourth decade of the present
century." Remains one of the most sweeping condemnations
made of both her person and her work, allowing her only skilled
workmanship. A similar but less harsh opinion is expressed in
an earlier edition, *The Contemporary French Novel*, 282-83.
New York: Oxford University Press, 1955. In later years,
Peyre's judgments of Colette once again became more moderate.

1968 Peyre, Henri. "On the Sapphic Motif in French Literature."
Dalhousie French Studies 1 (Oct. 1979): 27-28. In the course of
this survey of French fiction portraying lesbian relations, Peyre
expresses admiration for *Le Pur et l'impur* but regret that
Colette, whom he now terms one of the two most gifted
women writers of France in the twentieth century, did not write
a novel on the subject.

1969 Peyrefitte, Roger. In *L'Exilé de Capri*, 235-36. Paris: Flammarion,
1959. Trivial anecdote about Colette and Missy.

1970 Peytard, Jean. "Analyse structurale d'un texte de Colette." *Le
français dans le monde*, no. 77 (Dec. 1970): 67-74. Partial
sample structuralist analysis of three paragraphs from *Sido*,
intended for foreign students preparing the French *licence*.
Incorporated into item 1971.

1971 Peytard, Jean. "Essais d'analyse structurale des textes littéraires." In
*Syntagmes: linguistique française et structures du texte
littéraire*, 111-283. Paris: Belles Lettres, 1971. Linguistic
analysis of some aspects of *La Maison de Claudine*, *La
Naissance du jour* and *Sido*, and structural analysis of the last-

named work. Places particular emphasis on the relationship of writer to text and of the narrator Colette to the diverse fictional representations of "Sido." Concludes that *Sido* shows Colette continually weighing her reasons for writing the text as well as attempting to justify them. Remarks about Colette's use of appelations are especially interesting. Argues that they are chosen to express the notion that each character has possibilities for personal change, to reflect the way in which characters view one another, and to designate the functions with which each character is charged within the text. A fascinating article. Incorporates item 1970.

1972   Phelps, Robert. "Colette." *Observer Magazine*, 29 Oct. 1978, 60-65. Pictorial presentation of Colette's life and career.

1973   Phelps, Robert. "Colette, Cocteau and Proust." *Mademoiselle* 72 (Dec. 1970): 124-25, 155. Presents profiles of the public personas of three writers who admired one another's work but who had little in common except genius and a commitment to hard work.

1974   Phelps, Robert. "The Undying Fascination of Colette." *McCall's* 97 (Sept. 1970): 12-14, 136. Focuses on the popularity of the stage play "Colette," starring Zoe Caldwell, and of *Earthly Paradise*, Phelps' own collection of Colette pieces, on which the play was based. Contains chiefly anecdotes and biographical details. Asserts that Colette opened her cosmetic business in order to study other women at close range.

1975   Philbrick, Ann Leone. "The Ambiguist Despite Herself: How Space Nurtures and Subverts Identity in Colette's 'Le Toutounier'." *Modern Language Studies* 11 (Spring 1981): 32-39. Analyzes the significance of the womb-like spatial features of *Le Toutounier*, interpreting Alice and her sisters as both exploiters and victims of the refuge that they have created. A fine analysis of a little understood and seldom studied novel.

1976   Philbrick, Ann Leone. "Space and Salvation in Colette's 'Chéri' and 'La Fin de Chéri'." *Studies in 20th Century Literature* 8 (Spring 1984): 249-64. Analyzes the relationship of the main protagonists to the space they customarily frequent, and attempts to classify their attitude towards it as active or passive.

Insists on the apparent necessity, in Colette's novels, of active possession. Interprets the novels as two parts of the same one.

1977 Pichois, Claude. "Avant-propos." In *Lettres à ses pairs*, all eds. Questions the pertinence of the word *pairs* [peers] in the title, given that few of Colette's correspondents ever attained the public stature of Colette herself. Notes an evolution in her epistolary style over the decades and a desire to adapt her manner of writing to her speaker.

1978 Pichois, Claude. "Gide écrit à Colette." *Revue d'histoire littéraire de la France* 70 (March-April 1970): 193-95. Comments on item 1621, in which Gide bestows lavish praise on *Chéri*, and on item 1622, passage from Gide's journal of 1936 recording his reaction to *Mes apprentissages*.

1979 Pichois, Claude. "Introduction." In *Lettres de la vagabonde*, all eds. Succinctly outlines Colette's theatrical career and her relations with people involved in it.

1980 Pichois, Claude. "Introduction au Colloque: Colette aujourd'hui." *Cahiers Colette*, no. 3-4 (1981): 3-6. Notes that the 1979 Colloque de Dijon was the first university colloquium on Colette. Outlines recent current literary activity in the field.

1981 Pichois, Claude. "Littérature pour le trentième anniversaire de la mort de Colette." *Cahiers Colette*, no. 8 (1986): 5-14. Review essay. Discusses both primary and secondary material since 1984. Contains harsh words about several well-known publications. Reproaches writers for neglecting Colette's texts in favor of superficial aspects of her life and activity.

1982 Pichois, Claude. "Petite contribution à la connaissance des Œuvres complètes du Capitaine Colette." *Cahiers Colette*, no. 6 (1984): 20-23. Refutes popular notion that Colette's father and Willy's father knew each other during the Italian war or that they met through the Société de Géographie. Outlines the Captain's military career as evidence of this argument. A brief but valuable biographical contribution.

1983 Pichois, Claude. "Postface." In item 0739 *Douze dialogues de bêtes*, 221-29. Declares that Colette's gifts and training were

eminently suited to her development as an animal writer.
Contrasts her attitude towards animals with Léautaud's.
Suggests that her profound empathy and understanding of them
may have had its source in her presumed black ancestry.

1984   Pichois, Claude. "Préface." In item 0246 *Le Blé en herbe*, 17-26. A
       good all-round introduction to *Le Blé en herbe*. Provides general
       background material, including details surrounding the novel's
       first publication in *Le Matin* in 1923, and a brief interpretation
       of its ideas.

1985   Pichois, Claude. "Préface." In item 0588 *La Naissance du jour*, 5-
       15. Also, with fuller development of passages treating models
       for the love triangle and of Colette's fictionalization of her
       mother, in item 0592 *La Naissance du jour*, 21-29. Excellent
       interpretive introduction to the novel. Gives details about its
       genesis and its characters. Discriminates between aspects
       modeled closely on reality and those merely reflecting known
       situations or attitudes.

1986   Pichois, "Préface: Colette Willy devient Colette." In item 0053 *OP*
       2, ix-liii. Continues item 1987 for the years 1911-1923.
       Provides much detail about the peripetias of Colette's emotional
       life up to and after her separation from Willy, and again during
       the years preceding her divorce from Henry de Jouvenel. Paints a
       rare character sketch of the latter. Speculates on a possible
       connection between the death of Colette's mother and the birth
       of her child. Pichois is one of the few critics to discuss openly
       and objectively Colette's relations with Bertrand de Jouvenel.
       More than an introduction, this article provides a valuable
       appraisal of Colette's activities during some of her most
       productive years.

1987   Pichois, Claude. "Préface: de Claudine à la Vagabonde." In item
       0053 *OP* 1, ix-cxxii. Splendid complete introduction to
       Colette's life and work up to 1910. Assumes that the reader is
       already cognizant of its main lines. Gives illuminating details
       about life in Paris during the Belle Epoque, particularly those
       aspects which bear on Colette's early career. Distinguishes
       literary currents and factions, naming many persons in public
       and literary life. Corrects some popular misconceptions about
       Colette's childhood and marriage, and about Willy. Insists that

Colette was not nearly so unhappy in the early years of her marriage as she later claimed to have been. Includes interesting passages on the reasons for the marriage, as well as on the phenomenon of lesbianism in French society of the time. Ends with speculative comments on Colette's psychology, especially her stoicism and self-esteem. Quotes passages from many letters and articles.

1988 Pichois, Claude. "La princesse et l'écrivain: Marthe Bibesco, Henry de Jouvenel et Colette." *Cahiers Colette*, no. 9 (1987): 29-31. Notes on Henry de Jouvenel's liaison with Princess Marthe Bibesco, which began during the late winter of 1922-1923, and on Bibesco's attitude towards Colette.

1989 Pichois, Claude. "Le texte de Colette: à propos de l'édition de la 'Bibliothèque de la Pléiade'." In item 1077 *Colette, Nouvelles Approches Critiques*, 55-58. Declares that the Pléiade edition of Colette's complete works will be the essential edition for future study of her work, since it takes into acccount the variants and the manuscripts, and that the previously popular Le Fleuron edition is inadequate because it includes many late changes made by Colette for personal reasons.

1990 Pichois, Claude. In *Littérature et progrès: vitesse et vision du monde*, 102. Neuchâtel: La Baconnière, 1973. Brief comment, suggesting that Colette might be ranked among the *passéistes* of travel, that is, with those who tend to look backwards or who prefer the old.

1991 Pichois, Vincenette, and Alain Brunet. "Petit Complément à l' 'Album Colette'." *Cahiers Colette*, no. 7 (1985): 11-21. Corrections and addenda to item 1056.

1992 Picon, Gaëtan. "Songeant à l'œuvre de Colette..." In *Humanisme actif: mélanges d'art et de littérature offerts à Julien Cain*, vol. 1, 213-16. Paris: Hermann, 1968. Attempts to relate Colette to the nineteenth century novel tradition. Considers much of the interest of her books to have its source in the portrayal of the weak, and usually silent, partner of the couple. Asserts the presence of a cohesive vision in the totality of her work.

1993   Pierrefeu, Jean de. "D'Anatole France à Colette." *Journal des débats*, 9 Aug. 1922, 3. Extravagant praise for *La Maison de Claudine* leads Pierrefeu to the conclusion that the work of Anatole France, at that time considered by many to be the finest French writer alive, pales by comparison.

1994   Pierre-Quint, Léon. "Colette et Chéri." *Le Capitole*, 22 Dec. 1924, non-pag. [28-30]. Interprets Chéri as an animal and compares him to those of *Dialogues de bêtes*. Describes him as without sensibility or moral feeling, but admits his intelligence and sees him becoming a responsible male member of society at the end of the novel. Detects in Colette a tendency to treat alternately the themes of youth and age.

1995   Pintó, Alfonso. "La muerte de Colette." *Insula*, no. 105 (15 Sept. 1954): 8. Short eulogy, sketching Colette's life and work.

1996   Pirotte, Jacques. "Les images dans 'Beaujolais 1947'." *Revue des langues vivantes* 21:4 (1955): 316-21. Brief attempt to analyze thematic oppositions in the title work, an uncollected [but see item 1703 Hill-Marchand] radio talk, especially chains of images of hot-cold and motion-immobility.

1997   Piroué, Georges. "Le roman revendicatif féminin." *Table ronde* 99 (March 1956): 65-70. Sees in Colette an early example of a phenomenon common among post-World War II feminist writers: her works betray an essential dichotomy by which she uses her writing to express her sense of psychological fragmentation at the same time as she uses it as a therapeutic process by which she strives for wholeness.

1998   Pizzorusso, Anne-Marie. "G.A. Borgese et Colette." *Cahiers Colette*, no. 7 (1985): 23-35. Presents and analyzes item 1277. Includes summary of Borgese's career, character and attitude towards Colette.

1999   Pobé, Marcel. "Colette." *Schweizer Rundschau* 54 (Sept. 1954): 325-26. Brief but emotional eulogy.

2000   Polaire [pseud. of Emilie-Marie Bouchaud]. In *Polaire par elle-même*, 116-31, 142-45. Paris: Figuière, 1933. Because of her stage portrayal of Claudine, Polaire was at the height of her career in 1906, yet she died in poverty and obscurity at an early age. Colette remained in touch with her long after her separation from Willy. An entire chapter of these memoirs furnishes details and comments on Polaire's relations with both Colette and Willy. Fascinating biographical material, though some of the "facts" provided may be challenged.

2001 Ponchon, Raoul. "Langage des bêtes." *Le Journal*, 23 May 1904, 1. Also in item 1104 La Hire, 251-52. Thirteen four-line stanzas asserting that Colette is the first writer ever to understand and interpret the language of animals for other people. Obviously inspired by her just-published *Dialogues de bêtes*.

2002 Pons, Christian. "Centenaire de Colette." *Le Cerf-volant*, no. 85 (Jan. 1974): 62-63. Report of a talk on Colette by Madame Pin-Dabadie. Includes brief summary of Colette's life. Declares that, contrary to the opinion of some, she loved human beings since they were also part of nature.

2003 Porel, Jacques. "Souvenirs: une soirée avec Colette." *Revue de Paris* 58 (May 1951): 96-100. Also in *Fils de Réjane*, vol. 1, 99-105. Paris: Plon, 1951. Interesting account of a dinner with Colette and Prince Rainier of Monaco, also of Porel's first meeting with her and Jouvenel. Stresses her search for perfection in writing and her many-faceted personality. Book also includes passage comparing Colette's conscientious workmanship with that of Porel's mother, actress Réjane.

English translation [abridged]. "'Fils de Réjane'." Trans. Germaine B. Wilson. *Town & Country* 115 (Dec. 1961): 132-33, 176-79.

2004 Porte, Guy. "Quand Colette recopiait ses manuscrits pour un gigot." *Le Monde*, 13 Dec. 1973, 21. Main subject of article is actually the collection of bibliophile Richard Anacréon, who owned at the time one of the faulty first editions of *La Fin de Chéri*, from which 34 pages had been omitted. Colette copied out the missing chapter in her own handwriting for Anacréon. See also item 1718.

2005 Porter, Katherine Anne. [No title]. *Figaro littéraire*, 24 Jan. 1953, 5. Stresses Colette's original talent and fascinating personality.

2006 Pougy, Liane de [pseud. of Marie Chassaigne]. In *Mes cahiers
      bleus*. Paris: Plon, 1977. Considered by many critics to be one
      of the models for Léa in *Chéri*, Pougy's long-standing aversion
      for Colette is expressed in many passages of these memoirs, and
      in many different ways. Acknowledges Colette's talent but
      attributes to her all manner of negative motives for her actions.

      English translation: *My Blue Notebooks*. Trans. Diana Athill.
      New York: Harper & Row; London: Deutsch, 1979.

2007 Poulenc, Francis. "Le portrait." In *Journal de mes mélodies*, 29.
      Paris: Grasset, 1964. Also in *Diary of My Songs: journal de
      mes mélodies*, 44-45. London: Gollancz, 1985. Anecdote about
      the genesis of "Le portrait," a poem by Colette which Poulenc
      set to music. Gollancz edition is bilingual, with English trans.
      by Winifred Radford.

2008 Poulet, Marcel. "Colette et le terroir." *Bulletin de l'Association
      d'études, de recherches et de protection du Vieux Toucy*, no. 36
      (Feb. 1974): 13-26. Attempts to define Colette's ties to the
      Yonne, on the basis of the famous "J'appartiens à un pays que
      j'ai quitté" passage in "Jour gris" [*Les Vrilles de la vigne*].
      Stresses that the region was wild and well isolated in her
      childhood and little affected by city fashions. Identifies her
      interest in the supernatural as a taste typical of the area. This
      article offers no new facts but offers a fresh perspective and is
      written by a resident of the region.

2009 Poulet, Robert. "Colette." In *Partis pris*, 208-13. Brussels-Paris:
      Les Ecrits, 1943. General evaluation of Colette's major works,
      stating that if the intellectual dimension were not lacking in her
      work she would be the finest French writer ever. Ranks *Chéri* as
      her best work, but *La Jumelle noire* as unworthy of attention.

2010 Poulet, Robert. "Colette aurait cent ans." *Spectacle du monde*, no.
      133 (April 1973): 88-94. Poulet's fresh style makes this profile
      of Colette's life with summary assessments of major works an
      interesting article. Occasional inaccuracies and malicious jibes
      spoil the whole.

2011 Poulet, Robert. "Sur la littérature personnelle." *Ecrits de Paris*,
      March 1970, 92-99. Identifies *Claudine à l'école* as a major

factor in the popularity of autobiographic novels among modern female writers. Deplores this trend.

2012 Poupon, Pierre. "Colette ou l'art de la dégustation." *Revue vinicole*, Oct. 1955, 25-30. Also in *Mes dégustations littéraires*, 129-47. Dijon: Confrérie des Chevaliers du Tastevin, 1979. Searches in Colette's books for evidence of her wine-tasting talent. Attempts to measure her knowledge of the types of wines, their growing characteristics, the growing conditions producing them, and Colette's appreciation of their different aspects. The only article of its kind, by an expert in the field.

2013 Pourrat, Henri. "Colette." *J'ai lu*, no. 4 (Sept.-Oct. 1954): 3-5. Eulogy stressing Colette's ties with nature. A bit fanciful.

2014 Prieto Barral, María Fortunato. "Centenario de Colette." *Estafeta Literaria* 520 (15 July 1973): 27-28. Chiefly a report of activities in Spain celebrating the centenary of Colette's birth.

2015 Proust, Jacques. "Colette, ou la naissance du poème." *Travaux de linguistique et de littérature* 13 (1975): 741-51. Argues that *La Maison de Claudine*, *Sido* and *La Naissance du jour* furnish the key to all Colette's works. Interprets her message as an expression of the Epicurian *Carpe diem*. Quotes heavily from the three books.

2016 Proust, Marcel. In *Correspondence*, edited by Philip Kolb, vol. 12, 337-39, 353-54. Paris: Plon, 1984. Two letters of Nov. 1913 to Louis de Robert shed some light on the quarrel between the couples Colette-Willy and Madame Arman de Caillavet-Anatole France. In the first letter Proust confesses to having defended Colette in the quarrel, which had taken place several years earlier, but remains convinced that she has ever since considered him to be Madame de Caillavet's ally. The second letter, written after receiving Robert's response, expresses admiration for Colette's talent and pleasure at the other's offer to send her a copy of *Du côté de chez Swann*. In fact, the admiration soon became mutual. Colette's *Trait pour trait* contains a memorable portrait of Proust in which she describes the impression that Proust's novel made on her. The first of the two letters is also in item 2057 Robert, 68-69.

2017   Proust, Marcel. [Letter to Colette]. *Figaro littéraire*, 24 Jan. 1953,
       1. Also in *Nouvelles littéraires*, 18 June 1973, 8; *Lettres à ses
       pairs*, all eds.; item 1072 Chauvière, 146-48. Undated letter of
       1919. Proust comments on his own bad health, but expresses
       the pleasure he has received from reading *Mitsou*. He confesses
       to having wept over Mitsou's final letter to the Blue Lieutenant.

2018   Proust, Marcel. In item 1072 Chauvière, 88-89. In a letter, dated
       by Chauvière as of 1917, Proust thanks Colette for a copy of
       Les Heures longues. He declares that he was so much taken
       with the book that, despite his bad eyesight, he read it through
       without a stop.

2019   Pujade-Renaud, Claude. "La chimère maternelle et le sceau
       paternel." *Europe*, no. 631-32 (Nov.-Dec. 1981): 86-95.
       Interesting interpretation of *La Chatte*, based on unspecified but
       pro-Freudian hypotheses. Includes some analysis of the
       importance of incest in Colette's novels, and of the garden.
       Conclusions are sometimes strained.

2020   Queneau, Raymond. "Sagesse authentiquement féminine..." *Figaro
       littéraire*, 24 Jan. 1953, 7. Argues that Colette's works reveal an
       authentically feminine wisdom, expressed nowhere else in
       French literature. Considers her contribution to complement
       ideals expressed by Simone de Beauvoir and other intellectual
       feminists. Draws interesting parallels between Colette and Gide.

2021   Quennell, Peter. In *The Sign of the Fish*, 65-68. London: Collins;
       New York: Viking, 1960. Account of interview with Colette in
       which she ostensibly refers to a visit made to England in 1900.
       Quotes Goudeket's *Près de Colette* freely.

2022   Querlin, Marise. "Centenaire de la naissance de Colette." *Revue des
       lettres* 108 (Oct.-Dec. 1973): 7-14. Overlaps somewhat with
       item 2023, but contains excerpts of unpublished letters to
       Querlain from Colette's former schoolmistress, Olympe Terrain,
       in which Terrain comments on her relations with Colette.
       Colette's unkind portrait of her in *Claudine à l'école* hurt her
       deeply but the two became reconciled in later years. An
       extremely interesting and valuable biographical article.

2023 Querlin, Marise. "L'enfance de 'Claudine': Mademoiselle Sergent et son secret." *Artaban*, 12 April 1957, 1. Former student of the school Colette had attended at Saint-Sauveur comments on her relations with schoolmistress Olympe Terrain, on whom Colette modelled Mademoiselle Sergent of *Claudine à l'école*. The secret referred to in the title is the schoolmistress' son, whose existence became public knowledge only in her old age. Interesting biographical details.

2024 Quilliot, Claire. "Colette, 'La Chatte' et le métier d'écrivain." *Revue des sciences humaines*, no. 129 (Jan.-March 1968): 59-77. Analyzes Colette's techniques in *La Chatte*, asserting that it is a much more complex work than it is usually deemed to be. Attempts to define Colette's own attitude towards the main characters, especially the cat. Recent critical techniques will refute Quilliot's definitions, but will support affirmation of the novel's complexity.

2025 Raaphorst-Rousseau, Madeleine [signed: Madeleine Rousseau Raaphorst]. "Colette et sa mère 'Sido': lettres inédites concernant le premier mariage de Colette." *Rice University Studies* 59 (Summer 1973): 61-69. Brief comments on the letters to Colette from her mother published in item 1422 [*Figaro littéraire*, 24 Jan. 1953], followed by examination of four letters to Colette's half-sister Juliette and one to Juliette's husband, Dr. Charles Roché. These letters furnish valuable biographical details, since they refer to Achille's hospitality to the family after its financial ruin, the quarrel with Juliette's in-laws, and Colette's own activities at the time. Dating of the letters has been corrected in item 1987 Pichois, lix.

2026 Raaphorst-Rousseau, Madeleine. "Complexité de structure et ambiguïté de 'La Naissance du jour'." *Cahiers Colette*, no. 3-4 (1981): 56-68. Maintains that by 1928 Colette was aware of experimental techniques already current with other authors, notably Proust and Gide. Identifies the narrator of *La Naissance du jour*, published that year, as Colette the author relating fact but mixing in fiction and addressing the reader directly during her search for her future image as Sido's double. Identifies three sources of the complexity and ambiguity that render analysis of the novel difficult. Attempts to ascertain to what extent *La Naissance du jour* should be called a novel.

2027 Raimond, Michel. "L'expression de l'espace dans l'œuvre de
Colette." *Cahiers Colette*, no. 3-4 (1981): 69-77. Asserts that
space takes on values of prison-liberty, security-hostility in
some of Colette's writing and that her autobiographical works
reveal an existential experience of space. Analyzes *Noces* in the
context of these ideas. Identifies Sido as the principle governing
the expression of space in much of Colette's work.

2028 Rainier III, Prince of Monaco. In item 1095 *Hommage à Colette*,
non-pag. Brief expression of respect and admiration for Colette.

2029 Ranou, Annick. "Colette et Willy." *Historia*, no. 453 (Aug.-Sept.
1984): 81-88. Popular article which attempts to explain the
nuances and complexity of the love relationship between
Colette and her first husband. Summarizes known facts about
their courtship and marriage, as well as Colette's account of it
in *Mes apprentissages*.

2030 Rasson, Luc. "La critique littéraire d'un fasciste: Brasillach lecteur
de Colette." *Romanistische Zeitschrift für Literaturgeschichte*
10:3-4 (1986): 408-27. For some twenty years before his
execution as a collaborator at the end of World War II, French
writer and critic Robert Brasillach had expressed admiration for
Colette's work. Here, Rasson makes a bold attempt to identify
the reasons for this admiration and to relate them to Brasillach's
attraction to fascism. He rejects the common notion that
Brasillach's style was influenced by Colette, preferring instead
to identify common elements in their personalities and
backgrounds. He also asserts that Brasillach's sometimes
illogical loyalty to Colette's work was finally achieved by an
attempt to attribute fascist elements to it. An enlightening and
provocative article, even though its main subject is Brasillach
rather than Colette.

2031 Rattaud, Janine. "La littérature féminine." *La Classe de français* 7
(Sept.-Oct. 1957): 257-72. This survey of women's writing
ranks Colette as France's premier poet-novelist but considers her
best work to be her non-fiction.

2032 Ravner, Liv. "Colette." *Vinduet* 2 (Oct. 1948): 589-94. General
assessment of Colette's work, with particular reference to the
novels and descriptive works. Terms her a fine psychologist.

2033 Reboullet, André. "Colette y la esclavitud del amor." *Atenea* 32
      (April 1955): 29-40. General appraisal of Colette's life and
      works, with emphasis on her ideas about love as illustrated in
      the novels and on how she handled it in her own life.

2034 Reboux, Paul. "Comment ils écrivent: de Marcel Proust à Jean
      Cocteau. Réplique de Mme Colette." *Conférencia* 20 (1 April
      1926): 368-82. Text of an address given 4 Dec. 1925. After
      discussing the works of several modern French authors, Reboux
      calls on Colette to speak. In the *réplique* she carefully evades
      his inquiries about the work of others and replies only in a
      general way about her own. She insists on a need for spheres
      and curved lines as inspiration, a predilection she often
      mentions elsewhere. In dialogue form.

2035 Reboux, Paul. "La vertu de Colette." *Le Capitole*, 22 Dec. 1924,
      non-pag. [18-20]. Considers Colette the major French writer of
      her age, after Anatole France. Using as an example the bedroom
      scene in *L'Ingénue libertine*, Reboux offers an early attempt to
      analyze Colette's celebrated ability to portray equivocal subjects
      in a realistic but "chaste" manner. Later incorporated into his
      book *Colette ou le génie du style*.

2036 Relyea, Suzanne. "Polymorphic Perversity: Colette's illusory
      'Real'." In item 1076 *Colette: The Woman, The Writer*, 150-63.
      Uses Saussure's and Todorov's theories to demonstrate that
      Colette conveys a convincing image of materiality at the same
      time as she transforms matter into a hyperbole of sensual
      experience. Uses especially *Chéri* and the essay "Orchidée" to
      illustrate these ideas. Insists that, although Colette's female-
      oriented perspective is new, she "writes like a woman" because
      she focuses on desire and that, by doing so, she makes her work
      reflect the ideas and expectations of her class and sex.

2037 Relyea, Suzanne. "The Symbolic in the Family Factory: 'My
      Apprenticeships'." *Women's Studies* 8:3 (1981): 273-97.
      Compares Willy's stable of writers to the Marxian model of a
      factory, with Colette the only resident worker and Willy the
      capitalist owner-manager. Argues a central phœnix image in
      Mes apprentissages, suggesting a destructive multi-level
      oppression, out of which Colette finally escaped. Criticizes
      Lacan's theory of initiation into the symbolic order as not

applying fully to women in that it does not take women's
experience into account: Colette's case is an example. Contains
some inaccuracies but provides an interesting summary of the
ways in which Colette was legally and socially without power
in the society of the Belle Epoque.

2038 Remacle, Madeleine. "Une page de Colette." *Cahiers d'analyse
textuelle* 16 (1974): 71-79. Pedagogical analysis of three
paragraphs from Colette's famous passage "J'appartiens à un
pays que j'ai quitté" [*Les Vrilles de la vigne*]. Not an *explication
de texte* but a study of descriptive and evocative techniques.

2039 Rémy, Tristan. In *Georges Wague: le mime de la Belle Epoque*,
65-83, 177-78, 190-91. Paris: Georges Girard, 1964. This
biography of Colette's dance teacher, music-hall partner and life-
long friend is crammed with references to performances and
incidents of her music-hall years. Reveals how much Wague
remained a positive influence in Colette's life even after her
marriage to Henry de Jouvenel. Includes a good factual account
of the incident at the Moulin-Rouge. An excellent source of
details on Colette's music-hall career. Also casual allusions to
Colette throughout the book.

2040 Resch, Yannick. "Colette ou le plaisir-texte." In item 1077
Colette, Nouvelles Approches critiques, 167-74. Explores
Colette's relationship with her reader. Studies the description of
pythons in *Prisons et paradis*, as well as a passage on silk from
Le Voyage égoïste, to demonstrate that this relationship can be
defined in terms of rhythm. Notes that Colette does not provide
a representation of the object but floods it with secondary
details. An enlightening study of Colette's descriptive technique.

2041 Resch, Yannick. "Introduction." In item 0479 *La Fin de Chéri*, 5-
26. Excellent introductory analysis which attempts to relate
Chéri and *La Fin de Chéri* to literary, political and social
currents active in France just before and after World War I. Also
assesses the novels' place in the continuity of Colette's entire
output. Probably the best appraisal so far published of Chéri as
victim of the after-war malaise common to young men of his
generation.

2042 Resch, Yannick [signed: Yannick Resh]. "Le secret de Colette." In item 1057 *Album Masques: Colette*, 15-23. Summarizes legends attached to Colette, first as a woman living on the margins of respectable society, then as a writer of physical love and finally as a source of natural wisdom. Identifies Colette's "secret" as her capacity to make readers want to experience life as she does, and attributes the importance of memory in her work to its capacity to prolong that experience. Convincingly refutes the view that Colette ignored political events.

2043 Resch, Yannick. "Writing, Language, and the Body." In item 1076 *Colette: The Woman, The Writer*, 137-49. Maintains that Colette's fiction records the evolution of self and the search for a balance that would take into account the repressed paternal image. Explores this idea in terms of bodily language, and sets up a schema to illustrate it. Claims that Colette discovered her identity with *La Naissance du jour*.

2044 Rétif, André. "Colette et le terroir." *Vie et langage* 251 (Feb. 1973): 73-81. Delineates Colette's ties with her native region by noting the aspects she frequently mentions and the extent to which they seem to have influenced her.

2045 Réval, Gabrielle. "Colette." In *La Chaîne des dames*, 27-38. Paris: Crès, 1924. Mixture of fantasy and comment. Narrates Colette's early life in fairy-tale style, attempts to define her contribution to the Claudine novels, and briefly assesses her other works.

2046 Reymond, Evelyne. "Colette à Uriage." In *Les Heures dauphinoises des écrivains français*, 121-23. Grenoble: Didier Richard, 1984. Anecdotal account of Colette's visit to the baths at Uriage in 1946.

2047 Reymond, Evelyne. "Colette et les produits de beauté." *Pays de Bourgogne*, no. 125 (Jan.-March 1984): 215-18. In June 1932 Colette opened a shop in Paris for the sale of beauty products, and soon afterwards a second one at Saint Tropez. Although she worked hard, the business was not a success. This article provides a brief history of relevant events surrounding the venture and an assessment of factors contributing both to its initiation and to its decline.

2048 Ribadeau-Dumas, François. "Colette." *Revue mondiale* 180 (1 Dec. 1927): 286-89. Also in *Carrefour de visages*, 169-73. Paris: Nouvelle société d'édition, 1929. Profile of Colette as a person, based on repeated conversations and interviews and not a little fantasy. Includes much description of her physical self, her pets and her surroundings.

2049 Ricatte, Robert. "Bibliographie sommaire pour les agrégations de lettres et de grammaire: Colette: 'La Maison de Claudine', 'Sido'." *Information littéraire* 19 (Sept.-Oct. 1967): 181-82. Condensed primary and secondary bibliography for students. Includes brief annotations.

2050 Richard, Jean-Pierre. "L'ail et la grenouille." *Nouvelle Revue française*, no. 308 (1 Sept. 1978): 99-110. Also, under the title "Les deux demeures," in *Microlectures II: pages paysages*, 169-80. Paris: Seuil, 1984. Freudian-based discussion of the psychology of Colette and members of her family as portrayed in *Sido*, *La Maison de Claudine* and *La Naissance du jour*, with focus on the dwelling. Disappointing because it makes unjustified assumptions and draws no real distinction between real and fictional persons, with the result that the reader is never sure which is under discussion.

2051 Richard, Jean-Pierre. "Colette et le jour naissant." In *Mélanges littéraires François Germain*, 269-77. Dijon: Section de Littérature française de la Faculté de Lettres et Philosophie de Dijon, 1979. Also, under the title "Métamorphoses d'un matin," in *Microlectures II: pages paysages*, 181-91. Paris: Seuil, 1984. Freudian-based interpretation of *La Naissance du jour* in which all elements of the novel are interpreted in sexual terms. Basic analogy ties the longing for the dawn to the search for the womb.

2052 Richer, Julia. "Colette." *Notre temps*, 14 Aug. 1954, 5. Eulogy praises Colette's style but dismisses the substance of her work.

2053 Ritter, Raymond. "Avec Colette, un soir, à Pau..." *Pyrénées*, no. 19 (July-Sept. 1954): 129-32. Interesting reminiscences of an address given by Colette at Pau and an evening spent in her company about 1930. Recounts impressions of her as a profoundly sad person.

2054 Riverain, Jean. "Chez les poètes d'Auteuil." *Nouvelles littéraires,* 15 April 1948, 1, 6. Includes description of Colette's house in Auteuil during the second decade of the century.

2055 Robert, Jacques. "Colette." *Dictionnaire des Parisiens,* 88. Paris: Solar, 1970. Account of a brief inconsequential conversation with Colette shortly before her death. Book also has a section on Maurice Chevalier, quoting a dedication from her [p. 78].

2056 Robert, Jeanne de. In *Le Cœur a ses raisons,* 227, 278-79. Paris: Autoédition, 1987. Biography of Louis de Robert by his widow quotes Colette's praise of his work and recalls Robert's early recognition of her talent. Includes a letter from Colette to Robert from 1910.

2057 Robert, Louis de. In *Comment débuta Marcel Proust,* 68-69, 103-4. Paris: Gallimard, 1969. In her portrait of Marcel Proust in *Trait pour trait* Colette expresses gratitude to Louis de Robert for having introduced her to Proust's work. Here, Robert briefly gives his account of the incident. Also includes the letter of Nov. 1913 in which Proust expresses reluctance to contact Colette directly, because of her misunderstanding of his position in her quarrel with Madame Arman de Caillavet many years before.

2058 Robert, Louis de. In item 1072 Chauvière, 163-64. Undated letter, praising *La Vagabonde* extravagantly.

2059 Roberts, Nesta. "The Revelation of Colette." *Guardian,* 12 May 1973, 3. Brief, sympathetic overview of Colette's career and summary of events to be held in France for her centenary.

2060 Robida, Michel. "Colette." *Nouvelle Revue des deux mondes,* April 1973, 60-68. Interesting combination of reminiscences of Colette and critical evaluation of her work. Advances the hypothesis that Colette was the creator of a new literary genre, one which focuses on every-day things.

2061 Robinet, René. "L'Ascendance champenoise et ardennaise de Colette." *Etudes ardennaises,* no. 9 (April 1957): 9-12. Brief biographical article tracing Colette's maternal ancestors to seventeenth-century residents of Champagne and the Ardennes.

2062   Robinson, Lillian S. "Who's Afraid of a Room of One's Own?" In
       The Politics of Literature, edited by Louis Kampf and Paul
       Lauter, 354-411 [esp. 381-82]. New York: Pantheon, 1972.
       Includes an assessment of Colette's notion of the importance of
       sexuality in female identity. Terms her portrayal of these ideas a
       more realistic one than that of most female writers.

2063   Roge, Jeanne. "Les sources de Colette: souvenirs inédits de deux
       condisciples de Claudine." *La Grive*, no. 107 (July-Sept. 1960):
       11-13. A convincing account of reminiscences by the author's
       mother and aunt, models for the Jousserand girls in *Claudine à
       l'école*. Describes the visit Colette and Willy made to the school
       at Saint-Sauveur in the early years of their marriage, an event
       that has its counterpart in the visit by Claudine and Renaud in
       Claudine en ménage. Details provided and old letters render the
       identification certain.

2064   Roger-Marx, Claude. "Colette et ses illustrateurs." *Europe nouvelle*
       15 (24 Dec. 1932): 1495. High praise for editions of *La Treille
       muscate*, illustrated by Dunoyer de Segonzac, and *La Naissance
       du jour*, illustrated by Luc-Albert Moreau, as marvels of unity
       between text and illustrations. The locale and model for the
       illustrations for both books is Saint Tropez, where Colette and
       the two artists spent many summers.

2065   Rolfe, Bari. "Queens of mime." *Dance Magazine* 50 (Dec. 1976):
       68-73. Survey of performers includes brief summary of
       Colette's music-hall career. Interesting, though not without
       minor inaccuracies.

2066   Romain, Maurice. "De quoi le bonheur est-il fait?" *Les Annales*,
       25 March 1937, 281-86. Series of interviews on happiness
       includes one with Colette. One of the few in which Colette
       develops her opinion so fully on any abstract idea. Here she
       emphasizes the ambiguity of the word happiness but attempts
       to identify conditions necessary to achieve it.

2067   Romanowski, Sylvie. "A Typology of Women in Colette's
       Novels." In item 1076 *Colette: The Woman, The Writer*, 66-
       74. Attempts to show that Colette's novels form a coherent
       totality and that the characters bear a relationship to one other.
       Presents an initial typology based on the oppositions

adolescent-mature, positive-negative. Occasionally naive, especially with regard to Chéri.

2068 Rosasco, Joan Teresa. "'Chéri', ou le collier de Léa." *Teaching Language through Literature* 19 (Dec. 1979): 3-21. Excellent study of the mythological dimensions of *Chéri*, especially as it relates to the Demeter myth. Analyzes the importance of the seasons, their connection with the three women figures, Edmée, Léa and Lili. Successfully demonstrates that the basic structure depends on a tension between the cyclical eternal return of nature and the linear structure of human life. Detects both bipartite and tripartite elements in the work, each connected with a different mythological tradition, and develops their significance. A "must" both for those who wish to analyze Colette's fictional techniques and for those who merely wish to deepen their understanding of the novel's meaning.

2069 Rosello, Mireille. "Gigi et les *agents de change.*" *French Forum* 12 (May 1987): 203-13. Interprets *Gigi* as a struggle between pressures exerted by three units--Gaston, Gigi, and the couple Alicia-Madame Alvarez--with Gigi's future as the focus of pressure. Analyzes the sub-text conveying this idea, with emphasis on the financial aspects suggested at the different levels of narration.

2070 Rosenblum, Shari L. "The Demythification of Man in Colette: Seen as an Erotic Object, Coveted, but Secretly Scorned, in 'Chéri' and 'La Fin de Chéri'." *Centerpoint* 3 (Fall-Spring 1980): 52-56. Brief elaboration of statement made in the title.

2071 Rosny, J.-H. aîné. "Willy." In *Portraits et souvenirs*, 81-85. Paris: Compagnie française des arts graphiques, 1945. Reminiscences and opinions about Willy and Colette. Asserts that Colette was afraid of Willy.

2072 Rougemont, E. de. "Portraits graphologiques: Mme Colette Willy." *Mercure de France*, 16 Dec. 1912, 747-50. Analysis of Colette's handwriting deduces from it spontaneity, sincerity, sensitivity, generosity, a sense of discipline, willpower, charm, lucidity, remarkable intelligence and a prompt critical sense.

2073   Rousseaux, André. "A soixante-dix-sept ans Colette accueille Mac
       Orlan à l'Académie des Goncourt." *France-Illustration*, no. 226
       (11 Feb. 1950): 136-37. Pictorial article marking Colette's
       welcome of Pierre Mac Orlan to the Goncourt Academy. Colette
       was then president of the prestigious group. Excellent
       photographs.

2074   Rousseaux, André. "Colette au soleil du soir." *Littérature du
       vingtième siècle*, vol. 2, 7-20. Paris: Albin Michel, 1939.
       Ostensibly a study of *Duo*, *Le Toutounier* and *Bella-Vista*, but
       the last-named work is scarcely mentioned, and many of the
       ideas are obscured by the use of nebulous expressions such as
       âme de la chair [soul of the flesh], apparently intended to
       elucidate Colette's moral system. A much less satisfactory
       article than the following one.

2075   Rousseaux, André. "Colette ou le paradis perdu." *Revue de Paris* 40
       (15 Aug. 1933): 771-93. Also in *Ames et visages du XXe
       siècle: le paradis perdu*, 19-58. Paris: Grasset, 1936; and in
       Portraits littéraires choisis, 43-78. Geneva: Skira, 1947. Very
       readable major article, emphasizing the universal nature of
       Colette's work. Attempts to elucidate her thought by tracing
       themes to specific events in her life, particularly those of her
       childhood. Some analysis of her ideas about writing and of the
       way she portrays relations between men and women. Though
       Rousseaux does not always draw a distinction between Colette
       and her fictional namesakes, he does insist on the impossibility
       of ever completely knowing her through her books.

2076   Roux, François de. "Colette, sur les ondes enchante l'auditeur mais
       ne se livre pas." *Figaro littéraire*, 8 April 1950, 8. Brief but
       perceptive article focusing on André Parinaud's series of radio
       interviews with Colette. Implicitly reproaches Parinaud for
       concentrating on Colette's relations with Willy and on the
       identity of models for her fictional characters. Insists that readers
       are more interested in the books than in peripheral matters.

2077   Roux, Laurence de. "Les tentations de Colette." *Le Spectacle du
       monde* 278 (May 1985): 74-78. Interesting, if superficial and
       occasionally inaccurate, profile of Colette's life. Frequently
       mentions her age as if it were a significant factor in the context.
       Quotes her works freely.

2078 Rouzière, Jean-Michel. "Nous aurons bien servi Colette et le
      théâtre." *Avant-Scene Théâtre*, no. 708 (15 April 1982): 41.
      General comments about Colette and the theater. Rouzière
      directed the Théâtre du Palais-Royal for many years, including
      performances of *Gigi*, *De Molière à Colette*, *Notre Colette*, *Le
      Ciel de lit* and *Chéri*.

2079 Roy, Claude. "Classique Colette." *Le Point*, no. 39 (May 1951):
      25-37. Also, under the title "Colette," in *Descriptions critiques:
      le commerce des classiques*, 307-12. Paris: Gallimard, 1953.
      Attempts to define what a "classic" writer is and is not, and to
      explain why Colette is the only such writer of our time: she is
      not an imitator; she writes of things that everybody knows
      about but which she portrays as if seen for the first time; she is
      interested in everything; and she knows her limits. Detects
      traces of Horace, Catullus, Ovid and Tibelius in her prose and of
      Virgil in some of her characters. Terms her a Mediterranean
      writer. Accords to her qualities of intelligence, lack of
      pretention, and a desire for the natural. Concludes that Colette's
      popularity is logical because the classic writer speaks to all
      humanity.

2080 Roy, Claude. "Colette." *Poésie 47*, no. 40 (Aug.-Sept. 1947): 76-
      85. Also in *Descriptions critiques*, 107-18. Paris: Gallimard,
      1949. Traces the evolution of Colette's apparent revolt against
      love in the context of her awareness of society's rules--financial,
      legal, political and social--affecting the position of women over
      the years. Considers writing and the love of nature to be her
      antidotes against personal suffering.

2081 Roy, Claude. "De Claudine à Colette." *Lettres françaises*, 5 Feb.
      1948, 1, 4. Mostly a bouquet of compliments on the occasion
      of Colette's seventy-fifth birthday. Repeats some of the same
      ideas as items 2079-80.

2082 Roy, Claude. "La petite lumière de l'étoile vesper." *Bulletin de la
      Guilde du livre* 21 (Feb. 1956): 61-62. Emphasizes the
      impossibility of classifying *L'Etoile vesper* by genre. Considers
      its principal appeal to be in the music of the language.

2083 Roy, Jean-H. "De Colette Willy à Madame Colette." *Temps
      modernes* 6 (July 1950): 155-60. Terms Colette the first truly

sincere woman writer in French literature. Criticizes the structure of both *Chéri* and *Le Blé en herbe*, and ranks Colette's non-fiction as her best work.

2084   Roy, Jules. In item 1095 *Hommage à Colette*, non-pag. Brief passage claiming that, shortly before Colette's death, Roy sensed her already looking towards another world.

2085   Ruffini, Nina. "Addio a Colette." *Il Mondo*, 17 Aug. 1954, 8. In memoriam, stressing Colette's femininity and achievements.

2086   Ruggieri, Eve. "Colette." In *Eve Ruggieri raconte...*, vol. 1, 9-56. Paris: Mengès, 1980. Irresponsible but entertaining article. Imagines events in Colette's life, and relates both her words and thoughts as if they were true. Incidents mentioned appear to have been chosen for their piquancy rather than their importance. Although Ruggieri knew Colette personally, the article's lack of documentation and occasional inaccuracies render it next to useless as a biographical document.

2087   Rule, Jane. "Colette 1873-1954." In *Lesbian Images*, 126-38. Garden City, N.Y.: Doubleday; London: Davies, 1976. Superficial treatment of lesbianism in Colette's work. Views her portrayal of the Ladies of Llangollen in *Le Pur et l'impur* as hostile to Lady Eleanor Butler, and her attitude in general as condescending to women.

2088   Rupolo, Wanda. "La simbologia di Colette." *Nuova Antologia* 518 (1973): 53-60. Also, under the title "Colette e la poetica del 'double'," in *Il Linguaggio dell'immagine: saggi di letteratura francese contemporanea*, 84-92. Rome: Bonacci, 1979. Titles suggesting in-depth study of Colette's use of poeticization techniques, literary doubles or symbolic features are misleading. Points out passages indicating Colette's fascination with her own literary doubles as well as some revealing a preoccupation with shadow-figures or mirror-figures on the part of fictional characters, but makes no real attempt to analyze them.

2089   Russel, Dora Isella. "Colette: une experiencia de la vida." *Asomante* 16 (Oct.-Dec. 1960): 7-16. Speculates on connection between events and characters portrayed in Colette's work and those of her own life. Identifies her closely with her heroines.

2090 Sadoul, Georges. "Colette collaboratrice de Delluc." *Lettres françaises*, 12 Aug. 1954, 3. Calls Colette one of the great pioneers of film criticism. Briefly summarizes her work in film and quotes from her criticism to show that she was against war.

2091 Saint-George, Maurice-André. "Colette." *Revue nouvelle*, no. 33-34 (Aug.-Sept. 1927): 56-62. General assessment of Colette's publications to date. Remarks on an overriding sadness in her novels, attributing it to her "masculine" desire of an absolute, but in the form of love. Like many critics of the time, Saint-George judges her style so simple and pure that it defies analysis.

2092 Saint-Onge, Paule. "Colette aurait cent ans..." *Châtelaine* 14 (June 1973): 56-57. Thumbnail sketch of Colette as writer and woman. Stresses her esteem for women as a group.

2093 Saint-Paulien [pseud. of Maurice Ivan Sicard]. In *Don Juan: mythe et réalité*, 267-68. Paris: Plon, 1967. Brief allusion to Colette, accusing her of confusing Don Juan with Chérubin.

2094 Saix, Guillot de. "Ah! qu'on a 'du goût' en lisant Colette." *Figaro littéraire*, 17 April 1954, 9. Compendium of patois expressions used by Colette from the Puisaye region.

2095 Salacrou, Armand. "Vous aurez toujours tout deviné..." *Figaro littéraire*, 24 Jan. 1953, 3. Detects in Colette's theater criticism evidence of her aptitude to penetrate the performers' minds and to sympathize with their task.

2096 Sampelayo, Juan. "Un 28 de enero para Colette." *Estafeta literaria*, no. 507 (1 Jan. 1973): 19. Announcement to Spanish readers that Colette's childhood home at Saint-Sauveur will henceforth bear a plaque commemorating her birth one hundred years earlier.

2097 Sandel, Cora. "Colette." *Bonniers Litterära Magasin* 23 (Sept. 1954): 554-59. Writer Sandel translated Colette into Norwegian, and is considered by many to have been influenced by her. Here she blames Willy's publicity for Scandinavia's neglect of Colette, insisting that her work has more depth than she is generally given credit for.

2098   Sarde, Michèle. "La dame du Palais-Royal." *Bulletin du Club français de la médaille*, no. 88 (July 1985): 124-25. Succinct account of Colette's attachment to the Palais Royal, where she lived from 1927 to 1931 and from 1933 until her death in 1954, and of her relations with other people who lived there.

2099   Sarde, Michèle. "L'empire de Sido." In item 0013 *Sido: lettres à sa fille*, xi-xxiii. Comments on the relationship between Colette and her mother, and especially on those aspects which Sido's letters reveal. Emphasizes the demonstrated accuracy of Colette's fictional portrayal, the human weaknesses that the letters reveal in them both, and the evident depth of their attachment.

2100   Sarde, Michèle Blin. "The First Steps in a Writer's Career." In item 1076 *Colette: The Woman, The Writer*, 16-21. Asserts that the problem of economic domination is at the heart of female-male relationships portrayed in Colette's work and that it has its roots in Colette's own situation with Willy. Identifies Colette's world vision as that of a marginal group with no political entity.

2101   Sauvage, Marcel. "Colette." In item 0885 *Rêverie de Nouvel An*, 7-10. Flowery presentation of this early volume of personal essays. Attempts to relate Colette's work to her need to express a special sensibility.

2102   Scheffel, Helmut. "Die Erde ist mein Paradies." *Frankfurter Allgemeine*, 5 Aug. 1975, 14. Review of television film based on Phelps' *Earthly Paradise*.

2103   Schifres, Alain. "Colette sort du purgatoire." *Réalités*, no. 331 (Aug. 1973): 30-37. Presents brief extracts from *Sido* and *Mes apprentissages*, as well as the entire text of "Le cœur des bêtes" from *Journal à rebours*. Praises these as an antidote to the coldness and impersonal character of the industrial world.

2104   Schmidt, Albert-Marie. "Colette." *Réforme*, 14 Aug. 1954, 7. Attempts to define moral tenets implicit in Colette's work. Attributes to her an immediate intuition of nature, the legacy of her claimed black ancestor. Terms her misanthropic and her women characters generally egotistical, but asserts that towards the end of her career she recognized the destructive effects of such traits. Draws parallels with Gide's work.

2105　Séché, Alphonse. "Claudine-Polaire." In *Dans la mêlée littéraire (1900-1930)*, 29-38. Paris: Société française d'éditions littéraires et techniques, 1935. Anecdotes mostly about Willy's use of Polaire and Colette in the promotion of the Claudine novels. Emphasis is on Willy rather than on the two women.

2106　Secrest, Meryle. In *Between Me and Life: A Biography of Romaine Brooks*. Garden City: Doubleday, 1974; London: Macdonald & Jane's, 1976. Biography about lesbian painter Brooks contains many allusions to Colette as the friend of Natalie Clifford Barney. Includes several well-known anecdotes and frequently cites Colette's opinion.

2107　Senhouse, Roger. "Introduction." In *My Mother's House. Sido*, some eds. Provides background material for the two works, referring to them as if they were direct autobiography. Quotes passages of then-unpublished letters from Colette to her mother [later in item 0013 *Sido: lettres à sa fille*].

2108　Senhouse, Roger. "On translating Colette." *Time & Tide* 35 (16 Oct. 1954): 1380-82. Refutes statement by Bertrand de Jouvenel [in item 1743] that Colette had no curiosity about foreign languages. Senhouse declares that when he was translating her books into English Colette gave him advice. Compares old and new translations of *Chéri*.

2109　Sentein, François. "Sainte Colette." *Arts*, 11 Aug. 1954, 7. Unfavorable evaluation of Colette's work. Considers it out-dated and unsuitable for pedagogical study.

2110　Serra, Renato. "Un article inédit sur 'La Retraite sentimentale'." Trans. Anne-Marie Pizzorusso. *Cahiers Colette*, no. 6 (1984): 25-32. Also abbreviated version in the original Italian: "Per un libro che non ho letto: Pagine inedite su Colette." *Rivista di letterature moderne* 1 (1946): 137-47. Presentation and commentary by Alfredo Grilli. Written before World War I but not published during Serra's lifetime. Although Serra had not read the fifth novel in the Claudine series, he expresses opinions based on the comments of others. He declares that Colette's latest novel signals the end of the Willy-Claudine enterprises. He deplores Willy's publicity stunts and the commercialism founded on the Claudine image, but asserts that he detects among the dross a literary jewel, which is of Colette's creation. Ranks the creator of the Claudine and Minne novels scarcely behind Boccaccio and Rabelais. Interesting because Serra's observations are often similar to those of modern critics.

2111   Sert, Misia. In *Misia*, 39. Paris: Gallimard, 1952. Memoirs include brief passage on Colette and Willy.

2112   Sigaux, Gilbert. "Préface." In item 0620 *La Retraite sentimentale*, 7-26. Excellent introduction to the fifth and last Claudine novel, written by Colette alone. Sigaux attempts to assess its relation to the previous four, as well as the extent of Willy's contribution to them. Declares that together in this book Claudine and Annie speak with Colette's true voice.

2113   Simon, John. "Colette molested." *New York* 3 (25 May 1970): 58. Scathing review of *Colette*, Elinor Jones' stage adaptation of Phelps' *Earthly Paradise*.

2114   Simon, John. "Les poètes fantastiques." *Opera News* 45 (28 Feb. 1981): 25-34. Excellent account of Colette's and Ravel's collaboration on *L'Enfant et les sortilèges*, and a critic's assessment of the libretto. Points out that most criticism of the work focuses on the music and that opinion is divided on Colette's achievements as drama critic and playwright. Title refers to Apollinaire and Colette.

2115   Simon, Pierre-Henri. In *Histoire de la littérature française au XXe siècle*, vol. 1, 72-74, 158-59; vol. 2, 29-31, 162-63. Paris: Armand Colin, 1956. Sketches Colette's early rise to fame, identifying the publication of *Chéri* as marking the pinnacle of her achievement. Detects few flaws in her work. Considers her popular after her death because of a revival of the Stendhalian novel tradition.

2116   Sion, Georges. "Colette chez elle en Belgique." In item 1060 *Autour de Colette à Saint-Tropez*, non.-pag. [107-18]. General article about Colette's popularity and family roots in Belgium. Stresses the depth of her friendship with Queen Elisabeth of Belgium.

2117 Sion, Georges. "Discours." *Bulletin de l'Académie royale de langue et de littérature françaises* 51:3-4 (1973): 142-56. Also in item 1121 *Pour le centenaire de Colette,* 5-19. Text of address celebrating the one hundredth anniversary of Colette's birth. Draws on memories of others for a description of her reception at the Belgian Academy in 1936. Sketches her ties with Belgium and highlights of her life and career.

2118 Smith, Richard Langham. "Colette as critic." *Music and Musicians* 25 (Aug. 1977): 26-28. Analyzes music criticism published in *Gil Blas* in 1903 under the rubrics "Claudine au concert" and "Claudine au conservatoire," deemed by many scholars to be the work of Colette rather than of Willy, to whom it was long attributed. Compares the Claudine reviews with a parallel series by Debussy, declaring that Willy's influence can be seen in both. An important article by a well-informed critic.

2119 Solenière, Eugène de. In *Willy.* Paris: Sevin & Rey, 1903. 99p. Although this long homage to Willy contains no serious analysis, either of Colette's life or her work, it is an important reference for Colette scholars in that it provides a good picture of the measure of esteem in which Willy was held by many at the time of the first Claudines. Contains a long article on Willy, a brief one on Colette, an article entitled "Claudine à Marseille," allegedly written by Willy in collaboration with Colette, and articles on Willy by other critics. Excerpts from Willy's own criticism are liberally strewn throughout. Despite references to Colette as Willy's sometime collaborator, the two-page bibliography lists the Claudine novels among Willy's own publications and not among the "Ouvrages en collaboration."

2120 Soral, René. "Colette et l'homophilie." *Arcadie* 127-128 (July-Aug. 1964): 333-44. Summarizes incidents in Colette's books which depict homosexuality. Goal of article is to assess Colette's reaction to the subject of homosexuality, on the premise that her attitude is reflected in her works. Though mostly descriptive, the article provides a useful compendium of such passages for those who want one.

2121 Souday, Paul. "Madame Colette Willy." In *Les Livres du temps,* vol. 2, 289-304. Paris: Emile-Paul, 1914. One of the best early analyses of Colette's over-all output. Offers judgment of each publication to date, including the animal works. Asserts that, although Colette breaks new ground with *La Vagabonde*, in which Renée chooses freedom over love, its sequel, *L'Entrave*, which shows her submitting to domination of the male, is not convincing.

2122 Spacks, Patricia Meyer. "Free Women." *Hudson Review* 24 (Winter 1971-72): 559-73. Compares Colette with Anaïs Nin, Doris Lessing and Lillian Hellman, in the context of the three writers' commitment to writing and to personal liberty. Claims that Colette finds woman's most significant freedom to be in the act of writing itself.

2123 Spencer, Sharon. "The Lady of the Beasts: Eros and Transformation in Colette." *Women's Studies* 8:3 (1981): 299-312. Effort to demonstrate that Colette's writing about sex is revolutionary yet archaic because of its metaphors and images. Terms her a modern-day incarnation of the "lady of the beasts" or the Great Mother, and considers her fondness for cats proof of her desire to bring into consciousness the attributes of the archetypal feline. A not always convincing article, partly because of its frequent plot outlines, but one that does offer provocative ideas.

2124 Sprecher, A.-A. "Le capitaine Jules Colette." *Candide*, 21 Aug. 1930, 3. Account of an interview with a Colonel Godchot, who had been in correspondence with Captain Colette before his death. A short but significant biographical article, which confirms many details of Colette's portrait of her father.

2125 Springer, Mary Doyle. "Character Revelation in Colette's 'Julie de Carneilhan'." In *Forms of the Modern Novella*, 132-37. Chicago and London: University of Chicago Press, 1975. Classifies *Julie de Carneilhan* as a novel of "character," in which the development is not of the heroine herself, but rather of her own understanding of herself and parts of the world around her. Judges the novel to be a complex and in-depth presentation of the title character rather than a sketch. An interesting analysis of an oft-neglected or superficially viewed work of fiction. Also brief allusions to Colette in other sections of the book.

2126 Stansbury, Milton H. "Colette." In *French Novelists of Today*, 101-19. Philadelphia: University of Pennsylvania Press, 1935; Port Washington, N.Y.: Kennikat Press, 1966. Concise assessment of Colette's life and work for the general reader. The value of this otherwise fine article is flawed by paraphrase and the identification of Colette with all her heroines. Terms her a difficult person for the Anglo-Saxon reader to understand.

2127 Stary, Sonja G. "Memory in Colette's 'Chéri'." *Orbis Litterarum* 39:2 (1984): 114-22. Compares Colette's own use of recall with that of the protagonists in *Chéri*, and examines the role this activity plays in the development of the plots. Considers the two novels to be exercises in self-discovery by their author, and attempts to identify the conclusions to which she came after writing them.

2128 Stévo, Jean. "Colette." *Revue nationale* 43 (1971): 5-9. Reports conversations with Colette at her Palais Royal apartment. Describes the interior and cites Colette's remarks on Belgium, and especially on a visit to Brussels as a child.

2129 Stewart, Joan Hinde. "Colette and the Hallowing of Age." *Romance Notes* 20 (Winter 1979-80): 172-77. Examines *Chéri* and *La Fin de Chéri* as a demonstration of the dichotomy of the process of aging and old age itself. Asserts that Chéri is a metaphor for Léa's youth, but that he must die since he represents illusion. Contends that Léa's strength and lucidity are in direct contrast to the portrayals of aging women by male writers. Modified version was incorporated into Chapter 4 of Stewart's book on Colette.

2130 Stewart, Joan Hinde. "Colette: The Mirror Image." *French Forum* 3 (Sept. 1978): 195-205. Also, as "Colette and the Epistolary Novel," in item 1076 *Colette: The Woman, The Writer*, 43-53. Explores Colette's letter technique in *La Vagabonde* and *Mitsou*, as the expression both of an earlier literary tradition and of an experimental one. Studies these techniques in terms of the heroine's search for identity and her willingness to communicate with men. Concludes that the letter and the mirror serve similar functions. A valuable article, especially since *Mitsou* has so far been accorded little serious attention by critics. Modified version was incorporated into Chapter 3 of Stewart's book on Colette.

2131   Stewart, Joan Hinde. "Colette's Gynæceum: Regression and
       Renewal." *French Review* 53 (April 1980): 662-69. Analyzes
       Duo and its sequel *Le Toutounier*, in order to identify the
       significance of the *toutounier* itself. Modified version was
       incorporated into Chapter 5 of Stewart's book on Colette.

2132   Stewart, Joan Hinde. "The School and the Home." *Women's
       Studies* 8:3 (1981): 259-72. Analyzes affinities between
       Claudine à l'école and *La Maison de Claudine*, and the
       relationship of one as negative of the other. Studies especially
       the role of the school and the family home in this context, as
       well as the function of the mother and the re-creation of the
       past. An excellent article, which sees the two books as
       encompassing a totality of female experience. Some passages
       incorporated into chapters 1 and 2 of Stewart's book on Colette.

2133   Stewart, Joan Hinde. "Willy, Sido: une géographie morale."
       Europe, no. 631-32 (Nov.-Dec. 1981): 61-71. Examines a
       polarity, in both morality and geography, between the two
       works that Stewart deems Colette's two most important, *Sido*
       and *Mes apprentissages*. Studies these works in terms of
       opposition and compensation. A penetrating analysis of a
       polarity that has long been recognized in Colette's work but
       which has been neither well understood nor well defined.
       Modified version was incorporated into Chapter 6 of Stewart's
       book on Colette.

2134   Stimpson, Brian. "Introduction." In item 0255 *Le Blé en herbe*, 13-
       62. Detailled introduction to edition designed for British sixth
       form and university students. The best and most complete
       presentation of *Le Blé en herbe* so far published. Discusses
       publication history, structural patterns, characters, stylistic and
       other techniques, and reception by critics, before offering a
       useful interpretation. Attributes critics' tendency to under-
       estimate Colette's work to their ignorance of her non-fiction and
       their failure to recognize that her fiction should be read on more
       than one level. Contains perceptive remarks on Colette's prose
       technique. Terms *Le Blé en herbe* a major contribution to the
       twentieth-century novel because of the statement Colette makes
       in it and because of the depth of psychological insight it
       reveals. A significant article.

2135 Stirling, Monica. "Colette." *Atlantic Monthly* 178 (July 1946): 92-95. Comprehensive and appealing profile of Colette as she was in an interview just after World War II. Compares her work to Rebecca West's because of its passion, wit, use of vocabulary and commitment to truth. Includes brief summary of her life with Willy and assessment of her contribution to French literature.

2136 Stockinger, Jacob. "Colette Today." *San Francisco Review of Books* 4 (March 1979): 18-21. General assessment of the ways in which Colette's reputation has benefited from the feminist movement and of the ways in which her work expresses its beginnings. Briefly identifies salient features of her portrayal of homosexuality. Terms her a pioneer.

2137 Stockinger, Jacob. "Impurity and Sexual Politics in the Provinces: Colette's Anti-Idyll in 'The Patriarch'." *Women's Studies* 8:3 (1981): 359-66. Identifies *Le Sieur Binard* as an expression of social criticism, in which the two apparently unrelated incidents of the novella are actually essential to the expression of Colette's intention, which is to indicate that purity and impurity cannot be polarized geographically. A brief but valuable article on a much-neglected novella.

2138 Stockinger, Jacob. "The Test of Love and Nature: Colette and Lesbians." In item 1076 *Colette: The Woman, The Writer*, 75-94. Over-view of Colette's presentation of lesbianism. Notes a stylistic shift to a greater seriousness on the subject in *Claudine en ménage* and asserts that the five Claudines offer a complete sexual philosophy of tolerance. Judges *Le Pur et l'impur* to have broad metapsychological and sociological dimensions.

2139 Strowski, Fortunat. "Madame Colette." In *La Renaissance littéraire de la France contemporaine*, 83-93. Paris: Plon-Nourrit, 1922. Essentially an appreciation of *Chéri*, deploring the subject matter and plot, which Strowski finds unlikely. Frequently paraphrases and quotes from the novel. See item 1497 Doyon for reply.

2140 Suffel, Jacques. "Quelques dates et points de repère." *Journal de Genève*, 28 Dec. 1963, 12-14. Suggests that both Colette and Polaire should be grateful to Willy for the impetus that his

entrepreneurial skills gave to their careers. Reproaches Colette
for unkind treatment of Willy in *Mes apprentissages*. Gives
interesting details about the series of negative literary portraits
Willy and Colette made of each other.

2141   Sullerot, Evelyne. In *Histoire et mythologie de l'amour: huit
       siècles d'écrits féminins*. Paris: Hachette, 1974. This collection
       of poems, prose passages and comments by women on the
       subject of love contains many brief quotations from Colette's
       works. Arranged thematically. Interesting but without critical
       value.

2142   Supervielle, Jules. In item 1095 *Hommage à Colette*, non-pag.
       Praises Colette's concision and ability to capture the fleeting
       moment in a poetic and concrete way.

2143   Suther, Judith D. "The Concept of 'Kingdom' in Camus' 'La
       femme adultère' and Colette's 'La Vagabonde'." In *Selected
       Proceedings: 32nd Mountain Interstate Foreign Language
       Conference*, edited by Gregario C. Martin, 367-71. Winston-
       Salem: Wake Forest University, 1984. Insists that the meaning
       of the term *royaume* is the same in the two title works, and
       offers a definition of it. Compares it with elements found in
       work by Gide, Thoreau and Alain-Fournier.

2144   Tailhade, Laurent. "Colette (Colette Willy)." In *La Médaille qui
       s'efface*, 213-24. Paris: Crès, 1924. High praise for Colette's
       originality, daring and gift for descriptive detail, especially in
       Les Heures longues.

2145   Temkine, Raymonde. "L'ancienne et la nouvelle avant-gardes
       américaines." *Europe*, no. 599 (March 1979): 213-21. Includes
       brief review of *Dressed like an Egg*, English-language stage
       production based on the life of Colette. Terms it strange that
       Colette's memory should be kept alive largely through the
       efforts of Americans.

2146   Terrain, Olympe. [Letter to Claude Chauvière]. In item 1072
       Chauvière, 190-91. Colette's schoolteacher, the model for
       Mademoiselle Sergent in *Claudine à l'école*, recalls Colette as
       an excellent student, especially in composition, with a
       vivacious personality. Although this letter of 1930 contains no

negative comments, other correspondence reveals that she was
deeply hurt by Colette's first novel.

2147 Tesson, Eugène. "L'Eglise et le refus de funérailles religieuses."
Revue de Paris 61 (Oct. 1954): 108-12. An eminent member of
the Roman Catholic clergy defends the Church's decision to
refuse Colette a religious funeral. Elaborates official doctrines
supporting its position.

2148 Theis, Raimund. "Jugendstil und Heimkehr zur Natur: Colette." In
Die französische Autorin: vom Mittelalter bis zur Gegenwart,
edited by Renate Baader and Dietmar Fricke, 213-15. Wiesbaden:
Athenaion, 1979. Declares that Colette's feminism does not
reflect an ideological protest on her part but a personal quest,
and that it both resulted in a revolution in the perspective
through which fictional women characters are depicted and also
furthered the general emancipation of women in France.
Demonstrates how her vision went beyond that of the *Jugendstil*
or *Art nouveau* movement dominant during the early years of
her career.

2149 Thérive, André. "Colette." In *Galerie de ce temps*, 11-33. Paris:
Nouvelle Revue critique, 1931. This collection of three book
reviews published from 1920 to 1929 offers a good sample of
one critic's evolving opinion of Colette during her most prolific
decade. Includes comments not only about the specific novels
but about her entire output. Defends her against criticism of the
subject matter of *Chéri*. Offers a good early analysis of Chéri's
psychology in the sequel, *La Fin de Chéri*. Lauds courage of the
subject matter of *La Seconde*, ranking it equal to the other two
novels. Thérive is still one of the few critics to have detected
comic aspects in Colette's work.

2150 Thétard, Henry. "Colette et les fauves." *Revue des deux mondes*, 1
Sept. 1954, 76-81. Illustrates judgment of Colette as a premier
animal writer by relating incidents demonstrating her knowledge
of various types of animals and by quoting opinions of experts.

2151 Thiébaut, Marcel. "De Claudine à Colette." *Revue de Paris* 64
(Aug. 1957): 95-119. Also in *Entre les lignes*, 140-81. Paris:
Hachette, 1962. Extremely interesting over-all assessment of
Colette's work, despite some confusion between fact and fiction

and the occasional reliance upon details now known to be
inaccurate. Opinions expressed include many of those common
to critics of the middle decades of the century. Accords much
importance to the influence on Colette's work of her marriage to
Henry de Jouvenel. Claims to identify premonitory factors in
her novels, particularly in *Chéri*, as well as echos of atavistic
Celtic influences common to the Puisaye. Relates her work to
both primitivism and existentialism. The section on stylistic
techniques is the least satifactory.

2152 Thiry, Marcel. "Hommage à Colette et à Edouard Montpetit."
      *Bulletin de l'Académie royale de langue et de littérature
      françaises* 32 (Dec. 1954): 289-91. Text of a brief address, given
      9 Oct. 1954 to the Belgian Academy after Colette's death.
      Terms her a novelist of manners.

2153 Thomé, Jules-René. "André Jacquemin." *Courrier graphique* 15
      (May-June 1950): 17-24. Provides details of problems with the
      illustrations for the 1942 *La Naissance du jour*.

2154 Thomé, Jules-René. "Luc-Albert Moreau." *Le Portique*, no. 7
      (1950): 21-35. This assessment of Moreau's work includes a
      short commentary of the 1932 edition of Colette's *La Naissance
      du jour*, for which Moreau did the illustrations.

2155 Thoorens, Léon. "Grandeur et misère de Colette." *Revue générale
      belge* 90 (15 Sept. 1954): 1917-24. One of the best of the
      plethora of articles published just after Colette's death. Rejects
      works published during the last decade of her life as inferior to
      earlier ones. Identifies her place in twentieth century literature as
      at the center of a new literary current, whose writers depict a
      world in flux as seen from an individual perspective. Traces
      what Thoorens deems negative elements in her work to Willy's
      influence and to social injustices experienced by Colette because
      of the oppression of women. This is an important article
      because it supports a feminist viewpoint well before feminist
      critics became interested in Colette, and because Thoorens is
      one of the few early critics to attempt to assess Colette's work
      within the context of modern intellectual and literary currents.

2156 Thoraval, Jean, and Maurice Léo. "Colette: 'Les Vrilles de la
      vigne'." In *Le commentaire de textes littéraires*, 147-52. Paris:

Bordas, 1969. Analysis of paragraphs 2-5 of "Le dernier feu," in
order to elicit from it characteristics of Colette's personality and
talent. Stresses the universal application of its ideas. Contains
comments about other writers and works.

2157 Tinter, Sylvie. "Sexualité et écriture dans 'La Vagabonde'." *Hebrew
University Studies in Literature and the Arts* 9 (Spring 1981):
61-75. Interesting interpretation of Colette's portrayal of love in
La Vagabonde, the Claudine novels and parts of *Les Vrilles de
la vigne*. Asserts that Colette considers the source of problems
arising from relations between men and women to lie in the
nature of sexuality itself, and the three solutions possible to be
writing, memory and a retreat into nature. Concludes that all
three represent escape whereby love is directed away from the
sex-object and towards the self.

2158 Tinter, Sylvie. "Sidonie Colette ou le temps de la mère." *Hebrew
University Studies in Literature and the Arts* 14 (Spring 1987):
33-47. A not always convincing attempt to determine why
Colette waited thirteen years after her mother's death before she
wrote about her. Posits the view that writing the texts of *La
Maison de Claudine* marked a turning point in Colette's life,
when psychological factors obliged her to assess her past in
order to prepare for the future. Re-creating her childhood would
thus restore a damaged self-image and provide her with a
feminine model for her old age.

2159 Tortel, Jean. "Colette." *Cahiers du sud* 325 (Oct. 1954): 437-39.
Judges Colette's influence on French society to be greater than
either Gide's or Proust's because of her wide readership, and
criticizes the persistent indifference towards her work of many
otherwise serious critics.

2160 Tosi, Guy. "Colette et D'Annunzio." *Cahiers Colette*, no. 8
(1986): 15-23. Recounts Colette's few meetings with Gabriele
D'Annunzio beginning with their probable acquaintance in
1915. Quotes from their rare correspondence. D'Annunzio
admired Colette's work but their relations were sporadic and
apparently petered out altogether about 1928.

2161 Touquoy, Henry. "D'après son origine et son parler, Colette était
giennoise!" *Bulletin folklorique d'Ile-de-France* 19 (Oct.-Dec.

1956): 926-28. Reprinted from *Journal de Gien*, 21 June 1956. Offers geographical, historical, political and economic reasons for the view that Colette's birthplace of Saint-Sauveur is not truly Burgundian. Glosses *Claudine à l'école* and *Claudine à Paris* for patois terms ostensibly of Saint-Sauveur but which can also be traced to the region around the city of Gien.

2162 Tournier, Michel. "Colette ou le Premier Couvert." *Nouvelle Revue française* 324 (1 Jan. 1980): 84-94. Also in *Cahiers Colette*, no. 3-4 (1981): 78-88; and *Le Vol du vampire: notes de lecture*, 239-51. Paris: Mercure de France, 1981. Extracts in item 1057 *Album Masques: Colette*, 44. Comments on Colette's role in the Goncourt Academy, of which she became president. Compares her work with that of Proust and Céline, whom Tournier names as the two greatest French novelists of the century, as well as with that of Sartre, Valéry, Gide and Giono. Notes that Colette never won the Goncourt prize.

2163 Trefusis, Violet. In *Don't Look Round*, 88-90. London: Hutchinson, 1952. Brief but entertaining reminiscences of meetings with Colette. Includes much personal description. Also many casual references to Colette throughout the book.

2164 Trezza, Angela. "Colette." In *I Contemporanei Letteratura francese*, edited by Massimo Colesanti and Luigi de Nardis, 637-44. Rome: Luciano Lucarini, 1976. Brief biography and over-all assessment of Colette's work. Traces her originality to her portrayal of the female perspective on love and life, but draws a distinction between her and dedicated feminist writers.

2165 Trezza, Angela. "Dal realismo all'affabulazione." In *Il Mestiere di scrivere: Colette, Simone de Beauvoir, Marguerite Duras*, 63-88. Foggia: Bastogi di A. Manuali, 1983. Very good analysis of narrative techniques in *Chéri*, especially the use of zero and double focalization, by means of which Chéri is presented as love-object and product of Léa's creation. Makes perceptive remarks about Colette's methods of distancing and about the relationship of her techniques to those of impressionist painters.

2166 Triolet, Elsa. "La voix de nos maîtres ou les forces intérieures du roman (de Melville à Colette)." *Confluences* 3 (1943): 84-93. Also in *Problèmes du roman*, edited by Jean Prévost, 74-82.

Lyons: Confluences, 1943; Brussels: Le Carrefour, 1945.
Although the title indicates that this article treats the work of
many writers, references to Colette dominate the whole. Lauds
most aspects of her work, especially her "Frenchness."
Attempts to define her style and her appeal. Compares her with
Tolstoy in her ability to portray intimacy.

2167 Troyat, Henri. In item 1095 *Hommage à Colette*, non-pag. Brief
passage describing Colette's arrival at a hotel in Monaco.
Praises the magic of her style.

2168 Truc, Gonzague. "La sensibilité de Madame Colette, écrivain."
Revue hebdomadaire 47 (29 Jan. 1938): 554-71. Attempts to
define Colette's type of sensibility and to identify those areas of
her life and writing in which it plays a major role. Terms it
pagan but modern, in that it is little subject to recent traditions.
Later became chapter 5 of Truc's book on Colette.

2169 Truc, Gonzague. "L'unique héroïne de Madame Colette." *Revue
critique des idées et des livres*, no. 159 (25 Feb. 1920): 398-
410. Main idea of this article, written before publication of
Chéri, is that Colette's heroines are portraits of herself. Its
patronizing expressions of admiration for her work are typical of
Colette criticism of the period, which often consisted mostly of
paraphrase, quotation and rhetoric. Some passages of this article
were incorporated into chapter 2 of Truc's book on Colette but
his criticism of her became more perceptive with time.

2170 Truc, Gonzague. In *Classicisme d'hier et classiques d'aujourd'hui*,
30-32. Paris: Belles-Lettres, 1929. Criticizes Colette's fictional
characters as elementary and unilinear, devoted to the physical
life. Finds her celebrated style now heavy. These few paragraphs
were later incorporated into chapter 3 of Truc's book on Colette,
where the severity of the judgment is alleviated by other, more
favorable comments.

2171 Tusón, Vicente. "Colette o el hambre de vida." *Cuadernos
Hispanoamericanos*, no. 103 (July 1958): 59-63. Offers the
intriguing hypothesis that Colette's thirst for life can be
attributed to the trauma of the failure of her first marriage,
which transformed her feelings for men into a need for
possession, not only of physical objects but also of the past.

2172 Valéry, Paul. "'Colette qui, seule de son sexe...'" *Figaro littéraire*, 24 Jan. 1953, 1. Also in *Figaro littéraire*, 7 Aug. 1954, 4. Well-known dedication to Colette, saying that she, alone of her sex, knows that writing is an art, possesses that art and amazes many men who do not have it. The inherent sexism of this "compliment" has aroused the ire of many feminists.

2173 Vallentin, Antonina. "Colette hat einen Nebenberuf." *Frankfurter Zeitung*, 15 Jan. 1933, 9. Interesting evaluation of the pros and cons of Colette's latest venture, the sale of beauty products. Suggests several reasons for the move, including the necessity for Colette to have a second career in the event that a waning inspiration finds her no longer able to support herself by writing.

2174 van Casselaer, Catherine. In *Lot's Wife: Lesbian Paris, 1890-1914*, 71-80, 113-26, 145-46, 157-62. Liverpool: Janus, 1986. Includes many references to Colette and to passages in her books where lesbianism is mentioned. Chapter titled "I belong to Missy" is devoted completely to her relationship with the Marquise de Morny, with whom Colette lived after separating from Willy. Interesting and provocative but not reliable in its presentation of the facts.

2175 Vandérem, Fernand. In *Le Miroir des lettres*, vol. 2, 227-29; vol. 3, 157-60; vol. 6, 299-301; vol. 8, 193-98. Paris: Flammarion, 1920-29. Reviews of four novels--*Mitsou*, *Chéri*, *Le Blé en herbe*, and *La Fin de Chéri*--are typical of the decade. All are effusively laudatory, but one can detect, across the series, a subtle increase in the esteem in which Colette is held by Vandérem as her work matures. It is remarkable that, well before the dramatization of *Chéri*, Vandérem expresses a wish to see it performed on stage.

2176 Versini, Laurent. In *Le Roman épistolaire*, 236-37. Paris: Presses universitaires de France, 1979. Classifies *Mitsou* as a novel in the French epistolary psychological tradition, but offers no analysis of it.

2177 Viallet, Bice. "Colette." In *Il Romanzo femminile francese contemporaneo*, 161-77. Milan: Alpes, 1925. Early article attempting to situate Colette's work within the framework of a movement. Lists characteristics presumably distinguishing her from the mass of French female writers as well as from men writers. Judges severely her capacity for characterization, accusing her of lack of imagination, but praises highly the novels published before 1920. An interesting article offering some provocative opinions and conclusions, thus providing a useful balance against unreserved expressions of admiration or reproach made by many other critics of the time.

2178 Vignaud, Jean. "Colette, la sauvage." In *L'Esprit contemporain*, 92-98. Paris: Sagittaire, 1938. Unsatisfactory mixture of praise for Colette's originality and talent for depicting nature, and a tendency to characterize her as a primitive. Contains much paraphrase of *Sido* and *La Chatte*.

2179 Vigorelli, Giancarlo. "Colette, questa grande Fedra borghese." *Fiera letteraria*, 15 Aug. 1954, 1-2. Obituary and general homage. Develops a comparison between Colette and the notion of a "bourgois Phedra."

2180 Vildrac, Charles [pseud. of Charles Messager]. In *Pages de journal 1922-1966*, 44-45. Paris: Gallimard, 1968. Brief account of a visit to Colette with Georges Duhamel, during which all three writers trade compliments and puns.

2181 Villaret, Bernard. "Préface." In item 0008 *Lettres à Moune et au Toutounet*, 7-21. Brief biography of Hélène Jourdan-Morhange [Moune] and Luc-Albert Moreau [Le Toutounet] is provided by Moreau's nephew Villaret, who also includes anecdotes about his first meeting with Colette and their intermittent relations through the years. A very personal article.

2182 Villien, Bruno. "Colette et le cinéma." In item 1057 *Album Masques: Colette*, 174-75. A good summary, with comment, of Colette's film activity. Ranks *Lac-aux-dames* as the most "colettian" of all the films she directly inspired.

2183 Virmaux, Alain, and Odette Virmaux. "Le cinéma dans l'œuvre et la vie de Colette." In item 0980 *Colette: au cinéma*, 5-20. Succinct but comprehensive introduction to the first significant critical presentation of Colette's film work. Attempts to identify her ideas about film as an entertainment medium and to assess her contribution towards its ultimate development as a major industry in France. Also provides a summary of Colette's specific film activities.

English translation [abridged]: "Colette and the cinéma." Trans. Sarah W.R. Smith. In item 0984 *Colette at the movies*, 1-7.

2184   Virmaux, Alain, and Odette Virmaux. "Colette au cinéma." *Europe*, no. 631-32 (Nov.-Dec. 1981): 119-29. An important article, supplement to *Colette: au cinéma*, the Virmaux's seminal work on Colette's film writing. Identifies lost film scenarios and argues that Colette did not include her cinema work in the *OCLF* because she considered film to be an inferior genre. Argues that the new material demonstrates Colette's nostalgia and preference for silent films. Followed by six letters of 1916 to Madame Sigrist de Cesti in connection with film negotiations in Italy.

English translation: "Introduction: Colette and the cinema." Trans. Sarah W.R. Smith. In item 0984 *Colette at the movies*, 1-7.

2185   Virmaux, Alain, and Odette Virmaux. "Colette auteur de sous-titres." In item 0980 *Colette: au cinéma*, 99-102. Serves as introduction to Colette's text for *Jeunes filles en uniforme*, a German film for which she wrote the French sub-titles in 1931. Summarizes known details about the event.

2186   Virmaux, Alain, and Odette Virmaux. "Colette critique dramatique (sur 19 textes retrouvés à la faveur d'une recherche orientée vers 'Les Cenci' d'Antonin Artaud)." *Europe*, no. 631-32 (Nov.-Dec. 1981): 140-45. Details the discovery of 19 newly-discovered texts of theater criticism [annotated separately]. Compares texts in *La Jumelle noire* with texts written on the same plays for a different newspaper, noting that Colette is never repetitive.

2187   Virmaux, Alain, and Odette Virmaux. "Colette critique et chroniqueuse." In item 0980 *Colette: au cinéma*, 23-28. Introduces collection of film reviews which Colette published during the silent film era of 1914-1918 but which remained, for the most part, uncollected in book form until this volume appeared. It also attempts to identify the implicit criteria on which Colette's judgments were based.

English translation: "Colette the critic." Trans. Sarah W.R. Smith.
In item 0984 *Colette at the movies*, 9-13.

2188 Virmaux, Alain, and Odette Virmaux. "Colette dialoguiste." In
item 0980 *Colette: au cinéma*, 129-37. Also, under the title
"Colette et 'Lac-aux-dames'," in *Avant-Scène Cinéma*, no. 284
(15 March 1982): 4-7. Provides pertinent background
information about Colette's first real venture into dialogue
writing for the cinema, *Lac-aux-dames*, released in 1934. The
film was a great success.

English translation [abridged]: "Dialogue and Scenario by Colette:
'Lac-aux-dames'." Trans. Sarah W.R. Smith. In item 0984
Colette at the movies, 89-93.

2189 Virmaux, Alain, and Odette Virmaux. "Colette scénariste." In item
0980 *Colette: au cinéma*, 219-22. Traces the known history of
the film *Divine* (1935), which was not a success. Because the
manuscript of Colette's scenario and dialogue has been lost, the
text discussed in this introduction has been re-established from a
copy of the film itself.

English translation: "Dialogue and Scenario by Colette: 'Divine'."
Trans. Sarah W.R. Smith. In item 0984 *Colette at the movies*,
168-71.

2190 Vitoux, Pierre. "Le jeu de la focalisation." *Poétique*, no. 51 (Sept.
1982): 359-68. Critical discussion of item 1174, identifying
problems with Bal's theories and their application to *La Chatte*.

2191 Voisin, Joseph. "Colette." *Le Feu*, no. 78 (Oct. 1911): 406-12.
Unflattering but imaginative and entertaining parable, in which
Colette the barnyard hen falls victim to her own machinations.
Although this article has appeared in Colette bibliographies for
over fifty years, that the hen is actually meant to represent the
writer Colette, who in 1911 was still signing her work Colette
Willy, is open to question.

2192 Voisin, Marcel. "Théophile Gautier et Colette." *Bulletin de la
Société belge des professeurs de français*, no. 74-75 (1973) 28-
31. Analyzes *La Jumelle noire*, Colette's collection of theater
reviews, in order to demonstrate parallels with Gautier's

impressionist criticism. Judges her style of intuitive criticism
to be at least as sound as one based on dogma or the study of
techniques. An interesting assessment of a work on which little
serious research has so far been done.

2193   Vondrásková, Helena. "L'image de la femme dans l'œuvre de
       Colette." *Acta Universitatis Carolinæ. Philologica* 4 (1966):
       57-64. Attempts to define Colette's early notion of what women
       are. Concludes that she is alternately optimistic and pessimistic
       in her hope for a better life for women.

2194   Vondrásková, Helena. "Réflexions sur l'œuvre romanesque de
       Colette." *Acta Universitatis Carolinæ. Philologica* 6 (1969):
       87-99. Develops principles underlying Raaphorst-Rousseau's
       division of Colette's novels into autobiographical and objective,
       and defends Colette against the charge that her male protagonists
       are one-faceted. The attempt to situate her work in relation to
       artistic and literary currents of the late nineteenth and early
       twentieth centuries is only partly successful. Declares that
       Colette's novels constitute a social document depicting woman's
       consciousness under various conditions.

2195   Vondrásková, Helena. "Le roman de Colette, 'Le Blé en herbe',
       miroir de sa conception de la vie." *Acta Universitatis Carolinæ.
       Philologica* 3 (1959): 29-33. Argues that *Le Blé en herbe* is an
       expression of Colette's basic ideas about childhood and about
       the fundamental relationship between men and women, and that
       the novel demonstrates how firmly Colette is committed to the
       notion of the predominance of instinct over will.

2196   Wagner, Horst. "L'œuvre de Colette en Allemagne." In item 1077
       Colette, Nouvelles Approches Critiques, 189-203. Over-all
       assessment of the state of Colette research in Germany up to
       1984. Detects very little serious work, partly because of the
       difficulty of finding bibliography, partly because existing
       material is often inaccessible in any case. Delineates the image
       of Colette implicit in German criticism, noting that it remains
       at a cliché level because Colette is less popular than formerly
       and because she is still not accepted as a serious writer there.

2197   Wague, Georges. "Colette et le pantomime." *Le Capitole*, May
       1923, non-pag. [14]. Emphasizes Colette's professionalism

during the time they performed on tour together. Recalls her promptness, attentiveness and willingness, as well as the originality of her expression and her quickness to understand and execute new ideas.

2198 Wague, Georges."Elle savait ce qui ne s'apprend pas." *Lettres françaises*, 12 Aug. 1954, 4. Colette's former music-hall partner and long-time friend terms her an original performer, whose good humor and enthusiasm were great advantages. Looks back on fifty years of precious friendship.

2199 Wague, Georges. "Sur Colette et Sido." *Figaro littéraire*, 8 Dec. 1956, 4. Includes letter by Wague protesting against remarks by Escholier in item 1536. Insists that Escholier was wrong in stating that Colette spoke harshly of the music-hall.

2200 Walzer, Pierre-Olivier. "Colette." In *Le XXe siècle*, vol. 1, 324-31. Paris: Arthaud, 1975. Fine, dispassionate over-view of Colette's life and achievements. Attributes her apparently negative portrayal of men and her reputed amorality to events in her life. Lists characteristics of her attitude to life, her style and her sensuality.

2201 Walzer, Pierre-Olivier. "La révolution claudinienne." In *Autour de Colette à Saint-Tropez*, non-pag. [119-46]. Good attempt to demonstrate that Claudine represents a preliminary step towards feminine liberation in France. Considers her a bridge between the siren depicted by many symbolists, who viewed women as an inferior and negative influence in the life of the creative artist, and the natural but unhappy woman typical of naturalist literature. Notes that she was not the first literary example of that type, but was the first successful one. Gives Willy credit for having indirectly encouraged this contribution to the feminist cause.

2202 Warburg, Fredric. In *All Authors are Equal*, 149-54. London: Hutchinson, 1973. Fascinating summary of events leading up to the publication of the 21 volumes of Colette's works in English by Secker & Warburg, including negotations with American publishers. Warburg's account of a visit to the aged Colette for the signing of the contract is without doubt the most moving portrait ever written about her in English.

2203   Warburg, Fredric. In *An Occupation for Gentlemen*, 154. London:
       Hutchinson, 1959. Describes enthusiasm of Pamela Warburg
       for Colette's works. Fredric Warburg was instrumental in
       publishing the Secker & Warburg English translations,
       beginning in 1950.

2204   Watts, Janet. "Love your Subject, Marry your Subject." *Guardian*,
       27 Jan. 1973, 10. Curious article relating interview with
       Margaret Crosland quoting an interview with Colette.

2205   Wenger, Marguerite. "Bibliographie." *Das Buch* 3:10 (1951): 11-
       16. Detailed listing of editions of Colette's books followed by
       brief list of German translations to date.

2206   Werth, Léon. "Colette du XVIe siècle à nos jours." *Le Point*, no.
       39 (May 1951): 14-24. Recalls incidents of Colette's early
       career. Confesses to being fascinated with her style, because of
       its density of perfect images. Terms Colette's reputed amorality
       a type of purity, allied to observation touched with melancholy.
       Contrasts her apparent acceptance of all milieux with attitude of
       Neel Doff, a writer of pre-World War I.

2207   Wescott, Glenway. "A Call on Colette and Goudeket." In *Images
       of Truth: Remembrances and Criticism*, 142-48. New York:
       Harper & Row, 1962. Account of a long conversation with
       Colette's third husband and a subsequent interview with Colette
       herself, in which she insists on the feminine nature of her
       writing. Mostly personal impressions.

2208   Wescott, Glenway. "Colette." *Vogue* [U.S] 118 (Dec. 1951): 134-
       35, 186-91. General appreciation of the writer and the work.
       Most of this article was later incorporated into item 2207 or
       item 2211 or both.

2209   Wescott, Glenway. "Introduction." In *Break of Day* [trans. of *La
       Naissance du jour*], some eds. Interprets *La Naissance du jour* as
       an expression of Colette's effort to exorcise remnants of
       romanticism at the same time as she gave literary form to an
       alternative she rejected when she began her liaison with the
       youthful Maurice Goudeket. Surprisingly, Wescott identifies
       pantheism as the novel's transcendent emotion. Most of this
       introduction was later incorporated into item 2211.

2210 Wescott, Glenway. "Introduction." In item 0102 *Short Novels of Colette*, vii-lvii. Good general introduction to Colette's work. Includes biographical details, personal anecdotes, speculation on Colette's psychology, some publication information, a general analysis of the novels included in the volume, comments on Colette's style and remarks on her other works. An informal, entertaining article, which reveals Wescott's own reactions to the characters in the seven novels of the collection [*Chéri. The Last of Chéri. The Indulgent Husband. The Other One. Duo. The Toutounier. The Cat*].

2211 Wescott, Glenway. "An Introduction to Colette." In *Images of Truth: Remembrances and Criticism*, 86-141. New York: Harper & Row, 1962. Composite article, consisting of item 2210 edited and up-dated, combined with sections of item 2208. Result is a rambling but interesting article touching on a variety of topics.

2212 West, Paul. In *The Modern Novel*, vol. 1, 180-81. London: Hutchinson, 1963. Likens Colette to Camus in her refusal of absolutes, and Léa's stoicism to that of Mauriac's women characters.

2213 West, Rebecca. "Formidable." In *Ending in Earnest*, 180-81. Garden City, N.Y.: Doubleday, Doran, 1931. Reflections on an accidental meeting with Colette. Insists on the strength of her personality.

2214 West, Rebecca. [No title]. *Figaro littéraire*, 24 Jan. 1953, 5. Identifies Colette's contribution to the novel as a product of her attachment to reality and the brilliance and precision with which that reality is portrayed, especially in the creation of her most memorable characters.

2215 Whatley, Janet. "Colette and the Art of Survival." In item 1076 *Colette: The Woman, The Writer*, 32-39. Identifies the image of the porcelain repairer as a metaphor of Colette's art of survival and holds that her female characters all exhibit this principle, which Colette many times states is inherent in the female. Although the main idea of this article is not completely new, the demonstration it offers is a fine one.

2216 Whatley, Janet. "Colette's 'Le Pur et l'impur': On Real and Phony Mysteries." *Modern Language Studies* 13 (Summer 1983): 16-26. Draws an analogy between *Le Pur et l'impur* and a visit to a domain inhabited by the troubled spirits of bygone days, and analyzes Colette's suggestions of the occult in the work in the light of this analogy. Concludes that Colette offers her readers solutions to many small mysteries only to leave them with a major one at the end. An unusual and fascinating interpretation of Colette's most controversial work.

2217 Whittier, Gayle. "Nature as Birthright and Birthloss: Mary McCarthy and Colette." *Perspectives on Contemporary Literature* 5 (1979): 42-54. Interesting comparison of Colette's portrayal of childhood in *Sido* and *La Maison de Claudine* with Mary McCarthy's in *Memories of a Catholic Girlhood*. Focuses on their basic attitude towards childhood, as well as the function therein of mother, religion and art. Concludes that nature plays a positive role for Colette by permitting her to re-create and so recover her mother and her childhood, whereas no such process is possible for McCarthy, who must revise the past.

2218 Wickes, George. In *The Amazon of Letters: The Life and Loves of Natalie Barney*, 53-54, 90-99. New York: Putnam's, 1976. In this biography, Colette's name is frequently mentioned as a member of Barney's lesbian circle about 1910. Even after her second marriage the two women continued to be friends. Wickes declares that, contrary to the opinions voiced by some critics, Colette was never Barney's lover, but quotes Janet Flanner as saying that Barney was fonder of Colette than of any other woman in French society. Includes some well-known anecdotes.

2219 Willie, Josie. "Il manque Léa." *Gazette des lettres*, 29 Oct. 1949, 8. Attempts to define Chéri's modern counterpart. Concludes that such are plentiful while modern Léas are rare.

2220 Willy [pseud. of Henry Gauthier-Villars, writing as L'Ouvreuse]. "Claudine musicographe." *Mercure de France*, 15 Dec. 1927, 527-39. Presents a sheaf of selections from musical criticism published in *Gil Blas* in 1903 under the signature "Claudine." Researchers who consider these reviews to be all or mostly Colette's work rather than Willy's base their judgments partly on the style, which is very different from his, and partly on the content, since the musical preferences expressed therein reflect those known to be Colette's own.

2221 Willy [pseud. of Henry Gauthier-Villars]. "Une préface oubliée pour 'Claudine à l'école'." *Œuvres libres*, no. 161 (Oct. 1959): 278-80. Preface included in some of the early editions of *Claudine à l'école*. Emphasizes Claudine's "innocent perversity," and refers to Colette as amoral. This epithet was to be repeated by many later critics.

2222 Willy [pseud. of Henry Gauthier-Villars]. "Quelques détails sur la collaboration Colette-Willy." *Nouvelles littéraires*, 3 April 1926, 1. Protests against details furnished in an interview of Colette by Lefèvre [item 1787]. Insists that many of the equivocal elements of *Claudine à l'école* were not his invention but were rooted in the reality on which the novel was based, that he had met Luce personally, and that he and Colette had collaborated on the music reviews published in *Gil Blas* under the signature "Claudine au concert."

2223 Wiriath, Marcel. "Colette." *Ecrits de Paris*, no. 53 (March 1949): 25-26. Also in *Silhouettes*, 22-24. Paris: Self, 1949. Generally favorable assessment of Colette's work, without reference to specific titles, but declares that having little to say, she writes about herself.

2224 Wolfromm, Jean-Didier. "Colette nous a laissé son adresse." *Magazine littéraire*, no. 42 (July 1970): 11-14. Uses Colette's published correspondence to draw a portrait of Colette as letter-writer and friend. Emphasizes her willingness to help others and her courage at seeing her younger correspondents die before her.

2225 Wurmser, André. "Le respect fanatique de la vie." *Lettres françaises*, 12 Aug. 1954, 4. Emphasizes the importance of observation to Colette's art, insisting that she loved the world as she found it, that words were real objects to her, and that her example did much for the emancipation of women in France.

2226 Wyler, André. "Sido et Colette." *Figaro littéraire*, 22 Dec. 1956, 4. Letter to the editor from member of the Robineau-Duclos family, protesting against Escholier's statements about intrigues in the family [see item 1536].

2227   Yamata, Kikou. "Au Japon." In item 1072 Chauvière, 276-77.
       Praises Colette's non-anthropomorphic depiction of animals in
       La Paix chez les bêtes.

2228   Yamata, Kikou. "Une visite chez Colette." *France-Asie* 99 (Aug.
       1954): 1008-11. Account of a visit to Colette by the author, an
       admirer from Tokyo, about 1950. Personal impressions of
       Maurice Goudeket and of Colette, in whom Yamata observed
       much sadness, are particularly interesting.

2229   Zeisler, Marie-Claude. "Le thème de l'enfance chez Colette." *Ecole
       II* 67 (1 Feb. 1976): 2-8, 51. Thematic study in which Zeisler
       attempts to identify Colette's reasons for writing *Sido* and *La
       Maison de Claudine*, by defining the principal elements of her
       childhood as gleaned from those texts and analyzing her
       subsequent recapture of them through writing. Based on the
       premise that the two works are completely autobiographical.
       For students.

**Anonymous articles
arranged alphabetically by journal title**

2230   "Madame Colette." *Action française*, 3 Jan. 1929, 3. Impressions
       of Colette, in the Palais Royal and elsewhere. Compares her
       sensibility with Rousseau's.

2231   "Hommage à Colette." *Arcadie* 1 (Sept. 1954): 5-6. In memoriam,
       praising especially Colette's treatment of the various forms of
       homosexuality. Signed: Arcadie.

2232   "Hommage à Colette." *Bulletin de l'Institut français en Espagne*,
       no. 79 (Jan.-Feb. 1955): 9-16. General article sketching
       Colette's life and career, and assessing her place in French
       literature. Considers her interpretation of animal life even more
       original than her portrayal of love, but concludes that her vision
       is limited to the material world. Still one of the most impartial
       assessments of Colette's place in literature.

2233 "Bertrand de Jouvenel." *Cahiers Colette*, no. 9 (1987): 2. Notice of the death of Colette's step-son, 1 March 1987. Bertrand de Jouvenel, the eldest son of Colette's second husband, is considered by many to be the model for Phil in *Le Blé en herbe*. As one of the heirs to Colette's only daughter, he subsequently willed many of his step-mother's possessions to the future museum at Saint-Sauveur.

2234 "Colette au Palais." *Candide*, 15 Jan. 1925, 3. Announces Colette's first day as trial reporter and describes her peculiar manner of taking notes.

2235 "Great Age Ripened Colette's Talent." *Courier-Journal* [Louisville, Kentucky], 5 Aug. 1954, 4. In memoriam. Predicts increasing interest in Colette's non-fiction.

2236 "Claudine à Besançon." *Dépêche républicaine de Franche-Comté*, 23 Sept. 1903, non-pag. [1-2]. Account of an interview with Colette, in the absence of her husband Willy. Colette confesses to having collaborated on the Claudine novels and to having written articles of musical criticism for *Gil Blas*. This is one of the earliest public acknowledgments of Colette's share in work formerly attributed to Willy alone. Signed: L'Echo.

2237 *Figaro littéraire*, 14 Aug. 1954, 10. Six photographs of Colette's funeral, including the catafalque, the family, the mourners, and members of the Goncourt Academy.

2238 "Les ascendances de Colette." *Figaro littéraire*, 5 Jan. 1957, 11. Details about Colette's maternal ancestors.

2239 "L'hommage à Colette." *Gazette de Lausanne*, 14 Aug. 1954, 8. Brief account of Colette's funeral. Signed: Le promeneur des boulevards.

2240 *Illustrated London News* 225 (14 Aug. 1954): 269-71. Events reported include death of Colette, "the famous French novelist and great lover of animals," with photographs of the catafalque and the funeral procession.

2241   "Colette à l'Académie de Belgique." *Illustration*, no. 4858 (11 April 1936): 421. Report of Colette's reception at the Belgian Academy and of her acceptance address, 4 April 1936.

2242   "La Flecha en el Tiempo: Colette." *Insula*, no. 104 (1 Aug. 1954): 2. Obituary with brief account of Colette's life and career.

2243   "Colette joins France's Literary 'Ten'." *Life* 18 (28 May 1945): 47. Bird's-eye summary of Colette's career on the occasion of her election to the Goncourt Academy. Excellent portrait of her working in bed.

2244   "End of a Piquant Career." *Life* 37 (16 Aug. 1954): 77-83. Fine collection of photographs marking Colette's death and recording various stages of her career.

2245   "Conversation with Colette." *Living Age* 340 (May 1931): 265-68. "Interview" in which Colette confesses her likes and dislikes, and denies any wish to write. Trans. from the Vienna *Neue Freie Presse*.

2246   "Bibliographie des œuvres de Colette." *Livres de France* 5 (Oct. 1954): 10-12. Bibliography of editions of Colette's work, arranged chronologically.

2247   "Francis Jammes et Colette." *Mercure de France*, 1 Oct. 1954, 364-65. Brief comment on Jammes' preface to the *Sept dialogues de bêtes*, stressing his perspicacity in recognizing a deeper Colette behind her frivolous public image of 1905.

2248   "L'appartement de Colette au Palais-Royal ne deviendra pas un musée." *Le Monde*, 23 Dec. 1983, 12. Announces that furniture and other possessions left by Colette will go to the museum at Saint-Sauveur now that negotiations for one at the Palais Royal have failed.

2249   "Colette is dead in Paris at 81." *New York Times*, 4 Aug. 1954, 21. Sketches major incidents of Colette's life, and highlights, none too accurately, some of her works.

2250   "Colette is buried in saddened Paris." *New York Times*, 8 Aug. 1954, 85. Brief account of funeral.

2251 "Transition: Died." *Newsweek* 44 (16 Aug. 1954): 60. Obituary.

2252 "Une Proserpine de la Belle Epoque." *Nouvel observateur*, no. 83 (15 June 1966): 32-33. Questions whether the French still read Colette. Quotes brief remarks about her, particularly those of critic John Weightman.

2253 "Les dix sont sept." *Nouvelles littéraires*, 3 May 1945, 4. Brief announcement of Colette's election to the Goncourt Academy to replace La Varende, who had resigned after scandals at the end of World War II.

2254 "Colette et Lucie." *Nouvelles littéraires*, 12 July 1945, 4. Anecdote about Colette and Lucie Delarue-Mardrus and announcement of the first publication of *Gigi*.

2255 "Colette en promenade." *Nouvelles littéraires*, 11 Oct. 1945, 4. Brief account of a minor incident in which Colette has her photograph taken.

2256 "Les quatre-vingts ans de la Présidente." *Nouvelles littéraires*, 15 Jan. 1953, 7. Notice of Colette's eightieth birthday.

2257 "Sur le vif..." *Nouvelles littéraires*, 5 Feb. 1953, 7. Captioned photograph of Colette with members of the Goncourt Academy celebrating her eightieth birthday.

2258 "Colette grand officier." *Nouvelles littéraires*, 26 Feb. 1953, 7. Announcement of Colette's promotion to Grand Officer of the Legion of Honor.

2259 "Mieux vaut tard..." *Nouvelles littéraires*, 23 April 1953, 7. Brief anecdote about Colette's receiving the Grand Cross of the Legion of Honor.

2260 "La mort de Colette." *Nouvelles littéraires*, 5 Aug. 1954, 1. Stop-press announcement of Colette's death.

2261 "Profile--Colette." *Observer*, no. 8414 (7 Sept. 1952): 2. Brief but perceptive account of Colette's work for English readers. Stresses the difficulty of translating the subtleties of her style and the divergence between her views on love and those of the

English public. Terms her understanding of psychology superior to Aldous Huxley's. Wrongly assumes that she was still married to de Jouvenel in 1952.

2262 "Le cœur de Paris en deuil de Colette." *Paris-Match*, no. 281 (14 Aug. 1954): 14-21. Photographic report of Colette's lying-in-state at the Palais Royal and her subsequent burial at Père Lachaise cemetery. Particularly moving are photographs of some of the 10,000 people who filed past the catafalque.

2263 "Les grands de la littérature révélés par leur visage." *Paris-Match*, no. 993 (20 April 1968): 73-83. Series of close-up photographs of famous writers includes a splendid one of Colette from 1939.

2264 "La grande Colette n'a connu l'apothéose qu'à la fin de sa vie." *Paris-Match*, no. 1579 (31 Aug. 1979): 60-61. Fine photograph and comments stressing the honors of Colette's last years.

2265 "Arthritic Immortal." *Time* 45 (14 May 1945): 27. Frivolous notice of Colette's election to the Goncourt Academy.

2266 "Milestones." *Time* 64 (16 Aug. 1954): 71. Notice of death.

2267 "The Right to Rites." *Time* 64 (30 Aug. 1954): 42. Report of Graham Greene's letter to Cardinal Feltin after the Roman Catholic Church refused to allow Colette religious burial.

2268 "Le Dialogue des bêtes par Mme Gauthier-Villars." *La Vie heureuse* 3 (15 May 1904): non-pag. [100-1]. Also in item 1104 La Hire, 267-69. Interview in which Colette talks about the pets that served as inspiration for her newly published *Dialogues de bêtes*.

2269 "Hommage à Colette." *Vogue* [Paris], Sept. 1954, non-pag. Photograph and stop-press announcement of Colette's death.

2270 "Colette." *Wilson Library Bulletin* 6 (Sept. 1931): 86, 108. Profile emphasizing the autobiographical nature of much of Colette's work and the influence on her of her mother.

2271 "Obituaries." *Wilson Library Bulletin* 29 (Oct. 1954): 104. Notice of Colette's death.

APPENDICES

Appendix A

SPECIAL ISSUES ON COLETTE

Avant-Scène Théâtre, no. 708 (15 April 1982). Includes the text of *Chéri* as performed at the Théâtre des Variétés in 1982, a summary of the play's genesis, performances, metamorphoses and reception by critics. Interesting photographs. Also includes the text of "Notre Colette," presented at the Théâtre du Palais-Royal in November 1970 as part of the "Rencontres du Palais-Royal" series, as well as texts by Jean-Marie Fonteneau, Bernard Gavoty, Jean-Michel Rouzière, and Kitty Arnault. All annotated separately.

Cahiers Colette, no. 1 (1977). Articles by Gérard Bonal, Claude Mauriac, Maurice Goudeket, Françoise Mallet-Joris, Armand Lanoux, and J.-M. G. Le Clézio, as well as a previously unpublished theater review by Colette [«L'Accroche-Cœur» de Sacha Guitry], a bibliograpy of recent publications on Colette, and a list of theses. All annotated separately.

Cahiers Colette, no. 2: *Inédits en librairie* (1980). Contains 14 texts by Colette: Graphismes. «Un peu plus...» Le bois, le lac et les Français. Il fait froid. Le silence des enfants. «Saviez-vous, madame?...». Faits divers. Bricoleurs. Paresse. Paris vacances. Maurice Chevalier. M. Charles Boyer, d'Hollywood. Marseille. Carnaval brabançon. Also a list of theses on Colette compiled by Jeanne Contou. All annotated separately.

Cahiers Colette, no. 3-4: *Colloque de Dijon 1979* (1981). Papers given at the first university colloquium on Colette, at the University of Dijon. Introd. Claude Pichois. Articles by Francine Dugast, Nicole Ferrier, Christiane Milner, Mireille Gouaux-Coutrix, Madeleine Raaphorst-Rousseau, Michel Raimond, Michel Tournier, Jacques Dupont, Bernard Bray, Louis Forestier, and Michel Décaudin, also a list of theses compiled by Jeanne Contou. All annotated separately.

Cahiers Colette, no. 5 (1983). Articles by Alain Brunet, Elisabeth Charleux-Leroux, Jean Foyard, Jacques Dupont, and Jacques Frugier, as well as a list of theses compiled by Jeanne Contou. All annotated separately.

Cahiers Colette, no. 6: *Il y a trente ans, Colette...* (1984). Dominant theme is the thirtieth anniversary of Colette's death. Articles by Hervé Bazin, Jacques Dupont, Yvonne Brochard, Claude Pichois, Renato Serra, Elisabeth Charleux-Leroux and Marguerite Boivin, and Eleanor Reid Gibbard, as well as a list of theses compiled by Jeanne Contou. All annotated separately.

Cahiers Colette, no. 7 (1985). Articles by Edmonde Charles-Roux, Vincenette Pichois and Alain Brunet, Anne-Marie Pizzorusso, Guiseppe Antonio Borgese, Elisabeth Charleux-Leroux and Marguerite Boivin, Eleanor Reid Gibbard, and Alain Brunet, as well as a list of theses compiled by Jeanne Contou. All annotated separately.

Cahiers Colette, no. 8: *De Saint-Sauveur à Châtillon* (1986). Focuses on Colette's childhood home at Saint-Sauveur and her years at Châtillon-Coligny, where the family moved after their financial reverses. Articles by Henri Noguères, Claude Pichois, Guy Tosi, Alain Gaudard, Elisabeth Charleux-Leroux and Marguerite Boivin, Eleanor Reid Gibbard, and Marguerite Boivin (with Vincenette Pichois), as well as a list of theses compiled by Jeanne Contou. All annotated separately.

Cahiers Colette, no. 9: *La dame de 2h 15 du matin* (1987). Includes a letter from Colette to Yves Le Béchec as well as a radio address, "Colette parle aux Américains." Articles by Elisabeth Charleux-Leroux, Claude Pichois, Alain Brunet, Bernard Bray, Elisabeth Charleux-Leroux and Marguerite Boivin, Eleanor Reid Gibbard, and Marguerite Boivin (with Vincenette Pichois), as well as a list of theses compiled by Jeanne Contou. All annotated separately.

Cahiers Colette, no. 10: *Avers et revers* (1988). Articles by Michel del Castillo, Marie-Thérèse Colléaux (including correspondence from Colette to the *petites fermières*), Elisabeth Charleux-Leroux, Michèle Le Pavec, and Pierre Louÿs, as well as a list of theses compiled by Jeanne Contou. All annotated separately.

Le Capitole, May 1923. Homage issue containing articles by Henri Duvernois, Georges Delaquys, Léopold Marchand, Paul Blanchart, René Jeanne, Germaine Beaumont and Georges Wague; all are annotated separately but none are significant. Two pages bearing the title "Hommages à Colette" contain brief, effusive paragraphs signed Aurel, Gérard Bauër, André Billy, René Bizet, Jane Catulle-Mendès, Courteline, Fanny Clar, Lucie Delarue-Mardrus, Gérard d'Houville, Comtesse de Noailles, and Marcel Prévost; none are annotated separately. Also a selection of press notices. Not nearly as interesting as the later issue.

Le Capitole, 22 Dec. 1924. Almost a homage issue, rich in superlatives and clichés, poor in analysis, but interesting for its variety of topics and the over-all impression the reader has of critics' views. Texts by Robert de Flers, Henry Bernstein, Anna de Noailles, Pierre Benoit, Henri Béraud, Gérard Bauër, Lucie Delarue-Mardrus, René Gillouin, Paul Reboux, Charles Chassé, Léon Pierre-Quint, Henri Jeanson, Claude Chauvière, and Legrand-Chabrier. All annotated separately. Also contains a brief biography, photographs, a sketch by Léopold Marchand, and fac-similes of unidentified letters.

Europe, no. 631-32 (Nov.-Dec. 1981): 1-199. Articles by Michel Mercier, Mireille Gouaux-Coutrix, Jean Defoix, Francine Dugast-Portes, Chantal Paisant, Maurice Bouvier-Ajam, Henri Bordillon, Joan Hinde Stewart, Christiane Milner, Claude Pujade-Renaud, Brigitte Ferrand, Claudine Nast-Verguet, Odette and Alain Virmaux, Yannick Bellon, and Jacques Demy. Also includes some primary material: several unpublished letters by Colette, her comments on the Bellon film of 1950 [Commentaire pour Yannick Bellon], a series of unpublished drama criticism [Critiques pour *Sélection de la vie artistique*] and a chronology. All annotated separately.

Figaro littéraire, 24 Jan. 1953, 1-6. Issue celebrating Colette's eightieth birthday. Contains "Gîte d'écrivain" by Colette, excerpts from several letters to Colette from her mother, and a poem by her father. Texts by Jean Anouilh, Alexandre Arnoux, Gérard Bauer, André Billy, Francis

Carco, Paul Claudel, Dignimont, Roland Dorgelès, Dunoyer de Segonzac, Pierre Fresnay, André Gide, Philippe Hériat, Marcel Jouhandeau, Jacques de Lacretelle, Rosamond Lehmann, Henri Liebrecht, Pierre Mac Orlan, François Mauriac, Henri Mondor, Katherine Anne Porter, Marcel Proust, Armand Salacrou, Paul Valéry, and Rebecca West. All annotated separately.

Figaro littéraire, 7 Aug. 1954, 1, 4, 10. In memoriam issue. Texts by Gérard Bauër, Pierre Mazars, Paul Claudel, and Paul Valéry; all are annotated separately. Also photographs of relatives, friends and others present at Colette's lying-in-state and funeral.

Lettres françaises, 12 Aug. 1954, 1-6. In memoriam issue. Illus. Luc-Albert Moreau. Texts by Maurice Druon, Philippe Hériat, Hélène Jourdan-Morhange, Marcel Lherbier, Jean Marcenac, Musidora, Georges Sadoul, Georges Wague, André Wurmser, Louis Aragon, Claude Autant-Lara, and Julien Cain. Also includes the text of a passage recorded by Colette in 1951 [Colette devant sa mort]. All annotated separately.

Livres de France 5 (Oct. 1954): 3-12. In memoriam issue. Texts by Gérard Bauër, André Gide, Jean Cocteau, and Colette [Marcel Proust], illustrations and a long bibliography of Colette's work. All annotated separately.

Le Point, no. 39 (May 1951). Texts by André Gide, Gérard Bauër, Darius Milhaud, Léon Werth, Claude Roy, and Raymond Dumay, as well as four by Colette [Dans un cyprès. Marcel Proust. «Le veilleur». Orchidée]. All annotated separately. Excellent photographs.

Revue littéraire, no. 11 (March-April 1954). Includes extracts from *Le Blé en herbe*, *La Vagabonde* and *L'Etoile vesper*, each with a brief introduction by Léonce Peillard. Also "Colette un sage" by Robert Kemp. All annotated separately.

Women's Studies 8:3 (1981). Edited by Erica Eisinger and Mari McCarty. Feminist-oriented issue containing articles using a variety of methodologies. Articles by Erica Eisinger and Mari McCarty, Joan Hinde Stewart, Suzanne Relyea, Sharon Spencer, Donna Norell, Ann Cothran, Jacob Stockinger, and Mari McCarty. Graphics by Chris Ward. All annotated separately.

Appendix B

GERMAN TRANSLATIONS
of Colette's Works

Die Andere. Trans. Erna Redtenbacher. Berlin, Vienna, Leipzig: Zsolnay, 1930. 264p. [*La Seconde*].

Die Andere. Trans. Erna Redtenbacher. Vienna: Zsolnay, 1951. 242p. [*La Seconde*].

Die Andere. Trans. Erna Redtenbacher. Hamburg: Rowohlt, 1958. 151p. Coll. rororo-Taschenbuch 247. [*La Seconde*].

Die Andere. Trans. Erna Redtenbacher. Hamburg, Vienna: Zsolnay, 1959. 151p. [*La Seconde*].

Die Andere. Trans. Erna Redtenbacher. Berlin, Darmstadt, Vienna: Deutsche Buch-Gemeinschaft, 1959. 203p. [*La Seconde*].

Die Andere. Trans. Erna Redtenbacher. Hamburg: Rowohlt, 1984. 124p. Coll. rororo-Taschenbuch 5289. [*La Seconde*].

Annies Geständnisse. [Willy]. N.p.: Ebb, 1907. 213p. [*Claudine s'en va*].

Armande und andere Erzählungen. Trans. Doris Brehm and Luise Wasserthal-Zuccari. Berlin, Darmstadt, Vienna: Deutsche Buch-

Gemeinschaft, 1965. 183p. [*Armande. La Lune de pluie. Le Képi. Le Tendron*].

Bella-Vista und andere Erzählungen. Trans. Doris Brehm and Luise Wasserthal-Zuccari. Berlin, Darmstadt, Vienna: Deutsche Buch-Gemeinschaft, 1964. 177p. [*Bella-Vista. Gribiche. Le Rendez-vous. Le sieur Binard. La Cire verte*].

Blaue Flamme. Trans. Uli Aumüller. Pref. Angela Praesent. Hamburg: Rowohlt, 1979. 137p. Coll. rororo-Taschenbuch, Neue Frau 4371. [*Le Fanal bleu*].

Blumen und Jahreszeiten. Trans. Waltrud Kappeler. Illus. Pia Roshardt. Zurich: Büchergilde Gutenberg, 1953. 120p. [*Pour un herbier*].

Chéri. Trans. Hans Jacob. Leipzig, 1927. Berlin: Neff. 285p.

Chéri. Trans. Hans Jacob. Vienna: Zsolnay, 1955. 224p.

Chéri. Trans. Hans Jacob. Hamburg: Rowohlt, 1956. 146p. Coll. rororo-Taschenbuch 178.

Chéri. Trans. Hans Jacob. Munich: Droemer Knaur, 1985. 224p. Coll. Knaur-Taschenbuch 1345.

Chéri und Chéris Ende. Trans. Hans Jacob. Frankfurt: Büchergilde Gutenberg, 1960. 359p. [*La Fin de Chéri*].

Chéri und Chéris Ende. Trans. Hans Jacob. Hamburg, Vienna: Zsolnay, 1960. 316p. [*Chéri. La Fin de Chéri*].

Chéris Ende. Trans. Hans Jacob. Leipzig, Berlin: Neff, 1927. 223p. [*La Fin de Chéri*].

Chéris Ende. Trans. Hans Jacob. Leipzig: Weller, 1927. 222p. [*La Fin de Chéri*].

Chéris Ende. Trans. Hans Jacob. Vienna: Zsolnay, 1955. 206p. [*La Fin de Chéri*].

Chéris Ende. Trans. Hans Jacob. Hamburg: Rowohlt, 1957. 134p. Coll. rororo-Taschenbuch 229. [*La Fin de Chéri*].

Claudine. Trans. Lida Winiewicz. Hamburg, Vienna: Zsolnay, 1957. 664p. [*Claudine à l'école. Claudine à Paris. Claudine en ménage. Claudine s'en va*].

Claudine. Trans. Lida Winiewicz. Gütersloh: Bertelsmann-Lesering, 1960. 796p. [*Claudine à l'école. Claudine à Paris. Claudine en ménage. Claudine s'en va*].

Claudine. Trans. Lida Winiewicz. Stuttgart, Hamburg, Munich: Deutscher Bücherbund, 1978. 636p. [*Claudine à l'école. Claudine à Paris. Claudine en ménage. Claudine s'en va*].

Claudine erwacht. Trans. Lida Winiewicz. Hamburg: Rowohlt, 1960. 181p. Coll. rororo-Taschenbuch 281. [*Claudine à l'école*].

Claudine erwacht. Trans. Lida Winiewicz. Frankfurt: Fischer-Taschenbuch, 1976. 218p. Coll. Fischer-Bücherei 1723. [*Claudine à l'école*].

Claudine erwacht. Trans. Lida Winiewicz. Munich: Droemer Knaur, 1988. 239p. Coll. Knaur-Taschenbuch 1525. [*Claudine à l'école*].

Claudine findet zu sich selbst. Trans. Erika Danneberg. Hamburg: Rowohlt, 1963. 153p. Coll. rororo-Taschenbuch 397. [*La Retraite sentimentale*].

Claudine geht. [Colette Willy]. Trans. Geo. Nördlinger. Budapest: Grimm, 1903. 280p. [*Claudine s'en va*].

Claudine geht. Trans. Lida Winiewicz. Hamburg: Rowohlt, 1960. 146p. Coll. rororo-Taschenbuch 348. [*Claudine s'en va*].

Claudine geht. Trans. Lida Winiewicz. Frankfurt: Fischer-Taschenbuch, 1977. 119p. Coll. Fischer-Bücherei 1829. [*Claudine s'en va*].

Claudine in der Ehe. Trans. Lida Winiewicz. Hamburg: Rowohlt, 1960. 145p. Coll. rororo-Taschenbuch 322. [*Claudine en ménage*].

Claudine in der Ehe. Trans. Lida Winiewicz. Frankfurt: Fischer-Taschenbuch, 1976. 138p. Coll. Fischer-Bücherei 1808. [*Claudine en ménage*].

Claudine in Paris. [Willy]. Trans. Franz Hofen. Budapest: Grimm, 1901. 300p. [*Claudine à Paris*].

Claudine in Paris. [Willy]. Trans. Franz Hofen. N.p.: Ebb, 1902. 300p. [*Claudine à Paris*].

Claudine in Paris. Trans. Lida Winiewicz. Hamburg: Rowohlt, 1959. 147p. Coll. rororo-Taschenbuch 307. [*Claudine à Paris*].

Claudine in Paris. Trans. Lida Winiewicz. Frankfurt: Fischer-Taschenbuch, 1976. 154p. Coll. Fischer-Bücherei 1751. [*Claudine à Paris*].

Claudine in Paris. Trans. Lida Winiewicz. Munich: Droemer Knaur, 1988. 147p. Coll. Knaur-Taschenbuch 1524. [*Claudine à Paris*].

Claudines Ehe. [Willy]. Trans. Geo. Nördlinger. Budapest: Grimm, 1902. 303p. [*Claudine en ménage*].

Claudines Mädchenjahre. Trans. Erna Redtenbacher. Hamburg, Vienna: Zsolnay, 1960. 207p. [*La Maison de Claudine*]. Contains 29 texts.

Claudines Mädchenjahre. Trans. Erna Redtenbacher. Berlin, Darmstadt, Vienna: Deutsche Buch-Gemeinschaft, 1963. 176p. [*La Maison de Claudine*].

Claudines Retraite sentimentale. Trans. Erika Danneberg. Hamburg, Vienna: Zsolnay, 1958. 224p. [*La Retraite sentimentale*].

Claudines Schuljahre. [Willy]. Budapest: Grimm, 1902. 317p. [*Claudine à l'école*].

Claudines Schuljahre. [Willy]. Trans. Geo. Nördlinger. N.p.: Ebb, 1902. 317p. [*Claudine à l'école*].

Diese Freuden. Trans. Maria Dessauer. Frankfurt: Suhrkamp, 1982. 232p. Coll. Bibl. Suhrkamp 717. [*Le Pur et l'impur*].

Diese Freuden. Trans. Maria Dessauer. Frankfurt: Suhrkamp, 1983. 164p. [*Le Pur et l'impur*].

Drei... sechs... neun... Trans. Noa Elisabeth Kiepenheuer. Illus. Walt. Klemm. Weimar: Kiepenheuer, 1950. 94p. [*Trois... six... neuf...*].

Drei... sechs... neun... Trans. Noa Elisabeth Kiepenheuer. Hanau: Dausien; Weimar: Kiepenheuer, 1960. 116p. [*Trois... six... neuf...*].

Duett. Trans. Gertrud von Helmstatt and Gisela Bonn. Konstanz: Weller, 1948. 144p. [*Duo*].

Duett. Trans. Lida Winiewicz. Hamburg, Vienna: Zsolnay, 1959. 222p. [*Duo. Le Toutounier*].

Duett. Trans. Lida Winiewicz. Hamburg: Rowohlt, 1960. 152p. Coll. rororo-Taschenbuch 373. [*Duo. Le Toutounier*].

Duett. Trans. Lida Winiewicz. Berlin, Darmstadt, Vienna: Deutsche Buch-Gemeinschaft, 1962. 200p. [*Duo. Le Toutounier*].

Duett. Trans. Lida Winiewicz. Munich: Droemer Knaur, 1987. Coll. Knaur-Taschenbuch 1343. [*Duo. Le Toutounier*].

Eifersucht. Trans. Emi Ehm. Hamburg, Vienna: Zsolnay, 1959. 164p. [*La Chatte*].

Eifersucht. Trans. Emi Ehm. Berlin, Darmstadt, Vienna: Deutsche Buch-Gemeinschaft, 1961. 164p. [*La Chatte*].

Eifersucht. Trans. Emi Ehm. Frankfurt: Fischer-Bücherei, 1961. 165p. Coll. Fischer-Bücherei 407. [*La Chatte*].

Eifersucht. Trans. Emi Ehm. Vienna, Hamburg: Zsolnay, 1973. 173p. [*La Chatte*].

Eifersucht. Trans. Emi Ehm. Munich: Droemer Knaur, 1987. 112p. Coll. Knaur-Taschenbuch 1344. [*La Chatte*].

Eifersucht. La Vagabonde. Die Fessel. Mitsou. Trans. Alexander Auer, Elisabeth Roth, Grit Zoller. Hamburg: Zolnay, 1986. 640p. [*La Chatte. La Vagabonde. L'Entrave. Mitsou*].

Die Erde mein Paradies: Eine Autobiographie aus ihren Werken zusammengestellt von Robert Phelps. Trans. Gerlinde Quenzer, Justus

F. Wittkop et al. Frankfurt: Fischer, 1967. 487p. [*Autobiographie tirée des œuvres de Colette par Robert Phelps/Earthly Paradise*].

Die erste Madame d'Espivant. Trans. Ursula Seyffarth. Hamburg, Vienna: Zsolnay, 1960. 252p. [*Julie de Carneilhan*].

Die erste Madame d'Espivant. Trans. Ursula Seyffarth. Hamburg: Rowohlt, 1962. 155p. Coll. rororo-Taschenbuch 510. [*Julie de Carneilhan*].

Die erste Madame d'Espivant. Trans. Ursula Seyffarth. Hamburg: Rowohlt, 1982. 122p. Coll. rororo-Taschenbuch 4983. [*Julie de Carneilhan*].

Erwachende Herzen. Trans. Stefanie Neumann. Vienna: Zsolnay, 1952. 236p. [*Le Blé en herbe*].

Erwachende Herzen. Trans. Stefanie Neumann. Berlin, Darmstadt: Deutsche Buch-Gemeinschaft, 1955. 193p. [*Le Blé en herbe*].

Erwachende Herzen. Trans. Stefanie Neumann. Hamburg: Rowohlt, 1955. 154p. Coll. rororo-Taschenbuch 157. [*Le Blé en herbe*].

Erwachende Herzen. Trans. Stefanie Neumann. Munich: Deutscher Taschenbuch, 1986. 131p. [*Le Blé en herbe*].

Die Fessel. Trans. Erna Redtenbacher. Berlin, Vienna, Leipzig: Zsolnay, 1928. 299p. [*L'Entrave*].

Die Fessel. Trans. Erna Redtenbacher. Berlin: Neff, 1928. 223p. [*L'Entrave*].

Die Fessel. Trans. Erna Redtenbacher. Vienna: Zsolnay, 1950. 293p. [*L'Entrave*].

Die Fessel. Trans. Erna Redtenbacher. Hamburg: Rowohlt, 1954. 150p. Coll. rororo-Taschenbuch 120. [*L'Entrave*].

Die Fessel. Trans. Erna Redtenbacher. Illus. Sita Jucker. Zurich: Büchergilde Gutenberg, 1956. 266p. [*L'Entrave*].

Die Fessel. Trans. Erna Redtenbacher. Illus. Sita Jucker. Frankfurt: Büchergilde Gutenberg, 1957. 260p. [*L'Entrave*].

Die Fessel. Trans. Erna Redtenbacher. Munich: Deutscher Taschenbuch, 1984. 201p. [*L'Entrave*].

Frauen. Trans. Alexander Auer. Vienna, Hamburg: Zsolnay, 1986. 176p.

Die Freuden des Lebens. Trans. Erna Redtenbacher and Helene M. Reiff. Hamburg, Vienna: Zsolnay, 1961. 176p. [*La Naissance du jour*].

Die Freuden des Lebens. Trans. Erna Redtenbacher and Helene M. Reiff. Hamburg: Rowohlt, 1965. 123p. Coll. rororo-Taschenbuch 773. [*La Naissance du jour*].

Die Freuden des Lebens. Trans. Erna Redtenbacher and Helene M. Reiff. Munich: Droemer Knaur, 1986. 176p. Coll. Knaur-Taschenbuch 1346. [*La Naissance du jour*].

Die Freundin. Trans. Waltrud Kappeler and Louis Erlacher. Illus. Irene Zurkinden. Zurich: Büchergilde Gutenberg, 1956. 219p. [*La Seconde*].

Friede bei den Tieren. Trans. Erna Redtenbacher and Helene M. Reiff. Berlin, Vienna, Leipzig: Zsolnay, 1931. 191p. [*La Paix chez les bêtes*]. Contains 32 texts plus foreword.

Friede bei den Tieren. Trans. Erna Redtenbacher and Helene M. Reiff. Vienna: Zsolnay, 1953. 192p. [*La Paix chez les bêtes*].

Friede bei den Tieren. Trans. Erna Redtenbacher and Helene M. Reiff. Hamburg: Rowohlt, 1964. 120p. Coll. rororo-Taschenbuch 678. [*La Paix chez les bêtes*]. Contains 32 texts plus foreword.

Geträumte Sünden. Trans. Hans B. Wagenseil. Berlin, Dusseldorf: Transmare, 1949. 280p. [*L'Ingénue libertine*].

Geträumte Sünden. Trans. Hans B. Wagenseil. Hamburg, Vienna: Zsolnay, 1956. 269p. [*L'Ingénue libertine*].

Geträumte Sünden. Trans. Hans B. Wagenseil. Hamburg: Rowohlt, 1958. 155p. Coll. rororo-Taschenbuch 273. [*L'Ingénue libertine*].

Geträumte Sünden. Trans. Hans B. Wagenseil. Illus. Susanne Stolzenberg. Zurich: Buchclub Ex Libris, 1959. 287p. [*L'Ingénue libertine*].

Geträumte Sünden. Trans. Hans B. Wagenseil. Munich: Droemer Knaur, 1986. 156p. Coll. Knaur-Taschenbuch 1347. [*L'Ingénue libertine*].

Gigi. Trans. Stefanie Neumann. Pref. Rolf Italiaander. Vienna: Zsolnay, 1953. 287p. [*Gigi. L'Enfant malade. La Dame du photographe. Flore et Pomone*].

Gigi. Trans. Stefanie Neumann. Berlin, Darmstadt: Deutsche Buch-Gemeinschaft, 1953. 232p. [*Gigi. L'Enfant malade. La Dame du photographe. Flore et Pomone*].

Gigi, Erwachende Herzen und die Erzählungen. Trans. Stefanie Neumann and Emi Ehm. Illus. Rosemarie Joray. Zurich: Buchclub Ex Libris, 1962. 383p. [*Gigi. Le Blé en herbe. L'Enfant malade. La Dame du photographe. Flore et Pomone. Le Rendez-vous*].

Gigi und andere Erzählungen. Trans. Stefanie Neumann. Hamburg: Rowohlt, 1955. 151p. Coll. rororo-Taschenbuch 143. [*Gigi. L'Enfant malade. La Dame du photographe. Flore et Pomone*].

Gigi und andere Erzählungen. Trans. Stefanie Neumann. Hamburg: Rowohlt, 1960. 126p. Coll. rororo-Taschenbuch 143. [*Gigi. L'Enfant malade. La Dame du photographe. Flore et Pomone*].

Gigi und andere Erzählungen. Trans. Stefanie Neumann. Pref. Rolf Italiaander. Vienna: Buchgemeinschaft Donauland, 1961. 389p. [*Gigi. L'Enfant malade. La Dame du photographe. Flore et Pomone*].

Gigi und andere Erzählungen. Trans. Stefanie Neumann. Hamburg: Rowohlt, 1981. 137p. Coll. rororo-Taschenbuch 143. [*Gigi. L'Enfant malade. La Dame du photographe. Flore et Pomone*].

Gigi und Erwachende Herzen. Trans. Stefanie Neumann. Berlin, Darmstadt, Vienna: Deutsche Buch-Gemeinschaft; Gütersloh: Bertelsmann-Lesering; Stuttgart: Europäische Bildungsgemeinschaft; Vienna: Buchgemeinschaft Donauland, 1974. 285p. [*Gigi. Le Blé en herbe*].

Gigi und Erwachende Herzen. Trans. Stefanie Neumann. Vienna, Hamburg: Zsolnay, 1984. 288p. [*Gigi. Le Blé en herbe*].

Gribiche und zwei andere Erzählungen. Trans. Doris Brehm and Stefanie Neumann. Illus. Henri de Toulouse-Lautrec. Zurich: Diogenes, 1970. 277p. [*Gribiche* and two other stories].

Grüner Siegellack. Trans. Stefanie Neumann, Doris Brehm, and Luise Wasserthal-Zuccari. Frankfurt, Hamburg: Fischer-Bücherei, 1964. 163p. [*Bella-Vista. Gribiche. Le sieur Binard. Le Képi. Le Tendron. La Cire verte*].

"Die Heilung." Trans. Frantz Clément. *Das Tage-Buch* 7 (5 June 1926): 802-6. [Trans. of "La guérison" from *Les Vrilles de la vigne*].

Das Hotelzimmer. Trans. Brigitte Kahr and Luise Wasserthal-Zuccari. Vienna, Hamburg: Zsolnay, 1963. 240p. [*Chambre d'hôtel. La Femme cachée*].

Das Hotelzimmer. Trans. Brigitte Kahr and Luise Wasserthal-Zuccari. Hamburg: Rowohlt, 1968. 136p. Coll. rororo-Taschenbuch 909. [*Chambre d'hôtel. La Femme cachée*].

Daz Hotelzimmer und andere Erzählungen. Trans. Brigitte Kahr and Luise Wasserthal-Zuccari. Berlin, Darmstadt, Vienna: Deutsche Buch-Gemeinschaft, 1965. 188p. [*Chambre d'hôtel. La Femme cachée*].

Julie de Carneilhan. Trans. Ursula Seyffarth. Bad Wörishofen: Drei-Säulen, 1950. 252p.

Die Katze. Trans. Elisabeth Seeger. Vienna, Leipzig: Zeitbild, 1936. 247p. [*La Chatte*].

Die Katze aus dem kleinen Café. Trans. Gertrud Barnert. Vienna, Hamburg: Zsolnay, 1985. 184p.

Die Katze aus dem kleinen Café. Trans. Gertrud Barnert. Munich: Droemer Knaur, 1987. 179p. Coll. Knaur-Taschenbuch 1526.

Komödianten: Meine Gefährten und ich. Trans. Erna Redtenbacher. Berlin, Vienna, Leipzig: Zsolnay, 1931. 222p. [*L'Envers du music-hall*].

Mädchenjahre. Trans. Erna Redtenbacher. Hamburg: Rowohlt, 1963.
135p. Coll. rororo-Taschenbuch 547. [*La Maison de Claudine*].

Mein Elternhaus. Trans. Erna Redtenbacher. Berlin, Vienna, Leipzig:
Zsolnay, 1929. 232p. [*La Maison de Claudine*]. Contains 29 texts.

Meine Lehrjahre. Trans. Uli Aumüller. Hamburg: Rowohlt, 1980. 126p.
Coll. rororo-Taschenbuch, Neue Frau 4595. [*Mes Apprentissages*].

Minna. [Willy]. N.p.: Ebb, 1906. 263p. [*Minne*].

Minnas Eheirrungen. [Willy]. N.p.: Ebb, 1906. 234p. [*Les Egarements de
Minne*].

Mitsou. Trans. Erna Redtenbacher. Berlin, Vienna, Leipzig: Zsolnay,
1927. 148p.

Mitsou. Trans. Erna Redtenbacher. Vienna, Hamburg: Zsolnay, 1950.
154p.

Mitsou. Trans. Erna Redtenbacher. Frankfurt, Hamburg: Fischer-Bücherei,
1952. 148p. Coll. Fischer-Bücherei 11.

Mitsou. Trans. Erna Redtenbacher. Hamburg, Vienna: Zsolnay, 1958.
134p.

Mitsou. Trans. Erna Redtenbacher. Berlin, Darmstadt, Vienna: Deutsche
Buch-Gemeinschaft, 1963. 133p.

Mitsou. Trans. Erna Redtenbacher. Zurich: Buchclub Ex Libris, 1963.
133p.

Mitsou. Trans. Erna Redtenbacher. Hamburg: Rowohlt, 1980. 92p. Coll.
rororo-Taschenbuch 4578.

Neun von Colette. Trans. Stefanie Neumann, Doris Brehm, Emi Ehm,
and Luise-Wasserthal-Zuccari. Hamburg, Vienna: Zsolnay, 1962.
408p. [*Bella-Vista. Gribiche. Le Rendez-vous. Le sieur Binard. La
Lune de pluie. Le Képi. Le Tendron. La Cire verte. Armande*].

Paris durch mein Fenster. Trans. Gritta Baerlocher. Pref. Francis Carco. Illus. Jeanne-Marianne Moll. Zurich: Pan, 1945. 248p. [*Paris de ma fenêtre*].

Phil und Vinca. Trans. Lissy Radermacher. Berlin: Wegweiser, 1928. 128p. [*Le Blé en herbe*].

Phil und Vinca. Trans. Lissy Radermacher. Potsdam, Berlin: Kiepenheuer, 1928. 160p. [*Le Blé en herbe*].

Renauds Weib. Trans. Nina Carolus. Dresden, Berlin: Maschler, 1927. 273p. [*Claudine en ménage*].

Das Rendezvous: Drei Erzählungen. Trans. Emi Ehm and Luise Wasserthal-Zuccari. Frankfurt, Berlin: Ullstein, 1963. 143p. [*Le Rendez-vous. La Lune de pluie. Armande*].

Das Rendezvous. Trans. Doris Brehm. Hamburg: Rowohlt, 1981. 268p. Coll. rororo-Taschenbuch 4872. [*Le Rendez-vous. La Lune de pluie*].

Renée Néré: Das Schicksal einer Frau. Trans. Rosa Breuer-Lucka. Berlin, Vienna, Leipzig: Zsolnay, 1927. 349p. [*La Vagabonde*].

Renée Néré. Trans. Rosa Breuer-Lucka. Vienna: Zsolnay, 1951. 304p. [*La Vagabonde*].

Renée Néré. Trans. Rosa Breuer-Lucka. Frankfurt, Hamburg: Fischer-Bücherei, 1954. 221p. Coll. Fischer-Bücherei 69. [*La Vagabonde*].

Renée Néré. Trans. Rosa Breuer-Lucka. Gütersloh: Bertelsmann-Lesering, 1959. 303p. [*La Vagabonde*].

Sido. Trans. Doris Brehm. Hamburg, Vienna: Zsolnay, 1961. 131p.

Sido. Trans. Doris Brehm. Frankfurt, Hamburg: Fischer-Bücherei, 1963. 135p. Coll. Fischer-Bücherei 556.

Sido. Trans. Uli Aumüller. Hamburg: Rowohlt, 1982. 88p. Coll. rororo-Taschenbuch, Neue Frau 4905.

Sieben Tierdialoge. Trans. Emmi Hirschberg. Pref. Francis Jammes. Potsdam, Berlin: Kiepenheuer, 1928. 140p. [*Sept dialogues de bêtes*].

Tagesanbruch. Trans. Erna Redtenbacher and Helene M. Reiff. Berlin, Vienna, Leipzig: Zsolnay, 1928. 228p. [*La Naissance du jour*].

La Vagabonde. Trans. Ferdinand Hardekopf. Illus. Hanny Fries. Zurich: Büchergilde Gutenberg, 1954. 273p.

La Vagabonde: Renée Néré. Trans. Rosa Breuer-Lucka. Hamburg: Rowohlt, 1980. 182p. Coll. rororo-Taschenbuch 4651.

Das verzauberte Spielzeug. Trans. Evelyne Kolnberger. Illus. Gerard Hoffnung. Munich, Vienna: Langen Müller, 1974. [*L'Enfant et les sortilèges*].

Das verzauberte Spielzeug. Trans. Evelyne Kolnberger. Illus. Gerard Hoffnung. Vienna: Buchgemeinschaft Donauland; Gütersloh: Bertelsmann; Stuttgart: Europäische Bildungsgemeinschaft, 1975. [*L'Enfant et les sortilèges*].

Wir Komödianten vom Varieté: Meine Gefährten und ich. Trans. Erna Redtenbacher. Vienna: Zsolnay, 1952. 222p. [*L'Envers du music-hall*].

Wir Komödianten vom Varieté: Meine Gefährten und ich. Trans. Erna Redtenbacher. Vienna, Darmstadt, Berlin: Deutsche Buch-Gemeinschaft, 1964. 222p. [*L'Envers du music-hall*].

Zwiesprache mit Blumen. Trans. Hedwig Kehrli. Bern, Stuttgart, Vienna: Scherz, 1959. 77p. Coll. Parnass-Bücherei 111. [*Pour un herbier*].

Appendix C

ITALIAN TRANSLATIONS
of Colette's Works

L'Ancora. Milan-Verona: Mondadori, 1934. 300p. [*L'Entrave*].

L'Ancora. Tra le Quinte del Caffè-Concerto. Trans. C. Prosperi, E. Piceni. Milan-Verona: Mondadori, 1958. 234p. Coll. I Libri del pavone 153. [*L'Entrave. L'Envers du music-hall*].

Il Bambino e i Sortilegi. [Colette and Maurice Ravel]. Trans. Pietro Clausetti. Paris: Durand, 1925. [*L'Enfant et les sortilèges*].

Chéri. Trans. Lena Leva. Milan-Verona: Mondadori, 1949. 239p.

Chéri. Trans. Lena Leva. Milan-Verona: Mondadori, 1959. 216p. Coll. I Libri del pavone 182.

Chéri. Trans. Anna Maria Speckel. Rome: Casini, 1967. 187p. Coll. I Libri del sabato 60.

Chéri. Trans. Mella G. Arborio. Milan: Adelphi, 1984. 169p.

Chéri [theater]. [Colette and Léopold Marchand]. Trans. A. da Salvatore. *Il Dramma* 28 (15 Dec. 1951): 11-42.

Chéri. La Fine di Chéri. Trans. Mimmi Pasquali. Rome: Casini, 1955. 319p. [*Chéri. La Fin de Chéri*].

Claudina a Parigi. [Willy]. Florence: Salani, 1906. 260p. Coll. Biblioteca Salani Illustrata 120. [*Claudine à Paris*].

Claudina a Parigi. Trans. Laura Marchiori. Milan: Rizzoli, 1958. 175p. Coll. Biblioteca universale Rizzoli 1321-1322. [*Claudine à Paris*].

Claudina a scuola. [Willy]. Florence: Salani, 1906. 296p. [*Claudine à l'école*].

Claudina a scuola. Trans. Laura Marchiori. Milan: Rizzoli, 1955. 256p. Biblioteca universale Rizzoli 873-875. [*Claudine à l'école*].

Claudina maritata. [Willy]. Florence: Salani, 1906. 222p. Coll. Biblioteca Salani Illustrata 306. [*Claudine en ménage*].

Claudina se ne va. [Willy]. Florence: Salani, 1906. 215p. Coll. Biblioteca Salani Illustrata 308. [*Claudine s'en va*].

Claudina se ne va. Trans. Laura Marchiori. Milan: Rizzoli, 1958. 139p. Coll. Biblioteca universale Rizzoli 1345-1346. [*Claudine s'en va*].

Claudina se ne va. Trans. Elena Faber. Rome: Casini, 1966. 191p. Coll. I Libri del sabato 22. [*Claudine s'en va*].

Claudina sposata. Trans. Laura Marchiori. Milan: Rizzoli, 1958. 167p. Coll. Biblioteca universale Rizzoli 1333-1334. [*Claudine en ménage*].

Claudina sposata. Trans. Elena Faber. Rome: Casini, 1966. 220p. Coll. I Libri del sabato 18. [*Claudine en ménage*].

Claudine: Claudine a scuola. Claudine a Parigi. Claudine sposata. Claudine se ne va. Trans. Laura Marchiori. Rome: Casini, 1957. 516p. Coll. L'Arcobaleno 13. [*Claudine à l'école. Claudine à Paris. Claudine en ménage. Claudine s'en va*].

Claudine: Claudine a scuola. Claudine a Parigi. Claudine sposata. Claudine se ne va. Trans. Laura Marchiori. Milan: Rizzoli, 1986. 672p. [*Claudine a scuola. Claudine a Parigi. Claudine sposata. Claudine se ne va*].

Dalla mia Finestra. Trans. Elvira Petrucelli. Pref. Francis Carco. Milan: Garzanti, 1947. 228p. Coll. Vespa Blu, Scrittori Stranieri, new series no. 2. [*Paris de ma fenêtre*].

La Fine di Chéri. Trans. Levi A. Bassan. Milan: Adelphi, 1985. 154p. [*La Fin de Chéri*].

La Gatta. Sette Dialoghi di Bestie. [Colette Willy]. Trans. Enrico Piceni. Milan-Verona: Mondadori, 1935. 248p. Coll. Medusa, I grandi narratori d'ogni paese 55. [*La Chatte. Sept Dialogues de bêtes*].

La Gatta. Sette Dialoghi di Bestie. Trans. Enrico Piceni. Milan: Mondadori, 1959. 239p. Coll. I Libri del pavone 205. [*La Chatte. Sept Dialogues de bêtes*].

Gigi. Trans. Mimmi Pasquali. Rome: Casini, 1954. 99p. Coll. I Romanzi dell'Ambra 27.

Gigi e altri Racconti. Trans. M. Pasquali, M. Rivoire, A. Nigretti, G. Rossa. Milan: Mondadori, 1959. 228p. Coll. I Libri del pavone 196. [*Gigi. L'Enfant malade. La Dame du photographe. Flore et Pomone*].

Il Grano in erba. Trans. and pref. Roberto Ortolani. Modena: Guanda, 1945. 196p. Coll. Il Castello 20. [*Le Blé en herbe*].

Il Grano in erba. Il Mio Tirocinio. Trans. Sergio Miniussi, Marisa Ferro. Milan: Mondadori, 1964. 230p. Coll. I Libri del pavone 402. [*Le Blé en herbe. Mes apprentissages*].

Hotel Bellavista. Trans. M. Silvera. Milan: La Tartaruga, 1986. 80p. [*Bella-Vista*].

L'Ingenua Libertina. Milan: Ed. Milanese, 1948. 64p. Coll. I Libri di Afrodite 3. [*L'Ingénue libertine*].

L'Ingenua Libertina. Trans. Luigi Galeazzo Tenconi. Milan: Zibetti, 1959. 231p. Collano di romanzi per tutti 2. [*L'Ingénue libertine*].

L'Ingenua Libertina. Trans. Dianella Selvatico Estense. Turin: Edizioni dell'Albero, 1966. 222p. Coll. Letteratura d'amore 8. [*L'Ingénue libertine*].

L'Ingenua Libertina. Trans. Luigi Galeazzo Tenconi. Milan: Zibetti, 1966. 223p. Coll. Biblioteca universale Zibetti 12. [*L'Ingénue libertine*].

Julie de Carneilhan. Trans. M.L. Cipriani Fagioli. Milan-Verona: Mondadori, 1958. 147p. Coll. Romanzi e racconti d'oggi 17.

Il Mio Noviziato. Trans. Maurizio Andolfato. Milan: Adelphi, 1981. 142p. Coll. Biblioteca Adelphi 113. [*Mes apprentissages*].

Il Mio Noviziato. Trans. Maurizio Andolfato. Milan: Bompiani, 1986. 142p. [*Mes apprentissages*].

Mitsou. Trans. Maria Martone. Turin: Le grandi firme, 1929. 159p. Coll. del Cerchio blu 15.

La Nascita del Giorno. Trans. Levi A. Bassan. Milan: Adelphi, 1986. 148p. [*La Naissance du jour*].

"Proust al Ritz." *Paragone* 1 (Feb. 1950): 52-53. [Extract from *Flore et Pomone*].

Il Puro e l'impuro. Trans. Adriana Motti. Milan: Adelphi, 1980. 133p. Coll. Biblioteca Adelphi 98. [*Le Pur et l'impur*].

Il Puro e l'impuro. Milan: Bompiani, 1985. 144p. [*Le Pur et l'impur*].

Il Refugio sentimentale. Trans. Egidio Bianchetti. Milan: Martello, 1950. 224p. [*La Retraite sentimentale*].

La Vagabonda. [Colette Willy]. Trans. Virgilio Bondois. Milan: Facchi, 1920. 204p.

La Vagabonda. Trans. Carola Prosperi. Milan-Verona: Mondadori, 1936. 255p. Coll. Medusa: I grandi narratori d'ogni paese 16.

La Vagabonda. Trans. Luciana Nocioni. Rome: Casini, 1966. 189p. Coll. Grandi Romanzi 48.

La Vagabonda. Trans. Carola Prosperi. Milan: Mondadori, 1970. 253p. Coll. I Capolavori des Medusa.

La Vagabonda. Trans. and pref. Anna Banti. Milan: Mondadori, 1977. 197p. Coll. Gli Oscar 743.

La Vagabonda. Trans. Luciana Nocioni. Rome: Curcio, 1979. 181p. Coll. I Classici della narrativa 45.

La Vagabonda. Trans. Anna Banti. Milan: Mondadori, 1982. 208p.

La Vagabonda. Sette Dialoghi di Bestie. Trans. Carola Prosperi, Enrico Piceni. Milan: Club degli editori, 1966. x-263p. Coll. Collana '900, 105. [*La Vagabonde. Sept dialogues de bêtes*].

Appendix D

SPANISH TRANSLATIONS
of Colette's Works

Al rayar el día. Trans. E. Piñas. Barcelona: Argos-Vergara, 1982. 140p.
[*La Naissance du jour*].

El blat tendre. Trans. Ramón Folch i Camarasa. Barcelona: Plaza &
Janés, 1964. 148p. Coll. La rosa dels vents. [*Le Blé en herbe*]. Trans.
into Catalan.

El blat tendre. Trans. Ramón Folch i Camarasa. Barcelona: La Magrana,
1985. 120p. Coll. Llibres a ma 38. [*Le Blé en herbe*]. Trans. into
Catalan.

La casa de Claudina. [Colette (Colette Willy)]. Pref. A. Hernández Catá.
Madrid: Yagües-Mundo Latino, Libreria y Editorial Rivadeneyra, 1923.
266p. [*La Maison de Claudine*].

La casa de Claudina. Trans. María Luz Morales. Illus. Olga Sacharoff.
Decoration E. Mora. Barcelona: Mediterráneas, 1943. 177p. [*La
Maison de Claudine*].

La casa de Claudine. Trans. E. Piñas. Barcelona: Plaza & Janés, 1964.
169p. Coll. El Hipocampo. [*La Maison de Claudine*].

La casa de Claudine. Sido. Barcelona: Ed. B. [1988]. [*La Maison de Claudine*]. Coll. Libro amigo.

Chéri. Barcelona: Planeta, 1984. 224p. Coll. Grandes novelas de amor de la literatura.

Chéri. El fin de Chéri. Trans. Ramón Hernández and E. Piñas. Barcelona: Plaza & Janés, 1984. 256p. Coll. El ave fénix. [*Chéri. La Fin de Chéri*].

Chéri. El fin de Cheri. Gigi. Trans. Ramón Hernández and E. Piñas. Barcelona: G.P., 1967. 306p. Coll. Los Clásicos del Siglo XX 5. [*Chéri. La Fin de Chéri. Gigi*].

Claudine en la escuela. Trans. E. Piñas. Barcelona: Plaza & Janés, 1964. 207p. Coll. El Hipocampo. [*Claudine à l'école*].

Claudine en la escuela. Trans. José Batlió. Barcelona: Anagrama, 1986. 240p. Coll. Panorama de narrativas 78. [*Claudine à l'école*].

Claudine en la escuela. Claudine se va. La casa de Claudine. Trans. E. Piñas. Barcelona: G.P., 1967. 448p. Col. Los Clásicos del Siglo XX 13. [*Claudine à l'école. Claudine s'en va. La Maison de Claudine*].

Claudine en Paris. Trans. Josep Escué. Barcelona: Anagrama, 1988. 176p. Coll. Panorama de narrativas. [*Claudine à Paris*].

Claudine en Paris. Claudine y el matrimonio. El retiro sentimental. Trans. E. Piñas. Barcelona: G.P., 1968. 414p. Coll. Los Clásicos del Siglo XX 46. [*Claudine à Paris. Claudine en ménage. La Retraite sentimentale*].

Claudina en su casa. Buenos Aires: Sudamericana [1988]. Coll. pocket.

Claudine se va. Trans. E. Piñas. Barcelona: Plaza & Janés, 1965. 154p. Coll. El Hipocampo. [*Claudine s'en va*].

Claudine se va. Buenos Aires: Sudamericana [1988]. Coll. pocket. [*Claudine s'en va*].

Cuarto de hotel. Trans. Angel Samblencat. Mexico City: Ediciones Ibero-Americanas, 1943. 236p. [*Chambre d'hôtel*].

Cuarto de hotel. Trans. Angel Samblencat. Barcelona: Costa-Amic Editor, 1975. Coll. Libros de ayer y de siempre. [*Chambre d'hôtel*].

Cuentos de las mil y una mañanas. Trans. J. Ferrer Aleu. Barcelona: Plaza & Janés, 1973. 192p. Coll. Rotativa. [*Contes des mille et un matins*].

De la poesía moderna francesa: Colette. In *Poesia en el mundo*, no. 36 (1962): 4-23. Two texts from *Dialogues de bêtes*: Sentimentalismos. El primer fuego. Also French texts. [See item 0741].

La doña amagada. Trans. María-Merce, Marcal Serra. Barcelona: Mall, 1985. 170p. Coll. Sirie Oberta 21. [*La Femme cachée*].

Dúo. Trans. E. Piñas. Barcelona: Plaza & Janés, 1962. 148p. Coll. El Hipocampo.

Dúo. Trans. E. Piñas. Barcelona: G.P., 1964. 146p. Coll. Libros Plaza 334.

Dúo. Trans. E. Piñas. Barcelona: Anagrama, 1983. 136p. Panorama de narrativas.

El fin de Chéri. Trans. Ramón Hernández, E. Piñas. Barcelona: Plaza & Janés, 1984. 235p. Coll. El ave fénix 35. [*La Fin de Chéri*].

La gata. Trans. E. Piñas. Barcelona: Plaza & Janés, 1963. 137p. [*La Chatte*].

La gata. Trans. E. Piñas. Barcelona: G.P., 1964. 137p. Coll. Libros Plaza 330. [*La Chatte*].

La gata. Trans. E. Piñas. Barcelona: Círculo de lectores, 1970. 128p. [*La Chatte*].

La gata. Trans. E. Piñas. Barcelona: Plaza & Janés, 1976. 144p. Coll. Rotativa 151. [*La Chatte*].

La gata. Trans. E. Piñas. Barcelona: Orbis, 1982. 192p. Coll. Historia universal de la literatura 31. [*La Chatte*].

La gata. Trans. E. Piñas. Barcelona: La Oveja negra, 1983. 160p. Coll. Historia universal de la literatura. [*La Chatte*].

Gigi [theater]. [Colette and Anita Loos]. Trans. Victoria Ocampo. Buenos Aires: SUR, 1955. 157p.

Gigi. Trans. E. Piñas. Barcelona: G.P., 1965. 186p. Coll. Círculo de Lectores.

Gigi. Trans. E. Piñas. Barcelona: Plaza & Janés, 1977. 160p. Coll. Rotativa 173.

Gigi. El niño enfermo. La señora del fotógrafo. Flora y Pomona. Trans. E. Piñas. Barcelona: Plaza & Janés. 1962. 158p. Coll. El Hipocampo. [*Gigi. L'Enfant malade. La Dame du photographe. Flore et Pomone*].

Gigi. El niño enfermo. La señora del fotógrafo. Flora y Pomona. Trans. E. Piñas. Barcelona: G.P., 1963. 152p. Coll. Libros Plaza 309. [*Gigi. L'Enfant malade. La Dame du photographe. Flore et Pomone*].

Lo impuro. Trans. E. Piñas. Barcelona: Argos-Vergara, 1982. 149p. [*Le Pur et l'impur*].

La ingenua libertina. Trans. E. Piñas. Barcelona: Plaza & Janés, 1963. 175p. Coll. El Hipocampo. [*L'Ingénue libertine*].

La ingenua libertina. Trans. E. Piñas. Barcelona: G.P., 1964. 172p. Coll. Libros Plaza 331. [*L'Ingénue libertine*].

La ingenua libertina. Trans. E. Piñas. Barcelona: Círculo de Lectores, 1968. 232p. [*L'Ingénue libertine*].

La ingenua libertina. Trans. José Maria Aroca. Barcelona: Plaza & Janés, 1984. 224p. Coll. El ave fénix 30. [*L'Ingénue libertine*].

La ingenua libertina. Los zarcillos de la vid. La vagabunda. Trans. E. Piñas. Barcelona: G.P., 1969. 442p. Coll. Los Clásicos del Siglo XX 66. [*L'Ingénue libertine. Les Vrilles de la vigne. La Vagabonde*].

Mitsou. Trans. Jorge de Lorbar. Barcelona: Nuevo Arte Thor, 1985. 92p. Coll. El laberinto.

Mitsou o la iniciacíon amoroso. Trans. Julio Goméz de la Serna. Madrid: Ulises, 1929. 239p.

La Mujer oculta. Trans. E. Piñas. Barcelona: Anagrama, 1982. 176p. Coll. Panorama de narrativas 10. [*La Femme cachée*].

El niño y los sortilegios. [Colette and Ravel]. Madrid: Artes Graf. Ibarra, 1962. 14p. [*L'Enfant et les sortilèges*].

Obras completas. Barcelona: Plaza & Janés, 1963-1968. 4 vol. Coll. Los Clásicos del Siglo XX.
Contents of vol. 1 [trans. E. Piñas, José Maria Aroca]: *Junto a Colette. La Ingenua libertina. Los zarcillos de la vid. La vagabunda. El obstáculo. El reverso del music-hall. El viaje egoísta. El trigo verde. Sido. La gata. Dúo. Gigi. El niño enfermo. La señora del fotógrafo. Flora y Pomona. La flor de la edad.* [*Près de Colette* (by Maurice Goudeket). *L'Ingénue libertine. Les Vrilles de la vigne. La Vagabonde. L'Entrave. L'Envers du music-hall. Le Voyage égoïste. Le Blé en herbe. Sido. La Chatte. Duo. Gigi. L'Enfant malade. La Dame du photographe. Flore et Pomone. La Fleur de l'âge*]. 1537p.
Contents of vol. 2 [trans. E. Piñas]: *Claudine en la escuela. Claudine en Paris. Claudine y el matrimonio. Claudine se va. La casa de Claudine. La paz entre los animales. Al rayar el día. Prisiones y paraísos. Diario al revés. Desde mi ventana. Rasgo por rasgo. Diario intermitente. Nupcias.* [*Claudine à l'école. Claudine à Paris. Claudine en ménage. Claudine s'en va. La Maison de Claudine. La Paix chez les bêtes. La Naissance du jour. Prisons et paradis. Journal à rebours. De ma fenêtre. Trait pour trait. Journal intermittent. Noces*]. 1474p.
Contents of vol. 3 [trans. E. Piñas, R. Hernández]: *Chéri. El fin de Chéri. El retiro sentimental. Mitsou. El palomar. La segunda. Julie de Carneilhan. Lo puro y lo impuro. Doce diálogos de animales. Otros animales. La mujer oculta. La habitación iluminada. Bella-Vista. Cuarto de hotel. El quepis. El fanal azul.* [*Chéri. La Fin de Chéri. La Retraite sentimentale. Mitsou. Le Toutounier. La Seconde. Julie de Carneilhan. Le Pur et l'impur. Douze dialogues de bêtes. Autres bêtes. La Femme cachée. La Chambre éclairée. Bella-Vista. Chambre d'hôtel. Le Képi. Le Fanal bleu*]. 1571p.
Contents of vol. 4 [trans. Domingo Pruna, Guillermo Lledó, Manuel Rossell]: *La estrella vespertina. Mis aprendizajes. Tres... seis... nueve. Mis cuadernos. Para un herbario. Aventuras cotidianas. Al alcance de las manos. Desnudez. En tierra conocida. Entre la multitud. Hermosas estaciones. Miscelánea. Discurso de recepción. Paisajes y retratos. Las horas largas. La vagabunda* (teatro). *Camaradas* (teatro). *Chéri* (teatro). *La decapitada* (teatro). *El niño y los sortilegios* (teatro). *Los prismáticos negros.* [*L'Etoile vesper. Mes apprentissages.*

Trois... six... neuf... Mes cahiers. Pour un herbier. Aventures quotidiennes. Nudité. A portée de la main. En pays connu. Dans la foule. Belles saisons. Mélanges. Discours de réception. Paysages et portraits. Les Heures longues. La Vagabonde (theater). *En camarades* (theater). *Chéri* (theater). *La Décapitée* (theater). *L'Enfant et les sortilèges* (theater). *La Jumelle noire*]. 1771p.

El obstáculo. Trans. E. Piñas. Barcelona: Argos-Vergara, 1982. 200p. [*L'Entrave*].

El obstáculo. El reverso del music-hall. El viaje egoísta. Trans. E. Piñas. Barcelona: G.P., 1970. 316p. Coll. Los Clásicos del Siglo XX 77. [*L'Entrave. L'Envers du music-hall. Le Voyage égoïste*].

Paraíso terrenal: Una biografía de Colette basada en sus propios textos, recopilados por Robert Phelps. Trans. J. Ferrer Aleu. Barcelona: G.P., 1968. 441p. Coll. Libro documento 66. [*Autobiographie tirée des œuvres de Colette par Robert Phelps/Earthly Paradise*].

Querido. Trans. Julio Gómez de la Serna. Barcelona: Vergara [Miguza], 1963. 234p. Coll. Círculo de Lectores. [*Chéri*].

El retiro sentimental. Trans. E. Piñas. Barcelona: Plaza & Janés, 1966. 156p. Coll. El Hipocampo. [*La Retraite sentimentale*].

El reverso del music-hall. Trans. E. Piñas. Barcelona: Argos-Vergara, 1982. 128p. [*L'Envers du music-hall*].

La segunda. Trans. E. Piñas. Barcelona: Argos-Vergara, 1982. 164p. [*La Seconde*].

Sido. Trans. Julio Gómez de la Serna. Madrid: Literarias Sociedad General Española de Libreria, 1931. 182p.

Sido. Trans. Julio Gómez de la Serna. Barcelona: Sabadell, 1942. 143p. Coll. Cristal.

Sido. Trans. Julio Gómez de la Serna. Barcelona: G.P., 1957. 125p. Coll. Libros Plaza 87.

Sido. Trans. E. Piñas. Barcelona: G.P., 1972. 110p. Coll. Enciclopedia de Bolsillo Illustrado 1.

Trigo en ciernes. Trans. Ana Agudo. Madrid: Alfaguara, 1986. 168p. Coll. Juvenil 244. [*Le Blé en herbe*].

El trigo verde. Trans. E. Piñas. Barcelona: Plaza & Janés, 1971. 123p. Coll. Rotativa. [*Le Blé en herbe*].

La vagabunda. Trans. Miguel García Rueda. Paris: Ollendorff [1913]. 253p.

La vagabunda. Trans. E. Piñas. Barcelona: Plaza & Janés, 1965. 189p. Coll. El Hipocampo. [*La Vagabonde*].

La vagabunda. Trans. Mariano García. Barcelona: AHR, 1965. 287p. Coll. Larga vida. [*La Vagabonde*].

La vagabunda. Trans. E. Piñas. Barcelona: Argos-Vergara, 1981. 176p. [*La Vagabonde*].

La vagabunda. Trans. Hebe Monges. Buenos Aires: Centro Editor, 1983. Coll. Bibl. basica universal 248. [*La Vagabonde*].

Appendix E

Index of
BOOK TITLES OF COLETTE'S WORKS

[French and English editions]

Number indicates first item of that title

Amitié inattendue, Une	0001
Autobiographie tirée des œuvres de Colette	0057
Aventures quotidiennes	0696
Avril	0240
Barks and Purrs	0750
Bella-Vista	0226
Belles saisons	0697
Belles Saisons: A Colette Scrapbook	0066
Bêtes libres et prisonnières	0702
Blé en herbe, Le	0232
Blue Lantern, The	0135
Boy and the Magic, The	0954
Break of Day	0594
Broderie ancienne	0703

Captive, The	0466
Cat, The	0285
Cats, Dogs and I	0851
Celle qui en revient	0704
Ces plaisirs	0197
Chambre d'hôtel	0266
Chambre éclairée, La	0705
Chats	0712
Chats de Colette	0714
Chatte, La	0272
Chéri	0288
Chéri (theater)	0940
Chiens de Colette	0716
Ciel de lit, Le	0944
'Claudine,' Les	0059
Claudine à l'école	0326
Claudine à Paris	0360
Claudine amoureuse	0385
Claudine and Annie	0431
Claudine at School	0353
Claudine en ménage	0386
Claudine et les contes de fées	0416
Claudine in Paris	0379
Claudine Married	0407
Claudine Novels, The	0078
Claudine s'en va	0411
Colette	0060
Colette at the movies	0984
Colette: au cinéma	0980
Colette Omnibus	0069
Colette Omnibus, The	0070
Colette par Colette	0061
Collected Stories of Colette, The	0071
Complete Claudine, The	0075
Contes des mille et un matins	0718
Creatures Great and Small	0079
Dans la foule	0721
De Claudine à Colette	0175
De la patte à l'aile	0723
De ma fenêtre	0112
Découvertes	0724

Deuxième cahier de Colette	0830
Dialogues de bêtes	0725
Discours de réception	0751
Douze dialogues de bêtes	0733
Duo	0433
Earthly Paradise	0082
Egarements de Minne, Les	0447
En camarades	0946
En pays connu	0753
En tournée...	0002
Enfant et les sortilèges, L'	0948
Enfants dans les ruines, Les	0758
Entrave, L'	0448
Envers du music-hall, L'	0759
Etoile vesper, L'	0119
Evening Star, The	0127
Fanal bleu, Le	0130
Fanny and Jane	0643
Femme cachée, La	0776
Fin de Chéri, La	0467
Fleur de l'âge, La	0799
Fleurs, Les	0805
Fleurs du désert	0806
Flore et Pomone	0807
Florie	0809
Flowers and Fruit	0090
For a Flower Album	0869
Gentle Libertine, The	0535
Gigi	0484
Gigi and Selected Writings	0501
Gigi (theater)	0956
Heures longues, Les	0810
Histoires pour Bel-Gazou	0817
Indulgent Husband, The	0406
Ingénue libertine, L'	0506
Innocent Libertine, The	0537
Innocent Wife, The	0429

Journal à rebours	0822
Journal intermittent	0828
Journey for Myself	0092
Julie de Carneilhan	0543
Jumelle noire, La	0969
Képi, Le	0551
Last of Chéri, The	0480
Lesson in Love, A	0593
Letters from Colette	0050
Lettres à Hélène Picard	0003
Lettres à Marguerite Moreno	0006
Lettres à Moune et au Toutounet	0008
Lettres à ses pairs	0009
Lettres au petit corsaire	0010
Lettres de la vagabonde	0011
Looking Backwards	0095
Maison de Claudine, La	0139
Married Lover, The	0444
Mes apprentissages	0189
Mes cahiers	0833
Minne	0557
Mitsou	0558
Morceaux choisis	0062
Morning Glory	0600
Mother of Claudine, The	0183
Music-Hall	0771
My Apprenticeships	0193
My Mother's House	0179
Naissance du jour, La	0575
Notes algériennes et marocaines	0834
Notes marocaines	0835
Nudité	0836
Other One, The	0638
Other Woman, The	0794
Œuvres [Pléiade]	0053
Œuvres complètes de Colette [Centenaire]	0055

Œuvres complètes de Colette [Le Fleuron]   0054
Œuvres de Colette   0056

Pages choisies   0063
Paix chez les bêtes, La   0837
Paradis terrestre   0854
Paradis terrestres   0855
Paris de ma fenêtre   0113
Paysages et portraits   0857
Penguin Claudine Novels, The   0078
Places   0098
Plus belles pages de Colette, Les   0064
Pour Missy   0860
Pour un herbier   0861
Premier cahier de Colette   0829
Prisons et paradis   0871
Prrou, Poucette et quelques autres   0882
Pur et l'impur, Le   0200
Pure and the Impure, The   0206

Quatre saisons   0883
Quatrième cahier de Colette   0832

Rainy Moon and Other Stories, The   0111
Recaptured   0458
Recollections   0100
Regarde   0884
Renée, La Vagabonde   0685
Renée Néré (La Vagabonde)   0692
Renée Vivien   0213
Retraite sentimentale, La   0604
Retreat from Love   0624
Rêverie de nouvel an   0885
Ripening, The   0257
Ripening Corn, The   0262
Ripening Seed   0260
Ripening Seed, The   0258

Saha, The Cat   0287
Seconde, La   0628
Seconde, La (theater)   0964
Sept dialogues de bêtes   0727

Seven by Colette	0101
Shackle, The	0461
Short Novels of Colette	0102
Sido	0214
Sido et souvenirs d'enfance	0218
Sido: lettres à sa fille	0013
Six Novels	0103
Six Novels by Colette	0104
Splendeur des papillons	0888
Stories	0105
Stories of Colette, The	0109
Supplément à Don Juan	0221
Tender Shoot and Other Stories, The	0106
Tendron, Le	0647
Textes choisis de Colette	0065
These Pleasures	0209
Thousand and One Mornings, The	0719
Toutounier, Le	0649
Trait pour trait	0889
Treille muscate, La	0894
Trois... six... neuf...	0222
Troisième cahier de Colette	0831
Vagabond, The	0686
Vagabonde, La	0652
Vagabonde, La (theater)	0966
Vagrant, The	0691
Voyage égoïste, Le	0898
Vrilles de la vigne, Les	0916
Young Lady of Paris	0378

Appendix F

Index of
EDITORS, ENGLISH TRANSLATORS,
Illustrators and Other Contributors
to Colette's Books

	Item No.
Abastado, Claude	0059
Allier, Paul	0469
Auberjonois	0856
Aury, Dominique	0438
Baille, Hervé	0935
Ballivet, Suzanne	0336, 0513
Bardone	0055
Barret, Gaston	0402, 0529
Barye	0856
Beauclerk, Helen	0082-89, 0193-96
Bécat, Paul-Emile	0514
Benét, Rosemary Carr	0535-36, 0539, 0593, 0600, 0909-10
Bentinck, Morris	0102, 0285, 0287
Bérard, Christian	0334, 0367, 0393, 0418, 0487
Berg, Camille	0519
Berger, Yves	0756

Bernard, G.	0235
Berque, Jean	0238
Blossom, Frederick A.	0102, 0406, 0429-30, 0441
Blot, Gabrielle	0305
Bonal, Gérard	0349
Boncompain	0055
Bonfils, Robert	0607
Bonnard, Pierre	0698, 0856
Brasilier	0055
Braun, Georges	0527
Bray, Bernard	0053
Brayer, Yves	0056
Brianchon	0250
Briffaud, Daniel	0186, 0210
Briffault, Herma	0071-74, 0082-89, 0207-8, 0211-12
Brisson, Pierre	0618
Brunet, Alain	0053
Caillard, Christian	0697, 0806
Callimachi, Anne-Marie	0071-74, 0104, 0195-96, 0501, 0570-71
Carco, Francis	0113, 0117
Cardinal, Marie	0350
Carlègle	0836
Cathelin	0055
Cau, Véronique	0821, 0850
Cavaillès	0055
Chahine, Edgar	0562
Charmy, Emily	1043
Chastel	0723
Chimot, Edouard	0772
Cimière, Reine	1027
Clarac, Pierre	0063, 0065
Claveloux, Nicole	0745
Clouzot, Marianne	0239, 0256, 0895
Cochet, Gérard	0221
Cocteau, Jean	0346
Collins, Joseph	0206, 0209
Coltman, Derek	0082-89
Commère, Jean	0868
Cosgrave, J.O'H. II	0406, 0429
Courbouleix	0299
Coysens	0929

Creixams	0885
Crosland, Margaret	0098-99, 0442-43, 0445-46, 0624-27, 0719-20, 0793-98
Cura, Jacques	0241, 0300, 0489
Dally, Edith	0206, 0209
Damase, Jean-Michel	1030
Daragnès	0240, 0830
Dauchot, Gabriel	0376
Debraine, Paulette	0678
Debraine-Nemo	0249
del Castillo, Michel	0002
Delanoë, Léon	0053
Delaye, Alice	0614
Delcroix, Maurice	0053
Demazière, Albert	0478
Deslignères	0145
D'Hollander, Paul	0053, 0403
Dignimont	0056, 0222, 0450, 0510, 0561, 0658, 0829
Dufy, Raoul	0835, 0862
Dunoyer de Segonzac	0056, 0438, 0618, 0832, 0894, 0896
Dupas, Jean	1050
Dupont, Jacques	0053
Fabrice, Françoise	0398
Fermor, Patrick Leigh	0101, 0499, 0500, 0502, 0549-50
Flanner, Janet	0101, 0102, 105, 0207-8, 0211-12, 0313-4, 0319-20, 0353, 0357, 0569, 1053
Fontanarosa	0055
Forain	0621
Forbin, Roberte	0004-5, 0009-12
Fowlie, Wallace	0319
Fraipont, Gustave	0860
Frugier, Jacques	0053
Fry, Christopher	0954-55
Fusaro	0055
Gagarine, Princess Alexandre	0851
Garcia	0525

Garcia, Jean   0423
Garcia-Fons   0055
Garvin, Viola Gérard   0102, 0458-59, 0464, 0480, 0482,
                         0638, 0643
Genis   0055
Géol   0667
Gilot, Françoise   0599
Giroud, Françoise   0344
Gobô, Georges   0610
Goudeket, Maurice   0005, 0010, 0057-58, 0063, 0095-97, 0224,
                         0305, 0308, 0584, 0677, 0806, 0856
Grau Sala, Emile   0056, 0303, 0305, 0335, 0344, 0368, 0394,
                         0398, 0419, 0427, 0488, 0671, 0679
Grosjean, Claude-Michel 0347, 0375, 0400, 0426
Guérin, Charles   0898
Guillaume, André   0608
Guiramand   0055
Guyot   0274

Haramboure, Jean   0648
Hartog, Jan de   0944-45
Hennegan, Alice   0097, 0129
Henriot, Emile   0252
Hermann-Paul   0559, 0569
Hoffnung, Gerald   0954-55
Honeybourne, Rosemary   0186

Icart, Louis   0509
Izis-Bidermanas   0854

Jacquemin, André   0581
Jammes, Francis   0001, 0727-28, 0731-34, 0739-40, 0742-43,
                         0745-46, 0750
Jarach, Albert   0412, 0668
Jeanniot, Georges   0289
Jodelet   0663
Johnston, David McCall   0105
Jong, Erica   0070, 0795
Jouve   0855
Jouvenel, Bertrand de   0013

Jouvenel, Renaud de   0965
Jullian, Philippe   0324

Kelly, Maire   0750
King, Charles   0183
Kirby, Victoria Nes   0978
Kyria, Pierre   0253

Laborde, Chas   0328, 0362, 0390, 0413, 0507
Laboureur, J.-E.   0769
Laprade   0807
Laroche, Pierre   0956
Laurie, Marjorie   0444
Le Breton, Constant   0469
Lechantre, Jacques   0672
Lecoanet, S.   0844
Lelong, Pierre   0346
Lelong, René   0927
Le Petit, A.   0817
Le Vay, David   0092-100, 0127-29, 0719-20
Lindley, Denver   0802-3, 1054
Lobel-Riche   0290
Loos, Anita   0943, 0957-63
Lucien-Graux, Dr.   0416
Lydis, Mariette   0331, 0366, 0392, 0417, 0486

Malige, Jeannie   0013
Mallet, Robert   0001
Manet   0865-66, 0869-70
Marchand, Léopold   0940-42, 0964-65, 0966-68
Marquet   0123
Marks, Elaine   0501
Martin, Annie-Claude   0820
Matisse   0674, 0800
Mauriac, Claude   0061, 0175
McKenna, Edward L.   1055
McLeod, Enid   0070-74, 0079-89, 0101, 0103, 0179-82,
                           0184-88, 0501, 0594-99, 0601-2, 0686-90,
                           0693-94
Mégroz, Phyllis   0262

Méheut 0884
Mercier, Jean A. 0275
Mercier, Michel 0053
Métral, Maurice 0166
Meunier, Marcelle 0516
Meyer, Jean 0959
Mich 0656
Miller, Gilbert 0961
Mirande, Henri 0327, 0332, 0343, 0353, 0770
Molinard, Patrice 0740
Monnier, Paul 0301
Moreau, Luc-Albert 0578, 0753, 0831
Morin-Jean 0452, 0665
Morisot, Berthe 0724
Mortimer, Raymond 0322-23, 0325
Mourlot, Maurice 0737

Nam, Jacques 0712, 0728, 0750
Nicollier, Jean 0301

Oberlé, Jean 0560
Oudot, Roland 0056

Paradis, Madeleine 0756
Parinaud, André 0616
Pavie, Jean 0732
Perdriat, Hélène 0148
Pettier, Colette 0434
Phelps, Robert 0050-52, 0057-58, 0066-68, 0071-74,
0082-91, 0460, 0599
Picart le Doux 0705
Picasso 0252, 0856
Pichois, Claude 0003-7, 0009-12, 0053, 0246, 0588, 0592,
0739, 0959
Post, Herman 0313
Postgate, Raymond 0104, 0570-71, 0573-74
Poulenc 1031
Pouzet, Maurice 0521

Raaphorst-Rousseau,
  Madeleine   0053
Ramah   0647
Remfry-Kidd, Charlotte 0685, 0691-92
Rémy-Bieth, Michel   0002
Renefer   0234, 0661
Resch, Yannick   0053, 0479
Reschofsky, Jean   0818, 0845
Ringel, Renée   0341, 0371, 0396, 0422
Rose, Anna   0804
Roshardt, Pia   0864
Roubille, Auguste   0361, 0365, 0378, 0842
Routier, Jean   0333

Saint-André, Berthommé 0669
Sainte-Croix, G. de   0278
Sarde, Michèle   0013
Sauvage, Marcel   0885
Ségur, Adrienne   0953
Selz, Irma   0499
Senhouse, Roger   0070, 0082-89, 0101, 0103-4, 0135-38,
                     0179, 0181, 0184, 0186-87, 0258-61,
                     0263-65, 0315-18, 0321-25, 0481, 0483,
                     0499-505, 0596, 0639-42, 0644-45,
                     0869-70
Serraillier, Ian   0188
Serveau, Clément   0114, 0140, 0150, 0199, 0216, 0234, 0241,
                     0267, 0552, 0577, 0630, 0876, 0926
Seurat   0856
Shelley, Hugh   0168
Sigaux, Gilbert   0585, 0620
Sikorska, Andrée   0902
Smith, Sarah W.R.   0984
Stimpson, Brian   0255
Suba, Susanne   0285
Suter, André-Nicolas 0210

Taillefer, Jacques   0165, 0492
Tait, Elizabeth   0639-42, 0644-45
Tartas, Pierre de   0868
Térechkovitch, Constantin 0056, 0897

Terrasse, Michel   0887, 0952
Terry, Jane   0569, 0572
Thévenet, Jacques   0055, 0227
Thibaut, Danièle   0178
Thiébaut, Marcel   0218
Touchagues, Louis   0115, 0809
Troubridge, Una Vincenzo   0071-74, 0082-89, 0101, 0179-82,
                             0184-88, 0501

Valette   0731
Vallée, Armand   0158
Van Dongen   0056
Vertès, Marcel   0056, 0293, 0659
Villaret, Bernard   0008
Virmaux, Alain and Odette   0980, 0984
Vitale, Grazia   0819

Ward, Matthew   0071-74, 0090-91
Wescott, Glenway   0102, 0594-96
Whitall, James   0378, 0380, 0382
White, Antonia   0070-78, 0082-89, 0101, 0103, 0104,
                             0106-11, 0210, 0225, 0286, 0354-56,
                             0358-59, 0379, 0383-84, 0407-10, 0431-32,
                             0460-63, 0465-66, 0501, 0503-4, 0537-38,
                             0540-42, 0603, 0911-15
Wisbar, K.   0163
Wolff, Albert   0449, 0899-0900
Wolff, Kathleen   0951

Zbinden, Dr. Hans   0888
Zeitlin, Ida   0257